# NATIONAL LANDMARKS,
# AMERICA'S TREASURES

# NATIONAL LANDMARKS, AMERICA'S TREASURES

*The National Park Foundation's Complete Guide to National Historic Landmarks*

## S. Allen Chambers, Jr.

**JOHN WILEY & SONS, INC.**

New York • Chichester • Weinheim • Brisbane • Singapore • Toronto

Copyright © 2000 by The National Park Foundation. All rights reserved.

Published by John Wiley & Sons, Inc.

Published simultaneously in Canada.

This publication is designed to provide accurate and authoritative information in regard to the subject matter covered. It is sold with the understanding that the publisher is not engaged in rendering professional services. If professional advice or other expert assistance is required, the services of a competent professional person should be sought.

*Library of Congress Cataloging-in-Publication Data:*

Chambers, S. Allen.
        National landmarks, America's treasures : the National Park
    Foundation's complete guide to national historic landmarks / S.
    Allen Chambers, Jr.
            p.   cm.
        ISBN 0-471-19764-5 (pbk. : alk. paper)
        1. Historic sites—United States Guidebooks.   2. National
    monuments—United States Guidebooks.   3. United States Guidebooks.
    I. National Park Foundation.   II. Title.
    E159.C43   2000
    973—dc21                                                99-31114

Printed in the United States of America.

10 9 8 7 6 5 4 3 2 1

# CONTENTS

This historic moment in time, the approach of a new century and the next millennium provides us as Americans the opportunity to celebrate both our rich cultural diversity and our shared experiences.  It is a moment to reflect on those things that define us as a people.  To understand the people we have become, we have to look at the places, the books, the events, the photographs--all of the things--that form the heart of our cherished history.

Each of the more than 2000 places listed in this book reflects an historic moment in our past.  These American treasures include not only the homes of presidents, but also factories where our immigrant ancestors labored, places where our most talented writers, musicians and artists created, buildings designed by our greatest architects, examples of the technological innovations that propelled science and industry, and landscapes imprinted by those cultures indigenous to the land we call our home.  These places are found in America's largest cities and smallest towns--right next door and in the farthest outposts of our land.  They are part of our nation's collective memory and should be a part of our future.

The National Park Service is responsible under the 1935 Historic Sites Act for the identification of historic places of national importance for designation by the Secretary of the Interior.  Today, this work is carried out by the Park Service's National Historic Landmarks Survey in partnership with Federal, tribal, state and local government agencies; preservation professionals; nonprofit organizations; colleges and universities and private organizations and individuals. While some of these sites have become units of the National Park System, most remain in the hands of private owners--people and organizations that invest their time and resources to make certain they are preserved.  Each one of us must act as caretaker of this, our nation's precious history; we have a responsibility to keep it alive for ourselves and for future generations.

Some of the places in this book will be familiar, many will be new and exciting.  The stories of our past told in the places where history happened can be as compelling as the best fiction. I encourage you to let this book be the beginning of your journey to honor our past so that you can imagine our future.

Hillary Rodham Clinton

# PREFACE

While our National Parks contain some of America's most splendid natural and cultural resources, it would be impossible to incorporate every property important to the nation's history into the National Park System. Today the National Historic Landmarks Program of the National Park Service identifies potential landmarks and provides assistance to owners of nationally significant historic places that fall primarily outside the National Park System. Created by Congress in 1967 as the official nonprofit partner of the National Park Service, the National Park Foundation encourages and manages private donations "for the benefit of, or in connection with, the National Park Service, its activities, or its services, thereby furthering the conservation of natural, scenic, historic, scientific, or educational, inspirational, or recreational resources for future generations of Americans."

For this reason, the National Park Foundation is pleased to cooperate with John Wiley and Sons to produce the first comprehensive guide to National Historic Landmarks, places designated by the Secretary of the Interior as possessing exceptional value or quality in illustrating and interpreting the history of the United States. Proceeds from the sale of this book will be placed in the National Park Foundation's National Historic Landmarks Survey Fund to be used for the benefit of the program.

I urge readers to join the National Park Foundation in supporting the National Historic Landmarks Program. You help ensure the preservation of these outstanding historic places when you:

- Visit the places in this book that are open or accessible to the public, learn why they are important, and teach young people the value of their preservation.

- Make a contribution to National Historic Landmarks that serve as museums or historical societies by volunteering your time, becoming a member, or donating resources.

- Become familiar with historic preservation issues and encourage your elected officials to support legislation that protects significant historic places.

- Join the National Historic Landmark Stewards' Association—comprising National Historic Landmarks owners, managers, and friends groups—which advocates the preservation of National Historic Landmarks and works to promote public awareness of the program.

- Contribute to the National Historic Landmarks Survey Fund and the National Historic Landmarks Assistance Fund. Your donation on behalf of all National Historic Landmarks or those of your choice will aid the National Park Service in the identification and preservation of these irreplaceable resources.

We hope this book will help readers recognize the value these places have for us as Americans, and we are pleased to be a partner in this effort to help them discover and learn about these American treasures.

Jim Maddy
President, National Park Foundation

# ACKNOWLEDGMENTS

More than most books, this volume is the result of invaluable input from numerous individuals and institutions. Carol D. Shull, Robie S. Lange, and Kira Ramakrishna Badamo, of the National Park Service's National Historic Landmarks Survey, provided assistance from the initial concept through to publication. Their encouragement and expertise transformed what could have been an arduous task into a positive pleasure. While working with the NHL Survey, Barbara Copp, Andrea Harris, Ted Grevstad-Nordbrock, Robert L. Sandoval, and Edward Watkins provided critical assistance with various elements at crucial points in the preparation of the manuscript and illustrations. I am particularly indebted to Kira and Barbara for their adeptness with the computer—still more of a challenge than a companion to me—and to Larry Karr for technical support. After tapping various keys, it was always a pleasure and a surprise to see something pop up on the screen titled "Al's NHLs." Other staff, present and past, contributed important insights about various landmarks. Several helped draft the entries and supported the project in numerous other ways. Among these are Patty Henry, Benjamin Levy, Barry Mackintosh, George Mendez, Theresa Solury, and, especially, Carolyn Pitts. Several of those named above worked with the NHL Survey as contractors for the National Conference of State Historic Preservation Officers or as National Council for Preservation Education interns.

While working in something of a vacuum in the Washington headquarters office, I depended on numerous regional staff members of the National Park Service to review portions of the text. Among those who valiantly undertook to save me from egregious error are Mark Barnes, Linda Cook, Michael Crowe, Hank Florence, Rachel Franklin Weekley, Ann Huston, Alisa McCann, Cecil McKithan, Frank Miele, Diane Miller, Bill Nelligan, Becky Saleeby, Dena Sanford, Bob Spude, Stephanie Toothman, and Lysa Wegman-French.

I also thank the many professionals in the offices of the state historic preservation officers across the country. Among those who read draft descriptions of NHLs in their states and offered valuable suggestions and corrections are Eve Barsoum, Philip Bergen, John Bonafide, Bob Englert, Christine E. Fonda, Betsy Friedberg, Lynn Garofalini, Elsa Gilbertson, John F. A. Herzan, Katherine Jourdan, Terry Karschner, Pam Kennedy, Bob Kuhn, Peter Kurtz, Kathleen LaFrank, Calder Loth, Kirk Mohney, Mark Peckham, Greg Ramsey, Claire Ross, Gary Sachau, Ray Smith, Nancy Todd, and Jim Warren.

Historic American Buildings Survey/Historic American Engineering Record staff members David Barak, Catherine C. Lavoie, and Monica P. Murphy helped with the selection and preparation of illustrations. I also thank the individuals and organizations named in the credit lines of the illustration legends for granting permission to use their photographs and drawings.

I am indebted to the National Park Foundation for sponsoring the project and especially thank Megan Brand, Leslie Happ, and Todd McCreight for their assistance. Finally, special thanks to my editors at John Wiley & Sons: Jan Cigliano, David Sassian, and Amanda Miller.

# INTRODUCTION

Americans have long invested places with meaning. Thomas Jefferson was so impressed with Virginia's Natural Bridge that he purchased the property in 1774 with the hope that it would be forever preserved in the public trust. Such a magnificent natural feature, he and early visitors agreed, was symbolic of the bounty and splendor of America. Nearly a century and a quarter later, Natural Bridge was designated a National Historic Landmark for its role in the development of a national self-identity tied to the seemingly boundless landscape of the New World.

It is difficult to imagine that any one place could come to symbolize our nation today. The diversity that characterizes our nation's heritage is documented by nearly 2,300 National Historic Landmarks in the 50 states and 7 U.S. jurisdictions, reflecting almost every imaginable important aspect of our nation's history. The range of properties represented in the program reflects changing perceptions about which events, ideas, and experiences have most influenced American history.

National Historic Landmarks make tangible the American experience. They are places where significant historical events occurred, where prominent Americans worked or lived, that represent the ideas that shaped the nation, that provide important information about our past, or that are outstanding examples of design or construction. This book includes places reflecting our greatest achievements in areas such as science, literature, arts, architecture, and engineering, as well as places associated with struggles that profoundly affected our national course, such as those related to slavery, civil rights, the labor movement, and political reform. Taken as a whole, these historic places chronicle our most important archeological discoveries, chart our progress in areas such as transportation and industry, and document the people and ideas thought to have had the most profound influence on our nation. They reveal a landscape shaped by the multiplicity of cultures and traditions that compose our national identity.

Through the National Historic Landmarks Survey and the National Historic Landmarks Initiative, the National Park Service administers the National Historic Landmarks Program for the secretary of the interior. It is a cooperative endeavor of government agencies, professionals, independent organizations, and citizens, sharing knowledge with the Service and working jointly to identify and preserve National Historic Landmarks. The

National Park Service works alongside a host of partners to identify, evaluate, and document properties of national significance. It monitors the condition of existing Landmarks and provides technical assistance to the public to preserve them. The National Park Service supports the National Historic Landmarks Stewards Association—comprising Landmark owners, managers, and friends groups—which advocates the preservation of Landmarks and works to promote public awareness of the program.

## Origins of the Landmarks Program

The earliest legal recognition of the importance of historic preservation to the nation was the passage of the Antiquities Act of 1906, which authorized the president to proclaim as National Monuments places having significance in history, prehistory, or science. The first comprehensive effort to document the nation's most important historic places began in 1935 with the creation of the Historic Sites Survey. Although the program was primarily instituted to identify properties suitable for inclusion as units of the National Park System, in supporting the Act in his testimony before the House Public Lands Committee, Secretary of the Interior Harold L. Ickes stated that such a survey "would make it possible to call to the attention of States, municipalities and local historical organizations, the presence of historical sites in their particular regions which the National Government cannot preserve, but which need attention and rehabilitation."

Beginning in 1960, historic properties found nationally significant by the secretary of the interior received a new designation: National Historic Landmark. National Historic Landmark designation was seen as a way to encourage their owners to preserve important historic cultural properties. Although some of these places have been added to the National Park System, the National Park Service regards National Historic Landmark designation as an attractive alternative to federal acquisition of historic properties. Currently, a little more than 1 percent of National Historic Landmarks are located within National Park Service units.

The passage of the National Historic Preservation Act in 1966 greatly expanded the federal government's role in historic preservation. The Act established the National Register of Historic Places to recognize properties of state and local significance, as well as units of the National Park System. At that time all existing National Historic Landmarks and historic and cultural units of the Park System were listed in the National Register. Since then, any property not already listed in the National Register prior to its designation as a National Historic Landmark is listed when it is designated.

## Designating National Historic Landmarks

Potential National Historic Landmarks are identified in two ways: through theme studies that examine related properties within specific national historic contexts, and through special studies of individual properties with high integrity that appear to meet National Historic Landmarks Criteria (see "Specific Criteria for National Significance," pp. 4–5).

National Historic Landmark nominations may be prepared by interested individuals; by organizations; by state, federal, or tribal preservation officers; or by National Park Service staff. The National Historic Landmarks Survey staff provides information about theme studies and other comparable properties that may be relevant in the evaluation of particular properties and gives preliminary advice on whether a property appears likely to meet National Historic Landmarks criteria. National Park Service regional and support office staff who administer the National Historic Landmarks program in their areas also provide preliminary evaluations and assistance in preparing National Historic Landmark nominations.

Once a draft nomination is prepared, it is reviewed by the National Historic Landmarks staff. Following such reviews and any appropriate revisions, owners and elected officials are formally notified and given an opportunity to comment on those nominations that are likely candidates for National Historic Landmark designation. Owners of private property are given an opportunity to concur in or object to designation. In the case of more than one owner, if a majority of private property owners object, the secretary of the interior cannot designate the property but can determine whether it is eligible for designation. Proposed National Historic Landmarks are evaluated at meetings of the National Park System Advisory Board. Based on the recommendation of the Advisory Board, the secretary of the interior considers and designates National Historic Landmarks.

Once the secretary designates a Landmark, its owners may receive a bronze plaque attesting to its national significance. Owners of Landmarks may be able to obtain federal assistance from the Historic Preservation Fund (when available), federal investment tax credits for rehabilitation, and other federal tax incentives. Although the National Park Service encourages preservation of National Historic Landmarks, owners are free to manage their properties as they choose, as long as no federal license, funding, or permit is involved. If there is federal involvement, federal agencies must allow the Advisory Council on Historic Preservation an opportunity to comment on the project and its effects on the Landmark to ensure that historic values are considered in the planning of federally assisted projects.

## About This Book

The historic places listed in this book include all National Historic Landmarks designated through 1999. The official National Historic Landmark nomination on file at the National Park Service is the source of most of the information included in this publication. Collected over a period of several decades and prepared by countless individuals both within and outside the Park Service, this body of information reflects numerous approaches to and levels of information regarding the Landmarks. The documentation has been augmented with information of more recent vintage when available.

Entries are arranged in alphabetical order by county within each state to allow grouping by geographic proximity. The District of Columbia, Puerto Rico, and the Virgin Islands are alphabetized along with states, with other jurisdictions grouped together in the final section. Each entry is headed with the official Landmark name of the property, followed by the address (or location) and town or city. Some large cities, such as Richmond and Saint Louis, are not considered part of any county. In these cases, properties are alphabetized under the city name. An index by subject and National Historic Landmark name is included to help readers locate specific properties.

Location information is based on the National Register Information System (NRIS), the official database of all buildings, sites, districts, structures, and objects listed in the National Register of Historic Places. Many entries have no specific street address, but instead contain approximate location information. In some cases the National Park Service restricts certain information, such as property location, when it is necessary to prevent damage to the resource. In these cases, "Address Restricted" appears in the entry heading.

Landmarks included within units of the National Park System are identified by "(NPS)" following the property name. All National Park Service units are open to the public.

Although most National Historic Landmarks are in private hands or under state or local government ownership, many are also open to the public or can be viewed from a public thoroughfare. When available, information about public access has been provided. Readers should consult local sources to determine whether and when properties are open to the public.

## To Learn More

The records of the National Historic Landmarks program are open to the public. Information on Landmark designation is used for planning, public education, and interpretation. Copies of the documentation—including physical description, statement of significance, bibliography, photographs, and map—may be obtained from the National Park Service by writing to

National Historic Landmarks Survey
National Register, History and Education Division
National Park Service
1849 C Street, NW
Room NC400
Washington, DC 20240

To learn more about the historic preservation programs of the Park Service that include National Historic Landmarks, such as the National Register of Historic Places travel itineraries and Teaching with Historic Places lesson plans, and the Historic American Buildings Survey/Historic American Engineering Record documentation programs, visit the Park Service's Cultural Resources Programs website, "Links with the Past," at www.cr.nps.gov.

### Specific Criteria for National Significance:

The quality of national significance is ascribed to districts, sites, buildings, structures and objects that possess exceptional value or quality in illustrating or interpreting the heritage of the United States in history, architecture, archeology, engineering and culture and that possess a high degree of integrity of location, design, setting, materials, workmanship, feeling and association, and:

(a)(1) That are associated with events that have made a significant contribution to, and are identified with, or that outstandingly represent, the broad national patterns of United States history and from which an understanding and appreciation of those patterns may be gained; or

(a)(2) That are associated importantly with the lives of persons nationally significant in the history of the United States; or

(a)(3) That represent some great idea or ideal of the American people; or

(a)(4) That embody the distinguishing characteristics of an architectural type specimen exceptionally valuable for a study of a period, style or method of construction, or that represent a significant, distinctive and exceptional entity whose components may lack individual distinction; or

(a)(5) That are composed of integral parts of the environment not sufficiently significant by reason of historical association or artistic merit to warrant individual recognition but collectively compose an entity of exceptional historical or artistic significance, or outstandingly commemorate or illustrate a way of life or culture; or (a)(6) That have yielded or may be likely to yield information of major scientific importance by revealing new cultures, or by shedding light upon periods of occupation over large areas of the United States. Such sites are those which have yielded, or which may reasonably be expected to yield, data affecting theories, concepts and ideas to a major degree.

(b) Ordinarily, cemeteries, birthplaces, graves of historical figures, properties owned by religious institutions or used for religious purposes, structures that have been moved from their original locations, reconstructed historic buildings and properties that have achieved significance within the past 50 years are not eligible for designation. Such properties, however, will qualify if they fall within the following categories:

(b)(1) A religious property deriving its primary national significance from architectural or artistic distinction or historical importance; or

(b)(2) A building or structure removed from its original location but which is nationally significant primarily for its architectural merit, or for association with persons or events of transcendent importance in the nation's history and the association consequential; or

(b)(3) A site of a building or structure no longer standing but the person or event associated with it is of transcendent importance in the nation's history and the association consequential; or

(b)(4) A birthplace, grave or burial if it is of a historical figure of transcendent national significance and no other appropriate site, building or structure directly associated with the productive life of that person exists; or

(b)(5) A cemetery that derives its primary national significance from graves of persons of transcendent importance, or from an exceptionally distinctive design or from an exceptionally significant event; or

(b)(6) A reconstructed building or ensemble of buildings of extraordinary national significance when accurately executed in a suitable environment and presented in a dignified manner as part of a restoration master plan, and when no other buildings or structures with the same association have survived; or

(b)(7) A property primarily commemorative in intent if design, age, tradition, or symbolic value has invested it with its own national historical significance; or

(b)(8) A property achieving national significance within the past 50 years if it is of extraordinary national importance.

# ALABAMA

## ◼ Baldwin County

### BOTTLE CREEK SITE
**Address Restricted, Stockton vicinity**

This "type site" for the Pensacola culture of the Mississippian period on the northern Gulf Coast is a key to understanding the history and culture of the Mobile-Tensaw Delta in late prehistoric/protohistoric times. The site is believed to have been occupied as early as A.D. 1150, but its principal occupation is thought to have been from A.D. 1250 to 1550. It appears to have served as a major social, political, religious, and trade center for the region. The now isolated spot contains a number of mounds that served as platforms for houses and temples.

### FORT MORGAN
**Western terminus of Alabama Route 180, Mobile Point**

"Damn the torpedoes—full speed ahead!" Admiral David Farragut uttered his immortal command in August 1864 as his Union fleet attempted to capture this Confederate fort guarding Mobile Bay and to avoid the mines protecting it. When the fort surrendered, the bay was opened to the Union Navy and the port of Mobile sealed off from the Confederates. Union troops repaired the damage they had inflicted on the huge pentagonal brick stronghold. Fort Morgan was used as a training base in World War I, restored by the Public Works Administration in the 1930s, garrisoned in World War II, and is now a state park.

## ◼ Barbour County

### HENRY D. CLAYTON HOUSE
**1 mile south of Clayton**

This antebellum cottage was the home of Alabama congressman Henry D. Clayton, chairman of the House Judiciary Committee and author of the 1914 Clayton Anti-Trust Act. The Act, which created the Federal Trade Commission, was designed to outlaw a number of unfair trade practices and intended to strengthen the earlier Sherman Act.

## ◼ Colbert County

### BARTON HALL
**2.5 miles west of Cherokee on Route 72, 0.5 miles south of Route 72**

The exterior of this ca. 1847–1849 hipped-roof frame house is traditional in form but has exceptionally sophisticated Doric detailing on the entrance portico and in the entablature. Inside is a stunning, almost sculptural, double stairway that leads from the main hall to the rooftop deck in a series of flights, landings, and reverse flights. The house is not open to the public.

### IVY GREEN
**300 West North Commons, Tuscumbia**

Helen Keller, born in a cottage here in 1880, grew up in the 1820s main house, and learned to communicate at a water pump between the two buildings, thanks to the unceasing efforts of Anne Sullivan. Employing a finger lan-

*Ivy Green, Tuscumbia, Colbert County. Courtesy of NPS (Fred Myers).*

guage, Sullivan spelled out W-A-T-E-R as she pumped water over the hand of her seven-year-old charge, who was mute because of a childhood illness that left her deaf and blind. Helen Keller went on to teach and inspire humanity throughout the world. The house and cottage are now a museum dedicated to Helen Keller's life.

## WILSON DAM
### Tennessee River, Florence vicinity

Wilson Dam was begun by the U.S. Army Corps of Engineers in 1918 to harness energy at the Tennessee River's Muscle Shoals. The 4,535-foot-long concrete structure was completed in 1925 and became the first hydroelectric unit of the Tennessee Valley Authority (TVA) when it was created in 1933. One of TVA's cornerstones, Wilson Dam still has the largest hydroelectric-generating capacity of any of the Authority's 33 major dams. It is not open to the public. (Also in Lauderdale County.)

### ■ *Dallas County*

## BROWN CHAPEL AFRICAN METHODIST EPISCOPAL CHURCH
### 410 Martin Luther King, Jr. Street, Selma

Brown Chapel African Methodist Episcopal Church played a major role in events that led to the adoption of the Voting Rights Act of 1965. It was headquarters of the Selma Voting Rights Movement and the starting point for the three Selma-to-Montgomery marches. Media coverage of the violence during the marches showed that equal access to the ballot was far from being realized. The nation's reaction to Selma's "Bloody Sunday March" is widely credited with making the passage of the Voting Rights Act politically viable to an otherwise cautious Congress. Built in the early 20th century, Brown Chapel is an impressive edifice that displays Byzantine and Romanesque architectural influences.

### ■ *Elmore County*

## FORT TOULOUSE SITE
### 4 miles southwest of Wetumpka

From 1717 until 1763, this was French Louisiana's easternmost outpost. The fort was a stockade, built where the Coosa and Tallapossa join to form the Alabama River. The "Alabama Fort" also served as a trading post for commerce with Creek Indians living nearby. In 1814, General Andrew Jackson established Fort Jackson at the site, and the treaty ending the Creek War was signed here on August 9 of that year. The fort's reconstruction was one of Alabama's major projects honoring the nation's bicentennial in 1976. It is now a state park open to the public.

### ■ *Hale County*

## MOUNDVILLE SITE
### Near Moundville, Hale County

This site was a center for the southerly diffusion of Mississippian culture (A.D. 1000–1500) toward the Gulf Coast. The two dozen flat-topped mounds that survive served as substructures for temples, council houses, and homes of the rulers. The tallest mound rises 58 feet and covers two acres. A replica of a temple has been built on its top to assist in interpretation at the Mound State Monument.

## SAINT ANDREW'S CHURCH
### U.S. Highway 80, Prairieville

The sophisticated design of this board-and-batten Gothic Revival church is attributed to the influence of architect Richard Upjohn. Built by slave labor, it remains virtually unaltered since its completion in 1854. Vestibule, nave, and chancel, lit by narrow lancets and covered with steep gabled roofs, are arranged according to tenets espoused by the Ecclesiological movement. Interior woodwork is said to have been colored with a tobacco-based stain.

### ■ *Jefferson County*

## SLOSS BLAST FURNACES
### First Avenue and 32nd Street, Birmingham

This testament to the South's post–Civil War efforts to diversify its economy was erected in 1881–1882 by industrialist James Withers Sloss. Now a city-owned museum, the mammoth complex helped precipitate the industrial development of Birmingham, earning it the sobriquet "Pittsburgh of the South." Labor-intensive operations continued at the blast furnace until 1970.

Sloss Blast Furnaces, Birmingham, Jefferson County.
Courtesy of HAER (Jack E. Boucher).

## WILSON DAM
**Tennessee River, Florence vicinity (Colbert and Lauderdale Counties)**

(See entry under Colbert County.)

## ■ Macon County
### TUSKEGEE INSTITUTE (NPS)
**Vicinity of Tuskegee**

Indelibly associated with Booker T. Washington, who founded it in 1881, and George Washington Carver, chair of its Agriculture Department, Tuskegee Institute is one of the nation's preeminent African-American institutions of higher learning. Under Washington's aegis, the curriculum was designed to provide industrial and vocational education to ameliorate economic conditions of African Americans and improve their way of life. The Oaks, a Queen Anne style house built for Washington by students in the vocational training program, is part of the Tuskegee Institute National Historic Site.

## ■ Madison County
### EPISCOPAL CHURCH OF THE NATIVITY
**212 Eustis Avenue, Huntsville**

Described when completed in 1859 as "a splendid specimen of Gothic architecture," this Episcopal church was designed by English-born architect Frank Wills. A pristine example of a design based on ideals promulgated by the Ecclesiological movement to improve church architecture, it is distin-

guished by a tall, spired tower, a narrow nave flanked by low side aisles, and a polygonal chancel.

## NEUTRAL BUOYANCY SPACE SIMULATOR
**George C. Marshall Space Flight Center, Huntsville**

Designed to provide a simulated zero-gravity environment, this facility enabled researchers to gain firsthand knowledge of problems that would be encountered in space. The heart of the simulator is a water tank 75 feet in diameter and 40 feet deep, with portholes and four observation levels. Constructed in 1955, this was NASA's only such facility until the mid-1970s. The simulator contributed to the success of projects Gemini, Apollo, Skylab and the space shuttle. It is not open to the public.

## PROPULSION AND STRUCTURAL TEST FACILITY
**George C. Marshall Space Flight Center, Huntsville**

This concrete-and-steel test stand and support facilities were built in 1957. During the 1960s, under the direction of Dr. Werner von Braun, the Saturn family of launch vehicles was developed here. Continually used and modified to meet new demands, this installation has played a part in testing every important rocket developed by the Redstone Arsenal and, later, the Marshall Space Flight Center. Years of testing at this site have literally launched the American Space Program. The test facility is included on the U.S. Space and Rocket Center public tours of Marshall Space Flight Center.

## REDSTONE TEST STAND
**George C. Marshall Space Flight Center, Huntsville**

This oldest static firing facility at the Marshall Space Flight Center was instrumental in developing procedures that launched the nation's first satellite and the first American manned space flight. In 1953 the 75-foot-tall, steel-framed test stand was constructed of reused materials and cost only $25,000. A need for more sophisticated test sites resulted in its closing in 1961 and the removal of all

*Redstone Test Stand, Huntsville, Madison County. Courtesy of HAER (Jet Lowe).*

usable equipment. Today Redstone Test Stand is open to the public.

### SATURN V DYNAMIC TEST STAND
**George C. Marshall Space Flight Center, Huntsville**

This mammoth facility, 360 feet high, was built in 1964 to conduct mechanical and vibrational tests on fully assembled Saturn V rockets. Such testing was the last step before the vehicles were accepted for full flight status at the Kennedy Space Center in Florida. The Apollo and Skylab programs utilized Saturn V rockets, as did the first manned lunar landing, and none ever failed in its mission. The Saturn V Dynamic Test Stand is open for public tours.

### SATURN V LAUNCH VEHICLE
**Huntsville**

In January 1962, the United States launched its attempts to achieve a manned lunar landing by developing the Saturn V rocket under the direction of Dr. Werner von Braun. Seven years later, a Saturn V lifted off with Neil Armstrong, Edwin Aldrin, and Michael Collins aboard, and carried them to their rendezvous with destiny. This first Saturn V was the test vehicle at the Marshall Space Flight Center and is identical to the one that put man on the moon. On display since 1969, the three-stage rocket is a featured exhibit at the U.S. Space and Rocket Center.

### ■ *Marengo County*

### GAINESWOOD
**805 South Cedar Street, Demopolis**

Construction of this remarkable and complex house, one of America's most unusual Greek Revival style mansions, took 18 years, from 1842 to 1860. Nathan Bryan Whitfield, owner, architect, and builder, used architectural handbooks for inspiration, ordered ornaments from London, and fashioned much of the fabric on-site. The exterior is Doric, but the lavish multicolumned ballroom employs the more elaborate Corinthian order. Restored by the state, the house is now a museum, open to the public.

### ■ *Mobile County*

### *ALABAMA*
**Battleship Parkway, Mobile**

This 35,000-ton battleship, commissioned as the USS *Alabama* in August 1942, is one of only two surviving examples of the South Dakota class. *Alabama* gave distinguished service in the Atlantic and Pacific theaters of World War II. During its 40-month Asiatic-Pacific stint, it participated in the bombardment of Honshu, and its 300-member crew earned nine battle stars. Decommissioned in 1947, the ship was transferred to the state of Alabama in 1964 and is now a war memorial, open to the public.

### CITY HALL
**111 South Royal Street, Mobile**

Built in 1856–1857 to serve as city hall, armory, and market, this building is an impressive example of the 19th-century trend to combine several municipal functions within one building. Its expansive facade has

Drum, *Mobile, Mobile County. Forward torpedo room. Courtesy of the USS* Alabama *Battleship Commission.*

a twin-gabled main building connected to flanking wings by crenellated wing walls. Italianate features include broad, bracketed eaves and an octagonal cupola.

## DRUM
### Battleship Parkway, Mobile

This submarine was launched in 1941, at the outset of World War II, as the first of a type that became standard. Manned by a wartime crew of 85, it was swift and well suited to the lengthy underwater patrols typical of duty in the Pacific. *Drum* sank 15 enemy ships and was awarded 12 battle stars. It is now moored alongside the USS *Alabama* (see *Alabama*) as part of a war memorial, open to the public.

## GOVERNMENT STREET PRESBYTERIAN CHURCH
### 300 Government Street, Mobile

This exemplary Greek Revival church, completed in 1836 from designs by James Gallier in association with brothers James and Charles Dakin, exhibits an early American usage of a *distyle-in-muris* portico: a recessed porch with two columns between flanking end walls. This arrangement was adopted in a number of Greek Revival churches across the country. Interior details adhere to plates from a handbook by Minard LaFever, a famous 19th-century architect, with whom Gallier had worked in New York. The tower was toppled by a hurricane in 1852 and not replaced. Otherwise, the church is in largely original condition.

## ■ *Montgomery County*

## DEXTER AVENUE BAPTIST CHURCH
### 454 Dexter Avenue, Montgomery

This eclectically styled brick church, dating from 1878, played a pivotal role in the 1950s struggle for civil rights. Martin Luther King, Jr., then pastor, helped organize the Montgomery Improvement Association after Rosa Parks was arrested for refusing to obey segregationist policies requiring her to sit in the rear of a city bus. The Association, which held its meetings in the church, successfully boycotted the city's buses in 1955. Now called the Dexter Avenue King Memorial Baptist Church, it is open to the public.

## FIRST CONFEDERATE CAPITOL
### East end of Dexter Avenue, Montgomery

In February 1861, 37 delegates from six states that had seceded from the Union met here, adopted a constitution, elected and inaugurated Jefferson Davis as president, and flew the Confederate flag for the first time. In May 1861, the Confederate seat of government was moved to Richmond, Virginia. With several additions, this Greek Revival building continues to serve as the Alabama State Capitol.

## MONTGOMERY UNION STATION AND TRAINSHED
### Water Street, Montgomery

Built for the Louisville & Nashville Railroad in 1897–1898, this complex consists of a metal-and-timber-framed train shed and a

Montgomery, *Pickensville, Pickens County. Courtesy of the U.S. Army Corps of Engineers.*

handsome brick Romanesque station. The train shed is significant for its construction techniques. Trusses and metal eyebars were adapted from bridge-building techniques for a structure serving a different purpose, which represented an important step in the evolution of American civil engineering. The station and shed currently house a bank, restaurant, and the Hank Williams Museum.

### ■ *Pickens County*

### *MONTGOMERY*
**Tom Bevill Visitor Center, Pickensville**

Looking more like a showboat than the stalwart workhorse it actually is, this steam-propelled sternwheeler snagboat was designed and built in 1925. Snagboats cleared rivers of countless obstructions, opening previously inaccessible regions to navigation. One of the few of its type left, *Montgomery* played a key role in the well-known 1970s Tenn-Tom project that created a navigable route between the Gulf of Mexico and the Ohio River by deepening the Tennesee and Tombigbee Rivers. It now rests on its laurels, or at least on its steel-plated hull, at a Corps of Engineers visitor center.

### ■ *Russell County*

### APALACHICOLA FORT SITE
**Address Restricted, Holy Trinity vicinity**

The Spanish completed a wattle-and-daub blockhouse at this site in 1690 as their northernmost outpost on the Chattahoochee River. It was intended to prevent the English from gaining a foothold among the Lower Creek Indians, who had already accepted English traders and rejected Spanish missionaries. The post was garrisoned for only a year and was abandoned and destroyed by its builders in 1691. It is not open to the public.

### FORT MITCHELL SITE
**.25 miles east of Alabama Route 165, Phenix City vicinity**

Protecting an important Chattahoochee River crossing of the Federal Road, this site symbolizes three different policies relating to Native Americans during the early 19th century. The first Fort Mitchell (1813) was built during the period when the Creek Indian Nation was defeated and forced to make land concessions. The second Fort Mitchell (1825) and related structures represented the federal government's attempts to honor its treaty obligations. When the Indian removal policy of the 1830s resulted in a final deportation of the Creeks, Fort Mitchell was abandoned. The site is a historical park open to the public.

### YUCHI TOWN SITE
**Address Restricted, Fort Benning vicinity**

This is the largest known town site associated with the Yuchi tribe, who occupied it from ca. A.D. 1716 until they and their Creek neighbors were removed to Oklahoma in 1836. Before the Yuchi occupation, an Apalachicola (ancestral Creek) settlement had been here. William Bartram, noted explorer and naturalist, described the Yuchi town in the late 18th century as "the largest, most compact, and best situated Indian town [he] ever saw" and lauded its "large and neatly built" habitations. It is not open to the public.

■ *Talladega County*

## J.L.M. CURRY HOME
**Highway 21, 3 miles east from center of Talladega**

Jabez Lamar Monroe Curry was agent for both the George Peabody Fund, established in 1867 to promote education in "the more destitute portions" of the South and Southwest, and the John F. Slaytor Fund, founded in 1882 to help educate "the lately emancipated population of the southern

states." Through his able administration of these funds, Curry encouraged the expansion and improvement of the public school system and the establishment of normal schools for training teachers throughout the South. This antebellum Greek Revival cottage was his home from 1850 to 1865.

## SWAYNE HALL
**Talladega College, Talladega**

Swayne Hall, a three-story building with pedimented portico, was completed in 1857 by slave labor as a white Baptist school. It was purchased by the American Missionary Association, with assistance from the Freedmen's Bureau, in 1867 to form the nucleus of a black college. Unlike institutions that emphasized vocational training, Talladega established a liberal arts program in 1890, helping to create a black middle class that would lead in the civil rights movement. It is not open to the public.

# ALASKA

■ *Aleutian Islands Borough–Census Area*

## ADAK ARMY BASE AND ADAK NAVAL OPERATING BASE
**Adak Island, Adak Station**

Established in 1942, these World War II installations were the westernmost in the nation for a short while and provided a stage for strikes against the Japanese-held Aleutian Islands, Kiska and Attu. Until very recently, Adak, located about 1,400 air miles southwest of Anchorage, remained an active naval station.

## ANANGULA SITE
**Address Restricted, Nikolski vicinity**

This island site was of paramount importance in the peopling of North America and represents the earliest known occupation in the Aleutians. Archeologists have found evi-

dence of ancient stone core and blade tools, which were buried deep beneath many layers of volcanic ash. Radiocarbon tests in 1975 dated human occupation as having occurred about 8,400 years earlier. The occupants were Eskimo-Aleuts who had migrated along the Alaska Peninsula land bridge that connected the Asian and North American continents. The occupants' maritime cultural orientation, tool industry, and racial resemblance to Eastern Siberians set them apart from other aboriginal North Americans.

## ATTU BATTLEFIELD AND U.S. ARMY AND NAVY AIRFIELDS
**Attu Island**

Attu Island, westernmost of the Aleutians, was the scene of the only World War II battle fought on the North American continent. Japanese forces landed in June 1942, which

*Church of the Holy Ascension, Unalaska Island, Aleutian Islands Borough–Census Area, 1961. Courtesy of NPS (Charles W. Snell).*

marked the apex of their expansion in the North Pacific. American troops recaptured the island after fierce combat in May 1943. During the conflict many Japanese soldiers took their own lives. The island was subsequently used as a launching site for bombing missions to Japan's home islands.

## CAPE FIELD
### Northeast section of Umnak Island, Fort Glenn

Constructed between January and April 1942, Cape Field's first runway was then the U.S. Army's most westerly airfield in the Aleutian Islands. In June 1942 aircraft from Cape Field participated in a counterattack after the Japanese attacked the Dutch Harbor naval and army installations on nearby Amaknak Island. Several days later aircraft flew missions against the Japanese who had occupied Kiska, another Aleutian Island. By the close of 1942, Fort Glen had 10,579 personnel, but its role as an advanced air base had been supplanted by facilities on Adak Island farther to the west. Buildings, runways, and World War II artillery emplacements remain.

## CHALUKA SITE
### Address Restricted, Nikolski vicinity

This deeply stratified Aleut village site lies at the southern end of the modern village of Nikolski on Umnak Island in the Aleutian chain. The site has yielded records of approximately the last 4,000 years of Aleut history, from the time of early sea mammal hunters

to their modern descendants, who continue to hunt in the same waters.

## CHURCH OF THE HOLY ASCENSION
### Unalaska, Unalaska Island

One of the oldest, largest, and most impressive of Alaska's Russian Orthodox churches, this 1894 wood-frame building is fronted with a three-story bell tower capped with an onion-domed cupola. Unalaska had long been a center of Russian Orthodoxy in Alaska, and a predecessor church on the site was built by Father Veniaminov, a missionary assigned to this post in 1824. He translated the Bible into the Aleut language and recorded Aleut customs and material culture.

## DUTCH HARBOR NAVAL OPERATING BASE AND FORT MEARS, U.S. ARMY
### Amaknak Island, Unalaska

Dutch Harbor, the U.S. Navy's westernmost base in Alaska in the 1940s, and Fort Mears are on Amaknak Island in Unalaska Bay, off the northern coast of Unalaska Island. In early June 1942, Japanese aircraft attacked Unalaska in a fierce two-day bombardment that resulted in 43 American deaths. At the time of the Japanese attack on Pearl Harbor these two bases were the only U.S. defenses in the Aleutian chain, and they continued as important coastal defenses throughout the war. Fortunately, additional batteries installed in anticipation of future raids proved unnecessary.

## JAPANESE OCCUPATION SITE
### Kiska Island

Kiska, one of the westernmost of the Aleutian Islands, was, along with Attu Island, invaded and occupied by the Japanese in June 1942. In the months that followed, they constructed a number of military installations, but after the fall of Attu and successful American attacks on Japanese submarines, the enemy departed. Their undetected withdrawal in July 1943 proved an embarrassment when an American force of 34,000 troops arrived to invade a deserted island 18 days later.

## SEAL ISLAND HISTORIC DISTRICT
### Pribilof Islands, Saint Paul Island

Seal herds on the Pribilof Islands have long attracted fur hunters: first, the native peoples of the Bering Sea area, and since the 18th century, people of many other nationalities. An international conservation agreement between the United States, the United Kingdom, Russia, and Japan (1911) has ensured the preservation of the flourishing herds on the islands of Saint Paul and Saint George, an example of the importance of international arbitration.

## SITKA SPRUCE PLANTATION
### Unalaska vicinity, Amaknak Island

Early Russian explorers noted the absence of trees on the Aleutian Islands, and in 1805 two- and three-year-old spruce trees were shipped from Sitka and planted here on Amaknak Island. The project, undertaken to make the Unalaska colony more self-sufficient, is the first known afforestation project on the North American continent. The number of trees planted is not known. In 1834 there were 24 trees. Today, 6 original trees remain, augmented by hundreds of new seedlings.

### ■ Bristol Bay Borough–Census Area
## BROOKS RIVER ARCHEOLOGICAL DISTRICT (NPS)
### Address Restricted, King Salmon vicinity

Brooks River, less than two miles long, connects Brooks and Naknek lakes and has been a site of human habitation for many centuries. Twenty well-preserved sites with 960 depressions, many of them remains of substantial semisubterranean houses, span some 4,500 years and represent nine cultural phases. Included in the district is the greatest concentration of Arctic Small Tool Tradition (1800–1100 B.C.) artifacts known in Alaska, possibly in all of North America.

## KIJIK ARCHEOLOGICAL DISTRICT (NPS)
### Address Restricted, Nondalton vicinity

Located in southwest Alaska on the shore of Lake Clark, Kijik Archeological District comprises an extensive former village of Dena'ina Athabaskan Indians, dating from pre-European contact to the abandonment of Kijik village ca. 1910. These sites provide an incomparable opportunity to recognize and study complex Athabaskan settlements within a limited geographical area.

### ■ Fairbanks–North Star Borough–Census Area
## LADD FIELD
### Fairbanks vicinity

This first U.S. Army airfield in Alaska, just east of Fairbanks, was begun in 1938. The first Army Air Corps troops arrived in 1940. During World War II the facility served as a cold weather experiment station, air depot for repair and testing, and principal base for the Air Transport Command. This lend-lease program transferred nearly 8,000 aircraft to Russian crews for use on the Russian front. Renamed Fort Wainwright after 1961, it continues as an active base, and many of its World War II structures remain.

## NENANA
### Alaskaland Park, Fairbanks

SS Nenana, a five-deck sternwheel steamboat with a length of 237 feet and beam of 42 feet, exemplifies the vessels that played an important part in the exploration, growth, and settlement of vast stretches of America. Launched in 1933, Nenana was commissioned by the Alaska Railroad to ply the Yukon, Nenana, and Tanana rivers. Designed to carry both freight and passengers, it served

Nenana, *Fairbanks, Fairbanks–North Star Borough–Census Area, 1971. Courtesy of State of Alaska, Division of History and Archeology.*

during World War II by transporting military supplies. Honorably discharged, it now rests in drydock as an exhibit in Alaskaland Park.

## GEORGE C. THOMAS MEMORIAL LIBRARY
**901 First Avenue, Fairbanks**

This log bungalow, built for a library originally established by the Episcopal Church, housed a 1915 meeting between U.S. government officials and native Alaskans that attempted to settle land and compensation claims. The longstanding dispute that arose was not finally resolved until the Alaska Native Claims Settlement Act was passed in 1971.

■ *Haines Borough–Census Area*

### FORT WILLIAM H. SEWARD
**Port Chilkoot, Haines vicinity**

Fort Seward, established in 1898 as the last of 11 Alaskan military posts created in response to the 1897–1904 gold rushes, also served as a military presence during boundary disputes with Canada. Never fortified, it was renamed Chilkoot Barracks in 1922, served as Alaska's only active military post until 1940, and was sold to private owners after World War II. A number of large, frame

officers quarters and barracks still stand in military precision around the rectangular parade ground.

■ *Juneau Borough–Census Area*

### FORT DURHAM SITE
**Address Restricted, Taku Harbor vicinity**

Constructed in 1840, Fort Durham was a log stockade surrounding a number of log houses, one of three posts established by the British Hudson's Bay Company in Russian Alaska. The site represents the British role in the struggle for control of the North Pacific fur trade and was built on land leased from the Russian-American Company. After serving three years, the fort was abandoned in favor of yearly visits by a Hudson's Bay company ship.

■ *Kenai Peninsula Borough–Census Area*

### HOLY ASSUMPTION ORTHODOX CHURCH
**Mission and Overland Streets, Kenai**

Holy Assumption is the most enduring representation of Russian culture and architecture in south central Alaska. The church, dating from the 1890s, is fronted by a square tower base supporting an octagonal cupola and an onion dome. Behind the tower, the square nave and polygonal sanctuary also have onion domes. The church is of dovetailed-log construction but was covered with beveled siding soon after its completion. Inside, a richly appointed iconostas contains several icons that predate the church. Nearby are the 1881–1894 rectory and the small, onion-domed Saint Nicholas Chapel (1906).

### YUKON ISLAND MAIN SITE
**Address Restricted, Yukon Island**

First excavated in the 1930s, the Yukon Island Main Site in Kachemak Bay was the first to produce artifacts attributable to the Kachemak tradition of Pacific Eskimo marine mammal hunters. The Kachemak people occupied an area extending from Kodiak Island to Cook Inlet for about two millennia, from 1500 B.C. to sometime around A.D. 500. Recent excavations at the site have turned up evidence of an even earlier cultural tradition, Ocean Bay, previously known primarily from sites in the Kodiak Archipelago dated at ca. 2000–4000 B.C.

## ■ *Kodiak Island Borough–Census Area*

## KODIAK NAVAL OPERATING BASE AND FORTS GREELY AND ABERCROMBIE
### Kodiak vicinity

Kodiak Naval Operating Base and Fort Greely were Alaska's principal advance bases when World War II broke out. A joint operations center established here directed Alaskan operations in 1942–1943. Ships and submarines from Kodiak played a critical role in the Aleutian campaign, and Fort Greely stood ready to repel invaders. Fort Abercrombie, established in April 1943 as a subpost of Fort Greely, is now a state historical park.

## RUSSIAN-AMERICAN MAGAZINE
### Main and Mission Streets, Kodiak

Built prior to 1808, this is Alaska's oldest Russian building. It was built as a warehouse for the Russian-American Company, Russia's monopolistic trading company, and is constructed of logs chinked with moss, then clapboarded. After the United States acquired Alaska, it was purchased by the Alaska Commercial Company, which sold it in 1911 to W. J. Erskine. It served as the Erskine family home until 1948. Since 1967, it has been a museum.

## THREE SAINTS BAY SITE
### Address Restricted, Old Harbor vicinity

This was the site of the first permanent Russian settlement in North America, established in August 1784 by Grigorii Shelikhov, who named it after one of his ships. The settlement served as a base for further exploration, and in 1793 the colony moved to a better harbor, now the city of Kodiak. Like many other migrants, the Russians settled on land that had attracted prehistoric peoples. The site also represents the Three Saints phase of the Kachemak tradition, the zenith of this pre-Eskimo culture on Kodiak Island.

## ■ *Nome Borough–Census Area*

## ANVIL CREEK GOLD DISCOVERY SITE
### Combined with Cape Nome Mining District, Nome vicinity

Gold was discovered at Anvil Creek on September 20, 1898, the first large placer strike made on the Alaskan mainland. In October, the Cape Nome Mining District was organized and claims were filed on 7,000 acres. This gold rush, Alaska's greatest, centered on Nome, in a region previously occupied by only a handful of inhabitants. Anvil Creek was designated a National Historic Landmark (NHL) in 1965, and in 1978 it was incorporated into the larger Cape Nome District NHL.

## CAPE NOME MINING DISTRICT DISCOVERY SITES
### Nome vicinity

As noted in the discussion of the Anvil Creek Gold Discovery Site, gold was discovered there on September 20, 1898. Soon, over 12,000 people were in Nome—all hoping to strike it rich in one way or another. The fact that the gold fields yielded more than $57 million between 1898 and 1910 proved that many of them did. Anvil Creek was incorporated into the larger Cape Nome District as a National Historic Landmark in 1978.

## IYATAYET SITE
### Address Restricted, Cape Denbigh Peninsula

Located on the northwest shore of Cape Denbigh on Norton Bay, this stratified site produced the first evidence of the Denbigh Flint Complex (2000–3000 B.C.) and the Norton Culture (500 B.C.–A.D. 400), both pivotal for the understanding of Arctic prehistory. Both were first identified here, making this the type site for both. Many elements of earliest-level artifacts found at the site have affinities with Old World cultures.

## WALES SITE
### Address Restricted, Wales vicinity

Located on Cape Prince of Wales, this site contains material that spans the period from the Birnirk culture, the earliest recognizable manifestation of modern Eskimo culture in Alaska (A.D. 500–900), to that of the present Eskimo inhabitants of the modern settlement of Wales. The Wales Site includes mounds, a midden, a present-day native Alaskan community, and the first site of the Thule culture discovered by archeologists in Alaska.

### ◼ *North Slope Borough–Census Area*

## BIRNIRK SITE
### Address Restricted, Barrow vicinity

Sixteen mounds arranged in three rows parallel to the Arctic Ocean beach mark the type site for the Birnirk culture (A.D. 500–900). The site has yielded important information on the Birnirk and its successor, the Thule culture. Both belong to the North Alaskan branch of the Northern Maritime tradition, the earliest manifestation of Eskimo culture in North Alaska. The site is near Point Barrow, northernmost point in Alaska.

## GALLAGHER FLINT STATION ARCHEOLOGICAL SITE
### Address Restricted, Sagwon vicinity

This site was discovered in 1970 during reconnaissance surveys for the trans-Alaska pipeline. A hunting stand and lithic workshop, it represents one of the earliest dated archeological sites in Northern Alaska and demonstrates strong affinities between indigenous peoples of Alaska and Siberia. It is located on a prominent glacial kame, a sand-and-gravel mound that afforded a commanding view of the game-rich tundra, accounting for its repeated use and occupation by humans over time.

## IPIUTAK SITE
### Address Restricted, Point Hope vicinity

This site at Point Hope is the type site for the Ipiutak culture that flourished in northwestern Alaska at about the beginning of the common era. Some 575 house depressions were mapped at the site when it was first excavated in the early 1940s, thus establishing it as one of the largest known prehistoric settlements in the Alaskan Arctic. The site is also significant for its elaborate burial goods and its early evi-

dence of the use of iron. Along with other nearby sites, it represents 2,000 years of continuous occupation of Point Hope.

## LEFFINGWELL CAMP SITE
### 58 miles west of Barter Island on Arctic coast, Flaxman Island

This small barrier island off Alaska's Arctic coast served as headquarters for pioneer scientific researcher and explorer Ernest de Koven Leffingwell from 1906 to 1914. Leffingwell produced the first accurate map of the area and was the first person to study the phenomenon of ground ice, now known as permafrost. Eskimos living on the island shared their survival skills and acted as guides. Their descendants still use the island for subsistence hunting and fishing.

### ◼ *Northwest Arctic Borough–Census Area*

## CAPE KRUSENTERN ARCHEOLOGICAL DISTRICT (NPS)
### Address Restricted, Kotzebue

Several hundred sites compose this vast archeological district in northwestern Alaska. The sites are situated along a series of 114 beach ridges, horizontally stratified, with the oldest sites farthest from the present coastline and the youngest on the most recently formed ridges. The sweep of Arctic prehistory, dating from about 5,000 years ago through cultures ancestral to modern Inupiat Eskimo occupation of the area, has been documented on these ridges, with even earlier sites identified on the cliffs above.

## ONION PORTAGE ARCHEOLOGICAL DISTRICT (NPS)
### Address Restricted, Kiana vicinity

For thousands of years herds of caribou have traversed this bend on the Kobuk River during their seasonal migrations between taiga (subarctic evergreen forests) and the tundra. These animals were crucial to the lives of ancient hunters who once occupied the Onion Portage site. By virtue of its incredible stratigraphic sequence of cultures, spanning a period of nearly 10,000 years, the Onion Portage site has proven to be one of the most important in Alaska for documenting the progression of cultural change over a long expanse of time.

■ *Sitka Borough–Census Area*

## ALASKA NATIVE BROTHERHOOD HALL
### Katlean Street, Baranof Island

The Tlingits founded the Alaska Native Brotherhood/Sisterhood Society in Sitka in 1912 to oppose discrimination and to obtain compensation for their lands. In 1914 the Society built this large frame building as a meeting hall and headquarters. It remains a symbol of the political power the group attained.

## AMERICAN FLAG-RAISING SITE
### Lincoln and Katlean Streets, Baranof Island, Sitka

On October 18, 1867, the Russian flag was lowered on Castle Hill, home of Alaska's Russian governors, and the American flag was raised. With this ceremony, accompanied by a brief exchange of statements, Alaska was transferred to the United States. This was the nation's first expansion into noncontiguous territory. Alaska was admitted to the Union on January 3, 1959, and on July 4 of that year, the 49-star American flag was flown for the first time from the same site. Although no structures remain, the site, rich in historical archeology, is now a park commemorating these events.

## RUSSIAN-AMERICAN BUILDING NO. 29
### 202–204 Lincoln Street, Baranof Island, Sitka

This mid 19th-century log structure was labeled No. 29 on the 1867 map entitled "The Settlement of New Archangel" that documented Russian-American Company property transferred to the United States. With the Bishop's House, it is one of only two Russian–built structures remaining in Sitka, which, as New Archangel, had been the capital of Russian America. Built to house company workers, it testifies to Russian exploration and settlement in Alaska.

## RUSSIAN BISHOP'S HOUSE (NPS)
### Lincoln and Monastery Streets, Baranof Island, Sitka

In addition to housing the bishop, this two-story clapboarded log structure, built by the Russian-American Company between 1842 and 1844, served as a seminary and as offices for the Russian Orthodox Church in Alaska. A 1980s restoration by the National Park Service revealed that it had originally contained a sophisticated heating and ventilation system. Now a museum, the Bishop's House provides an unrivaled glimpse into the life and architecture of Russian Alaska.

## SAINT MICHAEL'S CATHEDRAL
### Lincoln and Maksoutoff Streets, Baranof Island, Sitka

Alaska's most famous and familiar "Russian" building, the Cathedral of Saint Michael the

*Russian Bishop's House, Baranof Island, Sitka Borough–Census area, 1959. Courtesy of NPS.*

Archangel was originally constructed between 1844 and 1848. Built of logs, covered with clapboards, it was an outstanding example of Russian church architecture and the embodiment of Russian cultural influence in North America. The church burned to the ground in 1966 but has since been reconstructed with fireproof materials. The restoration was based on documentation made in 1960–1961 by the Historic American Buildings Survey. Fortunately, the cathedral's priceless collection of icons was removed during the fire and once again embellishes the gilded iconostas.

## SITKA NAVAL OPERATING BASE AND U.S. ARMY COASTAL DEFENSES
**Baranof Island, Sitka**

Formally commissioned as the Sitka Naval Air Station in October 1939, this facility was redesignated the Naval Operating Base in July 1942. During the first months of World War II it was one of the few installations prepared to protect the North Pacific against enemy incursion. Planes from the base patrolled southeast Alaskan waters, tracking reported submarines and looking for other enemy activity.

■ *Skagway-Yakutat-Angoon Borough– Census Area*

## CHILKOOT TRAIL AND DYEA SITE (NPS)
**Dyea to the Canadian border, Taiya River Valley**

The 35-mile Chilkoot Trail, beginning at Dyea and following the Yukon River before ascending to its 3,500-foot summit at Chilkoot Pass, was the preferred route by which thousands of prospectors reached Canada's Klondike gold fields from 1897 to 1899. Chilkoot was far steeper than the White Pass Trail that began six miles southeast at Skagway. After the White Pass and Yukon Route Railway was completed in 1900, Chilkoot was virtually abandoned, and Dyea, once boasting Alaska's largest brewery, soon became a ghost town.

## NEW RUSSIA SITE
**Yakutat vicinity**

New Russia was established in 1796, apparently as an effort to create a more stable base for colonizing efforts than then existed at the empire's fur trading posts. In 1805, Tlingits, who had used the area for otter hunting, attacked and destroyed the stockade. According to a Russian hunter, they left "not one log... standing on another." This pivotal event postponed European intrusion in the region and helped keep it open for later American traders and explorers.

## SKAGWAY HISTORIC DISTRICT AND WHITE PASS (NPS)
**Skagway vicinity**

Skagway served as a point of entry for prospectors on their way to strike it rich in the Upper Yukon and Klondike gold fields. At first competing with nearby Dyea, Skagway overtook its rival in 1900 when the White Pass and Yukon Route Railway was completed. Once Alaska's largest city, the former boomtown contains the state's finest collection of turn-of-the-century commercial structures, many of them incorporated in the Klondike Gold Rush International Historical Park. White Pass Trail, northeast of Skagway, crests at the 3,000-foot pass at the Canadian border.

■ *Southeast Fairbanks Borough– Census Area*

## EAGLE HISTORIC DISTRICT
**Mile 0, Taylor Highway, Eagle**

Fort Egbert and the adjoining town of Eagle, on the Yukon River close by the Canadian border, were, at the turn of the 20th century, interior Alaska's windows on the world. They served as a military, judicial, transportation, and communications hub, and it was from here that Roald Amundsen announced the first successful navigation of the long-sought Northwest Passage in 1905. A number of structures from the historic era remain. Among them are the U.S. Customs House and U.S. Courthouse, both open as museums.

*Kennecott Mines, Kennecott, Valdez-Cordova Borough—Census Area. Concentration Mill. Courtesy of NPS (Robert L. Spude).*

## ■ *Valdez-Cordova Borough—Census Area*

### BERING EXPEDITION LANDING SITE
#### Kayak Island, Katalla vicinity

In July 1741, George William Steller disembarked from the *St. Peter* to step ashore on the northwest coast of Kayak Island. Here, in a mission to find plants to treat an outbreak of scurvy on board ship, he attempted the first contact between Europeans and Alaskan natives, having "found signs of people and their doings." Steller served as naturalist and surgeon on an expedition commanded by Vitus Bering, and his recorded observations are among the first contributions to the West's knowledge of the natural and human history of the region.

### KENNECOTT MINES
#### North Bank, National Creek, east of Kennecott Glacier, Kennecott

One of the largest copper mines in the nation, Kennecott contained some of the country's highest-grade ore deposits. Still remaining at the foot of Bonanza Ridge is a phenomenal industrial complex, little changed since it closed in 1938. Representative of mining processes of the era, the camp contains the powerhouse, tramway station, bunkhouses, and commissary, all dominated by a 14-story concentration mill. The world's first successful ammonia-leaching plant, greatly increasing the amount of recoverable copper ore, went into operation here in 1916.

### PALUGVIK SITE
#### Address Restricted, Hawkins Island

This well-defined area on Hawkins Island contains almost the full range of Pacific Eskimo site types in Prince William Sound. Located in the traditional cultural area of the Chugach Eskimo, this stratified midden, excavated in the 1930s, gives evidence of long-established population and cultural traditions.

■ *Wrangell-Peterburgh Borough–Census Area*

## KAKE CANNERY
**1.5 miles south of Kake**

Kake Cannery, containing more than a dozen buildings constructed from 1912 to 1940, demonstrates trends and technology in the Pacific salmon canning industry. Largely a self-contained facility, the cannery complex includes warehouses, cannery buildings, and housing for workers, all connected via boardwalks. Utilizing foreign contract labor, primarily Chinese, Japanese, Filipino, and, to a lesser extent, Korean, Mexican, and black workers, salmon canning became Alaska's largest industry in the first half of the 20th century.

■ *Yukon-Koyukuk Borough–Census Area*

## DRY CREEK ARCHEOLOGICAL SITE
**Address Restricted, Lignite vicinity**

The multilayered Dry Creek site, located near the northern flank of the Alaska Range in the interior of the state, is one of the oldest radiocarbon-dated sites in Alaska. Its earliest level, dated at more than 11,000 years ago, has produced bifacial projective points and the bones of Pleistocene elk. The overlying level dates back more than 10,000 years and has yielded a completely different type of stone tool technology, known primarily for its small microblades. This later technology appears to have ties with artifact assemblages excavated in Siberia.

# ARIZONA

■ *Apache County*

## CASA MALPAIS SITE
**Springerville vicinity**

Situated on terraces of a fallen basalt cliff along the upper Little Colorado River, the site dates from late Pueblo III to early Pueblo IV (A.D. 1250–1325) times. Casa Malpais appears to incorporate features of both early and late Mogollon culture settlement patterns. Tours are offered by the Casa Malpais Foundation.

## HUBBELL TRADING POST (NPS)
**Hubbell Trading Post National Historic Site, Ganado**

During the heyday of the Indian trader, this was one of the most important trading posts in the American Southwest. Established in the 1870s, the still-operating post represents the varied interactions of Navajos and traders on their reservation. In addition to the actual post, or store, this National Historic Site includes the 1890s Hubell house.

■ *Cochise County*

## DOUBLE ADOBE SITE
**Address Restricted, Douglas**

This is where the distinctive pre-ceramic Cochise culture, a hunting and gathering society, was first recognized. This culture was the base from which a number of ceramic cultures, particularly the Mogollon, developed. Double Adobe has yielded information on southern Arizona's prehistoric climate, ecology, and animal life, all quite different from what they are today.

## FORT BOWIE AND APACHE PASS (NPS)
**13–15 miles south of Bowie**

Commanding the eastern entrance to Apache Pass, Fort Bowie was built in 1862 and was replaced in 1868 by a larger post. The fort played a vital role in the U.S. Army's campaigns against Cochise, chief of the Chiricahua Apache, and later against Geronimo. Because spring water was available and reliable, the mountain crossing was used by early settlers

*Fort Huachuca, Cochise County. Administrative building (left) and barracks (right), ca. 1898. Courtesy of the Fort Huachuca Museum.*

and travelers in the region. Traces of the Butterfield Trail and adobe walls of the fort remain at this National Historic Site.

## FORT HUACHUCA
### 3.6 miles west of Sierra Vista

This sprawling cavalry outpost, founded in 1877 between Tombstone and the U.S.-Mexican border, played a prominent role in the 1886 subjugation of the renegade Geronimo's Chiracahua Apache, the last significant Indian group ranging free of reservation restraints. The fort was also headquarters for the Army's four all-black regiments: the 9th and 10th Cavalry and the 24th and 25th Infantry. Many 1880s adobe and frame structures remain. One now serves as a museum on this still-active military installation.

## LEHNER MAMMOTH-KILL SITE
### Address Restricted, Hereford

The Lehner site, excavated in 1955–1956, is one of the outstanding mammoth hunting sites in the Americas. Clovis fluted spear points and stone butchering tools uncovered indicate that hunters killed and butchered nine mammoths that were watering here. Radiocarbon dates for the artifacts and bones place the kills at some 11,000 years ago and have served as controls for several scientific studies.

## PHELPS DODGE GENERAL OFFICE BUILDING
### Copper Queen Plaza, Bisbee

From 1896 to 1961 this building served as the headquarters of the Phelps Dodge mining company, and it is the company's only important early office building existing in the United States. This structure symbolizes the company's pioneer role in western copper mining, as well as its growth and adaptation from a family-owned East Coast mercantile house of the 1830s into a modern corporation. The former office now houses a mining museum.

## SAN BERNARDINO RANCH
### 17 miles east of Douglas

At the turn of the 20th century, John H. Slaughter's cattle ranching empire, San Bernardino Ranch, encompassed 100,000 acres on both sides of the border between Arizona and Mexico. Prior to 1884, when Slaughter began operations with a land lease, the area had been subject to Apache raids. The sprawling adobe ranch house and outbuildings, among them a stone bunkhouse, are part of a ranch museum established in 1982. The complex illustrates the continuity of cattle ranching in the American Southwest.

## SIERRA BONITA RANCH
### 10 miles southwest of Bonita (Cochise and Graham Counties)

Founded in 1872 by Colonel Henry C. Hooker to supply beef to army posts, mining camps, and Indian agencies, this was the first permanent American cattle ranch in Arizona, as well as the first to introduce graded stock into the territory. On the site of a former Spanish hacienda that had been destroyed by the Apache in the early 1800s, Hooker erected an adobe fortress to fend off attacks by first the Apache and later the cut-throats and rustlers of Sulphur Springs Valley.

## TOMBSTONE HISTORIC DISTRICT
**U.S. Route 80, Tombstone**

The "town too tough to die" is one of the best-preserved western frontier mining towns of the 1880s. It developed as a boom-town after silver was discovered in 1877, but most of the important properties remaining postdate a May 1882 fire. Tombstone, renowned for the "gunfight at the O.K. Corral," epitomizes the legendary reputation of the "Wild West."

### ■ *Coconino County*
## MARY JANE COLTER BUILDINGS (NPS)
**South Rim, Grand Canyon National Park**

These four structures were designed by architect and interior designer Mary Jane Colter, built by the Atchison, Topeka, and Santa Fe Railway, and managed by its con-cessioner, the Fred Harvey Company. Hopi House (1905), modeled after a Hopi pueblo, was built to merchandise Indian handicrafts in a historically accurate environment. Hermit's Rest, a refreshment stand, and the

*Mary Jane Colter Buildings, Coconino County. Courtesy of NPS (Laura Soulliere Harrison).*

Lookout, both dating from 1914, were designed to appear as if they had grown out of the rocky landscape. Colter's last major structure on the South Rim, Desert View Watchtower, was completed in 1932, long after the establishment of Grand Canyon National Park. Modeled after an Anasazi tower, it has notable interior spaces based on circular forms. All four structures respect their incomparable settings and reflect the cultural heritage of the area.

## EL TOVAR (NPS)
**South Rim, Grand Canyon National Park**

This rambling stone, log, and frame hotel bridges the stylistic gap between Victorian-era resort architecture and the rustic mode later deemed appropriate for such spectacu-lar natural settings. Designed by a staff archi-tect of the Atchison, Topeka, and Santa Fe Railway, it opened to the public in 1905. Located at the edge of the South Rim, the hotel became the focal point for the railway's Grand Canyon resort; it continues to provide food and lodging to visitors at one of the country's most popular national parks.

## GRAND CANYON DEPOT (NPS)
**South Rim, Grand Canyon National Park**

Built in 1909–1910, this log depot, just south of El Tovar, gave visitors their first impression of the rustic sense of place the Atchison, Topeka and Santa Fe Railway intended for its Grand Canyon "destination resort." It was one of the very few rustic depots of its peri-od and is the only one remaining in which logs were used as actual structural members, not merely as decoration.

## GRAND CANYON LODGE (NPS)
**Bright Angel Point, North Rim, Grand Canyon National Park**

This U-shaped, stone-and-log lodge, with more than 100 attendant log cabins, is the most intact rustic hotel development remaining in the National Parks from an era when railroads, in this instance the Union Pacific, constructed "destination resorts." The 1927–1928 lodge was rebuilt in 1936 after a devastating fire, but the original scale, mate-rials, and ambiance remain. Like the lodge, the attendant cabins were designed to har-

Grand Canyon Park Operations Building, South Rim, Coconino County. Courtesy of NPS (Laura Soulliere Harrison).

monize with their rocky, forested setting on the canyon's North Rim.

## GRAND CANYON PARK OPERATIONS BUILDING (NPS)

**South Rim off West Rim Drive, Grand Canyon National Park**

This stone, log, and frame building, erected in 1929, took its architectural cues from its surroundings. Roughly textured stone piers at the corners imitate the canyon's rock formations, and the log pillars they support have the diameters of surrounding trees. The building, now a Park Ranger office, is a prime example of the purposely rustic style employed by the Landscape Division of the National Park Service.

## GRAND CANYON POWER HOUSE (NPS)

**South Rim off West Rim Drive, Grand Canyon National Park**

This 1926 masterpiece of trompe l'oeil employs overscaled elements to disguise its true size. Designed as a Swiss chalet, the building has a second-floor balcony that, from a distance, appears to be a likely spot to rest one's elbows. As the railing is actually five feet tall, it would be easier to rest a chin than an elbow. Inside, the diesel equipment that provided power to structures on the canyon's South Rim until 1956 remains in place.

## GRAND CANYON VILLAGE (NPS)

**Grand Canyon National Park**

This village complex is the largest and most ambitious "town" ever developed by the National Park Service to provide for the needs of visitors, park staff, and concessioners. In addition to the discrete areas for each of its major functions, the village is remarkable for the consistent architectural idiom its buildings and landscape features present. As a testament to the success of the early-20th-century plan, Grand Canyon Village has maintained its integrity over the years in spite of the ever-increasing numbers of visitors to this popular national park.

## LOWELL OBSERVATORY

**1 mile west of Flagstaff**

When this privately funded observatory was founded in 1894 by Percival Lowell, it was the only significant center of pure scientific research in the Southwest. Lowell studied Mars (theorizing that it was inhabited by intelligent beings) and performed computations leading to the discovery of Pluto. Other Lowell researchers developed the science of dendrochronology and discovered that the universe continues to expand, now a basic tenet of modern astronomy. Nearby are an administration building (1914) and Lowell's mausoleum (ca. 1916), both designed to connote Saturn and its rings. The observatory is still in operation.

## C. HART MERRIAM BASE CAMP SITE

**Coconino National Forest, Little Springs**

Operating from this camp in the San Francisco Mountains, Dr. C. Hart Merriam, America's first bioecologist, conducted investigations that led to his formulation of the

Life Zone Concept in 1889. Merriam concluded that forms of life are peculiar to given altitudinal areas, or zones, and that particular regions had flora and fauna not found in others. His work was seminal in the development of the science of ecology.

## WINONA SITE
**Address Restricted, Winona**

The Winona site has yielded considerable detail on cultural developments in the Flagstaff area during the period immediately following the eruption of Sunset Crater in A.D. 1066. Between A.D. 1070 and 1130, a span of a little more than two generations, new ideas brought into the area by immigrants from neighboring regions caused rapid change in the local culture, which gradually blended to form a new pattern of life that marked these people as distinct from others in the Southwest.

■ *Gila County*
## KINISHBA RUINS
**Address Restricted, Whiteriver**

This partially reconstructed complex on the Fort Apache Indian Reservation consisted originally of a large pueblo that contained two large and seven small masonry structures. During its peak population, ca. 1300, it may have housed a population of 1,000. The inhabitants, who abandoned the site at about 1400, represented a blend of Mogollon and Anasazi cultures.

■ *Graham County*
## POINT OF PINES SITES
**Address Restricted, Morenci**

This archeological site, within the present San Carlos Indian Reservation, contains a considerable number of ruins indicating occupation from ca. 2000 B.C. to A.D. 1400. University of Arizona excavations at the site have contributed to concepts about the culture of the area.

## SIERRA BONITA RANCH
**10 miles southwest of Bonita (Cochise and Graham Counties)**

(See entry in Cochise County.)

■ *Maricopa County*
## GATLIN SITE
**Address Restricted, Gila Bend**

Probably first occupied sometime before A.D. 900, the Gatlin Site contains one of the few documented Hohokam platform mounds. Associated with the mound are pit houses, ball courts, middens, and prehistoric canals. The mound is rare as an excavated and documented platform mound from the sedentary period of Hohokam development that is still relatively intact.

## HOHOKAM-PIMA IRRIGATION SITES
**Hohokam-Pima National Monument, Phoenix**

The Hohokam-Pima Irrigation Sites are remnants of the prehistoric (A.D. 1150–1450) canal system used to irrigate crops in the Salt River Valley. Nineteenth-century Anglo settlers used portions of this extensive and efficient network of canals in later expanded reclamation projects.

## PUEBLO GRANDE RUIN AND IRRIGATION SITES
**Pueblo Grande City Park, Phoenix**

The prehistoric platform mound and associated archeological remains at Pueblo Grande mark one of the last surviving urban architectural sites of its kind in the southwestern United States. There is evidence that between A.D. 1100 and 1400, Pueblo Grande served as a Hohokam administration center for a major irrigation canal system. Because of its prehistoric significance, preeminent archeologists have conducted research at Pueblo Grande since the 1880s. The site is now part of a municipal park.

## TALIESIN WEST
**Eastern outskirts of Scottsdale**

This stone, concrete, and frame complex, begun in 1937–1938 and developed and altered over many years, served as architect Frank Lloyd Wright's winter quarters, office, and school of architecture for his Taliesin Fellowship. One of his masterworks, Taliesin

Painted Desert Inn, Navajo County. Courtesy of NPS (Laura Soulliere Harrison).

West expresses not only Wright's mature architectural concepts but also his educational theories and visions of society. Like its Wisconsin counterpart, Taliesin East (see Taliesin East, Iowa County, Wisconsin), the property is owned by the Frank Lloyd Wright Foundation.

■ *Mohave County*

## HOOVER DAM
### Black Canyon of the Colorado River

This 726-foot-tall concrete arch-gravity storage dam, begun in June 1933 and dedicated in September 1935, was the greatest achievement in hydraulic engineering since the Panama Canal. Among the Bureau of Reclamation's earliest and largest multipurpose dams, it harnessed the Colorado River to provide flood control, irrigation, recreation, and electric power. Hoover Dam has had far-reaching consequences in the industrial, agricultural, and urban development of the southwestern United States. Architecturally, its Art Deco style details with Indian motifs are notable. The dam is open to the public for tours of its interior construction and electric plant (also in Clark County, Nevada).

■ *Navajo County*

## AWATOVI RUINS
### Keams Canyon vicinity

Located on the Hopi Indian Reservation, Awatovi Ruins is the site of one of the most important Hopi Indian villages encountered by Coronado's men in 1540. It contains the remains of a 500-year-old pueblo and a 17th-century Spanish mission complex. Excavations were conducted at the site by the Peabody Museum in the 1930s.

## OLD ORAIBI
### 3 miles west of Oraibi, Hopi Indian Reservation

Potsherds date the founding of this pueblo to ca. A.D. 1150, making it in all likelihood the oldest continuously occupied village in the United States. The pueblo, located atop the westernmost mesa in the Hopi Indian Reservation, documents Hopi culture and history from a time before European contact to the present.

## PAINTED DESERT INN (NPS)
### Off U.S. Route 40, Petrified Forest National Park

Designed by National Park Service architect Lyle E. Bennett and crafted by Civilian Conservation Corps workers, this former inn is a major example of the Pueblo Revival style. The Trading Post Room is lit by a translucent skylight with glass painted in designs found on prehistoric Pueblo pottery. Murals added in 1947 are by Hopi artist Fred Kabotie. The inn closed in 1963, and the building is now operated as a museum in the Petrified Forest National Park.

■ *Pima County*

## AIR FORCE FACILITY MISSILE SITE 8
### 1580 West Duval Mine Road, Green Valley

Between 1963 and 1987, 54 Titan II intercontinental ballistic missile (ICBM) complexes were constructed and placed "on alert." Designed to survive a first-strike nuclear attack and to launch warheads, these weapons were America's response to the "missile gap" panic of the late 1950s and early 1960s. This museum complex displays aboveground and belowground command

*Air Force Facility Missile Site 8, Green Valley, Pima County. Courtesy of Titan II Museum (David K. Stumpf).*

and control facilities, the silo, and the sole remaining Titan II missile.

## DESERT LABORATORY
### Off West Anklam Road, west of Tucson

A great deal of the science of plant ecology, especially desert ecology, was formulated at this laboratory, established in 1903 by the Carnegie Institution to study "methods by which plants perform their functions under the extraordinary conditions existing in deserts." Until it closed in 1940, the laboratory was the center for the study of North American desert ecology. The buildings are now used as classrooms and research facilities by the University of Arizona.

## SAN XAVIER DEL BAC MISSION
### 9 miles south of Tucson

One of the finest Spanish Colonial churches in the country, this spectacular baroque masterpiece was built between 1783 and 1797 of desert materials by Papago Indians supervised by Spanish-American master craftsmen. The mission, founded in 1700 by Jesuits, represents the northern thrust of Nueva España. The Jesuits were later replaced by Franciscans, who consecrated the present building, which now serves as an active parish church.

## VENTANA CAVE
### Address Restricted, Santa Rosa

This mountain cave, located on the Papago Indian Reservation and excavated in 1941–1942, contained stratified deposits dating from ca. 11,000 B.C. that illustrated early human association with extinct Pleistocene mammals. Subsequent levels demonstrated a history of continuous occupation from ca. 2000 B.C.–A.D. 1400.

## ■ *Santa Cruz County*

## MISSION LOS SANTOS ANGELES DE GUEVAVI (NPS)
### 6 miles north of the U.S.-Mexican border, Nogales

Adobe ruins mark the site of this Jesuit mission built in 1745–1751 and abandoned in 1773. It was the first *cabecera,* or head church, founded by the Jesuits in the area and represents the northernmost extension of the order's mission chain in New Spain. The

*Mission Los Santos Angeles de Guevavi, Santa Cruz County. Courtesy of the Archeological Conservancy.*

mission, a component of Jesuit efforts to Christianize and acculturate the Piman Indians, is now part of Tumacacori National Historical Park.

## SAN CAYETANO DE CALABAZAS
**Address Restricted, Santa Cruz Valley vicinity**

Founded in 1756 by priests from nearby Mission Guevavi, the *cabecera,* or headquarters for the area, this complex was part of the Jesuits' missionary effort to acculturate Native Americans. The site now consists of adobe and stone ruins and includes archeological deposits of the best example of a *visita,* or visiting mission, in the nation. The mission was abandoned in 1786 after Apache raids.

## TUMACACORI MUSEUM (NPS)
**Tumacacori National Monument, Tumacacori**

This thoughtfully designed museum grouping was the result of a careful decision not to attempt a conjectural restoration of the actual mission ruins at Tumacacori but to erect an interpretive center based on a typical mission complex. Built by the National Park Service between 1937 and 1939, the museum is a handsome example of Mission Revival architecture that replicates architectural elements typical of the Sonoran missions and helps to relieve pressure on the fragile adobe remains of the mission itself.

## ■ *Yavapai County*
## JEROME HISTORIC DISTRICT
**Jerome**

Perched precariously on a 30-degree slope of Mingus Mountain, Jerome was the center of one of America's richest copper-producing areas in the late 19th and early 20th centuries. After the mines closed in 1953, Jerome rapidly became "America's largest ghost city." Now a state historical park, the town and surrounding mining area illustrate the activities associated with copper production.

## ■ *Yuma County*
## YUMA CROSSING AND ASSOCIATED SITES
**Yuma and vicinity**

First used by Native Americans, this natural crossing served as a significant transportation gateway on the Colorado River during the Spanish colonial and U.S. westward expansion periods. The surviving buildings of the Yuma Quartermaster Depot and Arizona Territorial Prison are the key features on the Arizona side of the border; across the river, in California, stand the surviving buildings of Fort Yuma, an army outpost that guarded the crossing from 1850 to 1885. The three sites are operated as state parks. (Also in Imperial County, California.)

# ARKANSAS

## ■ *Arkansas County*
## ARKANSAS POST (NPS)
**8 miles southeast of Gillett on Arkansas Routes 1 and 169**

A trading post established in 1686 near the mouth of the Arkansas River by Henry de Tonti, one of La Salle's lieutenants, became the first successful French settlement in the Lower Mississippi Valley. Over subsequent years, it was abandoned, reclaimed by the French, and later still served Spanish, then American, settlers. The vagaries of the Arkansas River necessitated several changes of location. This final site is now a National Memorial.

## MENARD-HODGES SITE
**Address Restricted, Nady**

This late prehistoric, protohistoric, and historic site contains two large mounds and several house mounds. It has been identified as the site of "Osotouy," a Quapaw Indian village. Near the village, Henri de Tonti established a fur trading post, the Arkansas Post, in 1686.

## ■ Clark and Cleveland Counties

### CAMDEN EXPEDITION SITES
**(Clark, Cleveland, Grant, Hempstead, Nevada, Oachita, and Pulaski Counties)**

The Camden Expedition (March 23–May 2, 1864), named after the town of Camden on the Ouachita River, involved a series of engagements and marches in which Union forces stationed at Little Rock and Fort Smith were to proceed to Shreveport, Louisiana, and connect with an amphibious expedition that would advance up the Red River valley. Once joined, the combined forces planned to strike into Texas. The two pincers never converged, and the columns suffered major losses in a series of battles with Confederate forces along their line of march. Trenches and breastworks remain at several of the battle sites, and a number are open as units of the Arkansas State Park system.

## ■ Cross County

### PARKIN INDIAN MOUND
**Parkin**

This is the type site of the Parkin phase, a Late Mississippian and protohistoric phase dating from A.D. 1000–1650. Although late-19th- and early-20th-century accounts mention a number of small mounds, only one large mound and the ditch enclosing the village area are now visible. The site may be the town of Casqui mentioned in the narratives of 16th-century Spanish explorer Hernando De Soto. Recent archeological investigations undertaken in the 1990s help support this contention. The mound is open as Parkin Archeological State Park. (See Nodena and Eaker site, Mississippi County.)

## ■ Desha County

### ROHWER RELOCATION CENTER CEMETERY
**Arkansas Highway 1, Rohwer vicinity**

Rohwer Relocation Camp was constructed in late summer and early fall of 1942, follow-

*Rohwer Relocation Center Cemetery, Rohwer, Desha County. Soldiers Memorial. Courtesy of Arkansas Historic Preservation Program, Department of Arkansas History.*

ing dictates of Executive Order 9066, which directed relocation of more than 110,000 Japanese aliens and Japanese-Americans from the Pacific Coast. Ten relocation camps were established in remote areas far distant from the Pacific. Rohwer, the most intact camp remaining, housed more than 10,000 evacuees during its three-year existence. Memorials to those who died here provide a poignant record of a troubled period in American history. (See Manzanar, Inyo County, California.)

## ■ Garland County

### BATHHOUSE ROW (NPS)
**Hot Springs National Park, east side of Central Avenue, Hot Springs**

Eight closely spaced bathhouses and attendant fountains, promenades, and stairways constitute the nation's largest group of facilities illustrating the 19th- and 20th-century spa movement. They also include a fascinating and eclectic collection of architectural styles: Neoclassical, Renaissance Revival, Spanish, and Italianate. Hot springs in this mountain valley have been regarded as places for healing since prehistoric times. In 1832 the area was set aside as a federal reserve. It became a national park in 1921. Fordyce Bathhouse is

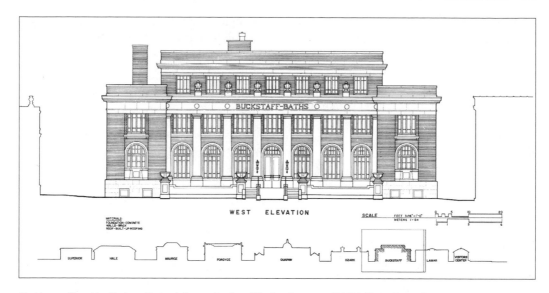

WEST ELEVATION

*Bathhouse Row, Hot Springs, Garland County. Buckstaff Baths. Courtesy of HABS (Dan Wininski).*

open to the public as a visitors' center and museum. Buckstaff Bathhouse still operates in its historic function as a public bathhouse.

### ◼ *Grant and Hempstead Counties*
### CAMDEN EXPEDITION SITES
**(Clark, Cleveland, Grant, Hempstead, Nevada, Oachita, and Pulaski Counties)**

(See entry under Clark County.)

### ◼ *Lee County*
### BEGINNING POINT OF THE LOUISIANA PURCHASE LAND SURVEY
**13 miles northwest of Marvell, Blackton vicinity (Lee, Monroe, and Phillips Counties)**

This is the initial point from which lands acquired in the Louisiana Purchase of 1803 were subsequently surveyed, beginning in 1815. From this spot, in an eastern Arkansas swamp, land surveys for all or parts of Arkansas, Louisiana, Oklahoma, Missouri, Kansas, Colorado, Nebraska, Iowa, Minnesota, North and South Dakota, Wyoming, and Montana were measured. The site was rediscovered in 1921 during a resurvey of local county lines, and a granite monument was erected in 1926. The site is now located in Louisiana Purchase State Park.

### ◼ *Lonoke County*
### TOLTEC MOUNDS SITE
**Southwest U.S. Route 165, Scott vicinity**

A large ceremonial complex and village site, Toltec Mounds represents occupation during the Coles Creek period (ca. A.D. 700–1000) and may yield information about the interaction between Lower and Central Mississippi Valley cultures. At the time the site was designated a National Historic Landmark in 1980, it was dedicated as Toltec Mounds Archeological State Park.

### ◼ *Mississippi County*
### EAKER SITE
**Address Restricted, Blytheville vicinity**

This is the largest and most intact Late Mississippian Nodena phase (ca. A.D. 1400–1700) village site within the Central Mississippi Valley. Containing some 50 acres, it is a protohistoric and historic period palisaded ceremonial mound and village complex with considerable research potential, especially in determining the relation between the Nodena phase and the historic Quapaw tribe. (See Nodena Site, Mississippi County, and Parkin Indian Mound, Cross County.)

## NODENA SITE
### Address Restricted, Wilson

Located on Nodena Plantation, from which it derives it name, Nodena is the type site for an important Late Mississippian cultural component, the Nodena phase, which dates from about A.D. 1400–1700 (contemporary with the Parkin phase). The first excavations here occurred in 1897. (See Eaker Site, Mississippi County, and Parkin Indian Mound, Cross County.)

■ *Monroe County*

## BEGINNING POINT OF THE LOUISIANA PURCHASE LAND SURVEY
### 13 miles northwest of Marvell, Blackton vicinity (Lee, Monroe, and Phillips Counties)

(See entry under Lee County.)

■ *Nevada and Oachita Counties*

## CAMDEN EXPEDITION SITES
### (Clark, Cleveland, Grant, Hempstead, Nevada, Oachita, and Pulaski Counties)

(See entry under Clark County.)

■ *Phillips County*

## BEGINNING POINT OF THE LOUISIANA PURCHASE LAND SURVEY
### 13 miles northwest of Marvell, Blackton vicinity (Lee, Monroe, and Phillips Counties)

(See entry under Lee County.)

■ *Pulaski County*

## CAMDEN EXPEDITION SITES
### (Clark, Cleveland, Grant, Hempstead, Nevada, Oachita, and Pulaski Counties)

(See entry under Clark County.)

## LITTLE ROCK CENTRAL HIGH SCHOOL (NPS)
### 14th and Park Streets, Little Rock

On September 24, 1957, President Dwight D. Eisenhower federalized the Arkansas National Guard and ordered the 101st Airborne Division to assist the desegregation of Little Rock Central High School. The next morning troops escorted nine black teenagers through an angry, jeering crowd to begin the fall semester. This was the first major confrontation in implementing the Supreme Court's 1954 *Brown v. Board of Education of Topeka* decision.

## OLD STATE HOUSE, LITTLE ROCK
### 300 West Markham, Little Rock

From 1912 to 1916, the Arkansas State Board of Health, in partnership with the University of Arkansas Medical School, worked from this building on successful campaigns to control or eradicate hookworm, a scourge of the South, and malaria, a disease that plagued much of the planet. Arkansas's drive to eradicate malaria in the rest of the United States and the world, carried out in the town of Crossett, constituted a success long acclaimed in the history of public health. The office of the surgeon general distributed nationwide a report of the Crossett experiment as *Public Health Bulletin No. 88,* and this detailed description became the formula for sanitation workers around the world. After restoration work is completed, the building will be open to the public.

## JOSEPH TAYLOR ROBINSON HOUSE
### 2122 Broadway, Little Rock

This early-20th-century frame house was the home of Joseph Taylor Robinson (1872–1937) from 1930 until his death. Taylor was Senate majority leader during the early days of Franklin D. Roosevelt's administration, and his ability to keep the "Senate's nose to the grindstone" played a major role in the successful passage of New Deal acts during the president's first "100 days." This was the period when such epochal laws as Emergency Banking, Civilian Conservation Corps, Federal Emergency Relief, Agricultural Adjustment, and Tennessee Valley Authority were passed. The house functions as Hope Lodge, a hospice for cancer patients.

■ *Sebastian County*

## FORT SMITH (NPS)
### Fort Smith

Established in 1817 near the confluence of the Arkansas and Poteau Rivers, the first fort at this site was among the earliest U.S. mili-

Fort Smith, Fort Smith, Sebastian County. Commissary Building, 1940. Courtesy of HABS (Lester Jones).

tary posts in the Missouri Territory. The fort's purpose was to control encroachment into Osage lands by both the Cherokee and westward-moving American settlers. A second fort, begun in 1838 a short distance from the site of the first, was garrisoned until the U.S. District Court for the Western District of Arkansas moved to the town of Fort Smith in 1871.

# CALIFORNIA

## ■ Alameda County

### CITY OF OAKLAND
**FDR Memorial Pier, Jack London Square, Oakland**

This steel-hulled tugboat was launched late in 1940 as the USS *Hoga* (after a Sioux word for "fish") and served heroically during the Japanese bombardment of Pearl Harbor the next year. *Hoga* fought fires on the battleships *Nevada* and *Arizona* and later participated in damage repair to keep the harbor open as an active naval base. At war's end it was leased to the City of Oakland, renamed, and served as a fireboat until its retirement in 1993. *City of Oakland* is the only surviving yard craft that was present at Pearl Harbor.

### FIRST CHURCH OF CHRIST, SCIENTIST
**2619 Dwight Way, Berkeley**

In 1910 five members of the Berkeley congregation asked architect Bernard Maybeck to design "a church that would look like a church" and be built of materials "that are what they claim to be, not imitations." His redwood-and-concrete response to the commission juggles stylistic elements from Byzantine, Romanesque, Gothic, and Japanese architecture, incorporating them in a wholly original manner. The church has been called one of the most extraordinary and charming ecclesiastical structures in America.

### HORNET
**USS *Hornet* Air, Sea and Space Museum, Pier 3, Alameda Point**

Launched in 1943, this Essex class aircraft carrier was part of the wartime buildup of the U.S. carrier force during World War II. *Hornet's* distinguished war career included participation in the invasion of Saipan and the Battle of the Philippine Sea; amphibious landings on Palau, the Philippines, Iwo Jima, and Okinawa; and strikes against the Japanese home islands. *Hornet* was later reactivated for

Hornet, *Alameda Point, Alameda County, 1943. Courtesy of U.S. Naval Institute.*

duty in both the Korean and Vietnam conflicts and gained fame in 1969 as the recovery vessel for the command modules and
crews of the first two manned landings on
the moon, the missions of *Apollo 11* and
*Apollo 12.*

## LAKE MERRITT WILD DUCK REFUGE
**Grand Avenue, Oakland**

This was America's first official wildlife
refuge, established March 18, 1870. It is a
small portion of Lake Merritt, a 160-acre
saltwater estuary surrounded by downtown
Oakland and maintained by the city. The
refuge is immensely popular with ducks and
people alike. Thousands of the former rest
and nest here, and tens of thousands of the
latter come to watch.

## LIGHTSHIP WAL-605, *RELIEF*
**Oakland Estuary in Brooklyn Basin, Oakland**

Built in 1904 and originally associated with
the Overfalls lightship station off the
Delaware coast, WAL-605 is the last steam-
powered lightship remaining in the United
States. From 1930 to 1950 it served as the
*San Francisco* and was renamed the *Relief* in
1951. *Relief* ended its career as a replacement
vessel at all Pacific Coast stations. Retired in
1975, *Relief* represents the end of more than
a century and a half of American lightship
operation.

## JOAQUIN MILLER HOUSE
**Joaquin Miller and Sanborn Drive, Oakland**

Joaquin Miller, "Poet of the Sierras," purchased property in the Oakland Hills in
1886 and built this small three-room frame
house, dubbing it the "Abbey." Miller, whose
writings deal with exploits of Indians, out-
laws, and pioneers, also erected stone monuments to Robert Browning, John C.
Fremont, and Moses on the property, which
is now an Oakland city park.

## PARAMOUNT THEATRE
**2025 Broadway, Oakland**

Oakland's Paramount Theatre is one of
America's greatest Art Deco movie palaces.
Designed by Timothy Pflueger of San
Francisco, it has an extraordinary tiled facade
dominated by two monumental Byzantine
figures, but it is the interior that is most
spectacular. The lobby contains a 40-foot-
high sculpture of leaves of frosted glass indi-
rectly lit, which Pflueger called a "fountain
of light." When the theater opened in
December 1931, it was the largest auditorium on the West Coast, seating 3,476 in gilded splendor. The Paramount was restored in
the 1970s as a community cultural center
and now presents symphony concerts, dance
recitals, variety shows, and, of course, movies.

## *POTOMAC*
**FDR Memorial Pier, Jack London Square, Oakland**

One of three surviving presidential yachts,
*Potomac* served only one president, Franklin D.
Roosevelt. From 1936 to 1945, it was a
major symbol of his presidency and served
him in the role of a "Camp David." *Potomac*
was docked 20 minutes from the White

*Paramount Theater, Oakland, Alameda County. Courtesy of HABS (Jack E. Boucher).*

House, and the president could go there to contemplate long-range decisions and hold meetings removed from day-to-day office pressures. Before being refitted as the *Potomac*, it was the Coast Guard patrol boat *Electra*. It is now operated by the nonprofit Potomac Association and is open year-round for dockside tours.

## ROOM 307, GILMAN HALL, UNIVERSITY OF CALIFORNIA
### University of California at Berkeley

On February 23–24, 1941, in this small research laboratory in the attic of Gilman Hall at the University of California at Berkeley, the man-made element plutonium was first identified. This momentous discovery led to the development of atomic explosives used in 1945 to end the war with Japan and in the subsequent development of nuclear energy reactors.

## ■ *Contra Costa County*
### JOHN MUIR HOUSE (NPS)
**440 Alhambra Avenue, Martinez**

This handsome Italianate house, built of redwood in 1882, was home to John Muir from 1890 until his death in 1914. Muir, famed conservationist and writer, founded the Sierra Club and has been referred to as the "father of the National Park System." It was designated a National Historic Site in 1964. The National Park Service has restored the mansion and the adjacent Martinez Adobe, the oldest building in Martinez. Both are open to the public.

### TAO HOUSE (NPS)
**Eugene O'Neill National Historic Site, Danville vicinity**

Eugene O'Neill, American playwright and winner of the Nobel Prize for literature in 1936, composed some of his most significant work here, including his autobiographical masterpiece, *Long Day's Journey into Night*. O'Neill and his wife lived in the comfortable "pseudo-Chinese" house from 1937 to 1944, naming it after a Taoist concept translated roughly as "the right way of life." Tao House became part of the Eugene O'Neill National Historic Site in 1976. (See Monte Cristo Cottage, New London County, Connecticut.)

*John Muir House, Martinez, Contra Costa County. Courtesy of NPS (Fred Mang, Jr.).*

■ *El Dorado County*

## COLOMA
**7 miles northwest of Placerville**

The discovery of placer gold at Coloma on January 24, 1848, resulted in the greatest series of gold strikes on the North American continent. The initial strike was at John A. Sutter's sawmill on the south fork of the American River. Coloma developed around the mill as a regional trading center when "forty-niners" flocked to the region's mining camps. Coloma declined after deposits were exhausted in the late 1850s, but the mill and most of the town are now a state park.

■ *Humboldt County*

## GUNTHER ISLAND SITE 67
**Address Restricted, Eureka**

When this huge shell mound, encompassing approximately six acres and attaining depths up to 14 feet, was excavated, it proved to typify the late prehistoric period and was instrumental in outlining the prehistory of the northern California coast. During historic times the site was occupied by a Wiyot Indian village.

■ *Imperial County*

## YUMA CROSSING AND ASSOCIATED SITES
**Yuma and vicinity**

First used by Native Americans, this natural crossing served as a significant transportation gateway on the Colorado River during the Spanish colonial and U.S. westward expansion periods. The surviving buildings of the Yuma Quartermaster Depot and Arizona

Territorial Prison are the key features on the Arizona side of the border; across the river, in California, stand the surviving buildings of Fort Yuma, an army outpost that guarded the crossing from 1850 to 1885. The three sites are operated as state parks (also in Yuma County, Arizona).

■ *Inyo County*

## BIG AND LITTLE PETROGLYPH CANYONS
**Address Restricted, China Lake**

These two canyons deep within the Coso Mountains are among the most spectacular petroglyph areas known in the western United States, exhibiting more than 20,000 designs. Among the most popular subjects depicted by primitive artists of at least two cultural phases were bighorn sheep, deer, and antelope.

## MANZANAR WAR RELOCATION CENTER
**Lone Pine vicinity**

Manzanar was the first of ten so-called American concentration camps in which people of Japanese descent, most of them American citizens, were taken from their West Coast homes as a security measure against possible sabotage and espionage during World War II. Some 10,000 people were herded into barracks at this camp in the Owens Valley desert, having been accused of no crime nor given any hearing or trial. The camp closed in 1945. (See Rohwer Relocation Center Cemetery, Desha County, Arkansas, and Harada House, Riverside County.)

*Manzanar War Relocation Center, Lone Pine, Inyo County. Military police post. Courtesy of HABS (Brian Grogan).*

## ◾ *Kern County*

### ROGERS DRY LAKE
**Edwards Air Force Base, Mojave Desert vicinity (Kern and San Bernardino Counties)**

This dry lake bed provided a natural laboratory for the flight testing of aircraft on the cutting edge of aerospace and aviation technology. First used in 1933, the lake bed forms the largest natural landing field in the world. It is the primary resource associated with establishment of Edwards Air Force Base, the world's premier flight testing and research center.

### WALKER PASS
**60 miles northeast of Bakersfield**

John Charles Fremont, returning in 1844 from his second topographical expedition to California, suggested that this pass through the southern Sierra Nevada be named for Joseph R. Walker, explorer, fur trapper, and guide, who led the first immigrant wagon train through it into California in 1843. Native Americans had shown the still remote pass to Walker in 1834.

## ◾ *Klamath County*

### LOWER KLAMATH NATIONAL WILDLIFE REFUGE
**Lower Klamath Lake, East of Dorris (Klamath County and Siskiyou County, Oregon)**

This first large area of public land to be reserved as a wildlife refuge was superimposed in 1908 on an existing federal reclamation project to drain the Klamath Basin wetlands for agricultural purposes. In 1940 measures were initiated to bring the refuge back to productivity, and with the introduction of scientific management principles into wildlife conservation, it again attracts migratory waterfowl in great numbers. The refuge provides an outstanding illustration of conflicts between reclamation and conservation interests and their potential resolution.

## ◾ *Los Angeles County*

### ANGELUS TEMPLE
**1100 Glendale Boulevard, Los Angeles**

Angelus Temple was completed in 1923 as the base of operations for Aimee Semple

*Bradbury Building, Los Angeles, Los Angeles County. Interior, 1965. Courtesy of HABS (Marvin Rand).*

McPherson, flamboyant pioneer in the field of radio evangelism. McPherson incorporated entertainment as part of her pentecostal "Foursquare Gospel" message. Calling herself "everybody's sister," she also preached a social ministry, and a temple commissary dispensed food to thousands of migrants to Los Angeles before, during, and after the Depression. The mammoth concrete-and-steel auditorium, half church and half theater, surmounted by a low saucer dome, continues as the home of the church McPherson founded.

### BRADBURY BUILDING
**304 S. Broadway, Los Angeles**

Completed in 1893, this unique five-story office building was designed by George H. Wyman, who had no formal architectural or engineering training at the time. The heavy sandstone exterior leaves one unprepared for the cage of light-filled glass within; the whole is a cobweb of cast iron covered with delicate Art Nouveau ornamentation.

### DAVID B. GAMBLE HOUSE
**4 Westmoreland Place, Pasadena**

Architect brothers Charles S. and Henry M.

Greene created one of America's finest expressions of the Arts and Crafts movement in this summer house, built in 1908. Structural woodwork is openly expressed and forms an essential element in the composition and design. Ralph Adams Cram once said of the Greenes and their California contemporaries that their work displays "an honesty that is sometimes almost brazen." The Gamble heirs presented the house to the city of Pasadena and the University of Southern California in 1966, and it is open to the public.

## HALE SOLAR LABORATORY
**740 Holladay Road, Pasadena**

Completed in 1925, Hale Solar Observatory is important for its association with George Ellery Hale, the person most responsible for the rise of the science of astrophysics in the United States. Hale's scientific contributions were numerous, especially in the area of astronomy. In the latter part of Hale's life, the laboratory was his office and workshop, where he studied the sun with instruments of his own design.

## EDWIN HUBBLE HOUSE
**1340 Woodstock Road, San Marino**

This two-story California Mission style stucco house was the home of one of America's greatest astronomers from 1925, when it was built, until his death in 1953. Among other accomplishments, Hubble discovered extragalactic nebulae, or galaxies, and their recession from each other.

## LANE VICTORY
**Berth S4, Port of San Pedro, San Pedro**

During World War II, 414 Victory Ships, designed to be faster and more efficient than Liberty Ships, were built to transport American supplies and troops to the European and Pacific theaters of war. *Lane Victory*, named for the black educator Isaac Lane, is the last of its class to retain integrity of original design, with all its wartime equipment intact. It is now docked in San Pedro as a memorial to Merchant Marine veterans of World War II.

## LITTLE TOKYO HISTORIC DISTRICT
**301–349 East First Street, 110–120 San Pedro, 119 Central Avenue, Los Angeles**

This small historic district, also known as Japantown, lies directly southeast of the Los Angeles Civic Center. Little Tokyo served as a haven and foothold for newly arriving Japanese and before World War II was the heart of America's largest Japanese–American community. It remains the historical focal point for Japanese-Americans in Los Angeles.

## LOS ANGELES MEMORIAL COLISEUM
**3911 South Figueroa Street, Los Angeles**

This world-renowned stadium was built in 1921–1923 to seat 75,000 and was later enlarged to a capacity of 101,574 for the 1932 Olympic Games. During that tenth Olympiad, the Olympic Village and victory podium, now standard features of the games, were introduced. The elliptical, reinforced concrete, cast-in-place structure was refitted as the centerpiece of the 1984 Olympics. Even with its changes, this huge sports facility retains the Art Moderne spirit envisioned by its original architects, John and Donald Parkinson.

## LOS CERRITOS RANCH HOUSE
**4600 Virginia Road, Long Beach**

This two-story adobe-and-frame ranch house, among the largest built in Mexican California, combines a traditional Spanish-Mexican hacienda plan with Monterey Colonial details. The U-shaped complex surrounds a large patio and is fronted by an expansive two-story porch. Built in 1844, the house was restored in 1930 and was purchased by the City of Long Beach in 1955. It is now operated as a museum by the city.

## RALPH J. SCOTT
**Berth 85, San Pedro**

On active duty since 1925, *Ralph J. Scott* is an excellent example of a high-speed, shallow-draft American fireboat, a type that has mostly been phased out of service. Operating out of a berth in San Pedro, the heart of the Port of Los Angeles, *Ralph* has fought many water-

Upton Sinclair House, Monrovia, Los Angeles County, 1971. Courtesy of NPS (Robert S. Gamble).

Twenty-Five-Foot Space Simulator, Pasadena, Los Angeles County. Courtesy of the JPL Facilities Office.

front fires during its long and distinguished career. Its name honors a former Chief Engineer of the Los Angeles Fire Department.

## ROSE BOWL
### 991 Rosemont Avenue, Brookside Park, Pasadena

The Rose Bowl, first and most renowned of the nation's postseason college football "bowl games," was established in 1916. Since 1922 this elliptical concrete stadium has hosted the game every New Year's Day except for one year during World War II. The Rose Bowl also commemorates the civic work of the Pasadena Tournament of Roses Association, which built the stadium and sponsors the annual flower festival, parade, and game. The Rose Bowl was also a venue for events of the 1932 and 1984 Olympics.

## SANTA MONICA LOOFF HIPPODROME
### 276 Santa Monica Pier, Santa Monica

This architectural fantasy was built by Charles Looff in 1916 to shelter one of his carousels. It is now the principal historic element of once-extensive amusement facilities at the Santa Monica Amusement Pier. It was restored in 1977–1981, and a carousel, although not the Looff original, still whirls around inside.

## UPTON SINCLAIR HOUSE
### 464 Myrtle Avenue, Monrovia

From 1942 until 1966 this was the principal home of Upton Sinclair, one of the most influential American novelists in the area of social justice. Virtually all of Sinclair's later works were written here in this neo-Mediterranean house, which is still privately owned.

## SPACE FLIGHT OPERATIONS FACILITY
### Jet Propulsion Laboratory, Pasadena

The Jet Propulsion Laboratory serves as the primary NASA center for the unmanned exploration of the planets. The Space Flight Operations Facility (1963) has as its hub the Network Operations Control Center, a vast complex of consoles, video displays, and various communication links, through which NASA controls and monitors its unmanned spacecraft flying in deep space.

## TWENTY-FIVE-FOOT SPACE SIMULATOR
### Jet Propulsion Laboratory, Pasadena

Constructed in 1961, this 85-foot-high, stainless steel cylindrical vessel at the Jet Propulsion Laboratory was designed to provide space simulation for testing spacecraft under conditions of extreme cold, high vacuum, and intense solar radiation. Ranger, Surveyor, Mariner, and Voyager are among the classes of spacecraft that have been tested here over the years.

## WATTS TOWERS
### 1765 East 107th Street, Los Angeles

These strange, intricate, and colorful constructions were an extraordinary incarnation of Italian immigrant Simon Rodia's memories of his homeland and a testimony to his affection for his adopted nation. He built the three tall towers (the tallest is almost 100 feet) and six short ones (the shortest is 15 feet) out of steel, reinforced concrete, and mosaic tile over a 33-year span from 1921 to 1954. Bridging gaps between architecture, engineering, and sculpture, they are among the nation's finest examples of naive art and have become a well-loved symbol of Los Angeles.

## WELL NO. 4, PICO CANYON OIL FIELD
### About 10 miles north of San Fernando

Pico Canyon, first explored for its oil potential in the 1860s, became the birthplace, and then the center, of California's petroleum industry in the 1870s and 1880s. On September 26, 1876, Well No. 4 was drilled to a depth of 370 feet and began producing a daily flow of 25 barrels. After deeper drilling, it produced 70 barrels per day. From the Pico Canyon field, oil industry pioneers went on to explore other fields, and by 1922 California had become the second-ranking oil-producing state in the nation.

■ *Marin County*
## MARIN COUNTY CIVIC CENTER
### San Rafael

This monumental, dramatically sited governmental complex is the last major work of architect Frank Lloyd Wright. The groundbreaking ceremony took place in 1960, a year after his death. One of the finest expressions of Wright's "organic architecture," the center has a rotunda from which two long wings extend at different angles. Repetitive arches establish a horizontal rhythm, coun-

tered by a 172-foot triangular tower. On the grounds is a U.S. Post Office, Wright's sole federal commission.

## POINT REYES LIFEBOAT STATION (NPS)
### Point Reyes National Seashore, Drakes Bay, Point Reyes

Heavy fog, high winds, and angry surf prompted the construction of a lifeboat station at the treacherous Point Reyes peninsula. Built in 1927 to replace a late-19th-century lifesaving station, this two-story frame boathouse is the only unaltered example of a once common type remaining on the Pacific coast. Thirty-six-foot motorized life-boats were launched from its railed launch ways, and after rescue missions were accomplished, hauled back with a winch. The officer-in-charge's quarters and other structures survive.

## UNITED STATES IMMIGRATION STATION, ANGEL ISLAND
### Angel Island State Park, Tiburon

The U.S. Immigration Station at Angel Island was the major West Coast processing center for immigrants from 1910 to 1940. What Ellis Island symbolizes to Americans of European heritage who immigrated on the East Coast, Angel Island symbolizes to Americans of Asian heritage on the West Coast. The largest island in San Francisco Bay, Angel Island was used as a prisoner of war camp during World War II. It was declared surplus in 1946 and since 1963 has been a California state park.

■ *Mariposa County*
## THE AHWAHNEE (NPS)
### Yosemite National Park, Yosemite Valley

This resort hotel at the eastern end of Yosemite Valley is named with a local Indian word meaning "deep, grassy meadow." Carefully constructed of rough-cut granite and concrete stained to imitate wood, designed to blend with its inspiring surroundings, the hotel opened in July 1927. Wrought-iron fittings, stained-glass windows, and murals based on Indian designs enhance its intentionally rustic atmosphere.

## LECONTE MEMORIAL LODGE (NPS)
### Yosemite National Park, Yosemite Valley

This small lodge was built in 1903, then moved a short distance west of its original site in 1919. It continues to serve as a reading room and information center maintained by the Sierra Club, which once thought of establishing headquarters in its namesake Sierra Nevada. The building relates handsomely to its setting, with rough stone walls and exaggeratedly steep roof lines suggestive of the cliffs that surround Yosemite Valley.

## RANGERS' CLUB (NPS)
### Yosemite National Park, Yosemite Valley

Stephen T. Mather, first director of the National Park Service, personally funded this U-shaped frame structure built to house rangers in Yosemite Park. The rustic chalet with board-and-batten siding is evidence of Mather's commitment to an architectural aesthetic appropriate for national parks.

## WAWONA HOTEL AND THOMAS HILL STUDIO (NPS)
### Yosemite National Park, Highway 41, Wawona

This seven-building group consists of the Wawona Hotel and annex, several cottages, manager's house, and the Hill Studio. Constructed between 1876 and 1918, the frame buildings with broad, encircling porches constitute the largest and best-preserved Victorian-era resort hotel complex within a National Park. Landscape painter Thomas Hill built his studio/sales room by 1886, and it served these uses until his death in 1908.

### ■ *Mendocino County*

## MENDOCINO WOODLANDS RECREATIONAL DEMONSTRATION AREA
### 11301 Little Lake Road, Mendocino vicinity

This is one of the best remaining examples of recreational demonstration area (RDA) planning and design in the country. The RDAs were a new kind of state park planned by the National Park Service during the New Deal. They accommodated private nonprofit organizations that operated sum-

*The Ahwahnee, Mariposa County. Courtesy of NPS (Laura Soulliere Harrison).*

mer camps for youths. Many rustic-style camp buildings built in the 1930s remain in a second-growth redwood forest, now part of the California state park system.

### ■ *Mono County*

## BODIE HISTORIC DISTRICT
### Bodie

Although only 5 percent of the buildings Bodie contained in its 1880s heyday remain, this is one of the finest examples of a mining "ghost town" in the West. Gold was discovered here on the western slope of the Sierra Nevada in 1859, and by 1880 the town had a population of 10,000. The town was abandoned in the 1940s, and its buildings in their isolated settings are now preserved in a state of "arrested decay" as a California state park.

### ■ *Monterey County*

## ASILOMAR CONFERENCE GROUNDS
### Asilomar Boulevard, Pacific Grove

Asilomar, its name freely translated from the Spanish as "refuge by the sea," was established in 1913 by the Young Women's Christian Association (YWCA). The center's first stone and/or shingle buildings were designed by Californian Julia Morgan, one of the nation's first prominent women architects. Asilomar is significant for its role in the work of the

YWCA and in the resort development of the Monterey Peninsula. Now a unit of the California state park system, it continues as a conference center.

## CARMEL MISSION
### Rio Road, Carmel

This stuccoed stone church and attendant buildings dating from 1793–1797 served as headquarters of the California missions under Father Fermin Francisco de Lasuen, "padre presidente." The mission was abandoned in the mid-19th century but partially rebuilt in 1884. The present restoration dates from 1924 and later. Still an active church, San Carlos de Borromeo at Carmel is one of the most familiar and popular of the California missions.

## LARKIN HOUSE
### 510 Calle Principal, Monterey

This structure, dating from 1835–1837, marked turning points in California architecture and history. Recognized as the prototype of the Monterey Colonial style, it ingeniously combines a timber frame (familiar to Thomas Oliver Larkin, its New England merchant/builder) with adobe blocks, the area's indigenous building material. The style, also typified by expansive two-story porches, was widely copied throughout California. The house is also significant because Larkin was U.S. Consul to Mexican California and was later instrumental in the annexation of this territory by the United States. The house was donated to the state in 1957 and is part of the Monterey State Historic Park.

## MONTEREY OLD TOWN HISTORIC DISTRICT
### Monterey

Founded in 1770, Monterey served as the Spanish, then Mexican, capital of California for most of the period from 1776 to 1848. It was also the social and economic center of early California and an outpost of European civilization during those years. A number of early adobes and Monterey Colonial buildings remain in this two-part, noncontinuous, historic district.

## OLD CUSTOM HOUSE
### 15 Alvarado Street, Monterey

Erected in 1827 by the Mexican government and enlarged in 1841–1846, this Monterey Colonial structure is the oldest public building on the West Coast. Until 1845 it was the only custom house north of Mexico, and all vessels plying the California coast had to record their cargo here. On July 7, 1846, Commodore John D. Sloat, commander of the U.S. Pacific Squadron, raised the American flag over the building and officially proclaimed California a part of the United States. It is now a museum.

## ROYAL PRESIDIO CHAPEL
### 550 Church Street, Monterey

Completed in 1795 by Indian labor from designs prepared in Mexico City, the Royal Presidio Chapel of San Carlos de Borromeo is the only remaining presidio chapel in California and the sole existing structure of the original Monterey Presidio. This was the state church of Spanish California, and its classic facade is the most elaborate of all the

Spanish-inspired churches in the state. It still houses an active parish.

## ■ *Napa County*

### ELMSHAVEN
**125 Glass Mountain Lane, Saint Helena**

This 1885 Victorian-era farmhouse was home to Ellen Gould White from 1900 to 1915. White was a cofounder of the Seventh Day Adventist Church and helped reorganize the church's administration while living here during the latter years of her life. Her numerous writings are still given "special authority" by church members. Elmshaven is now operated as a historic house museum.

## ■ *Nevada County*

### DONNER CAMP
**2.6 miles west of Truckee**

In the winter of 1846–1847, a group of 89 California-bound settlers from Illinois, under the leadership of brothers Jacob and George Donner, became trapped by heavy snows in the High Sierra. They built cabins near a lake, but only 47 members of the Donner party survived the ordeal. Rescuers arriving in late winter and spring found evidence of cannibalism. This tragic chapter in the saga of westward migration is commemorated at the campsite in Donner Memorial State Park.

## ■ *Orange County*

### MODJESKA HOUSE
**Modjeska Canyon Road, Modjeska**

This informal wooden cottage, enlarged from a pioneer cabin, served as the home of Madame Helena Modjeska from 1888 to 1906. One of the first "stars" to settle in southern California, the exiled Polish patriot was a noted Shakespearean actress and named her estate "Forest of Arden" after the locale in *As You Like It*. The house is now the centerpiece of a county park.

### RICHARD M. NIXON BIRTHPLACE
**18061 Yorba Linda Boulevard, Yorba Linda**

From his birth in 1913 to 1922, when the family moved to Whittier, this was the home of Richard Milhous Nixon, 37th President of the United States. Of his formative years here, and his parents' influence, he once said,

"It has certainly held me together at times when I have been under pressure. And it always will." Nixon is buried nearby, and the small 1½-story California bungalow, built by his father, is now operated by the Richard Nixon Library and Birthplace Foundation.

## ■ *Riverside County*

### HARADA HOUSE
**3356 Lemon Street, Riverside**

This architecturally undistinguished house, built in the 1880s, was the object of the first test of the constitutionality of an alien land law in the United States. In *California vs. Harada* (1916–1918) the court ruled that all native-born citizens, even minor children of immigrant parents, could own land. Later, during World War II, the Harada family was in-terned, illustrating another aspect of America's troubled dealings with its Japanese-American citizens. (See Manzanar, Inyo County.)

### MISSION INN
**Between Fifth, Seventh, Main, and Orange Streets, Riverside**

This largest Mission Revival building in California incorporates a gold altar from Mexico and Tiffany windows from New York among its many embellishments. The inn began in 1876 as a small hotel but evolved over the years into an almost overwhelmingly lavish complex that became one of the West Coast's best-known hostelries. Richard and Pat Nixon were married in the Mission Inn, and Ronald and Nancy Reagan honeymooned here.

## ■ *Sacramento County*

### BIG FOUR HOUSE
**I Street between Front and Second Streets, Sacramento**

Built in 1852 as three adjacent stores by Collis Huntington, Mark Hopkins, and Leland Stanford, this commercial structure served as offices when they, along with Charles Crocker, planned, financed, and built the Central Pacific Railroad, the western end of America's first transcontinental railway. The "big four" subsequently founded the Southern Pacific Railroad in these offices as well. The Big Four House was taken down in 1966–1967 and rebuilt on a new site in Old Sacramento.

## FOLSOM POWERHOUSE
### Off Folsom Boulevard, Folsom State Recreation Area, Folsom

In 1895 this hydroelectric generating plant sent high-voltage alternating current over long-distance lines for the first time, a major advance in the technology of electric power transmission and generation. The powerhouse and original generators are now exhibited and interpreted as part of Folsom Lake Recreation Area.

## LOCKE HISTORIC DISTRICT
### Bounded by the Sacramento River, Locke Road, Alley Street, and Levee Street, Locke

Locke, founded in 1915, is the largest and most intact example of a rural Chinese-American community in the nation. More than 50 closely spaced commercial and residential frame buildings make up what has been called "a frontier Chinatown." Locke is the only such community remaining in the Sacramento-San Joaquin River delta, in which a large number of Chinese immigrants settled.

## OLD SACRAMENTO HISTORIC DISTRICT
### Junctions of U.S. Routes 40, 50, 99 and California Routes 16 and 24, Sacramento

Sacramento emerged as the port and interior distribution center for the northern mines of the Mother Lode country in the Sierra Nevada in 1849–1850. The blocks immediately east of the Sacramento River became the business district, and a number of structures dating from the 1840s through the 1870s remain. Many have been restored and others have been reconstructed to recreate the Victorian-era flavor of the area's heyday.

## PONY EXPRESS TERMINAL
### 1006 Second Street, Sacramento

From April 1860 to March 1861 this structure housed the western terminal of the pony express. Other tenants included the California State Supreme Court and Wells, Fargo and Company. The two-story brick building was restored in the 1970s as part of the revitalization of the Old Sacramento Historic District and is now a museum.

## LELAND STANFORD HOUSE
### 800 N Street, Sacramento

In 1861, Leland Stanford purchased a substantial four-year-old house that served as the governor's mansion when he was elected California's first Republican executive in 1862. He and his successor, Frederick F. Low, to whom he leased the house, ensured that California remained loyal to the Union during the Civil War. In 1871, two years after driving the golden spike that marked completion of the transcontinental railway, Stanford enlarged the house, tripling its accommodations. The prodigious Second

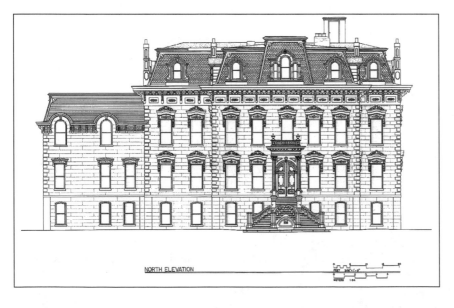

*Leland Stanford House, Sacramento, Sacramento County. Courtesy of HABS (Karen Cormier).*

NORTH ELEVATION

Empire mansion that resulted from the enlargements served as an orphanage after his death and is now operated by the California state parks.

## SUTTER'S FORT
**2701 L Street, Sacramento**

During the 1840s an adobe fort near the confluence of the Sacramento and American Rivers served as the focal point of John Augustus Sutter's far-flung enterprises. After the foreman at his sawmill near Coloma discovered gold there, workers from the fort joined the gold rush and eventually Sutter joined them. The fort deteriorated after 1849, but the central building survives. In 1937 the property became Sutter's Fort State Historical Monument.

### ■ *San Benito County*

## JUAN DE ANZA HOUSE
**Third and Franklin Streets, San Juan Bautista**

Erected ca. 1830 as a rectangular one-story, two-room adobe, the house was enlarged with a frame addition in the 1850s. The resulting building is typical of the "Americanization" of traditional Mexican houses by early American settlers in California.

## JOSÉ CASTRO HOUSE
**South side of the Plaza, San Jaun Bautista**

José Castro, commandant general of Northern California, built this adobe and timber structure in 1840–1841 to serve as his secretary's residence and his own office. Its horizontal massing and canopied second-story porch are typical features of early California architecture in the Monterey area. The house has been open to the public since 1935 as a unit in the San Juan Bautista State Historical Park.

## SAN JUAN BAUTISTA PLAZA HISTORIC DISTRICT
**Buildings surrounding the Plaza at Washington, Mariposa, and Second Streets, San Juan Bautista**

A striking example of a 19th-century village built on a traditional Spanish-Mexican Colonial plaza plan, the district is composed of five buildings, all facing the Plaza and all completed between 1813 and 1874. San Juan Bautista Church, on the west side of the Plaza, is the largest of the California missions.

### ■ *San Bernardino County*

## PIONEER DEEP SPACE STATION
**Goldston Deep Space Communications Complex, Fort Irwin**

Constructed in 1958, this was the first antenna to support the National Aeronautics and Space Administration's unmanned exploration of deep space. Essentially a polar-mounted parabolic dish, this became the prototype antenna for the entire Deep Space Network. Among the missions it tracked were Ranger, Surveyor, Apollo, and Voyager.

## ROGERS DRY LAKE
**Edwards Air Force Base, Mojave Desert vicinity (Kern and San Bernardino Counties)**

(See entry under Kern County.)

### ■ *San Diego County*

## BALBOA PARK
**1549 El Prado, San Diego**

This multibuilding complex, constructed for the 1915 Panama-California Exposition, includes some of America's finest examples

*Balboa Park, San Diego, San Diego County. Botanical Garden, 1971. Courtesy of HABS (Marvin Rand).*

of Spanish baroque architecture. Overall planning was by architect Bertram Goodhue, but local architects designed many of the individual buildings. The group was enlarged for the 1935 California-Pacific International Exposition and continues to serve as a San Diego park and cultural center.

## HUBERT H. BANCROFT RANCH HOUSE
**Bancroft Drive, Spring Valley**

Hubert Howe Bancroft, noted historian of the North American West, lived in this one-story adobe from 1885 until his death in 1918. From 1882 until 1890, Bancroft and 20 assistants compiled and published 39 volumes, uneven in quality but encyclopedic in detail, that remain authoritative histories of much of the Pacific slope. The house, now a museum of area history, was built in 1856 and incorporates curved oak timbers from the *Clarissa Andrews,* a trans-Atlantic steam packet, in its fabric.

## *BERKELEY*
**B Street Pier, San Diego**

Built in San Francisco in 1898, the *Berkeley* is the nation's oldest car and passenger ferry, remaining in essentially unmodified condition even to the retention of its unmodified 19th-century steam plant. *Berkeley* gave yeoman service during the San Francisco earthquake and fire of 1906, ferrying countless evacuees across the bay. After a 60-year career, it is now moored as part of the San Diego Maritime Museum.

## ESTUDILLO HOUSE
**4000 Mason Street, San Diego**

When this large adobe house was constructed in 1827–1829, it was one of the finest in Mexican California. Built in the shape of the letter U, it surrounds an inner patio or courtyard. Hand-hewn timbers and rafters were lashed together with rawhide thongs. The house was partially reconstructed in 1910 and restored in 1968–1969. It is part of the Old Town San Diego State Historic Park.

## GUAJOME RANCH HOUSE
**Vista vicinity**

Guajome Ranch House is one of Southern California's finest remaining examples of a Mexican-style ranch headquarters. A large adobe hacienda, it was built in 1852–1853. Living quarters were arranged on four sides of a patio surrounded by a veranda, and farming operations were accommodated around an attached carriage court. It is currently part of the Guajome Regional Park.

## HOTEL DEL CORONADO
**1500 Orange Street, Coronado**

This enormous 1887 frame hotel, rising from the Coronado peninsula beach like a castle, was designed by the Reid Brothers of San Francisco. Thomas A. Edison supervised the installation of the original electrical system, the world's first in a hotel. It was here that Edward, Prince of Wales, met Wallis Simpson during a 1920 banquet held in his honor. The Del was, and remains, one of the most architecturally interesting luxury hotels in the country.

## LAS FLORES ADOBE
**West side of Stuart Mesa Road, Camp Joseph H. Pendleton, Oceanside vicinity**

This is a prime example of the Monterey Colonial style of architecture. Like its prototype, the Larkin House, it combines Mexican adobe traditions with New England frame building habits. The expansive double porch is a typical feature of the style. Located within U.S. Marine Corps Camp Joseph H. Pendleton, the property is leased to the Orange County Council of the Boy Scouts of America as a campground. (See also Larkin House, Monterey County.)

## MISSION BEACH ROLLER COASTER
**3000 Mission Boulevard, San Diego**

Also known as the "Earthquake," this wooden-scaffolded roller coaster has dominated its low-lying surroundings since 1925. It is the only example remaining on the West Coast designed by Frank Prior and Frederick A. Church, among the most noted American builders of roller coasters. It is also the main survivor and most visible symbol of the Mission Beach Amusement Center, part of an ambitious early-20th-century recreational development.

## OAK GROVE BUTTERFIELD STAGE STATION
**13 miles northwest of Warner Hot Springs**

This small adobe building, now enlarged, was built as a way station on the Butterfield Overland Mail Route, which operated from 1858 to 1861. The first truly transcontinental stagecoach service, the Butterfield line was chartered when it became apparent that the transcontinent railroad would not be completed as early as expected. Although the Butterfield line was generally regarded as a successful frontier business venture, it was doomed when Congress approved another route for carrying the mail.

## OLD MISSION DAM
**North side of Mission Street–Gorge Road, San Diego**

Completed by 1817, this cobblestone and cement dam was one of the first major irrigation-engineering projects on the Pacific Coast of the United States. The dam, originally 220 feet long and 13 feet thick, impounded water that was released as needed for milling and for irrigating fields around Mission San Diego de Alcala, some five miles away.

## OLD SCRIPPS BUILDING
**8602 La Jolla Shores Drive, La Jolla**

Constructed in 1909–1910, the spare two-story, rectangular "Old Scripps" is the nation's oldest building in continuous use by a major oceanographic research institution. It was designed by California architect Irving J. Gill and is a notable example of his mature, utilitarian style, as well as an early example of reinforced concrete construction. It is now one of many buildings serving the Scripps Institution.

## SAN DIEGO MISSION CHURCH
**Mission Road, 5 miles east of San Diego**

Completed in 1813, this brick-and-adobe church served the mission founded by Father Junípero Serra in 1769, the first of the 21 California missions. The dominant feature of the complex is a tall campanario with five open arches holding bells. After serving as an Indian school and boys' home, the mission was restored in the 1930s and rededicated as a parish church in 1941.

## SAN DIEGO PRESIDIO
**Presidio Park, San Diego**

In 1769 the first permanent European settlement on the Pacific Coast of the present-day United States was established here. Father Junípero Serra founded the Mission of San Diego de Alcala, the first of the California missions, at the Presidio; however, it was later moved. The Presidio served as a base for expeditions exploring the interior and as Spanish military headquarters for southern California. The site is now a landscaped park and contains the mission-style Serra Museum, built in 1929.

## SAN LUIS REY MISSION CHURCH
**4 miles east of Oceanside**

Mission San Luis Rey de Francia was founded in 1798. The present church, the mission's

San Luis Rey Mission Church, San Diego County, 1968. Courtesy of NPS.

*Alcatraz Island, San Francisco, San Francisco County. Courtesy of NPS (Richard Frear).*

third, was built between 1811 and 1815 and forms part of California's most pristine mission complex. The baroque facade of the church was meant to be flanked by twin towers, only one of which was completed. In 1893, the Catholic Church rededicated the mission as a Franciscan college, a function it continues to serve, and began a long-term restoration.

## STAR OF INDIA
### San Diego Embarcadero, San Diego

Constructed in 1863 on the Isle of Man, this three-masted vessel is the oldest iron-hulled merchantman afloat in the world. From 1901 to 1923 the *Star* served in the salmon trade, carrying fishermen and cannery employees to the Alaskan fisheries. Restored between 1962 and 1963, the *Star* is now berthed as a museum ship at San Diego's Embarcadero.

## WARNER'S RANCH
### 4 miles south of Warner Hot Springs

Established in 1831, this pioneering cattle ranch served from 1848 to 1861 as a resting place for overland travelers after they had crossed the desert on the Gila River emigrant trail. From 1858 to 1861 the ranch served as a Butterfield Overland Mail stage station. Today two adobe structures—a house and a barn—remain, situated on 221 acres of rural grazing land.

## ■ *San Francisco County*
## ALCATRAZ ISLAND (NPS)
### San Francisco Bay, San Francisco

This sandstone island dominating the entrance to San Francisco Bay was the site of the first lighthouse on the Pacific Coast (1854), served as a Civil War bastion, and became the nation's first official army prison. "Uncle Sam's Devil's Island" was transferred to civilian authority in 1934 and became infamous as a place of incarceration for the nation's most hardened criminals. The prison was closed in 1963, and ten years later the island was opened to the public as the first unit of the Golden Gate National Recreation Area.

## *ALMA* (NPS)
### Hyde Street Pier, San Francisco Maritime National Historical Park, San Francisco

Built in 1891 by a German immigrant and named for his granddaughter, this "scow schooner" is the only survivor afloat of a once typical American vessel, known by different names in various parts of the country. By 1880 there were 150 of these flat-bottomed, shallow-draft workhorses in San Francisco Bay, plying their way between larger ships to deliver their bulk cargoes. *Alma* worked until 1957, was restored in the 1960s, and was transferred to the San Francisco Maritime National Historical Park in 1988.

Alma, *San Francisco, San Francisco County. Courtesy of NPS (Richard Frear).*

## AQUATIC PARK (NPS)
**San Francisco Maritime National Historical Park, San Francisco**

Aquatic Park, developed from 1936 to 1939, was one of California's largest Works Progress Administration (WPA) projects. The centerpiece of this group of "streamline-moderne" structures, all employing nautical metaphors, is a multipurpose structure containing the bathhouse, concession stand, and lounge. Its rounded walls, recessed upper stories, tubular steel railings, and porthole windows were purposely designed to create the illusion of an ocean liner. Murals and other artwork carry out the nautical theme. The main building, lifeguard stations, stadium, Sea Scout building, a seawall, and a semicircular pier form the Aquatic Park Historic District, now part of the San Francisco Maritime National Historical Park.

## *BALCLUTHA* (NPS)
**Hyde Street Pier, San Francisco Maritime National Historical Park, San Francisco**

Built in Glasgow, Scotland, in 1886, *Balclutha* sailed to San Francisco on its maiden voyage. It participated in the grain trade between California and England, then in the Pacific Coast lumber trade, and finally in the Alaska salmon industry, having been rechristened *Star of Alaska*. In 1934 it was renamed *Pacific Queen* and starred as an "extra" in several films. Now the last square-rigged sailing ship afloat on San Francisco Bay, *Balclutha* (restored and given back its original name in the 1950s) is a popular attraction at the San Francisco Maritime National Historical Park.

## BANK OF ITALY BUILDING
**552 Montgomery Street, San Francisco**

From 1908 to 1921 this ornate eight-story Second Renaissance Revival structure in San Francisco's financial district was headquarters of the Bank of Italy (later renamed the Bank

*Balclutha, San Francisco, San Francisco County, 1952. Courtesy of the National Maritime Museum.*

of America). Its founder, Amadeo Peter Giannini, son of immigrants, inaugurated the nation's first statewide branch banking system, creating one of the largest commercial banks in the world.

## C.A. THAYER (NPS)
**San Francisco Maritime National Historic Park, San Francisco**

This rare surviving example of a sailing schooner designed specifically for the 19th-century Pacific Coast lumber trade was built in California in 1895, appropriately, of native Douglas fir. It later participated in the Alaska salmon and Bering Sea codfish trades. Restored from 1959 to 1963, the *Thayer* is now on exhibit at the San Francisco Maritime National Historical Park.

## EUREKA (NPS)
**Hyde Street Pier, San Francisco Maritime National Historical Park, San Francisco**

The last intact wooden-hulled sidewheel steamer afloat in the continental United States, *Eureka* is significant as an example of a type of vessel that led U.S. inland waterborne commerce into the industrial era. Its 1890 "walking beam" marine steam equipment is the only operating example of this once common engine in North America. Launched as the *Ukiah,* it was rebuilt during 1920–1922 and relaunched as the *Eureka,* an auto-passenger ferry. *Eureka* is now exhibited at the San Francisco Maritime National

Historical Park, along with period automobiles evocative of its years of service.

## JAMES C. FLOOD MANSION
**Northwest corner of California and Mason Streets, San Francisco**

This Nob Hill mansion, faced with Connecticut sandstone carried round Cape Horn as ballast, was built by one of the bonanza kings, James C. Flood, a former bartender who struck it rich in Nevada's Comstock Lode. Stock value in the Comstock Mine, a syndicated venture, soared from $100,000 in 1870 to $159 million in 1874. Flood's San Francisco palace, completed in 1886, was the only mansion in its then-exclusive residential neighborhood to survive the 1906 earthquake and fire. It now houses a private club.

## HERCULES (NPS)
**Hyde Street Pier, San Francisco Maritime National Historical Park, San Francisco**

*Hercules* proved the validity of its name on its 1908 maiden voyage: towing brother tug *Goliath* through the Straits of Magellan from New Jersey to San Francisco. *Hercules* continued in service towing logs, sailing vessels, and disabled ships until 1962. The last remaining, largely unaltered, early-20th-century, ocean-going steam tugboat, *Hercules* rests from its labors at the San Francisco Maritime National Historical Park.

Hercules, *San Francisco, San Francisco County. Courtesy of NPS.*

## *JEREMIAH O'BRIEN* (NPS)
**Pier 3, Fort Mason Center, San Francisco Maritime National Historical Park, San Francisco**

During World War II, 2,751 Liberty Ships were built as an emergency response to a shortage of maritime cargo carriers. *Jeremiah O'Brien,* the only unaltered survivor still operative, participated in the D-Day invasion in 1944 and later carried cargo to various ports around the world. The ship is open to the public as the National Liberty Ship Memorial.

## OLD UNITED STATES MINT
**Fifth and Mission Streets, San Francisco**

Constructed between 1869 and 1874, this monumental granite-and-sandstone–faced Greek Revival building quickly became the principal mint in the country, as well as the federal depot for silver and gold. Designed by Alfred B. Mullett, it is one of the few downtown buildings that survived San Francisco's 1906 earthquake and fire. Its use as a mint ceased in 1937, and the building was threatened with demolition in 1969. Fortunately, it was preserved and is still owned by the federal government.

## *PAMPANITO* (NPS)
**Fisherman's Wharf–Pier 45, San Francisco Maritime National Historical Park, San Francisco**

Commissioned November 6, 1943, *Pampanito,* named for a fish found in the Pacific, was built at the Portsmouth, New Hampshire, naval shipyard and is representative of submarines that fought against Japan in World War II. It made six war patrols, is credited with sinking five Japanese ships, and earned six battle stars. *Pampanito* was decommissioned in 1945 and is now open to the public at the San Francisco Maritime National Historical Park.

## PRESIDIO OF SAN FRANCISCO (NPS)
**Northern tip of San Francisco peninsula, San Francisco**

Established by the Spanish in 1776 to guard the entrance to San Francisco Bay, this enormous military post was subsequently used by a sequence of nations: Spain, Mexico, and the United States. As Pacific Coast headquarters for the U.S. Army after 1849, the reservation exhibits military building, planning, and landscaping through many decades of historical development. Closure of the base was announced in 1989 and became effective in 1995. The 1,480-acre property is now part of the Golden Gate National Recreation Area and is administered by the private, congressionally chartered Presidio Trust.

## SAN FRANCISCO CABLE CARS
**1390 Washington Street, San Francisco**

Beloved symbols of San Francisco, these jaunty conveyances are the only cable cars still operating in an American city. Begun in

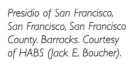
*Presidio of San Francisco, San Francisco, San Francisco County. Barracks. Courtesy of HABS (Jack E. Boucher).*

August 1873, the system of traction locomotion was designed to climb the steepest grades San Francisco had to offer, one reason that the cable cars and ten miles of track remain in this city of hills. The powerhouse and carbarn at Washington and Mason Streets, part of the designated landmark, contains a cable car museum.

## SAN FRANCISCO CIVIC CENTER
### Vicinity of Van Ness Avenue and Market Street, San Francisco

Of international importance, this monumental group of civic structures surrounding a plaza served as the birthplace of the United Nations and the setting for post–World War II peace treaties with Japan. The Civic Center is also the country's finest and most complete manifestation of the turn-of-the-century "City Beautiful" movement. Exposition Auditorium, one of the earliest components, is the only surviving building of the 1915 Panama-Pacific International Exposition.

## SAN FRANCISCO PORT OF EMBARKATION, U.S. ARMY (NPS)
### Fort Mason, Golden Gate National Recreation Area, San Francisco

During World War II this was the principal port on the West Coast for delivering personnel, material, weapons, and ammunition to the fighting fronts in the Pacific theater. Between December 1941 and August 1945, almost one and three-quarters of a million military personnel embarked here. The port, originally part of Fort Mason, is now part of the Golden Gate National Recreation Area, and its components house a multitude of community activities.

## WAPAMA (NPS)
### Hyde Street Pier, San Francisco Maritime National Historic Park, San Francisco

Launched in 1915, the wooden-hulled Wapama is the last survivor of more than 200 steam schooners that served the Pacific Coast lumber trade in the 19th and 20th centuries. These vessels formed the backbone of maritime trade and coastal commerce, ferrying lumber, general cargo, and passengers. Wapama is now on display at the San Francisco Maritime National Historical Park.

## ■ San Luis Obispo County
## HEARST SAN SIMEON ESTATE
### 3 miles northeast of San Simeon

Begun in 1919, this princely estate situated on La Cuesta Encantada (the name is translated as "The Enchanted Hill") near San Simeon was to be a permanent family residence, a place of retreat, and a showcase for the many art treasures amassed by publishing magnate William Randolf Hearst. With the assistance of architect Julia Morgan, a protégé of his mother and a graduate of the École des Beaux-Arts in Paris, Hearst constructed a cluster of buildings that includes the magnificent Hispaño-Moresque mansion, La Casa Grande. Hearst expanded the mansion steadily in order to display his ever growing collection of priceless artifacts. The property is now operated by the state of California as the Hearst San Simeon State Historical Monument.

## ■ San Mateo County
## WILLIAM C. RALSTON HOME
### College of Notre Dame, Belmont

William Chapman Ralston, "the man who built San Francisco," was an aggressive businessman who amassed a fortune financing silver mines of the Comstock Lode. From 1864 until his premature death in 1875 at age 49, he promoted California's potential to visitors at Ralston Hall, his palatial country estate. The 80-room Italian villa became the property of Notre Dame College in 1922.

## SAN FRANCISCO BAY DISCOVERY SITE
### 4 miles west of San Bruno

On November 4, 1769, from the crest of this ridge, the main body of the expedition led by Gaspar de Portola first sighted San Francisco Bay, the most important harbor on the Pacific Coast and one of the great anchorages of the world. On a clear day, you can still see forever from this unspoiled site, located within the boundaries of Golden Gate National Recreation Area.

■ *Santa Barbara County*

## GONZALEZ HOUSE
**835 Laguna Street, Santa Barbara**

Built ca. 1825 by Don Rafael Gonzalez, this one-story house with two one-room wings, covered verandas, and a tile roof is typical of Mexican-era adobe town houses of moderate size. Its main section is about 90 feet by 18 feet, the adobe walls at least 2 feet thick. Covered verandas extend along both long sides of the house.

## LA PURISIMA MISSION
**4 miles east of Lompoc**

La Purisima Concepcion Mission, founded in 1787, was moved to this site in 1813, and the complex was completed in 1818. After secularization in 1834, its adobe buildings fell into disrepair, not to be reconstructed until 100 years later. La Purisima was not one of the great California missions, but its authentic restoration, coupled with its expansive, unspoiled rural setting, make it one of the most representative and evocative of all. The mission is now a state historical monument.

## LOS ALAMOS RANCH HOUSE
**3 miles west of Los Alamos**

This one-story adobe-and-frame ranch house in its rural setting is one of the finest surviving examples of a traditional Mexican hacienda in California. Rancho Los Alamos was established in 1839, and the house served as a well-frequented lodging place for travelers on El Camino Real between Santa Barbara and Monterey.

## MISSION SANTA INÈS
**South of State Highway 246 on the east side of Solvang**

Mission Santa Inès is one of the best-preserved Spanish mission complexes in the United States, containing an unrivaled combination of setting, original buildings, extant collections of art and interior furnishings, water-related industrial structures, and archeological remains. The property is also important as the location of the start of the Chumash Revolt of 1824, one of the largest and most successful revolts of Native Americans in the Spanish West, representing indigenous resistance to European colonization. The mission also contains significant archeological potential for providing information on the critical period of accommodation between native peoples and European colonial powers.

## SANTA BARBARA MISSION
**2201 Laguna Street, Santa Barbara**

Built between 1815 and 1820, this is generally considered the most architecturally distinguished link in California's 21-mission chain. The classical lines of the church derive from Roman architectural precedent. Santa Barbara is the only California mission that survived in good condition and escaped secularization into the 20th century. An earthquake in 1925 damaged the building, and it was subsequently restored. In the 1950s further restoration work was undertaken.

## SPACE LAUNCH COMPLEX 10
**Vandenberg Air Force Base, Lompoc**

Built in 1958 for the U.S. Air Force's Intermediate Range Ballistic Missile (IRBM) testing program, this complex was rebuilt in 1963 and adapted for space launches. The last *Thor* space booster was launched from one of the installation's two pads in July 1980. The adjoining blockhouse contains one of the best existing collections of electronic equipment used to support launches of that era. The complex is a unique resource of technology dating from America's early efforts at space exploration.

■ *Santa Clara County*

## HANNA-HONEYCOMB HOUSE
**Stanford University Campus, Palo Alto vicinity**

Begun in 1937 and expanded over 25 years, this is the first and best example of Frank Lloyd Wright's innovative hexagonal design. Patterned after the honeycomb of a bee, the house incorporates six-sided figures with 120-degree angles in its plan, in its numerous tiled terraces, and even in built-in furnishings. The house is maintained by Stanford University.

*Lou Henry and Herbert Hoover House, Palo Alto, Santa Clara County. Courtesy of NPS (Richard Frear).*

## LOU HENRY AND HERBERT HOOVER HOUSE
**623 Mirada Road, Stanford University Campus, Palo Alto**

This large, rambling International style house, made to resemble "blocks piled up," was designed by Lou Henry Hoover. Her husband's contribution was to order that it be fireproof, and walls are constructed of hollow tiles. Built from 1919 to 1920, the house was the couple's first and only permanent residence, and it was here that Hoover awaited election returns in 1928 and 1932. After Mrs. Hoover's death in 1944, her husband deeded the house to Stanford to serve as the home of university presidents.

## NEW ALMADEN
**14 miles south of San Jose**

Mexican settler Antonio Surol first discovered ore deposits here in the 1820s, identified as quicksilver by Mexican Army officer Andreas Castillero in 1845. Long before, Santa Clara Indians had customarily used its solid ore, cinnabar, as paint to decorate their bodies. Until the cyanide process was discovered in 1887, quicksilver, or mercury, was the chief reduction agent for gold and silver, and New Almaden made possible the rapid development of California and Nevada mines. New Almaden was named for the world's largest quicksilver mine, Almaden, in Spain. The town, several mines, and several campsites are included in this large historic district.

## FRANK NORRIS CABIN
**10 miles west of Gilroy**

Benjamin Franklin (Frank) Norris has been called "the most stimulating and militant of the early American naturalist writers." His works reflect the individual's loss of identity in modern society. Something of the same "loss of identity" applies to this isolated cabin. Although Norris contemplated buying it, he never did. His friend, Mrs. Robert Louis Stevenson, lived on an adjoining property and erected a stone bench here in his honor after his early death in 1902 at the age of 32.

## UNITARY PLAN WIND TUNNEL
**Ames Research Center, Moffett Field**

Constructed between 1950 and 1955, this complex actually contains three wind tunnels. The research facility was created by the National Advisory Committee for Aeronautics (NACA), parent agency of the National Aeronautics and Space Administration (NASA). It was used extensively to design and test new generations of aircraft, both commercial and military, as well as NASA space vehicles, including the space shuttle.

## ■ *Santa Cruz County*

### SANTA CRUZ LOOFF CAROUSEL AND ROLLER COASTER
**Along Beach Street, Santa Cruz**

Built in 1911, the carousel is one of six essentially intact carousels in the United States manufactured by the Looff family, one of the earliest and most important makers of carousels. The "Giant Dipper" roller coaster (1924) is the older of the two large wooden scaffolded roller coasters remaining on the West Coast. Both are on the Santa Cruz Beach Boardwalk, one of the first amusement parks on the West Coast, patterned after New York's Coney Island.

## ■ *Siskiyou County*

### LOWER KLAMATH NATIONAL WILDLIFE REFUGE
**Lower Klamath Lake, Dorris vicinity**

(See entry in Klamath County, Oregon.)

## ■ *Solano County*

### MARE ISLAND NAVAL SHIPYARD
**Mare Island, Vallejo**

In 1854 this shipyard became the U.S. Navy's first permanent installation on the Pacific Coast. It thus serves to illustrate the nation's effort to extend its naval power into the Pacific Ocean. The first U.S. warship (1859) and first drydock (1872–1891) constructed on the West Coast were built here. The wood-shingled Saint Peter's Chapel (1901), with its signed Tiffany stained-glass windows, is the oldest Navy chapel in the country.

## ■ *Sonoma County*

### LUTHER BURBANK HOUSE AND GARDEN
**200 block of Santa Rosa Avenue, Santa Rosa**

Luther Burbank, known as the "Plant Wizard," experimented with thousands of plants in his goal to produce more and better varieties. Perhaps best known for his Shasta daisy, he also introduced more than 250 varieties of fruit during his long career as a horticulturist. He lived here the last 50 years of his life and in 1926 was buried under a Cedar of Lebanon that he had planted on the property. His home, and the gardens where he conducted much of his research, are open to the public.

### COMMANDER'S HOUSE, FORT ROSS
**North of the town of Fort Ross on California Route 1**

This rare and little-altered log house, constructed of large hand-squared redwood tim-

*Mare Island Naval Shipyard, Vallejo, Solana County. Drydock 1, ca. 1970. Courtesy of the U.S. Navy.*

bers mortised at the corners, was built in 1812. By 1818 glass for its windows had been imported from Russia. Fort Ross, now a state historic park, was a fur trading post established by the Russian-American Company and was occupied by Russians and Aleuts.

## FORT ROSS
### North of the town of Fort Ross

Founded in 1812, Fort Ross represented a Russian attempt to establish permanent trade relations with the Spanish in California. The post also supplied food for the Russian American Company's Alaskan operations but never proved successful economically; it was sold to John Sutter in 1841. The restored chapel, Commander's House (itself a National Historic Landmark) and reconstructed blockhouses, enclosed in a reconstructed stockade, form the Fort Ross State Historic Park.

## JACK LONDON RANCH
### Jack London Historical State Park, Glen Ellen vicinity

This state historical park commemorates popular writer Jack London (John Griffith London), who produced 51 books and numerous short stories during his prolific career. London lived here from 1905 until his death in 1916 and is buried on the property. His "Wolf House" burned in 1913 and is now a picturesque ruin, but his widow's "House of Happy Walls," built in 1919 as a memorial to London, survives.

## PETALUMA ADOBE
### Casa Grande Road, 4 miles east of Petaluma

Mariano Guadalupe Vallejo, commandant of the Sonoma Pueblo, built this huge U-shaped adobe structure as headquarters for his ranch over a ten-year period from 1836 to 1846. It was one of the showplaces of the province and remains the largest example of the Monterey Colonial style in the country. A fourth side that would have formed a quadrangle around a courtyard was never completed. The adobe is now a state historical monument.

## SONOMA PLAZA
### Center of Sonoma

Established in 1835 to check possible Russian expansion from Fort Ross and to control the Indians, Sonoma Pueblo was the Mexican government's chief military base in Alta California until 1846. On June 14 of that year the raising of the Bear Flag in the Plaza marked the beginning of the American revolt against Mexican rule. A number of restored adobe buildings, many included in the Sonoma State Historical Monument, surround the landscaped plaza.

## ■ *Tuolumne County*

## COLUMBIA HISTORIC DISTRICT
### 4 miles northwest of Sonora

Gold was discovered here in 1850, and three years later Columbia had become California's third-largest city. A fire in 1854 destroyed its frame buildings, but a rebuilding, mostly in brick, stood it in good stead when a second fire raged through in 1857. Although Columbia declined after 1860, it was never abandoned. It survives today, much of it in a state historic park, as one of the best-preserved mining towns of the California Mother Lode region.

## PARSONS MEMORIAL LODGE (NPS)
### Yosemite National Park, Tuolumne Meadows

Built in the summer of 1915 by the Sierra Club as an overnight shelter high in the Sierra Nevada, this rubble granite lodge was one of the first rustic stone buildings in a national park. The small building, named for an early director of the Sierra Club, combines the designer's thorough understanding of its harsh environment with an expressive use of natural materials.

■ *Yolo County*

## FIRST PACIFIC COAST SALMON CANNERY SITE
### On Sacramento River opposite the foot of K Street, Broderick

Here, between 1864 and 1866, William and George Hume and Andrew Hapgood of Maine perfected the canning techniques that led to the development of the multimillion dollar Pacific Coast salmon canning industry. The Hapgood, Hume & Company cannery was situated on a scow anchored in the Sacramento River.

# COLORADO

■ *Clear Creek County*

## GEORGETOWN–SILVER PLUME HISTORIC DISTRICT
### Interstate 70, Georgetown–Silver Plume

This district, perhaps the most scenic of all the Colorado mining areas, preserves much of the flavor of the mining era. Neighboring towns along Clear Creek, Georgetown and Silver Plume flourished with profits from silver and gold in the mid-to-late 19th century. Silver Plume was the working center of the fields, and Georgetown, once the state's second-largest city, was where miners who struck it rich, along with merchants and the middle class, chose to live. A number of impressive Victorian-era houses and commercial structures remain.

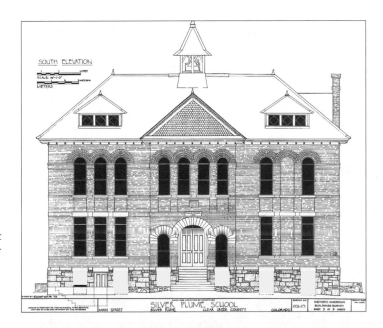

*Georgetown–Silver Plume Historic District, Clear Creek County. Silver Plume School, 1973. Courtesy of HABS (Richard Wolfe).*

■ *Conejos County*

## PIKE'S STOCKADE
**4 miles east of Sanford**

Here Zebulon Pike raised the American flag over Spanish soil during his 1807 expedition into territory acquired through the Louisiana Purchase. For this action, Spanish cavalrymen took him to Santa Fe, where he was interrogated and released. Pike left careful notes on the construction of the stockade, and these provided the basis for a 1960s replica built by the State of Colorado and administered by the Colorado Historical Society.

■ *El Paso County*

## PIKE'S PEAK
**Pike National Forest, 15 miles west of Colorado Springs**

Probably the best-known and most-visited mountain in the nation, Pike's Peak was named for explorer Zebulon Pike, the first American known to have viewed it. That was in 1806, and the first known ascent to its 14,110-foot summit was made in 1820. During the 19th century "Pikes Peak or Bust" became a familiar rallying cry for those heading west, and over the years the peak has assumed the role of a virtual icon of western exploration and settlement. The peak is within Pike National Forest, and a cog railway now takes visitors, numbering in the hundreds of thousands annually, to the top.

■ *Gilpin County*

## CENTRAL CITY/BLACKHAWK HISTORIC DISTRICT
**On Colorado Highway 119, Central City**

Central City/Blackhawk was the heart of the first great mining boom in Colorado (1860) and is at the center of one of the richest mining areas of the Rocky Mountain West. Discovery of gold here triggered the great Pike's Peak gold rush. The district encompasses hundreds of buildings, including rare examples of mining camp–era wooden structures and the famed Central City Opera House (1878), where stars such as Lillian Gish once performed. In 1932, the Opera House reopened for a summer music festival, which has now become an annual event.

■ *Kit Carson County*

## PHILADELPHIA TOBOGGAN COMPANY CAROUSEL NO. 6
**Kit Carson County Fairgrounds, Burlington**

Built in 1905 and moved in 1928 to the Kit Carson County fairgrounds, where it is still operating, this rare survivor was the sixth of 89 carousels built by the Philadelphia Toboggan Company. Its four chariots and individually carved 46-animal menagerie (camels, goats, horses, zebras, and others) revolve, three abreast, to music from a 1912 Wurlitzer Monster Military Band Organ. The carousel has recently undergone major restoration and is open during the summer. The animals have vibrant colors once again, and patrons can mount whichever animal they chose for only two bits ($.25).

■ *La Plata County*

## DURANGO-SILVERTON NARROW-GAUGE RAILROAD
**Between Durango and Silverton (La Plata and San Juan Counties)**

Completed in 1882, this 45-mile stretch of the Denver and Rio Grande Western Railway is one of the few narrow-gauge railroads surviving in the nation. It was built to haul ores from isolated areas to smelters and was also the main source of transportation and support for the mining community of Silverton, 45 miles from Durango. Covering a spectacularly scenic route, the railroad now operates as a popular tourist attraction during the summer.

■ *Lake County*

## LEADVILLE HISTORIC DISTRICT
**Town of Leadville**

Leadville's silver, gold, and zinc mines have yielded minerals of higher total value than those of any other mining district in the country. There were three major mining phases in the Leadville district, ranging from 1860 to 1917. A large number of early structures survive. The Healy House, a residential showplace built in 1878, and the Dexter Cabin, a miner's cabin of the same period, are now museums.

## ■ *Larimer County*

### LINDENMEIER SITE
**Address Restricted, Fort Collins vicinity, Larimer County**

Discovered in 1924, this was the first recognized and investigated campsite in the country where early man (the Folsom culture) had lived and worked. It was investigated from 1934 to 1940 by ethnologists from the Smithsonian Institution and the Colorado Museum of Natural History. Its two components, a campsite and a kill site, have provided glimpses into the life of the early hunters (9000–3000 B.C.) and have been of incalculable importance in developing archeological concepts.

## ■ *Las Animas County*

### RATON PASS
**Raton vicinity (Las Animas County, Colorado, and Colfax County, New Mexico)**

This mountain pass on the Santa Fe Trail was the shortest route between Colorado's upper Arkansas Valley and New Mexico. It played a crucial role in Stephen Watts Kearney's 1846 conquest of New Mexico and during the Civil War, when Confederate raiders and the threat of attack by southern Plains Indians halted traffic over the Cimarron cutoff.

## ■ *Montezuma County*

### LOWRY RUIN
**Pleasant View vicinity**

This 50-room pueblo (ca. A.D. 1100) is unusual in that it has a great kiva, a large underground ceremonial structure more commonly found in Arizona and New Mexico than in Colorado. The pueblo was constructed by the Anasazi (Old Ones) on foundations built by an earlier culture. Named after an early homesteader and investigated in 1930–1934, the pueblo ruins are on public land administered by the U.S. Bureau of Land Management.

### MESA VERDE ADMINISTRATIVE DISTRICT (NPS)
**Area at the head of Spruce Canyon, Mesa Verde National Park**

These 1920s core structures—park headquarters, museum, post office, and subsidiary buildings—were the first constructed by the

*Mesa Verde Administrative District, Montezuma County Park Headquarters building. Courtesy of NPS (Laura Soulliere Harrison).*

*Silverton Historic District, Silverton, San Juan County, 1971. Courtesy of HABS (William Edmund Barrett).*

National Park Service based on cultural traditions and designs represented in a particular park. Excellent examples of the Pueblo Revival style, they were the work of Jesse Nusbaum, archeologist and superintendent at Mesa Verde, who believed that appropriate designs would "help to preserve the Indian atmosphere which the ruins and environment create" and could be used to interpret and explain construction of the famous prehistoric dwellings built into the cliffs ca. A.D. 1100 to 1275.

■ *Otero County*

### BENT'S OLD FORT (NPS)
**West of Las Animas on Colorado Highway 194, La Junta vicinity**

Strategically located for trade with Southern Plains Indians, and the principal stop on the Mountain Branch of the Santa Fe Trail, this adobe post established by William and Charles Bent and Ceran Saint Vrain was the hub of a vast trading network ca. 1833–1849. In addition, during the Mexican War (1846–1848) Bent's Fort played a prominent role as a supply center for the U.S. Army. Now reconstructed on its original foundations, Bent's Old Fort is a National Historic Site.

■ *San Juan County*

### DURANGO-SILVERTON NARROW-GAUGE RAILROAD
**Between Durango and Silverton (La Plata and San Juan Counties)**

(See entry under La Plata County.)

### SILVERTON HISTORIC DISTRICT
**U.S. Route 550, Silverton**

As its name suggests, this was an important silver-producing area. Mining began in 1874, the year the town of Silverton was established. The town was connected to Durango by a narrow-gauge railroad in 1882. A number of significant buildings survive from the mining era, but the railroad (itself a National Historic Landmark) now transports tourists rather than miners. (See also Durango-Silverton Narrow-Gauge Railroad, La Plata County.)

■ *San Miguel County*

### TELLURIDE HISTORIC DISTRICT
**Route 145, Telluride**

Center of an extraordinarily rich gold mining area, Telluride was founded in 1878 and prospered after 1890, when the Denver and Rio Grande Railroad arrived. A number of buildings from its "boomtown" era remain, including the New Sheridan Hotel, where William Jennings Bryan once gave his "Cross of Gold" speech. Telluride now flourishes as a ski area and is consciously preserving its historic resources.

■ *Teller County*

### CRIPPLE CREEK HISTORIC DISTRICT
**Route 67, Cripple Creek**

One of the world's largest gold fields was discovered in 1891 along Cripple Creek. The town that sprang up was a Johnny-come-lately in the history of gold mining in Colorado, but by 1900, with a population of 25,000, it was the state's fourth-largest city. The next year, the area's gold fields yielded $25 million. After two fires in 1896 destroyed the formerly wooden town, rebuilding was done in brick and stone. A number of turn-of-the-century buildings remain, reflecting the character of the town's mining era.

# CONNECTICUT

■ *Fairfield County*

## BIRDCRAFT MUSEUM AND SANCTUARY

### 314 Unquowa Road, Fairfield

Mabel Osgood Wright helped resurrect the moribund Audubon movement at the end of the 19th century through her many writings and in 1898 organized the Audubon Society of Connecticut. In 1914 she established this sanctuary, named after one of her most popular books. Birdcraft displays another of her many contributions to ecology: "birdscaping," landscaping designed to attract birds. The museum contains dioramas depicting Connecticut wildlife.

## BUSH-HOLLEY HOUSE

### 39 Strickland Road, Greenwich

Three separate frame buildings were joined together at the end of the 18th century to form this house, which gained distinction between 1890 and 1920 as one of the nation's first summer art colonies. Distinguished figures in the development of American Impressionism taught and painted here. Many of them depicted the house, now a museum, in their works.

## OLIVER ELLSWORTH HOMESTEAD

### 778 Palisado Avenue, Windsor

From 1782 to 1807, Elmwood was home to Oliver Ellsworth, framer of the U.S. Constitution, author of the Judiciary Act of 1789 establishing the federal court system, and third chief justice of the United States. The house, a 2½-story clapboarded dwelling, is a museum.

## PHILIP JOHNSON'S GLASS HOUSE

### 798–856 Ponus Ridge Road, New Canaan

One of the masterworks of modern American architecture, Philip Johnson's 1949 Glass House epitomizes the International Style. It

*Philip Johnson's Glass House, New Canaan, Fairfield County. Courtesy of Bruce Clouette.*

and the subsequent additions Johnson made on his 16-acre estate provide an intimate glimpse into the work and thought of one of America's most influential 20th-century architects and critics. Features introduced here foreshadow elements in many of his major works. The property has been willed to the National Trust for Historic Preservation.

## LIGHTSHIP NO. 112, *NANTUCKET*
**Captain's Cove, Bridgeport**

Lightship No. 112, built in 1936 and best known by its former official designation, *Nantucket,* is one of a small number remaining of America's lightship fleet. For 39 years, *Nantucket* marked the dangerous Nantucket shoals and the eastern end of the Ambrose shipping channel into New York harbor. The station, established in 1854, was the most significant lightship station for transatlantic voyages. During its years of service, *Nantucket* was the last beacon seen by ships leaving the United States on the North Atlantic route, and the first seen by those entering. *Nantucket* is now a floating historic museum vessel.

## LOCKWOOD-MATHEWS MANSION
**295 West Avenue, Norwalk**

Erected between 1864 and 1868 from designs by Detlef Lienau, a Danish-born, French-trained New York architect, this is a prototypical example of the French Renaissance châteauesque style that came into full flower several decades later. Its scale and materials represented a new standard of opulent display, ushering in the Gilded Age. The mansion's rooms are arranged around a central octagonal rotunda lit by a skylight. The Lockwood-Mathews Mansion is now a house museum.

## STEPHEN TYNG MATHER HOME
**19 Stephen Mather Road, Darien**

Stephen Tyng Mather laid the foundations for the National Park Service as it operates today, serving as its first director from 1916 through 1929. His family's ancestral home was built in 1778 by his great-grandfather, and Mather regarded it as his home from 1906, when he became its sole owner, until his death in 1930. The house remains in family ownership.

## FREDERIC REMINGTON HOUSE
**154 Barry Avenue, Ridgefield**

For a brief period before his death, Frederic Remington, who realistically documented the life of the post–Civil War West in his artwork, lived in this house. Remington designed the gambrel-roofed, fieldstone-and-shingle Dutch Colonial house and produced his last works here. Theodore Roosevelt said of the artist's prodigious output, "The soldier, the cowboy and rancher, the Indian, the horses and the cattle of the Plains, will live in his pictures and his bronzes, I verily believe, for all time."

## JOHN ROGERS STUDIO
**10 Cherry Street, Ridgefield**

Sculptor John Rogers, once described as "honest and as inelegant as a stable boy," was one of America's most popular — and prolific — artists. During a 33-year career, he produced nearly 80,000 plaster copies of his 86 "Rogers Groups." These genre figures depicted "the little moments in life, humorous and sentimental, events which make up a lifetime." His statuettes *Coming to the Parson, Neighboring Pews,* and *The Checker Players* decorated Victorian parlors throughout the land. This little frame cottage that served as Rogers's studio from 1876 to his death in 1904 is now a museum displaying his works.

## JONATHAN STURGES HOUSE
**449 Mill Plain Road, Fairfield**

Built in 1840, this board-and-batten–sided building is one of the earliest and best-preserved architect-designed Gothic Revival cottages in the country. Extensive documentation relating to its building includes a color rendering by architect Joseph Collins Wells. Jonathan Sturges played an important role in promoting American art and served as patron to Asher Brown Durand. Later side and rear additions continued the board-and-batten motif of the original building.

## IDA TARBELL HOUSE
**320 Valley Road, Easton**

From 1906 to 1944 this was the home of Ida Tarbell, pioneer in the fields of contemporary journalism and literary biography. Working for *McClure's* magazine, she established her reputation with biographical series on Napoleon and Lincoln and sealed it with a series on Standard Oil that was later published in two volumes. Tarbell and journalists like Lincoln Steffens and Upton Sinclair, who focused on social problems from a stance of moral concern, were termed "muckrakers" by Theodore Roosevelt.

## ■ Hartford County

### A. EVERETT AUSTIN, JR., HOUSE
**130 Scarborough Street, Hartford**

Built in 1930, this Palladian style villa is the architectural embodiment of the achievements of A. Everett Austin, Jr., director of Hartford's Wadsworth Athenaeum from 1927 to 1944. Leigh French, Jr., was architect of record, but Austin supervised both design and construction. Interiors of the long, narrow house are particularly dramatic, ranging in stylistic influence from the baroque to the International. The house is now the property of the Athenaeum.

### HENRY BARNARD HOUSE
**118 Main Street, Hartford**

Henry Barnard, appointed first U.S. Commissioner of Education in 1867 by President Andrew Johnson, was born, lived, and died in this large brick house. Previous experience in promoting public educational policies in Connecticut and Rhode Island prepared him for the Washington position. From 1855 to 1882, Barnard published the 31-volume *American Journal of Education,* making material on educational practices and techniques available to teachers across the country.

### BUTTOLPH-WILLIAMS HOUSE
**249 Broad Street, Wethersfield**

Built in 1692, this is the oldest remaining house in Wethersfield, one of the oldest settlements in Connecticut. Now a museum, the restored 17th-century New England frame house with a two-room plan illustrates the range of architectural features and details that characterized the essentially medieval manner of building at the time.

### CHENEY BROTHERS HISTORIC DISTRICT
**Vicinity of Hartford Road and Laurel, Spruce, and Lampfield Streets, Manchester**

This 175-acre milling community commemorates the Cheney family's silk manufacturing enterprises. Included in the district are the 18th-century Cheney homestead (now a museum), several family mansions built by later generations, two dozen mill buildings, churches, and workers' houses. *Harper's Weekly* described the complex in 1890 as "in many respects…the most attractive mill village in the country." Technical innovations in spinning machinery helped the Cheney brothers achieve supremacy in the industry.

### SAMUEL COLT HOME
**80 Wethersfield Avenue, Hartford**

Armsmear is an extraordinarily large, rambling Italianate house dominated by a five-story tower. It was built by Samuel Colt, inventor of the Colt pistol and developer of mass production techniques. Colt's light and efficient revolver became popular during the war with Mexico, when the federal government ordered 1,000. As directed in his widow's will, the house is now a residence for widows of Episcopal clergymen and "impoverished but refined and educated gentlewomen."

### CONNECTICUT STATE CAPITOL
**Capitol Avenue, Hartford**

This ornate marble and granite edifice highlighted by a tall central dome was built in 1872–1880 and is considered one of the nation's finest examples of a monumentally scaled High Victorian Gothic building. Its eclectic nature is suggested by comments of a critic who declared that architect Richard M. Upjohn "had dined on Gothic, with an entrée or two of French chateaux and a dessert of Renaissance."

### SILAS DEANE HOUSE
**203 Main Street, Wethersfield**

Silas Deane, first envoy from the united American colonies, arrived in France in May 1776 at the behest of the Continental Congress. He was successful in negotiating French military and financial assistance that proved invaluable in the struggle for independence. Deane built this two-story frame house in 1766. Now a museum, it was restored in 1963–1965.

## FIRST CHURCH OF CHRIST, FARMINGTON
### 75 Main Street, Farmington

This handsome 18th-century New England meeting house played a role in the *Amistad* affair (1839–1841), foremost case in American history involving the foreign slave trade. In the summer of 1839, a group of Africans successfully mutinied against the crew of the slaveship *Amistad*. After numerous deliberations, they were declared free by the U.S. Supreme Court in 1841. They were transported to Farmington while awaiting transportation home, became active members of the community, and worshiped here. (See Austin F. Williams Carriagehouse and House.)

## HILL-STEAD MUSEUM
### 35 Mountain Road, Farmington

Hill-Stead, one of the country's foremost Colonial Revival houses, is the centerpiece of a large country estate. Built in 1901, the rambling frame house was designed by its original owner, Theodate Pope Riddle, in a unique collaboration with architects McKim, Mead & White. Now a museum, it remains as Mrs. Riddle left it upon her death in 1946. Hill-Stead contains an outstanding collection of French Impressionist paintings, assembled by Alfred A. Pope, the architect-owner's father.

## KIMBERLY MANSION
### 1625 Main Street, Glastonbury

Julia and Abby Smith, two elderly sisters, received an inequitable tax assessment on this large 18th-century farmhouse when they inherited it in the 1870s. Their vigorous and articulate protests against "taxation without representation" eventually secured a legal decision against the tax collector and, in the process, attracted international attention to their stand on women's rights.

## EDWARD W. MORLEY HOUSE
### 26 Westland Avenue, West Hartford

From 1906 to 1923 this unadorned frame house was the retirement home of chemist Edward W. Morley, who collaborated with Albert A. Michelson in measuring the speed of light (1887) and determining the atomic weights of hydrogen and oxygen.

## CHARLES H. NORTON HOUSE
### 132 Redstone Hill, Plainville

From 1922 until his death, Charles H. Norton, inventor and manufacturer of heavy-duty precision grinding machines that have become integral to modern industrial technology, lived here. His Plainville home, a handsome Georgian Revival house named Sharpenhoe, remains in private ownership.

## OLD NEW-GATE PRISON
### Newgate Road, Granby

Used from 1775 to 1782 for incarceration of Tories and other political offenders, New-

*First Church of Christ, Farmington, Hartford County. Courtesy of HABS (Jack E. Boucher).*

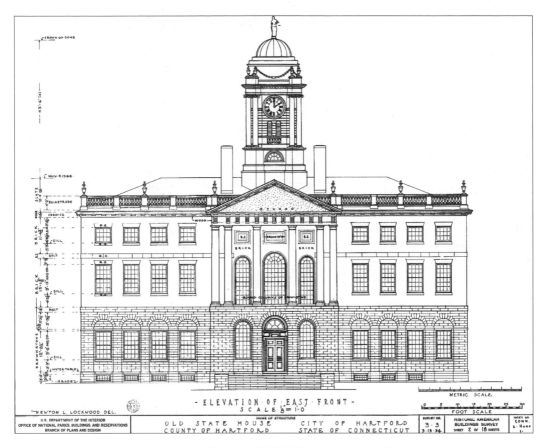

*Old Statehouse, Hartford, Hartford County. Courtesy of HABS (Newton L. Lockwood).*

Gate was undoubtedly the most horrendous prison in the North American colonies. Prisoners were housed deep underground and forced to work in copper mines that had operated at the site between 1707 and 1745. Stone and brick buildings at the prison, now a museum operated by the Connecticut Historical Commission, date mostly from 1790 to 1802, when New-Gate served as Connecticut's first state prison.

## OLD STATEHOUSE
### Main Street at Central Row

Designed in 1792 by Charles Bulfinch and erected in 1793–1796, this is the first of the great New England architect's public buildings in his dignified Adamesque Federal style. The Hartford Convention of 1814, one of the earliest debates on the sovereignty of states versus national sovereignty, was held here. After a new state capitol was built, this

became Hartford's city hall. It is now a museum.

## STANLEY-WHITMAN HOUSE
### 37 High Street, Farmington

This classic New England saltbox house, with its typical long, sloping roof to the rear, central chimney, framed second-story overhang with pendants, and diamond-paned sash windows, dates from 1720 but incorporates earlier features typical of late-17th-century work. A museum since 1935, the house was restored in the 1980s.

## MARK TWAIN HOME
### 351 Farmington Avenue, Hartford

From 1874 to 1891 this showy, idiosyncratic mansion was the residence of Samuel Langhorne Clemens, who assisted architect Edward Tuckerman Potter in its design. Clemens, a.k.a. Mark Twain, paid for it with

*Joseph Webb House, Wethersfield, Hartford County, 1960. Courtesy of NPS.*

proceeds from his *Innocents Abroad,* and it was here that he later wrote *The Adventures of Tom Sawyer* and *The Adventures of Huckleberry Finn.* Louis Comfort Tiffany helped decorate the house, which has been described as "part steamboat, part medieval stronghold, and part cuckoo clock."

## JOSEPH WEBB HOUSE
### 211 Main Street, Wethersfield

This handsome and conservative example of late Georgian design, a style used frequently in colonial Connecticut, was built in 1752. Its five days of fame came in May 1781 when General George Washington and the Count

de Rochambeau, French commander in America, held a conference here to plan a united offensive against the British. American and French troops moved south in conjunction with the arrival of the French fleet, and ultimately victory was achieved at Yorktown. The house is now a museum.

## NOAH WEBSTER BIRTHPLACE
### 227 South Main Street, Hartford

This classic early Connecticut saltbox was the birthplace of America's most famous lexicographer, or wordsmith. Noah Webster's two-volume *American Dictionary of the English Language* was published in 1828. His father had mort-

*Noah Webster Birthplace, Hartford, Hartford County. Courtesy of HABS (Robert Fulton III).*

gaged the farm, along with this farmhouse, to pay for young Noah's education at Yale, and it was obviously a case of money well spent. The house is now a museum.

## AUSTIN F. WILLIAMS CARRIAGEHOUSE AND HOUSE
### 127 Main Street, Farmington

Austin F. Williams, a leading abolitionist of his day, established a station on the Underground Railroad here and helped make Farmington a center of abolition activity in the Northeast. The property's particular significance derives from its association with the celebrated *Amistad* affair of 1839–1841. In a complex legal case arising from a slave revolt on the high seas in 1839, slavery as an institution was challenged for the first time in the U.S. Supreme Court. In March 1841, members of the Mende tribe of West Africa who had participated in the revolt were released from prison and housed in quarters that Williams provided. They remained in their temporary domicile, now incorporated in the carriagehouse, until they were returned to their homeland in November 1841. (See First Church of Christ.)

## ■ *Litchfield County*
### LITCHFIELD HISTORIC DISTRICT
### Vicinity of the Village Green, Litchfield

Probably the finest surviving example of a typical late-18th-century New England town, Litchfield was settled in the 1720s and named for an English cathedral city. During much of the 18th century the town was an outpost and trading center for Connecticut's northwest frontier. Litchfield contains impressive examples of architectural styles popular in the late 18th and early 19th centuries, as well as the later Colonial Revival.

## TAPPING REEVE HOUSE AND LAW SCHOOL
### South Street, Litchfield

Because so many of the approximately 1,000 graduates of this privately operated law school became prominent lawyers, judges, and politicians, it had a significant influence on the development of American jurisprudence. Founded in 1784 by Tapping Reeve and in operation until 1833, this was the first law school in the country not affiliated with any university. Aaron Burr, Reeve's brother-in-law, was the first student, and he and John C. Calhoun were among the school's well-known graduates. Both the house, built by Reeve in 1773, and the law building, added in 1784 as a library and lecture hall, are now museums.

## OLIVER WOLCOTT HOUSE
### South Street, Litchfield

From 1753 to 1797 this was the home of Oliver Wolcott, politician, soldier, and jurist.

Wolcott was a delegate to the Continental Congress, a signer of the Declaration of Independence, a state senator, and a governor of Connecticut. He built the frame Georgian style house in 1753. A descendant restored it ca. 1920, and it remains in private hands.

## ■ New Haven County

## RUSSELL HENRY CHITTENDEN HOUSE

**83 Trumbull Street, New Haven**

From 1887 to 1943 this Queen Anne style house was the residence of Russell Henry Chittenden, often known as the father of American biochemistry. Chittenden, director of Yale's Sheffield Scientific School, helped establish biochemistry as a major biological discipline.

## CONNECTICUT AGRICULTURAL EXPERIMENT STATION

**123 Huntington Street, New Haven**

In 1882 this property became the permanent home of the nation's first state agricultural experiment station, established by the Connecticut state legislature in 1875. Created largely because of the efforts of Professor W. O. Atwater, the station has consistently contributed to American agricultural development. The five-acre site contains several buildings, including Osborne Library, erected in 1882–1883 as the nation's first structure for a state agricultural experiment station.

## CONNECTICUT HALL, YALE UNIVERSITY

**Bounded by High, Chapel, Elm, and College Streets, New Haven**

Constructed in 1750–1752 with funds obtained through a lottery and with assistance from Connecticut's colonial legislature, this is the oldest surviving building at Yale, the nation's third-oldest institution of higher learning. When completed, it was described as "the best building in the colony," and it is now the only pre-Revolutionary building on campus. Although Yalies may not like to admit it, the conservatively styled Georgian structure was likely modeled on Harvard's Massachusetts Hall.

## JAMES DWIGHT DANA HOUSE

**24 Hillhouse Avenue, New Haven**

This villa was the home of James Dwight Dana, the Yale University geology professor who broadened the scope of his discipline from a study of rocks and minerals to a larger focus embracing the earth's geologic history and evolution. Dana developed his concepts while on the government-sponsored Wilkes Expedition that circled the globe in 1838–1842. New Haven architect Henry

*Othniel C. Marsh House, New Haven, New Haven County, 1963. Courtesy of NPS.*

Austin designed the house for Dana in 1848, and the family deeded it to Yale in 1962.

## OTHNIEL C. MARSH HOUSE
### 360 Prospect Street, New Haven

This fortresslike, red sandstone mansion was the residence of Othniel Charles Marsh, America's first professor of paleontology, whose studies and work supported Darwin's theory of evolution. Marsh also induced his wealthy uncle, George Peabody, to establish the Peabody Museum at Yale. Marsh, who lived here from 1878 until his death in 1899, willed his house and botanical gardens to the university. The Yale School of Forestry currently occupies the house.

## LAFAYETTE B. MENDEL HOUSE
### 18 Trumbull Street, New Haven

From 1900 to 1924 this was the home of Lafayette B. Mendel, the distinguished early-20th-century Yale biochemist. Mendel contributed to the identification of vitamins and performed pioneering research on proteins and nutrition in general.

## NEW HAVEN GREEN HISTORIC DISTRICT
### Bounded by Chapel, College, Elm, and Church Streets, New Haven

New Haven Green is significant because of three churches erected between 1812 and 1816 on its eastern side. The churches are remarkable for their individual architectural merit and as an outstanding 19th-century urban ensemble. The late Georgian/early Federal style Center Church (First Church of Christ, Congregational) was Connecticut's most monumental church of its time. United Church (Old North Church, Congregational) is a less exuberant example with similar lines, and Trinity Church (Episcopal) was one of the first major Gothic Revival structures in America.

## HENRY WHITFIELD HOUSE
### 248 Old Whitfield Street, Guilford

This much restored house, imbued with symbolism and sanctified by antiquity, represents important stages in America's attitude toward historic preservation, from an approach based largely on appearance and aesthetics to a more academic orientation. Said to date from ca. 1639–1640, the Whitfield House was remodeled in 1868 following a fire, heavily restored in 1902–1904, and restored again in the 1930s. It was opened to the public in 1899 as one of the first state-owned historical museums in New England.

## YALE BOWL
### Southwest of intersection of Chapel and Yale Streets, New Haven

This reinforced-concrete structure is one of the oldest active college stadiums in the country and was the largest in the nation when it opened in 1914. It was widely emulated because its "bowl" shape provided fine views for 71,000 spectators. It also commemorates Yale's influence in early college football because of its noted player-coach-official, Walter Camp.

## ◼ New London County
### CHARLES W. MORGAN
### Mystic Seaport, Mystic

Built and launched in 1841 in New Bedford, Massachusetts, this is the last of America's square-rigged wooden whaling vessels. Named after a principal owner, the *Morgan* made its last whaling voyage in 1921. During the 80 years it sailed, its crews killed more than 2,500 whales and brought more than 50,000 barrels of oil to port. The handsome three-masted *Morgan* is now a popular attraction at Mystic Seaport.

### EMMA C. BERRY
### Mystic Seaport Museum, Mystic

Known as a sloop smack and named for its captain's daughter, *Emma* was launched in 1866 in Noank, Connecticut, and joined others of its type in fishing for mackerel. Its graceful lines belie its workaday purpose. In fact, the year it was launched a local newspaper commented that such vessels "look more like small yachts or pleasure boats than fishing smacks." The wooden-hulled boats were designed to keep their catches alive in an internal "wet well" until reaching port. Now the last known survivor of its class, *Emma* is a

Emma C. Berry, *Mystic, New London County. Courtesy of the Mystic Seaport Museum, Inc., Mystic, CT (Mary Anne Stets).*

fully rigged floating exhibit at Mystic Seaport.

## FORT SHANTOK ARCHEOLOGICAL DISTRICT

**Address Restricted, Montville**

From 1636 to 1682 this was the most important Mohegan settlement and home of Uncas, tribal leader and statesman. Uncas helped Connecticut colonials defeat the Pequots in 1637 and in 1638 entered into a defense pact with Massachusetts Bay colonists in Boston. The site, always regarded as a sacred place by the Mohegans, became a state park in the 1920s, and professional excavations beginning in 1962 uncovered a wealth of artifacts. The Mohegan Nation was formally recognized as a tribe in 1994, and in 1995 the State of Connecticut returned Fort Shantok to it.

## FLORENCE GRISWOLD HOUSE

**96 Lyme Street, Old Lyme**

This elegant Federal style frame house, built in 1817, was operated as a boarding house

from 1899 through 1936 by Miss Florence Griswold. During that time it served as a center of American Impressionism, as artists who stayed there were among the leading practitioners in that style. Miss Griswold encouraged artists to paint panels of the dining room walls, and these remain a bravura testament to artistic talent and fellowship. The house is now the Florence Griswold Museum.

## L.A. DUNTON

**Mystic Seaport Museum, Mystic**

*L. A. Dunton,* launched in 1921, is the last surviving example of a once common early-20th-century New England fishing vessel. Built along the lines of the schooner *Jofre,* a vessel designed by Thomas J. McManus, prolific and influential planner of fishing schooners, *Dunton* incorporates features he introduced to improve safety and performance. A two-masted schooner, the fully restored, fully rigged ship is berthed at Mystic Seaport as a floating exhibit.

## MASHANTUCKET PEQUOT RESERVATION ARCHEOLOGICAL DISTRICT

**Address Restricted, Ledyard**

The Mashantucket Pequot Reservation Archeological District comprises nearly 1,638 acres of archeologically sensitive land in the northern portion of the uplands historically called Wawarramoreke by the Pequots. It is within the territory first chronicled as Pequot land in the earliest surviving map (1614) of the region.

## MONTE CRISTO COTTAGE

**325 Pequot Avenue, New London**

Eugene O'Neill, one of America's foremost dramatists, spent most of his first 21 summers in this frame house, the closest approximation to a home he ever knew in his youth. He likely wrote his earliest plays here, and the house later inspired the setting of his famous *Long Day's Journey into Night.* The house was named for a trite but profitable play in which his actor-father was a perennial star. (See Tao House, Contra Costa County, California.)

Nautilus, *Groton, New London County. Launching, 1954. Courtesy of the Department of Navy, Submarine Force Museum.*

## *NAUTILUS*

### Naval Submarine Base, Groton

The brainchild of Admiral Hyman G. Rickover, USS *Nautilus* was launched in 1954 as the world's first nuclear-propelled submarine. This pivotal achievement in naval engineering enabled *Nautilus* to remain submerged far longer than had previously been possible. *Nautilus* demonstrated its remarkable capabilities on its maiden voyage in 1955 when it set mileage and time records for sub-

mersion, and again in 1958 when it navigated beneath the Arctic icepack to the North Pole. Decommissioned in 1980, *Nautilus* rests in the Thames River in Groton as part of the Submarine Force Museum.

## CAPTAIN NATHANIEL B. PALMER HOUSE

### 40 Palmer Street, Stonington

This large Italianate house, now a museum, was the home of Nathaniel B. Palmer, the

*Captain Nathaniel B. Palmer House, Stonington, New London County. Courtesy of NPS (Janice Cunningham, Cunningham Preservation Associates).*

American mariner who discovered Antarctica in 1820. The Antarctican peninsula that Palmer found and mapped still bears his name. Palmer's achievements were not limited to exploration. He was also a noted ship designer and played a major role in the development of clipper ships. Fittingly, the house was capped by a large octagonal cupola, where Captain Palmer could look out on his beloved Stonington harbor.

## *SABINO*
**Mystic Seaport Museum, Mystic**

Launched in 1908 in Maine, *Sabino* is a rare surviving example of an excursion steamer, a boat designed to carry large groups of passengers on pleasure trips in inland waters. Thanks to a major restoration from 1975 to 1980, *Sabino* now carries passengers around Mystic Seaport, providing them with an open-deck experience similar to those enjoyed by past generations.

## JOHN TRUMBULL BIRTHPLACE
**Town Commons, Lebanon**

Joseph Trumbull built this classic New England early Georgian frame house (1735–1740) as a wedding present for his son, Jonathan Trumbull, who served as governor of Connecticut from 1769 to 1784. Jonathan's son, John Trumbull, was born here in 1756. A portraitist and painter of historical subjects, John was commissioned in 1817 to paint four Revolutionary War scenes for the rotunda of the U.S. Capitol. The house contains a number of original Trumbull family furnishings.

## WILLIAM WILLIAMS HOUSE
**Junction of Connecticut Routes 87 and 207, Lebanon**

William Williams, who served as a Connecticut delegate to the Continental Congress, was a signer of the Declaration of Independence, and helped frame the Articles of Confederation, lived in this shingle-covered house from 1755 to his death in 1811. Williams was son-in-law to Connecticut governor Jonathan Trumbull, whose house, also a National Historic Landmark, is close by.

## ◼ *Windham County*

## HENRY C. BOWEN HOUSE
**556 Route 169, Woodstock**

This is one of the best-documented, most fully developed, and most nearly intact Gothic Revival cottage-villas in the nation. Retaining its original interior and exterior architectural features, it was designed in 1845 by English-born architect Joseph Collins Wells. Although influences of architectural theories espoused by Andrew Jackson Downing and Alexander Jackson Davis are apparent, Wells deserves credit for the creative use of Gothic motifs and lively individualism. Also known as Roseland Cottage, Bowen House is now operated as a historic house museum.

## PRUDENCE CRANDALL HOUSE
**Southwest Corner of State Routes 14 and 169, Canterbury**

Prudence Crandall, American educator and reformer, lived in this elegant late-Georgian house for four pivotal years. She began teaching school here in 1831, but after admitting a young black girl in 1832, she lost local support. Instead of retreating, she reopened the school exclusively to teach "young ladies and misses of color"; however, after a mob attacked the house in 1834, she closed the academy, fearing for the safety of her students. Crandall became a symbol of the abolition movement, and her courageous stand helped the cause. The house is now operated as a museum by the Connecticut Historical Commission.

## SAMUEL HUNTINGTON BIRTHPLACE
**Connecticut Route 14, Scotland**

This early-18th-century saltbox was the birthplace and boyhood home of Samuel Huntington, a Connecticut signer of the Declaration of Independence, lawyer, politician, jurist, president of the Continental Congress from 1779 to 1781, and later governor of Connecticut. Little altered, the house is currently being restored.

Prudence Crandall
House, Canterbury,
Windham County.
Courtesy of Prudence
Crandall Museum
(Dennis Oparowski).

# DELAWARE

■ *Kent County*

## ASPENDALE

**1 mile west of Kenton**

Begun in 1771 and completed in 1773, this moderately sized brick farmhouse shows the persistence of early-Georgian architectural traditions in colonial Delaware. It utilizes the "Quaker plan," a single great room on one side, with two rooms sharing a chimney on the other. An older frame wing is attached to the house. Aspendale still presides over a rural landscape, with lanes and field divisions much as they were in the 18th century.

## JOHN DICKINSON HOUSE

**Kitts Hummock Road, southeast of Dover**

John Dickinson earned the title "Penman of the Revolution" through political writings such as *Letters from a Pennsylvania Farmer*

(1767) and lyrics to *The Liberty Song* (1768). Dickinson was one of Delaware's five delegates who signed the Constitution, and it was largely due to his influence that Delaware was the first state to ratify it, on December 7, 1787. Dickinson inherited the early Georgian style house in 1760 and constructed several additions prior to his death in 1808. Although a disastrous fire in 1804 consumed the original 1740 section, Dickinson reconstructed the dwelling. The property has been a state historic museum since 1956.

■ *New Castle County*

## JACOB BROOM HOUSE

**1 mile northwest of Wilmington, Montchanin**

Jacob Broom, signer of the U.S. Constitution served in the Delaware legislature and attended the Annapolis Convention in 1786. A

*Corbit-Sharp House, Odessa, New Castle County. 1967. Courtesy of NPS (Charles W. Snell).*

*John Dickinson House, Kent County. Courtesy of HABS (Jack E. Boucher).*

Georgia delegate to the convention called Broom "a plain good Man with some abilities, but nothing to render him conspicuous." He built this plain good stuccoed-stone house in 1795 and lived in it until 1802, when he sold it to E. I. du Pont, who expanded it.

## CORBIT-SHARP HOUSE
### Southwest corner, Main and Second Streets, Odessa

This elegant brick house, erected in 1772–1774, is one of the major examples of the mature Georgian style in the middle colonies. Its builder, William Corbit, had close economic ties with Philadelphia, and the architecture of that colonial metropolis obviously influenced the design of his house. The Henry Francis du Pont Winterthur Museum owns and operates the Corbit-Sharp house as a furnished historic house museum.

## ELEUTHERIAN MILLS
### North of Wilmington on Delaware Route 141 at Brandywine Creek Bridge, Greenville

Eleuthère Irenée du Pont established powder

mills here on Brandywine Creek in 1802-1803. For more than a century the black powder they produced helped the United States win its wars and established E. I. du Pont de Nemours & Co. as a major industrial corporation. The powder mills closed in 1921, but in 1952, as part of its sesquicentennial, the du Pont Company established the Eleutherian Mills-Hagley Foundation to restore and maintain the complex as a museum of early industry and as a research facility.

## FORT CHRISTINA
### Seventh Street and the Christina River, Wilmington

Built under the direction of Peter Minuit and named for the queen of Sweden, this first Swedish military outpost (1638) in the Delaware Valley was the nucleus around which the first Swedish settlement in North America developed. The fort fell into disrepair after the English conquest in 1664. In 1938, in commemoration of its tercentenary, the state of Delaware developed the site as a park. The site features an imposing sculpture including a representation of the *Kalmar Nyckel*, the ship that brought the first settlers. It was sculpted by Carl Milles and presented by the people of Sweden.

## HOLY TRINITY (OLD SWEDES) CHURCH
### Seventh and Church Streets, Wilmington

Built in 1698, this picturesque stone church is the most visible link with the Delaware Valley's early Swedish settlement. Although it was constructed after the fall of New Sweden, the church was built for a Swedish Lutheran congregation and services were held in the language of its members well into the 18th century. A parklike cemetery, older than the church, surrounds it and holds the remains of many Swedish settlers. Holy Trinity has housed an Episcopal parish since 1791.

## LOMBARDY HALL
### Concord Pike, Wilmington

Gunning Bedford, Jr., a Delaware delegate to the Continental Congress and the Annapolis Convention and a signer of the U.S.

Constitution in 1787, lived in this sturdy stone house, built of Brandywine granite, from 1793 to 1812. When the house was threatened with demolition in the 1960s, it was purchased by an affiliate of the Wilmington Masonic Order (Bedford was the first Grand Master of Masons in Delaware) and subsequently restored. It is currently operated as a house museum.

## NEW CASTLE HISTORIC DISTRICT
### Bounded by Harmony Street, The Strand, Third Street, and Delaware Street, New Castle

Founded by Peter Stuyvesant in 1651 to serve as New Netherland's capital on the Delaware, New Castle continued as the capital of colonial Delaware until 1776. With the growth of nearby Wilmington and the removal of the capitol to Dover, once busy New Castle became a quiet backwater. It survives as one of the nation's best-preserved colonial towns, with its original green surrounded by houses, churches, stores, and governmental buildings, a number of them open to the public.

## OLD COURTHOUSE
### Delaware Street, between Second and Third Streets, New Castle

This 1732 Georgian building was Delaware's colonial and early state capitol until 1777, when legislators decided to move to the more centrally located Dover. From 1777 to 1881 it was New Castle County's court house. The cupola served as the beginning point of the 12-mile radius that determines Delaware's curved northern boundary. Among the important events that took place here were Delaware's decision to separate from Great Britain and Pennsylvania and the writing and adoption of the first state constitution, both in 1776. The building was restored between 1955 and 1963 and is now a museum operated by the state.

## STONUM
### Ninth and Washington Streets, New Castle

Dating from the mid–18th century, Stonum was the country home of George Read. His accomplishments are neatly summarized in his epitaph, which reads: "Member of the

*Stonum, New Castle,*
*New Castle County.*
*Courtesy of HABS*
*(Jack E. Boucher).*

Congress of the Revolution, the Convention that framed the Constitution of the United States and of the first Senate under it. Judge of Admiralty. President and Chief Justice of Delaware and a Signer of the Declaration of Independence."

# DISTRICT OF COLUMBIA

### CLEVELAND ABBE HOUSE
**2017 I Street, NW**

From 1877 to 1909 this handsome Federal style town house was the home of Cleveland Abbe, a prominent meteorologist known as the father of the U.S. Weather Service. Timothy Caldwell built the house ca. 1802–1805 and rented it to James Monroe during the second decade of the 19th century. It served as the British legation in the 1820s and has been the private Arts Club of Washington since 1916.

### ADMINISTRATION BUILDING, CARNEGIE INSTITUTION OF WASHINGTON
**1530 P Street, NW**

Andrew Carnegie founded and endowed this Institution in 1902 to encourage scientific "investigation, research, and discovery" that would lead "to the improvement of mankind." The Beaux-Arts style building, designed by New York architects Carrère and Hastings, was completed in 1910. The building currently houses the administrative offices of the Carnegie Institution.

### AMERICAN FEDERATION OF LABOR BUILDING
**901 Massachusetts Avenue, NW**

On July 4, 1916, the American Federation of Labor (AFL) dedicated this imposing seven-story brick building as its new international headquarters. President Woodrow Wilson delivered the chief address for a building that, in the words of its founder Samuel Gompers,

*American Federation of Labor Building, 1973. Courtesy of NPS (Carol Ann Poh).*

symbolized the Federation's growth from "a weakling into the strongest, best organized labor movement of all the world." For years the building was known as the "national labor temple," but after the AFL merged with the CIO (Congress of Industrial Organizations) in 1955, it was sold. Although subsequently modernized, its exterior is largely unchanged. (See Samuel Gompers House.)

## AMERICAN PEACE SOCIETY
### 734 Jackson Place, NW

From 1911 to 1948, this Italianate town house facing Lafayette Square was headquarters of the nation's oldest organization dedicated solely to promoting international peace.

The Society was founded in 1828 by William Ladd, who sought to foster popular sentiment against war and attempted to persuade legislatures and individual leaders to organize an international court of arbitration as a logical alternative to war.

## AMERICAN RED CROSS NATIONAL HEADQUARTERS
### 17th and D Streets, NW

Constructed between 1915 and 1917, this monumental white marble Classical Revival building was designed to serve a dual purpose: as a memorial to women who served in the Civil War and as administrative headquarters of the nation's official relief organization.

*American Red Cross National Headquarters. Courtesy of the American National Red Cross.*

The Red Cross movement began in Europe to give aid on a neutral basis to the sick and wounded during wartime. Clara Barton founded the American Association of the Red Cross in 1881, and it was granted a congressional charter in 1900.

## ANDERSON HOUSE
**2118 Massachusetts Avenue, NW**

Designed by Boston architects Little & Browne and built between 1902 and 1905, this 50-room Late Renaissance Revival style building with its opulent interiors is an outstanding example of an early-20th-century urban mansion. Ambassador (ret.) Larz Anderson and his wife Isabel commissioned it as their home but planned for its eventual use as national headquarters, museum, and library of the Society of the Cincinnati. Anderson was a descendant of a founder of the nation's oldest patriotic order, composed of descendants of Revolutionary War officers. Except for brief periods during World War II, it has served its intended purpose since 1938.

## ARMY MEDICAL MUSEUM AND LIBRARY
**Walter Reed Army Medical Center, 6825 16th Street, NW**

Founded in 1862 "to collect and properly arrange...all specimens of morbid anatomy" that were accumulating during the Civil War, this was one of the nation's first organized medical/military research programs. The intent of assembling such a collection was to minimize loss of life among the wounded through a centralized study of specimens. The

collections were moved to the Armed Forces Institute of Pathology at the Walter Reed Army Medical Center in 1971 after the original building that housed the museum on the Mall was demolished.

## ARTS AND INDUSTRIES BUILDING, SMITHSONIAN INSTITUTION
**900 Jefferson Drive, SW**

Constructed between 1879 and 1881, this is the nation's best preserved example of 19th-century "world's fair" or "exposition" architecture. With its towers and pavilions faced in red brick and accents in yellow and blue polychrome brick, it presents a jaunty contrast to its more somber neighbors on the Mall. The building was designed by Adolph Cluss and Paul Schultze and constructed to house exhibits relocated from the Philadelphia Centennial Exhibition of 1876. The museum was rehabilitated in the 1970s as part of the nation's bicentennial celebrations.

## ASHBURTON HOUSE
**1525 H Street, NW**

Negotiations that took place here during a ten-month period in 1842 resulted in the Webster-Ashburton Treaty, settling the long-standing dispute with Great Britain over the U.S./Canadian boundary. At the time, the large town house was rented by Alexander Baring, Lord Ashburton, who had been appointed to negotiate with Secretary of State Daniel Webster. In 1954 the house was acquired by the neighboring Saint John's Episcopal Church, and it now serves as the parish house.

*Arts and Industries Building, Smithsonian Institution. Courtesy of HABS (Jack E. Boucher).*

## NEWTON D. BAKER HOUSE
**3017 N Street, NW**

From 1916 to 1920 this early Georgetown mansion was the residence of Newton Diehl Baker, U.S. secretary of war, who presided over the nation's World War I mobilization. Under his direction, the tide of battle on the western front turned in favor of the Allies. After the war Baker was a major proponent of Woodrow Wilson's concept of world involvement. The house had a second moment of fame after the assassination of President John F. Kennedy, when his widow purchased it and lived here for a year. It remains a private residence.

## BLAIR HOUSE
**1651–1653 Pennsylvania Avenue, NW**

This restrained town house, its first section built in the 1820s, has been enlarged and remodeled a number of times since. It has served as the federal government's official guest residence since 1942 and is significant for the great number of dignitaries who have resided or have been received within its walls. Blair House, named for Francis Preston Blair, Sr., who bought it in 1836, served as President Truman's home during the time the White House was being remodeled. The complex was restored in 1988 and enlarged yet again at the same time.

## WILLIAM E. BORAH APARTMENT, WINDSOR LODGE
**2139–2141 Wyoming Avenue, NW**

From 1913 to 1929 William E. Borah, leading Republican progressive senator from Idaho and a powerful force in promoting isolationist foreign policy during the 1920s, lived in apartment 21E in this early-20th-century co-op. Borah was a leader of the "irreconcilables," who defeated President Wilson's League of Nations.

## BLANCHE K. BRUCE HOUSE
**909 M Street, NW**

Republican Blanche Kelso Bruce, representing Mississippi, was the first African American to serve a full term in the U.S. Senate (1875–1881). He lived in this then-new Second Empire style brick house during his years in Congress. Prior to serving in the Senate, Bruce held various local elective and appointed offices. Afterward, he remained in Washington and was appointed D.C. Recorder of Deeds and Registrar of the U. S. Treasury.

## CARNEGIE ENDOWMENT FOR INTERNATIONAL PEACE
**700 Jackson Place, NW**

In 1910 Andrew Carnegie gave $10,000,000 to "hasten the abolition of war, the foulest blot upon our civilization." Carnegie stated that he was "drawn more to this cause than to any," and at his instigation, the Carnegie Endowment for International Peace was established in Washington. This red brick town house with Italianate detail, built in 1860 on Lafayette Square across from the White House, served as the endowment's headquarters until 1948.

## MARY ANN SHADD CARY HOUSE
**1421 W Street, NW**

From 1881 to 1885 this modest brick town house was the residence of Mary Ann Shadd Cary, writer, journalist, educator, and abolitionist. Cary lectured widely in the cause of abolition and after the Civil War became the nation's first African-American female lawyer.

## CITY HALL
**Fourth and E Streets, NW**

This imposing Greek Revival building, designed by architect George Hadfield, was constructed over a number of years, beginning in 1820. It served as city hall until the Civil War, when the federal government occupied it. It was converted into a courthouse, and among the trials of national interest held here was that of John Surratt, conspirator in Lincoln's assassination. The building was reconstructed in 1916–1918 and continues in governmental use.

## CONSTITUTION HALL
**311 18th Street, NW**

Designed by John Russell Pope and built in 1928–1929, this 4,000-seat hall accommodates annual Continental Congresses of the National Society of the Daughters of the American Revolution (DAR). These are held during the week of April 19 (the anniversary of the battles of Lexington and Concord). Constitution Hall, which augmented the DAR's adjoining headquarters building, Memorial Continental Hall, served for more than 40 years as an unofficial cultural center for the nation's capital. Its use was denied to singer Marian Anderson in 1939, a notable event in the national struggle for civil rights. (See Memorial Continental Hall.)

## CORCORAN GALLERY AND SCHOOL OF ART
**1700 New York Avenue, NW**

Chartered by Congress in 1870, the Corcoran Gallery is one of America's oldest art museums. It was founded by philanthropist William Wilson Corcoran, who contributed his collection and donated its first building, now the Renwick Gallery. At the turn of the century the gallery and school of art moved to this impressive Beaux-Arts building, designed by prominent New York architect Ernest Flagg. The Corcoran was the first of several monumental structures built to the southwest of the White House.

## ELLIOTT COUES HOUSE
**1726 N Street, NW**

From 1887 until his death in 1899, Elliot Coues, a leading 19th-century ornithologist, whose studies greatly expanded the knowledge of North American bird life, lived here. Coues helped found the American Ornithologists Union in 1883 and edited approximately 15 volumes of journals, memoirs, and diaries by famous western explorers and fur traders.

## DECATUR HOUSE
**748 Jackson Place, NW**

This brick town house was designed by Benjamin Henry Latrobe, one of America's first professional architects, for Commodore Stephen Decatur, suppressor of the Barbary pirates. The first private residence on Lafayette Square, it was built in 1818–1819. Decatur occupied it only shortly, dying in the house on the evening of March 22, 1820, after a fatal duel that day with Commodore James Barron. Later well-known residents included Henry Clay and Martin Van Buren. In 1956 the house was bequeathed to the National Trust for Historic Preservation, which used it for a time as its headquarters. It is now a historic house museum, with exhibits illustrating various epochs in its long and illustrious history.

## FRANKLIN SCHOOL
**925 13th Street, NW**

"Schools for all; good enough for the richest; cheap enough for the poorest." This was the motto the District of Columbia's school board took in planning for seven public schools built between 1862 and 1875. They were intended to be national models, and the Franklin School, dedicated in 1869, was the

*Franklin School, ca. 1900. Courtesy of the Library of Congress (Frances Benjamin Johnston).*

flagship of the endeavor. Adolph Cluss's design received awards at the 1873 International Exhibition in Vienna, the 1876 Centennial in Philadelphia, and the International Exposition in Paris in 1878. Alexander Graham Bell conducted "photopone" experiments here in 1876. The florid red-brick building, trimmed with stone and cast iron, served as an elementary school until 1925, as administrative offices from 1928 to 1968, and was restored in the 1990s.

## GALLAUDET COLLEGE HISTORIC DISTRICT
**Florida Avenue and Seventh Street, NE**

Established in 1864 by Abraham Lincoln as the National Deaf Mute College, this is the only institution of higher learning in America devoted specifically to the education of the deaf. Landscape designers Frederick Law Olmsted and Calvert Vaux planned the campus so that "the senses of sight and smell are gratified," and architect Frederick Clarke Withers designed its principal buildings in the High Victorian Gothic style.

## GENERAL FEDERATION OF WOMEN'S CLUBS HEADQUARTERS
**1734 N Street, NW**

Originally built as a private residence, this town house became the first permanent headquarters of the General Federation of Women's Clubs (GFWC) in 1922. Founded in 1890, GFWC is an umbrella organization for thousands of women's clubs across the country. After it acquired permanent headquarters, the federation became actively involved in conservation projects and community programs, including antidrug campaigns and adult literacy.

## GENERAL POST OFFICE
**E and F Streets between Seventh and Eighth Streets, NW**

This beautifully scaled and finely detailed building is a tour de force of restrained Neoclassical design. The first portion, facing E Street, was designed by Robert Mills and built in 1839–1844. The larger section fronting F Street was built in 1855–1856 from designs by Thomas U. Walter. The post office vacated the building in 1897, and after subsequent use by various federal agencies it is being rehabilitated in a public/private partnership.

## GEORGETOWN HISTORIC DISTRICT
**Georgetown, NW**

Founded in 1751, Georgetown grew as a Maryland tobacco port and as an independent entity until it became part of the federal district in 1790. The town immediately became the center of Washington's social and diplomatic life when government officials arrived in 1800, and it has maintained that position, to varying degrees, ever since. Now a pleasant residential neighborhood with a vibrant commercial core, Georgetown has a remarkable number of well-preserved 19th-century buildings of various sizes and types. Its pattern of narrow grid streets creates an intimate scale that contrasts with the broad avenues of L'Enfant's capital city.

## SAMUEL GOMPERS HOUSE
**2122 First Street, NW**

From 1902 to 1917 this three-story brick row house was the home of Samuel Gompers, president of the American Federation of Labor (AFL) from 1886 to his death in 1924. Gompers helped found the AFL, which became the largest trade union organization in the world. He directed his energies toward a realization of three goals for American workers: higher wages, shorter hours, and better working conditions. (See American Federation of Labor Building.)

## CHARLOTTE FORTEN GRIMKE HOUSE
**1608 R Street, NW**

From 1881 to 1886 this brick town house was the residence of Charlotte Forten Grimke, pioneer black female educator, early supporter of women's rights, writer, and abolitionist. After Union forces captured South Carolina's sea islands early in the Civil War, she taught former slaves at Port Royal on Saint Helena Island from 1862 to 1864. As the first black female to teach in the South, she paved the way for others to follow.

*Healy Hall, Georgetown University. Main stairway in north wing, 1969. Courtesy of HABS (Jack E. Boucher).*

## HEALY HALL
### Georgetown University, 37th Street, NW

Built from 1877 to 1909, this formidable Victorian structure is Georgetown University's beloved "Old Main." Containing classrooms, library, and auditorium, the huge building with its 334-foot clock tower marked the evolution of the school toward university status. Patrick Healy, S.J., the first African-American president of a major American university, selected architects Smithmeyer and Pelz, who also designed the Library of Congress. They faced Healy Hall with dark Potomac gneiss but used red brick on the rear elevations to harmonize with earlier college buildings.

## GENERAL OLIVER OTIS HOWARD HOUSE
### 607 Howard Place, Howard University, NW

This substantial Second Empire house, with mansard roof and tower, was built in 1867 as the residence of Oliver Otis Howard, Union general and commissioner of the Bureau of Refugees, Freedmen, and Abandoned Lands. He was also a member of Washington's First Congregational Church, which sponsored a school whose aim was to educate students regardless of sex or color, but with a special commitment to African Americans. From 1869 to 1874, General Howard served as the third president of the university named for him, and his house is the only one of its early buildings to survive.

## CHARLES EVANS HUGHES HOUSE
### 2223 R Street, NW

Charles Evans Hughes, a leader in the progressive movement, holder of important offices under several presidents, justice and chief justice of the U.S. Supreme Court, and Republican candidate for president in 1916, lived in this elegant palazzo from 1930 until his death in 1948. Located in Washington's Sheridan Circle embassy area, the house was designed by George Oakley Totten and built in 1907. It is now the Burmese chancery.

## HIRAM W. JOHNSON HOUSE
### 122 Maryland Avenue, NE

From 1929 to 1947 this was the residence of Senator Hiram W. Johnson, former governor of California and a leading voice of the Progressive movement. Johnson was instrumental in the formation of the Progressive Party in 1912 and was the party's vice presidential candidate when former President Theodore Roosevelt ran unsuccessfully on its ticket for president. The house was subsequently adapted to office uses.

## LAFAYETTE SQUARE HISTORIC DISTRICT (NPS)
### Bounded by H Street, Jackson Place, Madison Place, and Pennsylvania Avenue, NW

Designated as a portion of the President's Park when Washington became the U.S. capital in 1791, this greensward fronting the White House has also been called the nation's front yard. It was renamed in 1824 to honor the Marquis de Lafayette's visit. Houses fronting the park, which continues as a traditional site of national demonstrations, were among Washington's choice addresses throughout the 19th century. Beginning in President John F. Kennedy's administration, most of the remaining houses were restored and rehabilitated as governmental offices.

## LIBRARY OF CONGRESS
### First Street and Independence Avenue, SE

Established in 1800, the Library of Congress now ranks as one of the greatest libraries in the world. Founded primarily to serve Congress, its field of service has expanded to serve all government agencies, scholars, other libraries, and the public. The library was originally located in the U.S. Capitol building, but collections were moved in the 1890s to this magnificent Beaux-Arts-inspired building designed by architects Smithmeyer and Pelz. This is now designated the Jefferson Building and is one of the library's three adjoining buildings on Capitol Hill.

## ANDREW MELLON BUILDING
### 1785 Massachusetts Avenue, NW

This limestone-faced apartment building, very Parisian in appearance, was designed by J. H. deSibour and built in 1915 for upper-crust tenants. Millionaire industrialist Andrew Mellon lived in the top-floor unit during his term as U.S. secretary of the treasury (1921–1932). He authored the Mellon Plan, an early "trickle down" economic theory that helped stimulate the boom of the Roaring Twenties. The building was handsomely restored and adapted in the late 1970s to serve as headquarters of the National Trust for Historic Preservation.

## MEMORIAL CONTINENTAL HALL
### 17th Street, between C and D Streets, NW

The three-month Washington conference held here during the winter of 1921–1922 was a significant attempt to reduce global tension following World War I. Delegates from nine nations negotiated three treaties that stabilized the armaments race and helped maintain security in the Pacific, at least for awhile. The hall in which the conference was held was built between 1904 and 1910 as an assembly space and headquarters of the

Library of Congress. Rotunda in the main reading room. Courtesy of HABS (Jack E. Boucher).

National Society of the Daughters of the American Revolution (DAR). After Constitution Hall was built, the DAR converted Continental Hall into a library. (See Constitution Hall.)

## MERIDIAN HILL PARK (NPS)
### Bounded by 16th, 15th, and Euclid Streets and Florida Avenue, NW

This early-20th-century urban park is among the country's most ambitious and successful examples of neoclassical landscape design. Built on a hillside in 1915–1920, it was conceived as a Renaissance landscape with water features, including a cascade, terraces, and walls. Masonry is rendered in precast and cast-in-place concrete, early and important uses of these techniques. Horace W. Peaslee, architect, and Ferruccio Vitale, landscape architect, contributed their talents to produce this enduring urban amenity.

*Meridian Hill Park. Courtesy of HABS (Jack E. Boucher).*

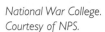

*National War College. Courtesy of NPS.*

## NATIONAL TRAINING SCHOOL FOR WOMEN AND GIRLS
### 601 50th Street, NE

Founded by Nannie Helen Burroughs in 1909, this school offered academic classes, religious instruction, and training in domestic arts and vocations to young black females. The school was set up under the auspices of the National Baptist Convention and was the first institution in America to offer all these opportunities within a single operation. The former Trades Hall, built in 1926 to replace the original classroom building, is now headquarters of the Progressive National Baptist Convention.

## NATIONAL WAR COLLEGE
### P Street, SW, within Fort Lesley J. McNair

President Theodore Roosevelt and Secretary of War Elihu Root established this college, which opened in 1907 and was based on

European prototypes, after the Spanish-American war exposed flaws in America's military forces. Courses in military strategy, tactics, logistics, and related disciplines were—and are—taught in the immense red-brick neoclassical building, designed by the well-known New York architectural firm of McKim, Mead and White.

## OCTAGON HOUSE
### 1799 New York Avenue, NW

Designed by William Thornton for the Tayloe family and completed in 1800, this splendid town house is one of the few houses in Washington that takes advantage of the angled lots created by L'Enfant's city plan. In spite of its name, the house is actually a hexagon with a rounded entrance bay. After the White House was burned in the War of 1812, the Madisons lived here from 1814 to 1815. The Treaty of Ghent that ended the

*Octagon House.
Courtesy of Octagon
House.*

war was signed in the second-floor circular room. The American Institute of Architects (AIA) purchased the Octagon in 1902 for its headquarters. After the AIA constructed a new headquarters on the site of the former stables in the 1970s, the Octagon became a historic house museum.

## OLD NAVAL OBSERVATORY
### 23rd and E Street, NW

Between 1844 and 1861, under the leadership of Matthew Fontaine Maury, the Naval Observatory became a world center for advances in oceanography and navigational information. Maury, considered the father of modern oceanography, made his greatest contributions during these years as superintendent of the Depot of Charts and Instruments, under whose organizational framework the observatory first operated. The observatory moved in 1893, and the old building, since enlarged, is now used as offices.

*Old Naval Observatory. 26-inch Great Equatorial telescope, ca.1873. Courtesy of the Library, U.S. Naval Observatory.*

## OLD PATENT OFFICE
### F and G Streets between Seventh and Ninth Streets, NW

Constructed in four sections over a 31-year period beginning in 1836, this is one of the nation's largest and most impressive Greek Revival buildings. Despite its long design and construction history (involving four architects), it is remarkable for its unity and its bold, simple monumentality—unsurpassed in 19th-century American civic architecture. The building now houses the National Portrait Gallery and National Museum of American Art.

## PENSION BUILDING
### Fourth, Fifth, F, and G Streets, NW

This immense red-brick Renaissance-inspired palazzo displays the architectural and engineering skills of Montgomery Meigs. Built between 1882 and 1887 to house the U.S. Pension Bureau, which had greatly expanded after the Civil War, it was also conceived as a memorial to those who fought in the conflict. A continuous 1,200-foot terra-cotta frieze on the exterior shows troops in various poses, and the interior courtyard is one of Washington's most impressive spaces. Rehabilitated in the 1980s, the structure now houses the National Building Museum.

## FRANCIS PERKINS HOUSE
### 2326 California Avenue, NW

From 1937 to 1940, Francis Perkins, the country's first female cabinet member, lived in this Georgian Revival brick town house. As secretary of labor throughout Franklin D. Roosevelt's presidency, Perkins was the prime mover in some of the Democratic Party's most lasting legislative accomplishments: the Social Security Act (Perkins chaired the committee that drafted the legislation) and the Fair Labor Standards Act, which created a minimum wage and restricted child labor nationwide.

## *PHILADELPHIA*
### Smithsonian Institution, National Museum of American History, Constitution Avenue between 12th and 14th Streets, NW

The only extant gunboat built and manned by Americans during the Revolutionary War, *Philadelphia* was hastily constructed and launched in the summer of 1776. As part of a fleet under the command of Benedict Arnold, it was sunk in a battle on Lake Champlain in October of the same year. Salvaged in 1935, *Philadelphia* was found to have been remarkably well preserved. In 1961 the gunboat was bequeathed to the Smithsonian and is now on exhibit at the Institution's National Museum of American History.

## RENWICK GALLERY
### 17th Street and Pennsylvania Avenue, NW

Built in 1859–1861 as the original Corcoran Galley of Art, this was the first major building in the nation designed in the Second Empire style, a French-inspired mode characterized by mansard roofs. James Renwick, the architect for whom the building is now named, and William Corcoran, the museum's patron, traveled to Paris beforehand to study architecture and museums. The gallery was commandeered in the Civil War to serve military purposes and later became home of the U.S. Court of Claims. After rehabilitations in 1967–1972, it was returned to gallery use by the Smithsonian Institution. A second rehabilitation dates from 1985–1986.

## ZALMON RICHARDS HOUSE
### 1301 Corcoran Street, NW

From 1882 until his death in 1899, Zalmon Richards, founder and first president of the National Teacher's Association (now the National Educational Association), lived in this Victorian-era brick row house. In 1867, Richards promoted passage of the bill that established the Federal Department of Education.

*Zalmon Richards House. Courtesy of NPS (Ronald S. Comedy).*

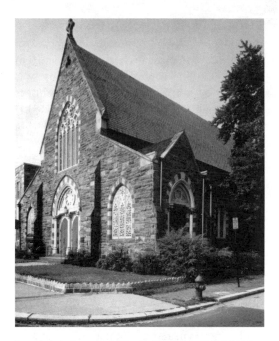

Saint Luke's Episcopal Church. Courtesy of NPS (Walter Smalling, Jr.).

## SAINT ELIZABETH'S HOSPITAL
**2700 Martin Luther King, Jr., Avenue, SE**

Founded in 1852, Saint Elizabeth's Hospital was the federal government's first hospital for the treatment of the mentally ill. Charles H. Nichols, first medical superintendent of the hospital, collaborated with social reformer Dorothea Dix to establish a model institution in the capital city. The 250-bed Center Building, designed in consultation with architect Thomas U. Walter, was one of the nation's first mental hospitals to utilize the Kirkbride plan, an arrangement allowing for patients to be housed in small wards or "families." The hospital has expanded over the years and contains many buildings on a handsomely landscaped campus.

## SAINT JOHN'S CHURCH
**16th and H Streets, NW**

This stuccoed-brick "Church of the Presidents" has graced Lafayette Square since it was first completed in 1816 from designs by Benjamin Henry Latrobe. The church was enlarged only four years later and has since undergone numerous alterations and additions, carried out by architects of the caliber of James Renwick and McKim, Mead and White. James Madison selected the Pres-

ident's Pew, and every subsequent president has used it while attending services in the church.

## SAINT LUKE'S EPISCOPAL CHURCH
**15th and Church Streets, NW**

Dr. Alexander Crummell, founder of the American Negro Academy and one of the most talented and articulate African-American scholars of the 19th century, founded this church in the 1870s. It stands as an embodiment of Crummell's view that churches should be advocates for social change, education, and self-help for their congregations and others. The first service was held in the stone Gothic Revival building on Thanksgiving Day, 1879. Calvin T. S. Brent, Washington's first African-American architect, designed the church.

## SEWALL-BELMONT HOUSE (NPS)
**144 Constitution Avenue, NE**

Since 1929 this house has served as the headquarters of the National Woman's Party. Alice Paul, the most significant figure in the final struggle for a constitutional amendment granting women the right to vote, founded the party. Robert Sewall built the house, one of Washington's oldest, in 1800. The second half of its hyphenated name honors Alva Belmont, staunch supporter of women's suffrage, who donated funds for the Woman's Party's earlier headquarters.

## SMITHSONIAN INSTITUTION BUILDING
**Jefferson Drive at Tenth Street, SW**

Designed by James Renwick when he was 29 and built between 1847 and 1855, this is the country's finest example of the Picturesque movement, not so much an architectural style as an approach that was the antithesis of classicism. Renwick provided Gothic and Romanesque designs, and the latter was selected. Constructed of locally quarried red Seneca sandstone, the "Castle," as it is popularly known, stands out among its marble neighbors on the Mall. The institution it houses, established by the bequest of James Smithson, English scientist and illegitimate son of the duke of Northumberland, was chartered by an Act of Congress in 1846.

## STATE, WAR, AND NAVY BUILDING
**Pennsylvania Avenue and 17th Street, NW**

This phenomenal granite pile took 17 years, from 1871 to 1888, to build. Designed by Supervising Architect of the Treasury Alfred B. Mullett in a flamboyant Second Empire style, it is noted for its complex mansard roof that caps multiple tiers of columns and hooded windows. Elaborate chandeliers, mantels, and spiral staircases give elegance to the interior. The building originally housed the three executive departments for which it was named. It now houses executive offices for the adjacent White House.

## MARY CHURCH TERRELL HOUSE
**326 T Street, NW**

This brick town house in Washington's LeDroit Park neighborhood was the residence of Mary Church Terrell, educator and civil rights leader. Mrs. Terrell was the first black woman to serve on an American school board (1895) and first president of the National Association of Colored Women (1896). Her fame achieved international proportions at the turn of the century when, in 1903, she spoke in Germany at the International Congress of Women on "The Progress and Problems of Colored Women." The acclaim she received from the speech started her on a lecture circuit in the United States, in which she tirelessly continued her fight against discrimination toward her race and her gender.

## TUDOR PLACE
**1644 31st Street, NW**

Among the foremost Federal-era mansions in the nation, this sophisticated building was designed by Dr. William Thornton, architect of the Capitol, and completed ca. 1815. Thomas Peter and his wife, Martha Washington's granddaughter, built it with funds from an inheritance from the first president. As home to generations of the Peter family of Georgetown, the house hosted dignitaries such as the Marquis de Lafayette and Robert E. Lee (a cousin). In 1966, Armistead Peter III, the last private owner, granted the nation's first easement under terms of the 1935 Historic Sites Act. In 1987 he endowed his family home as a historic house museum. Also known for its extensive grounds and gardens, Tudor Place is one of the showplaces of Georgetown, and of the nation's capital.

## TWELFTH STREET YMCA BUILDING
**1816 12th Street, NW**

Built in 1908–1912, this Renaissance Revival style building was the home of the nation's first African-American chapter of the Young Men's Christian Association (YMCA). Designed by African-American architect William Sidney Pittman, it came to be known as the "Bowen Y," after Anthony Bowen, who founded the black "Y" movement in the United States in 1853. John D. Rockefeller supported the cause by providing construction funds, and Theodore Roosevelt laid the cornerstone. The YMCA's existence

*Tudor Place, 1968.*
*Courtesy of HABS.*

in the nation's capital helped to stimulate such projects elsewhere in the country before it closed in 1985.

## OSCAR W. UNDERWOOD HOUSE
**2000 G Street, NW**

Arthur Underwood, U.S. congressman and senator from Alabama and Democratic presidential contender in the 1912 and 1924 elections, was the leading force behind the Underwood-Simmons Tariff of 1913, described as the most equitable tariff since 1861. From 1914 to 1925 this late-19th-century Second Empire town house was his residence. It is now used by George Washington University.

## UNITED STATES CAPITOL
**Capitol Hill**

The physical symbol of the United States, this magnificent structure housing the legislative branch of the government is familiar to everyone. President George Washington laid the cornerstone in 1793. The building was essentially completed in 1865, after President Abraham Lincoln directed that construction of the cast-iron dome continue as a symbol of the republic's endurance during the Civil War years. With but one interruption, after the British burned it in 1814, the capitol has housed Congress since 1800. The capitol serves as a fitting background for presidential inaugurations every four years and for Fourth of July celebrations every year.

## UNITED STATES DEPARTMENT OF THE TREASURY
**1500 Pennsylvania Avenue, NW**

This impressive Greek Revival building housing the Treasury Department was begun in 1836 from designs by Robert Mills and completed, wing by wing, by three other supervising architects of the Treasury, 35 years later. Its most imposing feature is a 466-foot Ionic colonnade along Fifteenth Street. Mills's design was originally executed in sandstone, but in 1908 this was replaced with granite.

## UNITED STATES MARINE CORPS BARRACKS AND COMMANDANT'S HOUSE
**801 G Street, SE**

This block-square urban complex, its site selected by President Thomas Jefferson, is the nation's oldest continuously active Marine Corps post. It served as headquarters for a century, from 1801 to 1901, and commandants have lived here since 1805. The barracks are home to the Marine Band, which has played for every president since John Adams. John Philip Sousa was band leader here from 1880 to 1892.

## UNITED STATES SOLDIERS' HOME
**Rock Creek Church Road, NW**

One of three similar institutions established in 1851, largely at the instigation of then-Senator Jefferson Davis, and now the only one remaining, this home was created for retired or disabled soldiers. Four pre–Civil

*United States Soldiers' Home. Courtesy of HABS (Jack E. Boucher).*

War buildings remain. Abraham Lincoln used the oldest, Anderson Cottage, or "Corn Riggs," as a summer White House during his presidency and wrote the second draft of the Emancipation Proclamation there.

## UNITED STATES SUPREME COURT BUILDING
**First and East Capitol Streets, NE**

Although the U.S. Constitution provided for a national judiciary, it took 145 years for the Supreme Court to find a permanent residence. Construction of this building for the Court's exclusive use reaffirmed the doctrine of judicial independence and separation of powers. The impressive Corinthian temple of justice, constructed of white Vermont marble and built between 1929 and 1935, is considered one of the masterpieces of well-known American architect Cass Gilbert.

## VOLTA BUREAU
**3417 Volta Place, NW**

In 1887, Alexander Graham Bell founded the Volta Bureau as an instrument "for the increase and diffusion of knowledge relating to the Deaf." In 1893 the institution moved to this yellow-brick and terra-cotta structure across the street from Bell's father's home and his laboratory. Boston architects Peabody and Stearns may have derived the design of the neoclassical building from the Italian Volta Temple, named for physicist Alessandro Volta. The Bureau continues its work in aiding the deaf.

## WASHINGTON AQUEDUCT
**MacArthur Boulevard, NW**

Built principally between 1853 and 1863 to supply water to the District of Columbia, the Washington Aqueduct is a testament to the engineering skills of Montgomery Meigs. Included in the system are a masonry dam at Great Falls, six bridges—one of them a 220-foot arch at Cabin John—a mile of tunnels, and 12 miles of conduit. Although the system has since been enlarged, Meigs's components continue to deliver water to the nation's capital. The aqueduct's construction was an early example of the Army Corps of Engineers' entry into public works projects (also in Montgomery County, Maryland).

## WASHINGTON NAVY YARD
**Eighth and M Streets, SE**

Built on an Anacostia River site purchased in 1799, the Washington Navy Yard was the first government-owned navy yard in the country. It served as the Navy's first home port and was the center of its early-19th-century operations during a critical period of expanding nationalism. Torpedoes, submarines, and ordnance have been tested here over the years. The yard now contains approximately 35 buildings erected between 1799 and 1920. Although now principally a naval administration center, the yard also houses the Navy Museum.

## WHITE HOUSE
**1600 Pennsylvania Avenue, NW**

The cornerstone of the White House, the first public building erected in Washington, was laid on October 13, 1792. Designed by James Hoban, the house was completed in 1800. It has been the home of every president of the United States since John Adams and is recognized around the world as the physical symbol of that office. The exterior, with additions and minor changes, remains much as Hoban intended. The interior has been completely renovated, but the historic floor plan remains.

## DAVID WHITE HOUSE
**1459 Girard Street, NW**

From 1910 to 1925 this brick row house, one of three units that C. L. Harding designed, was the home of David White, chief geologist of the United States Geological Survey. White is best known for his theories on the origin and evolution of oil distribution basic to the petroleum industry. His work in paleobotany also led him to make significant contributions to the study and understanding of coal formation.

## WOODROW WILSON HOUSE
**2340 S Street, NW**

Woodrow Wilson, 28th president of the United States, spent his last years (1921–1924) here as a semi-invalid, weakened by a stroke. Edith Bolling Wilson, his widow, lived in the handsome Kalorama-area town house, designed by Waddy B. Wood and built in 1915, almost 40 years. She donated it to the National Trust for Historic Preservation. Now a museum, it contains original Wilson furnishings and memorabilia.

## CARTER G. WOODSON HOUSE
**1538 Ninth Street, NW**

Carter Godwin Woodson, founder of black history studies in the United States, lived in this plain, Victorian-era brick row house from 1915 until his death in 1950. In attempting to correct widespread ignorance concerning black life and history, Woodson established the Association for the Study of Negro Life and History (1915), the Associated Publishers (1920), *The Journal of Negro History* (1916), and *The Negro History Bulletin* (1937). Woodson also created Negro

History Week (1926), now expanded to Black History Month.

## ROBERT SIMPSON WOODWARD HOUSE
**1513 16th Street, NW**

The first edition of *American Men of Science, a Biographical Directory* (1906) accompanied the names of those it considered most eminent in the profession with a star. Robert Simpson Woodward, astronomer, geologist, mathematician, and physicist, was given four stars and was the only person of the approximately 4,000 listed who received more than two. Woodward also served as the first president of the Carnegie Institution. During the time he held that position, he lived in this stone-faced Romanesque Revival town house from 1904 to 1914.

# FLORIDA

■ *Brevard County*

## CAPE CANAVERAL AIR FORCE STATION
**Cocoa vicinity**

Cape Canaveral, the most familiar name and site associated with America's Space Program, was selected in 1947 to become the center for launching operations. The National Historic Landmark consists of discontiguous sites within the Cape Canaveral Air Force Station and encompasses six launch pads, a

mobile service tower, and the original Mission Control Center that was used for all Mercury flights and the first three Gemini flights.

## WINDOVER ARCHEOLOGICAL SITE
**Address Restricted, Titusville vicinity**

This small, isolated peat deposit contains artifacts and human burials dating to the Early Archaic period, nearly 11,000 B.C. It represents one of the largest collections of

*Cape Canaveral Air Force Station, Brevard County. Launch Pad 36-B. Courtesy of U.S. Air Force, Eastern Space and Missile Center.*

human skeletal material from this time period and provided one of the largest collections of fiber arts yet found at any archeological site in the New World. The site, discovered in 1982 in connection with construction activities, also contained a diverse array of bone, antler, and wooden remnants. It is not open to the public.

### ■ Citrus County

## CRYSTAL RIVER SITE
**2.5 miles west of Crystal River**

This large and complex ceremonial center and burial site was occupied from ca. 200 B.C. to A.D. 1400. The site has played a significant role in the development of archeological method and theory by helping explain relationships between early mound-building groups on Florida's Gulf Coast and the Hopewellian cultures in the Ohio River Valley. Stelae (ceremonial stones) indicate contact with cultures in the Yucatan. The complex is maintained and interpreted as a state archeological site.

### ■ Dade County

## MIAMI-BILTMORE HOTEL AND COUNTRY CLUB
**120 Anastasia Avenue, Coral Gables**

The Miami–Biltmore Hotel and Country Club, one of the most luxurious hotels of its time, opened in 1926. Designed by New York architects Schultze and Weaver in the Mediterranean Revival style, the Miami-Biltmore is Coral Gables's chief reminder of the 1920s Florida land boom and is one of the most important monuments of this era in South Florida. It was commandeered into governmental service as a hospital from 1942 to 1968 but was rehabilitated as a luxury hotel in 1986.

## UNITED STATES CAR NO. 1
**Gold Coast Railroad Museum,**
**12450 Southwest 152nd Street, Miami**

Built in 1928 as the Pullman Company's *Ferdinand Magellan*, this private railroad car was armor plated and donated for use by President Franklin D. Roosevelt in 1942. It was also used by president Harry S Truman in his election campaign. The car is now housed in a railroad museum.

## VIZCAYA
**3251 South Miami Avenue, Miami**

Vizcaya, whose name means "an elevated place" in Basque, was completed in 1916 as the winter home of industrialist James Deering, who made his fortune producing farm machinery. New York painter and designer Paul Chalfin advised Deering, and the two created a 70-room melange of Renaissance, Baroque, Rococo, Mannerist, and Louis XIV styles that remains one of the most impressive examples of Gilded Age extravagance in the country. Vizcaya is a museum of the decorative arts.

### ■ Duval County

## MAPLE LEAF
**Address Restricted, Mandarin**

The sidewheeler *Maple Leaf*, launched in Canada in 1851, was sold to a Boston firm in 1862 and almost immediately became a U.S. Army transport ship. Laden with most of the baggage of three infantry units, including tents, equipment, and uniforms, it struck a Confederate torpedo, or mine, in Saint John's River on April 11, 1864, and sank, carrying five black crew members to their graves. After the war the wreck was moved to deeper water, where it lay forgotten until 1984. Subsequent archeological "dives" have uncovered much of its cargo, a veritable treasure trove of Civil War–era material culture. *Maple Leaf* now lies under several feet of mud.

### ■ Escambia County

## FORT SAN CARLOS DE BARRANCAS (NPS)
**Gulf Islands National Seashore, Pensacola**

This semicircular brick shore battery, built at the end of the 18th century, was an important element in the defenses of Spanish Pensacola. In 1814 it fell to Andrew Jackson, who invaded Florida in response to British-Spanish collaboration during the War of 1812. U.S. Army Engineers built Fort Barrancas on the site of Fort San Carlos in 1834–1844. Located at the Pensacola Naval

Air Station, the battery is part of Gulf Islands National Seashore.

## PENSACOLA NAVAL AIR STATION HISTORIC DISTRICT
### Pensacola

Established in January 1914 at the abandoned Pensacola Navy Yard, this was the United States' first permanent naval air station, the first Navy pilot training center, and the first U.S. naval installation to send pilots into combat. A Naval Aviation Museum is part of the still-active Naval Air Station. Although the museum is open to the public, access to the rest of the station is restricted.

## PLAZA FERDINAND VII
### Palafox Street between Government and Zaragossa Streets, Pensacola

This was the site of the formal transfer of West Florida from Spain to the United States on July 17, 1821. Andrew Jackson, then newly appointed governor, proclaimed the establishment of Florida Territory and set up a territorial government, with Pensacola as its temporary capital, four days later. The landscaped plaza, a portion of a city square laid out by the British in 1765 as a public park, is bordered by civic buildings.

### ■ Franklin County
## BRITISH FORT
### 6 miles southwest of Sumatra

This site, now Fort Gadsen Historical Site, is significant for its role in the First Seminole War. The British built a fort overlooking, and controlling, the Apalachicola River in 1814, during the War of 1812. After the war, it became known as "Negro Fort" because of the runaway slaves who received refuge here among the Seminoles. In 1816, the U.S. Army destroyed the fort, an action that precipitated the First Seminole War. A second fort built on the site and occupied by U.S. troops from 1818 to 1821 was known as Fort Gadsden.

## GOVERNOR STONE
### Apalachicola Harbor, Apalachicola

Built and launched in Pascagoula, Mississippi, in 1877 and named for that state's first governor, the *Stone* is the oldest surviving Gulf schooner. This two-masted type was vital to maritime commerce of the South and the Gulf Coast, where shallows and sandbars prevented larger vessels from coming into port. Schooners like the *Stone* have been called the "pickup trucks" of their day, transferring freight and goods. The restored schooner serves as a training vessel, and is available for excursions.

### ■ Hillsborough County
## EL CENTRO ESPAÑOL DE TAMPA
### 1526–1536 East Seventh Avenue, Tampa

An impressive example of Spanish, Moorish, and French Renaissance–influenced architecture, this massive masonry clubhouse dramatically illustrates the role of ethnic social and mutual assistance organizations in the daily life of immigrant populations in the late 19th and early 20th centuries.

## TAMPA BAY HOTEL
### 401 West Kennedy Boulevard, Tampa

This preposterous architectural fantasy combining Moorish and Turkish motifs was built in 1888–1891 as one of Florida's largest resort hotels. Its complex brick facade stretches 900 feet, and 13 crescent-capped minarets provide a bristling silhouette. In 1898 it became headquarters for U.S. Army forces that invaded Cuba in the Spanish-American War and a news center for journalists covering events of the conflict. Since 1933 it has served as classrooms and offices for the University of Tampa.

## YBOR CITY HISTORIC DISTRICT
### Roughly bounded by 21st and Nebraska Avenues, Frank Adamo Drive, and North 20th Street, Tampa

Developed in 1885–1886 by Vincente M. Ybor, this community named for him is significant in industrial and immigration history. In addition to the largest collection of buildings related to the cigar industry in America, and probably the world, it contains workers' housing and ethnic clubs organized by new arrivals of Italians, Germans, Cubans, and Spaniards. Ybor City was a rare multi-

*Tampa Bay. Hotel,
Hillsborough County.
Courtesy of HABS
(Walter Smalling, Jr.).*

*Ybor City Historic
District, Tampa,
Hillsborough County.
Courtesy of HABS
(Walter Smalling, Jr.).*

ethnic, multiracial industrial community in
the Deep South and illustrates manifold
aspects of the history of human relations.

### Indian River County

## PELICAN ISLAND NATIONAL WILDLIFE REFUGE
**South of Sebastian on Indian River**

This first federal sanctuary for the protection
of wildlife was established by President
Theodore Roosevelt in 1903. The refuge
consists of some 16 low-lying islands, covered
with mangrove, that serve as a rookery for
brown pelicans and other waterfowl. It is
open to the public.

### Leon County

## SAN LUIS DE APALACHE
**2 miles west of Tallahassee on U.S. Route 90**

By 1675 this Franciscan establishment was
the largest of 14 missions to the Apalache and
was the administrative center for the Spanish
Province of Apalache. In 1696, with the
threat of British and Indian attacks, a blockhouse and stockade were built, transforming
the mission into a fort. The Spanish abandoned and burned the post in 1704 when
news came of approaching British forces. The
site was near the place chosen for the new
capital of the American Territory of Florida:
Tallahassee. It is now a museum.

## Monroe County

### FORT ZACHARY TAYLOR
**U.S. Naval Station, Key West**

This massive brick fort, trapezoidal in shape and built at the westernmost tip of Key West, was a strong Union outpost in the South throughout the Civil War. It later became the most important naval base during the Spanish–American War (1898). Fort Zachary Taylor is a Florida state park.

### ERNEST HEMINGWAY HOUSE
**907 Whitehead Street, Key West**

This mid-19th-century house, built of limestone quarried on the site, stuccoed, and shaded by iron verandas, was the home of novelist Ernest Hemingway from 1931 to 1940. Hemingway, who won both the Pulitzer and Nobel Prizes for literature, wrote several works here, including *To Have and Have Not*. The house is a museum commemorating Hemingway and his work. (See also Ernest Hemingway cottage, Emmet County, Michigan.)

## Okaloosa County

### FORT WALTON MOUND
**Indian Temple Mound Museum, Highway 98, Fort Walton Beach**

This is the type site of the Fort Walton phase, an Indian culture present along the northwest Florida coast ca. A.D. 1200 to 1650.

Fort Walton is considered a manifestation of the southeastern spread of the Middle Mississippian culture. The first occupation of the site, however, occurred much earlier, perhaps in the first century A.D. The platform mound was excavated in 1901 and is now part of a city park.

## Okeechobee County

### OKEECHOBEE BATTLEFIELD
**4 miles southeast of Okeechobee on U.S. Route 441**

On Christmas Day 1837, U.S. troops under the command of Zachary Taylor engaged Seminole warriors in a three-hour battle. Although the two sides counted equal casualties, the Indians were driven from their position and the turning point in the Second Seminole War was decided in favor of the federal troops.

## Palm Beach County

### MAR-A-LAGO
**1100 South Ocean Boulevard, Palm Beach**

This sprawling Mediterranean style villa, with Hispanic and Moorish architectural overtones, exemplifies "Palm Beach" in the popular mind. It was built during the prosperous 1920s by Post cereal heiress Marjorie Merriweather Post, who designed it with architects Marion Wyeth and Joseph Urban. The estate had its own nine-hole golf course,

*Ernest Hemingway House, Key West, Monroe County, 1967. Courtesy of HABS (J. F. Brook).*

Mar-A-Lago, Palm Beach, Palm Beach County, 1967. Courtesy of HABS (Jack E. Boucher).

and Ocean Boulevard was depressed in front of it so the owner could enjoy an unobstructed view of the Atlantic. Donald Trump purchased the estate in 1985 for just $8 million of the $25 million asking price, and transformed the estate into a members-only club in 1995.

Bok Tower Gardens, Lake Wales, Polk County. Courtesy of The Bok Tower Gardens Foundation, Inc.

## ■ Pinellas County

### SAFETY HARBOR SITE
#### Philippe Park, Safety Harbor vicinity

This site dates from the late prehistoric and early historic periods, representing the Gulf Coast Timucua Indian culture at the time of contact with the Spanish (ca. 1500–1650). With its large platform mound, it is the Safety Harbor type site and may have been the capital of the Tocobago, a branch of the western Timucua. The site is preserved in Philippe Park, which is open to the public.

## ■ Polk County

### BOK TOWER GARDENS
#### Burns Avenue and Tower Boulevard, Lake Wales

Edward Bok, a native of the Netherlands, gained fame in his adopted country as editor of *The Ladies Home Journal,* the first national publication to exceed one million subscribers, and a primary force in the development of a middle-class culture in America. Bok became a Pulitzer prize-winning author, civic leader, and philanthropist. He presented this landscaped bird sanctuary, designed by Frederick Law Olmsted, Jr., and its "Singing Tower," a carillon tower designed by Milton B. Medary, to the people of America in gratitude for the opportunities they had provided him. President Calvin Coolidge dedicated the gardens on February 1, 1929. The tower and gardens are open to the public.

### ■ *Saint Johns County*

## CATHEDRAL OF SAINT AUGUSTINE

**Cathedral Street between Charlotte and Saint George Streets, Saint Augustine**

The Roman Catholic parish of Saint Augustine is the oldest in the United States, with records dating from 1594. This church, first built in 1793–1797 and elevated to cathedral status in 1870 when the Diocese of Saint Augustine was established, burned in 1887 and was enlarged afterward by architect James Renwick. Much of the baroque facade is original, but the tall campanile flanking the building is by Renwick.

## FORT MOSE SITE

**Address Restricted, Saint Augustine**

The Spanish established Fort Mose in the mid–18th century to help protect the northern approach to Saint Augustine. It was manned by black militia, mostly runaway slaves who had escaped from the British colonies of South Carolina and Georgia, and was the earliest known legally sanctioned free black community in the present United States. Its inhabitants emigrated to Cuba when Spain ceded Florida to Great Britain in 1763. The site is not open to the public.

## GONZALEZ-ALVAREZ HOUSE

**14 Saint Francis Street, Saint Augustine**

Popularly known as "The Oldest House," this is a good example of a "Saint Augustine style" town house, adapted to Florida's unique climatic conditions. The original one-story house (c. 1723), built during the Spanish period, has coquina (broken coral and shell) walls and floors of tabby (oyster shells mixed with lime). It was enlarged later in the 18th century during the British period and is now a historic house museum.

## LLAMBIAS HOUSE

**31 Saint Francis Street, Saint Augustine**

Among the few extant structures in Saint Augustine whose origins date to the first Spanish period, this house was built before 1763 but did not reach its final form until 1788, during the British period, when it was enlarged with a second story. Constructed on a variation of the "Saint Augustine Plan," it combines Spanish and English architectural details. The house is built of coquina and was restored in the 1950s. It is open to the public.

## SAINT AUGUSTINE TOWN PLAN HISTORIC DISTRICT

**Roughly bounded by Grove Avenue, the Matanzas River, and South and Washington Streets, Saint Augustine**

Saint Augustine, the oldest continuously occupied European settlement in the conti-

Gonzalez-Alvarez House, Saint Augustine, Saint Johns County, 1900. Courtesy of NPS.

nental United States, was founded as a Spanish military base in 1565. Although the city of today consists of old and new buildings in close proximity, the original street pattern established in Spanish times prevails. As typical in Spanish plans, narrow streets lead from a central plaza where religious and governmental structures are located.

■ *Saint Lucie County*

## ZORA NEALE HURSTON HOUSE
**1734 Avenue L, Fort Pierce**

Zora Neale Hurston, noted black writer of the mid-20th century, was also a folklorist and anthropologist. She neither romanticized nor condemned black folk life in her voluminous writings, which include four novels, two books on folklore, an autobiography, and more than 50 short stories and essays. Hurston lived in this modest concrete-block house while working as a reporter and columnist for the *Fort Pierce Chronicle* during the final years of her life.

■ *Sumter County*

## DADE BATTLEFIELD
**Bushnell vicinity**

This was the site of the first battle of the Second Seminole War (1835–1842). Of short duration, the battle was a complete Seminole victory, leaving only one American survivor. The Seminole ambush was part of Chief Osceola's plan of resistance to President Jackson's removal policies, a plan that was ultimately unsuccessful. The site is encompassed in Dade Battlefield Memorial State Park.

■ *Volusia County*

## MARY MCLEOD BETHUNE HOME
**Bethune-Cookman College, Daytona Beach**

This two-story Craftsman style frame house was built by Mary McLeod Bethune in the 1920s and was her home until her death in 1955. Bethune, one of America's best-known early 20th-century black leaders, was a civil rights advocate, administrator, educator, adviser to presidents, and consultant to the United Nations. Her house, on the campus of Bethune-Cookman College, successor to the Daytona Normal and Industrial Institute for Negro Girls that she established in 1904, is preserved as a museum and repository for her archives.

## PONCE DE LEON INLET LIGHT STATION
**4931 South Peninsula Drive, Ponce Inlet**

The nation's second-tallest brick lighthouse, this 175-foot tower was begun in 1884 to mark Mosquito Inlet on the Atlantic coast of Florida. The light station is significant for its association with federal efforts to provide an integrated system of navigational aids to insure safe maritime transportation. Ponce de Leon is one of the nation's best-preserved light stations, retaining not only its tower (complete with its original Fresnel first-order lens) but its three keepers' dwellings, oil house, and combination woodshed/privies. The light station has been restored and open to the public since 1982.

■ *Wakulla County*

## FORT SAN MARCOS DE APALACHE
**18 miles south of Tallahassee on U.S. Route 319 and Florida Route 363, Saint Marks**

Successive wooden and masonry forts strategically located at the confluence of the Saint Marks and Wakulla Rivers were occupied throughout the Spanish and British colonial periods and by U.S. troops during the Second Seminole War. Andrew Jackson's capture of the Spanish fort in 1818 was instrumental in the American acquisition of Florida in 1821. A federal marine hospital was built on the site in 1857, and a museum now stands on its foundations. Fort San Marcos is a state historic site.

# GEORGIA

■ *Baldwin County*

## GOVERNOR'S MANSION, MILLEDGEVILLE
**120 South Clark Street, Milledgeville**

This distinguished Greek Revival mansion, fronted by a giant-order Ionic portico, was designed by Charles B. McCluskey, who incorporated circular and octagonal spaces in its plan. It served as the home of Georgia governors from 1838, when it was completed, until 1868, when the state capital was moved from Milledgeville to Atlanta. The house is owned by the state and operated by Georgia College as a furnished house museum.

■ *Bartow County*

## ETOWAH MOUNDS
**3 miles south of Cartersville**

This site, containing three large platform mounds, two plaza areas, associated village remains, and an encircling dry moat, is important as an expression of the eastern expansion of Mississippian culture. Etowah also demonstrates the forms taken by Mississippian culture as a result of interaction with other Southeastern cultural traditions, especially that of the Gulf Coast. The mounds are owned by the state, and a museum at the site displays some of the extensive artifacts excavated over the years.

■ *Bibb County*

## CARMICHAEL HOUSE
**1183 Georgia Avenue, Macon**

This antebellum mansion exemplifies the variety and individuality possible within the generally static Greek Revival style. Classical details embellish the house, built on a modified Greek cross plan, and a spiral stairway leads to a third-floor octagonal belvedere where the arms of the cross intersect. The design derives from plans published in W. H. Ranlett's *The Architect*.

## HAY HOUSE
**934 Georgia Avenue, Macon**

This dramatic stuccoed brick Italian Renaissance villa, built in 1855–1860, provides a striking contrast to Georgia's more prevalent Greek Revival mansions. Heavy pedimented lintels top windows, and there is an octagonal cupola with consoles at the angles. Among the notable interior features are a ballroom and a carved mahogany staircase. The house, built by William B. Johnston after he and his wife returned from a honeymoon in Italy, is now a historic house museum.

■ *Chatham County*

## CENTRAL OF GEORGIA RAILROAD SHOPS AND TERMINAL
**West Broad Street at Liberty, Savannah**

This antebellum industrial district, established in the 1850s, is the nation's oldest surviving and best remaining example of an integrated, comprehensive railroad facility of its period. At the time it was built, the *New York Railroad Advocate* prophesied that Savannah was "likely to have the most complete and elegant railroad in the country." The complex presages the comprehensive industrial planning that became standard railroad practice in the last quarter of the 19th century. It is open to the public.

## GREEN-MELDRIM HOUSE
**Bull and Harris Streets, Madison Square, Savannah**

Completed in 1854, likely from designs by John S. Norris, the Green-Meldrim House, with oriel windows and crenellated parapet, is a splendid example of Gothic Revival architecture. The house was fitted with stylish and modern accouterments (including bathrooms with running water) and served handsomely as Union general William T. Sherman's headquarters during the winter of 1864–1865. It is now the parish house of the adjacent Saint John's Episcopal Church.

## JULIETTE GORDON LOW BIRTHPLACE

**10 Oglethorpe Avenue, Savannah**

This two-part National Historic Landmark includes an elegant Regency style mansion, built in 1818–1821, with a third story added in 1886, that was the birthplace and childhood home of the founder of the Girl Scouts in the United States, and a former carriage house several blocks away where the first troop met in March 1912. Mrs. Low's creation grew from 18 members to more than 148,000 at the time of her death in 1927. The house now serves as a national program center for the Girl Scouts of the United States of America and is open to the public as a historic house museum.

## OWENS-THOMAS HOUSE

**124 Abercorn Street, Savannah**

Designed in 1816 by English architect William Jay, who came to Savannah the next year to oversee completion of his commission, this elegant mansion of stucco-covered brick is considered America's finest example of Regency architecture. It was finished in 1819, and among its many outstanding features are indirect lighting in the drawing room, curved walls and doors, ornamental plasterwork, and an elegant central stairway. It is furnished and shown as a house museum.

## SAVANNAH HISTORIC DISTRICT

**Bounded by East Broad, Gwinnett, and West Broad Streets and the Savannah River, Savannah**

Savannah's unique city plan was devised by James Oglethorpe in 1733 and was followed in subsequent additions well into the 19th century. Each ward had its own square, with alternating through and local streets. Most of the parklike squares remain, surrounded by impressive houses and churches, many of them dating from the city's early years. Savannah is rightfully treasured as one of the country's premier examples of successful historic preservation.

## WILLIAM SCARBROUGH HOUSE

**41 West Broad Street, Savannah**

Built in 1819 for one of Savannah's early merchant princes, this monumental town mansion was designed by English-born William Jay, one of the most important architects practicing in early-19th-century America. The exterior employs the archaic Doric order, and a third story added in the mid–19th century respects the original proportions. The interior has innovative spatial arrangements and includes a two-story reception hall, or atrium. The Scarbrough House is now operated as the Ships of the Sea Museum.

## TELFAIR ACADEMY OF ARTS AND SCIENCES

**121 Barnard Street, Savannah**

Another example of architect William Jay's contributions to Savannah, this neoclassical building was built in 1818 as a private house for the Telfair family. In 1875, it was bequeathed to the Georgia Historical Society to serve as a public museum. Formally opened as a free art museum in 1886, the Telfair is now one of the oldest museums in the Southeast. It houses important collections of paintings and furnishings.

■ *Clarke County*

## HENRY W. GRADY HOUSE

**634 Prince Avenue, Athens**

This Greek Revival mansion, dominated by a giant-order Doric portico on three sides, was built in the mid-1840s and was the home of Henry W. Grady from 1863 to 1872. Grady became a prominent proponent of national reconciliation during the post–Civil War era, especially after his famous 1886 "New South" speech in New York. Grady promoted southern industry and agricultural diversification from his post as editor of the *Atlanta Constitution*. His former home in Athens was restored in 1977 and is now a historic house museum.

■ *Columbia County*

## STALLINGS ISLAND

**Address Restricted**

This Savannah River island, eight miles upstream from Augusta, contains one of the largest and most important shell middens in the Southeast. Three different cultural levels

*Telfair Academy of Arts and Sciences, Savannah, Chatham County, 1964. Courtesy of NPS (H. J. Sheely, Jr.).*

*Dixie Coca-Cola Bottling Company Plant, Atlanta, Fulton County, 1901. Courtesy of the Coca-Cola Company (Wilbur G. Kurtz, Jr.).*

are represented, one of which (ca. 1750 B.C.) has revealed the earliest use of pottery in the eastern United States. Numerous excavations conducted at various times have provided a great deal of information on Archaic Indians who lived in the Savannah River drainage area. The island is privately owned and not open to the public.

### ■ *Early County*

## KOLOMOKI MOUNDS
**Kolomoki Mounds State Park, 8 miles north of Blakely**

This is the type site of the Kolomoki culture (ca. A.D. 400–1400), thought to be a local variant of the Weeden Island culture. Excavations here revealed a great deal of information on burial practices and uncovered pottery of elaborate designs. Now a state park, the site contains the largest mound group in the Gulf Coast area.

### ■ *Floyd County*

## CHIEFTAINS
**80 Chatillon Road, Rome**

Sometime before 1819, Major Ridge, a Cherokee leader, purchased a log house that had been built ca. 1794 on the eastern bank of the Oostanaula River. Ridge, who operated a ferry and trading post at the site, made additions in 1827–1828. Ridge was the speaker of the Cherokee National Council and a significant advocate of modifying Cherokee ways with Anglo-American culture. In 1838 he was forced to accompany his people on the westward "Trail of Tears." The house is now a museum.

### ■ *Fulton County*

## DIXIE COCA-COLA BOTTLING COMPANY PLANT
**125 Edgewood Avenue, Atlanta**

This small brick building, irregularly shaped

to fit its angled corner lot, was built in 1891. From 1900 to 1901 it was the headquarters and plant of the Dixie Coca-Cola Bottling Company, parent of the Coca-Cola Bottling Company. The building is the oldest surviving structure associated with the early days of "Coke," the soft drink that has been called "the holy water of the American South," and represents its transformation from strictly a fountain treat to primarily a bottled drink.

## FOX THEATRE, ATLANTA
**660 Peachtree Street, Atlanta**

"The Fabulous Fox," one of the nation's largest and most extravagant movie palaces when it opened on Christmas Day, 1929, was designed in a neo-Moorish style, with onion domes, minarets, and horseshoe-arched openings. The auditorium, intended to appear as "a fortified courtyard within an ethereal city," continues the Arabian theme. Among the multitude of sounds the mighty Moller Organ can produce are exotic animal cries and thunder. The theater is still used for live performances and movie revivals.

## JOEL CHANDLER HARRIS HOUSE
**1050 Gordon Street, SW, Atlanta**

"The Wren's Nest," as Joel Chandler Harris called his then-rural frame house on "Snap Bean Farm," served as his home from 1881 until his death in 1908. Harris, editor and columnist with the *Atlanta Constitution,* authored the popular *Uncle Remus* tales but insisted that they were compilations of true folk tales, not his original creations. Uncle Remus and his critters, Br'er Fox, Br'er Rabbit, and the Tar Baby, remain popular with children of all ages. The house, now a museum, is remarkably unchanged from the time Harris lived and worked in it.

## MARTIN LUTHER KING, JR., HISTORIC DISTRICT (NPS)
**Bounded roughly by Irwin, Randolph, Edgewood, Jackson, and Auburn Avenues, Atlanta**

Honoring the nation's most prominent leader in the 20th-century struggle for civil rights, this urban area includes Martin Luther King, Jr.'s birthplace, the church he pastored, and his grave. The district, mainly along the east-

*Martin Luther King, Jr. Historic District, Atlanta, Fulton County. Martin Luther King, Jr. Birthplace. Courtesy of HABS (David J. Kaminsky).*

ern end of Auburn Avenue, a center of African-American life in Atlanta, was established as a National Historic Site in 1980.

## STATE CAPITOL
**Capitol Square, Atlanta**

Constructed between 1884 and 1889, this monumental neoclassical structure with its gilded dome is the perfect expression and symbol for the capital of the "New South," as Atlanta considered itself to be after Reconstruction. Along with many state capitols, its design and form follow architectural precedents established by the United States Capitol. Unlike all the rest, however, this one came in "under budget." A million dollars was appropriated for its construction, and $118.43 remained in the till when it was completed. The capitol continues in regular use and is now one of the city's oldest landmarks.

## STONE HALL, ATLANTA UNIVERSITY
**Morris Brown College, Atlanta**

Founded in 1866 by the American Missionary Association, Atlanta University was one of the few schools that offered quality academic education to African Americans in the late 19th century. Stone Hall, a three-story brick building with a tall clock tower centering its facade, was built in 1882 as the administration and main classroom building. Now, as Fountain Hall, it serves a similar role for Morris Brown College.

## SWEET AUBURN HISTORIC DISTRICT
**Auburn Avenue, Atlanta**

The center of black economic, social, religious, and cultural activities in Atlanta after the Civil War until the 1930s, this district centers on Auburn Avenue, east of the Martin Luther King, Jr., Historic District. As the major thoroughfare of one of the largest segregated urban areas in the South, Sweet Auburn was once considered the "richest Negro street in the world." Among its important institutions are the Big Bethel A.M.E. Church and the Butler Street YMCA.

### ■ *Glynn County*

## JEKYLL ISLAND
**Riverview Drive and Old Village Boulevard, Jekyll Island**

The Jekyll Island Club was established in 1886 to provide "profound seclusion and congenial companionship in one and the same spot." The club was envisioned as a winter Newport, and membership was limited to 100 people, among them the nation's wealthiest individuals. Few private cottages had dining rooms, as most members took meals at the clubhouse that centered the informally arranged grounds. The 1942 season was the last, and in 1946 the State of Georgia bought the island for development as a state park. Many club buildings have been restored and are open to the public.

### ■ *Gordon County*

## NEW ECHOTA
**Northeast of Calhoun on Georgia Route 225, Gordon**

This first national capital of the Cherokees, established in 1825, marked a turning point. Here the Indians adopted a republican legislature, published a newspaper, and established a supreme court, all based on Anglo-American precedent. In 1835 the infamous Treaty of New Echota was signed here, establishing the basic pretext for the final removal of the Cherokee to the West that resulted in the "Trail of Tears." Until research and subsequent archeological investigations confirmed the site in the 1950s, it was considered lost. Now a state park and museum, it contains the ca. 1827 Worcester House, home of a New England missionary, and several reconstructed buildings.

### ■ *Harris County*

## PINE MOUNTAIN STATE PARK
**2970 Georgia Highway 190, Pine Mountain vicinity**

Pine Mountain, with its phenomenal collection of facilities designed in an intentionally

*Pine Mountain State Park, Harris County. Pool and bathhouse. Courtesy of NPS (Ethan Carr).*

rustic style, is one of the nation's best examples of a Depression-era state park. It was developed collaboratively with the National Park Service, Civilian Conservation Corps (CCC), and Works Progress Administration (WPA) as a Recreational Demonstration Area. The park, now the western portion of Franklin D. Roosevelt State Park, is also significant because of its association with Roosevelt, who reviewed its progress and often made design suggestions during his visits to nearby Warm Springs. Of all the 1930s parks developed across the country, thanks to Roosevelt's New Deal agencies such as the CCC and WPA, this was the one with which he was most intimately connected. His Little White House at Warm Springs is included in the eastern half of the park. (See Warm Springs Historic District, Meriwether County.)

## ■ *Liberty County*

### SAINT CATHERINE'S ISLAND
**Off the Georgia coast, South Newport vicinity**

This privately owned coastal island was an important Spanish mission center for more than 100 years, from 1566 to 1684. Button Gwinnett purchased the island in 1765 and developed it as his plantation home. Saint Catherine's is the most significant site associated with this Georgia delegate to the Continental Congress and signer of the Declaration of Independence. Still privately owned, it was developed as a country estate and game preserve after 1876.

## ■ *Lumpkin County*

### CALHOUN MINE
**Address Restricted, Dahlonega vicinity**

This gold mine was discovered in 1828, and a year later more than 10,000 prospectors had swarmed to the site, across the Chestatee River from Cherokee country. The inevitable conflicts that arose drove the Indians from their land, ultimately to their expulsion west of the Mississippi. The mine, on private property, is virtually unnoticeable at the surface, although shafts and tunnels are still intact. Nearby Dahlonega is named after the Cherokee word for "golden," and from 1838 to 1861 a U.S. mint operated in the town. Access to the site is strictly controlled.

## ■ *McDuffie County*

### THOMAS E. WATSON HOUSE
**310 Lumpkin Street, Thomson**

Tom Watson, a founder of the Populist Party, urged a united front by white and black farmers, arguing that class interests "cut across racial lines." Embittered after defeat at the polls in 1892 and 1896, he reversed his racial attitudes and enjoyed a considerable following among rural Southern whites. He bought this house in 1900, added an impressive Corinthian portico, and lived here from 1905 until his death in 1922.

## ■ *Meriwether County*

### WARM SPRINGS HISTORIC DISTRICT
**Warm Springs vicinity**

This historic district is associated with Franklin D. Roosevelt, who first came to the small resort town's mineral waters in 1924, three years after being stricken with polio. The district includes the extensive campus-like facilities of the Warm Springs Foundation, which Roosevelt founded in 1927 to aid fellow victims of the disease. Roosevelt built the "Little White House" in 1932 and died there in April 1945.

## ■ *Muskogee County*

### COLUMBUS HISTORIC RIVERFRONT INDUSTRIAL DISTRICT
**East bank of the Chattahoochee River, 8th to 38th Streets North, Columbus**

Water power afforded by the 2½-mile falls of the Chattahoochee River made Columbus an early Southern manufacturing and textile center. Structures dating from 1844 to 1900 concentrated along the riverbanks document the evolution of hydromechanical and hydroelectrical engineering systems. Dams and their associated elements show the evolution of hydrotechnology. A great deal of original equipment remains in the several complexes that form this industrial district.

### OCTAGON HOUSE, COLUMBUS
**527 First Avenue, Columbus**

This unique house, consisting of two separate frame octagons, each a single story high, joined by a covered passageway, is likely the

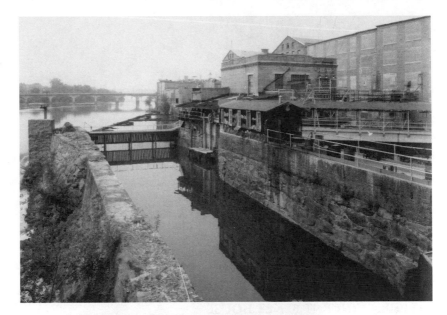

Columbus Historic Riverfront Industrial District, Columbus, Muscogee County. Courtesy of NPS (David Sharpe).

Octagon House, Columbus, Muscogee County. Courtesy of HABS (Jack E. Boucher).

only fully realized double octagon house in the country. Octagonal houses exemplify a short-lived fad that followed the 1848 publication of Orson Squire Fowler's *A Home for All; Or, The Gravel Wall and Octagon Mode of Building*. In his book, Fowler touted the octagonal form as providing more space than traditional square or rectangular buildings. It is not open to the public.

## SPRINGER OPERA HOUSE
### 105 10th Street, Columbus

A long three-story brick facade embellished with rudimentary Italianate details gives little clue to the elegant theater housed within. Opened in 1871, the Springer hosted celebrated entertainers in the late 19th and early 20th centuries, and the impressive list of performers who trod its boards gives it special significance. Among them were Buffalo Bill, Edwin Booth, Lillie Langtry, Will Rogers, and Irving Berlin. The Opera House was later converted to a movie house and after a period of neglect was restored to its original splendor—and use—beginning in 1964.

*Liberty Hall, Crawfordville, Taliaferro County, 1936. Courtesy of HABS (L. D. Andrews).*

## ■ *Richmond County*

### STEPHEN VINCENT BENÉT HOUSE
**2500 Walton Way, Augusta**

Stephen Vincent Benét, known for his poetry and short stories, began his writing career in this impressive house after moving here in 1911. At the time, the house was the commandant's house for the Augusta Arsenal, which his father commanded. The house, fronted by a two-tiered Tuscan portico, was built between 1827 and 1829 and now serves as the president's home for Augusta College, which took over the property after the arsenal was deactivated.

### COLLEGE HILL
**2216 Wrightsboro Road, Augusta vicinity**

The facade of this privately owned, two-story frame house is dominated by a two-tiered portico, covered by an extension of the roof. For a number of years it was thought that George Walton, Georgia signer of the Declaration of Independence, lived here, but another Augusta house was later determined to have been his home. (See George Walton House.)

### HISTORIC AUGUSTA CANAL AND INDUSTRIAL DISTRICT
**West bank of the Savannah River, Augusta**

This still intact nine-mile canal system, constructed in 1845–1846 and enlarged in 1874–1877, represents the South's attempts to industrialize both before and after the Civil War. Attendant textile mills along the canal date primarily from the 1870s and 1880s. They helped Augusta become one of the South's leading textile centers in the early 20th century.

### OLD MEDICAL COLLEGE
**598 Telfair Street, Augusta**

This was the first home of the Medical College of Georgia, founded in 1829 by Milton Anthony, who established the highest standards of education possible and attracted an impressive faculty. The college advocated national standards for medical education a full decade prior to the founding of the American Medical Association. The college, a handsome Greek Revival structure fronted by a monumental Doric portico, was designed by architect Charles Cluskey as a model for medical instruction. It is now a city museum.

### GEORGE WALTON HOUSE
**1230 Nelson Street, Augusta**

This 1½-story house, raised on a high basement, represents a regional architectural type known as a "Sand Hill Cottage." The older, smaller portion of the present building was the home of George Walton from 1791 to 1804. Walton, appointed to the Continental Congress in 1776 when he was 26 years old, was the youngest signer of the Declaration of Independence. After the war he served as Georgia's governor and as a U.S. senator. "Meadow Garden," as Walton called his home, is now a museum. (See College Hill.)

■ *Stephens County*

## TRAVELER'S REST

**6 miles east of Toccoa**

This fittingly named early-19th-century frame structure, one of the oldest houses in northeastern Georgia, was once regarded as the most popular inn and tavern on the Federal Post Road between Charleston and Chattanooga. It also served as a trading post for the Cherokees, a post office, and a home. Still in a rural setting, it was acquired by the Georgia Historical Commission in 1955 and was subsequently restored to serve as a museum.

■ *Taliaferro County*

## LIBERTY HALL

**Alexander H. Stephens Memorial State Park, Crawfordville**

Even though he supported moderate measures to stave off the splitting of the Union and voted against secession when the moment of decision arrived, Alexander H. Stephens was elected vice president of the Confederate States of America. This is the role for which he will forever be remembered, although he also enjoyed a remarkable political career both before and after the Civil War. Stephens, born two miles away in 1812 and orphaned at age 14, lived here from 1834 until his death in 1883. He built the main portion of the conservative frame house in 1875 to replace an earlier house on the site. Liberty Hall, a historic house museum, is located in this state park.

■ *Thomas County*

## LAPHAM-PATTERSON HOUSE

**626 North Dawson Street, Thomasville**

Built in the 1880s as a resort home for a Chicago businessman, this large frame mansion is the epitome of the eclectic, picturesque, romantic approach to design typical of the Victorian era. Its design and detailing are both exuberant and individualistic, and its plan is, in a word, idiosyncratic. None of the rooms on the U-shaped first floor are square or rectangular. The house is now a Georgia state park unit.

■ *Troup County*

## BELLEVUE

**204 Ben Hill Street, LaGrange**

Bellevue stands tall and proud as an exceptional architectural achievement, even in a state known for its many "white columns." A perfect high-style expression of the Greek Revival at the height of antebellum Southern affluence, it was built in the 1850s by Georgia statesman Benjamin Harvey Hill for his wife. The LaGrange Woman's Club maintains the house as a meeting place and as a memorial to Hill. It is open to the public.

■ *Walker County*

## JOHN ROSS HOUSE

**Lake Avenue and Spring Streets, Rossville**

This two-story, square-timbered log house was home to John Ross, whose 40-year reign as chief of the Cherokee nation began in 1828. Although Ross protested removal and led delegations of his people to argue against it, he was forced to lead them in their forced exile beyond the Mississippi—the infamous "Trail of Tears." The house is now a museum and a memorial to Ross.

■ *Wilkes County*

## ROBERT TOOMBS HOUSE

**216 East Robert Toombs Avenue, Washington**

After serving in both houses of the U.S. Congress, Robert Augustus Toombs became secretary of state of the Confederacy, then resigned that post to become a brigadier general in the Confederate Army. Known as Georgia's "unreconstructed rebel" after the war, Toombs lived here until his death in 1885. The house, an early-19th-century frame structure, is fronted by a later, almost ludicrously large Doric portico that attempts to provide an architectural image of the Old South. It is now a Georgia State Parks house museum.

## TUPPER-BARNETT HOUSE

**101 West Robert Toombs Avenue, Washington**

In 1860 a finely detailed, monumental Doric colonnade was built to surround all four sides of this ca. 1830s house. The house remains one of the finest examples of the numerous

transformations of Federal style houses to neoclassical mansions as cotton became king in the mid-19th-century American South.

This particular "white column" addition was made by a Baptist minister. The house remains privately owned.

# HAWAII

## ◼ *Hawaii County*

### HONOKOHAU SETTLEMENT (NPS)
**Kailua-Kona vicinity**

Because of its ideal landing places for canoes and its fishponds, the Honokohau coastal area was important to ancient Hawaiian Island chiefs as well as to their descendants. This settlement location includes numerous ancient house sites, temples, fishponds, a sled run, tombs, and scattered petroglyphs. It is now included within the boundaries of the Kaloko-Honokohau National Historical Park.

### KAMAKAHONU
**Northwest edge of Kailua Bay, Oahu,
Kailua-Kona vicinity**

Kamakahonu was the home of Kamehameha I, unifier of the Hawaiian Islands, from 1812 until his death in 1819. The residential compound included the Ahuena *heiau* (personal temple) of the king. It was here, within a year of Kamehameha's death, that the first missionaries to the Hawaiian Islands landed. The site is now within the grounds of a hotel,

and several of the buildings associated with Kamehameha have been reconstructed.

### KEAUHOU HOLUA SLIDE
**East of Hawaii 18, Keauhou vicinity**

This is Hawaii's largest and best-preserved *holua* (sled run). A dangerous pastime restricted to chiefs, Hawaiian-style sledding was accomplished by riding sleds down a rock track covered with earth and made slippery with wet grass. This steep slide, almost 4,000 feet long, perhaps longer originally, served as the site of contests that probably took place in connection with the annual religious festival, the Olakahiki. The contests have been described as the "Olympic games" of the Hawaiian people.

### MAUNA KEA ADZ QUARRY
**Address Restricted, Hilo vicinity**

Located at the top of Mauna Kea at an elevation of 12,000 feet, this is the largest primitive quarry in the world. Prehistoric Hawaiians obtained basalt here and fabricated it into stone implements, as evidenced by extensive heaps of chips. The archeological complex also contains religious shrines, trails, rock shelters, and petroglyphs.

## MOOKINI HEIAU
### Northern tip of Hawaii, Hawi vicinity

This massive platform with its open stone-paved court was a temple of the rulers—a state temple, or *luakini,* where human sacrifices were performed. It is one of the most important traditional sites in Hawaii because of its association with the legendary Polynesian priest Pa'ao, who is believed to have introduced new religious and social concepts to the islands ca. A.D. 1370. The landmark, a unit of Kohala Historical Sites State Monument, also contains the nearby birthplace of King Kamehameha I, who founded the Kingdom of Hawaii in 1795.

## PUUKOHOLA HEIAU (NPS)
### 0.9 mile southeast of Kawaihae, South Kohala District, Oahu

In the summer of 1791, King Kamehameha the Great sacrificed Keoua, his chief rival for the kingship of the Hawaiian Islands, at this temple. He had recently built it to honor his war god Kukailimoku and to ensure success in conquering all the islands to form a single kingdom under his rule. An older temple site and other ruins are included with Kamehameha's *heiau* in this National Historic Site.

## SOUTH POINT COMPLEX
### Address Restricted, Naaleu vicinity

This multifaceted site provides the longest and most complete archeological record of human occupation in the Hawaiian Islands. Fire hearths, a temple platform, canoe mooring holes, and salt pans are included in the complex. Through carbon 14 testing, a date of ca. A.D. 124 has been obtained at one house site, establishing it as one of the earliest recorded occupations in Hawaii.

## ◼ *Honolulu County*
### *ARIZONA* (NPS)
### Off Ford Island, Pearl Harbor, Oahu, Honolulu

Launched in 1915, the USS *Arizona* was moored at its Pearl Harbor berth when it was struck and sunk by a Japanese bomb on the morning of December 7, 1941, a day that President Franklin D. Roosevelt declared would "live in infamy." The *Arizona* and a shrine erected between 1961 and 1962 that straddles its submerged remains honor and commemorate the 1,177 members of the U.S. Navy and Marine Corps who perished on the battleship.

### *BOWFIN*
### 11 Arizona Memorial Drive, Pearl Harbor, Oahu, Honolulu

The World War II submarine *Bowfin* represents the role Pearl Harbor played in the sub-

Arizona, *Honolulu, Honolulu County. Courtesy of NPS (J. Livingston).*

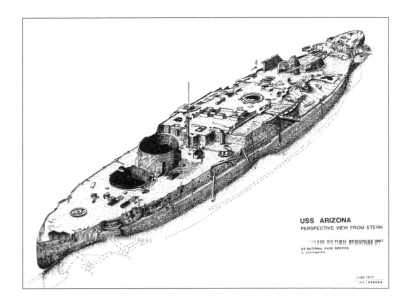

USS ARIZONA
PERSPECTIVE VIEW FROM STERN

US NATIONAL PARK SERVICE
J. Livingston

*Hickam Field, Honolulu County. Bullet-ravaged barrack walls. Courtesy of NPS (E. N. Thompson).*

## HICKAM FIELD
**Oahu, Honolulu vicinity**

Established in 1935 just to the southeast of Pearl Harbor and designed by Army Colonel J. Nurse, Hickam was Hawaii's largest and most important army airfield when World War II broke out. In their attack on Pearl Harbor, Japanese pilots destroyed numerous planes here, preventing their use in a retaliative strike, then proceeded to attack warships in the harbor. Several buildings still bear shell marks from the attack.

## HUILUA FISHPOND
**Kahana Bay, 13 miles north of Kanoehe on Hawaii Route 83, Oahu**

Huilua Fishpond, operational well into the 20th century, is one of the few surviving fishponds of an estimated 97 that once existed along the coast of Oahu. Fishponds, constructed for hatching and keeping fish, were unique achievements of the ancient Hawaiians in their extensive aquacultural practice.

marine war against Japan. Launched in 1942 and commissioned a year later, it sank 16 Japanese vessels and received eight battle stars, the Presidential Unit Citation, and the Navy Unit Commendation for service in World War II. The most completely outfitted submarine of its class in existence, the *Bowfin* is a popular attraction at Pearl Harbor.

## CINCPAC HEADQUARTERS
**Pearl Harbor Naval Base, Oahu, Honolulu vicinity**

This reinforced-concrete structure commemorates Admiral Chester W. Nimitz, commander in chief of the Pacific Fleet (CINCPAC) during World War II. Here, from 1942 through 1944, Nimitz commanded all American land, sea, and air forces in the Central and North Pacific. "A superb leader of men," Nimitz oversaw the Aleutians campaign, the Battle of Midway, and the liberation of Guam.

## FALLS OF CLYDE
**Pier 7, Honolulu**

Built in 1878 in Glasgow, Scotland, the four-masted tanker *Falls of Clyde* carried cement, wheat, sugar (from Hawaii), and petroleum during its many years of maritime service around the world. About to be scuttled at the end of its career, it was instead towed to Hawaii in 1963 and subsequently restored. Now remasted and rerigged as a floating exhibit, it is the only four-masted full-rigged ship afloat.

## IOLANI PALACE
**364 South King Street, Honolulu**

Termed "the only royal palace in the United States," this was the official residence of the last two rulers of the Kingdom of Hawaii, King Kalakaua and Queen Liliuokalani. As such, it is the most important surviving symbol of the days of Hawaiian independence. Designed and constructed from 1879 to 1882, it combines Italianate and Second Empire details with verandas appropriate to the local climate. In 1898 the formal transference of the sovereignty of the Hawaiian Islands to the United States took place on the palace steps. Iolani Palace is now a museum.

## KANEOHE NAVAL AIR STATION
**Vicinity of Kailua, Oahu**

Kaneohe was bombed by the Japanese seven minutes before the December 7, 1941, attack on Pearl Harbor, and again approximately an hour later. The Japanese goal, which was successful, was to destroy American planes before they could take to the air and interfere with the attack on Pearl Harbor. Hangar No. 1 and the seaplane ramps remain from 1941.

*Huilua Fishpond, Kahana Bay, Honolulu County, 1965. Courtesy of NPS (Walter Horchler).*

*Iolani Palace, Honolulu, Honolulu County, 1966. Courtesy of HABS (Jack E. Boucher).*

## KAWAIAHAO CHURCH AND MISSION HOUSES

**957 Punchbowl Street; 553 S. King Street, Honolulu**

This impressive stone church, dating from 1838–1842, is the "mother church" of Protestantism in Hawaii, as its congregation is an outgrowth of the original mission founded in Boston in 1819. As Hawaii's state church, it witnessed inaugurations and other services associated with the Kingdom of Hawaii. Earlier buildings associated with the missionary effort survive nearby. The earliest, a prefab dating from 1820, was built in Boston, disassembled, shipped to the "Sandwich Islands," and reerected "for the comfort of the ladies."

## OPANA RADAR SITE

**Kamehameha Highway, Oahu, Kawela vicinity**

At 7:02 A.M. on December 7, 1941, two U.S. Army technicians practicing with a new radar set at a portable unit here detected the approach of aircraft. They reported their findings, but it was determined that the blip indicated U.S. B-17 bombers, expected to arrive that morning. Only after the fact was it realized the radar had monitored Japanese planes on their way to Pearl Harbor. The tragic story of "what might have been" entered the mythology of World War II history, and radar's importance and potential in military operations became obvious to all.

## PALM CIRCLE
### Palm Circle Drive, Fort Shafter, Oahu, Honolulu

Palm Circle at Fort Shafter was World War II headquarters of the commanding general and his staff, U.S. Army forces, Pacific Ocean Areas. This command, responsible for supplying and administering all U.S. Army personnel in the Central and South Pacific, carried out logistical planning for the invasion of the Gilberts, the Marshalls, the Mariannas, Guam, Palau, and Okinawa.

## PUU O MAHUKA HEIAU
### 4 miles northeast of Haleiwa on Hawaii Route 83, Oahu

The largest surviving *heiau* on Oahu, this is a platform-type *luakini* temple with a low-walled court. Relatively intact, it measures approximately 570 feet by 170 feet. In 1792 three men from Captain George Vancouver's ship, HMS *Daedalus,* may have been sacrificed here. The property is now a state park.

## UNITED STATES NAVAL BASE, PEARL HARBOR
### 3 miles south of Pearl City on Hawaii Route 73, Oahu, Pearl City

Pearl Harbor's splendid anchorage was one of the principal reasons for early American interest in Hawaii, and the development of a station in the early 20th century was an important factor in the rise of U.S. naval power in the Pacific. Japan's 1941 attack on Pearl Harbor precipitated America's entry into World War II. Associated National Historic Landmarks located in this still vital naval installation include the ships *Arizona, Bowfin,* and *Utah.* National Historic Landmarks Hickam Field, Kaneohe Naval Air Station, the Opana Radar Site, Palm Circle, and Wheeler Field are also associated with the attack on Pearl Harbor.

## UTAH (NPS)
### Off Ford Island, Pearl Harbor, Oahu, Honolulu

Built in 1909, the first and only battleship to bear the name, the USS *Utah* was at its Pearl Harbor berth at the time of the Japanese air attack. It was hit by two torpedoes and capsized. Its rusting hulk, listing to port, now lies submerged in silt and water and serves as a memorial and tomb for the crew members who died in the attack.

## WHEELER FIELD
### Near Schofield Barracks, Oahu, Wahiawa

This airfield, established in 1922 in central Oahu, had become the Army Air Corp's principal fighter base in Hawaii by 1941. It was yet another target, and subsequent casualty, of the Japanese attack that December. With 83 of

*United States Naval Base, Pearl Harbor, Honolulu County, ca. 1941. Courtesy of the National Archives.*

its aircraft destroyed, 38 men killed, and 59 wounded, Wheeler was rendered helpless to retaliate for the attack on Pearl Harbor. The 1941 flight line, hangars, and barracks survive at this U.S. Air Force facility.

■ *Kauai County*

## COOK LANDING SITE
**2 miles southwest of Hawaii Route 50, Kauai, Waimea**

It is thought that Captain James Cook, first European known to have sighted the Hawaiian Islands, stepped ashore here for the first time on January 28, 1778. The site, on the southwestern coast of Kauai at the mouth of the Waimea River, is now a park.

## OLD SUGAR MILL OF KOLOA
**Maluhia and Koloa Roads, Kauai, Koloa vicinity**

Although native Hawaiians had grown sugar cane earlier, the first commercially successful sugar plantation was established here by Ladd & Company in 1835, marking the foundation of what became Hawaii's largest industry. Sugar long played a major role in Hawaii's economics and politics and was influential in the decision of the United States to annex the islands. The massive stone base of the chimney and stone foundations of the mill date from the early 1840s.

## RUSSIAN FORT
**On Hawaii 50, just southwest of the bridge over the Waimea River, Kauai**

Begun sometime in 1817, this large stone structure, in the form of an irregular octagon, is the most impressive reminder of the short-lived attempt by the Russian-American Company to gain a position of influence in the Hawaiian Islands. Evidently, the fort was incomplete when its commander's conduct alienated the Hawaiians, causing King Kamehameha to expel the Russians. Hawaiian troops later occupied the fort, which is now a state monument and park.

## WAILUA COMPLEX OF HEIAUS
**Wailua vicinity, Kauai**

This complex of five discontiguous properties includes a city of refuge, a petroglyph site, four important *heiaus,* a royal birth site,

and a bell stone. Together they form one of the most important complexes in the Hawaiian Islands, representing a long period of aboriginal cultural history. All of the sites are incorporated in Wailua River State Park.

■ *Maui County*

## HOKUKANO-UALAPUE COMPLEX
**Along Hawaii Route 45, Molokai, Ualapue vicinity**

These discontiguous sites form one of the most important and impressive archeological complexes in Hawaii. Six temple platforms and two fishponds are testaments to the architectural and engineering achievements, and to the political and economic power, that had evolved on Molokai between A.D. 1500 and 1778, when contact with the West was made.

## KALAUPAPA LEPROSY SETTLEMENT (NPS)
**Molokai, Kalaupapa vicinity**

This windswept peninsula on Molokai's northern coast was the site of a leper colony established in 1866 to curb an epidemic among native Hawaiians. Belgian priest Father Joseph Damien, "Martyr of Molokai," volunteered to minister here in 1873 and died a victim of the disease in 1889. The site, which includes Fr. Damien's Saint Philomena Church, became a National Historical Park in 1980.

## KAUNOLU VILLAGE SITE
**Address Restricted, Lanai City vicinity**

Remains of this former village on Lanai's leeward coast represent nearly all phases of Hawaiian culture. The state's largest surviving example of a prehistoric fishing community, Kaunolu included at least 86 house platforms, at a time when 10 was the norm in such communities. The village was a favorite deep sea fishing location for King Kamehameha I from ca. 1778 to 1810 but was abandoned in the 1870s.

## LAHAINA HISTORIC DISTRICT
**Island of Maui, Lahaina**

From time immemorial, Lahaina had been a favorite residence of Maui kings and chiefs,

*Kalaupapa Leprosy Settlement, Molokai, Maui County. Siloama Protestant Church. Courtesy of NPS (Russ Apple).*

and it was the royal residence during the time Hawaii changed from a traditional chiefdom to a constitutional monarchy. From ca. 1830 to 1860 the American whaling fleet made Lahaina an annual port of call. The core of the small town preserves the architecture and atmosphere of a mid–19th-century Hawaiian seaport.

## LOALOA HEIAU
### Island of Maui, Kaupo vicinity

This hillside temple site is one of Hawaii's many remaining intact examples of *luakini* sites, a state shrine where human sacrifices were made to implore success in warfare. Once the center of an important cultural complex, the raised platform is thought to have been built ca. A.D. 1730 by Kekaulike, king of Maui, who lived at Kaupo and died in 1736.

## PIILANIHALE HEIAU
### 4 miles north of Hana, near Kalahu Point, Island of Maui

Archeological excavations undertaken at this site revealed a court-type *heiau* and a chiefly residential area, the largest structural platform in the Hawaiian Islands. Its stone walls enclose a rectangle approximately 340 feet by 425 feet. The temple is believed to have been built in the 16th century by Piilani, one of Maui's greatest chiefs.

# IDAHO

■ *Ada County*

## ASSAY OFFICE
### 210 Main Street, Boise

Built by the federal government in 1870–1871 and constructed of local Boise sandstone, the Assay Office illustrates the importance of mining in the political, social, economic, and legal development of Idaho and the Far West. In operation from 1872 to 1933, the office is one of the most significant public buildings remaining from Idaho's territorial days. It now serves as offices for the Idaho State Historical Society.

■ *Bannock County*

## FORT HALL
### Fort Hall Indian Reservation, Fort Hall vicinity

Fort Hall, near the strategic junction of the Snake and Portneuf Rivers, was an early center of the fur trade and became one of the most important supply and trading centers on the Oregon Trail. During the period of Indian hostilities, from 1858 to 1883, it was an important military post. The first fort was built in 1834 and was sold to the Hudson's Bay Company in 1837. A historical marker identifies the site, and low grass–covered mounds mark the lines of the fort's adobe walls, now within the Fort Hall Indian Reservation.

■ *Butte County*

## EXPERIMENTAL BREEDER REACTOR NO. 1
### National Reactor Testing Station, Arco vicinity

This was the first reactor built by the Atomic Energy Commission in a program planned to derive electric power from atomic energy for civilian use. On December 20, 1951, Experimental Breeder Reactor No. 1 (EBR–I) produced the first usable amounts of electricity created by nuclear fission and proved that it could produce more fuel than it consumed.

SOUTH ELEVATION

UNITED STATES ASSAY OFFICE
210 MAIN STREET, BOISE, ADA COUNTY, IDAHO

HISTORIC AMERICAN BUILDINGS SURVEY
SHEET 5 OF 7 SHEETS

*Assay Office, Boise, Ada County. Courtesy of HABS (Mark T. Wellen).*

In July 1963 it was the first reactor to achieve a self-sustaining chain reaction using plutonium instead of uranium as the major fuel component. EBR-I is open to the public for tours.

### ■ *Cassia County*

## CITY OF ROCKS
### City of Rocks State Park, Almo vicinity

This site on the California Overland Trail was named for the numerous formations of eroded granite rocks that resemble a city skyline. A well-watered, relatively level area, in contrast to the extensive sagebrush plains surrounding it, City of Rocks was a popular stopping point and camping site for westbound pioneers from the 1840s to the 1880s. Wagon tracks, along with initials and inscriptions carved into the rocks, attest to the thousands who once passed this way. Most of the site is now incorporated within the City of Rocks National Reserve.

### ■ *Clark County*

## CAMAS MEADOWS BATTLE SITES
### East of Kilgore, Dubois vicinity

Two discontiguous sites in eastern Idaho, five miles apart, commemorate events that took place in August of the 1877 Nez Perce War. A predawn raid by Nez Perce warriors captured pack mules of a U.S. Army force that had been pursuing them, led by Major General Oliver O. Howard. The delay that ensued until a new pack train arrived allowed the Indians to escape into Yellowstone Park and Montana on their way to Canada. One of the sites marks the location of Howard's camp, the other where army troops endured a four-hour siege by the Nez Perce before being relieved.

### ■ *Clearwater County*

## LOLO TRAIL
### Beginning near Lolo, Montana, to Weippe Prairie, Idaho, Lolo vicinity

The 200-mile-long Lolo Trail is significant for two reasons, both based on its being a traditional Indian route through the Bitterroot Mountains. First, in September 1805, Toby, a Shoshoni guide, led the Lewis and Clark party through the passage. This would prove to be the single most arduous stretch of their entire journey, but was key to the expedition's reaching the Pacific side of the continent. Seven decades later hundreds of Nez Perce Indians used the trail when fleeing the U.S. Army during the Nez Perce War of 1877. (Also in Missoula County, Montana.)

## WEIPPE PRAIRIE
### South of Weippe and Idaho Route 11, Weippe vicinity (Clearwater and Idaho Counties)

On the morning of September 20, 1805, William Clark's advance party arrived here, at the western terminus of the Lolo Trail. Members of the Lewis and Clark expedition met the Nez Perce for the first time at this upland prairie, a favorite gathering spot for the tribe. The Nez Perce, who had never before seen white men, proved the most helpful of all the Indian tribes the expedition met in its journey.

*Cataldo Mission, Cataldo, Kootenai County, 1958. Courtesy of NPS (William C. Everhart).*

■ *Franklin County*

## BEAR RIVER MASSACRE SITE
**Preston**

On January 29, 1863, the California Volunteers under Colonel Patrick Edward Conner's command attacked a band of Northwestern Shoshoni here at their winter encampment. The culmination of 25 years of hostilities between the two, this bloodiest encounter between Native Americans and white men in the West between 1848 and 1891 resulted in the deaths of almost 300 Shoshoni and 14 soldiers. The strategy of attacking Indian winter encampments set a precedent that the U.S. Army repeatedly used in its Indian campaigns after the Civil War.

■ *Idaho County*

## LOLO TRAIL
**Beginning near Lolo, Montana, to Weippe Prairie, Idaho (Clearwater and Idaho Counties)**

(See entry under Clearwater County. Also in Missoula County, Montana.)

■ *Kootenai County*

## CATALDO MISSION
**Interstate 90, Cataldo**

Dating from the 1850s, this is the oldest

extant mission church in the Pacific Northwest. It was built by Jesuit missionaries in their efforts to convert the Coeur d'Alene Indians and was designed by Father Anthony Ravalli, a native of Italy. The impressive frame church is fronted with a Tuscan portico, above which is a baroque pediment decorated with a painted sunburst. The main altar, of wood painted to simulate marble, is attributed to Father Ravalli.

■ *Lemhi County*

## LEMHI PASS
**12 miles east of Tendoy**

The summit of this mountain pass marks the spot where the Lewis and Clark expedition crossed the Continental Divide in August 1805. It then formed the boundary between newly acquired Louisiana and Spanish territory to the West. The pass is in a remote section of the Beaverhead Range, at an elevation of 7,373 feet. Situated on U.S. property, the pass now marks the boundary between Idaho and Montana and is virtually unchanged from the time the expedition first crossed it (also in Beaverhead County, Montana).

# ILLINOIS

■ *Bureau County*

## OWEN LOVEJOY HOUSE
**East Peru Street, Princeton**

Owen Lovejoy, minister, abolitionist, U.S. congressman, and humanitarian, lived here from 1838 until his death in 1864. The house was a stop on the Underground Railroad, where Lovejoy harbored fugitive slaves on their way north to Canada and freedom. Elected to Congress in 1856, Lovejoy gained a national reputation through his congressional and party leadership and his fiery antislavery speeches. The house is operated as a museum.

■ *Champaign County*

## MORROW PLOTS, UNIVERSITY OF ILLINOIS
**Gregory Drive at Matthews Avenue, Urbana**

Begun in 1876, the Morrow Plots were the first soil experiment plots established by a college in the United States. The site has provided data on the effects of crop rotation and the impact of organic and chemical nutriment on plant yield. Experiments conducted here proved that rich prairie soil could be depleted by continuous crops of corn. In 1904 the plots were reduced in number from ten to three to provide space for college expansion.

## UNIVERSITY OF ILLINOIS OBSERVATORY
**901 South Mathews Avenue, Urbana**

Constructed by the State of Illinois in 1896, the University of Illinois Observatory is significant for its association with the development of the selenium cell and the photoelectric cell that revolutionized the measurement of celestial magnitudes. This research was conducted with a 12-inch refractor telescope independently mounted, for maximum stability, on a brick pier extending down to bedrock.

■ *Cook County*

## ROBERT S. ABBOTT HOUSE
**4742 Martin Luther King, Jr., Drive, Chicago**

Robert Sengstacke Abbott lived in part of this large Queen Anne style brick duplex from 1926 until his death in 1940. Abbott was the most successful black publisher of his era and through his newspaper, the *Chicago Defender* (est. 1905), encouraged African Americans to leave the South and settle in northern cities, particularly Chicago.

## ADLER PLANETARIUM
**1300 South Lake Shore Drive, Chicago**

This planetarium and astronomical museum were Max Adler's gift to the people of Chicago. The first institution of its type in the Western Hemisphere, it was intended to enable everyone to "observe the heavenly bodies as heretofore only astronomers could do." The still active planetarium opened in 1930 and was an attraction at the great Chicago exposition, "A Century of Progress" (1933–1934).

## AUDITORIUM BUILDING
**Roosevelt University, 430 South Michigan Avenue, Chicago**

One of the icons of American architectural history, this multipurpose building was conceived as a civic center housing an auditorium, space for political conventions, hotel rooms, and offices. It was built in 1886–1889 from designs by Dankmar Adler, who devised its daring and innovative solutions to engineering problems, and Louis Sullivan, who provided the proscenium-arched auditorium with a bravado performance of his signature foliate ornamentation. Roosevelt University restored the building, beginning in 1945, and it now serves as a city college and public theater.

## CARSON, PIRIE, SCOTT AND COMPANY STORE
**State and Madison Streets, Chicago**

Louis Sullivan, architect for the original (1899) section of this large department store, provided a logical and direct expression of function for his client and fully integrated his typical organic, Art Nouveau ornament into its design. The rounded corner bay is especially handsome and is the focal point of the ensemble. Later additions are in keeping with Sullivan's original concept.

## JAMES CHARNLEY HOUSE
**1365 North Astor Street, Chicago**

The Charnley House is important, both nationally and internationally, as one of the pivotal structures in the development of modernism in architecture. Its limestone and Roman brick walls are arranged with a strong sense of symmetry, but without any overt references to historical styles. Built in 1891–1892, it was one of the few major residential commissions of Louis Sullivan and a benchmark in the architectural development of Frank Lloyd Wright, who was then a draftsman and designer in the office of Adler & Sullivan. The house remains close to its original condition, both inside and out. In 1995, in an effort to safeguard its future, Seymour H. Persky purchased it and donated it to the Society of Architectural Historians (SAH). Now serving as the national headquarters of the SAH, this seminal monument in architectural history is open to the public.

## CHICAGO BOARD OF TRADE BUILDING
**141 West Jackson Boulevard, Chicago**

Established in 1848 as a response to the instability and chaos then existing in Chicago grain markets, this precedent-setting commodity exchange pioneered in establishing "futures" contracts. Its 45-story Art Deco headquarters, designed by the Chicago architectural firm of Holabird and Root, was erected in 1928–1930. The pyramidal roof is fittingly topped by a statue of Ceres, an ancient goddess of grain and harvest, sculpted by John H. Stoors.

## ARTHUR H. COMPTON HOUSE
**5637 Woodlawn Avenue, Chicago**

From the late 1920s to 1945 this was the residence of Arthur H. Compton, the distinguished physicist who discovered the "Compton effect," proving that light has both a particle aspect and a wave aspect. At the time Compton was a physics professor at the nearby University of Chicago. For his discovery, Compton received a Nobel Prize in 1927.

## AVERY COONLEY HOUSE
**300 Scottswood Road and 281 Bloomingbank Road, Riverside**

One of architect Frank Lloyd Wright's most famous designs, this long, low, multiwinged complex—essentially an enlarged "Prairie house"—was built in 1907–1909. Typical features include strong horizontal lines, stucco and wood construction, low-pitched roofs with broad eaves, impressive chimneys, and careful integration with its site. Wright considered it one of the best of his early buildings.

## CROW ISLAND SCHOOL
**1112 Willow Road, Winnetka**

This seminal International style building, jointly designed by Eliel and Eero Saarinen, and Perkins, Wheeler, and Will, opened in 1940 and served as the prototype for elementary schools across the country. Designed to embody the educational philosophy of Winnetka school superintendent Carleton Washburne, Crow Island incorporated progressive concepts such as child-scale furni-

*Crow Island School, Winnetka, Cook County. Courtesy of Betty Carbol.*

ture, self-contained classrooms with access to the outside, and flexible spaces—in short, the child-centered school. It still serves its original purpose.

## CHARLES G. DAWES HOUSE
### 225 Greenwood Street, Evanston

For almost a half century, from 1909 until his death in 1951, Charles Gates Dawes, first director of the budget (1921) and vice president of the United States under Calvin Coolidge, lived in this brick mansion. In 1924 an international committee he chaired produced the Dawes Plan, providing a rational payment schedule for Germany's World War I reparation. For his work Dawes received the 1925 Nobel Peace Prize. His house is now a museum and the Evanston Historical Society's headquarters.

## OSCAR STANTON DEPRIEST HOUSE
### 4536–4538 Martin Luther King, Jr. Drive, Chicago

In 1928, Oscar Stanton DePriest became the first African American elected to the U.S. House of Representatives from a northern state. A Republican, DePriest lost his seat in 1934 to the first black Democrat elected to Congress. From 1929 until his death in 1951, he lived in a second-floor apartment in this eight-unit building.

## JEAN BAPTISTE POINT DU SABLE HOMESITE
### 401 North Michigan Avenue, Chicago

This is the site of the home and trading post of Jean Baptiste Point Du Sable, black pioneer, fur trader, and entrepreneur. His establishment of a trading post ca. 1799 at a portage here marked the beginning of the city of Chicago. The site, on the northern bank of the Chicago River near its confluence with Lake Michigan, is marked in Pioneer Court Plaza, near the heart of Chicago's commercial district.

## JOHN FARSON HOUSE
### 217 Home Avenue, Oak Park

This is an early and distinguished example of the Prairie School, a regional expression of the Arts and Crafts movement that became one of America's greatest and most original contributions to architecture. Designed by George Maher, the house displays his unique combination of organic forms and classical detailing. Much of the original furniture, light fixtures, and art glass windows designed by Maher survive. Pleasant Home, as the Farsons named their house, is being restored by the Pleasant Home Foundation and serves as a historic house museum.

## JOHN J. GLESSNER HOUSE
### 1800 Prairie Avenue, Chicago

Completed in 1887, this massive granite-faced house was designed by the famous American architect Henry Hobson Richardson late in his career. It represents the height of his mature Romanesque style, a style he more often employed in religious and commercial structures than in residential work. The house was commissioned by John Glessner, then vice president of the International Harvester Company. It was threatened with demolition in the 1960s but was saved and subsequently restored by the Chicago Architecture Foundation. It is now a house museum.

## GRANT PARK STADIUM
### 425 East 14th Street, Chicago

Soldier Field, as it is popularly known, was dedicated as a memorial to World War I soldiers and is an imposing architectural presence on Chicago's lakefront. Holabird & Roche won the design competition and provided a classical composition with twin Doric colonnades. It was planned to be adaptable for a variety of public gatherings, and when it opened in 1924, the field was among the largest stadiums in the world. It has been the home of the Chicago Bears since 1971.

## GROSSE POINT LIGHT STATION
### 2601 Sheridan Road, Evanston

A coastal brick tower, Grosse Point Light Station was the lead navigational marker in Lake Michigan just north of Chicago Harbor. The light guided lake-borne traffic safely through one of America's most commercially important and highly traveled corridors, a route that connected the East Coast, Great Lakes, and Gulf Coast. In recognition

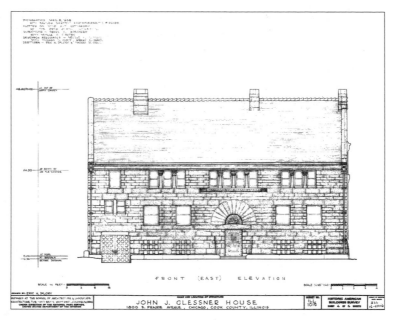

*John J. Glessner House, Chicago, Cook County. Courtesy of HABS (Eric N. DeLony).*

of its importance to maritime navigation, the Grosse Point lighthouse was fitted with the first second-order Fresnel lens on the Great Lakes. The station was decommissioned in 1941; however, the second-order Fresnel lens remains in place and all original buildings survive unaltered.

## HAYMARKET MARTYRS' MONUMENT
### 863 South Des Plaines Avenue, Forest Park

During a workers' rally held in Chicago's Haymarket Square in 1886 to protest police brutality against strikers at the McCormick Reaper Factory, a bomb exploded, killing several police officers who had come to demand an end to the meeting. Eight "anarchists" were arrested, and four were subsequently hanged. Ever since then the martyrs of this seminal event in U.S. labor history have served as an enduring symbol of workers' struggles. The monument marking the burial site of the victims in Forest Home/Walden Cemetery shows an allegorical female figure protecting a fallen laborer.

## HULL HOUSE
### 800 South Halsted Street, Chicago

Jane Addams, American social reformer and pacifist, moved into Hull House in 1889 and began to assist those living in the blighted area surrounding it. In her settlement house, she offered a wide variety of social services to Chicago's poor. Her work gained international attention, and in 1931 she became the first American woman to win the Nobel Peace Prize. In 1961 the former slum neighborhood was demolished and the Chicago Circle Campus of the University of Illinois built in its place. As part of the renewal, Hull House was reconstructed as a memorial to Addams.

## KENNICOTT GROVE
### Milwaukee and Lake Avenues, Glenview

This board-and-batten house and its associated nature preserve were home to Robert Kennicott, 19th-century naturalist, explorer, and curator and trustee of the Chicago Academy of Sciences. His career illustrates the development of American scientific research in the 19th century. Kennicott Grove, operated by the Glenview Park District as an interpretive center, has extensive nature trails.

## LEITER II BUILDING
### South State and East Congress Streets, Chicago

This pivotal building in the development of tall-building design dates from 1889–1891 and is the masterpiece of architect William Le Baron Jenney. It is outstanding for the clear expression of its skeletal construction, whereby load-bearing interior columns allow the greatest amount of natural light to enter from non-load-bearing exterior walls. Interiors were left open to be subdivided by tenants. The dimensions of the eight-story building were impressive for its time, and still are: 144 feet by 402 feet.

## FRANK R. LILLIE HOUSE
**5801 Kenwood Avenue, Chicago**

From 1904 until his death in 1947, Frank R. Lillie, the distinguished University of Chicago embryologist who served as director of Woods Hole Marine Biological Laboratory and president of the National Academy of Sciences, lived here. Lillie willed the house to the University of Chicago, and it now serves as an educational facility.

## MARQUETTE BUILDING
**140 South Dearborn Street, Chicago**

Built in 1893–1894 from designs by Holabird and Roche, this 16-story office tower is an exemplary manifestation of the then-new steel frame technology that demanded rethinking of architectural theories. Long horizontal bays of glass indicate that the masonry walls are non-load-bearing, and the gridlike pattern of narrow frames and spandrels proclaims the steel frame. Unlike many buildings of its time and place, the Marquette also contains important decorative detailing of the period.

## MARSHALL FIELD COMPANY STORE
**111 North State Street, Chicago**

Completed in 1907, this 12-story granite-faced building was designed by Daniel H. Burnham to house the retail operations of Marshall Field & Company. Containing nearly 35 acres of floor space, the building is notable for its light wells, one of which is covered with a Tiffany glass mosaic dome. Marshall Field & Company, a pioneer in customer-service concepts, was the nation's largest wholesaler and retailer in the early 20th century.

*Marshall Field Company Store, Chicago, Cook County, ca. 1960. Courtesy of Marshall Field & Company.*

## ROBERT A. MILLIKAN HOUSE
**5605 Woodlawn Avenue, Chicago**

From 1907 to 1921 this three-story brick house was the residence of Robert A. Millikan, one of America's best-known 20th-century scientists. In 1923, Millikan received the Nobel Prize in physics for proving that the electron is an elementary charge and for his work on the photoelectric effect.

## MONTGOMERY WARD COMPANY COMPLEX
**619 West Chicago Avenue, Chicago**

Since 1909 this expansive complex, constructed of reinforced concrete, has served as national headquarters for the country's oldest mail order firm. Founded in 1872 by Aaron Montgomery Ward, the company established high standards in consumer trust by supplying goods at fair value. The Mail Order House, identified by its ranks of horizontal "Chicago" windows, conforms to the shoreline of the North Branch of the Chicago River, on which it fronts.

## OLD STONE GATE, CHICAGO UNION STOCKYARDS
**Intersection of West Exchange Avenue and South Peoria Street, Chicago**

For almost a century, from ca. 1879 to 1971, this triple-arched, rough-faced limestone gate was the main entrance to the Chicago Union Stockyards, founded in 1865 to consolidate the city's many scattered stockyards into an efficient unit. Romanesque Revival in style, the gateway symbolizes Chicago's one-time role as the nation's largest meat-packer and is now the only surviving structure associated with the Union Stockyards.

## ORCHESTRA HALL
**220 South Michigan Avenue, Chicago**

Designed by Chicago architect Daniel Burnham in a Georgian Revival style, Orchestra Hall has hosted an incredible variety of performances since its dedication in 1904. The hall is home to the Chicago Symphony Orchestra, one of the first-ranked orchestras in the history of American music.

## PULLMAN HISTORIC DISTRICT
**Bounded by 103rd Street, railroad tracks, 115th Street, and Grove Avenue, Chicago**

Constructed between 1880 and 1884 as a model company town for industrialist George M. Pullman, for whom it was named, Pullman was a radical departure from the unhealthful, overcrowded working-class districts typical at the time. The town also played a pivotal role in the history of the American labor movement. In 1894 Pullman was the focal point of a violent strike that spread across the nation, prompting President Grover Cleveland to intervene with federal troops. This was the first time that provisions of the Sherman Anti-Trust Act played a part in smashing the unions. Many of Pullman's handsome Queen Anne and Gothic style buildings remain, and its Hotel Florence houses a museum. Unfortunately, a disastrous fire in the fall of 1998 damaged the clock tower and the factory where Pullman's railroad cars were built.

*Old Stone Gate, Chicago Union Stockyards, Chicago, Cook County. Courtesy of AASLH (Ralph J. Christian).*

*Frederick C. Robie House, Chicago, Cook County, 1963. Courtesy of HABS (Cervin Robinson).*

## RELIANCE BUILDING
**32 North State Street, Chicago**

Completed in 1895 from designs by Chicago architects John Root and Charles A. Atwood, this 15-story office building is a prime example of the "Chicago School" of high-rise design. Its iron-skeleton frame enables non-bearing exterior walls to be faced with expansive "Chicago window" bays, in which a large, fixed central pane is framed by narrow double-hung sash. The Reliance Building is also noted for its Gothic terra-cotta decorations and prominent vertical bays.

## RIVERSIDE HISTORIC DISTRICT
**Bounded by 26th Street, Harlem and Ogden Avenues, the Des Plaines River, and Forbes Road, Riverside**

Designed in 1868–1869 by Olmsted and Vaux, who were invited by the Riverside Improvement Company to plan a model community, Riverside is the nation's first development arranged so that open spaces and parkland are integral parts of the daily urban environment. Streets were planned to respect the dictates of topography, and deed restrictions ensured that fences would not mar the open, rolling landscape. Frederick Law Olmsted was virtually the father of landscape architecture as a profession, and Riverside remains one of the best testimonials to his genius.

## FREDERICK C. ROBIE HOUSE
**5757 South Woodlawn Avenue, Chicago**

One of architect Frank Lloyd Wright's most distinguished buildings, the Robie House epitomizes his Prairie Style. Its broad horizontal masses and planes, almost more sculpture than architecture, and its clean unadorned lines are recognizable by all familiar with modern architecture. It was designed and constructed in 1907–1909 and became one of the seminal buildings in 20th-century American architecture. The Robie House is now home to the University of Chicago Alumni Association. The entry hall, living room, and dining room are open to the public.

## ROOKERY BUILDING
**209 South LaSalle Street, Chicago**

Burnham and Root's Rookery Building, completed in 1886, combines a heavy Romanesque Revival masonry exterior with cast-iron skeletal construction. A prime example in the evolution of multistoried buildings, the 11-story Rookery is in the form of a hollow square, allowing light to penetrate interior offices. The expansive lobby was redecorated in 1905 by Frank

Lloyd Wright and is a veritable catalog of his early design motifs.

## ROOM 405, GEORGE HERBERT JONES LABORATORY, UNIVERSITY OF CHICAGO
**South Ellis Avenue between East 57th and 58th Streets, Chicago**

On August 18, 1942, in Room 405 of the George Herbert Jones Laboratory at the University of Chicago, a group of chemists first isolated a pure compound of the man-made element plutonium. This was a milestone in the development of nuclear energy, as plutonium is a basic fuel of nuclear reactors. Room 405, a small, narrow, pantrylike space, is maintained as it appeared in 1942 and can be viewed through a glass door.

## SEARS, ROEBUCK AND COMPANY
**925 South Homan Avenue, Chicago**

Only seven years after its founding in 1893, Sears, Roebuck and Company had become the country's largest mail order concern. This expansive four-building red-brick complex on Chicago's west side dates from 1905–1906 and contains the building that served as company headquarters until 1973. It also includes the printing plant that for many years produced the Sears Catalog, the company's principal selling instrument that was "required reading" in millions of American homes.

## SHEDD AQUARIUM
**1200 South Lake Shore Drive, Chicago**

The Shedd, appropriately located on the shore of Lake Michigan, was the nation's first inland aquarium to maintain a permanent collection of fresh and saltwater aquatic life. John G. Shedd, president of Marshall Field and Company, endowed the institution, which opened in 1930 to provide "instructive entertainment." The handsome marble building has Greek architectural details on the exterior and aquatic decorations inside.

## SITE OF FIRST SELF-SUSTAINING NUCLEAR REACTION
**South Ellis Avenue between East 56th and 57th Streets, Chicago**

Scientists at the University of Chicago, working under the supervision of Enrico Fermi, achieved a controlled release of nuclear energy for the first time on December 2, 1942. This first self-sustaining nuclear chain reaction took place in a converted squash court beneath the stands at the university's athletic field, and the group celebrated by drinking Chianti out of paper cups. The facility was demolished in 1958, and the spot is now marked by a bronze sculpture, *Nuclear Energy,* by Henry Moore.

## SOUTH DEARBORN STREET–PRINTING HOUSE ROW HISTORIC DISTRICT
**Bounded by Jackson Boulevard, Plymouth and Federal Courts, Dearborn and Congress Streets, Chicago**

This small area near the southeastern corner of Chicago's famous downtown "Loop" contains buildings pivotal in the city's growth and in American architectural history. The Manhattan (1891), the Old Colony (1894), and the Fisher (1896) buildings are all prime examples of the "Chicago School." The most famous is the 1889–1893 Monadnock Building. One of the largest masonry bearing-wall towers ever built, it is notable for its sheer unadorned stone and brick wall surfaces.

## LORADO TAFT MIDWAY STUDIOS
**6016 South Ingleside Avenue, Chicago**

This group of brick buildings contains a labyrinth of studios created by Lorado Taft, one of the country's most accomplished sculptors. Known for his realistic works in monumental scale, Taft maintained a studio here from 1906 to 1929, adding other facilities for his close-knit group of assistants and students. The Midway Studios appear much as they did in Taft's time and continue in use as an art facility of the University of Chicago.

## F. F. TOMEK HOUSE
**150 Nuttall Road, Riverside**

Frank Lloyd Wright's prairie house has been recognized by architects and scholars as his "greatest invention in [the] first phase of a long career." Constructed in 1907, the Tomek House, a well-preserved example of the type, is located in the Riverside National Historic

Landmark District. In addition to being a good example of the Prairie Style, the Tomek house documents the development of the style, which reached its clearest expression in Wright's Robie House.

## U-505
### Jackson Park, 57th Street and Lake Shore Drive, Chicago

When this German submarine was boarded off French West Africa on June 4, 1944, it was the first time since 1815 that the U.S. Navy had captured a foreign warship on the high seas. Subsequently brought to the United States, U-505 provided valuable intelligence about German naval equipment and codes. Now beached and berthed on concrete cradles at Chicago's Museum of Science and Industry, U-505 is a memorial to the 55,000 Americans who lost their lives at sea in World War II.

## UNITY TEMPLE
### 875 Lake Street, Oak Park

Designed in 1905 by Frank Lloyd Wright and completed in 1907, this well-known building marks the first time reinforced concrete was used on a monumental scale as its own architectural medium. In addition, the church represents a radical departure from traditional ecclesiastical design. Wright was a member of the congregation that still uses the building he designed "for the worship of God and the service of Man."

## THE WAYSIDE
### 830 Sheridan Road, Winnetka

This comfortable brick house facing Lake Michigan in an exclusive Chicago suburb was the residence of Henry Demarest Lloyd, a critic of the nation's industrial monopoly during the 1880s and 1890s. Lloyd was chief editorial writer for the *Chicago Tribune* from 1880 to 1885 and in 1894 authored *Wealth Against Commonwealth*, a landmark in the history of antimonopolism in America.

## IDA B. WELLS-BARNETT HOUSE
### 3624 South Martin Luther King, Jr., Drive, Chicago

From 1919 to 1929, this impressive Romanesque Revival town house, faced with rock-

Frank Lloyd Wright House & Studio, Oak Park, Cook County. Children's Playroom, 1967. Courtesy of HABS (Philip Turner).

faced granite blocks, was the home of Ida B. Wells, African-American teacher, journalist, and civil rights advocate. Almost single-handedly, Wells began the fight to awaken the world's conscience to the horrible realities of lynching—"our National crime," as she called it. Thanks in great measure to her pioneering efforts, the cause was afterward taken up by the National Association for the Advancement of Colored People (NAACP), which she had helped organize.

## FRANCES WILLARD HOUSE
### 1730 Chicago Avenue, Evanston

This diminutively scaled board-and-batten Gothic cottage, built in 1865, was the home of Frances Willard, "mother" of the Women's Christian Temperance Union (WCTU). Although she traveled extensively in her crusades against spirituous liquors, her "Rest Cottage," as she called the house her father built, was always home base. The National WCTU has carefully preserved the house and maintains it as a memorial to its founder.

## DANIEL HALE WILLIAMS HOUSE
### 445 East 42nd Street, Chicago

On the night of July 9, 1893, a patient was

rushed to Chicago's Provident Hospital with a stab wound that had almost punctured his heart. Dr. Dan Williams, the hospital's founder, was on duty, and successfully "sewed up the human heart" as a newspaper heralded his seminal operation. Considered to be the first fully successful heart operation, it was only one of many accomplishments of the outstanding black doctor who lived in this small Queen Anne house from ca. 1905 to 1929.

## FRANK LLOYD WRIGHT HOME AND STUDIO
**428 Forest Avenue and 951 Chicago Avenue, Oak Park**

An architect's own home and place of work provide insights into his ideals and practice that few commissions can emulate. This rambling building, built, rebuilt, and added to, served the architect from 1887 to 1909, the early years during which he formulated and refined his "Prairie Style." The complex was restored in the 1970s and 1980s and is now a museum and research center.

### Grundy County
## MAZON CREEK FOSSIL BEDS
**Benson Road, 3 miles southeast of Morris**

The Mazon Creek Fossil Beds are important in the history of U.S. geology. When they were discovered in the mid-19th century, the beds provided the best and earliest represen-

tations of some of the oldest plants and animals known. Sites where fragile fossils are common and well preserved (here in distinctive ironstone nodules) are exceedingly rare. The Mazon Creek beds continue to be a prolific source of fossils.

### Hancock County
## NAUVOO HISTORIC DISTRICT
**Nauvoo and its environs**

From 1839 to 1846, Nauvoo (from a Hebrew word meaning "beautiful place") was home to the Church of Jesus Christ of Latter Day Saints, or Mormons. At a time when prairie towns were typically ramshackle frame affairs, Nauvoo, then the largest urban center in Illinois, boasted fine masonry structures built under church auspices. Joseph Smith, church leader, was murdered in nearby Carthage in 1844, and in 1846 the Mormons left on their westward trek. Many of their buildings remain and are now museums.

### Henry County
## BISHOP HILL COLONY
**Off U.S. Route 34, Bishop Hill**

Founded in 1846 by religious dissidents who emigrated from Sweden to establish a new way of life on the Illinois prairie, the colony was run as a commune until its dissolution in 1861. Its archives, artifacts, and structures remain as important documents for the study

*Bishop Hill Colony, Bishop Hill, Henry County. Historic view. Courtesy of Bishop Hill Heritage Association.*

of immigration, ethnic heritage, architecture, and 19th-century communitarian societies. Portions of the former colony are now an Illinois State Historic Site.

### ■ *Jersey County*

## PRINCIPIA COLLEGE HISTORIC DISTRICT
### River Road, Elsah vicinity

The campus of Principia College, an institution of the Church of Christ, Scientist, contains eleven structures designed by noted California architect Bernard Maybeck. Built in 1931–1938, most are Tudor Revival brick and stone buildings with half-timbering, designed and placed to connote an English village. In contrast, Maybeck modeled the limestone chapel that dominates the campus after a New England meeting house.

### ■ *Jo Daviess County*

## ULYSSES S. GRANT HOME
### 511 Bouthillier Street, Galena

In 1865 the citizens of Galena presented this prominent two-story Italianate brick house to General U. S. Grant when he returned victorious to the town he had left four years earlier. Grant lived here until he became secretary of war in 1867 and again, briefly, following the end of his presidency. The house, restored in the 1950s from original drawings and spec-

ifications, is now maintained by the state as a historic house museum.

### ■ *Knox County*

## OLD MAIN
### Knox College, Galesburg

The oldest building at Knox College, this handsome Collegiate Gothic Revival structure is the best-preserved site associated with the famous Lincoln-Douglas debates of 1858. The fifth of the seven debates between Democratic senator Stephen A. Douglas and his Republican challenger, Abraham Lincoln, took place here on October 7. The debates highlighted the momentous issues carrying the nation toward disunion and civil war. Lincoln lost the election but achieved national attention because of his stance, expressed here, that slavery was a moral, not a political, issue.

### ■ *La Salle County*

## OLD KASKASKIA VILLAGE
### Address Restricted, Ottawa vicinity

First recorded in 1673 by Louis Joliet and Father Jacques Marquette, this is the best-documented historic Indian site in the Illinois River valley. The Kaskaskia, a band of the Illinois tribe, lived here, occupying hundreds of cabins on a 2½-mile stretch along the Illinois River. Excavations have provided

*Principia College Historic District, Elsah vicinity, Jersey County. Living room in Anderson Hall. Courtesy of the Principia (Frank Biggs).*

insight into native life and changes brought by early European contact.

## STARVED ROCK
### 6 miles west of Ottawa on Illinois Route 71
This prominent rock formation across the Illinois River from Old Kaskaskia Village (see Old Kaskaskia Village) marks the site of a palisaded fort established in 1683 by French explorers La Salle and Tonti. In 1691, the French abandoned the fort to follow the Kaskaskia, who moved south due to increasing pressure from the Iroquois. The site is now an Illinois State Park.

### ■ Lake County
## FORT SHERIDAN HISTORIC DISTRICT
### 25 miles north of Chicago along the shore of Lake Michigan, Lakeforest vicinity
Dating from a time when small frontier posts were being replaced by large garrisons at strategic points across the country, Fort Sheridan was constructed between 1889 and 1910. Unlike most forts, it was designed by a major architectural firm, Holabird and Roche. Although the Chicago architects were responsible for its major components, auxiliary buildings were constructed from standardized plans of the quartermaster general. O. C. Simonds landscaped the complex. Fort Sheridan was decommissioned in the 1990s.

### ■ Madison County
## LYMAN TRUMBULL HOUSE
### 1105 Henry Street, Alton
Lyman Trumbull, prominent Republican statesman from Illinois, chaired the U.S. Senate's Judiciary Committee from 1861 to 1871. He sponsored and secured passage of much Reconstruction legislation, including the Freedmen's Bureau Bill and the Civil Rights Act of 1866. From 1849 to ca. 1863, Trumbull lived in this Greek Revival brick and stone house, which is still privately owned.

### ■ Massac County
## KINCAID SITE
### Address Restricted, Brookport vicinity (Massac and Pope Counties)
This is one of the major temple mound sites in the Midwest. Research undertaken here has played a vital role in developing a chronology for dating pre-Columbian sites in the region. Its location suggests that the site was a major trade station along the Ohio River, and its extent and abundant refuse suggests a long period of occupancy.

### ■ McLean County
## DAVID DAVIS HOUSE
### 1000 East Monroe Street, Bloomington
An associate justice of the U.S. Supreme

*David Davis House, Bloomington, McLean County. Courtesy of NPS (George R. Adams).*

Court, David Davis is best known as author of the majority opinion in *Ex Parte Milligan,* an 1866 decision restricting the right of military courts to try civilians. "The Constitution of the United States," he argued, "is a law for rulers and people, equally in war and in peace." This elegant Italianate villa, designed by well-known Midwestern architect Alfred H. Piquenard, was his home from 1872 until his death in 1886. It is now a museum.

## ■ Ogle County

### JOHN DEERE HOME AND SHOP
**Near Grand Detour**

From 1836 to 1847 the small village of Grand Detour was home to John Deere, a skilled blacksmith who invented and manufactured a steel plow that could scour the tough prairie sod with a clean furrow, unlike other plows that quickly became clogged in the rich but sticky soil. Deere's farm implement made intensive cultivation of the Midwestern prairie possible. His house and a reconstruction of the blacksmith shop are maintained by the John Deere Foundation as a historic monument.

## ■ Pope County

### KINCAID SITE
**Address Restricted, Brookport vicinity (Massac and Pope Counties)**

(See entry under Massac County.)

## ■ Randolph County

### FORT DE CHARTRES
**Terminus of Illinois Route 155, West of Prairie du Rocher**

The third fort built by the French, near a site first fortified in 1720, was completed in 1756. One of the most complex fortifications in North America, it was the center of French civil and military authority in the Illinois country. The English replaced the French in October 1765, in accordance with terms of the treaty ending the French and Indian War. In 1772 the British destroyed the fort. The 20th-century reconstruction now on the site is a state park.

### PIERRE MENARD HOUSE
**Fort Kaskaskia State Park, Ellis Grove vicinity**

Built ca. 1802, this excellent example of a French Colonial raised cottage, more typical of the lower Mississippi valley than of this region, was the residence of Pierre Menard, a successful trader who was active in Illinois politics. Located at the base of the hill on which Fort Kaskaskia stood, the Menard House is a museum in Fort Kaskaskia State Park.

### MODOC ROCK SHELTER
**Address Restricted, Modoc vicinity**

Containing stratified deposits giving evidence of Archaic Indian occupation beginning ca. 7000 B.C., this rock shelter documents major changes in human subsistence and settlement practices. Modoc is also important in the development of American archeology, as method and theory shifted from a traditional classification approach to one indicating progressive evolution of cultural systems.

## ■ Rock Island County

### ROCK ISLAND ARSENAL
**Vicinity of Rock Island**

Established in 1862, this is one of the largest military construction projects of the late 19th century. The massive stone manufacturing shops and ancillary buildings remain as the administrative and technological core of the arsenal, and equally impressive stone officers quarters are still used for housing. General Thomas Rodman, a major figure in the history of American ordnance technology, outlined an ambitious construction program during his tenure as the arsenal's second commandant (1865–1871). Among Rock Island's significant contributions to U.S. ordnance technology is its leading role in the production of artillery carriages and recoil mechanisms.

## ■ Sangamon County

### SUSAN LAWRENCE DANA HOUSE
**301 Lawrence Avenue, Springfield**

This house with attached library (1902–1906) is one of the masterpieces of architect Frank Lloyd Wright's early period, and he lavished

*Susan Lawrence Dana House, Springfield, Sangamon County, 1970. Courtesy of Paul Sprague, Univ. of Wisconsin–Milwaukee.*

upon it all of his creative skills. In pristine condition, it also retains much of its original furniture and stained glass, made to the architect's designs and specifications. The Dana House was purchased by the State of Illinois in 1981, was subsequently restored, and is now a historic house museum.

## ABRAHAM LINCOLN HOME (NPS)
### Eighth and Jackson Streets, Springfield

The only house Abraham Lincoln ever owned, this frame building with rudimentary Italianate details was his family's home from 1844 to 1861, the years he advanced from small-town lawyer to president of the United States. Lincoln's son deeded the house to the State of Illinois in 1887, and in the 1970s it became the Lincoln Home National Historical Site. The restored house, now a museum, contains many original Lincoln furnishings.

*Abraham Lincoln Home, Springfield, Sangamon County. Courtesy of NPS (Richard Frear).*

## LINCOLN TOMB
### Oak Ridge Cemetery, Springfield

Dedicated in 1874, this is the final resting place of Abraham Lincoln, 16th president of the United States, his wife, and three of their four sons. The granite monument, centered by an obelisk above a raised platform, is embellished with bronze sculptural groups depicting Civil War–era infantry, cavalry, artillery, and navy, along with representations of the president.

## VACHEL LINDSAY HOUSE
### 603 South Fifth Street, Springfield

For most of his life Vachel Lindsay, a major figure in the American poetic renaissance of the early 20th century, lived in this simple frame house. Using emphatic rhythms and colloquial vocabulary, Lindsay created strikingly original verse. The house is similar to the nearby Abraham Lincoln House in its basic plan and architectural details.

*Old State Capitol, Springfield, Sangamon County, 1935. Courtesy of HABS (Clark Bullard).*

*Church of the Holy Family, Cahokia, Saint Clair County, 1968. Courtesy of NPS.*

## OLD STATE CAPITOL

**Fifth, Sixth, Adams, and Washington Streets, Springfield**

From 1839 to 1876 this notable Greek Revival structure, designed by John F. Rague, served as Illinois's fifth state capitol. Abraham Lincoln was a member of the first legislature that sat here (1840–1841) and in 1858 gave his "House Divided" speech in accepting the Republican nomination for the U.S. Senate. From 1876 until 1961 the former capitol was the Sangamon County Courthouse. Now a museum, it has been restored to its original appearance.

■ *Saint Clair County*

## CAHOKIA MOUNDS

**7850 Collinsville Road, Collinsville vicinity**

The largest community of the Mississippian Period in eastern North America, this site's occupation dates from approximately A.D. 800–1500. Among the prominent features are more than 100 mounds, varying both in size and in original function. Flat-top mounds were platforms for temples and houses of the leaders, and conical mounds marked burials. Monks Mound, the largest of all, covers 15 acres and rises in four terraces to a height of 100 feet. There is little doubt that this complex, supplemented with a surrounding group of satellite towns, sustained one of the largest populations in prehistoric North America. Major portions are included in Cahokia Mounds State Park. Cahokia Mounds was placed on the World Heritage List in 1982.

## CHURCH OF THE HOLY FAMILY
### East First Street, off Illinois Route 3, Cahokia

Catholic priests from Quebec founded the first mission here in 1699. The present structure, erected between 1786 and 1799, is typical of French Colonial *poteaux sur sole* (posts on sill) construction, in which logs, mortised into a sill, are placed vertically. A newer church now stands nearby, but the little-altered building still serves the parish.

## EADS BRIDGE
### Spanning the Mississippi River between Saint Louis, Missouri, and East Saint Louis, Illinois

This three-span, ribbed steel arch bridge crosses the Mississippi with an overall length of 6,442 feet and a clearance of 50 feet above high water. Dedicated on July 4, 1874, it was designed and built by Captain James B. Eads, who utilized an innovative cantilever support to produce spans larger than any previously constructed. The bridge was designed with two levels, the upper for a roadway, the lower

for a railroad. (Also in Saint Louis City, Missouri.)

### ■ *Tazewell County*

## FARM CREEK SECTION
### Highway 8 between School Street and Bittersweet Road, East Peoria vicinity

Frank Leverett, one of America's foremost glacial geologists, discovered this exposed face of a hill with its clearly defined stratifications in 1879 and described and pictured it in his monograph *The Illinois Glacial Lobe* in 1899. The site was used to help formulate regional and national stratigraphic classifications and has figured prominently in the study and development of glacial geology.

### ■ *Will County*

## ILLINOIS AND MICHIGAN CANAL LOCKS AND TOWPATH
### Channahon State Park, 7 miles southwest of Joliet

Begun in 1836 and completed in 1848, this canal linked Chicago to the Mississippi River and propelled the city into a position of commercial and industrial supremacy in the Midwest. Commercial use of the canal ended in the 1930s, but portions of it have been preserved and recognized by the establishment of the Illinois and Michigan Canal National Heritage Corridor.

# INDIANA

### ■ *Cass County*

## SPENCER PARK DENTZEL CAROUSEL
### Riverside Park, Logansport

From 1867 through 1929, Philadelphia's Dentzel Company supplied the country with top-of-the-line carousels. This, one of the three oldest that remain virtually intact, is thought to date from ca. 1903. According to the company's catalog, this particular model contains 42 animals (three abreast), and four "double-seated chariots, of fine

design and architecture, handsomely carved, fresco painted and upholstered in plush." In 1962 it was moved from its original location to Riverside Park, where it still operates.

### ■ *Dearborn County*

## THOMAS GAFF HOUSE
### 213 Fifth Street, Aurora

Lording over the city of Aurora and the Ohio River valley from its hillside perch, this extraordinary house designed by prominent

*Eleutherian College Classroom and Chapel Building, Lancaster, Jefferson County. Courtesy of NPS (Marsh Davis).*

*Charles L. Shrewsbury House, Madison, Jefferson County. Spiral staircase, 1971. Courtesy of HABS (Jack E. Boucher).*

mid-19th-century American architect Isaiah Rogers resembles nothing so much as a steamboat! Although its details are Italianate, it exemplifies the style popularly known as "Steamboat Gothic." Now a museum, it survives as a remarkable remnant of prosperous antebellum days along the Ohio River.

### ■ *Grant County*

## MARIE WEBSTER HOUSE
### 926 South Washington Street, Marion

This gambrel-roofed Colonial Revival house was the home and office of Marie Webster, master quilter and advocate of this traditional American craft. Webster began quilting when she was 50 years old, and in 1911 and 1912 the *Ladies Home Journal* featured her work. In 1915 she published *Quilts: Their History and How to Make Them,* the first how-to manual on quilting. She also sold patterns and kits and lectured on the subject, helping to popularize the craft throughout the country.

### ■ *Jefferson County*

## ELEUTHERIAN COLLEGE CLASSROOM AND CHAPEL BUILDING
### State Route 250, Lancaster

Constructed between 1854 and 1856, this three-story stone structure was the main building of a college established to provide education for all, regardless of race. Families affiliated with the school were involved in clandestine activities of the Underground Railroad, and the town of Lancaster was well known as a stopping point for slaves seeking freedom. In all likelihood, this building, now being restored, played an important role in their proceedings.

## LANIER MANSION
### 511 West First Street, Madison

This outstanding Greek Revival mansion, beautifully sited overlooking the Ohio River, was built between 1840 and 1844 for James Lanier, a prominent banker and financier who twice saved the State of Indiana from bankruptcy during the Civil War. Architect-builder Francis Costigan derived details from pattern books by architects such as Minard LeFever and Asher Benjamin and proudly inscribed his name on a silver plate set in the newel post of the three-story spiral staircase. Still containing many original furnishings, the Lanier House is open to the public.

## CHARLES L. SHREWSBURY HOUSE
**301 West First Street, Madison**

Ostensibly less showy than the nearby Lanier Mansion (see Lanier Mansion), at least on the exterior, this restrained Greek Revival house was built in 1846–1849 for a wealthy Madison merchant. Architect-builder Francis Costigan lavished the interior with classical trim, largely based on architect Minard LaFever's handbooks. The central hall contains a spectacular free-standing, self-supporting spiral staircase.

■ *Knox County*
## GROUSELAND
**3 West Scott Street, Vincennes**

William Henry Harrison lived here from 1804 to 1812, during the years he served as governor of Indiana Territory and defended American expansion into the former Northwest Territory. His efforts in the latter cause culminated in the Battle of Tippecanoe (see Tippecanoe Battlefield, Tippecanoe County). In 1840, Harrison was elected the ninth president of the United States but died shortly after assuming office. His handsome Federal style home on the Wabash has been restored and is a historic house museum.

■ *Marion County*
## BROAD RIPPLE PARK CAROUSEL
**Fifth Floor, Children's Museum at 30th Street, Indianapolis**

This wooden menagerie—one lion, one tiger, three giraffes, three goats, three reindeer, and thirty-one horses—provides a rare nostalgic treat at the Indianapolis Children's Museum. From 1917 to 1956 all but one of the animals were part of the city's Broad Ripple Park Carousel, one of the earliest surviving Dentzel menagerie carousels in the country. They were restored in 1975–1978

and reinstalled in a working carousel at the museum, where they prance once again to the sounds of a Wurlitzer organ.

## BUTLER FIELDHOUSE
**49th Street and Boulevard Place, Butler University Campus, Indianapolis**

Basketball and Indiana are inseparable. Butler University's field house, the oldest of the nation's major college basketball field houses, was built in 1928. It remains the largest such facility at a private institution, accommodating 15,000 spectators. For a number of years Hinkle Fieldhouse, as it is now named, housed the Indiana State High School Tournament, one of the most active and well known basketball tournaments in the country.

## BENJAMIN HARRISON HOME
**1204 North Delaware Street, Indianapolis**

Built in 1874–1875, when Benjamin Harrison was a prominent Indianapolis lawyer, this large Italianate brick house was his home until his death in 1901. Here he accepted the Republican party's nomination for the presidency, here he planned his campaign, and here he returned after serving as the nation's 23rd president. Now a museum, the restored house contains a number of original family pieces.

## INDIANA WORLD WAR MEMORIAL PLAZA HISTORIC DISTRICT
**Bounded by Saint Clair, Pennsylvania, Vermont, and Meridian Streets, Indianapolis**

This long rectangular plaza with its attendant buildings is a distinguished memorial to Indiana's war heroes and a notable example of the "City Beautiful" design movement of the early 20th century. Fittingly, the district also includes the national headquarters of the American Legion, formed in 1919 by veterans of World War I. Cleveland architects Walker and Weeks won the national competition for the design of the plaza, including the cenotaph and imposing War Memorial Building.

## INDIANAPOLIS MOTOR SPEEDWAY
**4790 West 16th Street, Speedway**

This is the home of the Indianapolis 500, held annually since 1911 and now one of the largest single-day sporting events in the world. The 2½-mile-long track, constructed in 1909, is the world's oldest continuously operating automobile race course and one of the premier auto racing sites in the United States. The Speedway has also made significant contributions to automobile design, performance, technology, and safety. A Hall of Fame museum adjacent to the course includes among its displays the Marmon Wasp that won the first "Indy 500."

## MADAME C. J. WALKER MANUFACTURING COMPANY
**617 Indiana Avenue, Indianapolis**

From her beginnings as a turn-of-the-century washerwoman and cook earning $1.50 per day, within 12 years Sarah Walker became the first millionaire black woman. This building, dating from 1927, was the hub of her lucrative cosmetology business. At one time the most successful black-owned industry in the nation, it employed 3,000 women. In addition to housing the office and factory, the structure also contained a restaurant, ballroom, and theater and served as a community cultural center.

## JAMES WHITCOMB RILEY HOUSE
**528 Lockerbie Street, Indianapolis**

James Whitcomb Riley, the "Hoosier poet," lived here as a paying guest during the last 23 years of his life, from 1893 to 1916. Riley was noted as a writer and lecturer, and Mark Twain once called one of his performances "about the funniest thing I ever listened to." The large brick Italianate house, built in 1872, was purchased the year of Riley's death by a group of friends and admirers and has been a museum since 1921.

■ *Miami County*

## WALLACE CIRCUS WINTER HEADQUARTERS
**2.5 miles southeast of city center, Peru**

Peru has been known as "Circus City" ever since Ben Wallace established his "circus farm" on its outskirts in the 1880s. The farm served as winter quarters for Wallace's Great World Menagerie and his successors, the American Circus Corporation and the Ringlings. Although winter was the off-season, the headquarters operated as a zoo, and on occasion Tom Mix and Clyde Beatty appeared as feature attractions. The headquarters was sold in the 1940s and is now part of a farm operation. A number of buildings from the heyday of the circus remain.

■ *Montgomery County*

## GENERAL LEW WALLACE STUDY
**Pike Street and Wallace Avenue, Crawfordsville**

Lew Wallace, now mostly remembered as the

*General Lew Wallace Study, Crawfordsville, Montgomery County. Courtesy of AASLH (George R. Adams).*

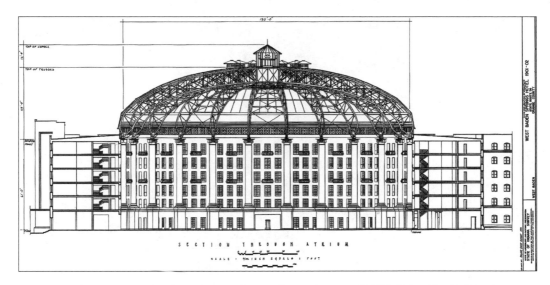

*West Baden Springs Hotel, West Baden Springs, Orange County. Courtesy of HAER (Roland David Schaaf).*

author of the popular novel *Ben Hur,* was also a Union general in the Civil War, governor of New Mexico Territory, and American minister to Turkey. In addition, he was an architect of sorts. The 1890s brick study he designed for his own use has been described as "the product of boyhood dreams, a vivid imagination, and impressions gathered from a lifetime of reading and travel." Combining Romanesque, Greek, and Byzantine motifs, it has a frieze with sculptured figures of characters from his novels. It is open to the public as a memorial to this multifaceted individual.

## ■ *Orange County*

### WEST BADEN SPRINGS HOTEL
**Off Indiana Route 56, West Baden Springs**

This astounding hotel is the focus of a spa town that dubbed itself the "Wiesbaden" (West Baden) or "Carlsbad" of America. Built in 1901–1902, the 708-room brick and concrete 6-story, 16-sided structure surrounds a vast circular atrium called the "Pompeian Court." The court is covered with a steel and glass dome 195 feet in diameter, which was the world's largest when it was built. In addition to its use as a hotel, the building has served variously as an army hospital, a Jesuit monastery, and a business college.

## ■ *Perry County*

### CANNELTON COTTON MILL
**Fourth Street between Adams and Washington Streets, Cannelton**

Construction on the Indiana Cotton Mills was begun in 1849, and the facility became operational in January 1851. One of the most impressive pre–Civil War mills in the Midwest, this large sandstone textile mill was the work of Rhode Island architect Thomas A. Tefft, who combined utility and aesthetics in his design. Financed by New Englanders, the mill contained 10,000 spindles and 372 looms and was intended to be the center of an industrial community rivaling those in the East. Although it operated for more than 100 years, it never achieved the goals of its founders.

## ■ *Porter County*

### JOSEPH BAILLY HOMESTEAD (NPS)
**West of Porter on U.S. Route 20**

Honore Gratien Joseph Bailly de Messein, also known as Joseph Bailly, was an independent fur trader and one of the earliest settlers in northwestern Indiana. Several log buildings remain from the trading post he established here in 1822. Bailly's home was an early center of culture in pioneer days, providing a meeting place for Indians and whites

*Cannelton Cotton Mill, Cannelton, Perry County. Courtesy of HAER (Jack E. Boucher).*

and a stopping place for travelers and missionaries. The property was purchased by the National Park Service in 1971 and is now part of Indiana Dunes National Lakeshore.

■ *Posey County*

## NEW HARMONY HISTORIC DISTRICT
**Main Street between Granary and Church Streets, New Harmony**

Utopian communities are rare enough, but New Harmony is unique: it was the site of not one, but two such settlements—one religious, one secular. In 1815, German religious refugees under the leadership of George Rapp established the first colony but stayed only a decade. In 1824, English industrialist and philanthropist Robert Dale Owen purchased "Harmonie" to establish a community based on "universal happiness through universal education." Buildings from both eras remain, many of them open to the public.

■ *Saint Joseph County*

## CLEMENT STUDEBAKER HOUSE
**620 West Washington Avenue, South Bend**

This baronial Richardsonian Romanesque mansion was the home of Clement Studebaker from 1889 until his death in 1901. In 1852, Studebaker and his brother founded a company that, by the 1890s, became the world's largest producer of horse-drawn vehicles. Studebaker Brothers was the country's only wagon-manufacturing firm that successfully converted to automobile production. Studebaker named his estate Tippecanoe Place to honor his close friend Benjamin Harrison.

■ *Spencer County*

## LINCOLN BOYHOOD HOME (NPS)
**On Indiana Route 345, near Gentryville, Lincoln City vicinity**

Abraham Lincoln's family lived in southern Indiana from 1816 to 1830, a period during which he grew to manhood and received his early instruction in reading the law. The reputed grave site of Lincoln's mother and the site of the Lincoln cabin, built by his father Thomas Lincoln, were part of the Nancy Hanks Lincoln State Memorial until 1962. They are now in the Lincoln Boyhood National Memorial.

■ *Tippecanoe County*

## TIPPECANOE BATTLEFIELD
**7 miles northeast of Lafayette on Indiana Route 225**

On November 7, 1811, a narrowly won victory at Tippecanoe Creek by a force of 1,000 under William Henry Harrison's command ended Shawnee chief Tecumseh's hopes of estab-lishing an Indian confederation to stem American encroachment into Indiana Territory. Because many believed Tecumseh's activities were sponsored by the British, the battle sparked agitation that eventually led to the War of 1812. Almost 30 years later, Harrison's recalling the victory in his campaign slogan "Tippecanoe and Tyler, too" helped propel him to the presidency. The battlefield is now a county park.

### ◾ *Vanderburgh County*

## ANGEL MOUNDS

**Angel Mounds State Memorial, 8 miles southeast of Evansville**

Located on an Ohio River bayou, this extensive site represents the northeasternmost extension of the Mississippian culture, which flourished from ca. A.D. 1000 to 1600. Named after a former owner of the property, the mounds and village site are now a state memorial. Several buildings and a portion of a stockade have been reconstructed.

### ◾ *Vigo County*

## EUGENE V. DEBS HOME

**451 North Eighth Street, Terre Haute**

"While there is a lower class, I am in it; while there is a criminal element, I am of it; while there is a soul in prison, I am not free." These were the beliefs of Eugene Victor Debs, founder of industrial unionism in the United States and the Socialist Party's candidate in five presidential elections between 1900 and 1920. This modified Queen Anne style house, where he lived from 1890 until his death in 1926, has been restored as a memorial to him.

### ◾ *Wayne County*

## LEVI COFFIN HOUSE

**115 North Main Street, Fountain City**

This two-story, Federal style brick house has been called the "Union Depot of the Underground Railroad." Levi Coffin, a Quaker abolitionist who lived in Fountain City from 1826 to 1846, is believed to have helped as many as 2,000 runaway slaves on their flight to freedom during these years. After emancipation, Coffin devoted much of his time and effort to improving the lot of freedmen. The house, constructed in 1839, is open as a memorial to Coffin and his work.

*Levi Coffin House, Fountain City, Wayne County. Courtesy of Pyle Photography.*

# IOWA

■ *Cedar County*

## HERBERT HOOVER BIRTHPLACE (NPS)
### Downey and Penn Streets, West Branch

Herbert Hoover, 31st president of the United States, was born on August 10, 1874, in this tiny two-room board-and-batten cottage. West Branch was a Quaker community, and Hoover's father was the village blacksmith at the time. The cottage was restored in 1938, the former president offering advice and providing recollections. It is now the centerpiece of the Herbert Hoover National Historic Site, which also includes the Hoover Presidential Library and the graves of the president and his wife, Lou Henry Hoover.

■ *Cherokee County*

## PHIPPS SITE
### Address Restricted, Cherokee vicinity

This is the type site of the Mill Creek culture, thought to have been a localized devel-

opment of the Middle Missouri Tradition influenced by the nearby Mississippian cultures. The village site, which dates from A.D. 900 to 1400, was not fortified, but accumulations of debris attest to a long and intense occupation. Artifacts uncovered at the site illustrate a combined hunting/agricultural subsistence pattern.

■ *Clinton County*

## VAN ALLEN AND COMPANY DEPARTMENT STORE
### Fifth Avenue and South Second Street, Clinton

This is one of the few remaining Midwestern buildings designed by architect Louis Sullivan in his later years that is still unaltered. The store is a four-story steel-frame skeleton, faced with brick, and has expansive plate glass windows on all levels. On the facade, three slender mullions extend from the second story almost to the cornice, where they terminate in exuberant vivid green terra-cotta foliate ornamentation.

*Van Allen and Company Department Store, Clinton, Clinton County. Courtesy of HABS.*

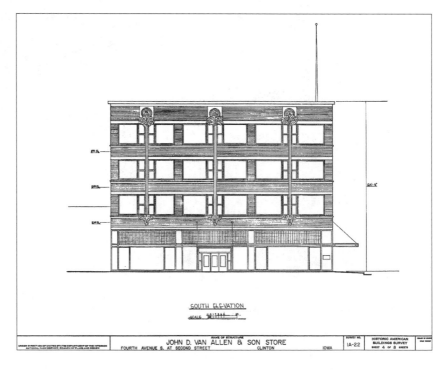

SOUTH ELEVATION

JOHN D. VAN ALLEN & SON STORE
FOURTH AVENUE S. AT SECOND STREET          CLINTON          IOWA

James B. Weaver
House, Bloomfield,
Davis County.
Courtesy of AASLH
(George R. Adams).

## ■ Davis County

### JAMES B. WEAVER HOUSE
**Weaver Park Road, Bloomfield**

During the last two decades of the 19th century, third-party movements exerted considerable influence in American politics. Few, if any, contributed as much to these movements as James B. Weaver, three-term congressman and Populist Party presidential candidate in the 1892 election. Weaver was an antimonopolist, a proponent of the graduated income tax, and a principal sponsor of the free coinage of silver. From about 1865 to 1890 he lived in this idiosyncratic brick house, easily identified by its overscaled lancet windows covered with brick hood molds. The house is operated as a bed-and-breakfast accommodation.

## ■ Dubuque County

### DUBUQUE COUNTY JAIL
**36 East Eighth Street, Dubuque**

Completed in 1858, this massive stone building was designed by Midwestern architect John F. Rague, who also designed two other National Historic Landmarks, the old Illinois and old Iowa state capitols. The jail is an interesting example of Egyptian Revival architecture, one of the rarest of America's

many 19th-century revival styles. In addition, the jail is significant in illustrating the antebellum penal reform movement in the United States, which helped make America's prisons models of design, planning, and organization.

### JULIEN DUBUQUE'S MINES
**Off Highway 52 South, south of Dubuque**

Lead was mined here from the 1780s through the Civil War. Indians told the French about lead deposits in the late 17th century, but it was not until trader Julien Dubuque negotiated an agreement with the Mesquakie tribe for exclusive rights that they were extensively developed. Dubuque obtained a Spanish land grant in 1796 stipulating that the 189-square-mile area be named "Mines of Spain." Dubuque established a trading post and engaged Indian and French laborers to extract the lead, which he annually transported to Saint Louis to exchange for trade goods. Today the site is part of the Mines of Spain State Recreational Area.

### WILLIAM M. BLACK
**Third Street at the Ice Harbor, Dubuque**

Constructed in 1934, this steam-propelled, sternwheel dredge is one of the few such vessels remaining in the country. *William M.*

*Black* played a major role in the improvement of the Missouri River system by dredging, deepening, and redirecting western rivers, fighting levee failures to prevent floods, and allowing navigation to regions that were previously inaccessible. The *Black* was decommissioned in 1973 and deeded to the Dubuque County Historical Society in 1979. It is now operated as a museum ship, associated with the Mississippi River Museum.

### ■ *Iowa County*

## AMANA COLONIES
### U.S. Route 151, Middle Amana

Incorporated in 1859, the Amana Society was the most successful utopian experiment in 19th-century America. An outgrowth of a German pietist movement that left the Lutheran Church in 1714, the group came to New York state in the 1840s and relocated to Iowa during the next decade. Eventually, seven villages were established on a 26,000-acre tract. At first, land and industries, owned in common, were managed by elders of the church, but in 1932 secular and religious matters were separated and ownership of private property accepted. The society is still active, and the villages still include buildings dating from the 1850s through the 1870s, many in active use as gift and craft shops, bed-and-breakfast accommodations, and museums.

### ■ *Johnson County*

## OLD CAPITOL
### University of Iowa, Iowa City

Built between 1840 and 1842 as the third capitol of Iowa Territory, this became the first state capitol when Iowa was admitted to the Union in 1846. When the state government moved to Des Moines in 1857, the former capitol became the first permanent building of the University of Iowa. Built of stone, fronted with a pedimented Doric portico, and topped with a dome, the capitol is a nationally important example of Greek Revival architecture. It was designed by architect John F. Rague and was meticulously restored in the 1970s. It is open to the public as the Old Capitol Museum.

### ■ *Lee County*

## GEORGE M. VERITY
### Keokuk River Museum, Victory Park, Keokuk

Built in Dubuque in 1927 and originally christened SS *Thorpe*, this is one of only three steam-powered towboats extant in the United States. *Thorpe* and its sister ships reopened barge service on the Upper Mississippi after World War I and helped to build a thriving industry. Renamed in 1940, the *George M. Verity* also saw service towing coal barges on the Ohio. The towboat is now on exhibit at the Keokuk River Museum.

### ■ *Louisa County*

## TOOLESBORO MOUND GROUP
### Iowa Route 99, Toolesboro vicinity

This is the best-preserved Hopewell site in Iowa and represents the westward extension of classic Hopewellian culture that flourished from ca. 200 B.C. to A.D. 300. The culture was noted for its burial mounds, and there were 12 of these when Toolesboro was first investigated in 1875. Excavations unearthed a variety of grave artifacts. The three mounds remaining are preserved and interpreted by the Iowa State Historical Society.

### ■ *Lyon County*

## BLOOD RUN SITE
### Junction of Blood Run Creek and the Big Sioux River

This extensive site, which also continues across the Big Sioux River into South Dakota, contains the remains of an Oneota Indian village and numerous conical mounds. Limited archeological investigations of the mounds indicate that the site may have been occupied as early as A.D. 1300. Occupation over many centuries by different tribes has left abundant cultural remains. (Also in Lincoln County, South Dakota.)

### ■ *O'Brien County*

## INDIAN VILLAGE SITE
### Address Restricted, Sutherland vicinity

This village, known to archeology as the Wittrock Site, contained about 20 dwellings surrounded by a palisade and ditch. It represents the Mill Creek culture, dating from ca. A.D. 1000–1300. Mill Creek culture was characterized by semisedentary people who followed an agricultural/hunting subsistence pattern. The site is protected as a state preserve but is undeveloped and surrounded by private lands.

## ■ Page County

### WILLIAM P. HEPBURN HOUSE
**321 West Lincoln Street, Clarinda**

In 1906, U.S. congressman William P. Hepburn of Iowa introduced and secured passage of the Hepburn Act, giving the Interstate Commerce Commission power to set railroad rates. This was an important precedent in federal regulation of private industry. For roughly a half-century, from the 1860s until his death in 1916, Hepburn called this frame house, highlighted with a prominent mansard-roofed tower, home, although during a great portion of that time he lived in Washington, D.C.

## ■ Polk County

### FORT DES MOINES PROVISIONAL ARMY OFFICER TRAINING SCHOOL
**Fort Des Moines Military Reservation, Des Moines**

Fort Des Moines, the third army installation with this name, was dedicated in 1903 as a cavalry post, but its fame came during World War I when it became a training camp for black officers. On October 15, 1917, 639 black men graduated from the fort's Provisional Army Officer Training School and embarked for the European theater of war the next year. Black units led by the officers trained here were assembled in France as the Ninety-second Division and performed gallant service. They received many citations and awards for meritorious and distinguished conduct in combat against the German army, primarily on the approaches to Metz in the Lorraine.

## ■ Pottawattamie County

### GRENVILLE M. DODGE HOUSE
**605 South Third Street, Council Bluffs**

As chief engineer of the Union Pacific,

Grenville M. Dodge supervised completion of the nation's first transcontinental railroad in 1869. That same year he completed this spacious Second Empire brick mansion, where he lived until his death in 1916. Considered one of Iowa's finest residences when built, it is now open as a historic house museum.

## ■ Poweshiek County

### MERCHANTS' NATIONAL BANK
**Fourth Avenue and Broad Street, Grinnell**

Small in scale, monumental in effect, this is among the best—and best preserved—of many Midwestern banks designed by Chicago architect Louis Sullivan. One of the fathers of modern American architecture, Sullivan designed the bank late in his career. Described as "Sullivan's jewel box," the Grinnell building is fronted by a terra-cotta sunburst displaying the architect's signature foliate ornamentation. The bank was completed in 1914 and still functions in its original use.

## ■ Scott County

### *LONE STAR*
**Buffalo Bill Museum, LeClaire**

Built as a short trade packet in 1868, *Lone Star* was converted to a towboat in 1876, lengthened in 1890, and rebuilt in 1922. It is the oldest of three remaining Western Rivers steam towboats and the only surviving example in the United States of a wooden-hulled boat built in the traditional Western Rivers fashion. The Western Rivers system, composed of the Mississippi, Ohio, and Missouri Rivers and their tributaries, carried most of the immigrants and freight that settled the Midwest. *Lone Star* is on display at the Buffalo Bill Museum.

### *PRESIDENT*
**500 North Leonor K. Sullivan Boulevard, Davenport**

Built in 1924 as the *Cincinnati*, an overnight packet boat, this steamship was renamed *President* in 1932 and converted to an excursion boat, the largest in America. The *President* is now the only remaining large

Woodbury County Courthouse, Sioux City, Woodbury County. Courtesy of HABS (Jack E. Boucher).

Western Rivers sidewheel excursion boat in the nation. In 1991 it was moved upriver from Saint Louis, Missouri, to Davenport, Iowa, where it is now operated as the *President* Riverboat Casino.

### ■ Story County

### THE FARM HOUSE
#### Iowa State University, Ames

This plain stuccoed-brick house, always called the Farm House, was completed in 1861 as the main building of a model farm for the Iowa State Agricultural College and Farm. From 1880 to 1885 it was the home of Seaman A. Knapp, noted agriculturist and teacher, and from 1891 to 1896 it was lived in by James Wilson, later U.S. secretary of agriculture under three administrations. Now surrounded by later buildings on the Iowa

State University campus, the Farm House is a historic house museum and is used for special events.

### ■ Woodbury County

### SERGEANT FLOYD
#### Mile Marker 730, Missouri River, Sioux City

Launched in 1932, *Sergeant Floyd* is one of only a handful of surviving U.S. Army Corps of Engineers vessels built to control the nation's inland waterways. It was instrumental in the Corps's mission to improve flood control and navigation along the Mississippi and Missouri Rivers. *Sergeant Floyd* carried supplies, helped in dredging operations, and carried engineers and visiting legislators on inspection tours. Retired in 1976, *Sergeant* was brought to Sioux City in 1983, subsequently restored, and is now a dry-berthed museum vessel and state welcome center.

### SERGEANT FLOYD MONUMENT
#### Glenn Avenue and Lewis Road, Sioux City

Sergeant Charles Floyd, the only member of the Lewis and Clark Expedition to lose his life during the journey, died on August 20, 1804, most likely of appendicitis. A 100-foot-high sandstone obelisk, standing on a bluff overlooking the Missouri River, marks the site where his remains were reburied in 1901.

### WOODBURY COUNTY COURTHOUSE
#### 620 Douglas Street, Sioux City

Constructed in 1916–1918, this is the nation's only major civic building in the Prairie style. Faced in Roman brick, with terra-cotta trim and ornaments, the four-story structure, with an eight-story tower rising from its central core, is also the largest example of its style. Initial plans were developed by local architect William M. Steele, who called in two colleagues formerly associated with him in the office of Louis Sullivan: Minneapolis architects William Purcell and George Elmslie. The courthouse survives in pristine condition, still fulfilling its original function.

# KANSAS

■ *Barber County*

## MEDICINE LODGE PEACE TREATY SITE
### Southeast of the town of Medicine Lodge

In October 1867, U.S. commissioners appointed by Congress met here with members of various southern Plains tribes to forge a peace treaty. Under its terms, the Indians gave up their nomadic life (and their claims to ancestral lands) in return for permanent reservations in Indian territory, and the government agreed to provide economic aid and other assistance. Many Indians refused to abide by the terms, but by the mid-1870s they had been subdued and relocated on their respective reservations.

## CARRY A. NATION HOUSE
### 211 West Fowler Avenue, Medicine Lodge

Carry Nation and her saloon-destroying hatchet resuscitated public interest in prohibition at the turn of the 20th century. While living in this small brick house in 1900, she received a "divine call" to "go to Kiowa," a nearby town, where she wrecked three saloons. She sold the house in 1902, using its proceeds to open a home for drunkards'

wives in Kansas City. She then continued on her crusading rampage; lecturing, touring, and smashing. Her Medicine Lodge house is now a museum.

■ *Bourbon County*

## FORT SCOTT (NPS)
### Town of Fort Scott

Established in 1842, Fort Scott served first as a frontier outpost, then as a Civil War garrison. During the Civil War, the fort was a major focal point of black troop activity and training. Later, Fort Scott served as a base of operations to quell Indian trouble from ca. 1869 to 1873. The fort, now a National Historic Site, consists of a number of restored structures around a central parade ground.

■ *Chase County*

## SPRING HILL RANCH
### North of Strong City on Kansas Highway 177

Spring Hill (Z Bar) Ranch represents the transition from open range to enclosed holdings of large cattle companies in the 1880s. The 10,894-acre empire and others like it transformed the cattle industry, one of the

Spring Hill Ranch, Strong City vicinity, Chase County. Dual-ramp barn. Courtesy of the National Park Trust (Brad Finch).

145

bases of Western settlement, from a primitive frontier activity into a modern industry. This virtually intact ranch contains an imposing Second Empire style ranch house, a school, a three-story barn, a chicken house, and corrals, all solidly constructed of stone, as well as vast expanses of southern Plains rangelands.

## ■ Dickinson County

### PARKER CAROUSEL

**412 South Campbell Street, Abilene**

Constructed ca. 1898–1901, this is the earliest of only three surviving carousels built by Abilene's Charles W. Parker Amusement Company, an operation that constructed some 68 carousels between 1896 and 1910. The carousel has 24 horses and four chariots (two of the latter are fittingly decorated with large yellow sunflowers, the Kansas state flower). The carousel was restored in the 1980s, when a new shelter was built to house it.

## ■ Douglas County

### HASKELL INSTITUTE

**Lawrence**

Founded in 1884, this was one of the first large off-reservation boarding schools established by the federal government for Indian students. The institute taught students from the southern Plains and upper Midwest. In 1965 it became Haskell Indian Junior College. Buildings of historic interest relating to the school's founding are scattered among a number of modern college structures.

### LECOMPTON CONSTITUTION HALL

**Elmore Street between Woodson and Third Streets, Lecompton**

"Bleeding Kansas" was the unintentional result of the Kansas–Nebraska Act of 1854, which allowed Kansans to determine whether their territory would become a free or slave state. Pro-slavery partisans met in this simple frame legislative hall in Lecompton, then the territorial capital, and drafted a constitution. President Buchanan supported it, but Congress rejected it, as did the people of Kansas when they voted in August 1858. (See Marais Des Cygnes Massacre Site, Linn County.)

## ■ Ford County

### SANTA FE TRAIL REMAINS

**9 miles west of Dodge City on U.S. Route 50**

From 1822 to 1873, until the railroad made it obsolete, the Santa Fe Trail was one of the West's great commercial, emigrant, and military routes. As such, it helped fuse the Southwest to the rest of the nation. The longest continuous stretch of clearly defined ruts made by countless thousands of wagons remains, nine miles west of Dodge City, in an area preserved by the city's Boothill Association.

## ■ Graham County

### NICODEMUS HISTORIC DISTRICT (NPS)

**U.S. Route 24, Nicodemus**

Established on homestead land and named after a legendary slave, the town of Nicodemus was officially founded on September 17, 1877. It is the only remaining town established by African Americans in the post–Civil War "Exoduster" movement, organized mainly through the efforts of Benjamin "Pap" Singleton, who founded 11 colonies in Kansas between 1873 and 1880. Nicodemus is a National Historic Site.

## ■ Grant County

### LOWER CIMARRON SPRING

**12 miles south of Ulysses on U.S. Route 270**

During the dry season, these springs afforded the only water on the 60-mile stretch of the Cimarron Cutoff of the Santa Fe Trail. The springs, a virtual oasis, were the object and stopping place of all who went over this desert route. One of the most dangerous and treacherous stretches on the way to Santa Fe, it had been called by the Spaniards *Jornada de la Muerte*, the journey of death.

## ■ Harvey County

### WARKENTIN FARM

**140 East North Street, Halstead**

Bernard Warkentin was a German Mennonite, born in the Ukraine, who immigrated to the United States in 1872 and promoted subsequent settlement of his brethren in the Great

*Nicodemus Historic District, Nicodemus, Graham County. A.M.E. Church. Courtesy of HABS (Clayton B. Fraser).*

*Warkentin Farm, Halsted, Harvey County. Courtesy of NPS (William Patrick O'Brien).*

Plains. Warkentin is also noted for introducing and improving central European wheat varieties, which revolutionized American grain production. He owned this property from 1874 until his death in 1908. The house he built in 1884 still stands, along with other farm buildings and plots used in his wheat hybridization experiments.

### ■ *Johnson County*

## SHAWNEE MISSION

### 53rd Street at Madison Road, Fairway

Among the earliest such institutions in the Louisiana Purchase area, the Shawnee Methodist Mission was established in 1830 by the Reverend Thomas Johnson and moved

to this site in 1839. Here children of many Indian tribes were taught English, manual labor, and agriculture. The first territorial governor of Kansas established an office at the Mission in 1854, and the first territorial legislature met here in 1855. The three original brick buildings, dating from 1839 to 1845, remain in a state park administered by the Kansas State Historical Society.

### ■ *Leavenworth County*

## FORT LEAVENWORTH
### Fort Leavenworth Military Reservation, Leavenworth

Fort Leavenworth has been in continuous occupation by the military since it was first established in 1827 to protect caravans on the Santa Fe Trail. Strategically located on a bluff overlooking the Missouri River, the fort was near the eastern termini of both the Oregon and Santa Fe trails. The fort also played a pivotal role in the Mexican War and in the Civil War, and it became the temporary capital of Kansas Territory in 1854. Many historic structures remain from various periods, and the Frontier Army Museum interprets the site.

### ■ *Linn County*

## MARAIS DES CYGNES MASSACRE SITE
### 5 miles northeast of Trading Post

On May 19, 1858, 30 pro-slavery sympathizers crossed into Kansas from Missouri, cap-

tured 11 free-state settlers, and shot them in this ravine near the state line. The massacre focused the nation's attention on "Bleeding Kansas," and the outcry following the episode helped defeat the pro-slavery Lecompton Constitution. The site is now a state park. (See Lecompton Constitution Hall, Douglas County.)

### ■ *Lyon County*

## WILLIAM ALLEN WHITE HOUSE
### 927 Exchange Street, Emporia

"Red Rocks," a handsome Tudor Revival house, was the home of William Allen White from 1899 until his death in 1944. White was an internationally renowned journalist and author whose writings had a marked effect on the political and social life of the country. His book *The Older Order Changeth* (1910) expressed the dominant view of the Progressive movement. A friend of Theodore Roosevelt's, White acted in the capacity of an unofficial Midwestern political adviser to the president.

### ■ *Morris County*

## COUNCIL GROVE HISTORIC DISTRICT
### U.S. Route 56, Council Grove

With abundant water, grass, and timber, Council Grove was a natural stopping place on the Santa Fe Trail. To the west, the Great Plains offered few provisions, so the town became an early supply center as well. It was named after treaties were made between government survey commissioners and the Osage that guaranteed Santa Fe caravans safe passage through the territory. Several well-marked sites and properties associated with the trail are located throughout the town.

## ■ *Pawnee County*

### FORT LARNED (NPS)
**5 miles west of Larned on U.S. Route 156**

From 1860 through the late 1870s, Fort Larned was the most important military post guarding the northern portion of the Santa Fe Trail. Abandoned in 1878, the fort became private property and the center of a large ranching operation. Now a National Historic Site, it survives as one of the nation's best-preserved mid-19th-century western military posts. Most of its stone buildings arranged around a quadrangle remain, and the barracks is a visitors center. Other buildings have been restored to their 1868 appearance and are open to the public.

## ■ *Rice County*

### TOBIAS-THOMPSON COMPLEX
**4 miles southeast of Geneseo**

This archeological district contains a cluster of eight related village sites located on the crests of ridges on both sides of the Little Arkansas River. Dating from A.D. 1500 to 1700, these villages are a link between prehistoric and historic periods, connecting the Little River Focus of the Great Bend Aspect and the Wichita Tribe. The villages may have been among those that Coronado visited in 1542.

## ■ *Saline County*

### PRICE WHITEFORD SITE
**3 miles east of Salina**

This prehistoric village and cemetery representative of the Smoky Hill Culture, which dates to about A.D. 1000–1350, provide a record of the early Central Plains Village period in Kansas. The unfortified village includes 12 to 15 known house sites, and the burial area contains remains of more than 140 individuals.

## ■ *Scott County*

### EL CUARTELEJO
**Address Restricted, Scott City vicinity**

This archeological district consists of more than 20 sites, mostly associated with the Dismal River/Plains Apache culture, dating from ca. A.D. 1650 to 1750. The principal site is a pueblo ruin thought to have been built by Taos Indians who sought refuge with the Apache during times of trouble with the Spanish. It is the northeasternmost example of a pueblo in the country. The site also illustrates Spanish explorations in the Plains that predated those of Americans by many decades. El Cuartelejo is within the boundaries of Lake Scott State Park.

## ■ *Shawnee County*

### SUMNER ELEMENTARY SCHOOL AND MONROE ELEMENTARY SCHOOL (NPS)
**330 Western Avenue/1515 Monroe Street, Topeka**

*Brown v. Board of Education of Topeka* was the 1952–1954 U.S. Supreme Court case that declared the country's "separate but equal" doctrine of segregated facilities for public schools unconstitutional. In 1952 the court's docket contained five separate cases challenging the doctrine. These were combined under the name of the Kansas case, in which Linda Brown, a student at the black Monroe Elementary School, had been refused admission at the white Sumner Elementary School. The Monroe School is now part of the Brown v. Board of Education National Historic Site.

## ■ *Washington County*

### HOLLENBERG PONY EXPRESS STATION
**1.5 miles east of Hanover**

This long frame structure commemorates one of the shortest-lived, yet most colorful and renowned, operations in the history of westward expansion: the Pony Express. The express operated from April 1860 to October 1861, carrying the U.S. mail at a rapid pace thanks to relay stations, where ponies were changed, and "home stations," where riders were replaced. This westernmost of the

*Hollenberg Pony
Express Station,
Washington County.
Courtesy of NPS.*

Kansas stations, now a museum, was one of the latter and is now the only unaltered Pony Express station still on its original site.

■ *Wilson County*

### NORMAN NO. 1 OIL WELL
**Mill and First Streets, Neodesha**

On November 28, 1892, oil flowing from this well signaled the beginning of production from the immense Mid-Continent field. By 1919 the field was producing more than half the nation's oil supply, and it continued to do so into the late 1930s. A replica of the derrick and a nearby museum, both in a city park, tell the story.

# KENTUCKY

■ *Boyle County*

### JACOBS HALL, KENTUCKY SCHOOL FOR THE DEAF
**South Third Street, Danville**

Established in 1823, the Kentucky School for the Deaf was the first publicly supported institution for the education of the deaf in the nation. Jacobs Hall, a four-story brick structure completed in 1857, is the oldest surviving building at the school. A notable Italianate structure, it housed the entire institution from the time it was completed until 1882.

### DR. EPHRAIM MCDOWELL HOUSE
**125–129 South Second Street, Danville**

This frame house and attached brick apothe-cary shop were the home and office of Dr. Ephraim McDowell, who performed the first successful ovariotomy here in 1809. The patient, 47-year-old Jane Todd Crawford, made a complete recovery and lived to the age of 78. The operation's success dispelled a then-common misconception—that exposing the inner wall of the abdomen invariably produced fatal infection—and led the way to a new era in surgical practice. The house was acquired by the Kentucky Medical Association in the 1930s and is open as a museum.

### PERRYVILLE BATTLEFIELD
**West of Perryville on U.S. Route 150**

The battle fought here in early October 1862 helped break a Confederate offensive

*Jacobs Hall, Kentucky School for the Deaf, Danville, Boyle County, 1960. Courtesy of Kentucky School for the Deaf.*

along a 1,000-mile front. For the number of men engaged, Perryville was one of the bloodiest battles of the Civil War. Nearly one-fourth of the 30,000 men who fought on both sides were killed or wounded. A portion of the battlefield is a Kentucky state park, with monuments and a museum.

■ *Butler County*

## GREEN RIVER SHELL MIDDENS ARCHEOLOGICAL DISTRICT

**Address Restricted, Logansport vicinity (Butler, Henderson, McLean, Muhlenberg, and Ohio Counties)**

Archeological investigations over the past 70 years at these shell middens, encompassed within a large, noncontiguous area extending through five counties, have contributed to the understanding of the Late Archaic Period (4000–1000 B.C.) in the eastern United States.

■ *Fayette County*

## HENRY CLAY HOME

**2 miles southeast of Lexington on Richmond Road**

From 1811 until 1852, Henry Clay, Kentucky's pre–Civil War politician who served as a U.S. senator, Speaker of the House of Representatives, and secretary of state, lived in a large five-part brick mansion, named Ashland. Clay's son had the house razed in 1857 because of structural problems, but reerected it on this site using the same plan and as much of the original materials as pos-

sible. Ashland is owned and operated by the Henry Clay Memorial Foundation, a private, nonprofit organization established in 1926 to maintain the estate as a historic shrine.

## KEENELAND RACE COURSE

**Off Versailles and Rice Roads, Lexington**

Keeneland is the most conspicuous manifestation of horse raising and racing in Lexington, "capital" of Kentucky's famous bluegrass country. The track was laid out in 1916 by Jack Keene, a preeminent figure in American racing, and the grandstand dates from 1936. Keeneland hosts the Phoenix Handicap and the Blue Grass Stakes, both dating from the track's opening season. The annual horse sales held here are among the most important of their kind in the world.

## OLD MORRISON, TRANSYLVANIA COLLEGE

**West Third Street between Upper Street and Broadway, Lexington**

Transylvania College, chartered by the Virginia Legislature in 1783 when Kentucky was still a part of the Old Dominion, is one of the oldest institutions of higher learning west of the Appalachians. Old Morrison, the college's impressive Greek Revival centerpiece, was built in 1831–1834 from designs by Gideon Shryock. Following a fire in 1969, the interior was reconstructed within the old shell, but the exterior, dominated by a pedimented Doric portico, is unchanged.

■ *Floyd County*

## MIDDLE CREEK BATTLEFIELD

**Intersection of Kentucky Routes 114 and 404, Prestonsburg vicinity**

During the Civil War, Abraham Lincoln once said that he would *like* to have God on his side, but he *must* have Kentucky. The state was then the ninth largest in population in the nation, and its strategic location was vital to the Union cause. The Northern victory here on January 10, 1862, with Colonel James A. Garfield in command, was vital in holding Kentucky for the Union and—following a string of Confederate victories—was an immense psychological boost. (See Mill Springs Battlefield, Pulaski and Wayne Counties.)

■ *Franklin County*

## LIBERTY HALL, FRANKFORT

**218 Wilkinson Street, Frankfort**

Constructed ca. 1796–1800, this two-story brick house was built by John Brown, a leading lawyer and politician who was instrumental in gaining statehood for Kentucky and who served as one of its first U.S. senators. Brown's house, superbly proportioned and detailed, is a notable example of Federal style architecture, remarkable for its time and place. It remained in Brown family ownership until 1955 and is now open for guided tours.

## OLD STATE HOUSE, FRANKFORT

**Broadway, bounded by Madison, Clinton, and Lewis Streets, Frankfort**

This solidly built structure, faced with marble quarried nearby and fronted with an impressive Ionic portico, introduced the Greek Revival style to Kentucky. It is the first major work of architect Gideon Shryock, pupil of William Strickland. The Kentucky legislature met here from December 1829 until 1910, when a new capitol was built. It is now operated as a museum by the Kentucky Historical Society.

■ *Harlan County*

## PINE MOUNTAIN SETTLEMENT SCHOOL

**State Routes 510 and 221, Bledsoe vicinity**

Construction of the Big Log House in 1913–1915 launched this important effort to adopt the concept of an urban settlement house to rural conditions. Founders Katherine Pettit and Ethel de Long sought to improve the lives of eastern Kentucky's miners and mountaineers by providing alternatives to one-room schools and primitive dwellings. The school offered instruction in traditional subjects to resident students, but also included classes in furniture making, home nursing, weaving, and stock raising. The study of ballads, folk songs, and dances

*Old State House, Frankfort, Franklin County, 1934. Courtesy of HABS (Theodore Webb).*

Belle of Louisville, *Louisville, Jefferson County. Courtesy of NPS (Kevin J. Foster).*

instilled a knowledge and appreciation of the mountain heritage. The complex now serves as an environmental educational center, building on the school's established traditions.

## ■ *Henderson County*

### GREEN RIVER SHELL MIDDENS ARCHEOLOGICAL DISTRICT

**Address Restricted, Logansport vicinity (Butler, Henderson, McLean, Muhlenberg, and Ohio Counties)**

(See entry under Butler County.)

## ■ *Jefferson County*

### BELLE OF LOUISVILLE

**45th Street and River Road, Louisville**

*Belle of Louisville,* launched in Pittsburgh in

1914 as the ferryboat *Idlewild,* is one of only two sternwheel river passenger boats operating under steam in the nation and is the sole remaining Western Rivers day packet boat. It also served as a towboat during World War II and is now an excursion boat. With its canopied pilothouse, jaunty stacks, and sternwheel, the *Belle* epitomizes the riverboat era on America's western waters.

### CHURCHILL DOWNS

**700 Central Avenue, Louisville**

Modeled after England's Epsom Downs, this racing track was established in 1874 in an attempt to stimulate the thoroughbred industry. Since 1875 it has been home to the Kentucky Derby, the internationally renowned race of three-year-old thorough-

*Churchill Downs, Louisville, Jefferson County. Courtesy of HABS (William G. Johnson).*

bred horses and the first phase of the Triple Crown. The original grandstands were replaced in 1894–1895 by the present structure. Its twin cupolas with their elongated spires have become the trademark of the Downs and of the Derby.

## LOCUST GROVE
### 561 Blankenbaker Lane, Louisville

George Rogers Clark, hero of the western theater of the American Revolution, defended Kentucky from the British and their Indian allies, then went on the offensive to force the surrender of Kaskaskia, Cahokia, and Vincennes. In 1809, after a stroke and amputation of his right leg, he moved to Locust Grove, home of his sister and brother-in-law, Lucy and William Croghan. He lived with them until his death in 1818. The handsome Federal style brick house, conservative in appearance and details, is now a historic house museum.

## LOUISVILLE WATER COMPANY PUMPING STATION
### Zorn Avenue, Louisville

This extraordinary Classical Revival outpouring of civic pride is one of the nation's finest examples of the symbolic and monumental function of industrial architecture. Built in 1858–1860, the engine and boiler rooms are disguised as a Corinthian temple, and the 169-foot standpipe tower appears as a triumphal Roman Doric column. A circular colonnade around its base is embellished with ten statues, including nine figures from mythology and an Indian and his dog. Instead of marble, as the Romans might have used for such construction, here the materials are brick, terra-cotta, and metal. The property is maintained by the Louisville Water Company.

## *MAYOR ANDREW BROADDUS*
### Fourth Street and River Road, Louisville

The United States Life-Saving Service was established in 1848 to assist shipwrecked mariners. Stations were set up near dangerous waters, and the first on the Western Rivers, guarding the treacherous Falls of the Ohio, dated from 1881. The *Life Saving Station Louisville*, now the *Mayor Andrew Broaddus*, was commissioned in 1928 as the third

lifeboat to fill the post. Now the only floating lifesaving station extant, the city-owned vessel serves as wharf boat, offices, and shops for Louisville's other historic nautical attraction, the *Belle of Louisville*. (See *Belle of Louisville*.)

## OLD BANK OF LOUISVILLE
### 320 West Main Street, Louisville

This architecturally sophisticated bank, built in 1837 of brick with a limestone facade, is distinguished by its Ionic *distyle-in-muris* portico and a coffered skylight dome over the central banking room. The structure's Greek Revival details derive from Minard LaFever's architectural style books. The bank is now the main lobby for the Actors Theater of Louisville.

## ZACHARY TAYLOR HOUSE
### 5608 Apache Road, Louisville

"Springfield," a two-story brick house built by Zachary Taylor's father, served as the future president's boyhood home from ca. 1790 to 1808. Taylor was married here in 1810, returned often during his military

*Louisville Water Company Pumping Station, Louisville, Jefferson County. Courtesy of HABS (Jack E. Boucher).*

career, visited before his short term as the 12th president of the United States began in 1849, and was brought back to the family cemetery for burial in 1850. The house, near the Zachary Taylor National Cemetery, is privately owned.

## UNITED STATES MARINE HOSPITAL
### 2215 Portland Avenue, Louisville

This hospital represents early federal efforts in health care and social welfare. In 1798, Congress established the Marine Hospital Fund, which, by 1912, evolved into the U.S. Public Health Service. The Louisville hospital was built between 1845 and 1852 and is the best of the few surviving examples of some 30 hospitals built before the Civil War, including 7 authorized by Congress in 1837 for construction on the "Western Waters." Built from standardized plans developed by architect Robert Mills, it exemplifies the latest ideas in hospital design of its time but is now used only for storage.

## ■ Kenton County

### DANIEL C. BEARD BOYHOOD HOME
#### 322 East Third Street, Covington

This was the boyhood home of Daniel C. Beard, author, illustrator, and a key figure in founding the Boy Scouts of America in 1910. "Uncle Dan" designed the Boy Scout uniform, wrote a monthly column for *Boy's Life,* and served as national Scout commissioner from 1910 until his death in 1941.

### COVINGTON AND CINCINNATI SUSPENSION BRIDGE
#### Spanning the Ohio River between Covington, Kentucky, and Cincinnati, Ohio

At the time of its completion in 1867, this suspension bridge, with its 1,057-foot span, was the longest in the world, taking the honor from the Wheeling Suspension Bridge upstream on the Ohio. It was designed by John A. Roebling, who went on to design an even longer span with his Brooklyn Bridge. Cables supporting the span are hung from huge stone towers with open arches 75 feet high and 30 feet wide. The bridge continues to provide a link between Kentucky and Ohio and is maintained by the Kentucky

Department of Highways (also in Hamilton County, Ohio.)

## ■ Leslie County

### WENDOVER
#### Frontier Nursing Services, Wendover Road, Wendover

In 1925, Mary Breckinridge established the Frontier Nursing Service, the first effort to professionalize midwifery in the United States, and built Wendover, a large log structure, for its headquarters. Until the 1930s, American women were more likely to die in childbirth than from any disease except tuberculosis. Breckinridge and her English-trained nurses provided prenatal and maternity care for residents in the isolated mountainous regions of eastern Kentucky.

## ■ Madison County

### FORT BOONESBOROUGH SITE
#### Fort Boonesborough State Park, off Kentucky Route 627, Richmond vicinity

Established by Daniel Boone in 1775, Fort Boonesborough was one of the earliest attempts at settlement in Kentucky. It served as a major military outpost during the Revolution, and although attacked and besieged by Indians, it stood firm, helping to secure and hold trans-Appalachian Kentucky for future American settlement and westward expansion. When peace was achieved, the fort's palisades were taken down and reused in new construction. The location of the fort is marked within Fort Boonesborough State Park.

### LINCOLN HALL
#### Berea College, Berea

Tracing its origins to 1855, Berea, named for a biblical town whose citizens were open-minded, is significant in the history of U.S. education as the nation's first college established specifically to educate African Americans and whites together. Lincoln Hall, a three-story brick building constructed in 1887, has significant associations with the school's history. Built to house classrooms, offices, a library, a museum, and laboratories, it is now the college's main administrative building.

*Burks' Distillery, Marion County. Still house. Courtesy of HAER (William Gus Johnson).*

■ *Marion County*

## BURKS' DISTILLERY
### About 3 miles east of Loretto

This is the oldest Kentucky distillery operating at its original site and the smallest legal distillery in the state. Whiskey making began here ca. 1805 in a small valley appropriately named "Happy Hollow." The site represents the growth of distilling as a major Kentucky industry and marks the development of bourbon into a distinctive American liquor marketed worldwide. Now home to "Maker's Mark," the distillery buildings are restored and open to the public.

■ *McLean County*

## GREEN RIVER SHELL MIDDENS ARCHEOLOGICAL DISTRICT
### Address Restricted, Logansport vicinity (Butler, Henderson, McLean, Muhlenberg, and Ohio Counties)

(See entry under Butler County.)

■ *Mercer County*

## SHAKERTOWN AT PLEASANT HILL HISTORIC DISTRICT
### Shakertown and vicinity

This Shaker community was begun in 1805, and by 1820 some 500 members of The United Society of Believers in Christ's

*Shakertown at Pleasant Hill Historic District, Mercer County. Spiral staircase, Trustees Office. Courtesy of HABS.*

Second Appearing were living and worshiping here and farming their 3,000 acres. Micajah Burnett was in charge of building operations, and most of his work—typical of the no-nonsense, straightforward Shaker style, wherein beauty is dependent on proportion and function—remains. Shakertown, one of the most successful of America's 19th-century religious communitarian settlements, was dissolved in 1910. The site is now preserved and open to the public.

■ *Muhlenberg County*

## GREEN RIVER SHELL MIDDENS ARCHEOLOGICAL DISTRICT
**Address Restricted, Logansport vicinity (Butler, Henderson, McLean, Muhlenberg and Ohio Counties)**

(See entry under Butler County.)

■ *Ohio County*

## GREEN RIVER SHELL MIDDENS ARCHEOLOGICAL DISTRICT
**Address Restricted, Logansport vicinity (Butler, Henderson, McLean, Muhlenberg and Ohio Counties)**

(See entry under Butler County.)

## INDIAN KNOLL
**Address Restricted, Paradise vicinity**

This site along the Green River is one of the most fully documented and largest of the Late Archaic shell midden sites in the eastern United States. Excavation has yielded vital scientific information on the Archaic Indian population that once inhabited the site.

■ *Pulaski County*

## MILL SPRINGS BATTLEFIELD
**Off Kentucky Route 90, Somerset and Nancy vicinity (Pulaski and Wayne Counties)**

The Confederate defeat at Mill Springs on January 19, 1862, following that at Middle Creek nine days earlier, led to an early collapse of the South's defensive line in Kentucky. The two battles were part of a string of Confederate setbacks that culminated in the Battle of Shiloh in April 1862, resulting in Union control of Kentucky and most of western Tennessee. The battle at Mill Springs occurred in three locations over a 320-acre landscape that remains much the same as it was then. Portions of the battlefield are open to the public. (See Middle Creek Battlefield, Floyd County.)

■ *Shelby County*

## WHITNEY M. YOUNG BIRTHPLACE AND BOYHOOD HOME
**Campus of Lincoln Institute, southwest of Simpsonville**

This plain two-story frame house was the birthplace and boyhood home of Whitney Moore Young, civil rights spokesman, adviser to three presidents, and leader in the cause of racial equality in the corporate marketplace. Young was executive director of the National Urban League from 1961 to 1971 and drew unprecedented support for the league's social and economic programs. The house is now used as part of a vocational-technical training center named for Young.

■ *Wayne County*

## MILL SPRINGS BATTLEFIELD
**Off Kentucky Route 90, Somerset and Nancy vicinity (Pulaski and Wayne Counties)**

(See entry under Pulaski County.)

# LOUISIANA

■ *Assumption Parish*

## MADEWOOD PLANTATION HOUSE
**East of Napoleonville on Louisiana Route 308**

The five-bay central block of this ca. 1845 Greek Revival plantation house is fronted by a giant-order hexastylar Ionic portico. To either side, short hyphens connect the main block with pedimented wings. The house was built by Thomas Pugh from designs by architect Henry Howard. Set in a grove of magnolias and oaks festooned with Spanish moss, Madewood is a picture-perfect representation of the popular image of the antebellum South. It is open as a historic house museum.

■ *Avoyelles Parish*

## MARKSVILLE PREHISTORIC INDIAN SITE

**Marksville Prehistoric Indian Park State Monument, Marksville**

This is the type site for the Marksville culture, a southern variant of the Ohio Hopewell. Its discovery in the 1930s led to the recognition that the Hopewellian culture was more widely spread than had previously been thought. A number of the culture's characteristic burial mounds remain, and there is also a museum at this Louisiana state park.

■ *Caddo Parish*

## SHREVEPORT WATERWORKS PUMPING STATION

**On Cross Bayou, off Common Street Extension, Shreveport**

Dating from the 1880s through 1921, this complex is a rare survival of an intact system of buildings, reservoirs, pipes, filters, boilers, pumps, and engines illustrating an early municipal waterworks. At first a private operation, the waterworks was purchased by the city in 1917 and was soon enlarged. In the 1970s new equipment was installed, but the original components, showing the history and evolution of engineering technology, were kept.

■ *East Baton Rouge Parish*

## KIDD

**Mississippi River near Government Street and River Road, Baton Rouge**

Representative of the Fletcher class of destroyers that were the backbone of U.S. naval forces during World War II, *Kidd* was named for Rear Admiral Kidd, who was killed aboard his flagship, the USS *Arizona,* during the attack on Pearl Harbor. *Kidd* saw heavy action in the Pacific theater, participating in nearly every important naval campaign and winning four battle stars. In 1982 the destroyer was towed from Philadelphia to Baton Rouge, restored, and opened as a major exhibit of the Louisiana Naval War Memorial.

## LOUISIANA STATE CAPITOL

**Capitol Drive, Baton Rouge**

This notable Art Deco style capitol stands as a monument to Governor Huey P. Long, Louisiana's famous "Kingfish." Intending the new capitol to be a symbol of the modern era, Long suggested that the old capitol (see Old Louisiana State Capitol) be turned over "to some collector of antiques." He gave the architects, the New Orleans firm of Weiss, Dreyfuss, and Seiferth, only two directives for the new: It should be a skyscraper and should depict the history of the state. Completed in only two years (1930–1932), the 34-story limestone-clad tower is decorated with significant sculptural groups, many by Loredo Taft and Lee Lawrie. Long was assassinated in the building in 1935, dying at age 42. A statue facing the capitol stands above his tomb on the grounds and shows him holding a model of his monument.

## OLD LOUISIANA STATE CAPITOL

**North Boulevard and Saint Philip Street, Baton Rouge**

This castellated Gothic building overlooking the Mississippi, designed by James H. Dakin, was castigated by Mark Twain, who put the ultimate blame on Sir Walter Scott for having inspired "this little sham castle" with his

*Shreveport Waterworks Pumping Station, Shreveport, Caddo Parish. Courtesy of HAER (Jet Lowe).*

*Shadows-on-the-Teche,
New Iberia, Iberia Parish,
1968. Courtesy of NPS
(Charles W. Snell).*

"medieval romances." The capitol was built in 1847–1849, and—Mark Twain aside—is considered one of the nation's finest examples of Gothic Revival architecture. Its dramatic interior rotunda dates from an 1880s reconfiguration. By the 1930s the capitol had become a symbol of the "old order" in Louisiana, and Governor Huey P. Long, definitely a member of the "new order," decreed that a new capitol (see Louisiana State Capitol) replace it. Restored in the 1990s, the former capitol is now a museum.

## ■ *East Feliciana Parish*

### THE COURTHOUSE AND LAWYERS' ROW
**Liberty, Saint Helena, Bank, and Woodville Streets, Clinton**

Except for a large octagonal domed cupola, this Greek Revival courthouse with surrounding Doric colonnade, completed in 1840, appears like many Louisiana plantation houses of its period. Five antebellum Greek Revival offices across Woodville Street from the public square constitute Lawyers' Row and add immensely to the overall architectural harmony of the East Feliciana parish seat.

### PORT HUDSON
**Along U.S. Route 61, Port Hudson**

In the spring of 1863 this Confederate stronghold on the Mississippi was the scene of bitter fighting. On May 27, the First and Third Regiments of the Louisiana Native Guards—the former composed of free blacks led by black officers and the latter of ex-slaves led by white officers—gave an unqualified affirmative answer to the question "Will the Negro fight?" When Port Hudson finally surrendered on July 8, 1863, Union forces took possession of the last Confederate bastion on the Mississippi. Part of the battlefield is a state commemorative area open to the public.

## ■ *Iberia Parish*

### SHADOWS-ON-THE-TECHE
**East Main Street, New Iberia**

Built between 1831 and 1834, this two-story porticoed house made of locally fired coral-colored brick is a superb combination of Greek Revival detailing with a traditional French Colonial Louisiana plan. Although large, it is relatively unpretentious, as it dates prior to the period when area planters sought to outdo each other with houses noted for their competitive ostentation. Shadows-on-the-Teche was bequeathed, with original furnishings and heirlooms intact, to the National Trust for Historic Preservation in 1958 and is maintained as a historic house museum.

## ■ *Lafourche Parish*

### EDWARD DOUGLASS WHITE HOUSE
**5 miles north of Thibodaux on Louisiana Route 1**

This frame 1½-story, raised cottage was birthplace, childhood home, and estate of Edward Douglass White, associate justice of the U.S. Supreme Court and, from 1910 to 1921, chief justice. His greatest impact resulted from his "rule of reason" for the enforcement of the Sherman Antitrust Act. The house, dating from ca. 1790, is now the focal point of a small Louisiana state park honoring White.

## ■ *Natchitoches Parish*

### KATE CHOPIN HOUSE
**Main Street, Cloutierville**

This Louisiana raised cottage, dating from the late 18th century, was the home of Katherine O'Flaherty Chopin from 1880 to 1883. A nationally significant novelist and short story writer, Chopin utilized the folk culture of the Louisiana bayou country around Cloutierville as background for many of her works. Her controversial novel *The Awakening* was chastised by reviewers because of its subject matter and sensual prose. The house now serves fittingly as the Bayou Folk Museum.

### LOS ADAES
**Northeast of Robeline off State Highway 6**

Founded in 1721 by the Spanish to check French expansion into east Texas, this presidio helped maintain the international balance of power between the two countries. Los Adaes served as capital of the Spanish province of Texas from 1751 to 1770. It was abandoned in 1774, never to be reoccupied. The sites of the hexagonal presidio and adjacent San Miguel mission are now part of a state commemorative park.

### NATCHITOCHES HISTORIC DISTRICT
**Roughly bounded by Second, Fourth, Jefferson, and Pavie Streets and Williams and College Avenues, Natchitoches**

Established by the French in 1714 to promote trade with the Spanish and Indians, Natchitoches was named for a tribe living along the Red River. Located at the head of navigation, the city became an important link in pack train trails between Louisiana and Texas. A number of early French buildings of *bousillage* construction (posts with interstices filled with mud strengthened with Spanish moss) remain, as do buildings of later periods.

### YUCCA PLANTATION
**Near the intersection of Louisiana Routes 119 and 493, Melrose**

Established in the late 18th century by Marie Therese Coin-Coin, a former slave who became a wealthy businesswoman, Yucca

*Yucca Plantation, Melrose, Natchitoches Parish. African House. Courtesy of HABS (Frank Hampson).*

Plantation (now known as Melrose) contains what may well be the oldest buildings of African design built by African Americans in the country. The African House, a unique, nearly square structure with an umbrella-like roof extending some ten feet beyond the exterior walls on all four sides, may be of direct African derivation. The "big house," French Colonial in style, dates from ca. 1833 and was built by Marie Therese's grandson. Yucca is a working pecan plantation, and the big house and outbuildings are open to the public.

■ *Orleans Parish*

## THE CABILDO
### Jackson Square, Chartres and Saint Peter Streets, New Orleans

This stuccoed-brick building, dating from 1795–1799, is the most important surviving monument representing Spanish domination of Louisiana. It was built to house the governing body, or *Cabildo,* and on December 20, 1803, the final transfer of Louisiana Territory from the French to the United States took place here. The mansard roof and cupola were added in 1847. At one time the New Orleans City Hall, it became the Louisiana State Museum in 1911 and was restored in 1966–1969. After a fire in 1988 the building was again restored and reopened to the public. (See The Presbytere.)

## GEORGE WASHINGTON CABLE HOUSE
### 1313 Eighth Street, New Orleans

George Washington Cable is known as the voice of the Louisiana Creoles. Through articles in *Scribner's* magazine and his own published works, he contributed to American regional literature with his stories of New Orleans and made the term *creole* better appreciated and understood. He entertained America's literary figures in his house, built in the city's Garden District in 1874 and modeled on early Louisiana Creole cottages. The house is privately owned.

## *DELTA QUEEN*
### 30 Robin Street Wharf, New Orleans

The best-known, best-loved riverboat on the Western rivers, *Delta Queen* recalls long-ago times when the cry went out: "Showboat's a'coming, there's dancing tonight!" One of only two remaining sternwheel passenger boats operating under steam, *Delta Queen* was built in 1927, served first on the Sacramento River in California, and then as a navy ferryboat on San Francisco Bay in World War II. After the war *Delta Queen* arrived via the Panama Canal, under tow, on the Mississippi. The 1966 Safety at Sea Law threatened its continued operation because of its wooden superstructure, but public outcry caused officials to grant an exemption. *Delta Queen's*

Delta Queen, *New Orleans, Orleans Parish. Courtesy of the Delta Queen Steamboat Company.*

steam calliope still announces its arrival in ports all along the Western rivers.

## DELUGE
### Mississippi River, New Orleans

In constant service since 1923, the *Deluge* is considered the nation's best-preserved example of an early-20th-century fireboat. When *Deluge* was christened, the *Times-Picayune* bragged that the appropriately named tug could "handle 10,000 gallons of water a minute" and "throw a stream of water 350 feet." Work-a-day fireboats like the *Deluge* remain an indispensable part of port activities, protecting life and property afloat and ashore, as they play their part in contributing to the nation's maritime trade and commerce.

## JAMES H. DILLARD HOME
### 571 Audubon Street, New Orleans

Educator James Hardy Dillard came to New Orleans in 1891 to teach Latin at Tulane University and soon became an administrator and a dean. From this base of authority, he became a trustee at two black colleges and, as president of the public library, promoted a Carnegie library for black citizens. He later directed philanthropic foundations supporting black education and training for teachers throughout the South. From 1894 to 1913 Dillard lived in this one-story frame house near Audubon Park in New Orleans.

## GALLIER HALL
### 545 Saint Charles Avenue, New Orleans

Among the major achievements of the Greek Revival in America, this is the finest remaining work of architect James Gallier, Sr. Constructed between 1845 and 1850, the structure first served as the New Orleans city hall. Its imposing Ionic portico with pediment containing sculptured figures of Liberty, Justice, and Commerce reflects "the majesty of the Law." Now renamed to honor its architect, Gallier Hall is used primarily for ceremonial events and exhibitions sponsored by the City of New Orleans.

## GALLIER HOUSE
### 1132 Royal Street, New Orleans

James Gallier, Jr., followed in his architect father's footsteps and obviously prospered in his profession. He built this imposing town house for himself and his family in the city's Vieux Carré in 1857–1860. Essentially, the Gallier House is a mid-19th-century American town house adapted to the physical and cultural conditions of the French Quarter. Like so many of its neighbors, it has a cast-iron gallery extending over the sidewalk in front, and subsidiary side and rear galleries provide access to many of its rooms. The house was restored in 1971, with Gallier's surviving plans used as a guide. It is now a historic house museum.

*Gallier House, New Orleans, Orleans Parish. Courtesy of HABS (Joseph Mistich).*

*Lafitte's Blacksmith Shop, New Orleans, Orleans Parish, 1968. Courtesy of NPS (Charles W. Snell).*

## GARDEN DISTRICT
**Carondelet, Josephine, and Magazine Streets and Louisiana Avenue, New Orleans**

This fashionable residential area had its beginnings in the 1830s, when American merchants began to build elegant houses on expansive lots upstream from the more crowded French-oriented Vieux Carré. A phenomenal number of important houses, representing architectural styles popular from antebellum days to the early 20th century, line the streets of this 80-block area. Churches, Lafayette Cemetery No. 1, cast-iron fences, and lush landscaping also contribute to an ambiance that is at once urbane and idyllic in this appropriately named district.

## HERMANN-GRIMA HOUSE
**818–820 Saint Louis Street, New Orleans**

This red-brick Federal style mansion, built in 1831, exemplifies the adaptation of American architecture to the New Orleans environment. Its elliptical fanlight and center-hall plan are typical of the former, and the wrought-iron balcony across the front and a recessed gallery across the rear illustrate the latter. The house was restored and opened to the public in 1971. One of its most popular attractions is the kitchen, restored to working condition in the late 1970s.

## JACKSON SQUARE
**Bounded by Decatur, Saint Peter, Saint Ann, and Chartres Streets, New Orleans**

Jackson Square, along with the notable buildings that flank it on three sides (the fourth opens on the Mississippi River levee) is the visual trademark of New Orleans. Hub of the Vieux Carre, it was laid out in 1721 as the "Place d'Armes." In 1803 the American flag was raised here for the first time over the newly purchased Louisiana Territory. An equestrian statue of Andrew Jackson, sculpted by Clark Mills and unveiled in 1856, stands at the center of the square.

## LAFITTE'S BLACKSMITH SHOP
**941 Bourbon Street, New Orleans**

This well-known charmer in the heart of the Vieux Carré was built of heavy timbers with brick infill and covered with plaster, sometime between 1772 and 1791. Although small, it displays such architectural refinements as a gracefully flared roofline and pedimented dormers. Supposed builders Jean and Pierre Lafitte are said to have posed as blacksmiths to mask their nefarious slave trading operations. The shop is now used as a bar.

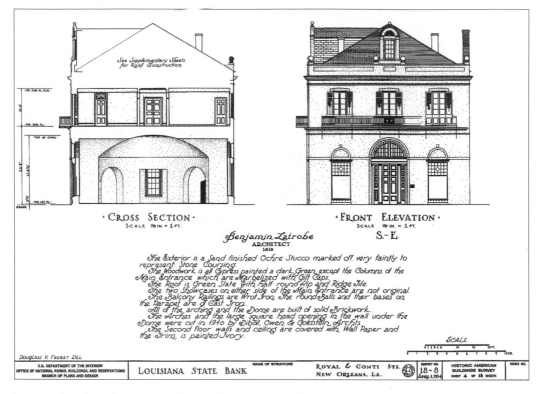

*Louisiana State Bank Building, New Orleans, Orleans Parish, 1954. Courtesy of HABS (Douglas V. Freret).*

## LOUISIANA STATE BANK BUILDING
### 403 Royal Street, New Orleans

Completed in 1822, this stuccoed-brick bank was the last structure designed by architect Benjamin H. Latrobe, who had moved to New Orleans to construct the city's waterworks. It housed the first bank incorporated (1818) in Louisiana after its admission to statehood. The building now serves as a shop, and the elegant circular banking room with saucer dome survives largely unaltered.

## MADAME JOHN'S LEGACY
### 632 Dumaine Street, New Orleans

Built in 1788, this is an outstanding example of a raised-cottage French Colonial town house. It obtained its unusual appellation when it served as the setting for George Washington Cable's story of the same name. The first floor contains offices and auxiliary rooms, and the second floor, fronted by a gallery, contains the main living spaces. Restored in the 1970s, Madame John's Legacy is maintained by the Louisiana State Museum as a historic house museum.

## MAYOR GIROD HOUSE
### 500 Chartres Street, New Orleans

This is one of the best examples of a large French Colonial town house in the country, illustrating the long-lived French architectural tradition in New Orleans. The two-story service wing was built in 1794, and the stuccoed-brick main block of 3½ stories dates from 1814. It is distinguished by its delicate iron balconies and domed octagonal cupola. The house is privately owned, but visible from the street.

## NEW ORLEANS COTTON EXCHANGE BUILDING
### 231 Carondelet Street, New Orleans

Organized in 1871, partly in response to changed economic conditions following the Civil War, the New Orleans Cotton Exchange soon became one of the leading institutions of its type in the world. The Exchange's success, which was instrumental in making New Orleans the nation's leading cotton port, was due in large part to its first superintendent, Henry G. Hester, whose careful analyses of crop conditions helped reduce investment risk. Since 1921, the Exchange has been housed in this eight-story neoclassical office building.

## PONTALBA BUILDINGS
### Jackson Square, New Orleans

Pacesetting examples of urban amenity and civic design, these identical red-brick apartment rows flanking Jackson Square (see Jackson Square) were built in 1849–1851 by Micaela Almonester, baroness de Pontalba. With shops on the ground floor and apartments above, the structures combine monumental Greek Revival architecture with ornamental ironwork typical of New Orleans. James Gallier, Jr. (see Gallier House) was the original architect, but after a falling out with his client, Henry Howard was commissioned to complete the drawings. The baroness herself designed the cast-iron balustrades, with the entwined letters *AP* forming a monograph of the Almonester and Pontalba initials. One of the units, 523 Saint Ann Street, is open as the 1850 House, a museum.

## THE PRESBYTERE
### 713 Chartres Street, New Orleans

Built ca. 1791–1813, this two-story stuccoed brick structure was designed to be the rectory of the adjoining Saint Louis Cathedral. Architect Gilberto Guillemard designed the Presbytere and the Cabildo (see the Cabildo), on the opposite flank of the cathedral, as matching structures, and they remain the finest examples of formal Spanish Colonial architecture in the country. The elaborate mansard roofs on both structures date from the 1840s. The Presbytere, which never served its intended function, is now a museum.

## SAINT ALPHONSUS CHURCH
### 2045 Constance Street, New Orleans

Saint Alphonsus, built by the Redemptorists in 1855–1857 for an Irish parish, was designed by Baltimore architect Louis L. Long. The Renaissance style exterior is notable for its excellent brickwork, and the polychromed interior presents an exuberant display of notable frescoes, stained-glass windows, statues, and furnishings. Saint Alphonsus

was one of three churches in a two-block area that served as the center of religious and community life for immigrants of French, German, and Irish origin. (See Saint Mary's Assumption Church.)

## SAINT MARY'S ASSUMPTION CHURCH
### 2039 Constance Street, New Orleans

Built by the Redemptorists in 1858–1860 for a German Catholic parish, this large brick church is a striking example of German Baroque architecture. The exterior is dominated by a massive tower, constructed independently of the church, and the interior is awash in ornamental plasterwork and woodwork, much of it obtained from Germany, as were the stained-glass windows. Even the pew ends display the Baroque fondness for curve and countercurve. Saint Mary's and Saint Alphonsus (see Saint Alphonsus Church), across the street, form an extraordinary complex of ecclesiastical architecture.

## SAINT PATRICK'S CHURCH
### 714 Camp Street, New Orleans

This large brick church is a notable, and early, example of the Gothic Revival style. Begun in 1837 from designs by James and Charles Dakin and completed in 1841 with James Gallier, Sr., as architect, it predates the better-known Trinity Episcopal Church in New York (see Trinity Church and Graveyard, New York County, New York), a comparable church in both size and cost. The sanctuary and altar are dramatically lit by stained-glass panels in the ceiling.

## UNITED STATES CUSTOMHOUSE, NEW ORLEANS
### 423 Canal Street, New Orleans

This huge granite structure provided an impressive architectural testament to the federal government's presence in 19th-century New Orleans. Begun in 1848, it took a third of a century to build. When completed in 1881, it was exceeded in size only by the U.S. Capitol among American buildings. Overall the style is Greek Revival, but each facade is centered by a pedimented pavilion with engaged columns showing Egyptian motifs.

## UNITED STATES MINT, NEW ORLEANS BRANCH

**420 Esplanade Avenue, New Orleans**

One of the first three branch mints authorized in the country, the New Orleans Mint was established in 1835 and became operational in 1838. It was housed in this handsome Greek Revival structure designed by architect William Strickland. The mint was seized by Confederate forces in 1861, but was returned to use after the war. In 1909 it became an assay office and was later used as a jail. It is now part of the Louisiana State Museum system and houses exhibits on the history of jazz and Mardi Gras.

## URSULINE CONVENT

**1114 Chartres Street, New Orleans**

This is the nation's finest surviving example of French colonial public architecture. It was built in 1748–1752 to house the Ursulines, whose dual mission was to establish a hospital for paupers and to teach young girls from well-do-do families. The stuccoed brick-building is Louis XV in style, typified by its formal, symmetrical facade and lack of extraneous ornamentation. When the Ursulines moved to another convent in 1824, they presented their former building to the bishop. After a variety of uses, it was restored in the 1970s and is now a museum and historical center.

## VIEUX CARRÉ HISTORIC DISTRICT

**Bounded by the Mississippi River, Rampart and Canal Streets, and Esplanade Avenue, New Orleans**

In extent, the Vieux Carré, or "French Quarter," coincides almost exactly with New Orleans's original city plan, platted in 1721. Within its 85 blocks are distinctive individual buildings, many designated separately as National Historic Landmarks. Even more characteristic of the "old quarter" are numerous vernacular structures that provide a unique ambiance and reflect the multinational heritage of New Orleans. With its wide range of attractions to suit all tastes, the well-preserved Vieux Carré is one of America's most popular tourist destinations.

■ *Plaquemines Parish*

## FORT DE LA BOULAYE

**Address Restricted, Phoenix vicinity**

Pierre Le Moyne, sieur d'Iberville, established a fort in 1700 as a formal act proclaiming physical possession of the mouth of the Mississippi in the name of France. The fort, a log blockhouse, was armed with six cannon. Hostile Indians forced its abandonment in 1707. The site, rediscovered in the 1930s when adzed logs and a cannonball were found, is not open to the public.

## FORT JACKSON

**West bank of the Mississippi River, 2.5 miles southeast of Triumph**

Constructed in 1822–1832 at the instigation of Andrew Jackson, this moated pentagonal brick fort guarded the Mississippi River approach to New Orleans, some 65 miles upstream. It saw no action until the Civil War, when it and the older Fort Saint Philip (see Fort Saint Philip) on the opposite shore fell after a six-day Union bombardment in April 1862. The Union navy, under David G. Farragut's command, then steamed to New Orleans, forcing its surrender and opening the Lower Mississippi to the Union. The fort is now a park and museum.

## FORT SAINT PHILIP

**East bank of Mississippi River, 2.5 miles southeast of Triumph**

Located on the east bank of the Mississippi River across from the later Fort Jackson (see Fort Jackson), Fort Saint Philip was built by the French in 1746, rebuilt by the Spanish in 1791, and finished by U.S. forces in 1812–1815. Like Fort Jackson, its surrender to Union forces after a six-day bombardment in April 1862 caused the subsequent Confederate surrender of New Orleans and the opening of the Lower Mississippi to the Union. The fort was sold to private owners in 1923.

■ *Pointe Coupee Parish*

## PARLANGE PLANTATION HOUSE

**Junction of Louisiana 1 and 78, Mix vicinity**

Erected ca. 1750, this is one of the finest and

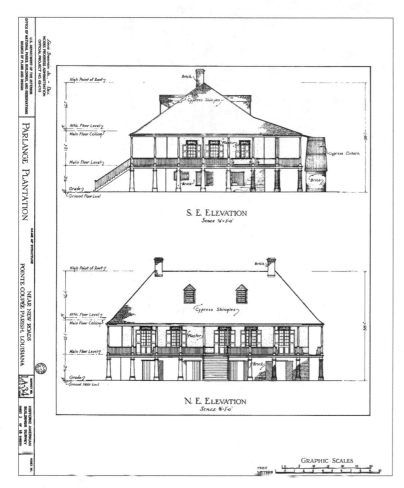

PARLANGE PLANTATION

POINTE COUPEE PARISH, LOUISIANA

NEAR NEW ROADS

*Parlange Plantation House, Pointe Coupee Parish, 1936. Courtesy of HABS (Louis Sarrazin, Jr.).*

least altered French Colonial plantation houses in the country. A classic example of a two-story raised cottage, it is surrounded by a veranda covered by an extension of the steeply pitched hip roof. The house, named after a later owner, faces False River, once the main channel of the nearby Mississippi. Surrounded by trees draped in Spanish moss, the privately owned Parlange maintains the serenity of an earlier era.

### ■ *Sabine Parish*

## FORT JESUP
### Fort Jesup State Monument, 7 miles northeast of Many

For a quarter century, from 1822, when it was established, until the time of the Mexican War, this was the most southwesterly military outpost in the United States. When Texas became a state, moving the frontier westward, its usefulness ceased. In 1850 the fort, then containing approximately 50 buildings, was auctioned. By 1929 only one building, a kitchen, remained. In 1957 the site was developed as a state park, the kitchen was restored, and one of the officers' quarters was reconstructed to serve as a visitor center.

### ■ *Saint Charles Parish*

## HOMEPLACE PLANTATION HOUSE
### 0.5 miles south of Hahnville

Erected in 1787–1791, this is an excellent and little-altered example of a large two-story French Colonial raised cottage. Its first-story walls are brick, while those of the second story are clapboarded over *bousillage* construction (cypress timbers infilled with mud and reinforced with Spanish moss.) Above, a steeply pitched hip roof with dormers extends on all four sides to cover two-story galleries. Homeplace remains in private ownership.

*Homeplace Plantation House, Saint Charles Parish, 1968. Courtesy of NPS (Charles W. Snell).*

## ■ *Saint James Parish*

### OAK ALLEY PLANTATION

**2.5 miles north of Vacherie**

The columns of Oak Alley, majestically framed by an 800-foot-long double row of giant live oaks, provide one of the most familiar and most treasured visual images of a southern plantation. The house, originally named Bon Sejour, was built in 1837–1839, and, with its surrounding colonnade of 28 Doric columns, is among the finest of the few of its type remaining. It is open to the public.

## ■ *Saint John the Baptist Parish*

### EVERGREEN PLANTATION

**Louisiana Highway 18, Wallace**

This remarkably well-preserved Mississippi River plantation contains more than 30 antebellum structures. The present appearance of the porticoed main house dates from 1832, when an earlier Creole building was remodeled in the fashionable Greek Revival style. Various outbuildings surround it, and a double row of 22 slave cabins stretches "back of the big house." Evergreen's buildings and fields, many still planted in sugar cane, the chief cash crop in antebellum times, provide an authentic image of the South's plantation landscape.

### SAN FRANCISCO PLANTATION HOUSE

**3 miles west of Reserve on Louisiana Route 144, Reserve**

One of the most ornate of Louisiana's great antebellum plantation houses, San Francisco, constructed in 1849–1850, exemplifies what has often been termed the "steamboat Gothic" style. Brackets and jigsawn decoration give it flair, especially at the roof line, but beneath it all, columned galleries relate San Francisco to other plantations along the Mississippi. The interiors of the house, which is open to the public, have notable painted ceilings and doors.

## ■ *Saint Martin Parish*

### ACADIAN HOUSE

**Longfellow-Evangeline State Park, Saint Martinville**

Constructed ca. 1765, this house, associated with the removal of the Acadians from eastern Canada to Louisiana, is an authentic survivor of a once common regional building type adapted to climate and available materials. The house has expansive galleries and is built of hand-hewn cypress with clapboarded walls over *bousillage* (an infilling of mud reinforced with Spanish moss). Since the early 1930s, the Acadian House has been a featured attraction at the Longfellow-Evangeline State Park.

## ■ *West Carroll Parish*

### POVERTY POINT

**12 miles north of Delhi on Bayou Macon**

The largest and most complex ceremonial earthworks of their kind yet found in North America, this Late Archaic/Transitional period complex is dominated by the huge Poverty Point Mound, which measures 640 feet by 710 feet at its base and rises nearly 70 feet high. The site was first mentioned in a publication in 1872, but it was not until the early 1950s, with aerial photography, that the giant geometric earthwork, composed of six ridges forming concentric octagons, became apparent. Poverty Point is a Louisiana State Commemorative Area and is open to the public.

# MAINE

## ■ *Androscoggin County*

### SABBATHDAY LAKE SHAKER VILLAGE
**Route 26, New Gloucester vicinity**

Formally organized in 1794, Sabbathday Lake survives as the last active Shaker community in the United States. Members of the celibate United Society of Believers were known for their self-sufficiency and practicality, with an unwritten adherence to the dictum "Nothing too much." Buildings at Sabbathday Lake reflect these principles and are characterized by a spare neatness and precision. The 1794 Meeting House has movable Windsor bench-es, allowing the floor to be cleared for spiritual exercises that appeared to nonbelievers as dancing, or "shaking." Sabbathday Lake is occupied by the Shaker Society, and many of the buildings are open as museums during summer months.

## ■ *Aroostook County*

### FORT KENT
**0.75 miles southwest of Fort Kent City on Maine Route 11**

Fort Kent, a two-story blockhouse constructed in 1838–1840, is the only extant fortification of the bloodless Aroostook "war"

Sabbathday Lake Shaker Village, Androscoggin County. Horse barn, 1973. Courtesy of NPS (Robert C. Post).

Fort Kent, Aroostook County. Courtesy of NPS.

*Morse-Libby Mansion, Portland, Cumberland County, 1970. Courtesy of NPS.*

(1838–1839), the conflict that climaxed the border disputes in the northeast with Great Britain following the War of 1812. The controversy was finally resolved by the Webster-Ashburton Treaty of 1842, after which Fort Kent was abandoned. It is now preserved as a state historic site.

■ *Cumberland County*

## NEAL DOW HOUSE
### 714 Congress Street, Portland

Neal Dow, the "Napoleon of Temperance," lived in this early-19th-century Federal style house for some 67 years. Dow authored the "Maine Law," passed in 1851 as the nation's first state temperance act, and also waged his campaign against "demon rum" in England. Dow was a candidate for the presidency in 1880 on the Prohibition Party ticket. The Dow family bequeathed the house to the Maine Women's Christian Temperance Union.

## HARPSWELL MEETINGHOUSE
### Harpswell Center on Maine Route 123, 9 miles south of Brunswick

Begun in 1757, this simple clapboarded two-story frame structure is a little-altered example of a small New England meetinghouse. The galleried interior features a high pulpit with sounding board. The building served in a dual capacity, as meetinghouse and town meeting hall, until 1844. It still serves in the latter capacity.

## WINSLOW HOMER STUDIO
### Winslow Homer Road, Prout's Neck, Scarborough

From 1884 until his death in 1910, Winslow Homer used this converted carriage house on his brother's property at Prout's Neck as a studio. One of America's best-known and best-loved artists, Homer once stated that he worked "in utter independence of schools and masters." He is known for his Civil War scenes, landscapes, genre paintings, and particularly for his powerful paintings of the sea.

## MCLELLAN-SWEAT MANSION
### 111 High Street, Portland

Built in 1800–1801 for wealthy Portland merchant Hugh McLellan, this superb and little-altered three story brick town house exemplifies the Federal Adamesque style in New England. It features a semicircular entrance portico with Doric pillars and pilasters, above which is a Palladian window. Interiors include Adamesque woodwork and a flying staircase. Mrs. Lorenzo de Medici Sweat, widow of a later owner, willed the house to the Portland Society of Art in 1908, and it is now part of the Portland Museum of Art.

## MORSE-LIBBY MANSION
**109 Danforth Street, Portland**

Designed by New Haven, Connecticut, architect Henry Austin and decorated with extraordinarily elaborate interiors by New York artist Giovanni Guidirini and his 11 assistants, this is one of the finest and least-altered Italian villas in the country. Built of brick, stuccoed, and embellished with brownstone trim, it has an asymmetrical facade, with a square tower containing the entranceway in its base. The house was constructed between 1858 and 1860 for Ruggles Sylvester Morse, a New Orleans hotel owner, who intended it as a summer residence. In 1943 it was donated to the Victoria Society, which maintains it as a historic house museum.

## THOMAS B. REED HOUSE
**30–32 Deering Street, Portland**

Thomas Brackett Reed, known as "Czar Reed" because of his power as the Republican Speaker of the U.S. House of Representatives during the 1890s, lived in one side of this large brick Victorian-era double house. In February 1890, a month after he assumed his position in Congress, Reed was responsible for the passage of new procedures known as the "Reed Rules," authorizing unprecedented power to the Speaker. Standing six feet, three inches tall and weighing close to 300 pounds, the "Czar" usually got what he wanted.

## HARRIET BEECHER STOWE HOUSE
**63 Federal Street, Brunswick**

From 1850 to 1852, this 2½-story frame house was the residence of Harriet Beecher Stowe, and it was here that she wrote *Uncle Tom's Cabin, or Life among the Lowly*. A scathing indictment of slavery, it was first published in serial form, became an instant success, and was eventually translated into 23 languages. The book had a direct impact on the course of American history. An idea of its influence can be garnered from Abraham Lincoln's salute to Stowe as "the little lady who started this great war."

## TATE HOUSE
**1270 Westbrook Street, Portland**

Built in 1755, this 5-bay, 2½-story frame house has a symmetrical Georgian facade and a clerestory gambrel roof that is one of only two extant examples of its type. The austere exterior and lavish interior trim reflect the colonial frontier economy. George Tate, for whom the house was built, was mast agent for the Royal Navy. As such, he was responsible for selecting the finest trees from American forests to be used as masts and spars on British ships. Resentment over this expropriation was a contributing cause of the Revolution. The Tate House is maintained as a historic house museum by the National Society of the Colonial Dames of America in the State of Maine.

## WADSWORTH-LONGFELLOW HOUSE
**487 Congress Street, Portland**

This was the boyhood home of the great American poet Henry Wadsworth Longfellow, who lived here from 1807 until he entered Bowdoin College, at age 14, in 1822. Despite frequent absences in subsequent years, he regarded this as his home until his second marriage in 1843, when he moved to Cambridge, Massachusetts. The brick house, quite restrained in its design, was originally built in 1785–1786 by Longfellow's grandfather, General Peleg Wadsworth. Longfellow's sister willed the house to the Maine Historical Society in 1901. The Society maintains it as a memorial to the two families whose names it shares.

### ■ *Hancock County*

### *BOWDOIN*
**Maine Maritime Academy, Castine**

The *Bowdoin*, built in 1921, was the brainchild of Admiral Donald Baxter MacMillan, who used it on 26 of his 29 voyages to the Arctic. Much of what is currently known about the Arctic derives from information gleaned on these voyages. Like the *American Eagle* (see *American Eagle*, Knox County), *Bowdoin* is an auxiliary schooner, utilizing both sail and motor power. *Bowdoin* served on the Greenland Patrol during World War II and was retired from service in 1954. It is now owned by the Maine Maritime Academy and used for educational purposes.

## DANIEL COIT GILMAN SUMMER HOUSE
### Off Huntington Road, Northeast Harbor

Daniel Coit Gilman summered here for more than 20 years, from the late 1880s until his death in 1908. Gilman was the first president of Johns Hopkins University, holding the post from 1875 to 1902. During that period he emphasized postgraduate study, and his success in the endeavor stimulated the rapid growth of postgraduate programs in other universities. The three-story shingled house is privately owned.

## PENTAGOET ARCHEOLOGICAL DISTRICT
### Address Restricted, Castine

Pentagoet was the most important trading post built by the French along the western Acadian frontier during the 17th century. Here Native Americans from as far away as the Saint Lawrence valley came to trade furs and pelts. Archeological excavations in the district's two discontiguous properties have uncovered well-preserved resources giving evidence of the full range of relations between French settlers and Native Americans during the period of Historic Contact (1635–1700).

■ *Kennebec County*

## JAMES G. BLAINE HOUSE
### Capitol and State Streets, Augusta

This expansive frame house served as the home of James G. Blaine for more than 30 years after he purchased it in 1862. Blaine was Speaker of the House of Representatives, twice a senator, twice secretary of state, and an unsuccessful presidential candidate in 1884. His forte was foreign affairs, and he helped establish the Pan-American Union in 1890. In 1919, the State of Maine obtained the house and renovated it as the governor's mansion, a purpose for which it is still used today. The house is open to the public for tours.

## CUSHNOC FORT WESTERN ARCHEOLOGICAL SITE
### Address Restricted, Augusta

This half-acre site on the banks of the Kennebec River, now planted as a lawn, contains the remains of Cushnoc, a mid-17th-century trading post established by the Plymouth Colony. Cushnoc, which may have been founded as early as 1628, was one of the most important English outposts along the Acadian frontier. It was abandoned by 1676, and the exact site, long the subject of speculation, was determined in the 1960s through archeological excavations. Fort Western (see Fort Western), built by British troops in 1754 during the Seven Years War, is nearby.

## FORT HALIFAX
### On U.S. Route 201, west of Winslow

Fort Halifax was built in 1754 for protection against Indian raids during the French and

Governor's House, Chelsea, Kennebec County, 1973. Courtesy of NPS.

American Eagle, *Rockland Harbor, Knox County. Courtesy of O.K. Barnes, Maine Windjammer Association.*

Indian War. A blockhouse, its hewn logs joined with dovetail notching, is the sole building remaining from the garrison and is the oldest structure of its type in the nation. The blockhouse is now owned by the State of Maine and is maintained as a state historic site.

## FORT WESTERN
**Bowman Street, Augusta**

Fort Western was built in 1754 as a fortified fur trading post. It was here, in September 1775, that Colonel Benedict Arnold began his unsuccessful march against Quebec. The main building, a long, shingled log structure that contained the trading post and living quarters, remains in largely unaltered condition. It was restored in 1920 and is open as a museum operated by the City of Augusta.

## GOVERNOR'S HOUSE
**Off Maine Route 17, Chelsea**

The National Home for Disabled Volunteer Soldiers was the nation's first veterans home. It was established immediately after the Civil War, and the 22-room Governor's House was completed in 1869. The mansard-roofed building now serves as the director's quarters for the Togus Veterans Administration Center, the country's oldest veterans facility.

## EDWIN ARLINGTON ROBINSON HOUSE
**67 Lincoln Avenue, Gardiner**

Edwin Arlington Robinson, one of America's major poets, lived and worked in this two-story clapboarded house from his infancy until his early twenties, when he left for college in the 1890s. Among his many honors, Robinson received three Pulitzer Prizes. One astute observer commented that Robinson was "the solitary poet who absorbed into his thought and art the best of the old in American poetry, and became the first of his generation to understand, however darkly, the new."

■ *Knox County*

### *AMERICAN EAGLE*
**Rockland Harbor, Rockland, Knox County**

Launched in 1930 as *Andrew and Rosalie*, this wooden-hull two-masted ship is of a type known as an auxiliary schooner, using both sail and motor power. *Andrew and Rosalie* was the last such schooner built in Gloucester, Massachusetts, home of one of the nation's largest fishing fleets. It was renamed *American Eagle* in 1941, and after 55 years in the fishing trade, was restored and placed in service in 1986 for summer cruises along the Maine coast as a windjammer (see *Bowdoin,* Hancock County).

## GRACE BAILEY
**Camden Harbor, Camden**

*Grace Bailey,* a two-masted coasting schooner, was built in 1882 in Patchogue, New York. At the time, such craft were the most common type of American vessel, carrying freight along the Pacific, Atlantic, and Gulf coasts, and on the Great Lakes. Now one of the few surviving examples of these nautical "freight trucks," *Grace* became a passenger-carrying windjammer in 1939.

## ISAAC H. EVANS
**Rockland Harbor, Rockland**

Built in 1886, *Isaac H. Evans* is the nation's oldest surviving oyster schooner, a two-masted type whose rig and centerboard made it easy to handle in shallow inlets and bays, and whose wide decks provided stability and space for freight. *Evans* spent most of its active career fishing and freighting on Delaware Bay; it currently serves as a windjammer, carrying passengers along the Maine coast during summer months.

## J. & E. RIGGIN
**Rockland Harbor, Rockland**

Built in 1927 in Dorchester, New Jersey, *J. & E. Riggin* represents the late and final form of the oyster schooner. In this type, the principles of naval architecture led to the designing of vessels with better hydrodynamic characteristics. Originally sail-powered, *Riggin,* named with the initials of Jacob and Edward Riggin, sons of the first owner, was converted to a motor vessel in 1946. In 1974 the schooner's sailing rig was restored for its service as a windjammer.

## LEWIS R. FRENCH
**Rockland Harbor, Rockland**

Launched in 1871, this is the oldest surviving sailing vessel built in Maine, the center for wooden shipbuilding in the United States after the Civil War. *French* worked mostly as a coasting schooner, carrying a variety of cargoes first as a sailing ship and later as a motor vessel. Restored in 1976, *Lewis R. French* currently serves as a Maine windjammer. Along with the *Stephen Taber,* this is the oldest known vessel that has been in continuous service since its launching.

## MERCANTILE
**Camden Harbor, Camden**

Launched in 1916 as a shoal-draft, centerboard two-masted schooner, *Mercantile* served the coasting trade until 1943, when it became part of the Maine windjammer fleet. *Mercantile* and other wooden windjammers serve as passenger vessels, teaching sail training and maintenance skills and helping to preserve traditional shipwright know-how.

## ROSEWAY
**Camden Harbor, Camden**

This wooden two-masted schooner, built in 1925, is the only known survivor of a type of vessel developed specifically to compete in yearly international races of fishing boats. In 1941, *Roseway* became a pilot boat in Boston, and during World War II served as a patrol vessel manned by the Coast Guard Reserve. *Roseway* has served as a passenger schooner since 1973. Meticulously maintained, *Roseway* still retains between 80 and 90 percent of its original hull fabric.

## STEPHEN TABER
**Rockland Harbor, Rockland**

From its launching in 1871 until 1920, this two-masted schooner plied the waters of New York Harbor and its environs, carrying all sorts of cargo. After 1920, *Taber* served similarly in Maine's Penobscot Bay, and in 1946 it became a Maine windjammer. *Taber* and *Lewis R. French,* both built in 1871, are the oldest documented American sailing vessels known to have been in continuous service since their launching.

## VICTORY CHIMES
**North End Shipyard, Rockland Harbor, Rockland**

The three-masted schooner *Victory Chimes* was launched in 1900 in Bethel, Delaware, as the *Edwin and Maud,* named for two children of its first captain. A well-preserved example of its type, *Victory Chimes* is the only surviving example of a "Chesapeake ram"—a flat-bottomed, shallow-draft schooner designed to pass through narrow canal locks—and one of only three surviving three-masted schooners in the United States. With a length of 132 feet, *Victory Chimes* is the largest member of

Maine's windjammer fleet that carries passengers along the coast during summer months.

## Lincoln County

### NICKELS-SORTWELL HOUSE
**Northeast corner, Main and Federal Streets, Wiscasset**

Built in 1807–1811 by Captain William Nickels, shipmaster, this large house is a splendid example of the Adamesque Federal style. Attenuated Corinthian pilasters mark vertical divisions of the flush-sided, three-story facade, which has details resembling plates in Asher Benjamin's *American Builder's Companion,* published the year before the house was begun. The house was restored in 1917–1918 and is preserved as a historic house museum by the Society for the Preservation of New England Antiquities.

### PEMAQUID ARCHEOLOGICAL SITE
**Off Route 130, Town of Bristol**

Pemaquid contains the remains of a colonial English settlement dating from ca. 1628 and occupied throughout the period of Historic Contact with Native Americans (1625–1759). The fortified settlement was on the frontier separating French Acadia from New England, and existed in part as a trading post, where manufactured goods were bartered for furs. Pemaquid was one of the first and most important centers of intercultural relations between Native Americans and English colonists in present-day Maine. Artifacts found among its fieldstone foundations, cellar holes, chimney bases, and hearths have yielded valuable information associated with this time period. Pemaquid is now a state historic site.

## Somerset County

### NORRIDGEWOCK ARCHEOLOGICAL DISTRICT
**Address Restricted, Madison and Starks**

Three discontiguous sites at the point where Sandy River flows into the Kennebec constitute this district. The Native American village "Naragooc," first mentioned by name in a European document dated 1625, was "the third town on the Kennebec" and was said to contain "fiftie households and one hundred and fiftie men." Although artifacts associated with nearly 6,000 years of human occupation have been found here, deposits dating from the period of Historic Contact with New England colonists (1614–1754) form the densest and most significant body of intact archeological resources.

## Waldo County

### FORT KNOX
**On U.S. Route 1 near Prospect**

Designed to protect Bangor and the Penobscot River valley from naval attack, Fort Knox is a huge granite pentagon that took a quarter-century to build. It was begun in 1844, and when work was halted in 1869, it was still incomplete. Fort Knox was garrisoned during the Civil War and in the Spanish-American War, but no enemy ships appeared on the Penobscot in either conflict. The fort, an excellent unaltered example of military architecture of its time, is now a state historic site.

## York County

### HAMILTON HOUSE
**Vaughn's Lane and Old South Road, South Berwick**

Beautifully sited on a hill overlooking the Salmon Falls River, this large Georgian style frame house was built in 1787–1788. Dormer windows, topped with broken swans-neck pediments, are particularly notable, and four massive chimneys hint at the spacious double-pile plan within. The house was willed to the Society for the Preservation of New England Antiquities in 1949, restored in 1950, and is now a historic house museum.

### SARAH ORNE JEWETT HOUSE
**5 Portland Street, South Berwick**

Sarah Orne Jewett lived and worked here for most of her life. Regarded as one of America's leading exponents of the local-color novel, she brought the genre to artistic perfection in her many depictions of the lives and landscapes of rural Maine in the late 19th century. In addition to their historical perspective, Jewett's works are important for their role in the development of women's literature. The house, built by Jewett's grandfather in 1774, is a historic house museum operated by the Society for the Preservation of New England Antiquities.

## LADY PEPPERRELL HOUSE
### Maine 103, Kittery Point

This distinguished example of high-style Georgian architecture was built between 1760 and 1765 by Lady Mary Pepperrell, widow of Sir William Pepperrell, wealthy businessman, military commander, and America's only designated baronet. The two-story frame house features a hipped roof, modillioned cornice, and gabled center pavilion with two-story Ionic pilasters. The house is maintained as a private residence.

## McINTIRE GARRISON HOUSE
### About 5 miles west of York on Maine Route 91

This is a notable example of a regional type of architecture known as a garrison house. Built of thick sawn logs, with a second-story overhang, the house has a large central chimney and is covered with a gable roof. Traditionally, such houses were single-family dwellings but were strongly built and could protect a number of families during times of danger from Indian attack. Clapboards and shingles now disguise the log construction and help to disguise its extraordinarily early date, ca. 1707.

## OLD YORK GAOL
### 4 Lindsay Road, York

This rare and well-preserved example of a substantial colonial prison served as the York County jail from ca. 1720 to ca. 1879. The original portion is an oak-lined stone cell, the "dungeon," the oldest-known instance of stone construction in the state. Several additions dating from ca. 1730 to 1806 gave the gaol its present appearance, that of a large, low, gambrel-roofed frame house with an exposed portion of stone wall on one elevation. The gaol was used during the 1890s as a school, but has been a museum since 1900.

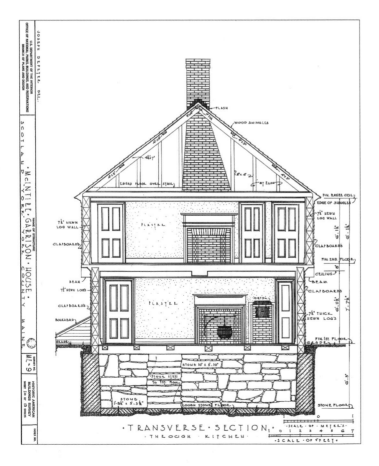

*McIntire Garrison House, York County. Transverse section, 1937. Courtesy of HABS (Joseph Depeter).*

# MARYLAND

## ■ *Anne Arundel County*

### BRICE HOUSE
**42 East Street, Annapolis**

Among the most imposing Georgian buildings in the country, this five-part brick mansion stands tall and proud on a terrace above street level. Its exterior is noted for the boldness of its design and the simplicity of its massing. In contrast, the interiors are quite sumptuous and have been attributed to William Buckland. James Brice, a leader in colonial Annapolis affairs, was the first owner of the house, which remained a private residence until the early 20th century. It was restored in the 1980s, and historic preservation easements were placed on both the exterior and interior. Currently, the International Masonary Institute owns the house.

### CHASE-LLOYD HOUSE
**22 Maryland Avenue, Annapolis**

One of the country's earliest and most elaborate three-story Georgian town houses, the Chase-Lloyd House was built between 1769 and 1774. Samuel Chase, soon to sign the Declaration of Independence, began construction but sold the incomplete house in 1771 to Edward Lloyd IV. Lloyd engaged architect William Buckland, then newly arrived in Annapolis, to finish it. A later owner bequeathed the house to the Episcopal Church as a home for elderly women in 1888. It continues in this use, and visitors are allowed to tour the house. (See Wye House, Talbot County.)

### COLONIAL ANNAPOLIS HISTORIC DISTRICT
**Annapolis**

In 1695 the capital of the colony of Maryland was transferred to this site on the Severn River. Sir Francis Nicholson, royal governor who decreed the move, was likely responsible for the town plan that eschewed the typical grid pattern. State and church circles form hubs from which streets radiate in spoke-like fashion. An impressive number of early structures remain, many of them listed individually as National Historic Landmarks. Annapolis was the nation's capital when it hosted the Continental Congress in 1783–1784. It continues as the capital of the State of Maryland.

### HAMMOND-HARWOOD HOUSE
**Maryland Avenue and King George Street, Annapolis**

This superb brick mansion is one of the most significant accomplishments of Georgian architecture in colonial America. A symmetrical five-part composition, it contains a two-story central block flanked by one-story hyphens that connect to polygonal-ended two-story dependencies. The interior contains notable woodwork that incorporates tobacco leaves in its carvings, an allusion to

*Chase-Lloyd House, Annapolis, Anne Arundel County, 1942. Courtesy of HABS (Charles E. Peterson).*

177

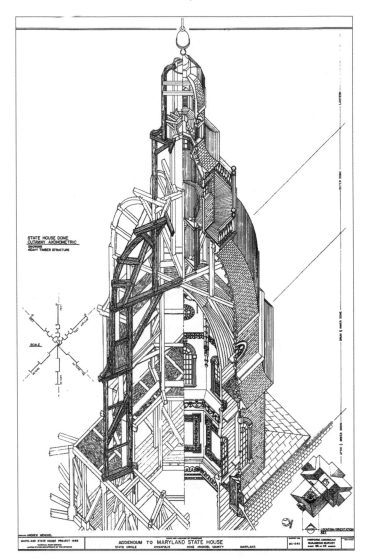

Maryland Statehouse, Annapolis, Anne Arundel County. Cutaway axonometric of dome. Courtesy of HABS (Andrew Wenchel).

the first owner's extensive plantations that provided the funds to build on such a scale. The house was designed by the accomplished colonial architect William Buckland and built in the 1770s. Charles Willson Peale's famous portrait of Buckland shows him holding a plan and elevation of the house, which has been open as a historic house museum since the 1940s.

## LONDON TOWN PUBLIK HOUSE
### Londontown Road, northeast of Woodland Beach

With obvious architectural affinities to the 18th-century Georgian mansions of nearby Annapolis, this large brick building was built as an inn. Located at a ferry crossing on the south bank of the South River, it was on one of colonial America's major north-south thoroughfares. Practically everyone coming from the south on the way to Philadelphia and points north passed this way. From 1828 to 1966, the building was the Anne Arundel County almshouse. Restoration began in the 1970s, and London Town is now a museum and archeological site.

## MARYLAND STATEHOUSE
### State Circle, Annapolis

This handsome Georgian structure with its tall dome dominates Annapolis from a commanding position on State Circle. It served as the nation's capitol from 1783–1784, and it was here, on December 23, 1783, that

George Washington resigned his commission as commander-in-chief of the Continental Army. On January 14, 1784, the Continental Congress, meeting in the building, ratified the Treaty of Paris, thus ending the Revolution. The Annapolis Convention, a forerunner of the 1787 Constitutional Convention, also met here. The Maryland Statehouse is the oldest building in the nation that remains in active use as the seat of a state government.

## WILLIAM PACA HOUSE
### 186 Prince George Street, Annapolis

This five-part Georgian mansion, built from 1763 to 1765, was the home of Maryland's famous patriot William Paca, signer of the Declaration of Independence, member of the state convention that ratified the U.S. Constitution, and three-time governor. In 1907 a hotel was built to the rear, and the Paca House was utilized to serve as its public rooms. The hotel was demolished in 1952, and the formal terraced gardens for which Paca's estate was noted have subsequently been recreated. The restored house and grounds are open to the public.

## PEGGY STEWART HOUSE
### 207 Hanover Street, Annapolis

Built in the 1760s, this brick Georgian house was owned and lived in by Daniel of St. Thomas Jenifer, member of the Continental Congress from 1778 until 1782. In 1787, Jenifer was a Maryland delegate to the federal Convention in Philadelphia and became a signer of the Constitution. The house achieved its popular name from another historic association. Anthony Stewart owned it in 1774, and when he paid the unpopular tea tax on the cargo of his vessel *Peggy Stewart*, Annapolis patriots forced him to burn his own ship.

## THOMAS POINT SHOAL LIGHT STATION
### Chesapeake Bay, Annapolis vicinity

Thomas Point Shoal Light Station is the last unaltered screwpile cottage-type lighthouse on its original foundation in the United States. Screwpile foundation technology greatly improved the U.S. aids to navigation

*Thomas Point Shoal Light Station, Anne Arundel County. Courtesy of U.S. Coast Guard (R. B. Ressler).*

system, allowing more than 100 lighthouses to be built in offshore locations that previously could only be marked by buoys or expensive lightships. Replacing an onshore station in 1875, the Thomas Point Shoal Light Station continues to serve as an active aid to navigation.

## TULIP HILL
### 2.5 miles west of Galesville on Owensville Road, Galesville

The central block of Tulip Hill, built in 1755–1756, is a finely designed example of an early Southern Georgian brick plantation house. With the wings and hyphens added between 1787 and 1790, the house became a distinguished example of a five-part country manor. Tulip Hill and its terraced landscape remain largely unaltered from the time they were completed and present a convincing portrait of the life-style that America's landed gentry enjoyed two centuries ago.

## UNITED STATES NAVAL ACADEMY
### Maryland Avenue and Hanover Street, Annapolis

Established in Annapolis in 1845, the U.S. Naval Academy has played a pivotal role in

American naval affairs, graduating career officers well versed in both military and academic studies throughout its history. In 1899, the navy commissioned New York architect Ernest Flagg to design a new academic complex, and the result is one of the country's finest expressions of monumental Beaux-Arts architecture. The domed chapel (1904–1908) rises 210 feet to the top of its lantern and, with the dome of the Maryland Statehouse, dominates the Annapolis skyline. John Paul Jones, "father of the American navy," is buried in the crypt.

## WHITEHALL
### Off Saint Margaret's Road, Annapolis

Colonial Maryland's governor Horatio Sharpe built this extraordinary brick Georgian villa in the 1760s as his private country retreat. The Corinthian portico that

*United States Naval Academy, Annapolis, Anne Arundel County. Chapel. Courtesy of HABS (Jack E. Boucher).*

*Whitehall, Annapolis, Anne Arundel County, 1968. Courtesy of NPS.*

centers the river facade of the five-part Palladian house is one of the earliest of its type in American architecture. Its details are taken from a 1742 English publication, *The Modern Builder's Assistant*. The notable interior woodwork is attributed to William Buckland.

## ■ *Baltimore County*
### COLLEGE OF MEDICINE OF MARYLAND
**522 West Lombard Street, Baltimore**

Constructed in 1812, the Medical College of Maryland, now known as Davidge Hall, is a handsome neoclassical structure fronted by a Doric portico and covered with a saucer dome. It is the oldest medical school building in continuous use in the United States and contains the nation's oldest anatomical theater. Essentially a circular amphitheater covered by a dome, the room allowed students to witness operations conducted by the faculty. In its plan, the theater harkens back to European anatomical halls dating from the Middle Ages.

### SHEPPARD AND ENOCH PRATT HOSPITAL AND GATE HOUSE
**Charles Street, Towson**

Moses Sheppard and Enoch Pratt founded this leading private institution for the treatment of the mentally ill in the mid-19th century. The gate house dates from 1860, and the two major hospital buildings, dramatic Norman Revival structures, were built from 1862 to 1891. Designed as the result of an architectural competition, they were based on ideas promulgated by Dr. Robert Kirkbride of Philadelphia. The buildings housed patients in separate wards, or wings, according to the nature and severity of their illnesses, and attempted to provide pleasant, self-contained, noninstitutional environments.

### THOMAS VIADUCT, BALTIMORE & OHIO RAILROAD
**Over the Patapsco River between Relay and Elkridge**

Completed in 1835 and named for the president of the Baltimore & Ohio Railroad, this is the world's oldest multiple-stone-arched railroad bridge. Civil engineer Benjamin H. Latrobe, son of the architect of the same name, designed it to carry trains across the Patapsco River. The route alignment necessitated building the bridge on a 4-degree curve, and skeptics, thinking it would collapse, dubbed the viaduct "Latrobe's Folly." Latrobe had the last laugh; the bridge, designed to carry six-ton engines of the 1830s, now carries their 300-ton descendants (also in Howard County).

## ■ *Baltimore City*
### BALTIMORE
**1415 Key Highway**

*Baltimore* is the oldest operating steam tugboat in the United States. Built in 1906 by Baltimore's Skinner Shipbuilding Company, *Baltimore* spent its career in and around the harbor of the city for which it was named, moving barges and work boats and going on inspection tours. On occasion *Baltimore* carried the mayor and other officials at maritime civic occasions, such as launchings of other vessels. At one of these events, in 1922, the vessel being launched capsized onto *Baltimore,* after which the tug was repaired and went back to work. *Baltimore* was restored in the 1990s for use as a working museum vessel. Licensed to carry passengers, it now steams around its old harbor haunts three or four times a year.

### BALTIMORE & OHIO TRANSPORTATION MUSEUM AND MOUNT CLARE STATION
**Pratt and Poppleton Streets**

The fledgling Baltimore & Ohio Railroad established its headquarters at Mount Clare in the 1830s, and the first regularly scheduled passenger trains in the nation carried customers from here to Ellicott City, 13 miles west (see Ellicott City Station, Howard County). In 1883 the huge "Passenger Car Roundhouse"—actually a polygonal brick building with 22 sides—was built adjoining the station. The structures now contain a transportation museum. A number of historic locomotives and railroad cars are among its exhibits.

## CARROLLTON VIADUCT
### Gwynn's Falls near Carroll Park

A monument in the history of American industrial architecture and civil engineering, this was the country's first masonry railroad bridge. It was completed in 1829 to carry the tracks of the Baltimore & Ohio Railroad over Gwynn's Falls. Carrollton Viaduct demonstrates the ability of early-19th-century builders to create new structures out of traditional building forms to serve entirely new functions. Still very much in use, the viaduct now supports far heavier loads than its original builders could ever have imagined. Or maybe they were more prescient than we know!

## CONSTELLATION
### Pier 1, Pratt Street

The U. S. frigate *Constellation,* launched from Baltimore on June 24,1798, became the first American ship to engage and defeat an enemy vessel. It fought the Barbary pirates and was the first ship to carry the American flag into Chinese waters. In the 1850s, *Constellation* was scrapped and a new ship, built at Gosport Navy Yard in Norfolk, Virginia, took the name. The new ship captured slave ships off the coast of Africa, saving more than 1,000 people bound for bondage. After serving as a training ship in the early 20th century, *Constellation* was decommissioned in 1955 and donated to the City of Baltimore for use as a museum ship and to become the symbol for the revitalization of the city's Inner Harbor. It was reconfigured to resemble the original 1797 frigate and was restored in 1996–1998. *Constellation* now welcomes visitors to its permanent berth in Baltimore Harbor.

## FIRST UNITARIAN CHURCH
### 2–12 West Franklin Street

Designed in 1817 by architect Maximilien Godefroy, a French emigré, and completed in 1818, this Neoclassical church was one of the first in the country to depart from the traditional meetinghouse-with-steeple that had dominated Protestant religious architecture for more than half a century. The church's design stresses the interplay of geometric forms and, with its low saucer dome, is essentially a hemisphere set on a cube. Unfortunately, the acoustics proved to be a failure, and the present interior, dating from 1893, was devised in an attempt to remedy the situation.

## HOMEWOOD
### North Charles and 34th Streets

Built between 1801 and 1803 by Charles Carroll Jr., Homewood is one of America's premier examples of late-Georgian, early-Federal architecture. The symmetrical five-part composition reflects Georgian precedent, but the delicately scaled, attenuated Adamesque details represent the Federal style at its most sophisticated. Carroll's father, Charles Carroll of Carrollton, footed the bills for the stone-trimmed brick house, and when they mounted far beyond what he had intended, he declared the project "a most improvident waste of money." Johns Hopkins University, whose campus surrounds it, has owned Homewood since 1902. First used as a faculty club, then as offices, it has been restored and is now a historic house museum.

## LIGHTSHIP NO. 116 *CHESAPEAKE*
### Baltimore Maritime Museum, Pier 4, Inner Harbor

Lightship No. 116, now known by the former designation *Chesapeake,* is the best-preserved representative of the third generation of American lightships: ships built during 1929–1930 that were powered by diesel-electric plants. Known as the 113-Foot Class, these were the last lightships built by the U.S. Lighthouse Service before it was absorbed into the U.S. Coast Guard. Now owned by the National Park Service, *Chesapeake* is on long-term loan to the City of Baltimore and is operated as a floating exhibit.

## ELMER V. MCCOLLUM HOUSE
### 2301 Monticello Road

This frame house in Baltimore's Windsor Hills neighborhood was the residence of Dr. Elmer V. McCollum for a decade, from approximately 1929 to 1939. McCollum had already discovered vitamin A by the time he moved to Baltimore as a biochemist at Johns Hopkins University's School of Hygiene and Public Health. While on the faculty, he discovered vitamins D and B. In addition,

Chesapeake, *Lightship No. 116, Baltimore City, 1936. Courtesy of the U.S. Coast Guard Historian's Office.*

McCollum outlined the roles that vitamins play in nutrition and their significant contributions to human health.

## H. L. MENCKEN HOUSE
### 1524 Hollins Road

This typical three-story Italianate style Baltimore row house, built in the 1880s to face fashionable Union Square, was the home of journalist-editor Henry Louis Mencken from his childhood until his death in 1956. A distinguished essayist and caustic critic of American society, Mencken was editor of *The Smart Set* (1914–1924), and cofounder and editor of the *American Mercury* (1914–1924). His home, "a larva of the comfortable and complacent bourgeoisie, encapsulated in affection and kept fat, saucy and contented," is little changed from the way he knew and described it. It is open to the public as a museum.

## MINOR BASILICA OF THE ASSUMPTION OF THE BLESSED VIRGIN MARY
### 401 Cathedral Street

This first Roman Catholic cathedral built in the United States was designed by architect Benjamin Henry Latrobe. Begun in 1806, it is constructed of granite hauled to the site by ox cart. Latrobe's sophisticated Neoclassical design employs a Latin cross plan and displays an intricate system of barrel vaults and shallow domes. When the cathedral was dedicated in 1821, it was one of the country's largest religious edifices. After a new cathedral was completed in suburban Baltimore in 1959, this building was designated a co-cathedral by papal decree.

## MOUNT CLARE
### Carroll Park

Mount Clare, dating from the 1760s, is a superior example of Georgian architecture. Built of brick, the house has a southern facade laid in all-header bond, an unusual pattern almost exclusive to Maryland architecture. The finest remaining colonial structure in Baltimore, this Carroll family home is embellished with Baltimore furnishings and portraits and is open as a historic house museum.

## MOUNT ROYAL STATION AND TRAINSHED
### 1400 Cathedral Street

Together, this granite-faced Renaissance style train station and its adjoining utilitarian steel-framed train shed display a felicitous marriage of architecture and engineering. A tall pyramidal-roofed clock tower that contains the main entrance in its base dominates the complex. Built in 1896 by the Baltimore & Ohio Railroad to provide an impressive

*Mount Royal Station and Trainshed, Baltimore City, 1971. Courtesy of the Library of Congress (William E. Barrett).*

entrance to the city, the station closed in 1961. It was subsequently remodeled to serve the Maryland Institute, College of Art.

## MOUNT VERNON PLACE HISTORIC DISTRICT
### Mount Vernon Place and Washington Place

Baltimore's Washington Monument, a 165-foot Doric column completed in 1829 from designs by Robert Mills, was the nation's first major memorial to the first president. It also serves as the focal point of this historic district. Four small parks, oriented to cardinal compass points, extend a block from the monument to form a Greek cross. Some of the city's, and the nation's, finest examples of urban architecture — domestic, ecclesiastical, and institutional — front the small parks. Mount Vernon Place and its monument form the symbolic heart of Baltimore.

## PEALE'S BALTIMORE MUSEUM
### 225 North Holiday Street

Rembrandt Peale opened the first building in the United States designed and erected exclusively as a museum and art gallery on August 15, 1814. According to an early advertisement, its first-floor rooms displayed "birds, beasts...Indian Dresses...and Miscellaneous Curiosities," and the second-floor gallery showed Peale's own works.

Visitors had to pay an extra quarter to see two wax statues, *The Grecian Beauty* and *The Dream of Love*. The museum, designed by Baltimore architect Robert Cary Long, Sr., resembles a three-story brick town house, but has a monumental frontispiece. It served as Baltimore's city hall from 1830 until 1875 and has been the city's municipal museum since 1931.

## PHOENIX SHOT TOWER
### Southeast corner of Fayette and Front Streets

Built in 1828, this tapering red brick tower is one of a very few shot towers left in the United States. Shot was manufactured by dropping molten lead from the top of the 14-story tower through a sievelike device. The lead formed itself into shot during its descent and hardened when it was quenched in a vat of cold water at the base of the tower. The shot tower was the tallest structure in the United States until work was resumed on the Washington Monument in the District of Columbia after the Civil War. It remained in operation until 1892 and continues as a major landmark in downtown Baltimore.

## EDGAR ALLAN POE HOUSE
### 203 Amity Street

Edgar Allan Poe lived in this small brick

town house with members of his family for two years, from 1833 to 1835. During this period, his short stories were beginning to attract favorable critical attention, and it was while living here that he courted his future wife, Virginia. The house, owned by the city and open as a museum, commemorates an important phase in the career of one of America's most famous writers.

## IRA REMSEN HOUSE
### 214 Monument Street

Researcher, author of seminal chemistry textbooks, chair of the chemistry department and later president of Johns Hopkins University, Ira Remsen was a major influence in American science at the turn of the century. A brilliant teacher, he followed his lectures on chemistry with laboratory exercises, a pedagogical technique that was adopted throughout the country. From ca. 1901 until 1925, this red-brick row house was his home.

## HENRY AUGUST ROWLAND HOUSE
### 915 Cathedral Street

This brick Baltimore row house was the home of America's best-known and most accomplished 19th-century physicist. Rowland's most important contribution to science was in the area of electromagnetism. A cohort stated that he "anticipated all others in the discovery and announcement of the beautifully simple law of the magnetic circuit." His work formed the foundation for the calculations necessary for designing dynamos and transformers. Rowland also shaped the Johns Hopkins Physics Department into a model that influenced other universities across the country.

## SAINT MARY'S SEMINARY CHAPEL
### 600 North Paca Street

Designed by French architect Maximilien Godefroy, at the time a resident of Baltimore, this is the nation's first neo-Gothic church. Built in 1806–1808, it started what became a virtual architectural avalanche of Gothic churches across the country. The small brick chapel was constructed for the Sulpician priests of Saint Mary's Seminary, founded in 1791 as the country's first Catholic seminary. A small Federal style brick house adjacent to

the chapel is also part of the Landmark designation. Elizabeth Ann Seton, sainted in 1975, organized the Daughters and Sisters of Charity while living here from 1808–1809.

## STAR-SPANGLED BANNER FLAG HOUSE
### 844 East Pratt Street

Baltimore had its own "Betsy Ross." It was in this small brick house that Mary Young Pickersgill, helped by her mother and her niece, designed and fabricated the huge American flag that flew over Fort McHenry during the British attack of September 13–14, 1814. Seeing that its "broad stripes and bright stars" still waved "in the dawn's early light," Francis Scott Key was inspired to compose "The Star-Spangled Banner." The house, now owned by the city, is maintained as a museum and contains Mary's $405.90 invoice for her work. The Star-Spangled Banner itself, measuring 42 by 30 feet and the world's largest flag when it was completed, now hangs proudly in the National Museum of American History in Washington, D. C.

## TANEY
### 1101 Key Highway, Inner Harbor

Commissioned as the *Roger B. Taney*, this is the only surviving warship afloat that was at Pearl Harbor on December 7, 1941, when the Pacific Fleet was attacked. *Taney* is one of two preserved Secretary class cutters, considered the most successful class of large cutters built by the U.S. Coast Guard. Secretary class cutters were named after secretaries of the U.S. Treasury, under whose jurisdiction the Coast Guard operates except during wartime. *Taney* steamed into the Atlantic for convoy duty in 1944, but returned to the Pacific in 1945 to participate in the Okinawa campaign and the occupation of Japan. After service in Vietnam, *Taney* was decommissioned in 1986 and is now an exhibit at the Baltimore Maritime Museum.

## TORSK
### Pier 4, Pratt Street

A World War II Tench class submarine that sank two Japanese coastal defense ships on August 14, 1945, *Torsk* is credited with firing the last two torpedoes and sinking the last combatant ships of the war. After the war, *Torsk*'s operations as a training vessel helped it establish a world record of 11,884 dives. *Torsk* is now a museum ship at the Baltimore Maritime Museum.

## WILLIAM HENRY WELCH HOUSE
**935 Saint Paul Street**

From 1884 to 1916, William Henry Welch was professor of pathology at Johns Hopkins University. During his tenure he transformed American medical research and teaching and became known as the dean of American medical science. Under his aegis at Hopkins, areas of investigation such as pathology and bacteriology became disciplines in their own right. Welch lived in an apartment in this Baltimore row house from ca. 1891 until 1908, the years during which he contributed so much to his chosen field.

### ■ *Calvert County*

## WILLIAM B. TENNISON
**Back Creek, Solomons Harbor, Solomons Island**

Built in 1899, *Tennison* is the last bugeye oyster buy-boat on the Chesapeake Bay, one of the first bugeyes to be converted to power, and one of the few log-hulled vessels remaining. Bugeyes dredged more oysters than any other vessel type in the world, but as the Chesapeake oyster harvest began to wane, smaller, more easily handled, and cheaper skipjacks replaced them. Bugeyes like *Tennison* then became buy-boats, purchasing catches from the skipjacks. Off-season, they hauled produce, lumber, and even livestock to markets in Baltimore, Norfolk, Richmond, and Washington. *Tennison* is now a floating exhibit at the Calvert Marine Museum.

### ■ *Carroll County*

## WHITTAKER CHAMBERS FARM
**East Saw Mill Road, Westminster**

In 1948, Whittaker Chambers, ex–Communist Party member and *Time* magazine editor, charged that former State Department official Alger Hiss had also been a Communist and an espionage agent during the 1930s. At his farm Chambers produced the famous "pumpkin papers," actually microfilmed copies of State Department papers he said Hiss had given him to pass to a Soviet agent, that he had hidden in a hollow pumpkin. Hiss was convicted of perjury in 1950. His trial polarized public opinion and hardened Cold War attitudes. The affair also brought young congressman Richard Nixon to national prominence and inspired senator Joseph McCarthy's excessive charges of Communist influence in the State Department. Chambers lived on the farm, where he also wrote his autobiography, *Witness,* from 1941 to his death in 1961.

### ■ *Cecil County*

## OLD LOCK PUMP HOUSE, CHESAPEAKE AND DELAWARE CANAL
**U.S. Route 213, Chesapeake City**

Built in 1837 to house a steam engine, boilers, and pumps to replace water lost in opening and closing a nearby canal lock, this pump house improved the operation of a key section of this vital transportation artery. Although the pump house has not been operational since 1926, the U. S. Corps of Engineers has preserved it virtually intact. It still contains two early steam engines (1851, 1854) and the great lift wheel. The pump house gains added distinction as one of the nation's first engineering monuments to be recognized and preserved.

### ■ *Charles County*

## HABRE-DE-VENTURE (NPS)
**Rose Hill Road, near the junction of Maryland Routes 225 and 6, Port Tobacco**

This informally arranged brick and frame house was the home of Thomas Stone, member of the Continental Congress and a signer of the Declaration of Independence from Maryland. The central section of the five-part structure that Stone began in 1771 burned in 1977 but has since been stabilized. In addition to the house, the property includes several early agricultural buildings and a small family graveyard where Stone is buried. The property is now the Thomas Stone National Historic Site.

## ■ Frederick County
### MONOCACY BATTLEFIELD (NPS)
**Southeast of Frederick**

Confederates under General Jubal Early repulsed Union troops commanded by General Lew Wallace during a three-day battle here in July 1864. Wallace's troops delayed Early's forces, however, thus giving the Union army time to prepare defenses around Washington and preventing it from falling into Confederate hands.

## ■ Garrett County
### CASSELMAN BRIDGE, NATIONAL ROAD
**East of Grantsville on U.S. Route 40**

The National Road, authorized in 1806 and completed from Cumberland to Wheeling in 1818, was the federal government's first experiment in public highway construction. It provided ready access across the formidable Appalachians and greatly stimulated the development of regions to the west. This 1813 bridge was an integral part of the road, carrying it over the Casselman River on a single stone arch, the largest in the country when it was built. U.S. Route 40 now supplants the National Road, and a later bridge carries it across the Casselman River just south of the old span. A park now surrounds the old stone bridge.

## ■ Harford County
### SION HILL
**2026 Level Road, Havre de Grace**

Beautifully sited overlooking the point where the Susquehanna River broadens to form the Chesapeake Bay, this privately owned early-19th-century Federal style brick mansion is the seat of the seafaring Rodgers family. Five generations of the clan, most of them named John, were involved in virtually every aspect of American naval history. Commodore John Rodgers fought the Barbary pirates during Thomas Jefferson's presidency. Later, Admiral John Rodgers brought wireless telegraphy to the Navy, and Commander John Rodgers was the first commandant of the air base at Pearl Harbor.

## ■ Howard County
### DOUGHOREGAN MANOR
**On Manor Lane, 8 miles west of Ellicott City**

From 1766 to 1832, Doughoregan Manor was the country home of Charles Carroll of Carrollton, a signer of the Declaration of Independence and delegate to the Continental Congress. A member of a wealthy Catholic family, Carroll lies buried in the chapel attached to the north end of the mansion. The Georgian brick plantation house, built by Carroll's father, was enlarged and remodeled by his son in the 1830s in the Greek Revival style. Doughoregan remains in Carroll family ownership and is the center of a large private estate.

### ELLICOTT CITY STATION
**South of the Patapsco River Bridge, Ellicott City**

Built in 1830–1831, this small cut-stone structure is the oldest railroad station in the United States still in use. It served as the western terminus of the original 13-mile section of the Baltimore & Ohio Railroad and has remained little changed since it was completed. The locomotive Tom Thumb raced a horse-drawn cart over the line in August 1830, but lost because of mechanical failure. Regularly scheduled service between Ellicott City and Baltimore in the 1830s provided passengers the exhilarating experience of traveling at speeds ranging from 18 to 20 miles per hour. (See Baltimore & Ohio Transportation Museum and Mount Clare Station, Baltimore City.)

### THOMAS VIADUCT, BALTIMORE & OHIO RAILROAD
**Over the Patapsco River between Relay and Elkridge**

(See entry under Baltimore County.)

## ■ Kent County
### CHESTERTOWN HISTORIC DISTRICT
**Bounded by the Chester River, Cannon Street, Maple Avenue, and Cross Street, Chestertown**

Chestertown flourished in the second half of the 18th century as the chief tobacco and wheat port of Maryland's Eastern Shore. During this prosperous period wealthy merchants, planters, and shippers constructed elaborate brick Georgian town houses that still dominate the townscape. Many of the best, and best preserved, are on Water Street, their back yards extending to the banks of the Chester River.

## NELLIE CROCKETT
### Sassafras River, Georgetown

Nellie Crockett, built in 1926 and named for a daughter of its first owner, is a classic example of a frame-and-plank buy-boat, a vessel type that has been termed the tractor-trailer of the Chesapeake. Captains of buy-boats bought oysters directly from dredges and transported them to the docks for sale. Before refrigeration, adequate roads, and railroads became the norm, buy-boats such as Nellie were indispensable to the economic life cycle of the Chesapeake, and to bringing America's favorite bivalves to market.

### ■ Montgomery County
## CLARA BARTON HOUSE (NPS)
### 5801 Oxford Road, Glen Echo

Clara Barton was the "Angel of the Battlefield" to both sides during the Civil War. Exhausted by her work healing the troops, she went to Switzerland to regain her health, but instead found herself on other battlefields, this time in the Franco-Prussian War. Impressed with the work of the International Red Cross during that conflict, she returned home with a mission: to per-

suade her country to establish an American Red Cross. This she did, and this large frame house, originally built to store Red Cross supplies, became Barton's home in 1897. It also served as the organization's headquarters until she retired in 1904. Barton continued to live here until her death in 1912. The home of this great humanitarian is now a National Historic Site and open to the public.

## RACHEL CARSON HOUSE
### 11701 Berwick Road, Silver Spring

Rachel Louise Carson, biologist, naturalist, writer, and poet, designed this one-story brick "ranch house" and lived in it from 1956 until her death in 1964. While here she wrote Silent Spring (1962). This seminal book helped to change the way Americans regard their natural environment and to inaugurate the modern environmental movement. Silent Spring sounded an alarm by drawing popular attention to the poisoning of the earth and showing how the indiscriminate use of chemical pesticides and herbicides can endanger public safety.

## GAITHERSBURG LATITUDE OBSERVATORY
### 100 DeSullum Avenue, Gaithersburg

This tiny frame observatory, 13 feet square, is one of six in the United States, Russia, Japan, and Italy that are associated with an important and long-lived program of international scientific cooperation. The International Polar Motion Service, established in 1899 by

Rachel Carson House, Silver Spring, Montgomery County. Courtesy of National Coordinating Committee for the Promotion of History (Page Putnam Miller).

Gaithersburg Latitude Observatory, Gaithersburg, Montgomery County, ca. 1910. Courtesy of the City of Gaithersburg.

the International Geodetic Association, was a cooperative effort among scientists from around the world to study Earth's wobble on its rotational axis. The obsolescence of man-operated telescopic observation forced its closing in 1982, but the city of Gaithersburg acquired it in 1986, restored it, and maintains it as a historic site.

## WASHINGTON AQUEDUCT
### Great Falls

Built principally between 1853 and 1863 to supply water to the District of Columbia, the Washington Aqueduct is a testament to the engineering skills of Montgomery Meigs. Included in the system are a masonry dam at Great Falls, six bridges—one of them a 220-foot arch at Cabin John—a mile of tunnels, and 12 miles of conduit. Although the system has since been enlarged, Meigs's components continue to deliver water to the nation's capital. The aqueduct's construction was an early example of the Army Corps of Engineers' entry into public works projects (also in the District of Columbia).

## ■ Prince George's County
### ACCOKEEK CREEK SITE (NPS)
**Address Restricted, Accokeek**

Occupied intermittently from about 2000 B.C., this National Historic Landmark, on a low, sandy Potomac River terrace opposite Mount Vernon, is remarkable for its variety and concentration of human occupation sites. Accokeek included a palisaded village

that was occupied from ca. A.D. 1300 to ca. 1630. Archeologists have used the Accokeek Creek Site to define a culture-history sequence in prehistoric archeology for the Mid-Atlantic region.

## GREENBELT, MARYLAND, HISTORIC DISTRICT
**Roughly bounded by Edmonston Road, Beltsville Agricultural Research Center, Baltimore-Washington Parkway, and Greenbelt Road, Greenbelt**

Greenbelt was the first and largest of three government-sponsored planned communities in the United States built on the "garden city" principles and architectural ideals of the mid-1930s. These were sponsored as part of Franklin D. Roosevelt's New Deal attempts to pull the country out of the Depression and to solve the nation's housing crisis. Greenbelt was also intended to be a low-cost suburban community that would help decentralize the population of Washington, D.C. It was never fully completed as envisioned, but most of its Depression-era houses survive, surrounded by open spaces and carefully separated pedestrian paths and roadways. The studies that produced Greenbelt helped to establish regional planning as a discipline.

## HIS LORDSHIP'S KINDNESS
### 3.5 miles west of Rosaryville

Also known as Poplar Hill, this brick manor is a prime example of a five-part Georgian country house. Maryland manors are known for their intriguing names, but few are as appropriate as His Lordship's Kindness. The earl of Shrewsbury built the central block, dating from the 1730s, as a wedding gift for his niece, Ann Talbot, when she married Henry Darnall III. The hyphens and dependencies date from the end of the 18th century. The privately owned manor also contains a rare collection of early agricultural outbuildings.

## MONTPELIER
### 2 miles east of Laurel on Maryland Route 197

Montpelier, begun in the mid-18th century, was added to in the 1770s when the symmetrical hyphens and wings were built. What emerged is a distinguished example of a late-Georgian, five-part Palladian mansion. Its exceptionally fine interiors date primarily from the second building campaign. Formal boxwood gardens surround the mansion, and a rare 18th-century summerhouse, hexagonal in plan, stands at the end of an allée. George Washington spent the night of May 9, 1787, here on his way to the Constitutional Convention in Philadelphia. Two years later, Martha Washington stopped to partake of Montpelier's hospitality. She was on her way to New York to attend her husband's inauguration as president.

## RIVERSDALE MANSION
### 4811 Riverdale Road, Riverdale

Dating from the beginning of the 19th century, Riversdale is one of the last of Maryland's great five-part Palladian mansions. Of stuccoed brick, it was built for Belgian émigré Henri Joseph Stier and was for a time the repository of the Stier family's collection of Old World master paintings, once the most outstanding collection of its type in the country. Riversdale is also significant for its association with Charles Benedict Calvert, Stier's grandson. Calvert helped establish the Maryland Agricultural College on part of Riversdale's extensive acreage and was instrumental in the establishment of the federal-level Bureau of Agriculture, now the U.S. Department of Agriculture. Riversdale has been restored and is open to the public as a historic house museum.

## SPACECRAFT MAGNETIC TEST FACILITY
### Goddard Space Flight Center, Greenbelt

The heart of this facility, built in 1966, appears to be straight out of *Star Wars*. It is a 42-foot diameter coil system that makes it possible to determine and minimize the magnetic movement of even the largest unmanned spacecraft, and thus maintain

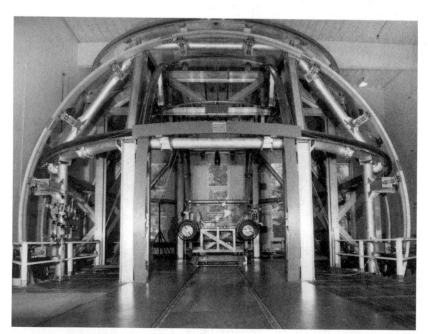

Spacecraft Magnetic Test Facility, Greenbelt, Prince George's County. Lunar Rover Vehicle Test, 1971. Courtesy of NASA, Goddard Space Flight Center Facilities Office.

satellites in orbit. The facility, the only one of its kind in NASA's inventory, is essential to the continuing success of the country's space program.

## ■ *Saint Mary's County*

### RESURRECTION MANOR
**4 miles east of Hollywood**

This venerable dwelling provides an excellent illustration of the evolution of a typical Southern one-room brick structure into a hall-and-parlor house. Located on one of the earliest manorial grants made in Maryland (1650), the first portion likely dates from ca. 1720. Resurrection Manor is a rare survival of post-Medieval architecture on the Mid-Atlantic seaboard. Unfortunately, as of this writing, it is neglected and deteriorated.

### SAINT MARY'S CITY HISTORIC DISTRICT
**Saint Mary's City**

Founded in 1634, America's third permanent English settlement served as Maryland's colonial capital until 1695. It is the only major 17th-century town site in the country that was never extensively built upon. Archeological excavations have uncovered a number of important vestiges of its history. A replica of

the 1676 State House was built in 1934, and plans call for the reconstruction of the brick chapel of 1638, the first Roman Catholic church built in the English colonies. Most of the site is included in the state-owned Historic Saint Mary's City.

### WEST SAINT MARY'S MANOR
**About 1 mile east of Drayden**

This brick-and-frame manor is a rare example of an early country house. Dating from the first third of the 18th century, it appears at first glance to be a small 1½-story cottage. Actually, it contains a double-pile plan: a broad central hall with two rooms on each side. West Saint Mary's represents the shift from earlier houses, with one- and two-room plans, to the more symmetrical arrangements of formal Georgian design. Located on the west bank of the Saint Mary's River, across from Saint Mary's City, the house is built on a portion of Maryland's earliest recorded land grant, dating from 1634.

## ■ *Talbot County*

### EDNA E. LOCKWOOD
**Navy Point, foot of Mill Street, Saint Michaels**

*Edna E. Lockwood* is the last Chesapeake Bay bugeye to retain its sailing rig and working

*Saint Mary's City Historic District, Saint Mary's County. Archeological remains of the Tolle-Tabbs House. Courtesy of Historic Saint Mary's City (Garry Wheeler Stone).*

appearance. Bugeyes are double-ended oyster dredges with hulls constructed of logs, a type unique to the Chesapeake Bay. *Edna's* hull contains nine heart-pine logs. The keel log is the heaviest, a design feature that aids in stabilization. Built in 1889 by master boat builder John B. Harrison, *Edna* dredged every oyster season from 1889 to 1967. *Edna* now serves as a floating maritime exhibit at the Chesapeake Bay Maritime Museum and on occasion sails around the bay as a museum ambassador, attending festivals and celebrations.

## HILDA M. WILLING
### Dogwood Harbor, Tilghman Island

Chesapeake Bay's skipjack fleet is the last commercial fishing fleet in North America that still uses sail power. The shallow-draft, centerboard skipjacks, specifically designed and adapted for use as oyster dredges in the Chesapeake Bay, were introduced in the late 19th century. Of the hundreds that once made up the fleet, only a handful remain. *Hilda M. Willing*, launched in 1905, retains its original appearance and is one of the best remaining representatives of its type.

## KATHRYN
### Dogwood Harbor, Tilghman Island

Soon after their introduction in the late 19th century, skipjacks became the preferred type of oyster dredges in the Chesapeake Bay. Their single-masted rigs and sharp-headed mainsails provided great power, even in light winds. During the first quarter of the 20th century, the skipjack fleet numbered in the hundreds. *Kathryn,* launched in 1901 at Chrisfield, is one of the earliest of the few that now survive.

## WYE HOUSE
### 7 miles northwest of Easton on Miles Neck Road

An outstanding example of a large Southern frame plantation house, this late-18th-century seven-part mansion illustrates the transi-

tion from late-Georgian to early-Federal architecture. The nearby orangerie, an extremely rare survival of an early garden structure where orange and lemon trees were cultivated, still contains its original 18th-century heating system of hot air ducts. Wye House was built for Edward Lloyd IV, a member of the family who obtained the property in 1658 and retained it for generations. (See Chase-Lloyd House, Anne Arundel County.)

### ■ *Washington County*

## FORT FREDERICK
### Vicinity of Big Pool

Built in 1756–1757 as a defense against French and Indian attack, this fort provided shelter for 700 people during the Pontiac uprising and was utilized as a prisoner of war camp during the Revolution. Fort Frederick was garrisoned again during the Civil War, but was never attacked throughout its long history of active service. In the 1930s, after archeological and historical research was conducted, the Civilian Conservation Corps restored the outer stone walls and the bastions at each of their four corners. The fort, now the centerpiece of a state park, survives as one of the largest and most complete frontier defenses in the South.

## KENNEDY FARM (NPS)
### Chestnut Grove Road, Samples Manor

During the summer and fall of 1859, "Isaac Smith" rented this vernacular stone, log, and frame farmhouse, five miles east of the U.S. Armory and Arsenal at Harpers Ferry. Smith, who soon revealed himself as John Brown, used it as his headquarters, stored arms in the house, and planned his October raid from here. Although Brown was captured, tried, found guilty, and hanged, his "soul is marching on." The house, now restored, is administered as part of the Harpers Ferry National Historical Park and is open to the public.

# MASSACHUSETTS

■ *Barnstable County*

## BLUE HILL METEOROLOGICAL OBSERVATORY
### East Milton

This observatory was founded in 1885 by meteorologist Abbott Lawrence Rotch as a weather station and research facility atop Blue Hill, the highest point in the greater Boston area. The site afforded a unique place for recording weather extremes, and Blue Hill soon took a leading role in the newly emerging science of meteorology. Many of the first scientific measurements of upper atmosphere weather conditions were accomplished here, and by 1895 weather forecasts based on wind velocities, air temperature, and relative humidity made at the observatory achieved remarkable accuracy. The observatory, its exterior resembling an ancient castle keep, is still in active use.

## LOUIS BRANDEIS HOUSE
### Neck Lane, off Cedar Street, Chatham

Louis Brandeis first gained public fame with his 1914 volume *Other People's Money and How the Bankers Use It,* a scathing attack on corporate power. His appointment by President Wilson to the U.S. Supreme Court two years later was an unequivocal endorsement of liberal reform and the worth of the individual. For 23 years, until his retirement in 1939, Brandeis often stood against the Court's majority opinions, proving "not only the right to dissent in America, but also that dissent can be constructive." This shingled Cape Cod cottage, forthright in its structure and style, was the Brandeis family's beloved summer retreat.

## KENNEDY COMPOUND
### Irving and Marchant Avenues, Hyannisport

This well-known family enclave consists of six acres of waterfront property, including several commodious summer and vacation residences belonging to the Kennedy clan. The compound served as a "launching pad" for John F. Kennedy's 1960 campaign for the presidency, and one of the houses served later as his summer White House. The compound is still privately owned and continues to serve as "home base" for one of 20th-century America's most influential families.

## NAUSET ARCHEOLOGICAL DISTRICT (NPS)
### Address Restricted, Eastham

The Nauset Archeological District consists of six discontiguous sites located within Cape Cod National Seashore that contain deposits dating to the Historic Contact period between Native Americans and Europeans. References to some or all of these sites are found in journals of European explorers who visited the area in the early 17th century. French explorer Samuel de Champlain's 1606 map of Nauset Bay depicts many of the sites.

■ *Berkshire County*

## ARROWHEAD
### 780 Holmes Road, Pittsfield

This late-18th-century farmhouse was the home of Herman Melville from 1850 to 1863. While living here, Melville wrote *Pierre* (1852), *Israel Potter* (1855), and *The Confidence Man* (1857) and—most important—completed his masterpiece, *Moby Dick* (1851). Melville named his home Arrowhead after finding numerous Indian relics on the property. The Berkshire County Historical Society purchased Arrowhead in 1975 and maintains it as its museum and headquarters.

## CRANE AND COMPANY OLD STONE MILL RAG ROOM
### Off Main Street on the Housatonic River, Dalton

Built in 1844, this little stone structure represents the nation's oldest paper manufactory in continuous operation at one site. Here rags were brought and sorted as the first step in the papermaking process. Since 1930 the building, which originally formed a portion

*Crane and Company Old Stone Mill Rag Room, Dalton, Berkshire County. Courtesy of Crane & Company, Inc., Dalton, Massachusetts.*

*Hancock Shaker Village, Hancock/Pittsfield, Berkshire County. Round barn. Courtesy of NPS (Polly M. Rettig).*

of a multisectioned structure, has housed the Crane Museum of papermaking, documenting the early development of the American paper industry.

## W. E. B. DU BOIS BOYHOOD HOMESITE
### Route 23, Great Barrington vicinity

Only ruins mark the site of the boyhood home of prominent sociologist and writer William Edward Burghardt Du Bois. A major figure in the civil rights movement during the first half of the 20th century, Du Bois helped found the NAACP. He authored more than 20 books and several hundred articles. Du Bois was the first African American to receive a Ph.D. degree from Harvard, and his dissertation, *The Suppression of the African Slave Trade,* became the first volume in the Harvard Historical Studies. Du Bois owned the house on the site from 1928 to 1954 and spent his spare time and quiet moments here.

## DANIEL CHESTER FRENCH HOME AND STUDIO
### 2 miles west of Stockbridge

American sculptor Daniel Chester French once said of his Berkshire summer home and studio, Chesterwood, "I live here six months of the year—in heaven. The other six months I live, well—in New York." His architect friend Henry Bacon designed both house and studio, which were built at the turn of the 20th century. Chesterwood is open to the public, and the studio contains casts of many of his famous works, among them the *Minute Man* statue in Concord and the seated figure of Lincoln in the Lincoln Memorial in Washington, D.C.

## HANCOCK SHAKER VILLAGE
### U.S. Route 20, 5 miles south of Pittsfield

The Hancock Shaker community was organized in 1790–1792 and flourished between 1820 and 1860. When the community was dissolved in 1960, the nonprofit Shaker Community, Inc., was formed to acquire and protect the property and open it to the public. Beautifully restored, furnished, and interpreted, the buildings and grounds provide an unrivaled glimpse into the lives and times of their fervent builders. The stone barn, dating from the 1820s, is thought to be the first round barn built in the country. It was constructed to house 52 milk cows and the hay necessary to feed them.

## MISSION HOUSE
### Main and Sargeant Streets, Stockbridge

This frame house, reconstructed in 1928, was originally built in 1739 by John Sergeant, first missionary to the Housatonic Indians. It stands as an important example of Georgian architecture on the New England frontier and is known for its exuberant swan's neck pediment above the front door, the sole exterior ornament. Inside, the plan reflects its dual use as Sergeant's home and a place to meet with his converts. Mission House is open to the public as a historic house museum.

## THE MOUNT
### South of Lenox on U.S. Route 7

This elegant Georgian Revival mansion was the home of author Edith Wharton from the time it was completed, ca. 1902, until 1911. During this time two of her best-known works were published: *House of Mirth* (1905) and *Ethan Frome* (1911). The latter, a stark tale of rural New England, is set in a countryside much like that surrounding The Mount. Wharton was the first woman to receive the coveted Pulitzer Prize for fiction, which she won in 1921 for *The Age of Innocence*. The Mount, at one time used as a girls school, was purchased in the 1990s by a nonprofit group that is in the process of restoring it. It is open to visitors daily from Memorial Day through October.

■ *Bristol County*
## PAUL CUFFE FARM
### 1504 Drift Road, Westport

Paul Cuffe, one of America's most prominent African-Americans at the turn of the 18th century, was a self-educated man who became a prosperous merchant and ship owner. A Quaker, he pioneered in the struggle for minority rights, and was active in the movement for black resettlement in Africa. He lived in this still privately owned, wood-shingled house near the site of the docks where he launched his ships.

## ERNESTINA
### Foot of Union Street, New Bedford

Built in 1894, *Ernestina* is the oldest surviving Grand Banks fishing schooner and one of only two remaining *Fredonia* style schooners, the most famous type of American fishing vessel. *Ernestina* is also one of two Arctic exploration sailing vessels left afloat in the United States. After such serious service, *Ernestina* now relaxes on regular sailings along the New England coast on educational cruises.

## JOSEPH P. KENNEDY, JR.
### Battleship Cove, Fall River

USS *Joseph P. Kennedy, Jr.*, named to honor President John F. Kennedy's older brother, is the sole remaining example of the *Gearing* class of destroyers. Although none in the *Gearing* class was built in time to see much World War II service, the class represented the ultimate stage in World War II destroyer design. After serving off Korea and with NATO forces, *Kennedy* steamed to Washington to participate in John F. Kennedy's inaugural festivities. *Kennedy* came to Fall River's Battleship Cove in 1974 and was commandeered to be headquarters of Tin Can Sailors, Inc., a national destroyermen's organization. The destroyer is currently on exhibit alongside naval National Historic Landmarks *Massachusetts, Lionfish*, PT 617, and PT 796.

## LIONFISH
### Battleship Cove, Fall River

USS *Lionfish* is an intact example of the standard fleet type, *Balao* class submarine that played an important part in World War II. *Lionfish* made two patrols in the Pacific during the war, receiving one battle star for its service. *Lionfish* is now on display at Fall River's Battleship Cove, along with National Historic Landmarks *Joseph P. Kennedy, Jr., Massachusetts*, PT 617, and PT 796.

## MASSACHUSETTS

### Battleship Cove, Fall River

One of two surviving *South Dakota* class battleships planned in anticipation of war during the 1930s, *Massachusetts* was built in the state for which it is named and was launched in 1941. *Massachusetts* saw action in both the European and Pacific theaters of World War II, and at war's end had earned 11 battle stars for combat service. The ship is the commonwealth's official memorial to its World War II casualties and is now the featured attraction at Battleship Cove in Fall River.

## NEW BEDFORD HISTORIC DISTRICT (NPS)

### Bounded by Water, Front, and Elm Streets, Acushnet Avenue, and Commercial Street, New Bedford

By 1840, New Bedford, located on the mainland, superseded Nantucket Island as the nation's leading whaling port. Within the subsequent decade, New Bedford became home port for half the nation's whaling ships and the wealthiest city in the country per capita. This nautically oriented historic district includes a number of 19th-century buildings attesting to the city's days of glory as a whaling port, including Seamen's Bethel, the chapel that Herman Melville described in Moby Dick. The area is now New Bedford Whaling National Historical Park.

## PT 617

### Battleship Cove, Fall River

Built in 1945 by the Electric Boat Company (Elco) at Bayonne, New Jersey, PT 617 is the only remaining 80-foot Elco type Patrol Torpedo boat, the most heavily used type of PT boat during World War II. Highly effective craft, PT boats were built in large numbers to harass enemy supply lines and shore installations. Involved in nearly every Pacific campaign, PT boats also participated in operations in the Aleutians, the English Channel, and the Mediterranean theater of war. PT 617 is now a museum vessel at Battleship Cove with the *Massachusetts, Joseph P. Kennedy, Lionfish,* and PT 796.

## PT 796

### Battleship Cove, Fall River

The best preserved of the three surviving Higgins type PT boats, PT 796 represents one of the two major types of Patrol Torpedo boats used in combat during World War II. PT 796 participated in President John F. Kennedy's inaugural parade in January 1961, playing the part of PT 109. PT 796 is on display at Battleship Cove with PT 617, *Massachusetts, Joseph P. Kennedy,* and *Lionfish.*

## H. H. RICHARDSON HISTORIC DISTRICT

### Bounded by Main Street, Elm Street, and the railway right-of-way off Oliver Street, North Easton

Thanks to the patronage of the Ames family, North Easton is a treasure trove of Henry Hobson Richardson's Romanesque Revival architecture. Included in this discontiguous historic district are his Oliver Ames Free Library, Oakes Ames Memorial Hall, Frederick Lothrop Ames Gate Lodge, F. L. Ames Gardener's Cottage, and Old Colony Railroad Station, all built between 1877 and 1885. The Ames family fortune stemmed in part from the California gold rush, when their already established shovel factory geared up production to supply their products to the miners.

## UNITED STATES CUSTOM HOUSE

### Southwest corner of Second and Williams Streets, New Bedford

Designed by nationally prominent architect Robert Mills and constructed in 1834–1836, this granite building achieves a monumentality through skillful handling of proportions and details. A pedimented Greek Doric portico centers the facade, and its full entablature continues around the building. The Custom House is symbolic of the era when New Bedford was a major port and adds architectural distinction to the New Bedford Historic District, another National Historic Landmark.

## ◼ *Dukes County*

## FLYING HORSES CAROUSEL

### 33 Oak Bluffs Avenue, Oak Bluffs

This is the oldest operating platform carousel in the country and may well be the oldest carousel of any type in the United States. It is one of two surviving examples built by carousel manufacturer Charles W. F. Dare

Company. Its 20 prancing horses and four chariots have delighted summer visitors of all ages to Oak Bluffs on Martha's Vineyard since 1884. The horses still prance during summer months.

## ■ *Essex County*

### ADVENTURE
**Harbor Loop, Gloucester**

*Adventure* is one of only two surviving dory trawling fishing schooners and represents the last group of vessels built in America for deep water sailing. Built in Essex in 1926, *Adventure* worked the North Atlantic banks until 1954. In 1943, its best year, *Adventure* landed a catch worth $364,000, making more profit than any other east coast fishing vessel of its time. *Adventure* was retired in 1954 and in 1988 was donated to Gloucester Adventure, Inc., a group formed to save the vessel. *Adventure* now regularly sails the Massachusetts coast, keeping its name and tradition alive.

### BOARDMAN HOUSE
**Howard Street, Saugus**

Built ca. 1687, this classic New England saltbox is typical of the late-17th-century, post-Medieval frame dwellings constructed by English colonists. The second floor has a pronounced overhang, and there is a massive central chimney. Much of the original framework and interior finishes remain, making the Boardman House a prime document for the study of early American architecture and construction methods. The house is open to the public.

### NATHANIEL BOWDITCH HOME
**9 North Street, Salem**

From 1811 to 1823 this three-story frame house was the home of Nathaniel Bowditch, a fascinating figure in the history of American science and navigation. Something of an "editor extraordinaire," he uncovered 8,000 errors in an 1800 English volume, *The Practical Navigator,* and two years later published *The New American Practical Navigator.* Not surprisingly, this supplanted the older work as a standard manual for seamen the world over. For years afterward sailors left port armed with a "Testament, a Bowditch, a quadrant, a chest of sea clothes, and a mother's blessing."

### PARSON CAPEN HOUSE
**Howlett Street, Topsfield**

This remarkable survivor, one of the best-preserved large 17th-century New England frame houses, has the date June 18, 1683, carved on a second-story beam, or girt. The mortised and tenoned oak frame, with its typical second-story overhang, rests on a foundation of unmortared fieldstones. "Parson" Capen—the Reverend Joseph Capen—was called to the pastorate at Topsfield in 1681, at the age of 23. His house was restored in 1913 and is operated as a historic house museum.

### CASTLE HILL
**Argilla Road, Ipswich**

Castle Hill is fittingly named. Overlooking the New England coast from its isolated hill, the baronial brick Georgian Revival mansion was built in the 1920s as a summer house for plumbing magnate Richard Teller Crane, Jr. It survives as a preeminent example of the American "country house," typically a large-scale complex with a main house surrounded by formal grounds, recreational facilities, greenhouses, and support buildings. Such establishments served the well-to-do as comfortable rural retreats from the increasingly crowded industrialized cities. Castle Hill is also significant for its well-preserved examples of the work of seven nationally known architects and landscape architects, including David Adler, Shepley, Rutan & Coolidge, Olmsted Brothers, Arthur Shurcliff, Ernest Bowditch, Edward Burnett, and Harriett Foote. The house and grounds, maintained by the Trustees of Reservations, are open to the public.

### CALEB CUSHING HOUSE
**98 High Street, Newburyport**

Caleb Cushing, President Tyler's commissioner to China, negotiated the 1844 Treaty of Wanghia, securing for the United States diplomatic and trade privileges by opening five major ports, establishing consular offices, and paving the way for American interests in the Far East. Cushing's three-story brick house is a fine example of New England Federal architecture and is maintained by the Historical Society of Old Newburyport.

## DERBY SUMMER HOUSE
### Glen Magna Estate, Ingersoll Street, Danvers

This delightful architectural confection is a rare American example of a formal 18th-century garden house, or tea house. Full of Federal style decoration, it was crafted in 1793–1794 by noted Salem designer and carpenter Samuel McIntire for wealthy Salem merchant Elias Hasket Derby. John and Simeon Skillen of Boston carved the two life-sized wooden figures that top its pedimented gable ends: a gardener on the east and a milkmaid at the west. The pavilion was moved from its original setting in 1901 but survives in a properly bucolic garden setting at the Glen Magna estate, maintained by the Danvers Historical Society.

## GARDNER-PINGREE HOUSE
### 128 Essex Street, Salem

This elegant Federal style three-story brick town house was built in 1804–1805 and is generally considered the masterpiece of Salem architect and carver Samuel McIntyre. Its attenuated proportions, clean, crisp lines, delicate white marble trim, and low hipped roof, hidden behind a balustrade, are archetypical features. John Gardner, for whom the house was built, was a Salem merchant and sea captain. Later owners, the Pingrees, gave the house to the Essex Institute, which maintains it as a museum.

## GENERAL JOHN GLOVER HOUSE
### 11 Glover Street, Marblehead

From 1762 to 1782 this two-story frame house was the home of John Glover, who progressed from shoemaker, fish vendor, and merchant to the position of brigadier general in the Continental Army. Glover and his regiment of Marblehead mariners were responsible for the evacuation of American troops from Long Island and were with Washington when he crossed the Delaware. Glover and his men led the advance on Trenton and took part in the battle of Princeton. Later, Glover participated in the sieges of Saratoga and Newport. In 1783 a grateful Congress brevetted him a major general in recognition of his many services to the cause of independence.

## HAMILTON HALL
### 9 Cambridge Street, Salem

This architecturally distinguished Federal style assembly hall and social center was designed by Samuel McIntyre and built in 1806–1807. Hamilton Hall resulted from a political schism between Salem's Federalists and Republicans in 1805. Federalists erected the three-story building and named it after their hero, Alexander Hamilton.

## OLIVER WENDELL HOLMES HOUSE
### 868 Hale Street, Beverly

This large informal clapboarded house of the Victorian era was the summer home of U.S.

*Oliver Wendell Holmes House, Beverly, Essex County, ca. 1972. Courtesy of NPS.*

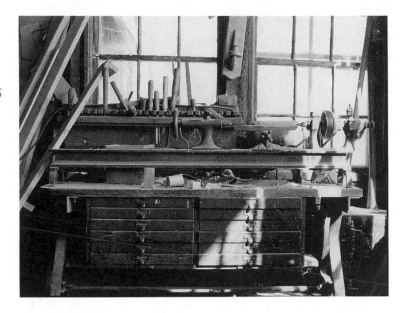

Lowell's Boat Shop,
Amesbury, Essex County.
Workbench. Courtesy of NPS
(J. Candace Clifford).

Supreme Court justice Oliver Wendell Holmes and his family. Holmes's eloquent minority opinions in decisions of the Supreme Court, on which he served from 1902 to 1932, earned him the title "The Great Dissenter." Those who admired him most dubbed him the "Yankee from Olympus."

## JEREMIAH LEE HOUSE
### 161 Washington Street, Marblehead

Built in 1768, the Jeremiah Lee House is one of the finest and most elaborate late-Georgian houses in the nation. Its frame exterior walls are scored, sanded, and painted to resemble ashlar stone blocks, and the interior contains finely carved woodwork. Mr. Lee, an ardent patriot during the Revolution, was a wealthy merchant-seaman. He undoubtedly enjoyed watching the activities of Marblehead's port from the glazed octagonal cupola astride the hipped roof of his mansion. The Marblehead Historical Society acquired the house in 1909 and maintains it as a house museum.

## HENRY CABOT LODGE RESIDENCE
### 5 Cliff Street, Nahant

Few congressmen have influenced the formulation of U.S. foreign policy as much as Henry Cabot Lodge, whose House and Senate career extended from 1887 to 1924.

Lodge advocated modernizing the navy, acquiring Hawaii, and building the Panama Canal and led the opposition to U.S. participation in the League of Nations. He always regarded Nahant as his place of residence. He first knew this stuccoed-brick villa in his youth, when his family used it as a summer home.

## LOWELL'S BOAT SHOP
### 459 Main Street, Amesbury

Established by Simeon Lowell in 1793, this oldest continuously operating boat shop in the nation remained in Lowell family ownership until 1976. Simeon Lowell is generally credited as designer and builder of the dory, America's most typical fishing boat throughout the 19th century and well into the 20th. Dories have been built at Lowell's, at the same site, in the same building, for more than 200 years.

## PEABODY MUSEUM OF SALEM
### 161 Essex Street, Salem

Founded in 1799 by the East India Marine Society at the height of Salem's maritime prosperity, this is the country's oldest continuously operated museum. East India Marine Hall, built in 1824–1825, along with an addition built in the 1970s, houses collections encompassing New England maritime history, Pacific ethnology, and the natural history of Essex County. By the mid–19th century Salem was no longer a major port, and in 1867, George Peabody provided a generous donation that enabled the Peabody Academy of Science to save the struggling East India organization and acquire its collections.

## PIERCE-NICHOLS HOUSE
**80 Federal Street, Salem**

This elegant late-Georgian house, begun in 1782, was the first important commission for 24-year-old Samuel McIntyre. In 1801, McIntyre remodeled some of the interiors, and together with his earlier work, the house illustrates his expertise in both Georgian and Adamesque decoration. The Essex Institute operates the house as a historic house museum.

## SAUGUS IRON WORKS (NPS)
**Central Street, Saugus**

The ironworks at Saugus, consisting of blast furnace, forge, and mill, operated intermittently from ca. 1648 to ca. 1670. Although ultimately not a financial success, it was one of the first such enterprises in the country, and workers and technicians trained at Saugus went on to establish other foundries. In the 20th century the site was excavated, the 17th-century ironmaster's house was restored, and other structures were reconstructed. Now the Saugus National Historic Site, the ironworks provides valuable insight into this early industrial venture.

## SPENCER-PIERCE-LITTLE HOUSE
**At the end of Little's Lane, Newbury**

Likely built ca. 1670, this is the best preserved of New England's few remaining 17th-century stone houses. The walls of the original cross-shaped building are two feet thick and are composed of granite interspersed with other stones and bricks, with a thick overlay of plaster. A frame wing dates from 1797. Along with an early barn on the property, this house with its accretions presents a rare glimpse of the continuum of New England life and architecture from earliest times to the present. The house is now a museum and is open in the summer.

## JOSEPH STORY HOUSE
**26 Winter Street, Salem**

As a Supreme Court justice from 1811 until his death in 1845, Joseph Story argued effectively for national supremacy over states' rights. His decisions helped consolidate the basis of the American nation, and he was widely regarded as the logical successor to become chief justice after John Marshall died in 1835. This was not to be, as Andrew Jackson, then president and a states' rightist, regarded him as "the most dangerous man in America." Also regarded as the father of Harvard Law School, Story lived in this mammoth Federal style brick house facing the Salem Common from 1811 until 1829. It is the only extant residence associated with the productive life of this remarkable jurist.

## ELIHU THOMSON HOUSE
**33 Elmwood Avenue, Swampscott**

English-born Elihu Thomson grew up in Philadelphia, where he and Edwin J. Houston developed a practical electric arc lighting system. Moving to New England when a group of businessmen offered to finance their work, Thomson continued to invent and develop new products. By 1890 the Thomson-Houston Electric Co. had become a leading manufacturer of electrical equipment. In 1892 the company merged with the Edison General Electric Company to become General Electric. Thomson built this imposing Colonial Revival mansion in 1889–1890 and lived here until his death in 1937. His family left the house to the town of Swampscott, which uses it as offices and an administration center.

## JOHN WARD HOUSE
**132 Essex Street, Salem**

Begun ca. 1684 and added to on several occasions by John Ward, its original builder and owner, this frame house is an excellent example of the organic, additive process by which most such dwellings developed: growing and changing as family needs and finances dictated. It was moved to the grounds of the Essex Institute in 1910 and restored in 1912. The Ward House is furnished and open as a historic house museum.

## JOHN WHIPPLE HOUSE
### 53 South Main Street, Ipswich

This venerable frame building with over-hangs, gables, and diamond-paned casement windows is one of New England's earliest houses. Begun ca. 1640, it is a remarkable example of the development of an early house over the years. Its three distinct units reflect the evolution of workmanship and detailing as Whipple descendants grew away from their English origins. The Ipswich Historical Society acquired the house in 1898, moved it to its present location on the Ispwich Green in 1927, and maintains it as a historic house museum.

## JOHN GREENLEAF WHITTIER HOME
### 86 Friend Street, Amesbury

John Greenleaf Whittier, author, editor, and abolitionist, lived and worked in this two-story frame house from 1836 until his death in 1892. Whittier composed a number of religious poems, many of which have been set to music and are sung as hymns. He is best known for his many short poems, such as "The Barefoot Boy" and "Barbara Frietchie," with their quotable lines. His most famous work is *Snowbound,* published in 1866. Whittier was also one of the most eloquent voices in the abolitionist cause, and on at least one occasion he was mobbed for his outspoken views. The Whittier Home Association maintains his house as a memorial to its famous occupant.

## ■ *Franklin County*

## OLD DEERFIELD HISTORIC DISTRICT
### Deerfield Village, Deerfield

When first settled in the 1660s, Deerfield was an extreme northern outpost of English America. Indian raids virtually destroyed the settlement on several occasions, but it was rebuilt each time, and by the 1750s Deerfield had become an important market town. Many of its colonial buildings have been preserved and are open to the public in one of America's most impressively restored and best-interpreted historic communities.

## ■ *Hampden County*

## EDWARD BELLAMY HOUSE
### 91–93 Church Street, Chicopee Falls

Journalist Edward Bellamy's historical significance lies in his 1888 book *Looking Backward.* An expression of utopian socialism, it has been called the "focus…of the whole movement of latter 19th century liberalism in America." Contradicting its title, the book describes a utopian American society in the year 2000. Bellamy's family moved to this frame house when he was two years old, and, except for occasional periods of absence, he lived here until his death in 1898.

## SPRINGFIELD ARMORY (NPS)
### Bounded by State, Federal, Pearl, and Byers Streets, Springfield

Even before Congress established this federal arsenal in 1794, it had played an important role in American military and industrial history. During the Revolution, arms were manufactured here and the facility served as a supply depot for the entire northeastern theater of war. Throughout the 19th century Springfield supplied the military with small arms, and when its companion armory at Harpers Ferry was destroyed during the Civil War, it became the nation's sole supplier. It remained so until 1904, when Rock Island Arsenal began to manufacture rifles. Springfield was phased out as a military installation in 1967–1968. The National Park Service now co-administers the property with a local community college and maintains a museum in the main arsenal building.

## ■ *Hampshire County*

## WILLIAM CULLEN BRYANT HOMESTEAD
### Bryant Road, 2 miles from Cummington

Poet, editor, and critic William Cullen Bryant lived in this rambling frame house until early manhood and made it his summer residence in the latter years of his life. It was here, at age seventeen, that he wrote the first version of his best-known poem, "Thanatopsis." The homestead, a late-18th-century farmhouse with Victorian additions and accretions, is open to the public during summer months.

## EMILY DICKINSON HOME
### 280 Main Street, Amherst

Emily Dickinson was born in this substantial brick house in 1830 and made her home here from 1855 until her death in 1886. More than most places associated with a particular person, the "mansion" and its grounds have an intensely intimate relationship with this reclusive poet. Contemporary reviewers were often bewildered by Dickinson's poems, with their metrical originality, fractured grammar, and obscure references, but over the years critical appreciation has steadily grown, and she is now recognized as a major figure in American literature. The house currently serves as a faculty residence for Amherst College but may be visited by appointment.

### ■ *Middlesex County*

## MARIA BALDWIN HOUSE
### 196 Prospect Street, Cambridge

Maria Louise Baldwin, one of America's most distinguished black educators of the late 19th and early 20th centuries, lived in this Greek Revival double house for 30 years, from 1892 to 1922. Baldwin established a national reputation as master of Cambridge's predominantly white Agassiz School. She was the only African American in New England to hold the position of school master during her years of tenure. Harvard University president Charles Eliot called her the best teacher in New England.

## GEORGE D. BIRKHOFF HOUSE
### 22 Craigie Street, Cambridge

George D. Birkhoff is regarded by many as the leading American mathematician of his generation. He began teaching at Harvard in 1912 and during his career earned practically every honor available in his field. Among his spectacular accomplishments was to solve Poincare's "last theorem," which his predecessor had posited but had been unable to answer. Birkhoff lived in this late-19th-century frame house from 1920 to 1928.

## BOSTON MANUFACTURING COMPANY
### 144 Moody Street, Waltham

This early-19th-century manufacturing complex of utilitarian brick structures represents the first truly modern factory in the United States. Here, for the first time, work was "integrated and mechanized...from raw material to finished product under a single management and within a single factory." This achievement signaled the birth of American industrialization and helped end U.S. dependence on British technology.

## PERCY W. BRIDGMAN HOUSE
### 10 Buckingham Place, Cambridge

Percy Bridgman lived in this early-20th-century house from 1928 until his death in 1961. Bridgman was a distinguished Harvard professor and physicist who received the 1946 Nobel Prize for his work. The Nobel citation acknowledged his "invention of [an] apparatus for obtaining very high pressures, and...the discoveries which he made by means of this apparatus in the field of high-pressure physics." Social scientists later adopted his concept of operational analysis.

## BUCKMAN TAVERN
### Hancock Street, east side of Lexington Green, Lexington

This frame tavern, already old at the time of the Revolution, not only heard "the shot heard round the world," it felt it. Because it was the local militia's headquarters, the British fired on it the morning of April 19, 1775, and it still bears scars left by their musket balls. This brief skirmish at Lexington marked the beginning of the armed struggle for American independence. John Buckman, proprietor of the tavern at the time, was one of the Lexington Minute Men. The town of Lexington acquired the tavern in 1913, and it is operated as a museum by the Lexington Historical Society.

## CHRIST CHURCH
### Garden Street

Christ Church was designed by Peter Harrison, one of colonial America's most skilled gentleman-architects. The frame Georgian structure was built between 1757 and 1761 and is one of the finest surviving 18th-century religious buildings in New England. The relatively simple exterior belies the refined elegance of the interior, where six

Ionic columns on each side support a tray ceiling. The church still houses an active parish.

## CONVERSE MEMORIAL LIBRARY
**36 Salem Street, Malden**

Henry Hobson Richardson's New England libraries are among the most notable expressions of his very personal version of Romanesque Revival architecture and are considered among his best works. The Converse Memorial Library, begun in 1884 and completed a year later, is the last of the group and the culmination of the type. Heavy archways and rows of windows are characteristic features, and an octagonal tower marks the juncture of the two arms of the L-shaped building. Richardson's libraries not only housed books, they functioned as community cultural centers, art and natural history museums, and lecture halls. One of the Converse's great treasures is its original Richardson-designed furniture.

## REGINALD A. DALY HOUSE
**23 Hawthorn Street, Cambridge**

Reginald Aldworth Daly, a native of Canada, earned a master's degree in geology from Harvard in 1893, and a doctorate in 1896. In subsequent years Daly investigated the entire spectrum of geology and became particularly noted for the application of physics and chemistry to his work. He died in 1957, having gained an international reputation for his contributions to the study of earth sciences. From 1920 until his death he lived in this frame and shingle-clad Queen Anne style house.

## WILLIAM M. DAVIS HOUSE
**17 Francis Street, Cambridge**

William Morris Davis was an outstanding geologist and geographer whose published works include more than 500 books and articles. In 1912, near the end of his career, he published a summation of his studies on the forces that shape the earth, essentially establishing the discipline of geomorphology. As one of his colleagues expressed it, Davis transformed the study of geography into a true earth science. A graduate and professor at Harvard, Davis lived in this shingled house, still a private residence, from ca. 1898 until his death in 1916.

## ELMWOOD
**Elmwood Avenue, Cambridge**

This three-story frame house, built in the late 18th century and altered early in the 19th, was the birthplace and lifelong home of James Russell Lowell. As first editor of the *Atlantic Monthly,* Lowell exerted a great influence on American literature. His literary achievements were matched by his diplomatic career, culminating with his appointment as ambassador to the Court of Saint James's in 1880. Before Lowell's occupancy, Elbridge Gerry, signer of the Declaration of Independence and vice president of the United States, but who will forever be remembered by the term *gerrymander,* lived in this house. It now serves handsomely as the residence of Harvard's presidents.

## RALPH WALDO EMERSON HOME
**Lexington Road and Cambridge Turnpike, Concord**

Ralph Waldo Emerson lived in this handsome, unpretentious frame house from 1835 until his death in 1882. After graduating from Harvard in 1821, Emerson became a minister, and although he left that calling in 1831, he continued to "preach" through poems, essays, and lectures. All his major works espousing and explaining his personal transcendental philosophy and his belief in the power of man to change for the better were prepared here. The house is maintained as a memorial to its famous occupant and is open to the public.

## REGINALD A. FESSENDEN HOUSE
**45 Waban Hill Road, Newton**

Reginald A. Fessenden, a multifaceted inventor, in 1906 became the first person to transmit the human voice and music by radio. He accomplished this through his spark transmitter, which he had developed and constructed in 1901. Fessenden also invented a fireproof insulation material, an early sonar system, and a gyrocompass. He lived in this three-story stuccoed-brick house from 1919 until his death in 1932.

## MARGARET FULLER HOUSE
### 71 Cherry Street, Cambridge

Margaret Fuller's *Woman in the Nineteenth Century,* published in 1845, has been called "the first considered statement of feminism" in America. Author, newspaperwoman, teacher, intellectual, and reformer, Fuller argued for the emancipation of women from every aspect of male domination. She once declared to Ralph Waldo Emerson, "I know all the people worth knowing in America, and find no intellect comparable to my own." She died with her Italian husband and two-year-old son in a shipwreck in 1850, when she was 40 years old. Fuller was born and reared in this house, which later became a settlement house called the Margaret Fuller Neighborhood House.

## GORE PLACE
### 52 Gore Street, Waltham

Built by Christopher Gore, prominent lawyer, soldier, signer of the Constitution, governor of Massachusetts, and U.S. senator, Gore Place is one of the nation's finest examples of a large country house of the Adam-esque Federal style. The five-part mansion, built in 1805–1806 from designs developed by Mrs. Gore and a Parisian architect, Jacques Guillame LeGrand, incorporates innovations seldom found in American architecture at the time. The entire west wing was the servants quarters, and the plan of the house is significant in demonstrating and interpreting the role and place of domestic labor. While employed by the Gores, African-American butler Robert Roberts codified rules and guidelines for household help in his publication *The House Servant's Directory,* one of the few guidebooks written by a domestic for other domestics. Gore Place is open to the public as a historic house museum.

## ASA GRAY HOUSE
### 88 Garden Street, Cambridge

Built in 1810 by the Massachusetts Society for Promoting Agriculture, this Federal style frame house is the earliest known work of architect Ithiel Town. Its primary significance derives from the fact that it was the long-term residence of Asa Gray: from 1842, when he became professor of natural history at Harvard, until his death in 1888. Gray was one of America's greatest botanists, and his writings launched the study of plant geography. In defending Charles Darwin's *Origin of Species,* Gray pleaded eloquently for scientific freedom. The house was moved from its original site in Harvard's Botanic Garden to its present site in 1910.

## HANCOCK-CLARKE HOUSE
### 35 Hancock Street, Lexington

The Reverend John Hancock built the rear ell of this frame structure in 1698, and his son Thomas added the front portion in 1734. Its designation as a National Historic Landmark derives from its association with Thomas's nephew, the great Revolutionary patriot John Hancock. When his father died in 1744, his uncle adopted him, and he lived here until 1750. Hancock, who would soon gain immortal fame for the size of his signature on the Declaration of Independence, and Samuel Adams happened to be spending the night of April 18, 1775, in the house, when Paul Revere came riding by around midnight. The revolutionaries were immediately whisked away to safety. The house was moved across the street from its original site in the 1890s, but was returned to its original foundations in the 1970s and is now open to the public.

## OLIVER HASTINGS HOUSE
### 101 Brattle Street, Cambridge

This handsome frame Greek Revival residence, with curved bays, elaborate cast-iron balconies, and low hipped roof crowned by a monitor, was built in 1844–1845. Originally the home of a Boston merchant, it now serves as apartments for the Episcopal Theological Seminary.

## LEXINGTON GREEN
### Massachusetts and Hancock Streets, Lexington

Sometime between midnight and one o'clock on the morning of April 19, 1775, Paul Revere arrived in Lexington, bringing word that British troops were on their way. The alarm thus sounded, Lexington's Minute Men assembled on the Green under the command of Captain Parker, whose orders were clear: "Stand your ground. Don't fire unless fired upon, but if they mean to have a war let it

*Oliver Hastings House, Cambridge, Middlesex County, 1970. Courtesy of NPS.*

*Longfellow House, Cambridge, Middlesex County, 1967. Courtesy of NPS (Charles W. Snell).*

begin here!" Gunfire ensued, and the Revolution had begun. Still a public space, the Lexington Green contains a number of memorials, among them the well-known bronze statue titled *Lexington Minute Man*.

## ARTHUR D. LITTLE, INC., BUILDING
### 30 Memorial Drive, Cambridge

Arthur D. Little, Inc., is the nation's first, and one of its most successful, independent commercial research laboratories. The company was founded in the late 19th century to advise on processes in the papermaking industry and has made numerous contributions to science and engineering over the years. This three-story building, located near the Massachusetts Institute of Technology

and resembling an early-20th-century school, was built in 1917 to contain administrative offices and laboratory facilities.

## LONGFELLOW HOUSE (NPS)
### 105 Brattle Street, Cambridge

This was the home of Henry Wadsworth Longfellow from 1837 to 1882. Widely regarded as one of America's greatest poets, Longfellow is remembered for "The Courtship of Miles Standish," "Evangeline," "Paul Revere's Ride," and "Hiawatha." His Cambridge home, a fine Georgian-style frame house, dates from 1759 and served as George Washington's Boston-area headquarters in 1775–1776. Now the major resource of the Longfellow National Historic Site, it is open to the public as a historic house museum.

## LOWELL LOCKS AND CANALS HISTORIC DISTRICT (NPS)
### Between Middlesex Street and the Merrimac River, Lowell

Lowell, founded in the 1820s, was one of the first cities in America to be developed entirely as an industrial community. Energy supplied by its abundant waterpower, carefully controlled by an intricate system of canals and locks, helped fuel the nation's industrial revolution. Lowell played a pivotal role in this growth and for years was the nation's center of cotton manufacturing. Lowell's virtually unaltered waterways, mills, and machinery constitute the most complete collection of early industrial structures and artifacts in the country. Those parts encompassed in the Lowell National Historic Park are open to the public.

## MASSACHUSETTS HALL, HARVARD UNIVERSITY
### Old Harvard Yard, Cambridge

As the oldest surviving building (1718–1720) at the country's first institution of higher learning (established in 1636), Massachusetts Hall is of undisputed national significance in the history of American education. Built as a dormitory, the early Georgian style brick building has three full stories and an attic fourth story lit by dormer windows in an expansive gambrel roof. Now surrounded by later, larger buildings at Harvard Yard, it remains the university's symbolic heart. America's oldest corporation, "The President and Fellows of Harvard College," meets within its walls.

## MEMORIAL HALL, HARVARD UNIVERSITY
### Cambridge and Quincy Streets, Cambridge

Memorial Hall is a bold, dramatic, and original example of a public building designed in the mature High Victorian Gothic style. The cathedral-like structure is identified by its polychromed brick walls and patterned slate roofs. Built in 1870–1878 as a living monument to Harvard's Civil War dead, it was designed by Boston architects William R. Ware and Henry Van Brunt to serve as a dining hall, theater, and memorial.

## OLD MANSE
### Monument Street, Concord

The Reverend William Emerson built this clapboarded house ca. 1770, and his family witnessed the opening salvos of the Revolution, fought at the nearby Old North Bridge, from its upstairs windows. Emerson's grandson, Ralph Waldo Emerson, lived here in 1834, and it was home to Nathaniel Hawthorne and his bride from 1842 to 1846. The house, with its many historical associations, is open to the public.

## ORCHARD HOUSE
### 399 Lexington Road, Concord

Amos Bronson Alcott, transcendentalist and educator, lived with his family in this unpretentious frame house for 25 years. During that time his talented daughter Louisa May wrote part of her best-known work here. *Little Women,* published in two volumes, was autobiographical in nature and an immediate success. After the second volume was published in 1869, Miss Alcott wrote in her journal, "Paid up all the debts...thank the Lord!...Now I think I could die in peace." Orchard House, which she dubbed "Apple Slump," is maintained as a historic house museum.

## ROBERT TREAT PAINE HOUSE
### 557 Beaver Street, Waltham

Henry Hobson Richardson's addition to Robert Treat Paine's summerhouse is one of the few surviving examples of his mature domestic style and is the largest and most monumental of his Shingle Style houses. The unique exterior combines a first floor constructed of glacial boulders with a shingle-clad second level. Expansive interiors predict the "open plans" more typical of modern architecture. Landscape architect Frederick Law Olmsted, who collaborated with Richardson, designed the extensive grounds of the estate. In 1974, Paine's grandson donated Stonehurst, as it was called, to the city of Waltham, and the property is now a house museum.

## THE PARSONAGE
### 16 Pleasant Street, Natick

"Virtue is always rewarded by wealth and

honor." Horatio Alger indoctrinated an enormous 19th-century juvenile audience with this comforting assurance in works such as *Ragged Dick* (1867) and *Tattered Tom* (1871). Alger's rags-to-riches stories reflected and reinforced the sentimental and materialistic values of his age. His father was pastor of Eliot Church in South Natick, and he summered here at the white-clapboarded parsonage for many years.

## REDTOP
**90 Somerset Street, Belmont**

William Dean Howells, prolific author, editor of *Atlantic Monthly,* and—most important—America's most influential literary critic at the end of the 19th century, lived here from 1878 to 1882. Howells inveighed against the typical romantic literature of his time, urging writers to espouse realism and to depict life as it was—warts and all. Nearly every important American author of the late 19th century visited this brick and stucco house that Howells commissioned architects McKim, Mead and White to design. The house is still privately owned.

## THEODORE W. RICHARDS HOUSE
**15 Follen Street, Cambridge**

Theodore Richards won the 1914 Nobel Prize for chemistry for his work in determining atomic weights. A Harvard professor, he was considered the foremost experimental chemist of his time. Also considered something of a "do-it-yourselfer," he assisted in building this idiosyncratic brick and shingled house, insisting on steel beams for strength and seaweed for insulation.

## ISAAC ROYALL HOUSE
**15 George Street, Medford**

What began ca. 1692 as a two-story brick house was transformed in the 18th century into what appears to be a large frame mansion. Isaac Royall began the process by remodeling and enlarging the house in 1733–1737, and his son finished the job in 1747–1750. The senior Royall's eastern facade displays rusticated quoins, and the son's western facade has fluted pilasters. Neither father nor son bothered to disguise the original southern brick end. No matter—the house, restored and open as a historic house museum, is an outstanding example of a 17th-century house transformed into a Georgian mansion.

## COUNT RUMFORD BIRTHPLACE
**90 Elm Street, Woburn**

Benjamin Thompson, born in Woburn in 1753, was a loyalist and became a British spy during the Revolution. Abandoning his American wife and child, he left Boston for England in 1775. There, and on the continent, he rapidly achieved fame and fortune. In 1784 he was knighted and honored as Count Rumford of the Holy Roman Empire. A man of many talents, he experimented with everything from stoves and fireplaces to carriages and coffee. He gained international recognition in 1798 when he disproved the then-prevailing caloric theory of the nature of heat. He also endowed a chair at Harvard and established the still-awarded Rumford Prize for "the most important discovery, or useful improvement, in any part of the continent of America, or in any of the American Islands on Heat or on Light." His birthplace, built by his grandfather in 1714, is a museum dedicated to his memory.

## SEVER HALL, HARVARD UNIVERSITY
**Harvard Yard, Cambridge**

Only a master architect such as Henry Hobson Richardson could design a building in his signature Romanesque Revival style and have it blend so well with its earlier Georgian and Federal style neighbors. Red brick, an overall horizontality, simple massing, and fenestration patterns—more formal here than Richardson generally employed—help make the 1878–1880 Sever Hall compatible with its Harvard Yard associates. Little altered, Sever still functions in its original use as a classroom building.

## MARY FISK STOUGHTON HOUSE
**90 Brattle Street, Cambridge**

This important example of H. H. Richardson's architecture is his most accomplished Shingle Style house, characterized by an overriding horizontality, informal fenestration, and

*Mary Fisk Stoughton House, Cambridge, Middlesex County, 1965. Courtesy of HABS (Jack E. Boucher).*

shingle-clad walls. As one of the architect's last works, it represents his mature style and indicates the stylistic directions he was taking before his untimely death. Mary Fisk Stoughton, widow of a former ambassador to Russia, who moved to Cambridge to live near her son, a member of the Harvard faculty, commissioned the house.

## PETER TUFTS HOUSE
### 350 Riverside Avenue, Medford

Built ca. 1678, this is an excellent example of a very rare New England building type: a 17th-century, pre-Georgian brick house. The house was extraordinarily large for its time, consisting of a double-pile plan: two rooms on each side of a central hall. Although there have been later alterations, the original fabric is still largely intact, and the house is open as a historic house museum.

## UNIVERSITY HALL
### Harvard Yard, Cambridge

A superb example of architect Charles Bulfinch's public architecture, this granite structure was built in 1813–1815 to serve primarily as Harvard's "Commons Hall." It originally contained four dining rooms— one for each class—all on the first floor, with a chapel and classrooms in the two stories above. Although the interiors have been altered over the years, the exterior remains largely as Mr. Bulfinch designed it.

## THE VALE
### Lyman and Beaver Streets, Waltham

Dating from 1793–1798, this is the finest extant example of an Adamesque Federal style country house designed by Salem architect Samuel McIntyre, and a rare remaining country house near Boston. A five-part composition, already quite ambitious, it was enlarged and remodeled in 1882 with the addition of another story atop each section. William Bell, an English gardener, designed the original landscaping, and his work remains largely intact. The original owner was Boston merchant Theodore Lyman, whose descendants maintained it until 1951, when they gave it to the Society for the Preservation of New England Antiquities. The Vale and its subsidiary buildings and grounds are open to the public.

## WALDEN POND
### 1.5 miles south of Concord

Henry David Thoreau, poet, philosopher, nature writer, and critic, spent the years 1845 to 1847 living in a simple one-room cabin on the shore of this 65-acre lake. His friend Ralph Waldo Emerson provided the property for Thoreau's experiment to "live away by the pond," where he hoped to meet "the great facts of his existence." Thoreau recounted his thoughts in the book *Walden, or Life in the Woods,* an American classic that tells of spiritual renewal achieved through contact with

*Walden Pond, Middlesex County. View across Deep Cove to Thoreau's cabin site. Courtesy of NPS (Polly M. Rettig).*

*The Wayside, Concord, Middlesex County, 1941. Courtesy of HABS (Frank O. Brazetti).*

nature. A rock cairn marks the cabin site. It and the pond are encompassed within the Walden Pond State Reservation.

## THE WAYSIDE (NPS)
### 455 Lexington Road, Concord

This rambling frame house, begun prior to 1717 but altered and extended over the years, was occupied by three acclaimed 19th-century authors and their families. From 1845 to 1848, Bronson Alcott's family, including his daughter Louisa May, lived here. Nathaniel Hawthorne and his family owned it from 1852 until 1868, and in 1883 Daniel and Harriet Lothrop bought it. Under the pseudonym Margaret Sidney, Harriet Lothrop wrote the *Five Little Peppers* series of juvenile fiction. The house, now part of Minuteman National Historical Park, is preserved and presented to the public as it appeared at the time of her death in 1924.

## WINN MEMORIAL LIBRARY
### 45 Pleasant Street, Woburn

Constructed from 1876 to 1879, this is the first in H. H. Richardson's series of New England libraries. Built of brownstone with sandstone and granite trim, the asymmetrical Romanesque Revival composition is dominated by a tall polygonal tower. A particularly ferocious gargoyle, an eagle with the mouth of a lion, guards the cavernous arched entrance alongside the base of the tower. The stack wing, with its barrel ceiling and arched alcoves, is among the most notable interior spaces.

## WRIGHT'S TAVERN
**Lexington Road, opposite the Burying Ground, Concord**

This colonial tavern witnessed two methods employed by American colonials in opposing English rule. The first was political: In October 1774, 300 delegates meeting here as the Provincial Congress of Massachusetts determined to cease paying taxes and to authorize provisions for armed forces. The second was military: On April 19, 1775, Minute Men gathered here in the morning, and British officers used it later in the day as a resting place. Amos Wright was the tavern keeper on that memorable day, and though he neither built nor owned the inn, it is named for him. The tavern is open to the public.

### ■ *Nantucket County*

## JETHRO COFFIN HOUSE
**Sunset Hill, Nantucket**

An archetypical example of a New England saltbox, this 1½-story frame dwelling with its tall central chimney dates from the late 17th century. Materials for its construction were shipped over to Nantucket from Exeter, New Hampshire, where Mr. Coffin's father owned timberland and a sawmill. The house was reconstructed in 1927 but survives as a text-book example of its type. It is open as a historic house museum.

## NANTUCKET HISTORIC DISTRICT
**Nantucket Island**

The name Nantucket derives from an Indian term meaning "far away land." During the century that lasted from ca. 1740 to 1840, "far away" Nantucket was the world's leading whaling port. Although the Nantucket Historic District encompasses the entire island, two major concentrations of historic interest are the towns of Nantucket, the finest surviving example of an early New England seaport, and Siasconset, where some of the island's earliest houses are located.

### ■ *Norfolk County*

## JOHN ADAMS BIRTHPLACE (NPS)
**133 Franklin Street, Quincy**

John Adams, signer of the Declaration of Independence, principal author of the Constitution, first vice president and second president of the United States, lived here from his birth (1735) until his marriage in 1764. Remarkably similar to the nearby birthplace of his son, it is a frame New England saltbox. Both properties are owned by the City of Quincy and maintained as museums by the Quincy Historical Society.

## JOHN QUINCY ADAMS BIRTHPLACE (NPS)
**141 Franklin Street, Quincy**

John Quincy Adams, sixth president of the United States, was born in this frame New England saltbox in 1767, next door to the birthplace of his father, John Adams. The elder Adams had moved here in 1764 and used one room as a law office for several years. In 1896, the Adams family restored the house for use as headquarters of the Quincy Historical Society and in 1940 deeded it to

*Nantucket Historic District, Nantucket Island, Nantucket County. The Old Mill. Courtesy of NPS (Patricia Heintzelman).*

*John Quincy Adams Birthplace, Quincy, Norfolk County, 1974. Courtesy of NPS (Polly M. Rettig).*

the city. The Society operates both houses as museums.

## ADAMS ACADEMY
### 8 Adams Street, Quincy

This rough granite building trimmed in brick is a superb example of the work of architectural partners William Robert Ware and Henry Van Brunt. Designed in 1869 in High Victorian Gothic style, it is the first American building based on principles established by French architect Viollet-le-Duc, whereby polychromed elevations are carefully arranged to reflect rational structural principles. Former president John Adams conceived the idea of the academy, gave the site, and provided the funds with which it was eventually built. The Academy was also designed to house a portion of his library, which he deeded to the town of Quincy in 1822. The building now serves as headquarters and library of the Quincy Historical Society and is open to the public.

## CRANE MEMORIAL LIBRARY
### 40 Washington Street, Quincy

Built in 1881–1882, this sturdy Romanesque Revival building is one of architect Henry Hobson Richardson's notable New England libraries. It is constructed of granite, with red sandstone trim delineating fenestration and floor levels. Eyebrow dormers punctuate the expansive slate roof. The sumptuous interior has handsome woodwork and notable stained-glass windows by artist John La Farge.

## FAIRBANKS HOUSE
### Eastern Avenue and East Street, Dedham

This picturesque dwelling lays claim to being the oldest frame house in the United States. Whether this is true or not, all three sections were built in the 17th century: the earliest ca. 1636, the second ca. 1641, and the last ca. 1654. Jonathan Fayerbanke [sic] built it, and his descendants have owned it ever since. The Fairbanks Family Association now maintains their remarkable house as a museum.

## CAPTAIN R. B. FORBES HOUSE
### 215 Adams Street, Milton

This three-story Greek Revival house, designed by Isaiah Rogers and built in 1833, stands as a testament to New England's extensive China trade during the early 19th century. Its owner, Robert Bennet Forbes, prospered during the Opium War, when the Chinese refused to trade with British vessels, but continued operations with American merchantmen. Inside, the Chinese Room is papered with imported wallpaper and furnished with Chinese pieces. In 1961 the house became the Museum of the American China Trade.

*Norfolk County Courthouse, Dedham, Norfolk County, 1972. Courtesy of NPS.*

## JOHN F. KENNEDY BIRTHPLACE (NPS)
### 83 Beals Street, Brookline

John F. Kennedy, 35th President of the United States, was born in this shingled frame house on May 29, 1917. His father had purchased the early-20th-century house soon after his marriage to Rose Fitzgerald in 1914 and sold it in 1921. In the 1960s, the Kennedy family repurchased it and furnished it to represent the time of the president's birth. The birthplace is now the John Fitzgerald Kennedy National Historic Site and is open to the public.

## GEORGE R. MINOT HOUSE
### 71 Sears Road, Brookline

George Richards Minot, one of the country's most distinguished pathologists, is noted for his discovery of a cure for pernicious anemia, a disease that previously had been considered almost invariably fatal. Minot's discovery that it could be cured by a diet rich in liver was the result of his long study of relationships between diet and disease. For his work, he and two colleagues shared the 1934 Nobel Prize in medicine and physiology. Minot lived in this handsome Brookline mansion from ca. 1929 until his death in 1950.

## NORFOLK COUNTY COURTHOUSE
### 650 High Street, Dedham

This Neoclassical granite courthouse, completed in 1827 and added to at the end of the 19th century, gained fame in 1921 as the scene of the notorious Sacco-Vanzetti trial. The trial was symbolic of the controversy aroused by rising American nativism and xenophobia in the post–World War I era. The guilt of the two men, both aliens and admitted anarchists, was presumed from the outset. Although evidence of their crimes — a robbery and murder — was largely circumstantial, they were convicted and sentenced to death. After six years of legal maneuvering, and despite massive public protests, they were electrocuted in 1927. The courthouse is open to the public.

## FREDERICK LAW OLMSTED HOUSE (NPS)
### 99 Warren Street, Brookline

Frederick Law Olmsted was America's preeminent landscape designer and environmental planner, and his designs became prototypes throughout the nation and beyond. He is perhaps best known for his design of New York's Central Park and Boston's "Emerald Necklace" of parks, but he also planned some 80 other urban parks, as well as parkways, suburban communities, and college campuses. In 1883 he moved to this small estate, which he named Fairsted, and lived and worked here until his death in 1903. The property, now open as the Frederick Law Olmsted National Historic Site, preserves a phenomenal collection of drawings and records of his numerous projects.

## JOSIAH QUINCY HOUSE
### 20 Muirhead Street, Quincy

The 1770 Josiah Quincy House is an outstanding example of New England Georgian architecture. The clapboarded frame house with quoined pilasters is noted for its delicate classical entrance portico and its monitor roof. Obscured from view behind a Chinese Chippendale balustrade, the monitor is the oldest known surviving example of this roof form in the country and was likely the seminal example from which others were modeled. The house, open as a historic house

*Old Ship Meetinghouse, Hingham, Plymouth County, 1967. Courtesy of NPS.*

museum, is also noted for its associations with four generations of Josiah Quincys and Eliza Susan Quincy, who helped shape the national political landscape and were prominent in education, commerce, history, and literature.

## UNITED FIRST PARISH CHURCH OF QUINCY (NPS)
### 1266 Hancock Street, Quincy

Designed by Alexander Parris and built in 1827–1828, this graceful church, constructed of Quincy granite, has one of the finest Greek Revival facades in New England. Behind and above its Doric portico, a square tower base containing a clock is topped by an open, circular belfry with a dome. Side walls, with arched windows, reflect earlier Georgian and Federal architectural traditions. Also known as the Stone Temple and the Church of the Presidents, this is the burial place of Presidents John and John Quincy Adams and their wives. John Quincy Adams was instrumental in its erection and bore most of the construction costs.

## ■ Plymouth County

## COLES HILL
### Carver, North, Water, and Leyden Streets, Plymouth

Coles Hill is the burial place of Plymouth colonists who died during the harsh first winter of settlement in 1620–1621, known as the "starving time." According to tradition,

burials took place at night, with graves disguised so that Indians would not know how dangerously weakened the colony was. Of the several sites associated with Plymouth's founding, only Coles Hill, named for a tavern keeper who had his business near Plymouth Bay, retains something of its original character. The hill slopes down to the bay, overlooking the traditional landing place of the *Mayflower.*

## GENERAL BENJAMIN LINCOLN HOUSE
### 181 North Street, Hingham

You lose some, you win some. In September 1778, after participating in a number of Revolutionary battles, Major General Benjamin Lincoln was appointed to the command of the American Army in the Southern department. He was forced to surrender Charleston, South Carolina, to the British in 1780, and after being exchanged as a prisoner of war, returned to service. In 1781, however, as Washington's second in command, Lincoln received the British sword of surrender at Yorktown. This expansive frame house was Lincoln's home from 1733 until his death in 1810.

## OLD SHIP MEETINGHOUSE
### Main Street, Hingham

This stalwart old building, begun in 1681 and enlarged in 1729 and 1755, is the country's only surviving example of a 17th-century Puritan meetinghouse. Built as the second meetinghouse of the First Parish in Hingham, it derives its name from the timber truss framing of its roof. Open to view from below, its many curved members resemble the inverted framework of a ship's hull, an appropriate design in this seafaring community.

## DANIEL WEBSTER LAW OFFICE
### Careswell and Webster Streets, Marshfield

Statesman, legal scholar, and orator Daniel Webster championed the Union throughout his multifaceted career. His famous Senate proclamation against nullification still rings loud and clear: "Liberty and Union, now and forever, one and inseparable." Webster used this one-room clapboarded building as his library and law office when he was away from Washington. Moved a half-mile from its original site in 1966, the law office contains Webster memorabilia and is open to the public.

### ■ Suffolk County

## AFRICAN MEETING HOUSE (NPS)
### 8 Smith Court, Boston

This brick meetinghouse was built in 1806 for the congregation of the "African Baptist Church," founded a year earlier. Built by black labor, the simple Federal style church was the first black church in Boston and is the oldest existing black church building in the United States. William Lloyd Garrison founded the New England Anti-Slavery Society here in 1832, and many leading abolitionists spoke from its pulpit. In 1987, the Meeting House was restored to its 1850s appearance. It is now the Museum of Afro American History and heart of the Boston African American National Historic Site.

## NATHAN APPLETON RESIDENCE
### 39–40 Beacon Street, Boston

Nathan Appleton was a pivotal figure in early American commerce and industry. In 1815, acting as agent for the Boston Manufacturing Company, he founded the first textile sales agency, establishing the precedent of separating manufacturing and marketing operations. Dubbed the "Great Manufacturer," Appleton helped shift New England's economy from its former commercial base to an industrial base after the War of 1812. His daughter Frances married Henry Wadsworth Longfellow at this residence. The elegant Beacon Street bowfront, one of twin town houses designed by architect Alexander Parris, was the home of the Women's City Club of Boston from 1914 to the 1990s.

## ARNOLD ARBORETUM
### 22 Divinity Avenue, Boston

This arboretum began as a tree farm for Harvard University in 1872 and is now considered by many to be America's greatest garden. It contains some 6,000 varieties of trees and plants that are hardy in the North Temperate Zone and is a preeminent institution for plant research. Harvard operates the 265-acre arboretum under provisions of a 999-year lease established in 1882 with the City of Boston. Forward-thinking as ever, Harvard's negotiators reserved the right to extend the lease for another thousand years when the current one expires. The Arboretum is open to the public.

## BEACON HILL HISTORIC DISTRICT
### Charles River Embankment, Beacon, Pinckney, Revere, and Hancock Streets, Boston

Platted and developed between 1795 and 1808, Beacon Hill remains one of the nation's finest and least-altered early urban environments. Primarily residential, the neighborhood contains elegant Federal and Greek Revival structures that have housed Boston's Brahmins for two centuries. Privately owned Louisburg Square is noted for its handsome bowfront mansions. Charles Bulfinch, who helped plan the original development and designed the Massachusetts State House that crowns the hill, also designed some of Beacon Hill's most important houses.

## BOSTON ATHENAEUM
### 10 Beacon Street, Boston

This is the largest of the nation's extant early proprietary libraries. Privately founded and funded in 1807, prior to the time free public libraries became the norm, it remains a leading research center for scholars of American history. Portions of the libraries of George Washington and John Quincy Adams, and—perhaps surprisingly—a huge collection of Confederate imprints, are among the Athenaeum's treasures.

## BOSTON COMMON
### Bounded by Beacon, Park, Tremont, Boylston, and Charles Streets, Boston

Set aside by the city of Boston in 1634, the 50-acre Common is considered the oldest public park in the United States. As early as 1660 it was used by citizens taking their evening strolls, until the nine o'clock bell "[rang] them home . . . [and] . . . the constables walked their rounds to see good orders kept, and to take up loose people." Some of the loosest people, or perhaps the loudest religious dissenters, were hanged here. The Common served as a political rallying point and military training field before and during the American Revolution and the Civil War. Later, a number of memorials and monuments were erected, including the well-known Robert Gould Shaw Memorial dedicated to the 54th Massachusetts Infantry, the Commonwealth's first regiment of free African Americans. With the adjoining Public Garden, also a National Historic Landmark, the Common remains one of Boston's most beloved civic amenities.

## BOSTON LIGHT
### Little Brewster Island, Massachusetts Bay, Boston

The southeastern tip of Little Brewster Island in Massachusetts Bay is the site of North America's first lighthouse. Built in 1716 by the Province of Massachusetts Bay, it was destroyed in 1776 by British forces evacuating Boston. The present 89-foot stone and brick tower, completed in 1783 by the Commonwealth of Massachusetts, incorporates parts of the original. Seven years later it was ceded to the federal government. The light is accessible from downtown Boston by boat, and visitors are welcome, but only during daylight hours.

## BOSTON NAVAL SHIPYARD (NPS)
### East of Chelsea Street, Charlestown, Boston

From 1800 to 1974 the Boston Naval Shipyard at Charlestown functioned as one of the most important shipyards in the country and as one of Boston's major employers. Its buildings, cranes, docks, and piers illustrate the industrial/technological revolution that established the United States as the world's greatest naval power. Modern ship design and construction were pioneered here, and for more than a century most of the Navy's rope was manufactured in the shipyard. The yard was decommissioned in 1974 and is now part of the Boston National Historical Park.

*Boston Light, Boston, Suffolk County. Courtesy of the U.S. Coast Guard.*

## BOSTON PUBLIC GARDEN
**Bounded by Beacon, Charles, Bolyston, and Arlington Streets, Boston**

In 1839 the first public botanical garden in the country was established on a portion of a large publicly owned tract of land immediately west of Boston Common. The 24-acre tract was landscaped during the 1860s and still retains the French Second Empire character established then. A six-acre pond is a principal feature, and in 1877 the famous Swan Boats, inspired by the *Schwanboot* in Wagner's opera *Lohengrin,* began plying its waters, using principles of bicycle propulsion. Like the Common, the Public Garden is a showcase of civic memorials and monuments. It is open to the public year-round, and the swan boats continue to operate daily during the summer.

## BOSTON PUBLIC LIBRARY
**Copley Square, Boston**

Built in 1888, this is the first major example of Beaux-Arts-inspired architecture in the country. Symmetrical in design, the monumental building resembles an Italian Renaissance palace. An unexpected feature behind its formal facade is the large interior courtyard. The Boston Library, designed by Charles Follen McKim and embellished with sculpture and murals by noted artists of the time, set a precedent for grand-scale urban libraries across the country. It is an architectural centerpiece of Copley Square.

## BROOK FARM
**670 Baker Street, Boston**

"Plain living and high thinking" were the aims of the Brook Farm Institute for Agriculture and Education, founded in 1841 by New England Transcendentalists as an experiment in communal living. The project was financed by a sale of stock, and Nathaniel Hawthorne was one of the shareholders. He left after six months, and the community was closed in 1847. Though short-lived, Brook Farm was one of the country's best-known communities of its type, largely because so many of New England's literary lights were associated with it. The property later became a Lutheran orphanage. No buildings remain from the Transcendental period.

## BUNKER HILL MONUMENT (NPS)
**Breed's Hill, Charlestown, Boston**

This monument marks the approximate center of a redoubt occupied by American forces during the June 17, 1775, Battle of Bunker Hill. Actually fought on Breed's Hill, where the monument is located, this was the first full-scale action between American militia and British regulars in the Revolution and proved to be the bloodiest single battle of the war. The British drove the colonials from their position, but their hard-wrought victory made them realize that the ensuing conflict would be longer and more difficult than they had envisioned. Solomon Willard designed the monument, a 220-foot granite obelisk, Lafayette laid its cornerstone in 1825, and it was completed in 1842. It is now part of the Boston National Historical Park. Visitors may climb to the top.

## CASSIN YOUNG
**Charlestown Navy Yard, Boston**

*Cassin Young* represents the many Fletcher class destroyers built by the Boston Navy Yard, exemplifying the intense military-industrial effort on the home front during World War II. The destroyer earned four battle stars and a Navy Unit Commendation at Okinawa and was the target of the last kamikaze (suicide) attack of World War II. *Cassin Young* is now a museum ship at Boston National Historical Park at Charlestown Navy Yard.

## CONSTITUTION
**Charlestown Navy Yard, Charlestown**

"Old Ironsides," the world's oldest commissioned warship, survives as a stirring symbol of early American naval skill and military might. Launched in 1797, it was one of six ships intended to protect America's growing maritime interests. *Constitution* fought French privateers in the Caribbean and Barbary pirates in the Mediterranean. The ship received its nickname in 1812 when it captured the British frigate *Guerriere*. One of its crew, seeing that shots fired from its opponent bounced off its heavy outer planking and fell into the sea, shouted, "Huzzah! her sides are made of iron!" *Constitution* fought in some 40 engagements without a loss and is now open to the public at the Charlestown Navy Yard in the Boston National Historical Park.

## ETHER DOME, MASSACHUSETTS GENERAL HOSPITAL
**Fruit Street, Boston**

This skylit operating theater on the top floor of Charles Bulfinch's Massachusetts General Hospital building derives its name and significance from an event that took place on October 16, 1846, that revolutionized the practice of medicine. Here ether gas was first successfully used in public to anesthetize a patient prior to surgery. When the patient recovered and reported he had felt no pain, the chief surgeon announced, "Gentlemen, this is no humbug!" The room served as the hospital's operating room from its 1821 opening until 1867. Classes and lectures are still held here, and it may be visited when not in active use. (See Massachusetts General Hospital.)

## FANEUIL HALL (NPS)
**Dock Square, Boston**

Given to the city by Peter Faneuil in 1740, Faneuil Hall, with its market and meeting hall, served as a focal point of Colonial protest against British rule. The hall was

Cassin Young, Charlestown, Suffolk County, 1944. Courtesy of the U.S. Navy.

Constitution, Charlestown, Suffolk County. Commodore's Quarters, 1934. Courtesy of HABS (Arthur C. Haskell).

enlarged from designs by Charles Bulfinch in 1805–1806 and later echoed the voices of leaders calling for the abolition of slavery. There are shops on its lower floor, and a public auditorium above still accommodates speakers of all causes. The "Cradle of Liberty," as the hall is familiarly known, is also the centerpiece of Faneuil Hall Market, Boston's impressive and successful renewal of its downtown commercial heart.

## FENWAY STUDIOS
### 30 Ipswich Street, Boston

One of the few studio buildings in the country designed and built expressly for the use of artists, and still serving its original function, Fenway Studios was conceived by Boston businessman and patron of the arts Eben Jordan. Built between 1904 and 1906 from plans by architects J. Harleston Parker and Douglas Thomas, the building met four requirements set out by the artists: north light, proper layout of rooms, a convenient location, and a sliding scale of rental fees. The exterior of the studios, still owned by the Fenway Trust that Jordan set up, followed tenets of the Arts and Crafts movement, with its commonsense design, respect for materials, and lack of historically inspired ornamentation. A number of prominent artists have been tenants here, among them Edmund Tarbell, Leslie P. Thompson, and Gardner Cox.

## FIRST HARRISON GRAY OTIS HOUSE
### 141 Cambridge Street, Boston

The first of three houses Charles Bulfinch designed for inveterate house builder Harrison Gray Otis, lawyer, mayor of Boston, and U.S. senator, this fine Federal style brick mansion dates from 1795–1796. It may be seen as the prototype for a distinguished series of three-story, three-bay Federal style mansions built throughout New England. Harrison sold the house in 1801 to build other houses, and the Society for the Preservation of New England Antiquities (SPNEA) acquired it in 1916. After a long-term restoration in the 1960s it was opened as a historic house museum. The Otis house also serves as headquarters for SPNEA.

## FORT WARREN
### Georges Island, Boston Harbor, Boston

This massive pentagonal fortification—its outer walls of Quincy granite are eight feet thick—was begun in 1834 to protect Boston Harbor. One of the nation's finest 19th-century coastal fortifications and the chief work of military engineer Sylvanus Thayer, it is strategically located on Georges Island, midway between the northern and southern arms of the harbor. Fort Warren is the most important Civil War site in New England, as it served as a prison for Confederate leaders and officers, including vice president Alexander Stephens. The fort, which can be approached only by boat, is open to visitors during summer months.

## WILLIAM LLOYD GARRISON HOUSE
### 125 Highland Street, Boston

William Lloyd Garrison was 19th-century America's most articulate and influential abolitionist. Through lectures and editorials in the *Liberator,* the newspaper he founded in 1831, he argued for immediate and unconditional emancipation for slaves. His unbending views earned him the title "Massachusetts Madman" from his foes, but by the time the Civil War broke out Garrison, more than anyone else, had established the moral nature of the conflict. He lived in semiretirement in this frame Roxbury house from 1864 to 1879, where he saw the ideals he had sought for so long take root. Formerly used as Saint Monica's Nursing Home, a facility for elderly women, the house is now part of the Saint Margaret Society Convent.

## CHESTER HARDING HOUSE
### 16 Beacon Street, Boston,

For four years, from 1826 to 1830, Chester Harding, one of the nation's great mid-19th-century portraitists, lived and worked in this brick house. Gilbert Stuart, himself an artist of no mean repute, complained of the "Harding fever" that temporarily eclipsed his own popularity. The house, four stories tall and quite large for its time, is now dwarfed by later commercial structures. It was renovated in 1963 as headquarters for the Boston Bar Association, which still occupies it.

## HARVARD STADIUM
### 60 North Harvard Street, Boston

Dating from 1903, this is the country's first college stadium. Its U-shape and arched openings became prototypes for other college stadiums, and its reinforced-concrete construction was a pioneering example of the use of that material. When completed, the stadium was the world's largest reinforced-concrete structure. Harvard played a major role in the development of intercollegiate football, and the stadium stands as a testimonial to generations of Crimson coaches and teams. It is still home to Harvard football and track events.

## SAMUEL GRIDLEY AND JULIA WARD HOWE HOUSE
### 13 Chestnut Street, Boston

During the three years the Howes lived here (1863–1866), they were key figures in Boston abolitionist circles and pursued other reform and humanitarian interests. Samuel Gridley Howe directed the Perkins Institution, formerly the New England Asylum for the Blind. Shortly after moving here, the couple went to Washington, and while staying at an army encampment, Julia composed a poem set to the rolling cadences of "John Brown's Body." It soon lived up to the title she gave it: "The Battle Hymn of the Republic." Their Chestnut Street house, built in 1804–1805 and privately owned, is typical of Beacon Hill's Federal style residences.

## KING'S CHAPEL
### Tremont and School Streets, Boston

Designed by Peter Harrison and built between 1749 and 1754, this is one of the most important surviving examples of ecclesiastical Georgian architecture in the nation. It was the first major building in British America to be built of stone and is the first recorded use of Quincy granite. The interior is particularly impressive with its fine Palladian proportions and elegant details. The church was built for Boston's Anglicans, but after the Revolution the congregation seceded from the Episcopal Church. In 1785 King's Chapel became the first Unitarian church in the country.

## LONG WHARF AND CUSTOM HOUSE BLOCK
### At the foot of State Street, Boston

Long Wharf, first built in 1710–1721, was the busiest pier in the busiest port in America during early colonial times. Nearly a half-mile long, the wharf epitomized colonial Boston's dependence on sea trade and travel. Custom House Block, a sturdy granite-fronted warehouse, was built on a portion of the wharf in 1848, at the zenith of Boston's 19th-century commercial prosperity. Together, the wharf and the block commemorate Boston's maritime and mercantile history. Today commuter boats and sightseeing tour vessels use the wharf.

## LUNA
### NDC Pier, Charles River, Boston

*Luna* is an early example of a diesel-electric-propelled vessel. Designed in Boston and built in Maryland in 1939, it was the flagship of the Boston Tugboat Company. *Luna* also saw service in New York, where it welcomed and docked famous ocean liners, among them *Queen Mary* on its maiden voyage. Now a museum vessel, *Luna* is being preserved and restored by the *Luna* Preservation Society in Boston.

## MASSACHUSETTS GENERAL HOSPITAL
### Fruit Street, Boston

Designed by Charles Bulfinch in 1817 and built by Alexander Parris in 1818–1823, this handsome Neoclassical granite structure is a rare surviving example of a major early American hospital. It was nearly doubled in size in the 1840s, and the greatly expanded institution for which it was built still uses it. One of its major rooms, the Ether Dome, is individually listed as a National Historic Landmark.

## MASSACHUSETTS HISTORICAL SOCIETY BUILDING
### 1154 Boylston Street, Boston

Founded in 1791, this is the oldest historical society in the United States. It was the brainchild of Reverend Jeremy Belknap, who—even before the society was organized—had

*Massachusetts General Hospital, Boston, Suffolk County, 1941. Courtesy of HABS (Frank O. Branzetti).*

persuaded Paul Revere to write an account of his ride. Its collections of manuscripts, maps, prints and drawings are now numbered in the millions and have been invaluable to American historical research and scholarship. The present brick and granite building, constructed in 1899, is the society's seventh home.

## MASSACHUSETTS STATEHOUSE
**Beacon Hill, Boston**

One of the country's most important examples of Federal style architecture in a public building, the Massachusetts Statehouse was completed in 1798 from designs by Charles Bulfinch. Additions have been made to the sides and rear, but the mostly original facade, dominated by the dome (originally shingled and whitewashed, but gilded since 1874), remains one of Boston's most familiar and best-loved architectural images.

## WILLIAM C. NELL RESIDENCE
**3 Smith Court, Boston**

This frame house on Boston's Beacon Hill was the home of William C. Nell, a leading black abolitionist and spokesman for civil rights from the 1830s to the end of the Civil War. In 1855, Nell published the first history of African Americans written by an African American, *The Colored Patriots of the American Revolution.*

## NEW ENGLAND CONSERVATORY OF MUSIC
**290 Huntington Avenue, Boston**

From its founding in 1867 as an independent music school, the New England Conservatory of Music has been preeminent in the field of classical music education and instruction in the United States. Its auditorium, Jordan Hall, completed in 1903, has long been regarded as one of the world's top concert halls and is noted for its superb acoustical qualities.

## NEW ENGLAND HOSPITAL FOR WOMEN AND CHILDREN
**55 Dimock Street, Boston**

Constructed from 1872 to 1930, the several buildings on this hilly, wooded campus constitute the oldest remaining hospital managed by and for women during the latter half of the 19th and early part of the 20th century. The hospital was established in an effort to overcome obstacles for women who wanted to enter the male-dominated practice of medicine. In recent decades the hospital has been reorganized as the Dimock Community Health Center.

## OLD CITY HALL
**School and Providence Streets, Boston**

One of the first major structures in the French Second Empire style in the United

Old City Hall, Boston, Suffolk County, 1961. Courtesy of HABS (Cervin Robinson).

States, this monumentally scaled four-story granite building was designed by Gridley J. F. Bryant and Arthur Gilman and constructed in 1862–1865. Its instant success contributed to the popularity of Second Empire style public buildings throughout the nation in the 1870s and 1880s. When a new city hall replaced this building in the 1960s, it was preserved and converted to commercial uses with a minimum of exterior alteration.

## OLD NORTH CHURCH (NPS)
### 193 Salem Street, Boston

Paul Revere's instructions to sexton Robert Newman on the eve of the Revolution, to "hang a lantern aloft in the belfry arch of the North Church tower as a signal light, one if by land, and two if by sea," along with Henry Wadsworth Longfellow's account, have made this building an icon in American history. Built from 1723 to 1740, Old North Church (officially Christ Church) was Boston's second Anglican church and is a superb example of colonial Georgian architecture. Its lines

and proportions show that its designer, William Price, was familiar with the work of English architect Christopher Wren. The famous tower has been rebuilt, and at a special service held on April 18 each year, two lanterns are hung and lit from its belfry. Open to the public, it is still an active Episcopal parish church as well as a museum.

## OLD SOUTH CHURCH IN BOSTON
### 645 Boylston Street, Boston

"Nature abhors a vacuum." So does High Victorian Gothic architecture, as the florid polychrome walls and extravagant details of this imposing stone church prove. Constructed in 1874–1875, it is among the finest ecclesiastical expressions of the style in the country. Modeled on northern Italian examples, the cruciform building is dominated by a tall campanile that anchors one corner of Copley Square. The church, also known as New Old South Church, was built for a congregation that formerly worshiped in another building that has also been designated a National Historic Landmark. (See Old South Meeting House.)

## OLD SOUTH MEETING HOUSE (NPS)
### Milk and Washington Streets, Boston

Built in 1729–1730, Old South combines a traditional meetinghouse plan with Georgian architectural styling. One of colonial Boston's largest buildings, Old South was used for mass meetings, including one in December 1773 to protest the tax on tea that launched the famous Boston Tea Party. Gutted by occupying British soldiers during the Revolution, it was used as a riding academy, infuriating American patriots. When the congregation moved to a new church (see Old South Church) in the 1870s, the Old South Association in Boston was formed to preserve it. The Association's efforts resulted in one of America's earliest preservation success stories. Old South is open to the public as a museum and is still used as a meeting place.

## OLD STATE HOUSE (NPS)
### Washington and State Streets, Boston

The Old State House, Boston's oldest public building, is a fine example of early Georgian architecture. It was built in 1712–1713 as Boston's second Town House and rebuilt in 1747 after a fire. It served as the seat of British colonial rule in Massachusetts, a fact attested to by the royal lion and unicorn on its east facade. On July 18, 1776, the Declaration of Independence was read for the first time in Boston from its balcony. From 1776 until 1798 it was the seat of government for the Commonwealth of Massachusetts, and from 1830 to 1840 it was Boston's city hall. It is now open to the public as a museum of Boston history.

## OLD WEST CHURCH
### 131 Cambridge Street, Boston

Built in 1806 as a Congregational meetinghouse, Old West is an early example of a monumentally scaled church in the then-new Federal Adamesque style. It was designed by Asher Benjamin and became the prototype for many other New England churches after the architect published its plans in *The American Builder's Companion*. The original congregation left in 1892, and after being used as a public library, the building was reopened in 1964 as a United Methodist Church.

## FRANCIS PARKMAN HOUSE
### 50 Chestnut Street, Boston

From 1865 to 1893, Francis Parkman, an early chronicler of American history, lived in this Federal style brick house on Boston's Beacon Hill. Believing that historical writing was a romantic art, Parkman used novelistic techniques to weave dramatic fabrics from basic historic facts. His best-known works are *The Oregon Trail* (1849) and his multivolumed magnum opus, *France and England in North America* (1851–1892).

## PIERCE-HICHBORN HOUSE (NPS)
### 29 North Square, Boston

This rare survivor, dating from ca. 1711, is one of the few pre-Georgian brick town houses remaining in New England. After serving as a tenement and store in the 19th century, it was restored in 1950–1951. Less than a stone's throw from the Paul Revere House, with which it shares a courtyard, the Pierce-Hichborn House is owned by the Paul Revere Memorial Association and is shown as a historic house museum.

## WILLIAM H. PRESCOTT HOUSE
### 55 Beacon Street, Boston

An accident while he was a student at Harvard left William H. Prescott virtually blind. In spite of that handicap, he pursued a career as a historian and writer. His forte was colonial Spanish history, and his *History of the Conquest of Mexico* (1843), and *History of the Conquest of Peru* (1847) place him among the first ranks of American historians. The four-story, bowfronted Beacon Street house where he lived from 1844 to 1859 is now state headquarters of the National Society of the Colonial Dames of the United States in the Commonwealth of Massachusetts.

## QUINCY MARKET
### South Market Street, Boston

Designed by Alexander Parris and sponsored in 1825–1826 by Boston's mayor Josiah Quincy, this is the country's most impressive large-scale urban market remaining from the early 19th century. It adjoins Faneuil Hall, another National Historic Landmark, and consists of a central granite mass flanked by rows of commercial blocks. The central market employs two major structural innovations of the period: cast-iron columns for interior support and a massive post-and-lintel system for exterior walls. The market was rehabilitated in the 1970s and forms a major component of one of America's most successful urban renewal projects.

## PAUL REVERE HOUSE (NPS)
### 19 North Square, Boston

When Paul Revere moved to this small frame house in Boston's North End in 1770, it was already almost a hundred years old. It is now the oldest remaining house in downtown Boston. Built soon after the Boston fire of 1676, it survives, thanks to a perhaps over-enthusiastic restoration/reconstruction, as a charming survivor of post-medieval Puritan architecture. It was from here that the patriot set out on his midnight ride in 1775 to warn his fellow patriots that the British were coming. The house served as Revere's home until 1800. The Paul Revere Memorial Association and the National Park Service maintain his house and the adjoining Pierce-Hichborn House as historic house museums.

## ELLEN SWALLOW RICHARDS RESIDENCE
**32 Eliot Street, Boston**

From 1876 to 1911 this was the home of Ellen H. Swallow Richards, founder of the domestic science movement. Her pioneering work in sanitary engineering and experimental research in domestic science widened professional opportunities for women. She was also instrumental in laying the foundations for the new science of home economics. Following their purchase of the house, Richards and her husband remodeled its water, sewage, and heating and ventilation systems, all reflections of her concerns as an early environmental scientist. Her domestic reforms contributed to the replacement of the cluttered and decorative Victorian dwelling that had previously typified American home life with more compact and efficient modern houses — the new American dream house

## SAINT PAUL'S CHURCH
**136 Tremont Street, Boston**

Saint Paul's is New England's first major building designed in the Greek Revival style. Alexander Parris and Solomon Willard received the commission in 1819, and the church was completed the next year. The church is constructed of sandstone shipped from Virginia, and its austere facade on Boston Common is fronted by an Ionic portico whose column capitals were carved by Willard. In 1912, Saint Paul's became the cathedral of the Episcopal Diocese of Massachusetts.

## DAVID SEARS HOUSE
**42 Beacon Street, Boston**

This elegant town house was begun in 1816 from designs by Alexander Parris and is a notable example of the Adamesque Federal style. It is also an early example of the use of granite in domestic building. Mr. Sears liked

it well enough to double its size in 1824. The private Somerset Club, which still owns it, acquired the house in 1875 and added the third floor.

## SHIRLEY-EUSTACE HOUSE
**31–37 Shirley Street, Boston**

From 1741 to 1756 William Shirley, twice royal governor of Massachusetts, built one of the most formal and imposing Georgian houses in New England as his country residence. Of frame construction, it was rusticated to appear like stone, and its giant pilasters, paired at the corners, were among the earliest in American architecture. A large octagonal cupola crowned its hipped roof. American forces confiscated the house during the Revolution for use as a barracks and hospital. It was later owned by William Eustace, another governor of Massachusetts. The house, no longer a country estate but surrounded by the inner city, is open to the public.

## CHARLES SUMNER HOUSE
**20 Hancock Street, Boston**

This Federal style Beacon Hill house was the residence of a pivotal figure in American politics during the Civil War era. Charles Sumner, the New England antithesis of "fire-eating" Southern secessionists (one of whom physically attacked him at his U. S. Senate desk), was an outspoken opponent of slavery. He represented Massachusetts in the Senate from 1851 until his death in 1874, and the polemics he delivered from the floor helped propel the nation toward the inevitable conflict. After the Civil War he was one of the leading figures in the radical wing of the Republican Party and played an influential role in foreign affairs.

## SYMPHONY HALL
**301 Massachusetts Avenue, Boston**

Symphony Hall was completed in 1900 by the nationally celebrated architectural firm of McKim, Mead & White as the permanent home for the Boston Symphony Orchestra (BSO). Symphony Hall remains, acoustically, among the top concert halls in the world. This achievement is primarily the result of the vision of BSO founder and longtime patron Henry Lee Higginson, pioneering Harvard physics professor Wallace Clement Sabine, and noted American architect Charles Follen McKim. Carefully following Sabine's specifications, McKim created a design that was subservient in all aspects to the needs of performing symphonic music.

## TREMONT STREET SUBWAY
### Beneath Tremont, Boylston, and Washington Streets, Boston

When the first unit of Boston's Tremont Street Subway, modeled after a system in Budapest, became operational on September 1, 1897, it was the first underground means of public transportation in the United States and the fifth in the world. It was an overnight success: approximately 50 million passenger miles were credited during the line's first year of existence. The original section of a now greatly enlarged underground system extended from the Public Garden to the Park Street Station. The original tunnel, constructed in 1895–1898, is still in use, as are the two original underground stations, Boylston and Park Street.

## TRINITY CHURCH, BOSTON
### Copley Square, Boston

This seminal building in the history of American architecture, built from 1872 to 1877, is one of the earliest works of H. H. Richardson. Even before it was completed, other architects were imitating it, but Trinity, with its rugged stone walls and massive central tower, remains the exemplar of the Richardsonian Romanesque style. John La Farge executed murals and some of the stained-glass windows in its magnificent interior. Trinity houses an active Episcopal parish that proudly maintains the building in pristine condition.

## WILLIAM MONROE TROTTER HOUSE
### 97 Sawyer Avenue, Boston

This late-19th-century house was the home of a noted African-American journalist and militant civil rights activist during the first decades of the 20th century. Trotter is best

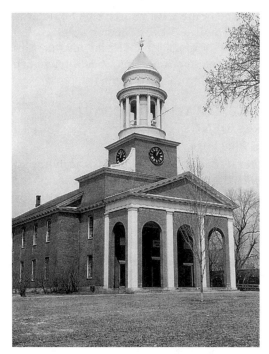

First Church of Christ, Lancaster, Lancaster, Worcester County, 1970. Courtesy of NPS (Charles W. Snell).

known for his opposition to Booker T. Washington, whom he regarded as an accommodationist because he supported and reinforced segregationist policies. Trotter graduated with highest honors from Harvard in 1895, and in 1901 he cofounded *The Guardian*, a weekly newspaper that espoused his views.

## ■ *Worcester County*

## AMERICAN ANTIQUARIAN SOCIETY
### 185 Salisbury Street, Worcester

This venerable institution, established in 1812, is the third-oldest historical society in the nation, and the first conceived on a national, rather than a statewide, level. Its third home, an early-20th-century Georgian Revival building, is impressive enough, but what it houses is truly remarkable: the single largest collection of printed source material relating to the early history, literature, and culture of the United States. As a noted historian remarked, without these resources, "our knowledge of the origins of this nation would for a long time have been composed of myths and legends. In a sense, the

American Antiquarian Society gave us our past." The Society is open to researchers.

## FIRST CHURCH OF CHRIST
### Facing the Common, Lancaster

Although closely associated with Boston architecture, Charles Bulfinch designed structures throughout New England. Constructed in 1816, this is probably the finest of his New England churches extant. A monumental pedimented portico, with Roman Doric pilasters separating brick arches and supporting a full entablature, fronts the building, and a circular tower with a domed cupola tops a square base. Except for the addition of a rear chapel and minor interior changes, the church appears as it did when it was dedicated on New Year's Day, 1817.

## FRUITLANDS
### Prospect Hill, Harvard, Worcester County

This vernacular New England farmhouse was the home of Bronson Alcott's short-lived "New Eden," an experiment in communal living. Alcott, a leading figure in education reform, a Transcendentalist, and a social philosopher, persuaded 15 others (including his family of six, one of them his daughter Louisa May) to join his community in June 1843. The group ate only fruits and vegetables, drank only water, and wore only linen clothing. His followers left after several months of this Spartan regime, and the Alcotts themselves departed in January 1844. Fruitlands is now a museum, open in the summer months.

## GODDARD ROCKET LAUNCHING SITE
### Ninth Fairway, between Tee and Green, Pakachoag Golf Course, Auburn

Dr. Robert H. Goddard launched the world's first liquid-propellant rocket here in 1926, setting the course for future developments in rocketry. At the time Goddard, who had many patents for rockets and rocket apparatus, was experimenting on the farm of a distant relative, and the launching site was an open field. His rocket, a slim, ten-foot cylinder, reached an altitude of 41 feet and a distance of 184 feet, and flew for 2.5 seconds. The site is now on the ninth fairway of the Pakachoag Golf Course, where balls fly that distance and height every day.

## JOHN B. GOUGH HOUSE
### 215 Main Street, Boylston

"The Apostle of Cold Water," as one historian dubbed John Gough, was a pivotal figure in the history of the American temperance movement. A former drunkard and victim of delirium tremens, Gough signed a pledge of total abstinence in 1842. For the next 44 years he captivated audiences here and abroad with his impassioned, and sometimes humorous, appeals for sobriety. He lived in this two-story frame house from 1848 until his death in 1886.

## LIBERTY FARM
### 116 Mower Street, Worcester

Abigail Kelly, once described by William Lloyd Garrison as "the moral Joan of Arc of the world," was one of the first American women to speak out publicly against slavery. Her husband, Stephen Symonds Foster, was also a reformer, and their Liberty Farm served as a station on the Underground Railroad, sheltering fugitive slaves on their way to freedom in Canada. The couple also participated in the struggle for women's rights, and in the 1870s, they withheld taxes on Liberty Farm to protest Abigail Kelly's inability to vote. They lived in this aptly named brick farmhouse from 1847 to 1881.

## GENERAL RUFUS PUTNAM HOUSE
### 344 Main Street, Rutland

Rufus Putnam, soldier during the French and Indian War, farmer and surveyor, entered the Revolution as a lieutenant colonel and was soon appointed chief engineer with the rank of colonel. He participated in numerous campaigns and after the war was instrumental in organizing the first settlement in the Northwest Territory, at Marietta, Ohio. President Washington appointed him U.S. surveyor-general in 1796. From 1781 until 1788, he lived in this farmhouse that the Commonwealth of Massachusetts had confiscated from its Tory owners during the Revolution.

# MICHIGAN

## ■ *Benzie County*

### CITY OF MILWAUKEE
**Marine Terminal Railyard, East Slip, Elberta**

This steel-hulled vessel, equipped to carry 22 railroad cars on its enclosed four-track deck, transported freight across Lake Michigan for more than a half century, from 1931 to 1982. It remains the sole surviving example of the pre-1940 "classic period" Great Lakes boxcar ferries, embodying the distinctive characteristics of these specialized craft.

## ■ *Calhoun County*

### MARSHALL HISTORIC DISTRICT
**Bounded by Plum Street, East Drive, Forest and Hanover Streets, Marshall**

The citizens of Marshall, founded in 1831 as a potential trading and manufacturing center, had high hopes of its becoming Michigan's capital city. These were dashed in 1847 when Lansing was selected. By the 1870s, Marshall had become a quiet backwater, and the manufacture of patent medicines became its main industry. Preservation efforts began in the 1920s when Mayor Harold C. Brooks began buying and restoring some of the town's early buildings. Today sensitive planning and preservation have combined to produce an overall quality of living found in all too few American towns of its size.

## ■ *Cheboygan County*

### FORT MICHILIMACKINAC
**At the terminus of U.S. Route 31, Mackinaw City**

Erected by the French early in the 18th century to control the important Straits of Mackinac, Fort Michilimackinac soon became a great fur trading center but was abandoned during the French and Indian War. Subsequently, it was occupied by the British and was their only garrison on the Great Lakes during the Revolution. The fort was eventually abandoned once more, but the site became a municipal park in 1857 and Michigan's second state park in 1904. The stockade and buildings representing its occupancy by French, British, and American troops have been reconstructed.

*Marshall Historic District, Marshall, Calhoun County. Pendleton-Alexander House, 1971. Courtesy of George Vallillee, Applied Photographics.*

*Saint Mary's Falls Canal, Sault Sainte Marie, Chippewa County, 1969. Courtesy of the U.S. Army Corps of Engineers.*

*Bay View, Bay View, Emmet County. Fairview Avenue. Courtesy of the Michigan Bureau of History (Brian Conway).*

■ *Chippewa County*

## SAINT MARY'S FALLS CANAL
### Saint Mary's River, Sault Sainte Marie

Until this mile-long canal was built, navigation—and, consequently, commerce—between Lake Huron and Lake Superior was blocked by the rapids of the Saint Mary's River. Two locks were built to accommodate the 22-foot difference in water level between the lakes, and after the canal was completed in 1855, development of the vast resources of the Lake Superior region soon followed. The "Soo locks," as the canal is popularly called, rank with the Erie and the Illinois and Michigan canals as one of the nation's most important and successful early waterways. Changes have been made over the years (there are now four locks), but only the icy grip of winter has hindered traffic to any extent for more than a century and a half.

■ *Emmet County*

## BAY VIEW
### Northeast of Petoskey on U.S. Route 31, Bay View

Bay View is one of the finest remaining examples of two uniquely American community forms: the Methodist Camp Meeting (begun in 1876) and the independent Chautauqua community (1885 to 1915). Instead of the grid plan typically utilized for campgrounds, Bay View's plat followed romantic landscape principals, with winding roadways taking advantage of the topography overlooking Little Traverse Bay. More than 400 buildings, mostly private frame cottages with Victorian-era trim, line the winding roads. Bay View still functions as a Methodist summer camp and is a major monument to American religious, cultural, social, and educational ideals.

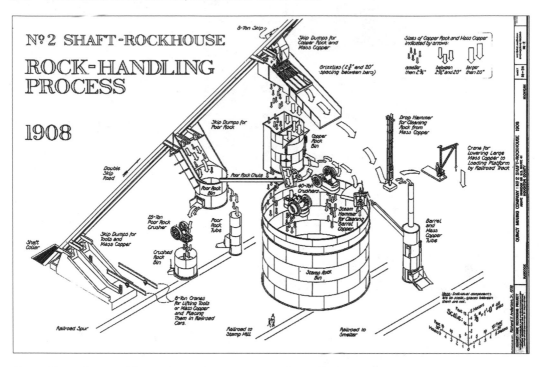

*Quincy Mining Company Historic District, Quincy, Houghton County. Rock-handling process, 1908. Courtesy of HABS (Richard D. Anderson, Jr.)*

## ERNEST HEMINGWAY COTTAGE

**Between the north shore of Walloon Lake and Lake Grove Road, Petoskey**

Ernest Hemingway spent his boyhood summers at "Windemere," a one-story frame cottage on the shore of Walloon Lake. His father built the house in 1900 when his son was a year old, and it was here the future author learned to hunt and fish and appreciate the outdoor life he came to celebrate in his writings. One of America's most influential and popular writers, Hemingway won the Pulitzer Prize in 1953 for his *Old Man and the Sea*. (See also Ernest Hemingway House, Monroe County, Florida.)

### ■ *Genesee County*

## DURANT-DORT CARRIAGE COMPANY OFFICE

**315 West Water Street, Flint**

William Crapo Durant was, quite simply, a business genius. By the turn of the 20th century his Durant-Dort Carriage Company was one of the nation's largest makers of horse-drawn vehicles. In 1904, Durant assumed control of the almost moribund Buick Motor

Car Company, and by 1908, when he founded General Motors, Buick was the best-selling car in the nation. From 1895 to 1913, Durant operated from this brick office building, the center of activities for his carriage and all-encompassing automobile enterprises. Considered the birthplace of General Motors, the office was restored after being designated a National Historic Landmark in 1978 and now serves as the focal point of an area called Carriage Town.

### ■ *Houghton County*

## CALUMET HISTORIC DISTRICT

**West of Michigan Route 26, south of Calumet Lake, Calumet**

Michigan's Keweenaw Peninsula was the first large area in the United States to be systematically mined and developed, and for a generation it was the most prolific source of copper in the world. During the 1870s, the Calumet and Hecla Mining Company mined 50 percent of America's copper. Calumet was its company town, and many of its important structures remain. They were designed by Shaw and Hunnewell of Boston (home to most of the company's original investors).

## QUINCY MINING COMPANY HISTORIC DISTRICT

**Between Portage Lake and Quincy Hill along U.S. Route 41, Hancock**

Along with the Calumet and Hecla Mining Company, the Quincy Mining Company properties represent the major elements of the Michigan copper industry. Between 1862 and 1868, Quincy was the nation's largest copper producer, and the company made singular contributions to the Northern effort during the Civil War by supplying raw materials for cannons, canteens, and naval equipment. A drop in copper prices in 1931 temporarily closed operations, and in 1957 mining ceased. Many company houses and structures associated with mining and smelting processes remain.

### ■ Ingham County

## MICHIGAN STATE CAPITOL

**Capitol Avenue at Michigan Avenue, Lansing**

Built between 1872 and 1878, the Michigan State Capitol was designed by Elijah E. Myers, one of the country's most successful architects of public buildings of his time. Myers was among the first to use the national capitol in Washington, D.C., as a model, and his design for Michigan helped to establish the standard for state capitols for decades to come. The building, particularly notable for its colorful High Victorian interiors, was restored in the 1990s.

### ■ Kent County

## NORTON MOUND GROUP

**Between Indian Mounds Drive and Interstate 196, Grand Rapids**

These are the most important and best preserved Hopewell mounds in the western Great Lakes region. The Norton Mound Group was the center of Hopewellian culture in the area from ca. 400 B.C. to A.D. 400. Early excavations (1874) revealed numerous burials rich in grave offerings, and later excavations (1963–1964) provided information on mound construction methods. At one time some 40 mounds were present, and although fewer than half remain today, these are well preserved in a Grand Rapids city park.

### ■ Leelanau County

## NORTH MANITOU LIFESAVING STATION (NPS)

**North Manitou Island, Sleeping Bear Dunes National Seashore**

This is the only surviving station of a network of nearly 200 that encompasses the entire lifesaving service history; the early volunteer efforts, the United States Life-Saving Service, and the United States Coast Guard. Because there was no interruption in service here from 1854, when the station was founded, until 1932, when it was discontinued, the well-used buildings retain a high degree of integrity in design, materials, and workmanship. The station is now part of the National Park Service's Sleeping Bear Dunes National Lakeshore.

### ■ Mackinac County

## GRAND HOTEL

**Grand Avenue, Mackinac Island**

This phenomenal building is one of America's major 19th-century "grand hotels." Built on a high bluff overlooking the Straits of Mackinac, the white clapboarded hotel is fronted by "the world's longest front porch," a 628-foot veranda extending the full length of its facade. Opened in 1887, the Grand continues in active use as a summer resort and continues to dominate Mackinac Island from its hillside perch.

## MACKINAC ISLAND

**Northeast across the Straits of Mackinac from Mackinaw City**

Now an idyllic summer resort (from which cars have been banned since early in the 20th century), this small island in the straits between Lakes Huron and Michigan was once the most important fur trading post and military center in the entire Great Lakes region. The British began Fort Mackinac in 1780. American control of the island was secured by the Treaty of Ghent in 1814, and John Jacob Astor's American Fur Company maintained its northern headquarters on the island until 1840. Mackinac's days as a summer resort date from the late 19th century, and in 1875, Mackinac National Park, the country's second National Park, was created.

*Grand Hotel, Mackinac Island, Mackinac County. Courtesy of the Grand Hotel.*

In 1895 the federal government transferred its holdings to the state, and most of the island is now the Mackinac Island State Park.

### SAINT IGNACE MISSION
**Marquette Park, State and Marquette Streets, Saint Ignace**

This site marks the location of a Huron Indian mission established by the indomitable Père Jacques Marquette ca. 1672. Although his travels took him far and wide throughout the Upper Mississippi basin in the next several years, he expressed a desire to be buried here, and in 1677 Indian converts and admirers carried out his wishes. A second mission, built close by in the 1830s, was moved to the site of the first in 1954. It now serves as a museum in a city park, and Marquette's grave is nearby.

### ■ *Midland County*

### ALDEN DOW HOUSE AND STUDIO
**315 Post Street, Midland**

The architecture of Alden B. Dow received national attention beginning with his early career through his late period, partly because he was associated with Frank Lloyd Wright. Dow was the first of Wright's Taliesin Fellows to design on his own, and his work combines an indebtedness to his mentor with an appreciation of European modernism, not to mention a healthy infusion of his own originality.

Midland has a number of examples of his work, but his house and studio, begun in 1933 and expanded over the years, are his most clearly acknowledged masterpieces.

### HERBERT H. DOW HOUSE
**1038 West Main Street, Midland**

Some time around 1890, chemist Herbert Dow discovered that bromine could be separated from raw brine by electrolysis. This was the first time an electrochemical process had been employed in the country, and Dow realized the great potential it offered. He moved to Midland, where he had noticed numerous brine deposits with large concentrations of bromine, and in 1897 founded the Dow Chemical Company. His expansive frame house dates from 1899, and its spacious and carefully landscaped grounds, evidence of Dow's great interest in horticulture, are open to the public.

### ■ *Muskegon County*

### *MILWAUKEE CLIPPER*
**Former Grand Trunk Western railroad car ferry docks, Muskegon**

The oldest passenger steamship on the Great Lakes, *Milwaukee Clipper* was launched in 1904 as *Junita*. In 1940, the Bureau of Marine Inspection and Navigation promulgated new rules that required a substantial rebuilding. Renamed the *Milwaukee Clipper*, the ship emerged from the dry dock as an Art Moderne vessel with "air-flow" streamlining, displaying a look still familiar in modern oceangoing passenger ships. Its quadruple-expansion steam engines, installed in 1905, were kept and are now the only known surviving examples of this important engine type. *Milwaukee Clipper* was refurbished again in the 1990s and is used as a museum and entertainment center.

## SILVERSIDES
**Naval Reserve Center, Fulton and Bluff Streets, Muskegon**

USS *Silversides* was commissioned in early December 1941, just eight days after Pearl Harbor. Its World War II mission was to stop raw materials and supplies—oil, bauxite, rubber, coal, food, and iron ore—from reaching Japan, which it accomplished with singular success. The "scourge of the Pacific" counted 23 confirmed sinkings and earned 12 battle stars for its exemplary service. After a postwar stint as a training ship in Chicago, the submarine came to rest in 1987 in Muskegon, where it is on exhibit.

## ■ Oakland County
## CRANBROOK
**500 Lone Pine Road, Bloomfield Hills**

This extraordinary enclave, where architecture, landscape, and sculpture blend in a seamless whole, resulted from a collaborative effort between its patrons, George and Ellen Booth, and its expatriate Finnish architect, Eliel Saarinen. Cranbrook was established in the first decade of the 20th century as an idealistic institution where art and handicrafts were taught as integral parts of the school curriculum. The goal was to combat shoddy machine-age goods by imbuing students with an appreciation of fine design in their everyday lives and providing them with the training necessary to create beautiful objects.

## ■ Saint Clair County
## LIGHTSHIP NO. 103, *HURON*
**Pine Grove Park, Banks of Saint Clair River, Port Huron**

Lightship No. 103, also known by its last official designation, *Huron*, is the only surviving example of a type of lightship built specifically for service on the Great Lakes. Below the waterline its hull is sharper than that of oceangoing lightships, a design modification enabling it to accommodate the shorter wave periods typical of the lakes. Lightships were vital partners in Great Lakes shipping, and the *Huron* served to mark an obstacle on the primary trade route, the treacherous Corsica Shoals near the southern end of Lake Huron. Built in 1920, *Huron* was the last lightship to serve on the Great Lakes and is now an outdoor exhibit.

## SAINT CLAIR RIVER TUNNEL
**Near Tenth Street, between Johnstone and Beard, Port Huron**

More than a mile long and 21 feet in diameter, the Saint Clair River Tunnel, linking Port Huron with Sarnia, Ontario, is North America's first subaqueous tunnel large enough to accommodate a railroad. It was completed in 1891, and during its construction new methods and uses of materials were developed that proved the efficacy of tunneling through the soft, porous ground commonly found beneath rivers. Tunnels such as the Saint Clair helped untangle railroad (and later vehicular) bottlenecks typical of most large urban centers located on wide waterways.

## ■ Wayne County
## COLUMBIA
**Nicholson Terminal, Ecorse**

*Columbia* is one of the last classic excursion steamers in the country. Designed by Frank E. Kirby, one of the leading naval architects of the time, it was built at the Detroit Dry Dock Company shipyard in 1902 and was used by the Detroit & Windsor Ferry Company to carry passengers to Bois Blanc (Bob-Lo) Island, a popular amusement park. Its captains have appreciated its fine machinery, much of which survives, and passengers enjoy its second-deck ballroom. (See *Sainte Claire*.)

## EDISON INSTITUTE
**Bounded by Michigan Avenue, Village Road, Southfield Expressway, and Oakland Boulevard, Dearborn**

Henry Ford contradicted himself! "History is more or less bunk" is one of his most famous utterances, but when he began planning The Edison Institute, he promised his secretary: "We're going to build a museum...and it won't be bunk." The Henry Ford Museum and Greenfield Village, as the Institute is popularly known, contains an unrivaled collection of American material culture representing Ford's interest in the history of transportation, agriculture and industry. The village, consisting of reconstructed historic structures, was one of the county's earliest outdoor, open-air museums. Ford named his project in honor of his friend Thomas Edison and first showed it to invited guests on October 21, 1929, on the 50th anniversary of Edison's invention of the first practical incandescent electric light bulb.

## FAIR LANE

### 4901 Evergreen Road, Dearborn

Henry Ford ushered in the automobile age when he began mass production of an inexpensive and reliable vehicle — the Model T. He introduced the "Tin Lizzie" in 1908, and in 1914 the Ford Motor Company sold 250,000 of these cars. In the same year he began construction of his 56-room Fair Lane, designed by Pittsburgh architect William Van Tine in a modified Scottish baronial style. Ford lived here from 1916 until his death in 1947. In 1956 the house and surrounding acreage were donated to the University of Michigan to develop its Dearborn campus.

The university currently uses Fair Lane as an administrative and conference center.

## FISHER BUILDING

### 3011 West Grand Boulevard, Detroit

The 1927–1928 Art Deco Fisher Building displays some of the most accomplished detailing of any American skyscraper ever built. The granite and marble exterior is emblazoned with solid bronze trim, and the vast arcade inside is embellished with 40 varieties of marble. Sponsored by the seven Fisher brothers, who manufactured automobile bodies and were part of the burgeoning automobile industry in Detroit, the 28-story skyscraper was intended both as an up-to-date office building and as a contribution to a more beautiful Detroit. It is one of the masterpieces of architect Albert Kahn, generally better known for his industrial buildings.

## FORD RIVER ROUGE COMPLEX

### 3001 Miller Road, Dearborn

Constructed mostly in a single decade, from 1917 to 1927, this is one of the industrial wonders of the world: a huge single plant encompassing all the basic steps in automobile production. It was here that Henry Ford achieved his dream of a nonstop, continuous production line, beginning with delivery of raw materials and ending with finished automobiles ready to be shipped to retailers. The

Ford River Rouge Complex, Dearborn, Wayne County. Glass plant. Courtesy of AASLH (Ralph J. Christian).

complex was designed largely by Albert Kahn, who purposefully planned it so that its components could be modified to take advantage of improved techniques as they were developed. (See Highland Park Ford Plant.)

## FOX THEATER
### 2111 Woodward Avenue, Detroit

This 1928 theater is the zenith of a particularly American, particularly exuberant, building type, the movie palace. Patrons enter the flamboyant Fox, designed by theater architect C. Howard Crane, though a five-story lobby, ascend a grand staircase guarded by plaster lions and dragons, and enter a 5,042-seat auditorium where monkeys, peacocks, serpents, horses, and strange deities cavort among Moorish arches under a "tented" ceiling. The decor and the sounds produced by the "Mighty Wurtlitzer" organ with its 2,700 pipes make the featured attraction—no matter what it is—take second billing.

## GENERAL MOTORS BUILDING
### 3044 West Grand Boulevard, Detroit

Ever since its completion in 1923, this huge office building has symbolized General Motors (GM), the largest manufacturing corporation in the world and a dominant player in the automobile industry. Albert Kahn designed the 15-story structure that contains 1,800 offices in addition to display rooms, shops, gymnasium, and auditorium. With a clearly defined base, shaft, and attic story, the tripartite vertical arrangement is typical of tall building design of its time. The plan has a central block with four projecting wings on each long side. In the 1990s, GM donated the building to the City of Detroit and moved its headquarters to a newer complex.

## GUARDIAN BUILDING
### 500 Griswold Street, Detroit

Completed in 1929, the Guardian Building is one of the most colorful and elaborate Art Deco skyscrapers in America. Its 36-story steel frame is covered with vibrant Arts and Crafts tile and orange brick. These warm tones symbolized the cordial, friendly image the Union Trust Company, for whom it was built, wanted to convey. Wirt C. Rowland, of the Detroit architectural firm Smith, Hinchman and Grylls, designed the building that became known locally as "the Cathedral of Finance."

## HIGHLAND PARK FORD PLANT
### 91 Manchester Avenue, Highland Park

Designed mostly by Albert Kahn, this plant is considered the birthplace of the moving assembly line. Techniques developed here revolutionized manufacturing methods throughout the world. The plant opened in

*General Motors Building, Detroit, Wayne County, ca. 1956. Courtesy of AASLH.*

1910 and expanded as Henry Ford and his colleagues developed new means of production to keep up with the ever-increasing demand for his popular Model T. Eventually, Highland Park was replaced by the River Rouge plant, and in 1927 the final assembly line here was moved to the new facility. (See Ford River Rouge Complex.)

## LINCOLN MOTOR COMPANY PLANT
**6200 West Warren Avenue, Detroit**

Automobile manufacturer Henry M. Leland resigned from Cadillac in 1917 after William C. Durant hesitated to focus his plants on the war effort. He established this plant in 1918, and here he produced Liberty engines, "one of America's greatest contributions to aviation during the war." At war's end, Leland introduced the precision-made Lincoln, along with the Mercury, and both automobiles were produced in this plant. Leland eventually lost out to Henry Ford, but he is remembered as the man who "created both of America's first-quality cars, Cadillac and Lincoln."

## PARKE-DAVIS RESEARCH LABORATORY
**At the foot of Joseph Campau Street at the Detroit River, Detroit**

This was the first industrial research laboratory in the country built for the specific purpose of conducting pharmacological research. Its 1902 construction marked the institutionalization of a pure-science research approach

that has been responsible for many of the modern "wonder" drugs that have been developed in subsequent years.

## PEWABIC POTTERY
**10125 East Jefferson Avenue, Detroit**

Founded in 1904 by Mary Chase Perry, Pewabic Pottery gained national recognition for its iridescent glazes and architectural tiles, used in murals and mosaics throughout the country. In 1907, William Stratton designed this half-timbered building, based on English cottage precedent, to house the pottery, and Miss Perry soon became Mrs. Stratton. An artist of the Arts and Crafts movement, Mary Stratton helped to raise the artistic standard of American ceramicists. The building, virtually unchanged, serves as a pottery, gallery, and classroom space for the Pewabic Society of Detroit.

## *SAINTE CLAIRE*
**Nicholson Terminal, Ecorse**

Designed by Frank E. Kirby, the steamer *Sainte Claire* was launched in Toledo, Ohio, in 1910 and entered service as part of the fleet operated by the Detroit & Windsor Ferry Company. *Sainte Claire* was *Columbia's* sister ship, and for 81 years the two shared the run from Detroit to Bois Blanc (Bob-Lo) Island, a record of service unequaled in U.S. maritime history. Along with the *Columbia, Sainte Claire* remains the country's best remaining example of a classic excursion steamer (See *Columbia.*)

# MINNESOTA

■ *Dakota and Hennepin Counties*

## FORT SNELLING
**Saint Paul vicinity (Dakota and Hennepin Counties)**

Commanding the bluff overlooking the confluence of the Minnesota and the Mississippi Rivers, Fort Snelling was begun in 1820 on property that Lieutenant Zebulon Pike purchased from the Sioux. It was the first

American fort in present-day Minnesota and occupied a leading position in the European-American settlement of the Old Northwest. When Minnesota Territory was created in 1848, the frontier had moved farther west, and Fort Snelling became a troop training center from the Civil War until World War II. Historic Fort Snelling is open to the public May through October.

## PEAVEY-HAGLIN EXPERIMENTAL CONCRETE GRAIN ELEVATOR
### Intersection of Highways 7 and 100, Saint Louis Park

Constructed in 1899–1900, this cylinder, 125 feet high with an inner diameter of 20 feet, is the first circular grain elevator built of poured reinforced concrete in the United States, and likely in the world. As such, it is

*Peavey-Haglin Experimental Concrete Grain Elevator, Hennepin County. Courtesy of HABS (Jet Lowe).*

the forerunner of a building type that has come to dominate the midwestern landscape wherever grain is grown and stored. The elevator was the idea of grain company owner Frank H. Peavey, who obtained the services of architect-builder-contractor Charles F. Haglin to construct it.

## PILLSBURY A MILL
### Main Street and Third Avenue, SE, Minneapolis

The immense water power provided by the Mississippi River's Saint Anthony Falls helped make Minneapolis the flour milling capital of the nation between 1880 and 1930. Of the giant flour mills built during those years, the Pillsbury A Mill is among the most impressive survivors. The largest, most advanced mill in the world when it was completed in 1881, the six-story, limestone A Mill was the standard by which all other mills of its time were measured.

## WASHBURN A MILL COMPLEX
### First Street South off Portland Avenue, Minneapolis

This industrial complex represents the growth and development of General Mills, Inc., and the radical transformations of the flour milling industry in the late 19th and early 20th centuries. The Washburn A Mill, a limestone structure with parts dating from 1874, stands across Saint Anthony Falls from the Pillsbury A Mill and is the only structure that remains from the original milling com-

*Fort Snelling, Dakota and Hennepin Counties. Commandant's house. Courtesy of HABS (Jet Lowe).*

Pillsbury A Mill, Minneapolis, Hennepin County. Courtesy of HABS (Jet Lowe).

plex established by Cadwallader C. Washburn. General Mills was an outgrowth of Washburn's enterprise, and the first of its famed "Betty Crocker" kitchens was installed here. Tragically, in 1991 an extensive fire destroyed much of the historic structure and milling machinery.

■ *Mille Lacs County*

## KATHIO SITE
### Address Restricted, Vineland

Occupied from archaic to historic times (3000 B.C.–A.D. 1750), this district was the ancestral homeland of the Dakota Sioux. In 1679, French explorer Sieur de Luth noted the existence of 40 Sioux villages in the vicinity. In the mid–18th century, the Chippewa, pressured by the westward expansion of European settlers, drove the Sioux westward and southward, where they later figured prominently in the history of the Plains and Rocky Mountain states. The district contains at least 17 sites of importance, some of which have been excavated, and is included within Mille Lacs-Kathio State Park.

■ *Morrison County*

## CHARLES A. LINDBERGH, SR., HOUSE
### County Road 52, Little Falls vicinity

From 1907 to 1920, Charles A. Lindbergh, Sr., who served in the U.S. Congress from

1907 through 1917, lived here. A reformer and independent, he was prominent in protest politics, opposing the nation's entry into World War I because he felt it was promoted by an "inner circle" of financiers who stood to profit. His famous aviator son, who has all but eclipsed his father in popular memory, also lived here. After completing the first nonstop flight across the Atlantic in 1927, "Lucky Lindy" immediately became an all-American hero. Like his father, he came to oppose America's entry into war (World War II). The Lindbergh family donated the house and farm to the State of Minnesota in 1931, and the property is now the Charles A. Lindbergh State Park.

■ *Olmsted County*

## MAYO CLINIC BUILDINGS
### 110 and 115 Second Avenue, Rochester

Brothers William J. and Charles H. Mayo were among the most innovative medical practitioners of the 20th century. At Rochester they established the first fully developed private practice of cooperative group medicine, the Mayo Clinic. This form of practice revolutionized health care in America and has since been emulated throughout the world. The 1914 building, the nation's first complete clinic and one of two buildings included in the National Historic Landmark, was demolished in 1986.

Charles A. Lindbergh, Sr., House, Morrison County. Courtesy of HABS (Jet Lowe).

The 1926–1928 Plummer Building, representing the continuing growth of concepts embodied in the earlier building, remains. A multistory skyscraper with impressive Art Deco sculptures and murals depicting medical themes, it contains "Dr. Will's" office and the meeting room of the clinic's board of governors, both open to the public.

## ■ Pine County

### SAINT CROIX RECREATIONAL DEMONSTRATION AREA
#### Off Route 48, Hinckley vicinity

This was the largest and remains one of the best examples of Depression-era recreational demonstration area (RDA) planning and design in the country. Forty-six RDA/state parks were planned by the National Park Service during the New Deal. In addition to providing recreation, RDAs were intended to "retire" marginal agricultural lands for this new and better use. The Saint Croix RDA became the Saint Croix State Park in 1943, and the many remaining structures built by the Civilian Conservation Corps typify the intentionally rustic style so popular for park design at the time.

## ■ Ramsey County

### F. SCOTT FITZGERALD HOUSE
#### 599 Summit Avenue, Saint Paul

Francis Scott Fitzgerald wrote several stories and his first published novel while living here. That novel, *This Side of Paradise*, pub-

F. Scott Fitzgerald House, Saint Paul, Ramsey County. Courtesy of HABS (Jet Lowe).

lished in 1920, established him as the spokesman for the emancipated but disillusioned youth of the Jazz Age. It was followed in rapid succession by *The Beautiful and the Damned* and *The Great Gatsby*. The house is the westernmost unit of Summit Terrace, a distinguished group of Victorian row houses located on Summit Avenue, Saint Paul's most prestigious residential street at the time the Fitzgerald family lived there.

## JAMES J. HILL HOUSE
### 240 Summit Avenue, Saint Paul

From 1891 until his death in 1916, James J. Hill, one of the great western railroad builders and one of the country's leading 19th-century financiers, lived here. Known as the "Empire Builder," Hill acquired railroads throughout the Northwest and merged several into the Great Northern Railway Company in 1890. His efforts helped bring the area it traversed, from Saint Paul to the Pacific, into the mainstream of American commerce. Hill's massive red-sandstone Richardsonian Romanesque mansion, with its own picture gallery and pipe organ, was designed by Peabody, Stearns, and Furber. It is now a historic site operated by the Minnesota Historical Society.

## FRANK B. KELLOGG HOUSE
### 633 Fairmont Avenue, Saint Paul

From 1889 until his death in 1937, Frank B. Kellogg, lawyer, U.S. senator and diplomat, lived in this large stone and shingle mansion. As secretary of state during the Coolidge administration, he negotiated the 1928 Kellogg-Briand Pact (1928), renouncing war as an international policy. Endorsed by 62 nations, the pact earned him the 1930 Nobel Peace Prize. Kellogg afterward served on the Permanent Court of International Justice at the Hague.

## ■ Rice County

## O.E. ROLVAAG HOUSE
### 311 Manitou Street, Northfield

Many adjustments, both psychological and physical, were necessary before pioneer immigrants to mid-America could find peace and prosperity in their new environment. No one understood this better than Norwegian-American novelist Ole Edward Rolvaag, who explored the process in his famous trilogy— *Giants in the Earth* (1927), *Peder Victorious* (1928), and *Their Father's God* (1931). From 1912 until his death in 1931, Rolvaag lived in this stuccoed and shingled bungalow.

## THORSTEIN VEBLEN FARMSTEAD
### Off Minnesota Highway 246, Nerstrand vicinity

Thorstein Bunde Veblen, economist, social scientist, and critic of American culture, lived on this farm as a youth and returned often as an adult. The product of an austere agrarian upbringing, Veblen is recognized as one of America's most creative thinkers. Of his 11 books, his *Theory of the Leisure Class* remains his best-known work. Published in 1899, its wicked satire and pungent observations were immediate "hits," and many of the phrases he coined, such as "conspicuous consumption," have since become everyday expressions.

*Frank B. Kellogg House, Saint Paul, Ramsey County. Courtesy of HABS (Jack E. Boucher).*

■ *Saint Louis County*

## HULL-RUST-MAHONING OPEN PIT IRON MINE
### Third Avenue, East, Hibbing

This is the largest open pit iron mine in the world. Begun in 1895, its immense output made Minnesota the leading producer of iron ore in the nation and helped to make the United States the world's leading producer of steel. It has proven the most productive mine on the rich Mesabi range, where deposits lie close to the surface. This condition fostered the development of open pit, or strip-mining, techniques, and the "mine" is actually nine or more open pits that appear as a single hole. Its scale and size can be gauged from the fact that it is frequently called "Minnesota's Grand Canyon."

## MOUNTAIN IRON MINE
### Off First Street and Mountain Avenue, Mountain Iron

Discovered in 1890, Mountain Iron Mine shipped its first ore in 1892 and from then until 1961 Minnesota's phenomenal Mesabi Range provided more than half the iron ore mined in the entire country. Thanks to the Mountain Mine, which proved the richness of the Mesabi, Minnesota became the leading supplier of iron ore in the nation. The Mountain Iron Mine closed in 1956, and the pit, which soon thereafter filled with water, is now a reservoir.

## SOUDAN IRON MINE
### Tower-Soudan State Park, off Minnesota Highways 1 and 169, Tower vicinity

This iron mine in the Vermilion Range is the oldest and deepest in Minnesota. Its 1884 opening marked the beginning of the exploitation of one of the richest iron ore deposits in the world. Soudan remained active until 1962, and in 1963 its owner, U.S. Steel, gave it and 1,000 acres of land to the state. Soudan Iron Mine now forms part of the Tower-Soudan State Park. A number of its original structures, as well as the underground workings, survive and are open to the public.

■ *Sherburne County*

## OLIVER H. KELLEY HOMESTEAD
### On U.S. Route 10, 2 miles southeast of Elk River

Minnesotan Oliver H. Kelley, appointed by President Andrew Johnson to study farm conditions in the post–Civil War South, was appalled by what he saw. To promote better agricultural practices and encourage communications among farmers, he founded the Order of the Patrons of Husbandry, familiarly known as the National Grange, in 1867. An important innovation of the order was the admission of women as full and equal members. From 1868 to 1870, Kelley's Minnesota farmhouse served as the organization's national headquarters. It is now a museum and operating farm, depicting the period when Kelley lived and worked here.

■ *Stearns County*

## SINCLAIR LEWIS BOYHOOD HOME
### 812 Sinclair Lewis Avenue, Sauk Centre

Sinclair Lewis, one of the country's best-known and most widely read novelists of the early 20th century, lived here from 1885 until 1902. His novel *Main Street*, published in 1920, was based in part on boyhood impressions of Sauk Center, a.k.a. "Gopher Prairie." *Main Street*, which satirized and exposed the smug provincialism of small town America, was followed by *Babbitt* and *Elmer Gantry*. In 1926 Lewis was offered the Pulitzer Prize for *Arrowsmith*, but refused the honor. In 1930 he was the first American to be given the Nobel Prize for literature. His boyhood home is open to the public.

■ *Steele County*

## NATIONAL FARMERS' BANK
### 110 North Cedar Street, Owatanna

Officers of this small-town bank were so impressed by Louis Sullivan's article "What Is Architecture" that they offered him the commission to design their proposed new bank. The building's success brought Sullivan other commissions and resulted in a stunning series of similarly scaled banks throughout the Midwest. The first of many, dating from

1907–1908, this one is often considered the finest. Although small in scale, the stone-and-brick bank, with its magnificent terra-cotta ornamentation, is formal and monumental, and—most notable—colorful. Inside are banking rooms, a farmers exchange room, and a private women's parlor. George Grant Elmslie shares credit with Sullivan for the building's design.

### ■ Washington County
### SAINT CROIX BOOM SITE
**On the Saint Croix River off Minnesota Highway 95, 3 miles north of Stillwater**

From 1856 to 1914, this site was the terminal point for the great Minnesota log drives down the Saint Croix River and its tributaries. Each year millions of logs were stored, then measured and sorted, and their ownerships determined, before being assembled into rafts for shipment downstream to the mills. This was the earliest, most important, and longest-lived of the major log storage and handling areas in Minnesota, which for a

number of years trailed only Michigan and Wisconsin as the nation's leading lumber producer. Nothing now remains of the boom site.

### ■ Yellow Medicine County
### ANDREW J. VOLSTEAD HOUSE
**163 Ninth Avenue, Granite Falls**

From 1894 to 1930, this Victorian-era frame house was the home of Andrew J. Volstead. Volstead, the man who "personified prohibition," served in the House of Representatives from 1903 to 1923. In 1919, after the states had ratified the Eighteenth Amendment, he drafted the National Prohibition Enforcement Act, which became known as the Volstead Act. With this act, Volstead conscientiously attempted to devise a bill that would secure "as much enforcement as the country would endure," but not so much as to cause "a public revulsion against national prohibition." The house is now owned by the city and used as offices, with one room devoted to Volstead's life and work.

# MISSISSIPPI

### ■ Adams County
### ANNA SITE
**Address Restricted, Natchez**

Anna Site is a major prehistoric ceremonial center. Construction of the mound complex coincided with the florescence of the Plaquemine culture (ca. A.D. 1200), which formed when indigenous cultures of the lower and middle Mississippi River valley began to interact. This is the type site of the Anna phase of the Plaquemine culture and contains eight truncated pyramidal platform mounds. Occupation of the site ended ca. A.D. 1500.

### ARLINGTON
**Main Street, Natchez**

An archetypical Southern mansion, fronted by a columned, pedimented portico and sur-

rounded by azaleas and magnolias festooned in Spanish moss, Arlington may be regarded as a prototype for many subsequent villas that embellished antebellum Natchez and the lower Mississippi. The brick house was built between 1816 and 1821, and its basic architectural details are in the Federal style that prevailed at the time.

### AUBURN
**Duncan Park, Natchez**

Levi Weeks, architect and builder of this elegant brick villa, was not the most modest of men. He described Auburn in 1812, when it was under construction, as "the most magnificent building in the Territory," especially for the Ionic columns of its portico and its "geometrical [spiral] staircase." Weeks noted that the owner, Lyman Harding (who was Mississippi's first attorney general), was a fel-

low "Yankey, a native of our own state, Massachusetts." The two northerners gave the South one of its handsomest early mansions, which served as a model for many others. It is now open to the public.

## COMMERCIAL BANK AND BANKER'S HOUSE
### Main and Canal Streets, Natchez

This is a superb example of a building type relatively common in the 19th century but all but vanished today: a combination bank and banker's residence. The Commercial Bank was chartered in 1833, and the stuccoed-brick building with marble facade was erected soon afterward. The bank portion is fronted by an imposing, monumental Ionic portico, and the residence, directly behind, has a domestically scaled Doric porch. Details of both were likely taken from published designs by Asher Benjamin. The building has been adapted, with minimal changes, to serve as the First Church of Christ, Scientist.

## DUNLEITH
### 84 Homochitto Street, Natchez

This is Mississippi's only remaining antebellum example of a full peripteral colonnaded mansion. Twenty-six giant-order Tuscan columns encircle the house, and cast-iron railings between them protect a first-floor porch and second-story gallery. Dunleith was built ca. 1855 by Charles C. Dahlgren, who later became a brigadier general in the Confederate Army of Mississippi.

Dunleith, Natchez, Adams County, 1973. Courtesy of NPS.

*Emerald Mound Site, Adams County. Courtesy of NPS (Mark R. Barnes).*

## EMERALD MOUND SITE (NPS)
### Natchez Trace Parkway, Stanton

This archeological site dates from the late Mississippian period (ca. A.D. 1200–1730). The platform mound is the second-largest late prehistoric earthwork in the country (after Monks Mound at Cahokia in Illinois). Emerald Mound has a flat top, or plaza, with two smaller secondary mounds at each end. The site demonstrates the influence of temple-building societies from the north among people of the lower Mississippi region. Adjoining the Natchez Trace, the mound was noted and described by a number of travelers in the early 19th century, many of whom cited adjoining mounds that have now disappeared. Emerald Mound was stabilized by the National Park Service in 1955.

## GRAND VILLAGE OF THE NATCHEZ
### 3 miles southeast of Natchez

This ceremonial mound center was the governmental and religious seat of the Natchez Indians during the late 17th and early 18th centuries and was described in accounts of the region by early French explorers. The Natchez culture developed directly from the prehistoric Plaquemine culture, and archeological evidence indicates that the site was occupied by the thirteenth century. Investigations have uncovered numerous artifacts, both native and European. Remnants of the three temple mounds, a plaza, and the village site are open and interpreted as the Grand Village of the Natchez Indians by the Mississippi Department of Archives and History.

## HOUSE ON ELLICOTT'S HILL
### North Canal Street at Jefferson Street, Natchez

This brick (first story) and frame (second story) house, ca. 1800, is among the oldest in Natchez. It was built soon after the Spanish platted a town on the bluffs above the Mississippi River. A two-story gallery fronts the house, whose plan is typical of Louisiana buildings of its period. There are no halls; instead, each room has direct access to the exterior. The house, also known as Connelly's Tavern, was restored in 1935–1936 for the Natchez Gar-den Club, which maintains it as a museum.

## LONGWOOD
### 1.5 miles southeast of Natchez

This eccentric brick house, its construction halted by the Civil War, is significant for several reasons. Begun in 1860, it is the country's largest and most elaborate octagonal house, representing a short-lived architectural fad promoted by phrenologist Orson Squire Fowler, who argued that the form provided more space than traditionally square or rectangular buildings afforded. Stylistically, Longwood is one of the finest surviving examples of the Oriental, or Moorish, Revival style, a short-lived architectural romanticism that flourished in the mid-19th century. Philadelphia architect Samuel Sloan designed the suburban villa for Haller Nutt, a wealthy cotton planter, whose fortune was devastated by the war. Also known as "Nutt's Folly," Longwood was acquired by the Pilgrimage Garden Club in 1970 and is open to the public.

## MELROSE
**Melrose Avenue, Natchez**

Jacob Byers's obituary, referring to him as "an eminent architect and builder," noted that he had planned and built "the palace mansion of J. T. McMurran, Esq., by many considered the best edifice in the State of Mississippi." Melrose, named by McMurran for Melrose Abbey in Scotland and completed in 1845, may be seen as the perfection of the Natchez villa. Greek Revival in style, it harkens back to earlier houses such as Auburn and Arlington, with its monumental portico and pristine setting. Melrose has never been compromised by accretions or alterations, and with its complete set of plantation outbuildings presents an unrivaled picture of antebellum prosperity. Melrose is open to the public.

## MONMOUTH
**East Franklin Street and Melrose Avenue, Natchez**

Another of the grand antebellum villas of Natchez, Monmouth was built ca. 1818 and brought to its present Greek Revival state of perfection ca. 1853 by John Anthony Quitman. Quitman, an outstanding Mexican War general, states' rights advocate, defender of slavery, and governor of Mississippi, bought the property in 1826 and lived here until his death in 1858. Monmouth stands as an eloquent testament to Quitman's economic and social status as a wealthy, influential lawyer and planter.

## ROSALIE
**100 Orleans Street, Natchez**

Built for a wealthy cotton broker in 1823, this handsome antebellum mansion stands at the site of the French Fort Rosalie, established in 1716 on a high bluff overlooking the Mississippi. Like so many Natchez houses, Rosalie is fronted by a monumental pedimented portico; here the architectural order is Tuscan. A sense of its scale and importance is afforded by the fact that it served as Union headquarters after the Confederate surrender at Vicksburg, although its pivotal location obviously played a more decisive role in its selection than any architectural merit. Rosalie was purchased by the Daughters of the American Revolution in 1938 and is a historic house museum.

## STANTON HALL
**High Street between Pearl and Commerce Streets, Natchez**

One of the largest and most ornate of Natchez's many imposing mansions, Stanton Hall represents the city's wealth and opulence on the eve of the Civil War. Built between 1851 and 1858 for wealthy cotton broker Frederick Stanton, the house has a monumental Corinthian portico sheltering a cast-iron second-floor gallery and is topped by a large belvedere above its hipped roof. The property occupies an entire city block and at one time housed the Stanton College for Young Ladies. In 1940, Stanton Hall was purchased by the Pilgrimage Garden Club and subsequently restored as the club's headquarters and a historic house museum.

### ■ *Alcorn County*

## SIEGE AND BATTLE OF CORINTH SITES
**Corinth vicinity (Alcorn and Corinth Counties)**

Two important trunk railroads passed through Corinth, making it a vital transportation hub of the western Confederacy. A Union siege, from April 28 to May 30, 1862, forced the Confederates to evacuate, and a Southern attack was also repulsed at the Battle of Corinth on October 3–4. This Union triumph, following a summer of Southern victories that appeared to presage recognition of the Confederacy by the United Kingdom, helped to end that prospect. Well-preserved earthworks, batteries, rifle pits, houses used as military headquarters, and the Corinth National Cemetery, with more than 5,600 Civil War interments, most of them unknown, remain. (Also in Hardeman County, Tennessee.)

### ■ *Bolivar County*

## I. T. MONTGOMERY HOUSE
**West Main Street, Mound Bayou**

Isaiah Thornton Montgomery and his cousin Benjamin Green, former slaves who had belonged to the family of Jefferson Davis, established the town of Mound Bayou in July 1887. One of a number of settlements founded during the post–Reconstruction period during which African Americans could exercise self-government, Mound Bayou prospered from its location on the railroad, the fertile Mississippi Delta, and Montgomery's leadership. He built this brick house in 1910 and lived in it until his death in 1924.

## ▪ Claiborne County

### OAKLAND MEMORIAL CHAPEL
**Alcorn State University, Alcorn**

Alcorn University, a product of Mississippi's Reconstruction legislature, was founded in 1871 as the nation's first land-grant college intended specifically to educate African Americans. Its first president was Hiram R. Revels, the first African American elected to the U.S. Senate. The site chosen was the campus of Oakland College, a defunct white Presbyterian institution that had prospered before the Civil War. Oakland Chapel, a distinguished Greek Revival building with an imposing pedimented portico, was built in 1838. It is the only unaltered structure associated with both Oakland College and the fledgling days of Alcorn University. Like most buildings of its caliber and of its time and place, it was built by slave labor.

## ▪ Clay County

### WAVERLY
**10 miles east of West Point, Clay County**

This Greek Revival mansion, begun in the 1840s and completed in 1852, is distinguished by an immense octagonal rotunda that projects through the roof as a cupola. Inside, double curved stairways and railed balconies on three levels add to the dramatic effect. The open cupola, also acting as a ventilator, carried off vapors from the gas lighting system. Waverly is open to the public as a historic house museum.

## ▪ Corinth County

### SIEGE AND BATTLE OF CORINTH SITES
**Corinth vicinity (Alcorn and Corinth Counties)**

(Also in Hardeman County, Tennessee — see entry under Alcorn County.)

## ▪ Hancock County

### ROCKET PROPULSION TEST COMPLEX
**National Space Technology Laboratories, Bay Saint Louis**

This complex was built in 1965 to support the mission of the National Space Technology Laboratories for rocket propulsion systems. It is important for its role in testing several stages of the Saturn V rocket, crucial steps in the effort to put astronauts on the moon. In essence, this complex was the critical final step in certifying the Saturn V rocket ready for flight.

## ▪ Harrison County

### BEAUVOIR
**200 West Beach Boulevard, Biloxi**

Jefferson Davis, president of the Confederate States of America, lived at Beauvoir from 1877 until 1889, the year of his death. It was at this place of retirement that he wrote *The Rise And Fall of The Confederate Government,* which was in part a summation of his eventful life. Architecturally, Beauvoir is a fine example of a Gulf Coast "raised cottage." A veranda extends across the front and halfway along the sides; the arrangement is calculated to take advantage of winds from the adjacent Gulf to provide natural ventilation. Beauvoir is open as a memorial to its most famous occupant and owner.

## ▪ Hinds County

### CHAMPION HILL BATTLEFIELD
**4 miles southwest of Bolton**

The battle at Champion Hill was a crucial Union victory in the Vicksburg campaign, itself a turning point in the Civil War. Troops led by General Ulysses S. Grant forced the retreat of General John C. Pemberton's Confederate forces on May 16, 1863. The siege of Vicksburg followed, and on July 4, 1863, the Confederates surrendered the city and its garrison. It has been said that "the drums of Champion Hill sounded the doom of Richmond." Champion Hill is owned and administered by the Mississippi Department of Archives and History.

*Rocket Propulsion Test Complex, Hancock County. A-1 Test Stand with Saturn V second stage, ready for firing, 1967. Courtesy of NASA, Marshall Space Flight Center Facilities Office.*

*Old Mississippi State Capitol, Jackson, Hinds County. Senate Chamber. Courtesy of Tom Joynt.*

## MISSISSIPPI GOVERNOR'S MANSION

### 316 East Capitol Street, Jackson

Mississippi's Governor's Mansion was built in 1839–1841 and has been continuously occupied ever since. Only the Virginia governor's mansion enjoys a longer record of continuous occupancy by a state's chief executives and their families. The mansion, a monumental Greek Revival brick building with a rounded entrance portico that recalls the south facade of the White House, was designed by English-born architect William Nichols. The building was enlarged in 1908–1909 and refurbished and restored in 1972–1975.

## OLD MISSISSIPPI STATE CAPITOL

### East side of State Street at the head of Capitol Street, Jackson

Designed by William Nichols and built between 1836 and 1840, this impressive Greek Revival building served as Mississippi's state capitol until 1903. Architecturally, it is notable for its rational interior plan and architectural details. Historically, it is noted for witnessing the 1839 passage of the Married Women's Property Act, the first law passed by any state to protect the property rights of married women. The capitol also witnessed the passage of Mississippi's 1890 Constitution, which disenfranchised African Americans and served as a model soon emulated by other southern states. Restored in 1959–1961, the old capitol now serves as the State Historical Museum.

## ■ Humphreys County

### JAKETOWN SITE
**Address Restricted, Belzoni vicinity**

This deeply stratified habitation site on an old meander ridge of the Mississippi River in the northwestern portion of the state was occupied ca. 2000–600 B.C. It served as a regional trading center between the Poverty Point culture area of the lower Mississippi River valley and cultures to the east. Excavations undertaken in the 1940s and 1950s recovered thousands of ceramic sherds that provide a quantitative understanding of the ceramic chronology in the region. Archeologists also found more than 10,000 other Poverty Point artifacts. Many of the items traded were produced here as well. The well-preserved earthen mounds and middens indicate that the site was occupied over a long period.

## ■ Lafayette County

### AMMADELLE
**637 North Lamar Street, Oxford**

Constructed between 1859 and 1861, this red brick Italian villa is a prime example of the architectural talents of Calvert Vaux, perhaps better known for his work in landscape design. Vaux's original drawings survive and show that the house remains little changed from his original conception. An intended wine cellar and balconies were never built, as the Civil War interrupted their installation. The picturesque curves defining lawns and plantings of the seven acres surrounding the house were also devised by Vaux.

### WILLIAM FAULKNER HOUSE
**Old Taylor Road, Oxford**

William Faulkner is a major figure in American literature. Characters inhabiting his not-so-fictional Yoknapatawpha County illustrate the decay and sterility of the old aristocracy, the crassness and amorality of the rising commercial class, the burden of guilt in race relations, and the courage and endurance of African Americans. Faulkner was awarded the Nobel Prize in 1950 and was awarded the Pulitzer twice, in 1955 and posthumously in 1963. He purchased this frame antebellum Greek Revival house in 1930, named it Rowan Oak, and lived in it until his death in 1962. Now owned by the University of Mississippi, the house is virtu-

*Ammadelle, Oxford, Lafayette County. Courtesy of HABS (Jack E. Boucher).*

*William Faulkner House, Oxford, Lafayette County. Courtesy of HABS (Jack E. Boucher).*

ally unchanged from Faulkner's time and is open to the public.

## LUCIUS Q. C. LAMAR HOUSE
### 616 North 14th Street, Oxford

From about 1868 to 1888 this frame cottage was the home of Lucius Quintus Cincinnatus Lamar, one of the most versatile statesmen Mississippi—or any other state—ever produced. In 1861, Lamar resigned his seat in Congress and drafted the Mississippi Secession Ordinance. During the Civil War he served the Confederacy as a soldier and commissioner to Russia. After the war, he became a leading Southern spokesman for reconciliation during Reconstruction, an exponent of Southern industrial progress, and a leader of the "New South" movement. Later in his career he served in the U.S. Senate, as secretary of the interior, and on the U.S. Supreme Court.

### ■ *Lauderdale County*

## HIGHLAND PARK DENTZEL CAROUSEL
### Highland Park, Meridian

This wooden carousel, dating from the 1890s, is likely the oldest of the three earliest Dentzel menagerie carousels that remain virtually intact. The other two, in Indiana, are also designated National Historic Landmarks. In addition to its carved animals, the Highland Park Carousel still has its original oil "scenery" paintings—some showing animals, others landscapes, all framed in gilded wooden frames—and is the only one of the three still covered by a historic "shelter," or carousel house, built from plans furnished by the Dentzel Company. Dentzel, founded in the mid-19th century by the son of a German carousel maker, produced more than 100 carousels. The Highland Park Carousel was restored as a Bicentennial project in the 1970s.

### ■ *Noxubee County*

## DANCING RABBIT CREEK TREATY SITE
### Address Restricted, Macon vicinity

On September 27, 1830, a forced treaty was signed at this traditional Choctaw gathering place, by which the tribe gave up all claims to land east of the Mississippi River, and which ultimately led to their removal. The infamous treaty—it later served as a model for similar pacts of removal for the Chickasaw, Cherokee, Creek, and Seminole nations—also opened up large parts of eastern Mississippi and western Alabama to settlement. A historical marker and a later Choctaw cemetery mark the site.

### ■ *Warren County*

## PEMBERTON'S HEADQUARTERS
### 1018 Crawford Street, Vicksburg

The siege of Vicksburg, one of the most

strategic campaigns of the Civil War, lasted 47 days, from May 18 to July 4, 1863. During most of this time, Confederate commander Lieutenant General John C. Pemberton and his staff were headquartered in this two-story brick house. On July 3, the same day that marked the Confederate defeat at Gettysburg, Pemberton held a council with his officers to discuss capitulation and the next day surrendered to Union forces led by Major General U. S. Grant. The loss of Vicksburg severed the Confederacy geographically and may be seen as the beginning of the end of the Southern cause.

## WARREN COUNTY COURTHOUSE
### Court Square, Vicksburg

This impressive Greek Revival civic building served as a symbol of Confederate resistance in the Vicksburg campaign of 1862–1863. Standing tall, proud, and new (it was finished in 1861) on a high bluff, it was easily visible to Union troops camped on the floodplain across the Mississippi River. In May 1863, Grant's army lay siege to Vicksburg, and on July 4, after 47 days, the city surrendered. Soldiers of the 75th Illinois and 4th Minnesota proudly unfurled the colors from the courthouse cupola, symbolizing their victory. The courthouse is now a museum.

## ■ Washington County
## WINTERVILLE SITE
### Along State Highway 1, Winterville vicinity

This prehistoric ceremonial mound complex is one of the largest of its type in the Mississippi valley. The mounds were constructed between A.D. 1000 and 1400, and constitute the type site of the Winterville phase of the Mississippian period (A.D. 1200–1400). There were some 23 truncated pyramids arranged to form two large plazas, with the largest earthwork, the Great Temple Mound, in the center. The 18 mounds remaining are maintained and interpreted as the Winterville Mounds State Park.

## ■ Yazoo County
## HOLLY BLUFF SITE
### Address Restricted, Holly Bluff

This fortified ceremonial mound complex, with 20 earthworks remaining, is one of the largest prehistoric Mississippian centers in the lower Mississippi River Valley. It contains evidence of continuous occupation dating back to the Poverty Point Culture (ca. 2000–500 B.C.), and is the type site for the Lake George phase (A.D. 1400–1600). The site marks the southern margin of the Mississippian cultural advance down the Mississippi River and the northern edge of the Cole's Creek and Plaquemine cultures of the South.

# MISSOURI

## ■ Boone County
## SANBORN FIELD AND SOIL EROSION PLOTS
### University of Missouri, Columbia

Established on the University of Missouri campus in 1888, Sanborn Field is the country's second-oldest experimental field for soils and crops. The nearby Soil Erosion Plots, first in the country to measure runoff and erosion caused by different crops, were created in 1917. Research conducted at both sites have led to improvements in agricultural practices and techniques, as well as providing solid foundations for America's soil conservation movement.

## ■ Buchanan County
## PATEE HOUSE
### 12th and Penn Streets, Saint Joseph

John Patee completed this huge U-shaped

hotel in 1858, intending it to be the finest in the West. He also intended it to be across the street from an anticipated railroad terminal. When the terminal was built several blocks away, Patee's visions of financial security faded. No matter. Fame was ensured when the hotel became the eastern terminus of the Pony Express, and housed the business offices of its owners. A cannon announcing the inauguration of this early-day rapid delivery mail service between Saint Joseph and Sacramento, California, was fired in front of the hotel on April 3, 1860. After serving once as a factory and twice as a women's college, the hotel was partially restored in 1975. It is now a museum with a wide assortment of collections, many focused on transportation.

## ■ Callaway County

### RESEARCH CAVE
**Address Restricted, Portland**

Similar to Graham Cave in many respects, the rock shelter known as Research Cave was a significant prehistoric Indian site containing deposits that reflected an intermittent occupation over a period of at least 8,000 years. The cave was especially important to research, as its name indicates, because it contained three major cultural complexes — Archaic, Middle-to-Late Woodland, and Middle Mississippian — in relatively undisturbed sequence. Adding to its importance, many normally perishable items had been preserved here. Unfortunately, much of the cave has been destroyed and its integrity severely compromised. (See Graham Cave, Montgomery County.)

## WESTMINSTER COLLEGE GYMNASIUM
**Westminster College, Fulton**

"From Stettin in the Baltic to Trieste in the Adriatic an iron curtain has descended across the Continent." Winston Churchill made his famous assessment of conditions in post–World War II Europe in his "Sinews of Peace" speech, delivered in the gymnasium of this small liberal arts college on March 5, 1946. Immediate reaction to his conception of a figurative iron curtain was negative on both sides of the Atlantic, as few then realized the seriousness of the Soviet threat. Events soon vindicated Churchill's position, and his speech helped prepare the way for the Truman Doctrine and, later, for the North Atlantic Treaty Organization.

## ■ Clay County

### WATKINS MILL
**6 miles northwest of Excelsior**

Built in 1859–1860 as the central feature of a self-sufficient community on Missouri's western frontier, this three-story brick building is a wonderfully preserved example of a mid-19th-century woolen mill, complete with original machinery and business records. The property became a state park in

*Patee House, Saint Joseph, Buchanan County. Courtesy of HABS (Jack E. Boucher).*

*Harry S Truman Historic District, Independence, Jackson County. Truman House. Courtesy of HABS (Jack E. Boucher).*

1962, and a number of surrounding buildings, including the Watkins farmhouse, have since been rehabilitated or reconstructed. They and the mill are open to the public.

### ■ *Jackson County*

### FORT OSAGE
**North edge of Sibley on the Missouri River, Sibley**

Fort Osage, the country's first military outpost in the area acquired in the Louisiana Purchase, was established in 1808 by General William Clark for the protection and promotion of trade with the Osage Indians. It soon became one of the most successful of the 28 government-supervised trading posts that functioned from 1795 to 1822. These operated under a "factory" system intended to prevent exploitation of Indians by individual traders. In 1825, Fort Osage became the point from which distances were measured on the Santa Fe Trail. Over the years its buildings were dismantled, but beginning in 1947 reconstruction was undertaken. The fort is open to the public as a unit of the Jackson County Parks and Recreation Department.

### MUTUAL MUSICIANS ASSOCIATION BUILDING
**1823 Highland Avenue, Kansas City**

From the 1920s to the 1940s this building was the home of American Federation of Musicians Local 627, whose members created the Kansas City style of jazz, one of America's truly indigenous musical expressions. The simple masonry building served as a second home and training ground for such greats as Count Basie, Hershel Evans, Lester Young, Charles "Bird" Parker, and Hot Lips Page. During the 1930s and 1940s the sounds emanating from this location were "all the rage" throughout the country. The building is still used as a practice hall and concert venue for jazz musicians.

### HARRY S TRUMAN FARM HOME (NPS)
**12301 Blue Ridge Boulevard Extension, Grandview**

This vernacular farmhouse was President Harry S Truman's home from 1907 to 1917, and he later recalled that those years were among the best of his life. Here, from ages 23 to 34, Truman developed abilities that would serve him throughout his career, and his intimate knowledge of farming appealed to the rural vote during the close-fought election of 1948. During his presidency, experience gained at the farm helped Truman shape his federal farm programs. The house was restored in the 1980s and became part of the Harry S Truman National Historic Site in 1992.

### HARRY S TRUMAN HISTORIC DISTRICT
**Delaware Street area, Independence**

From the time of his marriage in 1919 until

his death in 1972, Harry S Truman was intimately associated with North Delaware Street in Independence. Bess Truman's family home at 219 North Delaware became the couple's home and remained their primary residence throughout their lives. After he retired from the presidency, Truman maintained an office at the Harry S Truman Library that adjoins the upper-middle-class residential neighborhood, often arriving after a brisk morning walk, just as had been his habit in Washington. The house, an elaborate Victorian-era frame house with scroll-sawn trim, and the library/museum, where the Trumans are buried, are major components of the Harry S Truman Historic District and are open to the public.

## ■ *Linn County*

### GENERAL JOHN J. PERSHING BOYHOOD HOME
**Worlow and State Streets, Laclede**

From 1866 to 1877 this was the home of John Joseph Pershing. In 1917, as commander of the American Expeditionary Force to Europe, Pershing exercised the greatest authority of any American general since U. S. Grant and organized what was then the largest army in American history. His forces were instrumental in ending World War I. In 1919 a grateful Congress made Pershing General of the Armies, a title previously held only by George Washington. Later, as chief of staff, Pershing laid the groundwork for the reorganization and modernization of the army that would help prepare it for another conflict: World War II. This frame Victorian-era house, now a Missouri state park, is open to the public as a museum honoring its boyhood occupant.

## ■ *Marion County*

### MARK TWAIN BOYHOOD HOME
**206–208 Hill Street, Hannibal**

Often considered the Midwest's outstanding literary shrine, this small frame house was the boyhood home of Samuel Langhorne Clemens, better known as Mark Twain. The people and places he knew during the first two decades of his life in this Mississippi River town had a great influence on the career of this eminent American novelist and humorist. Huckleberry Finn was modeled on a childhood chum, Becky Thatcher resembled his teenage heartthrob, and Tom Sawyer was "a combination of three boys whom I knew." The house—its dining room the scene of Tom Sawyer's Painkiller Patent Medicine episode with Peter the cat—is open to the public. The famous fence with "three coats of whitewash on it" that Tom conned his bud-

*General John J. Pershing Boyhood Home, Laclede, Linn County. Courtesy of HABS (Anthony Apostolarus).*

dies into painting for him, is still here. (See Mark Twain House, Hartford County, Connecticut.)

### ■ *Montgomery County*

### GRAHAM CAVE
**0.5 miles north of Mineola**

When Graham Cave was excavated in 1949–1955, archeologists from the University of Missouri found deposits dating back to 8,000 B.C. and spanning much of the Archaic period until about 4,000 B.C. Remains from the Early and Middle Archaic times give the rock shelter its importance and illustrate a merging of Eastern and Plains influence in Missouri. The shallow cave is not accessible to the public, but is visible, and forms the centerpiece of Graham Cave State Park. (See Research Cave, Callaway County.)

### ■ *Pike County*

### "CHAMP" CLARK HOUSE
**204 East Champ Clark Drive, Bowling Green**

James Beauchamp "Champ" Clark, Speaker of the House of Representatives from 1911 to 1919, lived here from 1899 until his death in 1921. Clark played a major role in the campaign to replace Speaker Joseph G. Cannon and his arbitrary control of legislative procedure, known as "Cannonism." He was also Woodrow Wilson's leading competitor for the Democratic presidential nomina-

tion in 1912. Clark named his comfortable Victorian-era frame farmhouse "Honey Shuck" after the honey locust trees in the yard. It is now a historic house museum.

### ■ *Saint Louis City*

### ANHEUSER-BUSCH BREWERY
**721 Pestalozzi Street**

This huge complex represents the influence of German immigrants on the beer brewing industry in America. Eberhard Anheuser started the brewery in 1852 and was joined by his son-in-law, Adolphus Busch, in 1865. Busch pioneered new methods of production and distribution, including use of the refrigerated railroad car. The buildings, dating mostly from the last quarter of the 19th century, combine utilitarian plans with ornamental brick and stonework.

### CHRIST CHURCH CATHEDRAL
**1210 Locust Street**

Constructed between 1859 and 1867, this Gothic Revival masterpiece is one of the few remaining examples of the work of architect Leopold Eidlitz. A native of Prague who trained in Vienna, Eidlitz practiced in New York, where he obtained a number of important commissions. Through his work and his writings, he brought new attitudes to American design, which had traditionally looked to England for inspiration. Eidlitz worked in a variety of styles and proved here that he was capable of designing a Gothic

*Anheuser-Busch Brewery, Saint Louis, Saint Louis City. Brew house, 1942. Courtesy of HABS (Piaget-van Ravenswaay).*

Revival church equal to any in the country. The church became the cathedral of the Episcopal Diocese of Missouri in 1888.

## EADS BRIDGE
### Spanning the Mississippi River between Saint Louis, Missouri, and East Saint Louis, Illinois

This three-span, ribbed steel arch bridge crosses the Mississippi with an overall length of 6,442 feet and a clearance of 50 feet above high water. Dedicated on July 4, 1874, it was designed and built by Captain James B. Eads, who utilized an innovative cantilever support to produce spans larger than any previously constructed. The bridge was designed with two levels, the upper for a roadway, the lower for a railroad. (Also in Saint Claire County, Illinois.)

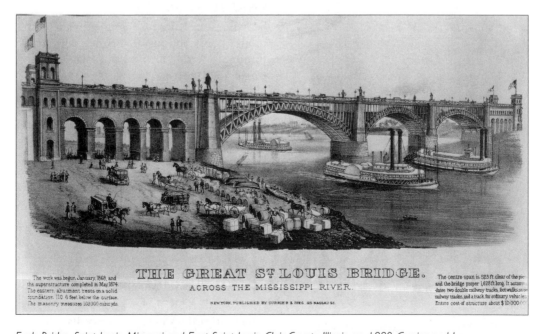

*Eads Bridge, Saint Louis, Missouri and East Saint Louis, Clair County, Illinois, ca. 1880. Currier and Ives.*

## JOSEPH ERLANGER HOUSE
**5127 Waterman Boulevard**

From 1917 until his death in 1965, Joseph Erlanger, graduate of the Johns Hopkins Medical School and one of the leading American physiologists of the first half of the 20th century, lived here. Erlanger shared the 1944 Nobel Prize in medicine and physiology for his discovery of the electrical nature of the human nervous system. His work demonstrated that American medicine had definitely come of age.

## GATEWAY ARCH (NPS)
**Memorial Drive between Poplar Street and Eads Bridge**

This 630-foot catenary arch is the tallest monument in the United States. Designed by Eero Saarinen in 1947, it was not built until the 1960s. At the time the complicated, yet subtle, design and unique structural system had never been attempted on such a large scale. Towering over downtown Saint Louis and the Mississippi River, the shining stainless steel arch symbolizes the city's role as the Gateway to the West and has become its easily recognized logo. Part of the Jefferson National Expansion Memorial, the arch is open to the public.

*Gateway Arch, Saint Louis. Courtesy of HABS (Jack E. Boucher).*

## GOLDENROD
**400 North Wharf Street**

When *Goldenrod* was built in 1909, it was the largest showboat ever constructed. Its exterior was relatively plain, but its 1,400-seat theater was lavishly decorated with gilt, red velour, and bright carpets. The theater has been altered, but *Goldenrod* still serves up melodrama and vaudeville to appreciative audiences. (See *Majestic,* Hamilton County, Ohio.)

## INAUGURAL
**300 North Wharf Street**

One of two surviving Admirable class fleet minesweepers, the largest and most successful class of American minesweepers, *Inaugural* (1944) was fitted for both wire and acoustic sweeping and could double as an antisubmarine warfare platform. The Admirable class minesweepers were also used as patrol and escort vessels. After distinguishing itself in the bloody battle of Okinawa, *"Augie"* remained in the dangerous waters off that island until the war's end. It then swept the seas off Japan, clearing 82 mines for the occupation forces. Unfortunately, *Inaugural* sank in the Mississippi during the flood of 1993 and is no longer accessible.

## SCOTT JOPLIN RESIDENCE
**2685-A Morgan Street**

Scott Joplin, "King of Ragtime," made enormous contributions to American music through a prodigious output that included single hits such as "Maple Leaf Rag" and "Sunflower Slow Drag" and the full-scaled opera *Treemonisha*. His syncopated rhythms, unique combinations of Midwestern folk and African-American melodic traditions, continue to provide foundations for modern compositions and listening pleasure for millions. From 1900 to 1903, Joplin lived in this brick row house. The house was restored in the 1990s and is open to the public as a Missouri state park.

## MISSOURI BOTANICAL GARDEN
**2345 Tower Grove Avenue**

Established in 1859, this is among the oldest botanical gardens in the country. Its founder, Henry Shaw, intended the 75-acre garden to show the public the ornamental delights of plants, to educate the average citizen in basic botany and horticulture, and to be a center for scientific botanical research. Shaw and his successors have succeeded on all counts: the Garden is recognized as one of the foremost institutions of its kind in the world.

## SHELLEY HOUSE
**4600 Labadie Avenue**

One-half of a typical Saint Louis two-family flat built in 1906, the Shelley house is important in African-American history and in law. It was the home of the plaintiffs in *Shelley v. Kraemer* (1948), in which the U.S. Supreme Court ruled that enforcement of racially restrictive housing covenants was unconstitutional. This decision led to substantial changes in housing patterns throughout the country in succeeding decades. The house is still privately owned.

## TOWER GROVE PARK
**4255 Arsenal Street**

Officially opened to the public in 1872, Tower Grove is among the nation's largest and best-preserved 19th-century city parks designed in the "gardenesque style." Unlike the picturesque landscapes of Frederick Law Olmsted that depend primarily on plant material, gardenesque parks add a variety of structural elements—gates, pavilions, picnic shelters, and bandstands—to make a more formally organized landscape. Like the adjoining Missouri Botanical Garden, the 285-acre Tower Grove Park was a gift to Saint Louis by merchant philanthropist Henry Shaw, who was largely responsible for its design.

## UNION STATION
**18th and Market Streets**

Designed by Saint Louis architect Theodore C. Link and erected in 1892–1894, Union Station and its Terminal Hotel are among the most monumental examples of their type in the country. Details reflect the Richardsonian Romanesque style, and the overall form and complex rooflines resemble those of a huge château. The adjoining single-vault steel train shed, designed by engineer George H. Pegram to cover 32 tracks, was America's

largest. In the 1980s the structures were restored, remodeled, and reopened. With its operating hotel and "festival market place" that now occupies much of the station, this is one of America's most impressive and imaginative revitalizations of a historic complex.

## UNITED STATES CUSTOMHOUSE AND POST OFFICE, ST. LOUIS
**Olive, Locust, Eighth and Ninth Streets**

Constructed between 1873 and 1884, this is one of two major surviving examples of federal buildings in the French Second Empire style designed by Alfred B. Mullet, supervising architect of the U.S. Treasury. Along with the Old Executive Office Building in Washington, D.C., it represents a high-water mark in America's interpretation of this 19th-century architectural style. The building is now enveloped by later, taller downtown structures, but its sturdy granite walls, pilasters, quoins, and mansard-roofed dome still dominate their surroundings. Threatened with demolition in the 1960s, the building was instead rehabilitated and adapted for various commercial uses.

## WAINWRIGHT BUILDING
**709 Chestnut Street**

This 10-story, iron-and-steel–framed office building, pivotal in the history of tall building design and construction, was built in 1890–1891 from designs by Louis Sullivan. Before the Wainwright, surfaces of tall buildings had been covered with architectural cliches that bore no relation to their structure. Here Sullivan articulated a tripartite division of base, shaft, and capital that—with carefully orchestrated fenestration patterns and rhythms of piers and spandrels—masterfully reflects and respects the metal-frame skeleton beneath. The Wainwright was threatened with demolition in the 1970s, but was saved when the State of Missouri purchased it and converted it for use as a state office building.

## WASHINGTON UNIVERSITY HILLTOP CAMPUS HISTORIC DISTRICT
**Lindell and Skinker Boulevards**

The district is associated with the Louisiana Purchase Exposition, held in Saint Louis in 1904, and with the third modern Olympic

Games held in conjunction with the Exposition. The Exposition, the largest in area and scope of World's Fairs up to that date, used the newly emerging university campus as its site. Although the buildings included in the landmark designation were not specifically designed as Exposition structures, they remain the largest extant group from the heyday of World's Fairs. Francis Gymnasium and Francis Field, provided for in the campus plan, were completed specifically to house the Olympics, at which Alice Roosevelt, the president's daughter, handed out the medals.

## ■ *Saint Louis County*

### WHITE HAVEN (NPS)
**9060 Whitehaven Drive, Grantwood Village**

Ulysses S. Grant first came to White Haven in 1844 as a guest of his West Point roommate, Frederick Tracy Dent. At the time the family's eldest daughter, Julia, was away, but during subsequent visits she was home, and as Grant later recalled, his trips soon became far "more enjoyable." They were married in 1848 and lived here for a short period in the 1850s. Grant had originally planned to retire to White Haven, before the political scandals of his administration and financial difficulties made that impractical. The handsome frame house, fronted by a double gallery, is now the U. S. Grant National Historic Site.

## ■ *Sainte Genevieve County*

### LOUIS BOLDUC HOUSE
**123 South Main Street, Sainte Genevieve**

Built ca. 1785, this is an excellent example of a unique method of construction employed by the French in North America: *poteaux-sur-sole.* Posts, or logs, arranged vertically, are set on sills, with clay and grass *(bouzillage)* filling. A wide *galerie,* or veranda, surrounds the house. Canadian-born Louis Bolduc was a prosperous lead miner, merchant, and planter, as well as a leading figure of the French village of Sainte Genevieve. His house was restored in the 1950s and is now a historic house museum.

### SAINTE GENEVIEVE HISTORIC DISTRICT
**Sainte Genevieve**

First settled in the mid-18th century on lower ground, where it was frequently flooded, Sainte Genevieve was relocated to its present site after the flood of 1785. The principal seat of government during Spanish control of western Louisiana territory, the town gradually declined after the Louisiana Purchase and the emergence of Saint Louis as the area's major port and commercial center. Sainte Genevieve has retained much of the atmosphere of its missionary, fur trading, mining, and military eras, and a number of its earliest buildings survive.

## ■ *Saline County*

### ARROW ROCK
**Arrow Rock State Park**

Arrow Rock was one of the early starting points of the Santa Fe Trail. Long before, the Missouri River crossing here had been noted by French cartographers (1723) and Lewis

*Louis Bolduc House, Sainte Genevieve, 1968. Courtesy of NPS.*

and Clark (1804) and had figured prominently in the earliest trailblazing expeditions that opened the West. A permanent ferry was established in 1817. The cliff known as Arrow Rock, remains of the ferry road, Santa Fe Spring, and buildings are preserved in Arrow Rock State Park, adjacent to the small well-preserved town.

## GEORGE CALEB BINGHAM HOUSE
**First and High Streets in Arrow Rock State Park**

From 1837 to 1845 this was the residence of George Caleb Bingham, American portrait and landscape painter. It was during his years at Arrow Rock that Bingham began his sketches of the Missouri River and frontier life that developed into his famous genre paintings. The little brick-and-frame house that he built soon after his marriage was restored in 1936, and again in 1964–1965. It is now a historic house museum within the Arrow Rock State Park.

## UTZ SITE
**Address Restricted, Marshall**

Located on bluffs known as "The Pinnacles," overlooking the Missouri River, this site was occupied from ca. A.D. 1400 to the late 1700s. The summit was likely the principal village area the Missouri Indians occupied at the time of their first contact with Europeans. The site was known to early French explorers, beginning with Père Marquette, whose 1673 map noted "Messourit" Indians here. Artifacts uncovered during archeological investigations indicate that as early as 1724 the Indians were trading at nearby Fort Orleans, the first European outpost on the

Missouri River. Part of the site is within Van Meter State Park and is open to the public.

### ■ *Vernon County*

## CARRINGTON OSAGE VILLAGE SITES
**Osage Village State Historic Site, Nevada**

Occupied from about 1775 to 1825, this was one of the last dwelling places of the Big Osage Indians in southwest Missouri, prior to their removal to Kansas. The site was visited in 1806 by Zebulon Pike. Excavations at the site uncovered large numbers of trade goods, interpreted as illustrating the rapid assimilation achieved by the Osage.

### ■ *Wright County*

## LAURA INGALLS WILDER HOUSE
**1 mile east of Mansfield on U.S. Business Route 60**

Laura Ingalls Wilder created the famous *Little House* series. Classics of children's literature, the stories record the joys and struggles of frontier life—seen through the eyes of Laura as a young girl between the ages of five and eighteen—during the years her family homesteaded in Wisconsin, Kansas, Minnesota, and Missouri. Wilder began writing at the age of 65 while living in this modest frame house. Her daughter Rose Wilder Lane, who urged her mother to record her memories, handled negotiations with her publisher, and edited the manuscripts, has recently been credited with much of the actual writing. The Wilder books have been translated into 26 languages and into other media as well. The house is now a museum.

# MONTANA

## Beaverhead County

### BANNACK HISTORIC DISTRICT
**Off Montana Route 278, Bannack**

Gold was discovered on Willards (now Grasshopper) Creek in July 1862, and soon prospectors swarmed to find their bonanza. Bannack, named for a nearby Indian tribe, sprang up almost overnight. When Montana Territory was established in 1864, Bannack became its first capital. By then, richer deposits had been discovered at Virginia City, and at their first assembly the state legislators voted to move the capital there. Now a state park, Bannack is preserved as a Western ghost town that retains a great deal of character reflecting its brief moment in the sun.

### LEMHI PASS
**12 miles east of Tendoy**

The summit of this mountain pass marks the spot where the Lewis and Clark Expedition crossed the Continental Divide in August 1805. It then marked the boundary between newly acquired Louisiana and Spanish territory to the west. The pass is in a remote section of the Beaverhead Range at an elevation of 7,373 feet. Situated on U.S. property, the pass now marks the boundary between Idaho and Montana and is virtually unchanged from the time the expedition first crossed it. (Also in Lemhi County, Idaho.)

## Big Horn County

### CHIEF PLENTY COUPS (ALEK-CHEA-AHOOSH) HOME
**0.5 miles west of Pryor, at the intersection of Bureau of Indian Affairs Roads 5 and 8**

The homestead of Chief Plenty Coups, one of the last and most celebrated traditional chiefs of the Crow Indians, includes his house, an adjacent log store he operated, and the Plenty Coups Spring, a site of historic and cultural significance to the Crow people. Chief Plenty Coups established the homestead in 1884 and lived there until his death in 1932. One of the most important Native American leaders of the transitional period and an ambassador and negotiator for the Crow, Chief Plenty Coups advocated the adoption of those aspects of American culture necessary to succeed on the reservation while maintaining traditional religious beliefs and cultural values.

*Bannack Historic District, Bannack, Beaverhead County. Abandoned commercial building on Main Street. Courtesy of NPS (Blanche Higgins Schroer).*

## ■ *Blaine County*

### CHIEF JOSEPH BATTLEGROUND OF BEAR'S PAW
#### Approximately 15 miles south of Chinook

"From where the sun now stands, I will fight no more, forever." The battle and siege that took place here from September 30 to October 5, 1877, ended when Chief Joseph uttered those words at this place. He and more than 400 Nez Perce Indians, exhausted from a 1,700-mile trek to escape confinement on a reservation, surrendered to U.S. troops. Even General of the Army William T. Sherman lauded the Nez Perce as displaying "a courage and skill that elicited universal praise." More than a battle was lost at Bear's Paw. It signaled the end of the Nez Perce's existence as an "independent Indian people." Henceforth, they lived as a group of displaced persons — in the white culture, but not of it. Interpretive signs and exhibits mark the undisturbed site of this poignant episode in American history.

## ■ *Broadwater County*

### RANKIN RANCH
#### Avalanche Gulch

Jeanette Rankin, elected in 1916, was the first woman elected to serve in the U.S. House of Representatives, an achievement all the more remarkable for occurring at a time when most states did not allow women to vote. Rankin served two terms, 1917–1919 and 1941–1943, and is best remembered for her pacifism. She opposed America's entry into both world wars and was the only member of Congress to vote against the declaration of war against Japan in 1941. She also played an important role in women's rights and in the social reform movement. From 1923 until 1956 this dynamic figure spent almost all her summers in this frame house, owned by her brother and originally the headquarters of a 2,000-acre ranch.

## ■ *Cascade County*

### GREAT FALLS PORTAGE
#### South of Great Falls

Meriwether Lewis and William Clark, on their famous expedition, were likely the first white men to view the Great Falls of the Missouri River. They were also likely the first white men to curse this 14-mile stretch of falls and rapids, as it took them a full month, from June 13 to July 13, 1805, to accomplish an 18-mile overland portage around the mammoth obstacle. It was one of the most difficult ordeals of their momentous journey.

### CHARLES M. RUSSELL HOUSE AND STUDIO
#### 1217–1219 Fourth Avenue, Great Falls

Charles Russell was a cowboy with a pur-

*Chief Plenty Coups (Alek-Chea-Ahoosh) Home, Pryor, Big Horn County. Courtesy of Thomas H. Simmons.*

pose. Witnessing and participating in the waning days of the legendary American West, he recorded what he saw in paintings and sculpture. He became one of America's most popular and successful artists, and in 1911 his adopted state commissioned him to paint Lewis and Clark's meeting with the Oollashoot Indians for the state capitol in Helena. Russell was honored further when he was selected to be one of Montana's representatives in Statuary Hall at the U.S. Capitol. The frame house where the artist lived from 1900 to 1926 was moved a short distance in 1973. The adjacent log studio he built in 1903 is a museum honoring him.

## ■ Chouteau County

### FORT BENTON
**Town of Fort Benton**

Established as a fur trading center in 1847 at the head of navigation on the Missouri, Fort Benton flourished after 1859 with the growth of steamboat traffic on the river. At one time it was the largest fur trading center in the Northwest and the major distributing point on the Northern Plains. Discovery of gold in Montana in 1862 added to its prosperity, but the arrival of the railroad in 1887 heralded a decline in the water-borne traffic that created it. The old fort is being reconstructed and is now located within Fort Benton City Park.

## ■ Dawson County

### HAGEN SITE
**Address Restricted, Glendive**

The Hagen site represents a pre-horse transition from a sedentary to a nomadic life-style. The Mountain Crow settled at Hagan late in the 1400s after separating from the Awatixa Hidatsa (who remained at Knife River on the Missouri River). The large amount of prehistoric pottery found here is unusual for the Northwestern Plains. The plentiful use of cord-wrapped-rod ceramic decoration suggests that nomads from the north joined the Mountain Crow at Hagen. Hoes and squash knives found here indicate that the inhabitants practiced horticulture.

## ■ Flathead County

### GOING-TO-THE-SUN ROAD (NPS)
**Glacier National Park, West Glacier vicinity (Flathead and Glacier Counties)**

"Landscape engineering" is an essential component in making scenic areas accessible to the motoring public without marring the very features that people come to see and without destroying natural ecological systems. When Glacier National Park's Going-to-the-Sun Road was begun in 1921, it was the most ambitious road construction project ever undertaken by the Bureau of Public Roads and the National Park Service. The innovative agreement between two federal bureaus, along with the rugged topography that had to be traversed, made the road an early laboratory for policies and practices in other road engineering projects. Going-to-the-Sun Road still defines the basic circulation pattern in Glacier National Park.

### GREAT NORTHERN RAILWAY BUILDINGS (NPS)
**West of Babb, Glacier National Park (Flathead and Glacier Counties)**

Following similar cooperative arrangements between railroads and the National Park Service at Yellowstone and Grand Canyon establishing "destination resorts," the Great Northern Railway undertook this operation at Glacier. Built during the "teen" years of the 20th century, these stone, frame, and log buildings—the Many Glacier Hotel, two chalets, and a store—form what is likely the largest collection of Swiss style buildings in the country. The architectural style was deemed appropriate, as Glacier National Park was touted in railroad and park advertisements as "the Switzerland of America." The buildings were carefully sited to be a single day's journey apart and represent the only example of this European arrangement in the country.

### LAKE MCDONALD LODGE (NPS)
**Off Going-to-the-Sun Road, Glacier National Park, West Glacier**

Planned to rival the accommodations being built contemporaneously at Glacier National Park by the Great Northern Railway, Lewis Glacier Hotel is one of the finest examples of

Going-to-the-Sun Road, West Glacier vicinity, Flathead and Glacier Counties. West side tunnel. Courtesy of NPS (Ethan Carr).

the Swiss chalet style in the country. Above a stone ground floor the upper stories are frame, and interior spaces use natural materials to create a purposely rustic, frontier atmosphere. Begun in 1913, the hotel opened in 1914, and its name was changed to Lake McDonald Lodge in 1957. It still serves its original purpose, and the lobby floor still contains inscribed Indian messages translated as "New life to those who drink here" and "Big feast."

## ▪ Gallatin County

### THREE FORKS OF THE MISSOURI
**On the Missouri River, northwest of the town of Three Forks**

On July 25, 1805, Captain William Clark of the Lewis and Clark Expedition arrived at this site and concluded that the Missouri River originated here at the confluence of three smaller rivers. To honor their sponsors, the explorers noted in their journal that they "agreed to name [the rivers] after the President of the United States and the Secretaries of the Treasury and state": Jefferson, Madison, and Gallatin. The site is within the Missouri Headwaters State Park.

## ▪ Glacier County

### CAMP DISAPPOINTMENT
**12 miles northeast of Browning, Blackfoot vicinity**

This pristine site on Cut Bank Creek in the Blackfoot Reservation marks the northernmost point reached by the Lewis and Clark Expedition, important because Meriwether Lewis, who camped here in July 1806, hoped to find that the headwaters of the Marais River arose north of the 49th parallel. Had this been the case, the boundaries of the Louisiana Purchase would have been extended. From the site he observed that the headwaters of the river arose in the west, not in the north. That disappointment, and four days of rainy weather that prevented him from taking the latitude, gave the site its name. Lewis recorded on July 26 that he was "bidding a lasting adieu to this place which I now call camp disappointment."

### GOING-TO-THE-SUN ROAD (NPS)
**Glacier National Park, West Glacier vicinity (Flathead and Glacier Counties)**

(See entry under Flathead County.)

### GREAT NORTHERN RAILWAY BUILDINGS (NPS)
**West of Babb, Glacier National Park (Flathead and Glacier Counties)**

(See entry under Flathead County.)

## ▪ Madison County

### VIRGINIA CITY HISTORIC DISTRICT
**Wallace Street, Virginia City**

Virginia City was founded in 1863 and became a boomtown when gold was discov-

261

ered along Alder Gulch. The gold strike became one of the largest in the northern Rockies, and within a few years a 12-mile stretch was lined with prospecting camps. From the beginning, Virginia City, which became Montana's territorial capital in 1865, was the center of activity. The capitol was moved to Helena in 1875, but Virginia City remains the seat of Madison County. Today it has the appearance of a classic Western ghost town, with false-fronted buildings lining the main street. Many are open as museums and tourist attractions.

## ■ *Missoula County*

### LOLO TRAIL

**Beginning near Lolo, Missoula County, Montana, to Weippe Prairie, Idaho**

The 200-mile-long Lolo Trail is significant for two reasons, both based on its being a traditional Indian route through the Bitterroot Mountains. First, in September 1805, Toby, a Shoshoni guide, led the Lewis and Clark party through the passage. This would prove to be the single most arduous stretch of their entire journey, but was key to the expedition to reach the Pacific side of the continent. Seven decades later hundreds of Nez Perce Indians used the trail when fleeing the U.S. Army during the Nez Perce War of 1877. (Also in Clearwater and Idaho Counties, Idaho.)

### TRAVELER'S REST

**1 mile south of Lolo near U.S. Route 93**

This level lowland, near the spot where Lolo Creek enters the Bitterroot River, was a pivotal stop during the Lewis and Clark Expedition. The explorers camped here from September 9 to 11, 1805, before beginning the most arduous part of their journey over the Lolo Trail. Meriwether Lewis recorded that he determined to stop to "rest our horses and take some scelestial [sic] observations." On their return, the travelers again rested here, from June 30 to July 3, 1806. This time William Clark recorded the event: "We arrived at our old encampment... with a view to remain two days in order to rest ourselves and horses." The site, near U.S. Route 93, is marked with interpretive signs.

## ■ *Park County*

### NORTHEAST ENTRANCE STATION (NPS)

**Vicinity of Cooke City and Silver Gate, Yellowstone National Park**

This rustic entrance building and the adjacent ranger station/residence mark the northeastern entrance to Yellowstone National Park. They not only delineate a physical boundary but also mark a psychological separation between the rest of the world and an area set aside as a permanent wild place. The log structures, with their exaggerated saddle notches, were purposely designed to appear as if they had been executed by pioneer craftsmen with limited hand tools. The buildings remain virtually unchanged from the time they were built in 1935.

## ■ *Powell County*

### GRANT-KOHRS RANCH (NPS)

**Edge of Deer Lodge**

John Grant, who established this ranch in 1853, is often credited with founding Montana's range cattle industry, and Conrad Kohrs, who purchased the spread in the 1860s, was one of the foremost "cattle kings" of his era. The original ranch house and a number of subsidiary structures essential to their far-flung ranching operations remain and are open to the public as the Grant-Kohrs Ranch National Historic Site.

## ■ *Silver Bow County*

### BUTTE HISTORIC DISTRICT

**Butte city limits**

Butte was settled after gold was discovered in 1864, then prospered on silver in the 1870s. In 1880, Marcus Daly, an Irish emigrant, struck copper—a vein of unparalleled richness 50 feet wide. Butte soon became the center of the largest copper mining region in the world, with more than $2 billion worth of minerals produced from "the richest hill on earth." Butte, once characterized as "a bully of a city, stridently male, profane and blustering and boastful," is less boisterous now than in its heyday, but a number of buildings and sites readily call those times to mind.

## BURTON K. WHEELER HOUSE
### 1232 East Second Street, Butte

During the 1920s and 1930s, Burton K. Wheeler was one of the "most formidable of the Senate radicals." He first gained attention in the Teapot Dome scandal in 1924, and he became the first prominent Democrat to support Franklin Delano Roosevelt for the presidency. Later, Wheeler broke with Roosevelt because he believed the president was too conservative. From 1908 until he went to Washington in 1923, Wheeler lived in this modest bungalow. The house is still privately owned.

■ *Yellowstone County*

## PICTOGRAPH CAVE
### 7 miles southeast of Billings

This large, deep rock shelter is one of the key archeological sites used to determine the sequence of prehistoric occupation on the Northwestern Plains. Deposits indicate four periods of occupation, dating from 7000 B.C. to after A.D. 1800. The 100 red, black, and white pictographs that gave the cave its name

were recorded before vandals took their toll. Even so, at this rare dry cave, artifacts perishable elsewhere permit a view of the past that is little possible elsewhere. The site is now a Montana state park.

## POMPEY'S PILLAR
### West of town of Pompey's Pillar on U.S. Route 10

William Clark noted in his journal that he "arrived at a remarkable rock" at 4:00 P.M. on Friday, July 25, 1806, as the Lewis and Clark Expedition was returning from its epic journey to the Pacific. Clark ascended the massive sandstone formation and "from its top had a most extensive view in every direction." He named it "Pompey's Tower," after the 18-month-old son of their Indian guide, Sacajawea, and "marked [his] name and the day of the month and year" on its surface. Still visible, his mark is probably the only extant on-site evidence of the entire expedition. The site is owned by the Bureau of Land Management and is open to public visitation.

*Pompey's Pillar, Yellowstone County, 1954. Courtesy of NPS (Ray H. Mattison).*

# NEBRASKA

■ *Cass County*

## WALKER GILMORE SITE
### Address Restricted, Murray vicinity

This extreme eastern Nebraska site is a key
archeological property for outlining the prehistoric cultural stages represented in the
Central Plains, and the type site of the
Stearns' Creek Woodland culture, likely dating
from the first millenium. Extensive remains of
vegetation and the relative absence of arrow
points and flint flakes point to a primarily
horticultural orientation of this culture.

■ *Dawes County*

## FORT ROBINSON AND RED CLOUD AGENCY
### 2 miles west of Crawford on U.S. Route 20 (Dawes and Sioux Counties)

These two sites were focal points during the
last phases of Indian resistance to American
expansion on the Northern Plains. In 1873,
Chief Red Cloud and his large band of
Cheyenne, Arapaho, and Sioux were moved
to the White River area and required to live
within three miles of the Agency. The Indians
objected to the stipulation, and in 1874,
Camp Robinson, renamed Fort Robinson in
1878, was established to protect government
agents and property from their harassment.

The fort also served as a base for army campaigns and as a frontier outpost. During the
20th century, Fort Robinson was at one time
a Quartermaster Remount Depot and served
as a prisoner of war camp during World War
II. A number of buildings that survive have
been refurbished and opened as museums by
the Nebraska Historical Society.

■ *Douglas County*

## FATHER FLANAGAN'S BOYS' HOME
### West Dodge Road, Boys Town

In 1921, Father Edward Joseph Flanagan
established Boys Town for homeless boys on a
farm outside Omaha. With its homelike environment and the morally upright atmosphere
it fosters, this "City of Little Men" has
become a prototype in the development of
20th-century juvenile care around the world.
Boys Town became familiar to many
Americans through the 1938 movie of that
name starring Spencer Tracy and Mickey
Rooney. A 1943 statue at Boys Town shows
two boys with the famous legend, "He ain't
heavy, Father, he's m' brother."

## *HAZARD*
### 2500 North 24th Street (East), Omaha

*Hazard* is one of two surviving Admirable

*Father Flanagan's Boys' Home, Boys Town, Douglas County. Courtesy of NPS (Duane R. Noecker).*

William Jennings Bryan House, Lincoln, Lancaster County. Courtesy of NPS (Stephen Lissandrello).

class fleet minesweepers, the largest and most successful ships of their type in the American navy. Extraordinarily versatile, *Hazard,* built in 1944, was fitted for wire and acoustic sweeping and could double as either an anti-submarine or antiaircraft ship. Along with other Admirable vessels, *Hazard* also served in patrol and escort duties. *Hazard* is now on exhibit at Freedom Park in Omaha, where it is maintained as a World War II museum and memorial.

## ■ Garden County
## ASH HOLLOW CAVE
### Address Restricted, Lewellen vicinity

The several groups of people who occupied this cave for more than 1,700 years left behind evidence that has helped provide a relatively complete picture of aboriginal cultural changes in the Central Plains. It is of primary importance in placing major cultures of the Ceramic Period (A.D. 1000–1700) in proper chronological order. The cave is in Ash Hollow State Historical Park.

## ■ Howard County
## COUFAL SITE
### Address Restricted, Cotesfield vicinity

Coufal, dating from ca. A.D. 1130 to 1350,

was a major settlement of the Central Plains tradition. Excavations have uncovered 22 earth lodges, 30 cache pits, and more than 17,000 artifacts. The site bridges the gap between late prehistoric villagers and the origins of the Pawnee.

## PALMER SITE
### Address Restricted, Palmer vicinity

First reported by Lewis and Clark in 1804, this is a Skidi Pawnee Indian village site. A later visitor noted that the village had 120 lodges, or houses, but by 1836 only 70 were reported. The village was abandoned by 1844, when the Skidi moved downstream on the Loup River. The settlement gained fame when Man Chief, son of the Skidi chieftain, rescued a Comanche girl about to be sacrificed. His heroism earned him a silver medal, on which was inscribed "Bravest of the Brave." Much of the village site remains uninvestigated.

## ■ Lancaster County
## WILLIAM JENNINGS BRYAN HOUSE
### 4900 Sumner Street, Lincoln

From 1902 to 1921, Fairview was the home of William Jennings Bryan, who won the Democratic presidential nomination in 1896 at the age of 36. A leader in the free silver

movement during the gold standard controversy, he is remembered for his "Cross of Gold" speech at the Democratic National Convention. Twice again, in 1900 and 1908, Bryan became the losing nominee of his party, and from 1913 to 1915 he served as secretary of state under Woodrow Wilson. Bryan had hopes that his fine brick home would become "the Monticello of the West," but after his defeats in the political arena, this never happened. After his death it became a nursing home, and in 1961 it became a historic house museum.

## NEBRASKA STATE CAPITOL
### 1445 K Street, Lincoln

One of America's most distinctive state capitols, this limestone-faced building is the masterpiece of architect Bertram Grosvenor Goodhue. Built from 1922 to 1932 in the Art Moderne style, it was intended to symbolize Nebraska's heritage and aspirations, and under Goodhue's guidance, it incorporated work by some of the finest American artisans and craftsmen of their time. A 400-foot domed tower rising from its center dominates the structure. At the apex of the dome is a 19-foot bronze statue, *The Sower*, by sculptor Lee Lawrie, whose work is found

throughout the building. Few American buildings combine the rugged strength, monumental size, and robust simplicity of the Nebraska State Capitol, which remains in virtually pristine condition.

### ■ *Nemeha County*

## *CAPTAIN MERIWETHER LEWIS*
### Southeast of Brownville

One the few surviving U.S. Army Corps of Engineers vessels built to control the nation's inland waters, *Captain Meriwether Lewis* (1931) is also one of the country's best-preserved examples of a cutterhead dredge. The *Captain* helped to keep the Missouri River deep and clean until retiring in 1965. In 1977 the dredge was towed to Brownville to become a dry-berthed museum vessel on the banks of the river it had helped to keep clear for so long. Since 1981, *Captain Meriwether Lewis* has housed the Museum of Missouri River History.

### ■ *Otoe County*

## J. STERLING MORTON HOUSE
### Centennial Avenue, Nebraska City

In 1874, at the urging of J. Sterling Morton,

the State of Nebraska proclaimed an annual Arbor Day, with prizes to be awarded to those who planted the most trees. The movement soon spread across the country—and around the world. In 1893, President Cleveland appointed Morton secretary of agriculture. In that post he introduced new areas of research, among them the study of soil and crop production. From the time he arrived in Nebraska in 1855 until his death in 1902, Morton lived on this farm just outside Nebraska City. After his death, his son remodelled the house into a large Colonial Revival mansion and in 1923 donated it to the state. It is now open to the public as part of Arbor Lodge State Historical Park, honoring the founder of Arbor Day.

## ◼ Red Willow County
### GEORGE W. NORRIS HOUSE
**706 Norris Avenue, McCook**

Progressive Republican George W. Norris served in the U. S. House of Representatives from 1903 to 1912, and in the Senate from 1913 to 1943. He authored the Twentieth Amendment, abolishing lame-duck sessions of Congress, and introduced the bill establishing the Tennessee Valley Authority. Franklin Roosevelt, whose programs he fostered, called him "a gentle knight of progressive ideals." Norris lived here from 1899 until his death in 1944. The house, virtually unchanged from the time Norris remodeled it in 1930–1931, was acquired by the Nebraska State Historical Society in 1968 and is now a museum.

## ◼ Richardson County
### LEARY SITE
**Address Restricted, Rulo vicinity**

This large prehistoric village and burial site of the Oneota culture is the largest and richest of the few that occur west of the Missouri River. William Clark, on his way west with Meriwether Lewis in 1804, was likely the first white person to notice the site. He correctly opined that the several mounds were man-made and were constructed for human burials.

## ◼ Scotts Bluff County
### ROBIDOUX PASS
**9 miles west of Gering**

At the summit of this important pass on the Oregon Trail, pioneers traversing the dry, flat prairie had their first glimpse of Laramie Peak. The pass, used primarily between 1843 and 1851, provided a good supply of fresh water and wood, and in 1848 an Indian trader named Robidoux established a trading post that supplied additional amenities. Robidoux Pass fell into disuse after the opening of Mitchell Pass in 1851. Trail ruts can still be seen, however, and several markers commemorate the pass and the trading post.

### SIGNAL BUTTE
**Gering vicinity**

Identified in 1931, Signal Butte was the first site of the middle prehistoric period in the Central and Northern Plains to be excavated by archeologists. The high density of artifacts have led to the speculation that the area served as a well-protected bison butchering and drying area, high above the easy reach of preying bears and wolves. It is also possible that it was a habitation and workshop site. Carbon dating places the earliest occupations about 2590 to 2210 B.C.

## ◼ Sioux County
### FORT ROBINSON AND RED CLOUD AGENCY
**2 miles west of Crawford on U.S. Route 20 (Dawes and Sioux Counties)**

(See entry under Dawes County.)

## ◼ Thurston County
### DR. SUSAN LAFLESCHE PICOTTE MEMORIAL HOSPITAL
**505 Matthewson Street, Walthill**

Dr. Susan LaFlesche Picotte, first licensed Native American physician, pioneered in providing health care for her people. Born on the Omaha Indian Reservation, she was the youngest child of Chief Joseph LaFlesche (Iron Eye), the last recognized chief of his tribe. Picotte studied at Hampton Institute in Virginia and received her medical degree from the Woman's Medical College of Pennsylvania. She returned to the Omaha Reservation in 1890 as physician at the government boarding school, became physician for the entire tribe, and served as teacher, social worker, adviser, and interpreter. This hospital, a 1½-story Craftsman style frame building constructed in 1912–1913, fulfilled her lifelong dream that all people should have access to quality medical care.

### ■ Valley County

### SCHULTZ SITE
**Address Restricted, North Loop vicinity**

This site serves as the type site for one of the earliest, if not the first, Woodland culture manifestations in the Central Plains: the Valley focus. It is the only excavated village of that focus and has yielded a number of artifacts providing a picture of a stable, sedentary population. The site suggests a trade or cultural network emanating from the Midwest's Hopewell culture, which linked other groups from the eastern seaboard to the Gulf of Mexico and to the northern Rocky Mountains.

### ■ Washington County

### FORT ATKINSON
**1 mile east of Fort Calhoun**

Though short-lived, Fort Atkinson, established in 1820, was of great importance in America's military history and in its westward expansion. Intended as one of a chain of forts designed to guard the Western frontier and protect U.S. fur trade after the War of 1812, it was the only one built, and for a time was the westernmost outpost of the United States. As the frontier moved westward, Fort Atkinson became redundant, and in 1827 it was abandoned. The site is now Fort Atkinson State Historical Park, and a number of features have been reconstructed.

### ■ Webster County

### WILLA CATHER HOUSE
**Corner of Third and Cedar Streets, Red Cloud**

Willa Cather captured the pioneer spirit of the West as few other writers have. Her works—local in scope, national in significance—include such favorites as *O Pioneers!*, *My Antonia*, and *Death Comes for the Archbishop*. Cather once recalled that the "years from eight to fifteen are the formative period in a writer's life." These were the years, from 1884 to 1890, when she lived in Red Cloud. Her comfortable childhood home is now preserved as a museum honoring Cather and her work.

### PIKE PAWNEE VILLAGE SITE
**Address Restricted, Guide Rock vicinity**

This is the site of the Pawnee village that Lieutenant Zebulon Pike visited in late September 1806 on his mission to secure territory acquired through the Louisiana Purchase. A 350-man Spanish force, departing the week before, had left their flag, which the Pawnee were flying. Although Pike had only 20 men, he persuaded the chief to take down the European emblem and replace it with the American flag. After this was accomplished, the diplomatic Pike returned the Spanish flag to the chief, but advised him, "It should never be hoisted during our stay."

# NEVADA

### ■ Clark County

### HOOVER DAM
**Black Canyon of the Colorado River**

This 726-foot-tall concrete arch-gravity storage dam, begun in June 1933 and dedicated in September 1935, was the greatest achievement in hydraulic engineering since the Panama Canal. Among the Bureau of Reclamation's earliest and largest multipurpose dams, it harnessed the Colorado River to provide flood control, irrigation, recreation, and electric power. Hoover Dam has had far-reaching consequences in the industrial, agricultural, and urban development of the southwestern United States. The dam is open to the public for tours of its interior construction and electric plant. (Also in Mohave County, Arizona.)

## ■ Lyon County

### FORT CHURCHILL
**U.S. Route 95A, Weeks vicinity**

Although it lasted only a decade, from 1860 to 1870, Fort Churchill was an important post that guarded the Central Overland Mail Stage, the Pony Express, and the line of the first transcontinental telegraph. Built of adobe, the fort also provided protection for the emigrant trail to California. As the frontier era passed and Nevada became a state, the fort was abandoned, and in 1871 the buildings were auctioned. Now a state park, the fort contains interpretive markers alongside adobe reconstructions built by the Civilian Conservation Corps in the 1930s.

*Hoover Dam, Clark County, Nevada and Mohave County, Arizona. Courtesy of the Bureau of Reclamation, Lower Colorado Region.*

*Fort Churchill, Lyon County, 1958. Courtesy of NPS.*

## ■ *Pershing County*

### LEONARD ROCKSHELTER
**Address Restricted, Lovelock**

The significance of this site was realized in 1936 when, during the course of a bat guano mining operation, several ancient artifacts were uncovered. In later investigations, radio-carbon samples determined that the site had been occupied from ca. 6710 B.C. to ca. A.D. 1400. Leonard Rockshelter is significant for the long continuum of sporadic cultural occupations recorded in its stratigraphy, representing one of the oldest and longest records of human occupation in the western Great Basin.

## ■ *Storey County*

### VIRGINIA CITY HISTORIC DISTRICT
**Virginia City**

Virginia City grew atop the phenomenally rich Comstock Lode, discovered in 1859. The Comstock surpassed earlier California strikes in all dimensions, dictating large-scale industrial and corporate enterprises. As the first silver boomtown, Virginia City became the prototype for subsequent western mining towns in other states. The National Historic Landmark includes the contiguous settlements of Virginia City, Gold Hill, Silver City, and Dayton, as well as surrounding hillsides that still show evidence of mining activities. The ambiance of Virginia City remains very much that of a mining boomtown, and many of its buildings are open to the public.

## ■ *Washoe County*

### FRANCIS G. NEWLANDS HOME
**7 Elm Court, Reno**

This large Shingle Style house overlooking the Truckee River was the home of Francis Griffith Newlands from the time he built it in 1890 until his death in 1917. Newlands served Nevada in the U.S. House of Representatives from 1892 to 1903 and in the Senate from 1903 until his death. He authored the Reclamation Act of 1902, which put the federal government in the irrigation business and opened up vast areas of the formerly arid West to profitable agricultural production. The house is well maintained under private ownership.

## ■ *White Pine County*

### FORT RUBY
**West side of Ruby Lake near Hobson**

Fort Ruby was established in the eastern Nevada wilderness in 1862 to protect the coaches of the Central Overland Mail and became a critical transportation and communication link between Union states of the East and West at the onset of the Civil War. The fort also protected pioneers on the Overland Trail from Indian attack, but after the transcontinental railroad was completed in 1869, it no longer had a useful purpose. The remaining buildings are among the oldest examples of log construction in the state.

# NEW HAMPSHIRE

## ■ *Carroll County*

### E.E. CUMMINGS HOUSE
**Salter Hill Road, Silver Lake**

"Joy Farm," a white-clapboard farmhouse set in an unspoiled wooded countryside, is associated with one of the most innovative American poets of the 20th century. e. e. cummings summered here from 1923 until his death in 1962. Using few capitals, coining new words, and punctuating according to his own rule or whim, cummings broke almost every grammatical and structural convention in the English language. These innovations would be of little interest had he not used them in the service of a genuine poetic sensibility.

## ■ *Cheshire County*

### HARRISVILLE HISTORIC DISTRICT
**Town of Harrisville and its environs**

Harrisville provides an unrivaled glimpse

into the life and times of early-19th-century New England industry and community life. A center for the manufacture of woolen goods since 1799, the town has maintained mills, stores, boarding houses, dwellings, churches, and other structures that reflect the myriad levels of society and their relationships. It is, according to one authority, "the only industrial community of the early 19th century in America that still survives in its original form."

### ■ Coos County

## MOUNT WASHINGTON HOTEL
**Off Route 302, Carroll**

When this large frame resort hotel opened in 1902 on a remote 10,000-acre tract, it was the largest in New Hampshire's White Mountains. Its size and isolation made it an ideal choice to host the 1944 Bretton Woods Conference, an international gathering of economists, lawyers, and politicians who met to chart a blueprint for the world's monetary system. The International Monetary Fund and World Bank were created at the conference.

### ■ Hillsborough County

## MACDOWELL COLONY
**West of U.S. Route 202, Peterborough**

Marian Nevins MacDowell established this camp in 1908 as a living memorial to her husband, Edward MacDowell, one of America's first great composers. Mrs. MacDowell had purchased the property in 1896, and it proved a welcome retreat for the couple. The colony now contains some 42 buildings on 400 acres of forest and meadow land and has become an internationally known retreat where gifted artists enjoy ideal conditions for creative work.

## FRANKLIN PIERCE HOMESTEAD
**3 miles west of Hillsborough on New Hampshire Route 31**

Franklin Pierce, 14th president of the United States, occupied this comfortable two-story clapboarded house from infancy until his marriage in 1834. Pierce held the presidency from 1853 to 1857, a critical period during which sectional differences escalated, eventually resulting in the Civil War. His father, Benjamin Pierce, who was New Hampshire's governor from 1827 to 1829, built the house in 1804. The homestead was donated to the State of New Hampshire in 1925, and is open to the public during summer months.

### ■ Merrimack County

## CANTERBURY SHAKER VILLAGE
**288 Shaker Road, Canterbury**

Designed, built, and inhabited by Shakers from its founding in 1792 until the 1990s, Canterbury is considered among the most intact and authentic of this group's surviving villages. Shakers—the United Society of Believers in Christ's First and Second

*Canterbury Shaker Village, Canterbury, Merrimack County. Courtesy of HABS (Bill Finney).*

Appearing—were the most numerous, most successful, and best known of America's 19th-century utopian communal societies. The stark harmony of the practical structures at Canterbury, along with their furnishings and handicrafts, illustrates Shaker principles of simple beauty through function. Canterbury is open to the public.

## DANIEL WEBSTER FAMILY HOME
### South Main Street, West Franklin

The Elms, the Webster family home, is a frame dwelling that Daniel Webster loved for more than 50 years as a vacation retreat, home, and "solace to the end of his days." An eloquent champion of preserving the Union, Webster served his nation in the political arena from 1812 until his death in 1852. His last words were "I still live." The grave sites of his parents and siblings are located here.

### ■ *Rockingham County*

## *ALBACORE*
### Portsmouth Maritime Museum, Portsmouth

*Albacore,* an experimental diesel-electric submarine launched at Portsmouth in 1953, represents a revolution in naval engineering. Designed to be a true submarine, its surface characteristics subordinated to underwater performance, it was quieter, faster, and more maneuverable than any of its predecessors. *Albacore* became the model for all future U.S. Navy submarines, and for most foreign submarines as well. *Albacore* returned home in 1984 and is now moored in a permanent dry berth as a prime exhibit at the Portsmouth Maritime Museum.

## JOSIAH BARTLETT HOUSE
### Main Street, Kingston

From 1774 until his death in 1795, Josiah Bartlett, physician, Revolutionary patriot, signer of the Declaration of Independence and the Constitution, chief justice and governor of New Hampshire, lived here. His frame house, still a private residence, is identified by a historical marker that notes yet another accomplishment of this multitalented man: He also founded the New Hampshire Medical Society.

## ROBERT FROST HOMESTEAD
### 2 miles southeast of Derry on New Hampshire Route 28

From 1900 to 1909, this 13-acre farm was the home of Robert Frost, one of the few 20th-century poets to command both critical respect and wide readership. Frost authored 11 volumes of poetry and won the Pulitzer Prize four times. Much of his style and strength emanated from this homestead, and he once remarked, "The core of all my writing was probably the free years that I had there." The New Hampshire Division of Parks acquired the property in 1965, restored it, and opens it to the public. (See Robert Frost Farm, Addison County, Vermont.)

*Robert Frost Homestead, Rockingham County. Courtesy of the New Hampshire Division of Parks and Recreation (Eric M. Sanford).*

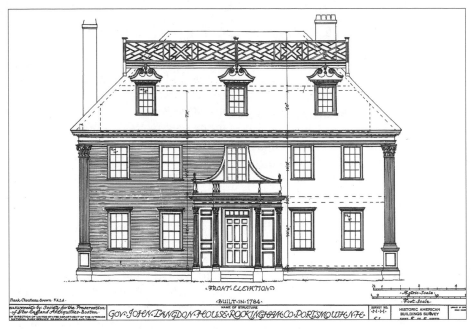

·FRONT·ELEVATION·

·BUILT·IN·1784·

GOV·JOHN·LANGDON·HOUSE·ROCKINGHAM·CO·PORTSMOUTH·N·H·

*Governor John Langdon Mansion, Portsmouth, Rockingham County. Courtesy of HABS (Frank Chouteau Brown).*

## RICHARD JACKSON HOUSE
### Northwest Street, Portsmouth

Built in 1664 by a shipbuilder, this fine example of a New England saltbox is Portsmouth's oldest dwelling and likely the oldest house in the state. The steeply gabled dwelling has a heavy structural frame sheathed with vertical planks and covered with clapboards. The Society for the Preservation of New England Antiquities acquired the house in 1927, and it is open to the public as a historic house museum.

## JOHN PAUL JONES HOUSE
### Middle and State Streets, Portsmouth

John Paul Jones, born John Paul in Scotland, became a naval officer and hero of the American Revolution. Had he said nothing else, his retort to an English commander who called on him to surrender gives him everlasting fame: "I have not yet begun to fight." Thanks to that attitude, it was the British *Serapis,* not Jones's *Bonhomme Richard,* that struck her colors. Jones was grounded on terra firma for two years (1781–1782) as a boarder in this imposing gambrel-roofed mansion. The only surviving structure with significant Jones associations, the house was acquired by the Portsmouth Historical Society in 1919 and is open to the public.

## LADD-GILMAN HOUSE
### Governors Lane and Water Street, Exeter

This well-preserved house was the birthplace and home of Nicholas Gilman, Jr., one of New Hampshire's delegates to the Constitutional Convention of 1787 and a signer of the Constitution. Gilman also served in the U.S. House and Senate. His rambling homestead was begun in 1721 by Nathaniel Ladd and was later enlarged and altered by Gilman's father. Since 1902, the Society of the Cincinnati in New Hampshire has owned and maintained the house, which is open to the public.

## GOVERNOR JOHN LANGDON MANSION
### 143 Pleasant Street, Portsmouth

One of the great Georgian houses of America, this frame mansion was built in 1784 as the home of John Langdon, a leading figure in mercantile, military, and political affairs in New Hampshire. Langdon was a delegate to the 1787 Constitutional Convention and was the first president pro tem of the United States Senate. It was he who notified George Washington of his election as president of the new nation. Langdon's house is open to the public.

## MACPHEADRIS-WARNER HOUSE
**Daniel and Chapel Streets, Portsmouth**

Constructed in 1718–1723 for local merchant Archibald MacPheadris, this is one of New England's finest early Georgian brick houses. It was also one of the most ambitious houses of its time and place. Its lightning rod, likely the first in the area, was installed under the direction of Benjamin Franklin, and the stair hall contains unusual wall murals depicting Native Americans. Royal Governor Benning Wentworth lived here from 1741 to 1753. The house is now maintained as a historic house museum.

## MOFFATT-LADD HOUSE
**154 Market Street, Portsmouth**

Built in 1763, this grand three-story frame house is one of New England's most important late-Georgian mansions. It gains added significance in that it served as the residence of William Whipple from 1768 to 1785. Whipple, sea captain, merchant, politician, general, and jurist, was a signer of the Declaration of Independence. Beautifully restored and maintained, the house and its well-documented early garden are open to the public.

## MATTHEW THORNTON HOUSE
**2 Thornton Street, Derry Village**

From about 1740 to 1779 this two-story New England saltbox was home to Irish-born Matthew Thornton, physician, politician, and jurist. Thornton helped prepare a constitution for New Hampshire and was elected Speaker of its House of Representatives in January 1776. Later that year he served in the Continental Congress and signed the Declaration of Independence.

## WENTWORTH-COOLIDGE MANSION
**Little Harbor Road, 2 miles south of Portsmouth**

Standing near the water's edge, this rambling, 42-room house was the home of Royal Governor Benning Wentworth from 1753 until his death in 1770. Wentworth was appointed by King George II in 1741, and his 26-year term was the longest of any of America's colonial governors. The clapboard-ed mansion was constructed in three stages (ca. 1695, 1730, and 1750). Wentworth built the last portion to serve as his official residence and office and typically summoned councillors to "come to Little Harbor to drink the King's Health." The house, donated to the state in 1954, is open to the public.

## WENTWORTH-GARDNER HOUSE
**140 Mechanic Street, Portsmouth**

Built in 1760, this is an exceptionally handsome example of a late-Georgian New England town house. It is particularly notable for its classical proportions, its rusticated wooden facade, and its interiors, where a spacious stair hall and carved woodwork add to its distinction. Wallace Nutting, a pioneer in the historic preservation movement, restored the house in the early 20th century. The house, which fronts on the water, is open to the public.

### ◼ Strafford County

## JOHN SULLIVAN HOUSE
**23 New Market Road, Durham**

John Sullivan, a major general during the Revolution, was one of Washington's ablest officers, participating in numerous battles in New England and the Middle Colonies. In December 1774, leading 400 Portsmouth Sons of Liberty, Sullivan captured Fort William and Mary, which guarded the entrance to Portsmouth Harbor. Sullivan purchased this frame house in 1764 and called it home until his death in 1795. He is buried in the family cemetery on the property.

### ◼ Sullivan County

## SALMON P. CHASE BIRTHPLACE AND BOYHOOD HOME
**Route 12-A, Cornish**

This frame New England farmhouse was the birthplace and childhood home of Salmon P. Chase, one of those rare individuals who held important positions in all three branches of the federal government. He served Ohio in the U.S. Senate from 1849 to 1855, and as its governor from 1855 to 1859. A second term as an Ohio senator was cut short when Abraham Lincoln selected him to become secretary of the treasury. He served in that

Augustus Saint-Gaudens Memorial, Cornish, Sullivan County. Courtesy of NPS (Richard Frear).

capacity from 1861 to 1864, then became chief justice of the Supreme Court, where he presided from 1864 until his death in 1873. In his last post Chase administered the impeachment trial of President Andrew Johnson.

## AUGUSTUS SAINT-GAUDENS MEMORIAL (NPS)
### Cornish

Augustus Saint-Gaudens, one of the nation's most talented sculptors, lived and worked here during the last 22 years of his life. After his death in 1907 his widow and son deeded the property to a group established to maintain it as a memorial. Casts of some of his most noted works are displayed in the studio. The property became the Saint-Gaudens National Historic Site in 1965 and is open to the public.

# NEW JERSEY

## ▓ Atlantic County

### ATLANTIC CITY CONVENTION HALL
#### Pacific, Florida, and Mississippi Avenues and the Boardwalk, Atlantic City

This vast edifice, 650 by 350 feet, fronts Atlantic City's Boardwalk with a dramatically curved limestone exedra, a covered double row of columns. Of all the city's buildings, it best recalls Atlantic City's heyday as a seaside resort. When completed in 1929, the extraordinary Great Hall was the largest room in the world with unobstructed views and contained the world's largest pipe organ, a gargantuan instrument of 33,000 pipes. For many years this is where 40,000 spectators— 30,000 seated on the main floor, 10,000 in the mezzanine—annually heard Bert Parks sing, "Here she comes, Miss America."

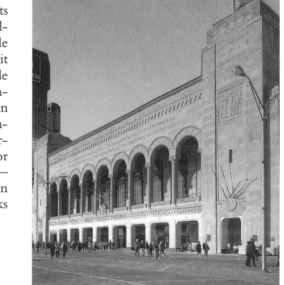

Atlantic City Convention Hall, Atlantic City, Atlantic County. Courtesy of HABS (Jack E. Boucher).

*Lucy, the Margate Elephant, Margate City, Atlantic County. Courtesy of HABS (Jack E. Boucher).*

## LUCY, THE MARGATE ELEPHANT
### Decatur and Atlantic Avenues, Margate City

Lucy, 75 feet long and 65 feet tall (counting her howdah, or canopied saddle), is America's largest pachyderm. She is also the oldest, having stood, albeit in several locations, on the Margate beachfront since 1881. A true American "folly," the frame-and-tin elephant was a real estate promoter's brainchild, and was built to spur development in what was then South Atlantic City. Lucy contains rooms reached via stairways in her hind legs; her trunk, submerged in a trough, is actually a chute built to connect "with a sewer or other conduit for conveying slops, ashes, etc." Lucy was restored in the 1970s and remains one of the strangest and best-loved attractions on the Jersey shore.

### ▪ *Bergen County*

## HERMITAGE
### 335 North Franklin Turnpike, Hohokus

Almost completely rebuilt and enlarged in 1845 from an 18th-century structure, this charming sandstone cottage is the only remaining Gothic Revival house definitely attributable to architect William Ranlett.

Ranlett considered his work to be "after the Old English style," and the house remains an outstanding example of the early Gothic Revival in American domestic architecture. The home of the Rosencrantz family for years, it is now a historic house museum.

## PALISADES INTERSTATE PARK
### West bank of the Hudson River

This park represents an early cooperative effort between two states. After the Civil War, quarrying threatened to destroy the Palisades, the imposing stone cliffs that line the western bank of the Hudson River opposite New York City. In the 1890s the states of New Jersey and New York formed commissions to attempt to save them, and an Interstate Park Commission was the result. J. P. Morgan made the first contribution, and in 1901 the state of New York appropriated $50,000 to buy property in the state of New Jersey! By 1914 the initial goal of acquiring a 14-mile stretch of the Palisades had been accomplished. Additional land has been incorporated on both sides of the Hudson in subsequent years. (Also in Orange and Rockland Counties, New York.)

## ELIZABETH CADY STANTON HOUSE
### 135 Highwood Avenue, Tenafly

From ca. 1868 to 1887, this two-story frame house was the residence of Elizabeth Cady Stanton, early leader in the women's rights movement. Called "the leading intellectual force in the emancipation of American women," Stanton delivered the call for female suffrage at the Seneca Falls (New York) Convention of 1848. Her home there is also a National Historic Landmark, but she spent her most active years working for women's rights here in Tenafly. (See Elizabeth Cady Stanton House, Seneca County, New York.)

### ▪ *Burlington County*

## BURLINGTON COUNTY PRISON
### High Street, Mount Holly

This stone prison accepted its first felons in 1811 and was the oldest prison in continuous use in America when it ceased to serve its original function in 1966. Part of its longevity was due to the fact that Robert Mills

*Burlington County Prison, Mount Holly, Burlington County. Courtesy of HABS.*

designed it to embody the most modern correctional methods of the time. Mills also suggested the motto that was placed over the entrance: "Justice Which, While it Punishes, Would Endeavor to Reform the Offender." The former jail has been adapted to its present museum use with little alteration.

## FRANCIS HOPKINSON HOUSE
### 101 Farnsworth Avenue, Bordentown

Francis Hopkinson was a man of many talents. A lawyer, judge, politician, poet, satirist, composer, artist, and inventor, he made his home in this red-brick Bordentown house from 1774 until his death in 1791. It was during this time that he went to Philadelphia to sign the Declaration of Independence. He also designed the Great Seal of the United States, and in 1781 composed *Temple of Minerva*, a cantata celebrating the alliance between France and the United States.

## NEW SAINT MARY'S EPISCOPAL CHURCH
### Broad Street between Talbot and Wood Streets, Burlington

This pivotal building in the history of the Gothic Revival style was the first American attempt to imitate a specific English medieval church. Modeled on the early 14th-century church of Saint John the Baptist at Shottesbrooke in Berkshire, its design and construction were milestones in the career of Richard Upjohn, who used English architect William Butterfield's drawings of the church of Saint John. Saint Mary's was severely damaged by fire in 1976 but has since been restored and refurbished.

## PAULSDALE
### 126 Hooton Road, Mount Laurel Township

Paulsdale, a stuccoed-brick farmhouse, was the childhood home and permanent "home base" of Alice Paul, a leader in the woman's suffrage movement. Paul's Quaker heritage influenced her views on equality of the sexes and prepared her to work for securing passage of the Nineteenth Amendment in 1920. She also drafted the Equal Rights Amendment in the 1920s and was instrumental in having the sex equality clause included in the United Nations Declaration of Human Rights.

## ◼ Camden County

## *HADROSAURUS FOULKII LEIDY* SITE
### Maple Avenue, Haddonfield vicinity

Discovered in a marl pit on this site in October 1858, *Hadrosaurus Foulkii Leidy* was the first relatively complete dinosaur skeleton found in North America, or, for that matter, anywhere in the world. Realizing the significance of his find, William Parker Foulke asked Joseph Leidy and Isaac Lea of the Academy of Natural Sciences of Philadelphia to evaluate it. Presentation of the discovery to the scientific world, and Leidy's reconstruction of the skeleton, revolutionized the understanding of dinosaurs and brought countless thousands to the Academy to see it.

## WALT WHITMAN HOUSE
### 330 Mickle Street, Camden

This simple tin-roofed frame house served as Walt Whitman's home from 1884 until 1892, the last eight years of his life. "The poet of democracy," Whitman is remembered for his *Leaves of Grass,* a work whose great merit was recognized only after his death. His modest Camden home contains a number of furnishings and Whitman memorabilia and is open to the public.

## ■ *Cape May County*
## CAPE MAY HISTORIC DISTRICT
### Cape May

Cape May proclaims itself the nation's oldest seashore resort. It began to flourish after the War of 1812 and by the mid–19th century was considered the nation's summer capital, where presidents and congressmen mingled among its crowds. The city maintains one of the largest extant collections of mid- and late-19th-century frame buildings in the country, with more than 600 seashore houses and hotels providing an almost complete showcase of Victorian-era architecture.

## ■ *Essex County*
## JOHN BALLANTINE HOUSE
### 43 Washington Street, Newark

This elegant late-19th-century mansion was built in 1894 for the wealthy owner of a Newark brewery. All the drawings and specifications by New York architect George Edward Harney survive, providing a remarkably detailed record of design and construction during the Victorian era. Maintained by the Newark Museum of Art as a historic house museum, the Ballantine House vividly evokes the life-style of a prosperous family of its period.

## GRACE CHURCH, NEWARK
### 950 Broad Street, Newark

Consecrated October 5, 1848, Grace Church was commissioned by Bishop George Washington Doane of New Jersey, one of Richard Upjohn's most important patrons and a proponent of "high church" Episcopalianism. The early–English Gothic church, with its corner tower and spire, is built of brownstone and remains an excellent and little-altered example of the work of mid-19th-century America's foremost Gothic Revival architect.

## ■ *Gloucester County*
## RED BANK BATTLEFIELD
### East bank of the Delaware River at the west end of Hessian Avenue, National Park

On October 22, 1777, Americans successfully defended Fort Mercer, an earthen fort at Red Bank that guarded the Delaware River approach to Philadelphia. This victory delayed opening the river as a supply route for General Howe's army, which occupied Philadelphia. Portions of the earthworks remain in the park that now occupies the site. Nearby, and also part of the park, the James Whitall, Sr., house is a 1748 brick building that served as a hospital during the battle.

## ■ *Hudson County*
## CLARK THREAD COMPANY HISTORIC DISTRICT
### 900 Passaic Avenue, East Newark

Founded in 1864, the Clark Thread Company and its successor firms led the nation in the manufacture of cotton thread from the 1870s through the first half of the 20th century. This large but "close-knit" industrial complex, contained within a large city block, includes most of the company's principal late-19th-century mill buildings.

## GREAT ATLANTIC AND PACIFIC TEA COMPANY WAREHOUSE
### Provost Street between First and Bay Streets, Jersey City

A and P are two of the most familiar initials in American commerce. From its beginnings in 1859 as a leather and tea importing business in New York, to its position as the nation's largest retailer by the mid-20th-century, A&P symbolizes every major phase of chain-store history in America. This early-20th-century warehouse, a little-altered nine-story reinforced-concrete structure on Jersey City's waterfront, was part of the chain's manufacturing and distribution center for the New York–New Jersey area.

## HOLLAND TUNNEL
### Between New York, New York County, New York, and Jersey City

Until the Holland Tunnel was opened in 1927, all vehicular traffic coming to the nation's largest city from the west had to cross the Hudson River by ferry. The Holland Tunnel was the first subaqueous tunnel in the world specifically designed for automobile traffic. Before it was constructed, engineers conducted an extensive research program to determine the effects of auto emissions and to ascertain the most efficient methods of ventilation. Virtually all subsequent subaqueous automobile tunnels have based their ventilation systems on the findings obtained here. (Also in New York County, New York.)

## ◼ Mercer County

## ABBOTT FARM HISTORIC DISTRICT
### Address Restricted, Trenton

This is the largest known Middle Woodland (ca. 500 B.C.–A.D. 500) village site in the coastal Mid-Atlantic/New England region. The property, on the east bank of the Delaware River about two miles downstream from the falls at Trenton, became the focal point of a famous 40-year controversy about the antiquity of human occupation of the New World. More than 100 books and articles have been published on Abbott Farm, one of the country's most famous archeological sites.

## GROVER CLEVELAND HOME
### 15 Hodge Road, Princeton

Before they left Washington and the White House in 1897, Grover and Frances Folsom Cleveland decided to make Princeton their retirement home. Mrs. Cleveland selected this Italianate mansion, located in the fashionable western section of the college town and appropriately named "Westland." Until his death in 1908, the two-term president,

known for his earnestness and incorruptibility, lived here. The house, still privately owned, remains much the same as the Clevelands knew it.

## ALBERT EINSTEIN HOUSE
### 112 Mercer Street, Princeton

From 1936 until his death in 1955, Albert Einstein, German-born theoretical physicist and 1921 Nobel Prize winner, lived in this unpretentious frame house. Einstein is best remembered for his achievements in three theoretical directions: the special theory of relativity, with its famous $E = MC^2$ formulation, the general theory of relativity, and the unified field theory. Einstein did most of his work in his study in this house or at Princeton's Institute for Advanced Studies, a short walk away.

## JOSEPH HENRY HOUSE
### Princeton University, Princeton

Joseph Henry lived in this brick house from 1832 to 1846, when he taught at the College of New Jersey, now Princeton University. Henry, who had already developed the electromagnet by this time, also built the first electric motor and helped Morse make the telegraph a success. After his Princeton years, he became first secretary of the Smithsonian Institution (1846–1878) and president of the National Academy of Sciences (1868–1878). Henry was a pivotal figure in the history of American science but never obtained a patent for his work. Instead, he rested secure that he had "added by [his] investigations to the sum of human knowledge."

## LAWRENCEVILLE SCHOOL
### Main Street, Lawrenceville

The campus of this private college-preparatory school is a rare surviving example of the successful collaboration of architects and landscape planners. The school was founded in 1810, but major campus development dates from the 1880s, when Boston architects Peabody and Stearns designed its major buildings and Frederick Law Olmsted devised the landscape. Little changed since, the campus is still characterized by solid Romanesque Revival buildings arranged informally around an open green.

## MAYBURY HILL
### 346 Snowden Lane, Princeton

This Georgian stone farmhouse, built ca. 1725 and enlarged in 1753, was the boyhood home of Joseph Hewes, who served as a member of the Continental Congress from North Carolina and was a signer of the Declaration of Independence. Neither his Edenton, North Carolina, home nor office survives, and Maybury Hill, recently restored, remains the only place with close associations to Hewes.

## MORVEN
### 55 Stockton Street, Princeton

Morven is a handsome Georgian style brick house that was begun in the mid–18th century, then added to and remodeled several times. It was the homestead of the prominent Stockton family and was home to Richard Stockton, lawyer, judge, and signer of the Declaration of Independence. Between 1954 and 1982, Morven was the official residence of New Jersey's governors. In the late 1980s it came under the direction of the New Jersey State Museum. A multiphased restoration project began in the fall of 1998.

## NASSAU HALL
### Princeton University, Princeton

When Nassau Hall, literal and figurative heart of Princeton University, was completed in 1756, it contained the entire College of New Jersey: classrooms, dormitories, library, and dining room. It was then the largest college building in colonial America and later served as the prototype for a number of other colleges. During the Revolution it was used as a barracks and hospital and was the scene of the last British stand during the Battle of Princeton. For several months in 1783, Nassau Hall served as the nation's capitol. Reconstructed and remodeled after several fires, its original sturdy stone walls survive. It remains just as sturdy in the hearts of all Princetonians when they rise to sing "In Praise of Old Nassau."

## OLD BARRACKS
### South Willow Street, Trenton

This 2½-story fieldstone structure is the only surviving barracks of five that New Jersey's colonial legislature authorized in 1758. They were intended to provide housing for troops during the French and Indian War, thus ending the quartering of soldiers in private homes. Hessian mercenaries were the unfortunate occupants on Christmas night, 1776, when Washington crossed the Delaware to take the Trenton garrison by surprise the next morning. Now virtually surrounded by later structures, the only colonial barracks surviving in the country is open to the public as a museum.

*Morven, Princeton, Mercer County. Courtesy of HABS (Jack E. Boucher).*

## PRESIDENT'S HOUSE
### Nassau Street, Princeton

This two-story brick house next to Nassau Hall was built in 1756 to serve as a home for presidents of the College of New Jersey. John Witherspoon, who became president in 1768, lived here until 1779. Witherspoon was a New Jersey delegate to the Continental Congress and a signer of the Declaration of Independence. The Georgian style house adds a charming domestic note to the Princeton University campus and is currently used as offices for the Alumni Council.

## PRINCETON BATTLEFIELD
### Princeton Battlefield State Park

The battle that began at sunrise on January 3, 1777, on a field outside Princeton ended when British troops who were barricaded in Nassau Hall surrendered. This, the second American victory in New Jersey (after Trenton), helped to raise the morale of the colonists at the time they most needed it. Washington's victory at Princeton also helped to strengthen his position at home and abroad. A portion of the battle site is now a state park.

## PROSPECT
### Princeton University, Princeton

Prospect is significant for many reasons. Perhaps the finest residence designed by Philadelphia architect John Notman, who helped introduce the Italianate style to America, the stone mansion was built in 1851–1852 for Thomas F. Potter. It was purchased privately in 1878 and given to the College of New Jersey to be used as the new president's house. Woodrow Wilson, who served as Princeton's president from 1902 to 1910, was its third occupant. It was at Prospect that Wilson accepted the Democratic nomination for governorship of New Jersey. Prospect's use as the president's home ceased in 1968, and it is now a university club.

## WILLIAM TRENT HOUSE
### 15 Market Street, Trenton

Built in 1719 by the founder of Trenton, this early-18th-century brick house is a distinguished example of the early-Georgian style, with its classic simplicity and straightforward proportions. Slightly arched windows, a bold cornice, and an octagonal cupola (from which Trent could look up and down the Delaware River) are its major ornaments. The Trent House later served as the home of several governors of New Jersey and is now open to the public as a historic house museum.

## WASHINGTON'S CROSSING
### Delaware River, Titusville

Here, on Christmas night, 1776, General George Washington and his troops crossed the Delaware River on their way to capture Trenton, then held by British forces. The success of Washington's carefully planned maneuver gave the colonials a much-needed taste of victory at the war's lowest ebb. Thanks largely to the famous painting by Emanuel Leutze, the crossing has assumed almost legendary proportions in American history. State parks on both banks of the river, one in New Jersey, one in Pennsylvania, now memorialize the event, as does an annual reenactment. (Also in Bucks County, Pensylvania.)

## ■ *Middlesex County*

## OLD QUEENS, RUTGERS UNIVERSITY
### Rutgers University, New Brunswick

Begun in 1809, this handsome Federal style fieldstone building was designed by John McComb, Jr., one of early America's most important architects. Like Princeton's Nassau Hall, which served as a model, it contained virtually the entire institution when it was built. Students and faculty moved in before it was completed in 1825, the year Queens College was renamed Rutgers College. Now housing administrative offices, Old Queens remains the heart of Rutgers University.

## ■ *Monmouth County*

## ALL SAINTS' MEMORIAL CHURCH
### Navesink Avenue and Locust Road, Navesink

Modeled on a chapel on the Isle of Wight in England, this small Gothic Revival stone church was built in 1864 from designs by Richard Upjohn. Then the most prestigious practitioner of the Gothic Revival style in America, Upjohn intended the church and its attendant schoolhouse and parsonage to replicate the type of ecclesiastical complex often associated with medieval English manors. The interrelated Stephens and Milnor families sponsored the project.

## FORT HANCOCK AND SANDY HOOK PROVING GROUND HISTORIC DISTRICT (NPS)
**New Jersey Route 36, Sandy Hook**

Even before Fort Hancock was built as a military defense post just prior to the Civil War, Sandy Hook, a fishhook-shaped promontory guarding New York City and its harbor, had been recognized for its strategic position. British troops used it as a rendezvous point during the Revolution, and U.S. troops occupied it during the War of 1812. Some 110 historic buildings (including the Sandy Hook Light) and 16 coastal defense batteries dating from ca. 1857 to 1950, attest to its development over the years. The Proving Ground was established in 1874 and operated until 1918–1919. It played a key role in the development of coastal and field artillery, as well as radar. Sandy Hook now comprises the New Jersey side of the Gateway National Recreation Area.

## T. THOMAS FORTUNE HOUSE
**94 West Bergen Place, Red Bank**

During the early 20th century this was the home of T. Thomas Fortune, a crusading journalist who articulated the cause of African-American rights and provided a national forum for black causes in his newspapers. Born a slave in Florida, Fortune left his native state in 1876 to enter Howard University and began his first newspaper, *The New York Globe,* in 1881. He purchased this house in Red Bank in 1901 and later enlarged it. Fortune's last editorial appeared in the June 9, 1928, issue of *Negro World,* the same issue that carried his obituary.

## HORN ANTENNA
**Crawford Hill Facility, Holmdel**

"We live in an ocean of whispers left over from our eruptive creation." Few listened to this pronouncement of the "Big Bang" theory of the creation of the universe until 1965, when two researchers at the Bell Telephone Laboratories were experimenting with the Horn Antenna, originally constructed to support a satellite project. After suppressing all interference from the antenna, Drs. Arno A. Penzias and Robert A. Wilson still heard a constant noise 100 times more intense than they had expected. The noise was the microwave background radiation that permeates the universe and was evidence confirming the "Big Bang" theory. The whispers, or at least their discovery and interpretation, earned the scientists the 1978 Nobel Prize for physics.

## MONMOUTH BATTLEFIELD
**Freehold vicinity**

The June 28, 1778, Battle of Monmouth marked the combat debut of the Continental army after a hard winter of training at Valley Forge. Here, on a hot summer day, Washington's troops attempted to disrupt British General Henry Clinton's march from Philadelphia to Sandy Hook. Clinton escaped, but both sides realized that the colonials could now engage British regulars on even terms. Monmouth also marked the debut of "Molly Pitcher," the American heroine who carried water to her husband and other American artillerymen during the sweltering battle. A major portion of the battlefield is preserved and interpreted in a state park.

## SANDY HOOK LIGHT
**Fort Hancock Military Reservation, Sandy Hook**

When erected in 1764, this nine-story brick tower, octagonal in section, was the fifth lighthouse built in America. Originally called the New York Lighthouse, it guided vessels to and from the nation's major port, steering them away from Sandy Hook's treacherous shoals. New York merchants financed the lottery that secured funds for its construction, and in 1789 it was deeded to the federal government. Today it remains the oldest lighthouse in the United States.

## SEABRIGHT LAWN TENNIS AND CRICKET CLUB
**Rumson Road and Tennis Court Lane, Rumson**

Seabright Lawn Tennis and Cricket Club, organized in 1877 and incorporated in 1886,

*Sandy Hook Light, Sandy Hook, Monmouth County. Courtesy of NPS (R. E. Greenwood).*

is one of the nation's oldest continuously active tennis clubs. The club has hosted many of the world's best-known amateur tennis players. The Seabright Invitational Tournament, held annually from 1884 to 1950, was a major event on the eastern U.S. tennis circuit and the traditional prelude to national championships in Boston and New York.

## SHADOW LAWN
### Cedar and Norwood Avenues, West Long Branch

This palatial manor house was built in 1927 for Hubert T. Parsons, president of the F.W. Woolworth Company. Faced with Indiana limestone, the rather somber exterior hides a three-story interior courtyard covered with a skylight. Horace Trumbauer, Philadelphia's master of the Gilded Age, was architect of record, but in all likelihood his able chief designer, Julian Abele, America's first professional black architect, deserves equal credit. Parsons lost his fortune in the Depression, and in 1939, Shadow Lawn, which had cost millions, was sold for $100. In 1956 it became the central building of Monmouth College.

## ■ *Morris County*

## CRAFTSMAN FARMS
### Route 10 and Manor Lane, Parsippany-Troy Hills

Craftsman Farms was the home, school, and workshop of Gustav Stickley, a leader in the American Arts and Crafts movement. The buildings and furniture—the latter known as Mission Style—that Stickley and his cohorts sponsored and produced influenced the nation's taste in the early 20th century. He established Craftsman Farms in 1908, intending it to be a farm-school where children would learn from master craftsmen. Although Stickley went bankrupt in 1916 and sold the farms in 1917, the site is still replete with the spirit of its taste-making founder. The complex was threatened with development in 1989 but was saved by the Township of Parsippany-Troy Hills and is open April through October.

## THE FACTORY, SPEEDWELL VILLAGE
### 333 Speedwell Avenue, Morristown

Samuel F. B. Morse developed and first suc-

The Factory, Speedwell Village, Morristown, Morris County. Courtesy of the Speedwell Village.

cessfully demonstrated the telegraph in this simple early-19th-century mill building. The year was 1838, and the mill was owned by Stephen Vail, proprietor of the Speedwell Iron Works and one of Morse's partners. The message Morse delivered here, "Railroad cars just arrived 345 passengers," was admittedly not as memorable as the one he sent from Washington to Baltimore in 1844: "What hath God wrought." The factory is part of a restored 19th-century ironworks complex, open to the public.

## THOMAS NAST HOME
### MacCulloch Avenue and Miller Road, Morristown

From 1873 to 1902, Villa Fontana was the home of Thomas Nast, German-born cartoonist whose devastatingly funny and accurate drawings in *Harper's Weekly* contributed to the downfall of New York's corrupt Boss Tweed–Tammany Hall ring. Not only did Nast "invent" the Tammany Tiger, his fertile mind also created Santa Claus (as American children visualize him), the Democratic donkey, and the Republican elephant. His Second Empire–style Villa Fontana now wears a Colonial Revival veneer, but its dormered mansard roof remains as evidence of its earlier incarnation, when Nast knew it.

■ *Ocean County*

## GEORGIAN COURT
### Lakewood Avenue, Lakewood

Bruce Price designed this lavish mansion for George Jay Gould, wealthy eldest son of Jay Gould. The Georgian Revival house, completed in 1898 and now converted to college use, contains marble of almost every known variety, including Black Egyptian and Royal Irish Green. The surrounding estate contained stables, a gatekeeper's lodge, and even a private casino. Price was one of the most talented architects in America in the last quarter of his generation and was the father of Emily Post, the next generation's arbiter of taste.

## HANGAR NO. 1
### Lakehurst Naval Air Station, Manchester Township

Commissioned in 1921, Lakehurst Naval Air Station became the hub of the U.S. Navy's lighter-than-air experiments. Two years later, inside Hangar No. 1, engineers assembled *Shenandoah*, America's first rigid airship, or helium-filled dirigible. Lakehurst became the American Airship Center and was the only stopping place in the country for commercial airships. Its moment in history came in 1937, when the huge German zeppelin *Hindenburg*, the largest airship ever built, burned as it attempted to land.

## ◼ *Passaic County*

## PIETRO AND MARIA BOTTO HOUSE
**83 Norwood Street, Haledon**

The 1913 Patterson Silk Strike began on January 27, when 800 workers at the Henry Doherty plant left their looms to protest low wages and long hours. Patterson was then the country's silk-manufacturing capital, and soon 25,000 other workers joined the rebellion. Leaders of the Industrial Workers of the World (IWW, or "Wobblies") addressed as many as 15,000–20,000 workers at a time from the balcony of this home of a weaver, Pietro Botto. The restored house now serves as a museum commemorating the event and is furnished to represent the home of a working-class family of the time.

## GREAT FALLS OF THE PASSAIC SOCIETY FOR UNIVERSAL MANUFACTURING
**Paterson**

In the 1790s, the Society for Useful Manufactures selected the Great Falls of the Passaic River as the site for a development intended to free America from dependence on English manufacturers. Alexander Hamilton was among the organizers, and French engineer/planner Pierre Charles L'Enfant designed the system, which was the first attempt in the country to harness the entire power of a major river for industrial purposes. An original underground canal, mill buildings—including the original Colt gun facility—and a later hydroelectric plant remain.

## RINGWOOD MANOR
**Ringwood Manor State Park, Ringwood Borough**

This large, rambling brick-and-frame structure is associated with one of America's earliest and most important iron producing enterprises. A charcoal iron furnace was established here in 1739, and except for a hiatus after the Revolution, manufacturing continued until 1890. Nearby mines were worked until 1931. The manor, begun ca. 1810 as the ironmaster's residence, was pre-

sented to the state in the 1930s and now, as a historic house museum, is the major attraction at Ringwood Manor State Park.

## ◼ *Sussex County*

## MINISINK ARCHEOLOGICAL SITE
**Address Restricted, Bushkill vicinity**

Minisink was the most important Munsee Indian community during most of the 17th and 18th centuries. The Munsee lived in an area stretching from southern New York across northern New Jersey to northeastern Pennsylvania. Archeological resources found on this upper Delaware River island site have yielded information on their contact with colonial traders and settlers. Minisink is one of the most extensive, best-preserved, and most intensively studied archeological sites in the Northeast. (Also in Pike County, Pennsylvania.)

## ◼ *Union County*

## BOXWOOD HALL
**1073 East Jersey Street, Elizabeth**

Elias Boudinot, elected president of the Continental Congress in 1782, purchased this shingle-covered house in 1772 and owned it until 1795, when he sold it to Jonathan Dayton. Dayton, youngest signer of the Constitution, was Speaker of the U.S. House of Representatives when he moved in and remained here until his death in 1824. Boudinot entertained George Washington before his inauguration in New York in 1789, and Dayton entertained Lafayette in 1824. The house, with its appreciable historic associations, is open to the public as a historic house museum.

## WILLIAM LIVINGSTON HOUSE
**Morris and North Avenues, Union**

William Livingston built Liberty Hall in 1772–1773 and made it his home until his death in 1790. Livingston was a major figure during the Revolutionary period. He served as governor of New Jersey from 1776 to 1790 and was a signer of the Constitution. His fine frame house has been greatly enlarged since his time but is still intact beneath and behind its accretions. In 1997 the house was donated to the Liberty Hall Foundation. It is open to the public as a house museum.

# NEW MEXICO

## ■ *Colfax County*

### RATON PASS
**Raton vicinity**

This mountain pass on the Santa Fe Trail was the shortest route between Colorado's upper Arkansas Valley and New Mexico. It played a crucial role in Stephen Watts Kearney's 1846 conquest of New Mexico, as well as during the Civil War, when Confederate raiders and the threat of attack by southern Plains Indians halted traffic over the Cimarron Cutoff. (Also in Las Animas County, Colorado.)

## ■ *Dona Ana County*

### MESILLA PLAZA
**2 miles south of Las Cruces on New Mexico Route 28**

This geographically challenged little town was founded in 1848 by the Mexican government for the purpose of resettling Mexican citizens from territory that had been ceded to the United States by the Treaty of Guadalupe-Hildago. Five years later, according to the terms of the 1853 Gadsden Purchase Treaty, Mesilla became part of the United States. Although it has now been part of the United States for almost all of its corporate existence, Mesilla still retains the flavor of a Mexican village, with its major buildings arranged around a central plaza.

### WHITE SANDS V-2 LAUNCHING SITE
**White Sands Missile Range**

This site is closely associated with U.S. testing of the German V-2 rocket, the origins of the American rocket program, and Dr. Werner von Braun's leadership of the nation's space program. The V-2 Gantry Crane and Army Blockhouse represent the first generation of rocket testing facilities that provided the foundation for the nation's exploration of space. The site is still used for weapons tests. White Sands Missile Range Museum offers many exhibits tracing the history of missile and space flight testing.

## ■ *Eddy County*

### CARLSBAD RECLAMATION PROJECT
**North of Carlsbad**

One of the most extensive private irrigation projects in the American West—where adequate water supply has always been a concern—was undertaken in the Carlsbad area in the 1880s. Inhabitants of the Pecos Valley built stone dams to form a series of reservoirs. Soon the formerly arid basin became a rich garden and stock raising area. After a series of floods damaged the system, the federal government stepped in under provisions of the Reclamation Act of 1902. Many of the

*White Sands V-2 Launching Site, Dona Ana County. Hermes missile in V-2 gantry. Courtesy of U.S. Army White Sands Missile Range.*

early stone dams and canals, and the original concrete flume, remain.

### ■ *Lincoln County*

## LINCOLN HISTORIC DISTRICT
**U.S. Route 380, Lincoln**

La Placita del Rio Bonito, "the little town by the beautiful river," was founded in the 1850s by Hispaño farmers. In 1869, when Lincoln County was formed, it was renamed and became the county seat. Unlike a rose, it did not smell as sweet with its new name in the years following, when cowboys, badmen, rustlers, lawmen, and gunfighters drifted in. Disputes over land and water rights and government beef contracts erupted in a three-day gun battle, known as the Lincoln County War of 1878, in which "Billy the Kid" participated. Now considerably quieter, Lincoln survives today as one of the best-preserved cow towns that sprang up along the cattlemen's frontier in the years following the Civil War.

### ■ *Los Alamos County*

## BANDELIER CCC HISTORIC DISTRICT (NPS)
**Bandelier National Monument (Los Alamos and Sandoval Counties)**

This impressive group of 31 Pueblo Revival buildings, mimicking a small New Mexico village, dates from the 1930s. Designed by National Park Service architects and built by members of the Civilian Conservation Corps, the adobe-washed stone group is the largest unaltered collection of such structures in any National Park. The buildings were erected as the administrative, residential, and maintenance core of Bandelier National Monument and, for the most part, still serve their original purposes.

## LOS ALAMOS SCIENTIFIC LABORATORY
**Central Avenue, Los Alamos**

Los Alamos was founded January 1, 1943, on the isolated Pajarito Plateau, for a single purpose: to develop an instrument of war—the nuclear fission, or atomic, bomb. In subsequent years the hydrogen bomb was also developed here. The laboratory continues to be a center for research on nuclear weapons and peaceful applications of atomic energy. Much of Los Alamos is off limits to visitors, but a museum explains the purposes and history of the site. (See Trinity Site, Socorro County.)

### ■ *Luna County*

## VILLAGE OF COLUMBUS AND CAMP FURLONG
**Portions of Columbus and Pancho Villa State Park, Columbus**

This small border village achieved its moment of fame, or infamy, early in the morning of March 9, 1916, when approximately 485 Mexican revolutionaries led by General Francisco "Pancho" Villa crossed into the United States. Before the town was fully awakened by his attack, ten civilians and eight soldiers had been killed. Without consulting the Mexican government, President Wilson ordered General John J. Pershing to lead a punitive expedition into Mexico to capture Villa and prevent further raids across the international border. A portion of the site is commemorated in Pancho Villa State Park.

### ■ *McKinley County*

## MANUELITO COMPLEX
**Address Restricted, Manuelito**

This rocky valley exhibits evidence of continuous Anasazi occupation from about A.D. 700 to 1350. Among the most impressive of its many sites is the ruin of a large pueblo that extends from the valley floor up a talus slope to the top of a mesa. Some 1,500 rooms have been counted in this structure. With its long span of use, Manuelito yields valuable information on Anasazi development.

### ■ *Mora County*

## WAGON MOUND
**East of Wagon Mound on U.S. Route 85**

Wagon Mound, a lone stone butte, was the last great landmark on the westward journey across the plains of northeastern New Mexico. It was a guidepost seen by all travelers on the High Plains section of the Cimarron Cutoff of the Santa Fe Trail. Santa Clara Spring, a natural camping spot two

*Watrous, Watrous, Mora County. William Tiptons's store. Courtesy of the New Mexico State Historic Preservation Office (Betsy Swanson).*

miles northwest of the mound, became the site of frequent Indian ambushes. Wagon Mound thus began to serve not only as a guide, but as a warning to travelers. Extensive ruts remain as evidence of the route of the trail.

## WATROUS
### U.S. Route 85, Watrous

Here, at the settlement of La Junta de Los Rios Mara y Sapello — the confluence of the Mora and Sapello Rivers — the Mountain and Cimarron Cutoff routes of the Santa Fe Trail joined, or separated, depending on which way one was traveling. It was here that wagons organized into trains before entering hostile Indian territory. In 1879, the Santa Fe Railroad laid out the present town of Watrous and wrote finis to the glory years of the trail by supplanting it with the Iron Horse. Trail remnants, along with several historic buildings, survive.

## ◼ *Rio Arriba County*

## GEORGIA O'KEEFFE HOME AND STUDIO
### County Road 164, House No. 13, Abiquiu

Georgia O'Keeffe occupies a pivotal, pioneering position in American art. She created her own style by adapting early modernist tenets to quintessentially American motifs. Her stark paintings of cattle skulls bleached by the desert sun are familiar to all. From

1949 until her death in 1984, O'Keeffe lived and worked here at Abiquiu. The buildings and their surroundings, along with the views they command, inspired many of her paintings and continue to provide great insight into her vision. The home and studio are maintained by the Georgia O'Keeffe Foundation and are open to the public.

## PUYE RUINS
### Address Restricted, Española

Puye, "assembling place of cottontail rabbits," in the Tewa Indian tongue, is the name of one of the largest prehistoric Indian settlements on the Pajarito Plateau. Established in the late 1200s or early 1300s, it was abandoned ca. 1600. Ruins at the site, including a pueblo atop the mesa, display a variety of architectural forms and building techniques. Puye is located on the Santa Clara Indian Reservation.

## SAN GABRIEL DE YUNQUE-OUINGE
### Address Restricted, Española

This was the first European settlement established in New Mexico and consequently served as the first Spanish capital. It was founded within an abandoned Tewa pueblo and was occupied by Spanish colonists from 1598 until about 1609. It was from San Gabriel that the Spanish set out to explore the country and to find the mythical gold-rich Quivira, always *poco mas alla* ("a little further on"). In 1610, the Spaniards themselves moved a little farther on, and established their new capital at Santa Fe.

## ■ Roosevelt County

### BLACKWATER DRAW
**Address Restricted, Clovis**

Blackwater Draw, an extinct riverbed, contains two separate sites of great archeological significance. Both have yielded information about the nature of humans and their environment at the end of the last period of glaciation. Blackwater Draw Locality No. 1 is the type site of the Clovis Culture. Both it and Locality No. 2 (Anderson Basin) were discovered when wind erosion exposed remains of extinct Pleistocene animals. A hand-dug well at Locality No. 1 represents one of man's earliest known attempts in the New World to control water. Eastern New Mexico State University owns and interprets the site.

## ■ San Miguel County

### GLORIETA PASS BATTLEFIELD (NPS)
**10 miles southeast of Santa Fe on U.S. Route 84-85 (San Miguel and Santa Fe Counties)**

In February 1862, a Confederate brigade of 2,500 Texans marched up the Rio Grande valley with the intention of driving through Albuquerque and Santa Fe and on to Denver. Federal soldiers moved to intercept them, and the two armies met at Glorieta Pass in the Sangre de Cristo Mountains. The battle took place on March 26–28, 1862, ending the Confederate invasion and forcing the rebels to abandon their campaign in the Southwest. The battlefield became a part of Pecos National Historical Park in 1993.

### PECOS PUEBLO (NPS)
**South of Pecos on New Mexico Route 63**

Pecos, east of Santa Fe, was one of the largest pueblos in New Mexico and an outstanding landmark for early Spanish explorers. Here Coronado's men found "the Turk," an Indian guide who led them on their search for Quivira, one of the legendary "Seven Cities of Gold." A mission was established at the pueblo by 1620, but was abandoned in 1782. By then the pueblo had begun to decline, and it was abandoned in 1838. Pecos National Historical Park manages the site.

## ■ Sandoval County

### BANDELIER CCC HISTORIC DISTRICT (NPS)
**Bandelier National Monument (Los Alamos and Sandoval Counties)**

(See entry under Los Alamos County.)

### BIG BEAD MESA
**Address Restricted, Casa Salazar**

This is the site of an impressive Navajo village, occupied from about 1745 to 1812. After moving into the Big Bead Mesa area,

*Pecos Pueblo, San Miguel County, 1946. Courtesy of NPS (George Grant).*

the Navajo formed an alliance with the Gila Apaches and established a stronghold that menaced the Laguna and Acoma pueblos. The site, dotted with remains of stick-and-stone–walled hogans, demonstrates patterns of trade and raiding that characterized Navajo relations with Pueblo, Apache, and Hispanics.

## SANDIA CAVE
### Address Restricted, Bernalillo

Sandia Cave's artifacts, originally believed to be the earliest evidence of North American settlement, were composed predominantly of projectile points, reflecting the Folsom tradition and the Solutrean tradition and suggesting that prehistoric North Americans were of European descent. The site's authenticity has come under question, and several scientific tests have reassessed the earlier interpretations. Despite the reassessment, Sandia is significant for its impact on both popular and professional opinions of early prehistoric settlement in North America.

## ■ *Santa Fe County*
## BARRIO DE ANALCO HISTORIC DISTRICT
### Bounded by East De Vargas and College Streets, Santa Fe

First settled in 1620, the Barrio de Analco (meaning "on the other side of the water") is unique because it represents an active working-class neighborhood of Spanish colonial heritage. The district, across the Santa Fe River from Santa Fe proper—where officials resided around the central plaza—contains numerous examples of Spanish Pueblo architecture, characterized by the adobe construction indigenous to the Southwest. The focal point of the barrio was the Chapel of San Miguel, described in 1626 as serving the laborers, artisans, and Indian servants of the growing suburb.

## EL SANTUARIO DE CHIMAYO
### 1 mile northwest of Santa Cruz Reservoir Dam, Chimayo

Completed in 1816 as a private chapel, this is a well-preserved adobe church. Twin bell towers flank its entrance, and the interior is especially notable for its original decorations, including numerous religious paintings and statuary. El Santuario became a place of pilgrimage soon after its construction. The chapel centers the small village of El Potrero, one of several settlements in the Santa Cruz Valley collectively called Chimayo.

## GLORIETA PASS BATTLEFIELD (NPS)
### 10 miles southeast of Santa Fe on U.S. Route 84-85 (San Miguel and Santa Fe Counties)

(See entry under San Miguel County.)

## NATIONAL PARK SERVICE REGION III HEADQUARTERS BUILDING (NPS)
### Old Santa Fe Trail, Santa Fe

This largest known adobe building in the United States is a masterpiece of Spanish Pueblo Revival architecture. Hand-built furniture and hammered-tin light fixtures add to the authentic period flavor, as does an outstanding art collection, ranging from Pueblo

*El Santuario de Chimayo, Chimayo, Santa Fe County. Courtesy of NPS (Walter Smalling, Jr.).*

pottery and Navajo rugs to works provided by members of Santa Fe's art colony in the 1930s. Cecil Doty, then a National Park Service regional architect, designed the head-quarters, which was built during the Depression by Civilian Conservation Corps workers.

## PALACE OF THE GOVERNORS
### Santa Fe Plaza, Santa Fe

Erected in 1610–1612 as part of the royal presidio of Santa Fe, the adobe Palacio Real is the oldest public building built by European settlers in the continental United States. It served as the residence of Spanish, then Mexican, and finally American, gover-nors of New Mexico until 1907. Architecturally, the palace combines Pueblo Indian and Spanish methods of construction and design and has influenced buildings throughout the Southwest. The restored building, occupying an entire side of the Santa Fe Plaza, is open to the public as a museum.

## SAN LAZARO
### Address Restricted, Cerrillos vicinity

San Lazaro consists of the ruins of two pueb-los: one prehistoric and the other a planned historic pueblo with four house blocks around a central plaza. A Spanish chapel was established at the pueblo, but after the Pueblo Rebellion of 1680, the Spanish abandoned the site. San Lazaro constitutes the largest ruins in the area and has provided informa-tion on the development and history of Puebloan peoples in the Galisteo Basin.

## SANTA FE PLAZA
### Santa Fe

As in most towns established under Spanish influence, Santa Fe's plaza is the city's physi-cal, cultural, and economic center. Santa Fe was established in the winter of 1609–1610, and its plaza served as the center of defense against Indian attack in its early years. It soon became the central marketplace and, later, the final goal of travelers on the Santa Fe Trail. In 1846, General Stephen Watts Kearny raised the American flag over the plaza, announcing New Mexico's annexation by the United States. Although smaller now than in Spanish times, the plaza is still the heart of one of America's most historic places.

## SETON VILLAGE
### 6 miles south of Santa Fe off U.S. Route 84

Ernest Thompson Seton, artist, author, scien-tist, and one of America's greatest naturalists, chaired the committee that brought the Boy Scout movement to the United States, served as Chief Scout, and wrote the first Scout manual. He settled here in 1930 and estab-lished Seton Village as the summer center for the American Woodcraft League, which had more than 80,000 members at the time. Seaton's own house, a 45-room adobe "cas-tle," is the most impressive building in the village.

## ■ Socorro County

## TRINITY SITE
### White Sands Missile Range, Bingham vicinity

Here, at the White Sands Missile Range on the bleak and barren desert crossed by the Jornada del Muerto ("Journey of Death") trail, the world's first nuclear device (code name "Trinity"), which had arrived from Los Alamos, was exploded. The "unprecedented, magnificent, beautiful, stupendous, and terri-fying" detonation, far more powerful than had been expected, took place on July 16, 1945, at 0529:45. On August 6, 1945, a sec-ond bomb, "Little Boy," was dropped on Hiroshima, Japan. On August 9, the third device, "Fat Man," was detonated above Nagasaki; Japan surrendered five days later. Trinity's Ground Zero is marked by a lava-stone monument. The site in this still-active missile range is open to the public twice a year. (See Los Alamos Scientific Laboratory, Los Alamos County.)

## ■ Taos County

## ERNEST L. BLUMENSCHEIN HOUSE
### Ledoux Street, Taos

In 1919 painter Ernest L. Blumenschein pur-chased this one-story, 11-room adobe dating from Spanish times and adapted it as his home and studio. In 1898, Blumenschein had cofounded the Taos Art Colony, which became the most important art center west of the Mississippi in the early 20th century.

The house is open as a museum dedicated to Blumenschein.

## KIT CARSON HOUSE
**Kit Carson Avenue, Taos**

Kit Carson, fur trader and mountain man, has become a legendary hero of the "Old West." A contemporary who knew him well once said that he was "first in every quality which constitutes excellence in a mountaineer." Carson bought this U-shaped Spanish Colonial adobe in 1843 when he married Josefa Jaramillo, and the two lived here until 1868, the year both died. The house has been a museum since 1952.

## LAS TRAMPAS HISTORIC DISTRICT
**On New Mexico Route 76, Las Trampas**

First settled in 1751 by 12 Spanish families from Santa Fe, Las Trampas flourished despite Comanche and Apache raids. The village, a Spanish-American agricultural community, preserves significant elements of its 18th-century heritage in appearance and culture. It is one of the few Spanish-influenced settlements in the state that retains its distinct plaza plan. The adobe church of San José de Gracia, facing the plaza, is one of the state's architectural treasures.

## MABEL DODGE LUHAN HOUSE
**Morada Lane, Taos**

Mabel Ganson Evans Dodge Stern Luhan, an important patron of the arts, nurtured the famous artistic community that centered on her Taos home for 40 years. She arrived in town in 1917, and even before she completed her Pueblo Revival adobe house in 1922, artists and writers had come to visit and work in it. Among the many pilgrims were D.H. Lawrence, Mary Austin, Willa Cather, Robinson Jeffers, Ansel Adams, Edward Weston, and Georgia O'Keeffe.

## SAN FRANCISCO DE ASSISI MISSION CHURCH
**The Plaza, Ranchos de Taos**

More sculptural than architectural, the massive adobe walls of this Spanish Colonial church were built between 1772 and 1816. The facade is flanked by twin belfries, but the almost bru-talistic forms of the rear walls—chancel and transepts—provide the most lasting impression. Thanks to paintings by Georgia O'Keeffe and photographs by countless others, this is perhaps the best known of all of New Mexico's colonial mission churches.

## SAN JOSÉ DE GRACIA CHURCH
**North side of the Plaza, Las Trampas**

Erected between 1760 and 1776, this is one of the best-preserved and least-altered Spanish Colonial pueblo churches in New Mexico. Projecting buttresses flanking the facade terminate in small towers and enclose a recess with an outdoor balcony. Interior decorations include paintings and a carved wooden reredos. Like many New Mexico churches of its time, the sanctuary at San José is "mysteriously" lit by a transverse clerestory window invisible from the nave.

## TAOS PUEBLO
**3 miles north of Taos**

Taos Pueblo was first visited by Europeans in 1540, when Coronado's expedition arrived. The Spaniards were mightily impressed by the Tigua Indian habitation, with its five-story communal dwellings, and in 1598 established a mission. Over subsequent centuries Taos borrowed from Spanish-American and Anglo-American cultures but retained its integrity and identity as an independent community. Its great significance is attested to by the fact that the United Nations International Educational, Scientific, and Cultural Organization designated it as a World Heritage Site in 1982.

### ■ *Torrance County*

## ABO (NPS)
**3 miles west of the town of Abo on U.S. Route 60**

Occupied from late prehistoric times through the Spanish occupation, this pueblo typifies the period in which acculturation began in the American Southwest. A large mission church of red sandstone with adobe mortar was built in the 1630s to serve the Tompiros tribe, but by the 1670s the village was deserted because of the increasing strength of the Apache in the area. Ruins of the pueblo and mission are preserved in Salinas Pueblo Missions National Monument.

## QUARAI (NPS)
### 1 mile south of Punta de Agua

Ruins at this site help document the acculturation processes that occurred during the early period of contact between Native Americans and the Spanish. Missionary work began at the Quarai pueblo ca. 1620, and at one time Mission La Purisima Concepcion de Cuarac was headquarters of the Holy Office of the Inquisition in New Mexico. By 1678, owing to Apache raiding and severe famines, Quarai was abandoned. Ruins of the pueblo, church, and monastery remain, and there is a museum at this component of Salinas Pueblo Missions National Monument.

## ■ Union County

## FOLSOM SITE
### Address Restricted, Folsom

Few, if any, sites can compare with this bison killing and processing area in the contributions it has made to the advance of knowledge about prehistoric humans in the Western Hemisphere. Dating to approximately 8285 B.C., it is the type site of the Folsom Culture. In 1926 scientists made the dramatic find of flint spear points embedded in the ribs of an extinct species of bison, confirming what had previously been only suspected regarding the early advent of humans in the Americas.

*San José de Gracia Church, Las Trampas, Taos County. Courtesy of NPS (Walter Smalling, Jr.).*

*Abo, Torrance County, 1940. Courtesy of NPS (E. K. Reed).*

*Acoma Pueblo, Valencia County, 1934. Courtesy of HABS (M. James Slack).*

*Zuni-Cibola Complex, Valencia County. Prehistoric rock carvings, Village of the Great Kivas. Courtesy of NPS (Roger Anyon).*

## RABBIT EARS
### Clayton vicinity

Nothing on the Cimarron Cutoff of the Santa Fe Trail was more important to travelers than this conspicuous double-peaked mountain. Rising high above the plains, it served as a four-day guide on the journey, promising well-watered campsites at its base.

Rabbit Ears and nearby Round Mound, along with three campsites located between them—McNees Crossing, Turkey Creek Camp, and Rabbit Ears Creek Camp—are together known as the Clayton Complex. The area is used for grazing, and significant remnants of the trail may still be found.

## ■ *Valencia County*
### ACOMA PUEBLO
**13 miles south of Casa Blanca on New Mexico Route 23**

Acoma Pueblo, built on top of a giant, craggy mesa, is one of the oldest continuously occupied settlements in the United States. Founded as early as A.D. 1100, its location made it virtually impregnable in early times. The Mission of San Estevan del Rey, built to the side of the pueblo ca. 1629–1642, adds to the impressiveness of the site with its battered adobe walls and bold silhouette, a near-perfect blend of Indian and Spanish influences. The Acoma Indians still use the pueblo and still maintain their identity here as a separate community with distinctive cultural systems.

### HAWIKUH
**Zuni Indian Reservation**

Established in the 1200s and abandoned in 1680, this Zuni pueblo was the largest of the fabled seven golden "Cities of Cibola" and the first one seen by Spanish explorers. In 1539, the Black Moorish scout Estevan (Estevanico) became the first non-Indian to reach the area but was killed for his trouble by the inhabitants a day after he entered their city. A year later, when the Coronado Expedition reached the pueblo, its members found not gold but a small, crowded, dusty village. Now only ruins remain.

### SAN ESTEVAN DEL REY MISSION CHURCH
**On New Mexico Route 23, Acoma**

The Spanish padres erected churches wherever they settled in the New World, and in New Mexico they established a unique architectural style that blended native construction and detail with European plan and form. This grand adobe building, constructed by Franciscans between 1629 and 1642 and repaired in 1799–1800, is the finest and most impressive of all. Standing to one side of the Acoma Pueblo, the church and its adjoining buildings provide an incomparable glimpse of a long-ago age.

### ZUNI-CIBOLA COMPLEX
**Address Restricted, Zuni**

These four noncontiguous archeological sites contain house ruins, kivas, pictographs, petroglyphs, trash mounds, and a mission church and convent. They have proven to be an important source of material providing evidence for the fusion, in prehistoric times, of Mogollon and Anasazi traits that led in subsequent centuries to a distinct Zuni culture.

# NEW YORK

## ■ *Albany County*
### FORT ORANGE ARCHEOLOGICAL SITE
**Address Restricted, Albany**

Dutch West Indian Company employees built Fort Orange, a half-acre earthen fort surrounded by a wooden palisade, in 1624. The site was a flat, narrow plain along the western shore of the Hudson River, downstream from the head of navigation and astride major overland Indian routes. First as Beverwyck, then as Albany, it was a logical center for trade and diplomacy. Salvage archeology was undertaken in the 1970s, and many artifacts were uncovered.

### JAMES HALL OFFICE
**Lincoln Park, Albany**

James Hall, one of the country's best-known 19th-century geologists, conducted much of his research in this office. The expertise he showed in his 1830s survey of New York state led to other commissions in the fields of geology and paleontology. Hall became the first president of the Geological Society of America and a charter member of the

National Academy of Sciences. His cohort, James Dwight Dana, lauded him by stating that without Hall, "the geological history of the North American continent would not have been written."

## HARMONY MILLS
### Cohoes

From the late 1860s through the 1880s, the Harmony Mills Company was one of the largest American producers of cotton fabric for printed calicoes and fine cotton muslins. Harmony Mill No. 3 was the largest individual cotton factory in the world when it was completed in 1872 and was acknowledged as representing the state of the art at that time.

## NEW YORK STATE CAPITOL
### Capitol Park, Albany

Erected between 1867 and 1899, this is one of the nation's most lavish, architecturally significant, and idiosyncratic state capitols. It was begun in the Italian Renaissance style, but was completed in the Romanesque Revival style. Thomas Fuller, Leopold Eidlitz, and H. H. Richardson contributed their architectural talents to the melange. Construction of the building marked a period of great prosperity and confidence in post–Civil War New York, whose sobriquet, the Empire State, is well reflected in this building that still houses a portion of its government.

## SAINT PETER'S EPISCOPAL CHURCH
### 107 State Street, Albany

This French Gothic style church was designed by noted architect Richard Upjohn in concert with his son, Richard M. Upjohn. The stone church was built in 1859–1860, but the 180-foot tower, one of its most striking elements, was not completed until 1876. The basilican plan incorporates a shallow polygonal chancel, and the interior is lit by stained-glass windows, many of English design and manufacture.

## SCHUYLER FLATTS ARCHEOLOGICAL DISTRICT
### Address Restricted, Town of Colonie

Schuyler Flatts, the largest expanse of arable sandy loam along the Hudson River north of Albany, contains the archeological remains of 6,000 years of human occupation. Astride the main communications corridor connecting the Hudson and Champlain Valleys, this strategic position commanded the northern and western approaches to the Fort Orange–Albany area during the Historic Contact period, the early 17th century. The district contains intact features and artifactual evidence dating from that time.

## PHILIP SCHUYLER MANSION
### Clinton and Schuyler Streets, Albany

Constructed in 1761–1762, this was the home of Philip Schuyler, a general in the Revolutionary War and a member of the Continental Congress. The elegant brick mansion is one of the finest Late Georgian houses in the Middle Colonies, and the delicate Chinese balustrade around the eaves of its hipped roof is one of the earliest uses of such a feature in the country. Alexander Hamilton married Schuyler's daughter in the parlor in 1780, and Schuyler lived here until his death in 1804. The State of New York purchased the mansion early in the 20th century, restored it, and maintains it as a state historic site.

## WATERVLIET ARSENAL
### South Broadway, Watervliet

"The principal establishment for making fixed ammunition and all the articles of equipment for a train of artillery will be near Albany." So Decius Wadsworth, chief of ordnance, decreed in 1813, the year the arsenal was founded. Watervliet is now the oldest arsenal in continuous operation in the United States. During its peak development, from the 1820s through World War II, it was the U.S. Army's most important center for developing and producing large-caliber weapons. During peacetime, Watervliet is responsible for maintaining large-weapons capability. Buildings representing all but the earliest period of operations remain, most in active use.

■ *Bronx County*

## BARTOW-PELL MANSION
### Pelham Bay Park, Shore Road near Bartow Circle

A description of this house published in a

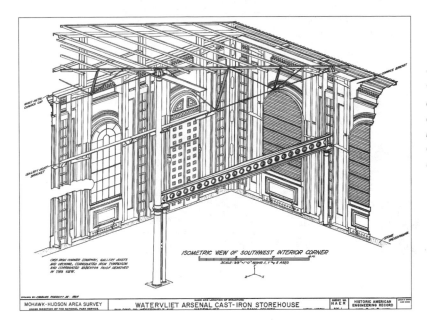

*Waterlviet Arsenal,
Waterlviet, Albany
County. Isometric view
of the cast-iron store-
house, 1969. Courtesy
of HAER (Charles
Parrott, III).*

*Croton Aqueduct (old),
Croton to New York
City, Bronx, New York,
and Westchester
Counties. Original con-
figuration of Saw Mill
River Culvert, ca. 1843.
Wiley and Putnam.*

guidebook in 1842, the year it was completed, still applies: "a fine stone house in the
Grecian style, which presents a neat front,
with projecting wings." It was influenced by
the work of prominent architect Minard
Lafever and has notable interiors. Robert
Bartow built the house on the site of an earlier house erected by his ancestor, Sir John
Pell. The house and its extensive grounds are
open to the public.

## CROTON AQUEDUCT (OLD)
### Between Croton and New York City (Bronx, New York, and Westchester Counties)

Built between 1837 and 1842, this aqueduct
was New York City's first planned water supply system, a model that other cities soon
emulated. The 40-mile-long, masonry-lined
conduit, 8½ feet high, led from a dam on the
Croton River to central Manhattan. Some
parts are tunneled through solid rock, others

*Van Cortlandt House, Bronx County, 1967. Courtesy of NPS (Charles W. Snell).*

are carried across rivers and valleys on bridges and berms, but most of the line rests on stone foundations immediately below grade. Portions of the aqueduct's route now serve as a recreational trail.

## LORILLARD SNUFF MILL
### New York Botanical Gardens

Constructed ca. 1840 by the P. Lorillard Company, this fieldstone mill is one of the nation's oldest extant tobacco factories. It symbolizes the importance of tobacco in the development of American commerce and industry and a time when snuff outranked chewing and smoking as the preferred method of use. Tobacco was colonial America's first principal export, ranking second only to cotton as late as 1860. After serving a number of capacities, the former mill is now a restaurant and meeting facility at the New York Botanical Gardens.

## NEW YORK BOTANICAL GARDENS
### Southern and Bedford Park Boulevards

Established in 1896, this exemplary institution soon became one of the leading botanical gardens in the world, a position it still maintains. Within its 230 acres are one of the world's largest herbariums, research laboratories, an extensive botanical library and museum, and an extraordinary Victorian-era glass conservatory. A portion of the gardens occupies the former estate of tobacconist Peter Lorillard.

## VAN CORTLANDT HOUSE
### Van Cortlandt Park at 242nd Street

Erected between 1748 and 1749, this is one of the most notable early-Georgian manor houses of the middle colonies. It is significant architecturally for its beautiful, and unusual, stone and brick masonry. Walls are stone, windows are framed in brick, and keystones are carved with satyrlike faces, a unique feature in American colonial architecture. The interior is noted for its woodwork and refined paneling. The Van Cortlandt family lived here until 1889, when they deeded the house and its extensive grounds to the City of New York. The grounds now form Van Cortlandt Park, and the house is a historic house museum.

## ■ Broome County

## NEW YORK STATE INEBRIATE ASYLUM
### 425 Robinson Street, Binghamton

The New York State Inebriate Asylum was constructed between 1858 and 1866 as the United States Inebriate Asylum, the first single-purpose hospital in the country designed and built for the treatment of alcoholism as a disease. The asylum was an outgrowth of a developing attitude in 19th-century America, that drunkenness was the cause of nearly all social and economic problems and that its cure — temperance — would result in their eradication. Isaac Gale Perry designed the castellated Gothic Revival structure, which is now encompassed within a late-19th-century health facility.

## ■ Cayuga County

## WILLIAM H. SEWARD HOUSE
### 33 South Street, Auburn

As U.S. secretary of state from 1861 to 1869, William Seward negotiated the purchase of Alaska from Russia, which denigrators castigated variously as "Seward's Folly" or "Seward's Icebox." His position as secretary of state capped a long career of public service. He was governor of New York from 1839 to 1843 and U.S. senator from 1848 to 1861. His Auburn house, built in 1816–1817 by his father-in-law, was his permanent residence from 1824 until his death in 1872. It is now open as a historic house museum.

## HARRIET TUBMAN HOME FOR THE AGED
### 180–182 South Street, Auburn

Harriet Tubman spent almost a third of her long life as a slave. In 1849 she escaped over the Underground Railroad from Maryland's Eastern Shore to Philadelphia and then devoted the next decade of her life to assisting others to achieve the same goal. One of the most famous "conductors" on the Underground Railroad, she guided more than 300 slaves, including her aged parents, to freedom. Long before she established this home for aged and indigent African Americans in 1908, Harriet Tubman had become an American folk hero. She died here in 1913 at the age of 93.

## JETHRO WOOD HOUSE
### Poplar Ridge Road, Poplar Ridge

Today's American agricultural machines are models of efficiency—not so at the beginning of the 19th century. Before Jethro Wood patented his first successful cast-iron plow in 1819, farmers relied on cumbersome, inefficient wooden implements or on metal plows that were little better. Wood's plows produced cleaner furrows, and three separate standard parts made repairs and replacements easier

than ever before. From 1800 until his death in 1834 this great benefactor of American agriculture lived in this two-story clapboarded farmhouse, which is still a private residence.

## ■ Chautauqua County

## CHAUTAUQUA HISTORIC DISTRICT
### Bounded by Chautauqua Lake, North and Lowell Avenues, and New York Route 394, Chautauqua

Beginning in 1874 as a Methodist Sunday school teachers' assembly, the Chautauqua Institution developed into one of America's most popular educational programs. Typically held in summer months in wooded retreats, Chautauquas across the country sponsored innovative secular programs long before colleges and universities accepted similar ideas. The movement began and grew in this wooded area on the shore of Lake Chautauqua, and the district retains a remarkable degree of integrity. Fanciful wooden cottages with ample porches that provided lodging for families participating in the program virtually define the term *Victorian* and typify the sort of housing erected at many other Chatauquas.

## LEWIS MILLER COTTAGE
### Asbury Avenue, Chautauqua

The Chautauqua Institution was founded in 1874 and flourished through its innovative summer programs that contributed to America's growing appetite for knowledge. Lewis Miller, a cofounder, suggested a Methodist campground for the site that became Chautauqua. As the program continued to expand, Miller organized a four-year study program and created the Chaugauqua Press. His cottage, one of the earliest in this still functioning summer educational retreat, is still privately maintained.

## ■ Chemung County

## NEWTOWN BATTLEFIELD
### New York Route 17, 6 miles southeast of Elmira

This now peaceful mountaintop was the scene of a battle between American forces and Indians on August 29, 1779. The battle, won by the colonials, was a result of the Sullivan Expedition, an operation involving almost 4,000 troops led by Major General John Sullivan at Washington's command. The expedition was a counteroffensive against the Iroquois, who, as British allies, had raided settlements in upstate New York and western Pennsylvania. A portion of the battlefield is included in the Newtown Battlefield State Park.

## Clinton County

### ADIRONDACK FOREST PRESERVE
**(Clinton, Essex, Franklin, Fulton, Hamilton, Herkimer, and Saint Lawrence Counties)**

This huge area became the first state forest preserve in the nation when New York State established it as a wilderness area in 1885. The act of establishment encompassed all state-owned lands in the Adirondack region, along with those in three counties in the Catskills, and directed that they be forever kept as a wilderness. By the time the preserve was declared a National Historic Landmark in 1963, some 2,500,000 acres had been incorporated.

### PLATTSBURGH BAY
**Cumberland Bay, east of Plattsburgh**

A decisive American naval victory here on Lake Champlain on September 11, 1814, destroyed the invading British fleet and halted a major thrust into the United States during the War of 1812. The invading British troops were compelled to withdraw to Canada, and the war soon ended. This National Historic Landmark also includes the remnants of Fort Brown, where a simultaneous land battle took place.

### VALCOUR BAY
**4 miles south of Plattsburgh on the west shore of Lake Champlain**

On October 11, 1776, a naval engagement occurred at this narrow channel on the western shore of Lake Champlain. American forces under Benedict Arnold's command engaged the British, led by General Sir Guy Carleton, who was on his way to establish control of the Lake Champlain–Hudson River waterways in hopes of severing the

middle colonies from New England. The British won, but the Americans inflicted sufficient damage to delay their effort. When the British resumed their march the next year, Americans were better prepared to repulse them, which they did at Saratoga. Arnold's little navy had accomplished far more than its sailors had imagined possible.

## Columbia County

### FREDERIC E. CHURCH HOUSE
**At the east end of Rip Van Winkle Bridge, Church Hill**

Olana, beautifully sited overlooking the Hudson River, is a masterful mix of Persian, Moorish, Italian, and East Indian architectural styles. Designed by Church with help from Calvert Vaux, it reflects the noted artist's love of travel and his flair for the dramatic. Primarily a landscape painter, Church was among the ablest of American 19th-century artists. Olana, its name taken from an Arabic word meaning "our place on high," is open to the public as a state historic site.

### CLERMONT
**Clermont State Park, Germantown**

Clermont, built in 1728 and rebuilt after the British burned it in 1777, was the country home of Robert Livingston, delegate to the Continental Congress and first secretary of foreign affairs under the Articles of Confederation. Later known as Chancellor Livingston, he was an able jurist and diplomat. As minister to France during Jefferson's administration, he negotiated the terms of the purchase of the Louisiana Territory from Napoleon. Also an inventor, Livingston helped Robert Fulton perfect the steamboat. Named after the estate, Fulton's *Clermont* steamed by the property on its 1807 maiden voyage. The house is open to the public as a state historic site.

### HUDSON RIVER HISTORIC DISTRICT
**East side of the Hudson River between Germantown and Staatsburg (Columbia and Dutchess Counties)**

This 30-square-mile district on the eastern shore of the Hudson River, midway between

New York City and Albany, is composed of several villages and a number of country houses. With its Dutch colonial origins and its remarkably diverse ethnic populations, the region holds a unique position in the settlement and social history of the nation. Sedate Dutch homesteads, rustic German farms, industrious Yankee towns, and Gilded Age mansions all contribute to a rich landscape fabric, remarkable for its integrity and its preservation.

## LINDENWALD (NPS)
**On New York Route 9H, east of Kinderhook**

Martin Van Buren, eighth president of the United States, purchased this late-18th-century brick house in 1839. After leaving the White House, he said, "[I spent] the last and happiest years of my life, a farmer in my native town." During Van Buren's occupancy, architect Richard Upjohn remodeled and enlarged the original Federal style house, giving it an Italianate appearance. Lindenwald is now open to the public as the Martin Van Buren National Historic Site.

## MOUNT LEBANON SHAKER SOCIETY
**U.S. Route 20, New Lebanon**

Mount Lebanon was the second and principal community of 19 settlements the Shakers established in the United States, and it was here that the central ministry resided. Shakers at Mount Lebanon were organized into groups, or "families," each consisting of 60 adults divided as equally as possible between the sexes. Each family had its own dwelling house (or houses), workshops, and outbuildings, and, as would be expected, all were characterized by simplicity of form and honesty of expression. Construction virtually ceased after 1876, but some 34 original buildings now remain, many of them part of the Darrow School. Mount Lebanon is open to the public on summer weekends.

## STEEPLETOP
**444 East Hill Road, Austerlitz**

Feminist, agnostic, and political radical, Edna St. Vincent Millay was a leader in the Bohemian cultural movement of the 1920s, centered in New York's Greenwich Village. She was also an important literary figure and received the 1923 Pulitzer Prize for *The Harp Weaver,* a collection of sonnets. Except for periods of travel and visits to New York City, Millay and her husband lived at this secluded Columbia County farm from 1925 until his death in 1949, and hers the next year. Located just outside Austerlitz, Steepletop is now the Millay Colony for the Arts.

## VAN ALEN HOUSE
**New York Route 9H, 2 miles south of U.S. Route 9, Kinderhook vicinity**

The Van Alen House, built in two stages in 1737 and 1750, is an important and rare example of the type of Dutch Colonial architecture that emerged in the northern counties of the Hudson Valley. Luycas Van Alen's house has the characteristic features of steep, sharply pitched gable roofs, rooms aligned in a row, and fine cross-bond brickwork with glazed headers. This last feature produces a diamond, or diapered, pattern that adds immensely to the design. The house was acquired by the Columbia County Historical Society in 1961, was subsequently restored, and is open to the public.

## ■ *Delaware County*

## WOODCHUCK LODGE
**2 miles from Roxbury**

John Burroughs, America's first important nature writer, is commemorated by three National Historic Landmarks. From 1908 until his death in 1921, he used this rustic lodge on the family farm as his summer home and study. During these years Burroughs was the nation's recognized authority on the out-of-doors, instilling in his readers "a deep affection for nature seasoned by genuine understanding." He is buried nearby. (See John Burroughs Riverby Study and Slabsides, Ulster County.)

## ■ *Dutchess County*

## HUDSON RIVER HISTORIC DISTRICT
**East side of the Hudson River between Germantown and Staatsburg (Columbia and Dutchess Counties)**

(See entry under Columbia County.)

## HUDSON RIVER STATE HOSPITAL, MAIN BUILDING
### Route 9, Poughkeepsie

This is the country's first significant example of the High Victorian Gothic style applied to an institutional building. Dating from 1867 to 1871, it was designed by Frederick C. Withers and established his reputation as one of the finest practitioners of an architectural style characterized by strong contrasts in materials and colors. The facility was modeled on principles promoted by Dr. Thomas Kirkbridge for treatment of the insane, and the grounds were developed by landscape architect Frederick Law Olmsted. The building is deteriorated, and only two floors are currently in use.

## MONTGOMERY PLACE
### River Road, Annandale

This elegant country estate, overlooking the Hudson River and the Catskill Mountains beyond, is a unique survival of the Romantic vision of mid-19th-century America. Architect Alexander Jackson Davis transformed a staid, formal Federal style house, built in 1805, into a handsome Neoclassical composition during the mid–19th century. At the same time, Andrew Jackson Downing helped transform the surrounding landscape into a pleasure ground with numerous subsidiary buildings. Historic Hudson Valley acquired the estate in 1986 and subsequently restored the house. Montgomery Place is open to the public.

## SAMUEL F. B. MORSE HOUSE
### 370 South Street, Poughkeepsie

Samuel Finley Breese Morse purchased "Locust Grove" in 1847, three years after transmitting his famous telegraphic message, "What hath God wrought!" from Washington to Baltimore. He engaged architect Alexander Jackson Davis to transform the house into a Tuscan villa and used it as his summer home until his death in 1871. Along with his telegraph, Morse invented the Morse code, and he is also recognized as an important 19th-century American artist. The Huguenot Historical Society acquired the property in 1975, and it is open as a historic house museum.

## OLD MAIN, VASSAR COLLEGE
### Vassar College campus, Poughkeepsie

Matthew Vassar, "Squire of Poughkeepsie," grew wealthy from the brewery business and determined to use his fortune to found and endow an educational institution "more lasting than the pyramids." He realized his lofty aspiration with Vassar College, one of the first women's colleges in the country. Old Main, constructed between 1861 and 1865 from designs by James Renwick, remains one of the earliest, largest, and most successful expressions of the Second Empire style in the United States. Designed to accommodate 400 students and the entire faculty and their families, and to contain classrooms, library, and chapel, Old Main housed all of the college— in fact *was* the college—for many years.

## SPRINGSIDE
### Academy and Livingston Streets, Poughkeepsie

In 1850, Matthew Vassar hired Andrew Jackson Downing to plan his country estate. Downing is recognized as America's first landscape architect, and he exerted a profound influence through his work and writings. Until the 1980s, Springside was the sole example of his work that had survived almost intact in its entirety. Such is no longer true, but twenty acres of the historic "pleasure grounds" were protected from development when Springside Landscape Restoration acquired them in 1990.

## TOP COTTAGE (NPS)
### 24 Potters Bend Road, Hyde Park

Constructed in 1938, during Franklin Delano Roosevelt's second term in office, this small stone cottage served as his private country retreat for the rest of his presidency. Architect Henry Toombs designed the cottage under Roosevelt's direction, and it embodies the president's strong interest in the early history and architecture of the Hudson Valley. Many features were specifically designed to accommodate Roosevelt's need for wheelchair accessibility. Consequently, of all the buildings associated with Roosevelt, Top Cottage is the most poignant and personal reminder of his private life while he was president of the United States. The house

Buffalo State Hospital, Buffalo, Erie County. Administration Building, 1965. Courtesy of HABS (Jack E. Boucher).

is open to the public as part of the Roosevelt-Vanderbilt National Historic Site.

## VASSAR COLLEGE OBSERVATORY
### Raymond Avenue, Poughkeepsie

In 1865, Matthew Vassar built this observatory for Maria Mitchell on the campus of the college he had recently founded. Astronomer, professor, and crusader for higher education and professional advancement for women, Mitchell was the first woman elected to both the American Academy of Arts and Sciences and the American Philosophical Society. Vassar had the observatory custom-designed for her. It contained the country's third-largest telescope at the time, Mitchell's classroom and laboratory, and rooms that served as home for her and her father. Mitchell's emphasis on high scientific standards and feminist ideals made her a role model for those she taught and those who followed.

■ *Erie County*

## BUFFALO AND ERIE COUNTY HISTORICAL SOCIETY BUILDING
### 25 Nottingham Court, Buffalo

The only structure surviving from the Pan-American Exposition of 1901, this Neoclassical marble building has a portico based on the Parthenon. The exposition was held to encourage economic ties between North and South America after the Spanish-American War, but is now remembered chiefly because President McKinley was assassinated while visiting the fair. Designed by locally prominent architect George Cary, this structure served as the New York State Building during the Exposition and has been the home of the Buffalo and Erie County Historical Society since 1902.

## BUFFALO STATE HOSPITAL
### 400 Forest Avenue, Buffalo

Begun in 1872, this huge complex represents an important transition in the developing architectural talents of H. H. Richardson. Cohesive massing characterizes the design and hints at Richardson's soon-to-be-perfected Romanesque style. Richardson collaborated with partners Frederick Law Olmsted and Calvert Vaux, who sited the buildings and landscaped the property. The hospital is also significant in the history of treatment for the mentally ill, as its plan followed Dr. Thomas Kirkbridge's system, whereby patients were placed in wards according to their specific illnesses and needs.

## *EDWARD M. COTTER*
### Michigan and Ohio Streets on the Buffalo River, Buffalo

Built in 1900 and launched as *W.S. Gratan,* the *Edward M. Cotter* is an operating fireboat of the Buffalo Fire Department. As such, *Cotter* is the oldest fireboat still in service in the country. *Cotter*'s lines conform to the general image of fireboats, but it has features specific to use on the frequently frozen waterways where it serves. The boat exploded in July 1928 when flames overcame it, but it was rebuilt in 1930 and has been in full service ever since.

## MILLARD FILLMORE HOUSE
### 24 Shearer Avenue, East Aurora

Millard Fillmore, 13th president of the United States, built this house in 1826, when he was first married and was the only lawyer in East Aurora. A state legislator, U.S. congressman, and vice president, he became president in 1850 after Zachary Taylor died in office. Although his career as chief executive was undistinguished, he met the nation's need for a conservative president during a time of increasing sectional differences. His simple frame house, reflecting the modest aspirations of his early career, has been moved from its original site but retains its early form and structure.

## KLEINHANS MUSIC HALL
### Symphony Circle, Buffalo

One of three commissions given to the new architectural firm of Eliel and Eero Saarinen after the Great Depression, this music hall ranks among this father-and-son team's finest work. Built in 1938–1940, it is a coherent expression of Eliel's late work and also shows the growing influence of the younger Eero. The main auditorium seats 3,000 and, in addition to its clean, rational design, is noted for its acoustics and lighting system.

## DARWIN D. MARTIN HOUSE
### 125 Jewett Parkway, Buffalo

Built in 1904–1906, this is one of the earliest, most impressive, best-preserved examples of architect Frank Lloyd Wright's Prairie Style. In typical fashion, the house is faced with Roman brick and covered with broad-hipped roofs. Flowing horizontal lines, open plan, and integration between exterior and interior spaces are also prominent and characteristic features. The State University of New York at Buffalo acquired the house in 1967.

## PRUDENTIAL BUILDING
### Church and Pearl Streets, Buffalo

The last collaborative effort of its architects, Dankmar Adler and Louis Sullivan, the 1895 Prudential Building is considered a masterpiece of early skyscraper design. The clarity of its steel-frame skeleton is clearly expressed, and the tile and terra-cotta sheathing are covered with Sullivan's familiar flowing ornamentation: a perfect marriage of realism and romanticism. The exterior remains largely in its original condition, and because the surroundings are unencumbered, its soaring quality can still be appreciated and understood.

## ROYCROFT CAMPUS
### Main and South Grove Streets, East Aurora

Roycroft, founded by Elbert Hubbard in 1895, is the most famous of several late-19th-century Arts and Crafts "guilds" — communities established as part of an artistic revolt against the mass production of applied arts. Here craftsmen could live and work in a

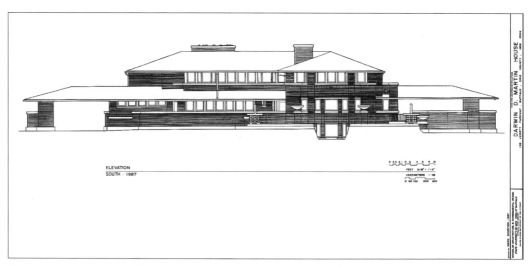

*Darwin D. Martin House, Buffalo, Erie County. Courtesy of HABS (Mark Schryver).*

medieval setting, making beautiful objects by hand in the manner that craft-guilds had done ages ago. Hand-painted and hand-bound books, paintings, carvings, metalwork, and ceramics—all were produced here during the first third of the 20th century. The Depression wrote finis to Roycroft, however, and in 1938 creditors took possession of the property. Many of the medieval styled buildings of the campus survive, now in multiple private ownership.

## SAINT PAUL'S CATHEDRAL
### 139 Pearl Street, Buffalo

Richard Upjohn received the commission to design Saint Paul's largely because of the reputation he had gained with his Trinity Church in New York City. Constructed between 1849 and 1851, Saint Paul's again proved his mastery of the Gothic Revival style. Modeled on English architectural precedent, it is an excellent example of the sort of "correct" church design that mid-19th-century ecclesiologists advocated. Saint Paul's, built of local red Medina sandstone set in a random ashlar pattern, was located a few blocks from the western terminus of the Erie Canal. It soon became a symbol of Buffalo's progressive spirit and aspirations and in 1866 became the Cathedral of the new Diocese of Western New York.

## THE SULLIVANS
### 1 Naval Cove Park, Buffalo

Named for five brothers who lost their lives in the Battle of the Solomon Islands, *The Sullivans* is an excellent example of the Fletcher class. This was the largest and most important class of U.S. destroyers in World War II and the backbone of destroyer forces throughout the conflict. It took part in intense combat, rescuing downed aviators and earning nine battle stars for its service. *The Sullivans* is now open to the public at the Buffalo and Erie County Naval and Military Park.

■ *Essex County*

## ADIRONDACK FOREST PRESERVE
### (Clinton, Essex, Franklin, Fulton, Hamilton, Herkimer, and Saint Lawrence Counties)

(See entry under Clinton County.)

## JOHN BROWN FARM AND GRAVESITE
### John Brown Road, Lake Placid

Few of those who have sung, "John Brown's body lies a-moldering in the grave," know that his grave is here in upstate New York. It was from his small, plain, unpainted frame farmhouse that the famous and controversial abolitionist set forth, first to Kansas, then to Harpers Ferry, with his plan to exorcize slavery from America by armed confrontation. At his request, his body was returned here for burial after he was tried for treason and executed in 1859. From the moment he was interred, the farmhouse and grave site were regarded as a shrine. The property was deeded to the State of New York in 1896 and is open to the public as a state historic site.

## FORT CROWN POINT
### Crown Point

French, British, and Americans have all laid claim to Crown Point, a strategic peninsula jutting into southern Lake Champlain. The French and British constructed forts here, and ruins of both remain in this state historic site. The huge British fort, Fort Crown Point, was damaged by an explosion in 1773, captured by Americans in 1775, and abandoned in 1777. Also known as Fort Amherst, it was built on the most up-to-date military principles of its time, and—in its ruinous but unaltered state—is considered one of the finest colonial-era fortifications in the country.

## FORT SAINT FREDERIC
### Junction of New York Routes 8 and 9N, Crown Point

Control of Lake Champlain was a key objective for the French and English in the 18th century. With construction of Fort Saint Frederic in 1731 at the narrowest point of the lake, the French gained the upper hand. A limestone fort with 62 mounted guns, it blocked the use of Lake Champlain as a possible avenue for British invasion into Canada. In 1759, facing attack from Sir Jeffery Amherst, the French retreated, burning the fort as they left. The British then began a new fort on higher ground nearby. Stabilized ruins of both forts are open to the public at this state historic site.

## FORT TICONDEROGA
**On New York Route 22, 2.5 miles south of Ticonderoga**

Control of Lake Champlain and its valley, the natural trade and transportation route from the upper Hudson region to Canada, was vital to the French, the English, and—in their turn—the Americans. The French built the stone Fort Vaudreuil at this narrow point in 1755. The British captured it in 1759 and renamed it Fort Ticonderoga. On May 10, 1775, Ethan Allen and 83 three of his "Green Mountain Boys" took it in one of the most famous exploits of the gathering Revolution. The British returned in 1777 and destroyed Fort Ti after Burgoyne's surrender at Saratoga. Reconstruction was begun in the early 20th century. The fort is open to the public.

## ELKANAH WATSON HOUSE
**3 miles east of U.S. Route 9, Port Kent**

All those blue ribbons won at America's state and county fairs throughout the years can be traced to one man. Elkanah Watson was a diplomat during the Revolution—he delivered the final peace treaty to King George III in 1782—a canal promoter, educator, businessman, banker, and agriculturist. Watson organized his first fair in 1810; the idea being to promote better crops and livestock through a spirit of competition. Winners in each category received ribbons as prizes. His

house, overlooking Lake Champlain, was built in 1828 at Port Kent, a town he helped found.

### ■ *Franklin County*

## ADIRONDACK FOREST PRESERVE
**(Clinton, Essex, Franklin, Fulton, Hamilton, Herkimer, and Saint Lawrence Counties)**

(See entry under Clinton County.)

### ■ *Fulton County*

## ADIRONDACK FOREST PRESERVE
**(Clinton, Essex, Franklin, Fulton, Hamilton, Herkimer, and Saint Lawrence Counties)**

(See entry under Clinton County.)

## JOHNSON HALL
**Hall Street, Johnstown**

This imposing Georgian frame mansion flanked by stone dependencies was the home of Sir William Johnson, superintendent of Indian affairs in the northern British colonies and a frontier leader in pre-Revolutionary New York. A trusted and respected negotiator, Johnson played a major role in establishing and maintaining relations with the Iroquois Confederacy, which had far-reaching effects on the settlement of the country. Johnson Hall, built in 1763, has been restored and is open as a historic house museum. (See Fort Johnson, Montgomery County.)

Johnson Hall, Johnstown, Fulton County, 1967. Courtesy of NPS (Charles W. Snell).

■ *Genesee County*

## HOLLAND LAND OFFICE
**West Main Street, Batavia**

In 1796 six Dutch banking houses that had acquired vast tracts of land in western New York and northern Pennsylvania incorporated the Holland Land Company. The company surveyed its property and sold directly to homesteaders, playing a major role in the settlement and expansion of this northern frontier until its operations ceased in 1856. This stone structure, the third and final land office the company built, dates from 1815. It now houses the Genesee County Museum.

■ *Greene County*

## BRONCK HOUSE
**On the west side of U.S. Route 9W, 2 miles west of Coxsackie**

Built in three stages, this manor house illustrates the architectural evolution of Dutch Colonial dwellings from the earliest periods of settlement to the years immediately following the American Revolution. The first section, of stone, was built in 1663, the second, of brick, was added in 1738; and the last, a stone rear wing, was built in 1792. The house was presented to the Greene County Historical Society in 1938 and is now open as a historic house museum.

## THOMAS COLE HOUSE
**218 Spring Street, Catskill**

Thomas Cole was a founding figure of the Hudson River school, one of America's first recognizable schools of painting. The school, which glorified and often romanticized natural beauties of the landscape, sprang up largely because of Cole's work. The family lived in this brick house, built by Mrs. Cole's uncle in the early 19th century, from 1836 to 1848. Cole's frame studio stands in the yard.

■ *Hamilton County*

## ADIRONDACK FOREST PRESERVE
**(Clinton, Essex, Franklin, Fulton, Hamilton, Herkimer, and Saint Lawrence Counties)**

(See entry under Clinton County.)

■ *Herkimer County*

## ADIRONDACK FOREST PRESERVE
**(Clinton, Essex, Franklin, Fulton, Hamilton, Herkimer, and Saint Lawrence Counties)**

(See entry under Clinton County.)

## MOHAWK UPPER CASTLE HISTORIC DISTRICT
**Address Restricted, Town of Danube**

Archeological and architectural resources located in this district are associated with Nowadaga, western settlement of the 18th-century Mohawk Indian community of

Canajoharie. Its inhabitants belonged to the easternmost constituency of the Iroquois Confederacy. The term *castle* refers to the fact that their settlement was a fortified, palisaded community. Included in the district is the Indian Castle Church, a wooden-framed Anglican chapel built in 1769.

### ■ *Kings County*

## BROOKLYN BRIDGE

**Over the East River connecting Brooklyn and Manhattan (Kings and New York Counties)**

In 1867, two years before work on the Brooklyn Bridge commenced, its designer John Roebling predicted, "When constructed in accordance with my designs, [it] will not only be the greatest bridge in existence, but will be the greatest engineering work of the continent, and of the age. Its most conspicuous features, the towers, will serve as landmarks to the adjoining cities, and they will be entitled to be ranked as national monuments." Completed in 1883 by Roebling's son, Washington A. Roebling, this remained the world's longest suspension bridge for 20 years. Later bridges have stolen that distinction, but the senior Roebling's superlatives still provide an accurate assessment of this renowned landmark, loved throughout the world.

## BROOKLYN HEIGHTS HISTORIC DISTRICT

**Bounded by Atlantic Avenue, Court and Fulton Streets, and the East River, Brooklyn**

Brooklyn Heights, with its phenomenal views of Lower Manhattan across the East River, was one of New York's most prestigious 19th-century addresses. Houses and churches remain in excellent condition and present an almost complete architectural catalog of the variety of styles available during its heyday. Brooklyn Heights, still a popular residential area, became New York City's first designated historic district in 1965. Examples of early ironwork, flagstone sidewalks, and other embellishments add to its charm and to its significance.

## BROOKLYN HISTORICAL SOCIETY BUILDING

**128 Pierrepont Street, Brooklyn**

The Neoclassic facade of this 1881 building hides an innovative structural system behind its brick walls and terra-cotta trim. The fourth floor is suspended from iron rods extending from iron trusses, allowing an open two-story library to occupy the second and third floors. Built for the Long Island Historical Society, predecessor of the present institution, it was designed by architect

*Brooklyn Bridge, Kings and New York Counties. Courtesy of HAER (Jet Lowe).*

George B. Post and is one of the few remaining intact examples of his work. Interiors are in the Queen Anne style and display hand-carved woodwork, custom bronze hardware, stained glass, and Minton tile floors.

## PLYMOUTH CHURCH OF THE PILGRIMS
### 75 Hicks Street, Brooklyn

Between 1849 and the outbreak of the Civil War, this plain brick church was one of the nation's foremost centers of antislavery sentiment. Its minister at the time was Henry Ward Beecher, and William Lloyd Garrison and John Greenleaf Whittier were among other abolitionists who preached from its pulpit. The church, established as Brooklyn's Second Congregational Church, was designed specifically to accommodate the crowds that came to hear Beecher and his cohorts. Its simple design reflects the Puritan ethic of plain living and high thinking, and the walls that once rang to the sound of abolition oratory remain largely unchanged.

## QUARTERS A, BROOKLYN NAVY YARD
### U.S. Naval Facility, Brooklyn

Built in 1805–1806 as quarters for commanders of the Brooklyn Navy Yard, this handsome Federal style frame house served in that capacity until the 1960s. Matthew C. Perry occupied it from 1841 to 1843, and it was his association with the house that earned its designation as a National Historic Landmark. Perry was commissioned to undertake the difficult position of attempting to open Japan to Western trade for the first time, and he carried out his duties with aplomb and success. The treaty he signed at Yokohama in 1854 not only opened Japan to trade, it began a new epoch in the history of the world.

## JOHN ROOSEVELT "JACKIE" ROBINSON HOUSE
### 5224 Tilden Street, Brooklyn

Jackie Robinson was the first African American to play on a major league baseball team, thus breaking the color barrier in professional team sports. Branch Rickey, president of the Brooklyn Dodgers, who purposefully scouted for an athlete to work his

way to the top through the ranks of the minor leagues, aided Robinson in the milestone accomplishment. Robinson's first year as a major leaguer was 1947, and it was also the year that the Dodgers won the National League pennant. Robinson and his family lived in this Brooklyn duplex from 1947 to 1950.

## SAINT ANN–HOLY TRINITY CHURCH
### 157 Montague Street, Brooklyn

Minard Lafever, one of mid-19th-century America's leading architects, secured his reputation with the design of this outstanding Gothic Revival church. Built in 1844–1847, it was largely funded by Edgar John Bartow, who had dreamed of building the finest church in New York City. The windows, by brothers William and John Bolton, comprise the earliest complete set of stained glass designed and fabricated in this country. The sandstone spire that once soared above the tower has been removed.

## WYCKOFF HOUSE
### 5902 Canarsie Lane, Brooklyn

This house is a major and little-altered example of the sort of vernacular frame house built by Dutch settlers on western Long Island. Pieter Claesen Wyckoff built the original section ca. 1652, and this is now the oldest known house surviving in New York City. Several 18th-century additions and an alteration in 1819 brought it to its present form. Members of the Wyckoff family lived in the house until 1902. It was donated to the city in 1970, was restored, and is now open as a historic house museum.

## WYCKOFF-BENNETT HOMESTEAD
### 1699 East 22nd Street, Brooklyn

This superb example of the Dutch Colonial style has miraculously survived with little change since its construction ca. 1766. Even the names that Hessian soldiers, quartered here during the Revolution, inscribed on the windowpanes remain. The house is of frame construction, mostly shingled but partly clapboarded, and contains handsome paneled woodwork. In the late 1890s the house was turned 90 degrees and placed on a brick foundation. It remains privately owned.

### ■ Lewis County

## FRANKLIN B. HOUGH HOUSE
**Collins Street, Lowville**

Franklin B. Hough is the father of American forestry. He first noted a decline in forest production while comparing figures of the New York State censuses of 1855 and 1865, both of which he supervised, and quickly moved to encourage curbing the rapid destruction of the nation's forests. Hough wrote the first American book on forestry, and his work in the Department of Agriculture laid the groundwork for the U.S. Forest Service. In 1885, the year of his death, Hough wrote the bill creating New York's vast Adirondack Forest Preserve. From 1863 to 1885 he lived in this Italian villa, which is still privately owned.

### ■ Livingston County

## GENESEO HISTORIC DISTRICT
**Along Main Street at Court and North Streets, Geneseo**

One of the most remarkably preserved villages in western New York, Geneseo was founded in 1790 and prospered in the 19th century as the trading center of the Genessee Valley. The town benefited from the largesse of founders William and James Wadsworth and from later generations of the family. Andrew Jackson Downing knew Geneseo well and wrote of it in *The Horticulturalist*. Buildings in this picturesque and sophisticated community display the full panoply of 19th-century architectural styles.

### ■ Madison County

## ONEIDA COMMUNITY MANSION HOUSE
**Sherrill Road, Oneida**

Oneida, founded in 1848 by John Humphrey Noyes, was one of America's most radical and most successful experimental communities. Perfectionism and a form of communism governed its activities, and the community practiced complex marriages and selective breeding. Industries, including a silverware factory, fueled the economy, and when the community dissolved in 1881, business operations continued as a joint-stock company.

This rambling U-shaped brick building housed the entire community. It is now maintained as a museum by Oneida Ltd., the famous silver firm that grew from one of the commune's major industries.

### ■ Monroe County

## SUSAN B. ANTHONY HOUSE
**17 Madison Street, Rochester**

Active in numerous reform movements, Susan B. Anthony entered the fight for women's rights in 1851 after meeting Elizabeth Cady Stanton. She was especially effective in garnering legislative petitions and in accompanying them with as many signatures as possible. In 1869 she played the leading role in organizing the National Woman Suffrage Association. This brick house, now a museum, was her home for 40 years, from 1866 until her death in 1906.

## GEORGE EASTMAN HOUSE
**900 East Avenue, Rochester**

George Eastman made photography a popular pastime and amassed a fortune in the process. He had developed flexible film by 1885, and in 1888 he first marketed the portable Kodak camera, packaged with a 100-exposure roll. Now everyone could participate in a process that had formerly been the sole province of those with formidable, expensive equipment and infinite patience. Eastman's Georgian Revival mansion, built in 1905, has been said to reflect "the inventor's desires as much as it does the architect's design." It served as Eastman's home until his death in 1932 and now, greatly enlarged, fittingly houses a museum of photography.

### ■ Montgomery County

## ERIE CANAL
**Fort Hunter**

Completion of the Erie Canal in 1825 was one the nation's most dramatic and significant achievements. Uniting the Great Lakes and the Atlantic seaboard, it opened the Old Northwest Territory—as well as central and western New York State—to settlement, provided distribution for raw materials and manufactured goods, and bonded the North and the West. It also ensured the growth of New

Fort Johnson, Montgomery County, 1967. Courtesy of NPS (Charles W. Snell).

York City as the nation's dominant urban center. The landmark designation encompasses a three-and-a-half-mile section of the canal that is protected and open to the public as the Schoharie Crossing State Historic Site.

## FORT JOHNSON
### Junction of New York Routes 5 and 67, Fort Johnson

This impressive stone manor, a fine example of early-Georgian architecture, was built by Sir William Johnson in 1748–1749. Johnson was appointed superintendent of Indian affairs of all the British colonies in North America while living here and held many councils in the house. Originally, Fort Johnson was surrounded by a log stockade. It later became home to Johnson's Loyalist son, Sir John Johnson, who spent a portion of the Revolution in his fortified mansion guarded by 150 Scottish Highlanders and a number of Mohawks. Fort Johnson is open to the public as a historic house museum. (See Johnson Hall, Fulton County.)

## FORT KLOCK
### On New York Route 5, 2 miles east of Saint Johnsville

Standing near the northern bank of the Mohawk River, this vernacular stone structure is a rare example of a mid-18th-century fur trading post and fortified house. The house was built over a spring, making the fort a logical place for settlers to seek refuge in time of war. It served this purpose during the Revolution, when a log stockade surrounding the house was built to give further protection. Fort Klock was restored in the 1960s and is open to visitors during the summer.

## ◼ *Nassau County*

## *CHRISTEEN*
### Oyster Bay

Built in 1883 to work in Long Island Sound, *Christeen* is the country's oldest surviving working example of an oyster sloop, a round-bottomed, gaff-rigged, one-masted vessel used to pull oyster dredges or to serve as a platform for tonging. At the turn of the century, oysters were America's chief seafood, requiring large fleets to work the beds and satisfy the nation's insatiable appetite for bivalves. Currently, the *Christeen* is being rebuilt for use as a floating classroom in Oyster Bay by the *Christeen* Oyster Sloop Preservation Corporation.

## FORT MASSAPEAG ARCHEOLOGICAL SITE
### Address Restricted, Massapequa

Fort Massapeag, a Dutch outpost on Long Island's southern shore, was built, occupied, and abandoned during the mid-17th century.

It served briefly as a trading post with the Massapeag Indians and as a frontier refuge. The site is preserved in a municipal park and contains archeological deposits preserving evidence of military and economic ties during the Historic Contact period of the 17th century.

## JOHN PHILIP SOUSA HOUSE
### 14 Hicks Lane, Sands Point, Port Washington

John Philip Sousa, known far and wide as "the March King," became the director of the United States Marine Corps Band in 1880. During the succeeding 12 years he composed numerous marches for the unit, among them "Semper Fidelis" and the "Washington Post March." His "Stars and Stripes Forever" remains his best loved and most often played composition. Its stirring sounds have become an almost de rigeur accompaniment for Fourth of July fireworks celebrations across the nation. Sousa lived at this rambling stuccoed house overlooking Manhasset Bay from 1915 until his death in 1932.

### ■ New York County

## 7TH REGIMENT ARMORY
### 643 Park Avenue, New York

Built in 1877–1880 in what could be described as a mock-military style, this massive structure occupies an entire city block on Manhattan's Upper East Side. Like the 69th Regiment Armory, it was built to serve in the dual capacity of drill hall and clubhouse. A three-story building with a one-story drill shed behind, it contains one of the nation's most significant groups of 1880s "high-style" interiors and furnishings. Individual regimental companies chose the design and the decorator to embellish their rooms, or parlors, and vied with each other to attain the most beautiful space. The most elaborate interior is the Veterans' Room, designed by Stanford White and decorated by Louis Comfort Tiffany.

## 69TH REGIMENT ARMORY
### 68 Lexington Avenue, New York

This formidable brick mass represents a type of building that served in the dual capacity of military facility and social clubhouse for units of the National Guard. The type was popular in late-19th-century America, but this particular armory is nationally significant for another reason. It was the site of the Armory Show—the 1913 International Exhibition of Modern Art. This was the first major exhibit of contemporary art in America, and it revolutionized the nation's artistic tastes and perceptions. Some 1,300 works of art were displayed, and here for the first time many Americans saw the works of Cezanne, Van Gogh, Matisse, and Picasso.

## AFRICAN BURIAL GROUND
### Broadway and Reade Streets, New York

Excavations for new construction in lower Manhattan in the early 1990s revealed the presence of burials dating as early as 1712. Throughout the 18th century, African Americans, both free and slave, were buried in ground that was then part of New York's "common" land. Remains of more than 400 individuals have been recovered. Over the years topographical changes occurred; most of the burial ground is far below present grades and far beneath New York's skyscrapers. Signs that provide historic perspective on the cemetery and those who were buried here mark the site.

## AMERICAN STOCK EXCHANGE
### 86 Trinity Place, New York

This handsome Art Deco building, erected in 1921 and enlarged 1929–1931, houses one of the nation's important securities exchanges. Tracing its origins to 1849, when the discovery of gold in California precipitated an increase in securities trading, the exchange remained an outdoor "curb" market—"the most picturesque, exciting, and incomprehensible segment of American business"—until it moved to this building, its first, and thus far only, permanent home.

## CHESTER A. ARTHUR HOUSE
### 123 Lexington Avenue, New York

Chester Alan Arthur brought a sense of duty and integrity to the White House following the assassination of President Garfield in September 1881. Although his career had been bolstered by a powerful Republican machine dependent on spoils, once the former "veep" was catapulted into the presidency, he emerged as a dignified and honest chief executive and a major supporter of civil rights reform. He lived in this five-story Manhattan brownstone row house both before and after his rise to national prominence.

## BAYARD-CONDICT BUILDING
### 65–69 Bleecker Street, New York

Built in 1897–1899, this 12-story building is one of New York's first "skyscrapers." Midwesterner Louis Sullivan was its architect, and, along with the Prudential Building in Buffalo, this is his only eastern work. The piers and mullions of its terra-cotta facade emphasize the vertical nature of the building, an accomplishment most architects of early high-rise buildings failed to achieve. The top stage is embellished with the bold and lavish ornament typical of Sullivan's work.

## BELL TELEPHONE LABORATORIES
### 463 West Street, New York

For almost a century, from 1898 to 1966, this solid 13-story building was the home of Bell Telephone Laboratories, America's largest industrial research laboratory. One of four major components of the Bell System, the laboratories were responsible for pioneering work in telecommunications technology.

*Bayard-Condict Building, New York City, New York County. Detail of Sullivan's cornice ornamentation, 1964. Courtesy of HABS (Cervin Robinson).*

Television transmission, including color TV, digital computers, direct distance dialing, and satellite communications were developed here. In the late 1960s, under direction of architect Richard Meir, the building was converted into low-cost studio and loft housing for artists.

## BROOKLYN BRIDGE
### Over the East River, connecting Manhattan and Brooklyn (Kings and New York Counties)

(See entry under Kings County.)

## CARNEGIE HALL
### Seventh Avenue, between 56th and 57th Streets, New York

Constructed in 1891 and named for its principal investor, Andrew Carnegie, this utilitarian building is one of America's best-known musical venues. In addition to its concert hall, known for its near-perfect acoustics, Carnegie Hall houses studios and a recital hall. These, and its crowded calendar of concerts drawing thousands of patrons, established the surrounding area as the major musical center of the country.

## ANDREW CARNEGIE MANSION
### 2 East 91st Street, New York

Andrew Carnegie, who arrived in the United States from Scotland at age 13, became one of the nation's richest men, establishing an industrial empire that included coal mines, steel mills, and steamship and rail lines. In 1901 he began construction on this 64-room brick mansion, which he intended to be "the most modest, plainest, and roomiest house in New York." From it, he devoted the rest of his life to philanthropic enterprises, in particular the establishment of public libraries across the nation. Carnegie died in 1919, and in 1972 the Carnegie Corporation gave the house, neither the city's most modest nor its plainest, to the Smithsonian Institution. It now serves as the National Design Museum.

## CENTRAL PARK
### Bounded by Central Park South, Fifth Avenue, Central Park West, and 110th Street, New York

Manhattan without Central Park would be unthinkable. This huge green space, first conceived by farsighted city fathers in the 1840s, has become an ever more appreciated and vital urban amenity over the years. Planned by the winning team of Frederick Law Olmsted and Calvert Vaux, it was the first large-scale public park in the nation designed and constructed according to a well-developed concept, that of a forest in the city. The basic framework of the park survives remarkably unchanged, even though it now accommodates people, pets, and traffic in numbers that its founders could scarcely have imagined.

## CENTRAL SYNAGOGUE
### 646–652 Lexington Avenue, New York

Designed by Henry Fernbeck and erected in 1871–1872, this large brownstone temple is an outstanding example of the Moorish Revival, an architectural style deemed particularly appropriate for synagogue architecture in the 19th century. Resembling the earlier Plum Street Temple in Cincinnati, the building is noted for the dramatic octagonal towers capped with bulbous globes that flank its horseshoe-arched entrances. Central Synagogue, in continuous use longer than any other synagogue in New York City, is currently being restored after a devastating fire in 1998.

## CHRYSLER BUILDING
### 405 Lexington Avenue, New York

This extraordinary Art Moderne skyscraper, designed by William Van Alen, was built in 1928–1930 by Walter Chrysler, who dedicated it to "world commerce and industry." Until the Empire State Building was completed a few blocks away, the Chrysler was for several months the world's tallest building. Noted for its "machine age" design and decor, it has gargoyles modeled on winged radiator caps, emblematic of the automobile that was the foundation of its builder's fortune. The steel-covered dome and spire provide a dramatic punctuation mark on Manhattan's skyline and stand as an enduring and popular symbol of New York in the Roaring Twenties.

## CHURCH OF THE ASCENSION
### 36–38 Fifth Avenue, New York

Built in 1840–1841, this is one of the earliest churches designed by Richard Upjohn, done at about the time he designed Trinity Church

on Wall Street. This smaller and more austere English Gothic building is well known for its sumptuous fittings, added in later years. Stanford White designed the chancel and reredos, John LaFarge the stained-glass windows and mural of the Ascension, while Louis Saint-Gaudens sculpted the flying angels at the altar.

## CITY HALL
### Broadway and Chambers Street, New York

Completed in 1811, New York's City Hall is significant both in the history of civic administration of the nation's most populous city and for its architectural merit. Architects John McComb and Joseph Mangin, a Frenchman, gave the building a strong French character. Although most of the city's day-to-day administrative tasks are now undertaken in expanded quarters nearby, City Hall is still home to the mayor and the president of the city council.

## WILL MARION COOK HOUSE
### 221 West 138th Street, New York

"The master of all masters of our people." High praise, indeed, coming from Duke Ellington, who was referring to Will Marion Cook, noted black composer, songwriter, and orchestra conductor. Although he was classically trained, Cook turned his attention to "ragtime" and helped spread the gospel of black-inspired music through his compositions and musical comedies. From 1918 to 1944 he lived in this impressive brick town house in Harlem, part of a late-19th-century development that came to be known as Strivers Row.

## COOPER UNION
### Cooper Square, Seventh Street and Fourth Avenue, New York

This institution fulfilled philanthropist Peter Cooper's dream to "improve and elevate the working classes of the City of New York." It opened in 1858, offering instruction in chemistry, physics, math, and music, and housing the only well-stocked free library in the city. Soon, as many as 3,000 people a week passed through its doors. In February 1860, Abraham Lincoln delivered the keynote address of his 1860 campaign in the lecture hall. The six-story brownstone building housed "state-of-the-art" mechanical systems that Cooper designed. The Cooper Union now grants bachelor's degrees in architecture, art, and engineering.

## CROTON AQUEDUCT
**Between Croton and New York City (Bronx, New York, and Westchester Counties)**

(See entry under Bronx County.)

## DAKOTA APARTMENTS
**1 West 72d Street, New York**

Completed in 1884 on the west side of Central Park, this huge edifice is one of the earliest large-scale apartment houses in the country. It was designed by Henry J. Hardenbergh and received its unusual name because it was considered so far from the heart of Manhattan that it might as well have been in Dakota Territory. A "communal palace" of brick with stone and terra-cotta trim, it exemplifies the German Renaissance style and combines the conveniences of a private home with the services of a luxury hotel. The Dakota remains the home of many celebrities.

*Dakota Apartments, New York City, New York County. ca. 1970. Courtesy of HABS.*

## DYCKMAN HOUSE
**4881 Broadway, New York**

This remarkable relic survives as the only 18th-century farmhouse on Manhattan Island. A notable example of Dutch Colonial architecture, it employs fieldstone, brick, and clapboard in its construction and has a low-pitched gambrel roof that curves out to cover front and rear porches. Built in 1783 near the northern tip of the island, the house fronts Broadway, then the main road leading from New York northward. The restored Dyckman House is open as a historic house museum.

## *EDSON*
**Intrepid Air-Sea-Space Museum, New York**

The Forrest Sherman class of destroyers was developed by the U.S. Navy after World War II and reflected lessons learned during that conflict. *Edson,* launched in 1958, is one of two surviving members of the type and was built to be an effective antisubmarine warfare platform and screening escort vessel. It participated in the Vietnam conflict and later functioned as a training vessel in Newport, Rhode Island. Decommissioned in 1989, *Edson* was placed on display at the Intrepid Sea-Air-Space Museum, along with *Intrepid.*

## ELDRIDGE STREET SYNAGOGUE
**12–16 Eldridge Street, New York**

Most eastern European Jews who came to America in the late 19th century arrived in New York and settled in the city's Lower East Side. Most practiced Orthodox Judaism, and the Eldridge Street Synagogue was their first—and finest—place of worship. Built in 1886–1887, it has a facade that bristles with horseshoe arches and other Moorish-inspired ornamentation, and a virtually unaltered interior. The synagogue and the experience of its founding generation represent crucial times in the development of Judaism in America.

## EDWARD KENNEDY "DUKE" ELLINGTON RESIDENCE
**935 Saint Nicholas Avenue, Apartment 4A, New York**

"Duke" Ellington, regarded as one of the most creative American composers of the 20th century, and one of the leaders in developing and expanding jazz, lived from 1939 to

1961 in an apartment in this six-story building on Saint Nicholas Avenue in Harlem. Ellington, who composed more than 1,500 pieces, began his career as a ragtime pianist in his native Washington, D. C., where he also acquired his nickname because of his impeccable dress and sophisticated manner. He received the Medal of Freedom in 1969.

## EMPIRE STATE BUILDING
### 350 Fifth Avenue, New York

Although it is no longer the world's tallest building—a title it held for 40 years—this famous 102-story skyscraper remains New York's most widely recognized architectural symbol. Designed by Shreve, Lamb & Harmon and constructed in 1930–1931 as a speculative office building, it is beautifully finished in the Art Deco style. The building rises one-fifth of a mile high, supported on an elastic steel skeleton that is an engineering masterpiece. Its prominent spire, or "mast," was designed to be a mooring mechanism for dirigibles. It is better known for serving as a perch for King Kong when he challenged the world in the famous 1933 film.

## EQUITABLE BUILDING
### 120 Broadway, New York

This lower Manhattan skyscraper was headquarters of one of America's leading insurance companies. On the site of Equitable's previous home office, it also commemorates Henry Baldwin Hyde, the company's founder and prime mover in the post–Civil War expansion of the insurance industry. Equitable was organized in 1859 and by 1886 was the world's largest life insurance company. The 40-story steel-and-masonry building, erected in 1914–1915, is in the Second Renaissance Revival style.

## HAMILTON FISH HOUSE
### 21 Stuyvesant Street, New York

This Federal style brick town house was the birthplace and residence of Hamilton Fish, scion of a distinguished New York family. After serving as governor of New York and as a U.S. senator, Fish became, at age 60, President Grant's secretary of state. There he provided stability and gained a modicum of respect for an otherwise demoralized and scandal-ridden administration. Fish's grandfather, Petrus Stuyvesant, built the house and once hosted General Lafayette for dinner here.

## FLATIRON BUILDING
### Fifth Avenue, Broadway and 23rd Street, New York

The Flatiron Building—its name deriving from the shape its triangular lot dictated—has been compared to a ship sailing up Broadway. Its bold silhouette is one of Manhattan's familiar forms, and its steel-framed structure is handsomely sheathed in limestone and brick with classically inspired terra-cotta trim. Architect Daniel Burnham was influential in the development of skyscrapers in Chicago and New York, and for ten years after its completion in 1901, his 21-story Flatiron was the world's tallest building. It still stands tall and proud, a symbol of America's turn-of-the-20th-century energy and imagination.

## FOUNDER'S HALL
### 66th Street and York Avenue, New York

Chartered in 1901, this institute for medical research was the first of John D. Rockefeller's great philanthropic foundations. With it, Rockefeller sought not simply to relieve the needy, but to "attack misery...through the weapon of research." "Don't be in a hurry to produce anything practical," he advised its staff. "If you don't, the next fellow will. You, here, explore and dream." In 1954 the institute assumed the status of a graduate university and in 1965 was named the Rockefeller University. Founder's Hall, the first laboratory, was opened in 1906 and still serves its original function.

## GOVERNORS ISLAND
### New York Harbor, New York

In 1652, Governors Island, a half-mile from Manhattan's southern tip, was reserved as a private estate for New Amsterdam's Dutch governors. It later served similarly for New York's English governors, but it became a vital component in the defense of New York Harbor beginning with the Revolution. Forts

Governors Island, New York City, New York County. Fort Jay. Courtesy of the U.S. Coast Guard Third District (Jet Lowe).

Jay and Williams became the nuclei of a number of buildings erected over the years. The island served as an army post until 1966 and then became the world's largest U.S. Coast Guard base. After the Coast Guard vacated, the U. S. General Services Administration took over. This agency is currently developing plans for the island's reuse.

## GRACE CHURCH
### Broadway, 10th Street, and Fourth Avenue, New York

Constructed from 1843 to 1846, the white marble Grace Episcopal Church is the first masterpiece of James Renwick Jr., who would become one of the foremost practitioners of the Gothic Revival style. The commission, executed when he was only 25, established his reputation, although critics thought the detail far too fussy and flamboyant. Grace Church is located where Broadway changes direction, and its tower and spire constitute one of New York's most impressive urban vistas from several directions.

## GRAND CENTRAL TERMINAL
### 71–105 East 42nd Street, New York

Constructed early in the 20th century, this monumental Beaux-Arts structure is a triumph of architecture, planning, and engineering. Its dramatically lit grand concourse centers a complex transportation network and provides an unrivaled first impression of New York to countless commuters and travelers. Grand Central made preservation history in 1978, when—thanks to efforts of Jacqueline Kennedy Onassis and others—the U.S. Supreme Court decreed that its status as a New York City Landmark protected it from demolition. This decision upheld the rights of local authorities across the country to protect and preserve their landmarks. The terminal was restored in 1998 and now appears every bit as grand as it did when it first opened.

## HAMILTON GRANGE (NPS)
### 287 Convent Avenue, New York

This Federal style frame mansion is the only house ever owned by Alexander Hamilton, proponent of the Constitution, chief organizer of Washington's administration, and first secretary of the treasury. It was completed in 1802 from designs by New York architect John McComb, but Hamilton enjoyed it only a few short years. In July 1804 he spent the night before his fatal duel with Aaron Burr in the study, writing a farewell letter to his wife. The house was moved some 500 feet in 1889. It became a unit of the National Park Service in 1962.

## HENRY STREET SETTLEMENT AND NEIGHBORHOOD PLAYHOUSE
### 263–267 Henry Street and 466 Grand Street, New York

Lillian Wald, trained as a nurse, came to New

York's Lower East Side, which she described as "a vast crowded area, a foreign city within our own," in 1893. In order to visit and minister to the area's sick, she moved to a tenement that July. Two years later she moved to larger quarters at 265 Henry Street, where she lived and worked for nearly 40 years. Wald organized her settlement house to meet the social and educational needs of immigrant families, and it became one of the leading institutions of its type in the country. The Neighborhood Playhouse was built in 1915 as an integral part of her efforts. Both continue the good works Lillian Wald started.

## MATTHEW HENSON RESIDENCE
### 246 West 150th Street, New York

On April 6, 1909, Matthew Henson, an African-American trailblazer on Robert Peary's expedition, became the first man known to reach the North Pole. On the trip, he saved Peary's life on several occasions, conversed with the Eskimo in their language, and made the sledges that carried the team to the Pole. Peary remarked, "I couldn't get along without him." From 1929 until his death in 1955, Henson lived in an apartment in the Dunbar Apartments. Named for black poet Paul Laurence Dunbar, it was the first large black cooperative in the city. A tablet at the entrance commemorates Henson's occupancy.

## HOLLAND TUNNEL
### Between New York, New York County, and Jersey City, Hudson County, New Jersey

(See Hudson County, New Jersey.)

## *INTREPID*
### Intrepid Square, New York

The third Essex class aircraft carrier built in the United States, *Intrepid*, launched in 1943, represents the class that formed the core of the fast carrier task forces in the Pacific war. *Intrepid* won fame in the Pacific in World War II as the "Fighting I" and received five battle stars. The Essex class formed the core of the postwar carrier fleet. Modernized in 1954, *Intrepid* is now the centerpiece of the Intrepid Sea-Air-Space Museum in New York City, along with another National Historic Landmark vessel, *Edson*.

## JAMES WELDON JOHNSON RESIDENCE
### 187 West 135th Street, New York

James Weldon Johnson lived in this five-story Harlem apartment from 1925 to 1938. A versatile and talented individual, Johnson was a crusading spokesman for full equality for African Americans. He became field secretary of the National Association for the Advancement of Colored People in 1925, the year he moved into his apartment, and later became general secretary of the organization. During the years he contributed his talents to the cause of civil rights, he wrote songs, poems, and essays, winning prizes and awards until his death in 1938.

## *LETTIE G. HOWARD*
### South Street Seaport Museum, New York

This wooden fishing vessel, built in 1893, is

*Holland Tunnel, New York and New Jersey. Courtesy of HAER (Jet Lowe).*

one of only two remaining examples of a "Fredonia" schooner, once the standard fishing boat type in North America's offshore fisheries. Named for the daughter of its captain, *Lettie* spent much of its career fishing for red snapper off Yucatan. The ship was rehabilitated between 1968 and 1972, extensively restored in 1991, and is currently operated by the South Street Seaport Museum as a working museum ship and training vessel.

## LIGHTSHIP NO. 87 *AMBROSE*
**South Street Seaport Museum, New York**

Now known by its last official designation, *Ambrose, No. 87* was built in 1907 to serve as the first lightship on the newly established Nantucket station, to help guide mariners into the nation's busiest port, New York. No. 87 is also important in the history of radio, as it was equipped with the first successful shipboard radio beacon. After years of meritorious service, *Ambrose* was decommissioned in 1968 and is now a floating historic museum vessel at South Street Seaport, providing pleasure and instruction for visitors to the port it served so well.

## LOW MEMORIAL LIBRARY
**Columbia University, West 116th Street, New York**

Built in 1895–1897, this is one of the most important Neoclassical structures in America and one of architect Charles Follen McKim's masterpieces. Centerpiece and symbol of Columbia University, it was the first major building erected on the present campus and was conceived as the visual and academic focal point of the plan. Ancillary buildings are carefully placed around the domed library, and the campus it centers is recognized as a classic of Beaux-Arts planning and design.

## R. H. MACY AND COMPANY STORE
**151 West 34th Street, New York**

When this huge structure on Herald Square was completed in 1902, it boasted 42 miles of wiring, 33 hydraulic elevators, and 1,000 tons of ornamental iron and bronze. After a major addition was built in the 1920s, Macy's proclaimed that it was the "world's largest department store under one roof." R. H.

Macy founded the store in the 1850s, pioneered the one-price system, introduced varied merchandise, advertised extensively, and always refused to be undersold. The history of Macy's is the history of the American department store, a major chapter in the story of American retailing.

## MCGRAW-HILL BUILDING
**326 West 42nd Street, New York**

The 35-story McGraw-Hill Building, completed in 1931, is the last of architect Raymond Hood's pace-setting New York skyscrapers and is a unique blend of the International Style and Art Moderne. It is notable for its blue-green color—made possible by the largest application of glazed terracotta blocks ever undertaken—its spare, clean lines, and its prominent setbacks, the last feature mandated by New York zoning laws.

## CLAUDE MCKAY RESIDENCE
**180 West 135th Street, New York**

Perhaps not as well known as some of his cohorts, Claude McKay is often called the "father of the Harlem Renaissance," the notable black literary movement of the 20th century. McKay gained fame in 1919 with publication of his explosive poem "If We Must Die," an eloquent statement on post–World War I racial conditions, which Winston Churchill once read to the British Parliament. A native of Jamaica, McKay also wrote *Home to Harlem,* the first book by an African American to reach the bestseller lists. From 1941 until 1946 he lived in this impressive brick structure that was built as the Harlem Branch of the YMCA.

## METROPOLITAN LIFE INSURANCE COMPANY BUILDING
**1 Madison Avenue, New York**

Completed in 1909 from designs by Pierre and Michel LeBrun, this 50-story tower was modeled after the campanile in Venice and for four years was the world's tallest building. It marked the culmination of a major building program for Metropolitan Life and is symbolic of the company that represents the growth and development of the American life insurance industry. Metropolitan became the world's largest private investor and introduced a number of innovations in the industry. A likeness of its tower headquarters has appeared on countless insurance forms through the years.

## METROPOLITAN MUSEUM OF ART
### Fifth Avenue at 82nd Street, New York

Known throughout the world for its unparalleled art collections, the Metropolitan occupies a mammoth structure whose origins date back to 1874. Expanded over the years, the museum is identified most closely with its dramatic Fifth Avenue facade and Great Hall, designed by Richard Morris Hunt in the Beaux-Arts style and built in 1895–1902. With elegant spaces providing grand and opulent settings for its treasures, the Metropolitan is truly one of the world's greatest museums.

## FLORENCE MILLS HOUSE
### 220 West 135th Street, New York

Florence Mills was one of the most acclaimed entertainers of the Roaring Twenties, starring in such productions as *Shuffle Along,* the first large-scale musical composed, directed, and performed by African Americans. With her performance, she became the "toast of Broadway" overnight and was soon regarded as a success symbol and role model for African Americans. Mills's death at age 32 cut short her burgeoning career and her efforts to improve race relations. From 1910 to 1927, the years of her greatest achievements, she lived in this Harlem row house.

## J. PIERPONT MORGAN LIBRARY
### 33 East 36th Street, New York

John Pierpont Morgan exemplifies the emergence of the financier as a force in American industry. He ushered in the "era of Morgan" with his investments in the New York Central Railroad and eventually controlled 100,000 miles of American track. He also organized U.S. Steel, and in 1907 helped the nation avert a financial panic by persuading bankers and financiers to support institutions in need. Morgan was also an art collector and bibliophile. In 1900 he commissioned McKim, Mead and White to build this Renaissance style library adjacent to his house. Thanks to his generous endowment, its collections are—as he directed—"permanently available for the instruction and pleasure of the American people."

## MORRIS-JUMEL MANSION
### 160th Street and Edgecombe Avenue, New York

This elegant Georgian country manor is the major surviving landmark of the September 16, 1776, Battle of Harlem Heights. This American victory restored the offensive spirit of the colonial troops and served as a warning to the British that their campaign would not be an easy one. General Washington made his headquarters in the mansion from September 14 to October 18, 1776. The house was acquired by the City of New York in 1903 and is maintained as a historic house museum.

## NATIONAL CITY BANK BUILDING
### 55 Wall Street, New York

This solid Neoclassical building on New York's Wall Street housed one of the country's most influential financial institutions. First known as City Bank of New York, National City was one of several banks formed in 1812 to fill the void created by the demise of the First Bank of the United States a year earlier. Under the leadership of James Stillman, who became president in 1891, the bank began a meteoric rise. Stillman commissioned McKim, Mead and White to remodel and enlarge the old New York Merchant's Exchange, which he had purchased in 1899, into the present building. It now serves as a restaurant/banquet house, and plans call for its conversion to a hotel.

## NEW YORK AMSTERDAM NEWS BUILDING
### 2293 Seventh Avenue, New York

Founded in 1909 "with six sheets of paper, a lead pencil and a dressmaker's table," the *New York Amsterdam News* became one of the country's best-known black newspapers. Between 1916—when it moved to this central unit of five 4-story row houses—and 1938, the paper's circulation, coverage, and reputation grew, as it expanded from a local

*Morris-Jumel Mansion, New York City, New York County, 1967. Courtesy of NPS (Charles W. Snell).*

*National City Bank Building, New York City, New York County. Courtesy of NPS (George A. Adams).*

Harlem community paper to one with a national scope and concerns.

## NEW YORK CHAMBER OF COMMERCE
### 65 Liberty Street, New York

The first organization in the country established to promote trade and commerce traces its founding to a meeting held in Fraunces Tavern in 1768 and to the charter King George III granted it two years later. In the years since, the Chamber has continued to promote New York City and State, and has served as the organizational prototype for similar institutions across the country. The Chamber of Commerce Building dates from 1901–1902 and was dedicated by Theodore Roosevelt. A prime example of the Beaux-Arts style, it now houses the International Bank of China, which rehabilitated the building in 1991.

## NEW YORK COTTON EXCHANGE
### 1 Hanover Square, New York

The second exchange of its kind in the world, the New York Cotton Exchange was founded in 1870, only months after the Liverpool Cotton Association, and was the first regularly organized commodity market in America to deal with contracts for future delivery. Its establishment marked the end of the factorage system for marketing America's most important 19th-century domestic crop and the beginning of today's futures trading system for buying and selling commodities. India House, a handsome brownstone structure built in the 1850s for the Hanover Bank, first housed the exchange.

## NEW YORK LIFE BUILDING
### 51 Madison Avenue, New York

The New York Life Insurance Company, founded in 1841 as the Nautilus Insurance Company, has played a major role in the development of life insurance policies and practices. One of the nation's most innovative firms, it was the first to establish a branch office system and pioneered a widely copied actuarial method of insuring individuals based on medical studies. In 1928 the firm moved to this 34-story skyscraper designed by noted architect Cass Gilbert. Its Gothic lines and prominent pyramidal tower sheathed in gold leaf make it a prominent architectural presence in midtown Manhattan.

## NEW YORK PUBLIC LIBRARY
### Fifth Avenue and 42d Street, New York

One of the most stolid and reassuring architectural elements along Manhattan's famous Fifth Avenue, this Beaux-Arts masterpiece was completed in 1911 from designs by architects Carrère and Hastings. On either side of a monumental stairway, two stone lions, sculpted by Edward Clark Potter, guard the main entrance to one of the world's great research institutions. The library was formed when several libraries consolidated at the turn of the 20th century. Generous bequests from New Yorkers over the years have endowed it with operating funds and with priceless collections of manuscripts and rare books.

## NEW YORK STOCK EXCHANGE
### 11 Wall Street, New York

The New York Stock Exchange, virtually synonymous with "Wall Street," is the nation's largest securities market. It began in 1792 in the Tontine Coffee House, and after a number of temporary locations, moved into the first section of its present building early in the 20th century. Designed by architect George Post, the Exchange is fronted by an imposing Corinthian portico on a high podium, a fitting architectural symbol for the ultimate "temple of finance."

## NEW YORK STUDIO SCHOOL OF DRAWING, PAINTING, AND SCULPTURE
### 8 West Eighth Street, New York

Until 1954 this was the home of the Whitney Museum of American Art, the first museum devoted exclusively to American art of the 20th century. The result of a partnership between two extraordinary women, Gertrude Vanderbilt Whitney and Juliana Rieser Force, the studio functioned as a hive of working and living spaces for painters, sculptors, and composers. The studio school was the locus of an unrivaled program of exhibitions and philanthropy that has helped shape American art and artists ever since.

## NEW YORK YACHT CLUB BUILDING
### 37 West 44th Street, New York

One of New York's greatest visual delights is the sight of three stone sterns, dripping with garlands of shells and seaweed, waves and dolphins, on this 44th Street building. These nautical motifs fittingly mark the home of the New York Yacht Club, America's oldest and foremost yachting organization. The club was established in 1844 as a private gentlemen's club and moved to this neo-Baroque clubhouse designed by Whitney Warren of Warren & Wetmore in 1900. Highly evocative of the Gilded Age, the building is also renowned as the long-time home of the America's Cup.

## THE NEWS BUILDING
### 220 East 42nd Street, New York

Built in 1929–1930, this 36-story building was the first modernistic freestanding skyscraper designed by Raymond Hood. Marking one of the high points in skyscraper design, it is notable for the vertical "soaring" quality of its uncluttered exterior and for the Art-Deco bas-relief ornamentation of its entrance. The frontispiece depicts the building itself surrounded by clouds and sunbeams, and one can easily picture mild-mannered reporter Clark Kent walking through its portals. Captain Joseph Patterson, founder of the tabloid *Daily News,* which long had the largest circulation of any daily newspaper in America, commissioned the building.

## OLD MERCHANT'S HOUSE
### 29 East Fourth Street, New York

Built in 1832 and bought in 1835 by Seabury Tredwell, this three-story brick town house provides a remarkably authentic picture of the life and times of a prosperous mercantile family. Tredwell's daughter lived in the house from her birth in 1840 until her death in 1933, saving everything and changing nothing. Although the house itself is a good representative of the transition between Federal and Greek Revival styles of architecture, the collections it houses make this property truly remarkable. The house was restored in the 1970s and is open as a house museum with furniture, fabrics, clothes, and carpets remaining just as the Tredwells left them.

## OLD NEW YORK COUNTY COURTHOUSE
### 52 Chambers Street, New York

Some buildings are famous; others are infamous. The Old New York County Courthouse is one of the latter. It stands as a monument to the machinations of William Marcy ("Boss") Tweed, who ran one of the most infamous political machines in American history, and who has become *the* symbol of graft and corruption in American annals. Tweed owned the quarry that supplied the marble, and the "Tweed Ring" profited from a 65 percent commission on each shady contract awarded during its construction. When the ring was broken in 1871, $13 million had been expended on a courthouse that was still unfinished! Notwithstanding, the building is a handsome Renaissance Revival structure that provides a nice architectural complement to nearby City Hall.

## THE PLAYERS CLUB
### 16 Gramercy Park, New York

Actor Edwin Booth, recognizing the low esteem in which Victorian society held his fellow thespians, founded the Players: "[It will be] a beacon to [lift them] up to a higher social grade than the Bohemian level that so many worthy members of my profession grovel in." He purchased this handsome brownstone residence in 1888 and commissioned architect Stanford White to transform it into a clubhouse. Booth also contributed his books and memorabilia, which became the nucleus of one of the nation's finest collections of material relating to the theater.

## PLAZA HOTEL
### Fifth Avenue at 59th Street, New York

Designed in the French Renaissance style by Henry Hardenbergh, this opulent 18-story white-brick and marble structure is an outstanding example of American hotel architecture. The building cost $12 million, and when it opened—fully booked—on October 1, 1907, its luxury was unmatched in the nation. Set back from Fifth Avenue at the southeastern corner of Central Park, it occupies one of the finest sites in the city, and although now surrounded by taller buildings, the Plaza still outshines them all. It continues as a familiar symbol of elegance; in fact, many would argue that its turn-of-the-century luxury remains unrivaled.

## PUPIN PHYSICS LABORATORY, COLUMBIA UNIVERSITY
### Broadway and 120th Streets, New York

On January 25, 1939, a uranium atom was split for the first time in the New World in a basement laboratory here. Dr. Enrico Fermi, then a new member of Columbia University's faculty, having heard of a successful splitting of the atom in Copenhagen ten days earlier, determined to verify it by conducting an identical experiment. In a masterpiece of understatement, a colleague wrote, "Believe we have observed new phenomenon of far-reaching consequences."

## PAUL ROBESON RESIDENCE
### 555 Edgecombe Avenue, New York

Paul Robeson lived in this Harlem apartment building from 1939 to 1941. A famous black actor, singer, scholar, and athlete, Robeson was widely acclaimed for his artistic talent but suffered public condemnation for his political sympathies in the 1940s and 1950s. Because of his communist leanings, the U.S. State Department revoked his passport in 1950, but in 1958 the Supreme Court restored it. Robeson is remembered for his rendition of "Ole Man River" in the musical *Showboat* and for his performance in Othello. His unyielding conviction to stand firm for his belief in human dignity is a more enduring legacy.

## ROCKEFELLER CENTER
**Bounded by Fifth Avenue, West 48th Street, Seventh Avenue, and West 51st Street, New York**

Rockefeller Center changed the form of midtown Manhattan. Conceived and built between 1930 and 1939, it was one of the most successful urban projects in America. It integrated architecture, city planning, landscape architecture, entertainment, art, and sculpture on a scale never achieved before— and very seldom since. The vast project, developed by John D. Rockefeller, Jr., provided thousands of jobs during the Depression and restored the image of New York as America's premier city. It remains one of New York's most popular and most admired attractions and a vivid lesson to urban planners.

## SAINT GEORGE'S EPISCOPAL CHURCH
**Third Avenue and East 16th Street, New York**

For 52 years, beginning in 1894, the stone walls of this massive mid-19th-century Romanesque Revival church reverberated to the music of Harry Thacker Burleigh. He was the sole African American among 60 applicants for the position of baritone soloist at this wealthy parish, and senior warden J. P. Morgan, Sr., cast the vote that decided his appointment. A composer and arranger as well as singer, Burleigh took the spiritual to new heights. He transformed these formerly simple, unaccompanied tunes, all the while maintaining their dignity and the pathos of their origins. His rendition of "Deep River" captures the yearnings of those who first sang it, and of the man who preserved and improved it.

## SAINT PATRICK'S CATHEDRAL
**Fifth Avenue between East 50th and East 51st Streets, New York**

Saint Patrick's Roman Catholic Cathedral represents the Gothic Revival at its grandest. It is the first medieval-inspired church in the country built on the scale of a cathedral. Architect James Renwick skillfully wove elements of French, German, and English Gothic into his plans, indicating the diverse nationalities represented in the diocese. The cornerstone of the white marble cathedral was laid in August 1858, it was opened in 1879, and the twin spires were completed in 1888. It remains an ornament to the city and an inspiration to those who worship within.

## SAINT PAUL'S CHAPEL
**Broadway between Fulton and Vesey Streets, New York**

This handsome stone church is Manhattan's only religious edifice remaining from colonial times. Built in 1764–1766, it is one of the most accomplished examples of ecclesiastical Georgian architecture in the country. Both American and British military officers worshiped in Saint Paul's during the American Revolution, and Washington attended services here after his inauguration in 1789. Later, funeral services for two presidents, James Monroe in 1831 and William McKinley in 1901, took place here. The interior is especially noteworthy, with its original wineglass pulpit, Waterford chandeliers, and altar designed by Pierre Charles L'Enfant.

## MARGARET SANGER CLINIC
**17 West 16th Street, New York**

From 1930 to 1973 this 19th-century brick row house served as a clinic established by Margaret Higgins Sanger, a pioneer in birth control. According to a biographer, Sanger dispensed "safe, harmless information" about contraception to the working classes to whom her clinic administered. In coining the term *birth control,* she did not invent a new practice but introduced a new frankness to the subject of sexuality. As a speaker and writer on sexual reforms, she dedicated her life to winning reproductive autonomy for women and to giving them a choice about parenthood.

## GENERAL WINFIELD SCOTT HOUSE
**24 West 12th Street, New York**

Winfield Scott, victorious general in the Mexican War and Whig presidential candidate in 1852, lived in this Manhattan brownstone from 1854 to 1855. Scott has been described as "something of a mirror of the Army itself. His flaws were great, but he had large virtues as well." Not only a brilliant military leader in the field, he is also remembered for his achievements as a peacemaker in resolving the nullification crisis. His former home now serves as the center for Italian studies at New York University.

## HARRY F. SINCLAIR HOUSE
**2 East 79th Street, New York**

From 1918 until 1930, a period encompassing both the height of his economic power and the depth of his disgrace, Harry F. Sinclair lived in this mock French chateau, one of the most imposing of Fifth Avenue's many mansions. Sinclair is a pivotal figure in the history of the American oil industry. Two years before he moved here, he had formed the Sinclair Oil Corporation, which became the nation's largest independent oil company. Sinclair's acquisition of drilling rights in the Teapot Dome oil reserve in 1922 brought him down. Although eventually acquitted of charges of bribery in this famous political scandal, public opinion judged him guilty.

## ALFRED E. SMITH HOUSE
**25 Oliver Street, New York**

This three-story Victorian brick row house in Lower Manhattan was the home of Alfred E. Smith from 1907 to 1923. Smith's life and career mark a critical juncture in the evolution of American politics. Four-term governor of New York, he created a loyal, honest government and in 1928 was nominated as the Democratic candidate for president. Unfortunately for Smith, there were already three strikes against him: "The Happy Warrior" was a "city boy" and a Catholic, and no Democratic candidate stood a chance of being elected during the heady, prosperous late twenties. As one commentator observed, "Al Smith arrived too early on the political scene to be accepted as a national symbol."

*Soho Cast-Iron Historic District, New York City, New York County. Haughwout Building, 1967. Courtesy of HABS.*

## SOHO CAST-IRON HISTORIC DISTRICT
**Bounded by West Broadway and Houston, Crosby, and Canal Streets, New York**

Soho, an acronym for "South of Houston (Street)," developed as a major textile center in the latter half of the 19th century. Large buildings whose structural systems and cast-iron facades allowed the greatest possible penetration of light characterize the area. As New York expanded northward, the area was virtually forgotten until the 1960s, when artists discovered that the well-lit lofts were as perfect for their purposes as they had been for the textile industry. Soho contains what is likely the largest group of cast-iron buildings in the world and is a virtual textbook of the commercial architecture and technology of its time.

## A. T. STEWART COMPANY STORE
**280 Broadway, New York**

Alexander Turney Stewart is generally credited for creating the first department store in the United States. Thanks to him, the status of retailers rose from "monger" to "merchant," and soon John Wanamaker, Marshall

Field, and others were able to stand on the foundations he firmly established. Stewart erected his "Marble Palace" in 1845–1846, and it has been fittingly termed "the cradle of the department store." Although the top two stories postdate Stewart's era, the building is otherwise remarkably unchanged from the time he enlarged it in 1850–1853. It now serves as municipal offices.

## SURROGATE'S COURT
### 31 Chambers Street, New York

This monumental structure, dating from 1899–1907, was built as New York City's Hall of Records but was designed for its main courtroom to house the Surrogate's Court— established under Dutch rule in 1656 to administer property of "orphans and minor children." Architect James R. Thomas designed an American version of a French Hôtel de Ville, an eight-story granite-faced structure with Beaux-Arts grandeur and French Renaissance detailing. Philip Martin embellished it with notable sculptural groups.

## TENEMENT BUILDING AT 97 ORCHARD STREET
### 97 Orchard Street, New York

This six-story brick building of the Civil War era housed immigrants, perhaps as many as 10,000 during the 72 years it served as a tenement. Rooms on the top two floors are an urban time capsule, with wallpaper, plumbing, and light fixtures dating from 1931, when the apartments were boarded up and declared vacant. They were "discovered" in 1988 and now—open to the public as the Lower Manhattan Tenement Museum— impart an unforgettable sense of the living conditions that so many new Americans experienced during their first years in the land of opportunity.

## THIRD JUDICIAL DISTRICT COURTHOUSE
### Sixth Avenue at 10th Street, New York

This familiar Greenwich Village structure is the best-known and most exuberant work by architect Frederick Clarke Withers. Built in 1874–1877, it is designed in the "Ruskinian" or "Venetian" style, often known by the rubric High Victorian Gothic. Typical of its

*Third Judicial District Courthouse, New York City, New York County, 1960. Courtesy of HABS (Cervin Robinson).*

kind, it is faced with bright red brick with a plethora of stone trim contrasting in color. Part of its charm is its triangular shape, dictated by the angles of the lot on which it stands. The silhouette includes a number of gables and spikes, and the clock tower that dominates the composition rises in successive polygonal, circular, and square stages to terminate in a pyramidal roof.

## TIFFANY AND COMPANY BUILDING
### 401 Fifth Avenue, New York

Completed in 1905 from designs by McKim, Mead and White, this copy of a 16th-century Venetian palazzo served until 1940 as the home of Tiffany and Company. Tiffany is arguably the most famous jewelry store in the world, and its name is a virtual synonym for quality and luxury. The company traces its founding to 1837 and over the years has won countless awards for its designs and merchandise. Tiffany was designated Queen Victoria's jeweler in 1883, and there is even a gem, tiffanyite, named for the company. To call a company "the Tiffany of its industry" is an unsurpassed accolade.

## SAMUEL J. TILDEN HOUSE
**14–15 Gramercy Park South, New York**

Samuel J. Tilden, a wealthy corporation lawyer and former New York State legislator, is a foremost representative of the conservative political reformers of the 1870s. He came to national prominence during his successful campaign to reform Tammany Hall and the Tweed Ring. Tilden was one of the two central figures in the disputed Tilden-Hayes presidential election of 1876 and the resultant compromise of 1877, events that essentially ended the post–Civil War Reconstruction era in the South. From about 1860 until his death in 1885 he lived in this Gramercy Park town house, now occupied by the National Arts Club.

## TRIANGLE SHIRTWAIST FACTORY BUILDING
**23–29 Washington Place, New York**

On the afternoon of March 25, 1911, one of the worst industrial disasters in American history took place when fire swept through the Triangle Shirtwaist Factory. One hundred forty-six workers, most of them young women, were killed. Many suffocated, others were trapped behind crowds or locked doors, and more than a third leapt to their deaths. The factory occupied the eighth, ninth, and tenth floors of this loft building, and windows at these levels were beyond the reach of fire truck ladders. The fire is credited with changing both factory and fire prevention laws throughout the country. The building—now equipped with adequate exits—serves as classrooms and office space for New York University.

## TRINITY CHURCH AND GRAVEYARD
**Broadway at Wall Street, New York**

Trinity Church, one of the early triumphs of the Gothic Revival style in America, houses a parish chartered in 1697, making it the oldest Episcopal parish in New York City. The present church, third on the site, was completed in 1846 from designs by Richard Upjohn, and the admiration he received because of his success catapulted him to national fame. The surrounding churchyard predates the church, and Alexander Hamilton, Robert Fulton, and Albert Gallatin are among the notables buried in it. Through no fault of its own, but because it stands at the head of, and on an axis with, Wall Street, Trinity has become something of a symbol for the financial heart of America.

## UNION SQUARE
**Bounded by East 14th and East 17th Streets, Union Square West and Union Square East, New York**

Located in lower midtown Manhattan, Union Square is nationally significant for its role in American labor history. Although the park has been the focal point for well over a century for parades, mass gatherings, soapbox orations, and demonstrations, its particular moment in history occurred on September 5, 1882, when the first Labor Day parade took place. This marked the beginning of organized labor's 12-year effort to secure passage of national legislation that would set aside one day each year to recognize the contributions and achievements of American workers.

## UNITED CHARITIES BUILDING
**105 East 22nd Street, New York**

Completed in 1893, its costs borne entirely by wealthy businessman John S. Kennedy, this building was intended to provide convenient, rent-free office space to four specific charitable groups—the Charities Organizations Society, the Association for the Improvement of the Condition of the Poor, the Children's Aid Society, and the New York City Mission and Tract Society. Offices for other benevolent groups were let at lower rentals than prevailing on the open market. The building continues in its original use as a headquarters office building for charitable and social service organizations and occupies a pivotal spot in the history of the nation's social reforms.

## UNITED STATES CUSTOM HOUSE
**1 Bowling Green, New York**

Constructed from 1900 to 1907, this is an outstanding example of the use of Beaux Arts elements in a government structure and one of Cass Gilbert's finest buildings. It is embellished with allegorical sculpture by

Daniel Chester French and murals by Reginald Marsh. The Custom House faces Bowling Green at the southern tip of Manhattan and occupies a site intended in the 1780s for a presidents' house when it was thought that New York would be the nation's permanent capital. The Bureau of Customs vacated the building in 1973, and it now serves as the home of the National Museum of the American Indian.

## WOOLWORTH BUILDING
**233 Broadway, New York**

From its completion in 1913 until 1930, this was the world's tallest building. It stands as a monument not only to Frank W. Woolworth, originator of the variety chain store and the building's sponsor, but also to its architect, Cass Gilbert, who won acclaim for his brilliant adaptation of Gothic architecture and detail to a skyscraper. It was a New York clergyman who first called it "the Cathedral of Commerce," a nickname it still bears. Although it has long since lost its crown as the world's tallest, the Woolworth Building has seldom been surpassed in proclaiming the tall-building ethic with such soaring verticality.

■ *Niagara County*

## ADAMS POWER PLANT TRANSFORMER HOUSE
**Off 15th Avenue near Buffalo Avenue, Niagara Falls**

Built in the last decade of the 19th century, this electric-power-generating facility retained its position as the largest hydroelectric power plant in the world well into the 20th century. When it became operational, long-distance commercial electrical transmission became a reality. The transformer house, an impressive stone structure built in 1895 from designs by McKim, Mead and White, is the only surviving building of the original plant, which has been hailed as "the birthplace of the modern hydroelectric power station."

## COLONIAL NIAGARA HISTORIC DISTRIC
**Near the Niagara River, Lewiston and Youngstown**

During the century leading up through the

American Revolution, this area was the key strategic portage route linking interior North America with the Atlantic seaboard. It contains important archeological remains and standing structures associated with alliances and conflicts between various Indian and European groups. One of these sites, the restored Old Fort Niagara, is a state historic site.

## NIAGARA RESERVATION
**Niagara Falls**

Created in 1885 by the State of New York, this reservation is the first instance in the nation in which the legal doctrine of eminent domain was employed to acquire land for aesthetic purposes. Consisting of more than 400 acres along the eastern shore of the Niagara River, the reservation preserves and enhances views of Niagara Falls unencumbered by commercial enterprises. Under Frederick Law Olmsted's guidance, some 150 structures, mostly tawdry eyesores, were removed. Niagara Reservation was a tremendous step forward in the organized movement to protect America's scenic and historic resources and set precedents that other states have followed.

■ *Oneida County*

## ROSCOE CONKLING HOUSE
**3 Rutgers Park, Utica**

From all accounts, Roscoe Conkling was a man everyone loved to hate. Quite the dandy, "Lord Roscoe" was recognized by the single blond curl he trained to dangle over his broad forehead. He was aloof and arrogant and a powerful Republican political "boss"— dominant during the Grant administration, defiant in the Hayes and Garfield years. His posturing led to the highly charged political atmosphere that resulted in President Garfield's assassination, an event that spelled an end to Conkling's own political life. Conkling's house has been altered since his time, but its original lines are still discernible.

## WILLIAM FLOYD HOUSE
**West side of Main Street, Westernville**

William Floyd, a wealthy Long Island landowner before the Revolution, was a New York delegate to the Continental Congress.

Although he played a minor role in the debates that shaped the nation, he proved his mettle by signing the Declaration of Independence. In 1803, at age 69, Floyd left Long Island with his family to establish a new home in western New York. He built this large frame house in 1803–1804 and lived in it until his death in 1821. Little altered, it remains in private ownership.

## FORT STANWIX (NPS)
### Dominick, Spring, Liberty, and North James Streets, Rome

This was the setting of the 1768 Treaty of Fort Stanwix, by which the Iroquois ceded a vast territory south and east of the Ohio River, clearing the way for a surge of new settlers. During the Revolution colonial troops garrisoned the fort and withstood an English siege in August 1777, thus preventing reinforcements from reaching Burgoyne at Saratoga. Fort Stanwix was razed after the war, and buildings were subsequently erected on its site. These were removed in a 20th-century urban renewal project and now—as Fort Stanwix National Monument—the site is open to the public.

## ORISKANY BATTLEFIELD
### 5 miles east of Rome on New York Route 69

The August 6, 1777, Battle of Oriskany was an engagement between American militia attempting to relieve besieged Fort Stanwix and a combined force of British Loyalists and Indians. Although the Americans failed in their goal, the unseasoned militia's unwillingness to retreat after an ambush led to the abandonment of the siege and ultimately to the removal of the British threat in the Mohawk Valley. The battlefield is now a state historic site, and the marshy ravine where the ambush occurred has been preserved.

## ELIHU ROOT HOUSE
### 101 College Hill Road, Clinton

Elihu Root was secretary of war under Presidents McKinley and Theodore Roosevelt and later became Roosevelt's secretary of state. Military organization was one of his many talents, and he has been called "the father of the modern American army." Root was among the first statesmen to grasp the implications of America's becoming a world power, and his effective military reforms stood the nation in good stead in later years. Root purchased this rambling Federal style frame house in 1893 and considered it his permanent home throughout his years of government service. He died here in 1937.

## UTICA STATE HOSPITAL MAIN BUILDING
### 1213 Court Street, Utica

This mammoth building opened in 1843 as the first "state asylum for the insane poor" in New York. It was then, and remains, one of the largest and most powerful architectural statements of the Greek Revival in the country. Designed in an archaic Doric mode, apparently not by an architect but by the chairman of the Board of Trustees, the hospital has a massive portico whose fluted columns rise four full stories. Although the design harkens back to ancient Greek principles, the building's heating and ventilating systems were quite modern for their time.

## ▪ Ontario County
## BOUGHTON HILL
### Address Restricted, Victor

Boughton Hill marks the site of Gannagaro, the "great town" of the Seneca Indians, who were the westernmost, and most powerful, of the Five Nations in the League of the Iroquois. At the height of its occupancy, the stockaded settlement likely had several thousand inhabitants, occupying 150 multifamily longhouses. It was destroyed in 1687 by the French, and the Seneca subsequently abandoned their village life-style for one of small family groups. The site is now Ganondagan State Historic Site.

## ▪ Orange County
## DELAWARE AND HUDSON CANAL
### (Orange, Sullivan, and Ulster Counties)

Completed in 1828, this 108-mile canal was the main waterway connecting the anthracite coalfields of northeastern Pennsylvania with the furnaces of New York. Enormously profitable, the canal helped fuel America's industrial growth when coal was the nation's major source of power, but growth of the railroads led to the canal's demise in 1899. A

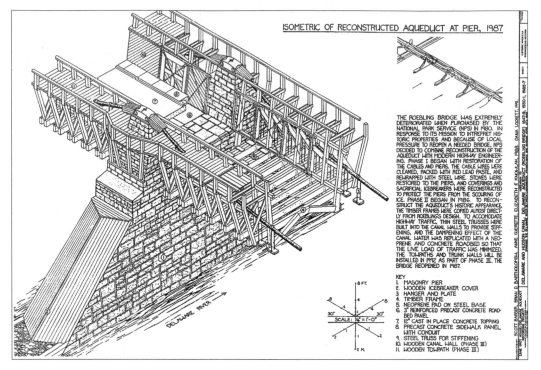

ISOMETRIC OF RECONSTRUCTED AQUEDUCT AT PIER, 1987

THE ROEBLING BRIDGE WAS EXTREMELY DETERIORATED WHEN PURCHASED BY THE NATIONAL PARK SERVICE (NPS) IN 1980. IN RESPONSE TO ITS MISSION TO INTREPRET HISTORIC PROPERTIES AND BECAUSE OF LOCAL PRESSURE TO REOPEN A NEEDED BRIDGE, NPS DECIDED TO COMBINE RECONSTRUCTION OF THE AQUEDUCT WITH MODERN HIGHWAY ENGINEERING. PHASE I BEGAN WITH RESTORATION OF THE CABLES AND PIERS. THE CABLE WIRES WERE CLEANED, PACKED WITH RED LEAD PASTE, AND REWRAPPED WITH STEEL WIRE. STONES WERE RESTORED TO THE PIERS, AND COVERINGS AND SACRIFICIAL ICEBREAKERS WERE RECONSTRUCTED TO PROTECT THE PIERS FROM THE SCOURING OF ICE. PHASE II BEGAN IN 1986. TO RECONSTRUCT THE AQUEDUCT'S HISTORIC APPEARANCE, THE TIMBER FRAMES WERE COPIED ALMOST DIRECTLY FROM ROEBLING'S DESIGN. TO ACCOMODATE HIGHWAY TRAFFIC, THIN STEEL TRUSSES WERE BUILT INTO THE CANAL WALLS TO PROVIDE STIFFENING, AND THE DAMPENING EFFECT OF THE CANAL WATER WAS REPLICATED WITH A NEOPRENE AND CONCRETE ROADBED SO THAT THE LIVE LOAD OF TRAFFIC WAS MINIMIZED. THE TOWPATHS AND TRUNK WALLS WILL BE INSTALLED IN 1992 AS PART OF PHASE III. THE BRIDGE REOPENED IN 1987.

KEY
1. MASONRY PIER
2. WOODEN ICEBREAKER COVER
3. HANGER AND PLATE
4. TIMBER FRAME
5. NEOPRENE PAD ON STEEL BASE
6. 3" REINFORCED PRECAST CONCRETE ROADBED PANEL
7. 12" CAST IN PLACE CONCRETE TOPPING
8. PRECAST CONCRETE SIDEWALK PANEL WITH CONDUIT
9. STEEL TRUSS FOR STIFFENING
10. WOODEN CANAL WALL (PHASE III)
11. WOODEN TOWPATH (PHASE III)

SCALE: ¼" = 1'-0"

DELAWARE RIVER

*Delaware and Hudson Canal, Orange, Sullivan and Ulster Counties, New York, and Wayne County, Pennsylvania. Isometric drawing of reconstructed aqueduct and masonry pier. Courtesy of HAER (Scott Barber, Brian D. Bartholomew, Anne Guerette, Elizabeth F. Knowlan).*

number of vestiges, including locks and the Roebling Aqueduct spanning the Delaware River, remain in this discontiguous National Historic Landmark. (Also in Wayne County, Pennsylvania.)

## FORT MONTGOMERY
### Address Restricted, Fort Montgomery

Sir Henry Clinton's brilliant attack on Forts Montgomery and Clinton on October 6, 1777, destroyed the twin Hudson River defenses on which colonial troops had been working since March 1776. Although Clinton's campaign ultimately failed in its primary objective—to relieve Burgoyne's army on the upper Hudson—it likely enabled him to obtain easier terms of surrender. Clinton dismantled both forts, but extensive and unaltered earthen ruins remain, along with brick foundations that have been excavated and stabilized.

## E. H. HARRIMAN ESTATE
### New York Route 17, Harriman

Arden was the country estate of Edward

Henry Harriman, a preeminent organizer and builder of railroads. He obtained control of the Union Pacific in 1897 and used it as a stepping stone to control the Southern Pacific, which he acquired in 1901. The merger that soon followed made this the largest railroad of its time. Harriman commissioned the prominent New York firm of Carrere and Hastings to design Arden. Built of granite, it is in the style of a French château, and was completed in 1909, a few months before Harriman's death. It is now owned by Columbia University, which uses it as a conference center.

## HISTORIC TRACK
### Main Street, Goshen

Harness racing developed in the United States, and early races in Goshen took place on its main street. The first race on this site occurred in 1838. The half-mile oval track, along with grandstand and judges' platform, assumed their current appearance by 1911. It remains one of the oldest (if not the oldest) active trotting tracks in the country.

E. H. Harriman Estate, Arden, Orange County, 1962. Courtesy of NPS.

General Henry Knox Headquarters, Vails Gate and Cornwall, Orange County, 1967. Courtesy of NPS (Charles W. Snell).

Messenger and his famous descendent Hambletonian are among the trotters associated with Historic Track.

## KNOX HEADQUARTERS
### Quassaick Avenue and Forge Hill, Vails Gate

This stone farmhouse served four times during the Revolution as headquarters for General Henry Knox, Washington's artillery chief. A brilliant military strategist, Knox designed and built gun carriages that allowed light cannon to keep pace with marching regiments. He participated in battles on Long Island, Trenton, and Germantown, and was also at the siege of Yorktown. At war's end, Knox conceived and organized the Society of the Cincinnati and became the new nation's first secretary of war. His headquarters is now a state historic site.

## PALISADES INTERSTATE PARK
### West bank of the Hudson River (Orange and Rockland Counties)

This park represents an early cooperative effort between two states. After the Civil War, quarrying threatened to destroy the Palisades, the imposing stone cliffs that line the western bank of the Hudson River opposite New York City. In the 1890s the states of New Jersey and New York formed commissions to attempt to save them, and an Interstate Park Commission was the result. J. P. Morgan made the first contribution, and in 1901 New York appropriated $50,000 to buy property in New Jersey! By 1914 the initial goal of acquiring a 14-mile stretch of the Palisades had been accomplished. Additional land was incorporated on both sides of the Hudson in subsequent years. (Also in Bergen County, New Jersey.)

## UNITED STATES MILITARY ACADEMY
**New York Route 218, West Point**

Troops have been stationed at this pivotal spot guarding the Hudson River since January 1778, making West Point the oldest permanently occupied military post in the country. Benedict Arnold commanded the post during the Revolution and attempted to betray it to the British in 1780. Congress established the U.S. Military Academy here in 1802. Buildings and memorials at the Academy attest to its long history, and its list of graduates reads like a "Who's Who" in American military service. Twentieth-century buildings, mostly Gothic Revival in style, are dominated by the Cadet Chapel, built in 1910 and standing high above the academic cluster and the parade ground.

## WASHINGTON'S HEADQUARTERS
**Liberty and Washington Streets, Newburgh**

George Washington used this Dutch Colonial fieldstone residence as headquarters from

*Cobblestone Historic District, Childs, Orleans County. First Universalist Church, 1965. Courtesy of HABS (Jack E. Boucher).*

April 1, 1782, to August 19, 1783, during the closing days of the Revolution. Here he drafted crucial documents that laid the foundation for the new nation's orderly transition from war to peace. The house is also noteworthy for its role in historic preservation. In 1850 it became the first building in the country purchased by a state for the specific purpose of preserving it as a historic property. Washington's Headquarters is open to the public as a state historic site.

### ■ *Orleans County*

## COBBLESTONE HISTORIC DISTRICT
**Ridge Road, Childs**

This historic district marks the epicenter of a particular method of American vernacular construction that seems to have begun in New York State. The three buildings that constitute the district are all built of cobblestones—glacially rounded stone residue from the Ice Age. The buildings date from 1834 (First Universalist Church), ca. 1840 (the parsonage), and 1849 (District 5 Schoolhouse). Some 700 cobblestone buildings have been counted in New York, and those in other states were mostly built by emigrants from this area of the Empire State.

### ■ *Oswego County*

## *NASH* (HARBOR TUG)
**H. Lee White Marine Museum, at the foot of West First Street, Oswego**

Launched in 1943 as *Major Elisha K. Henson* (LT-5), this vessel is typical of the several hundred large harbor tugs (LTs) used by the U.S. Army Corps of Engineers in every theater of World War II operations. In 1944, *Henson* supported amphibious landing operations and invasions. It is the only known surviving army service craft associated with the Normandy D-Day landings. *Nash* remains essentially unmodified, is still operational, and is a popular attraction at the H. Lee White Marine Museum.

## HYDE HALL
**Glimmerglass State Park, south of Springfield Center**

This remarkable limestone manor, begun in 1817, combines the high style grace of an

Nash, Oswego, Oswego County. Courtesy of the H. Lee White Marine Museum (Mercedes A. Niess).

English country house with the solidity and ingenuity of an American dwelling. It also happens to be one of early America's most thoroughly documented buildings. Phillip Hooker designed it for George Hyde Clarke, and both the architect's drawings and the owner's bills survive. Architecturally, as a student of the house has aptly stated, Hyde Hall "stands with one foot in the English Regency and the other in the American Greek Revival." It has been restored and is open to the public as a major attraction in Glimmerglass State Park.

## ■ Queens County

### LOUIS ARMSTRONG HOUSE
**3456 107th Street, Corona**

Louis Armstrong — "Satchmo" to his world-wide legion of fans — lived in this house from 1940 to 1971. One of America's most creative, influential, and popular musicians, he arranged, composed, and played blues and jazz like no one else during his 55-year career. In the 1950s and 1960s, Satchmo took his trumpet around the world, giving concerts and serving as a goodwill ambassador sponsored by the U. S. Department of State. When his house was designated a National Historic Landmark, his widow wrote, "I'm sure Louis is looking down on us with a content smile of happiness."

### RALPH JOHNSON BUNCHE HOUSE
**115–125 Grosvenor Road, Kew Gardens**

As undersecretary general, Ralph Johnson Bunche was the highest-ranking African American in the United Nations Secretariat. He negotiated the Israeli-Arab Truce of 1949 and was consequently awarded the Nobel Peace Prize, becoming the first African American to receive that honor. Bunche was also instrumental in settling the Suez Canal crisis in 1956. Later, President Kennedy bestowed the nation's highest civilian award, the Medal of Freedom, on this dedicated public servant. From 1952 until his death in 1971, he lived in this stuccoed Tudor Revival house in Kew Gardens.

### KING MANOR
**150th Street and Jamaica Avenue, Jamaica**

Rufus King lived in this shingled, gambrel-roofed mansion intermittently from 1806 until his death in 1827. A distinguished public servant, King sat in the Continental Congress (1784–1786), signed the U.S. Constitution (1787), served as U.S. senator (1789–1795), and was minister to Great Britain (1796–1803). The last nationally prominent Federalist, he was twice the party's vice presidential nominee (1804 and 1808) and once its presidential candidate (1816).

## OLD QUAKER MEETINGHOUSE
### South side of Northern Boulevard, Flushing

This two-story shingle-clad, hipped-roof structure seems an architectural anomaly in its present urban setting. The oldest portion dates from 1694, making it New York's single surviving example of a 17th-century ecclesiastical building. The meetinghouse was enlarged to its present size in 1716–1719, and except for the years from 1776 to 1783, when the British commandeered it as a prison, hospital, and stable, it has been used continuously for religious services. In its proportions and framing system, it stands as a prime example of the survival of postmedieval design and building techniques.

■ *Rensselaer County*

## BENNINGTON BATTLEFIELD
### New York Route 67 near the Vermont state line, Walloomsac

The American militia's victory at the Battle of Bennington on August 16, 1777, contributed significantly to the defeat of British general Burgoyne's army at Saratoga two months later. The defeat also discouraged Burgoyne's already uneasy Indian allies and encouraged enlistments in the American army. The battlefield, close to the Vermont border, is preserved and open to the public.

## FORT CRAILO
### On Riverside Avenue south of Columbia Street, Rensselaer

This brick manor house was built by Hendrick Van Rensselaer, grandson of Killiaen Van Rensselaer, who founded the 700,000-acre patroonship of Rensselaerwyck. Under this Dutch system of land tenure devised to encourage settlement, patroons (proprietors) were granted tracts if they provided passage for tenants to occupy their lands. Killiaen never visited America, but counted the guilders that enriched his coffers as profits from settlement, farming, and fur trading increased. The house, built ca. 1712 and enlarged ca. 1768, preserves the story of the greatest of the patroonships and is open to the public as the Crailo State Historic Site.

## W. & L. E. GURLEY BUILDING
### Fulton Street, between Fifth and Union, Troy

This factory was built in 1862 by the W & L. E. Gurley Company, known worldwide for the design and manufacture of precision mathematical and engineering instruments. The firm first made surveying equipment, and by 1900 was the nation's largest manufacturer of such products. Gurley soon began manufacturing weights and measures for the National Bureau of Standards, and later, as Teledyne Gurley, produced instruments used during the Apollo program. The U-shaped four-story brick building now houses a wondrous museum collection of instruments.

## KATE MULLANY HOUSE
### 350 Eighth Street, Troy

Kate Mullany, who organized and led Troy's all-female Collar Laundry Union in the 1860s, was America's most prominent female labor leader. Male unionists recognized her group as the only bona fide female union in the country and applauded her success in bargaining with laundry owners for her objectives. Mullany and her cohorts also supported other working unions and labor activity. She lived in this typical working-class brick row house from 1869 until her death in 1906.

## TROY SAVINGS BANK AND MUSIC HALL
### 32 Second Street, Troy

Constructed in 1871–1875 to house a rare combination of functions—music and mammon—this building contains a bank on the first floor and a 1,250-seat concert hall above. The idea came from the bank's board of directors, and architect George B. Post gave concrete, or rather stone, expression to its members' public-spirited thoughts. His French Renaissance building is one of the finest 19th-century auditoriums in the United States. It continues to dominate downtown Troy and—recently restored—continues to provide an exceptional venue for musical events.

*Alice Austen House, Staten Island, Richmond County. Courtesy of the Library of Congress.*

## ■ *Richmond County*

### ALICE AUSTEN HOUSE
**2 Hylan Boulevard, Staten Island**

Elizabeth Alice Austen lived in this house overlooking the Narrows of New York Harbor for 78 years. She began her career as a photographer in the 1880s, taking pictures that displayed realistic images and natural edges, rather than the blurry, romantic views generally advocated in photography's early years. Austen also preferred photographing people engaged in normal activities, instead of in stilted studio poses. "Clear Comfort" began as a one-room farmhouse ca. 1700 and emerged as a charming Gothic Revival dwelling during the Austen ownership. It has been restored and is open to the public.

### CONFERENCE HOUSE
**Hylan Boulevard, Tottenville, Staten Island**

This impressive stone house, its architectural lines clearly revealing its Dutch heritage, was almost a century old when its "fifteen minutes of fame" occurred. On September 11, 1776, Lord Howe, commander in chief of British forces in America, invited representatives of the Continental Congress to meet and discuss terms of peace to end the fledgling American Revolution. Ben Franklin, John Adams, and Edward Rutledge came and exchanged pleasantries, but informed his Lordship that they would stand by their Declaration of Independence. The Billopp Mansion, or Conference House, has been restored and is now a museum.

### FIREFIGHTER
**Saint George Ferry Terminal, Staten Island**

When *Firefighter* was designated a National Historic Landmark in 1989, it was one of only ten surviving fireboats in the country that were 50 years of age or older. The best-known fireboat associated with the Port of New York, *Firefighter* was launched in 1938 by Mayor Fiorello LaGuardia and was a popular exhibit at New York's 1939 World's Fair. *Firefighter*'s long service without modification indicates its proven position as the culmination of American fireboat design.

### SAILORS' SNUG HARBOR
**Richmond Terrace, New Brighton, Staten Island**

Captain Robert Richard Randall established this wonderfully named institution, which opened in 1833 "for the purpose of maintaining and supporting aged, decrepit and worn-out sailors." Randall's estate provided sufficient income to build one of the nation's finest Greek Revival institutional complexes to house the "snug harbor." Overlooking New York Harbor, the huge complex remains a rare surviving example of mid-

*Sailors' Snug Harbor, New Brighton, Richmond County. Courtesy of NPS.*

19th-century urban planning, architecture, and landscaping, scarcely equaled in the nation. The City of New York purchased the property in 1973, relocated the sailors to a new home in North Carolina, and began restoration in 1976 to transform the home into the Snug Harbor Cultural Center.

## THE VOORLEZER'S HOUSE
### Arthur Kill Road, Staten Island

The *voorlezer* was an important figure in Dutch communities, both in the Old and the New Worlds. He was a layman who assisted pastors in church services, led the singing, kept records, taught school, catechized, and, in general, looked out for the community's cultural and spiritual well-being. This unique example of early Dutch architecture, built ca. 1695, served Staten Island's *voorlezer,* and consequently the community, as residence, church, and school. It is thought to be the oldest elementary school building in the country. The simple two-story frame house is open to the public.

## WARD'S POINT ARCHEOLOGICAL SITE
### Address Restricted, Tottenville vicinity

Ward's Point is the largest, best-preserved, and most intensively studied archeological site associated with Indian people in today's metropolitan New York area. Knowledge of the site dates to 1858, when workmen excavating foundations for a new house unearthed the first reported human interments in the area. The site's archeological resources chronicle contact between Munsee people and Europeans along the Atlantic Coast during the late 16th and early 17th centuries.

### ■ *Rockland County*

## DE WINT HOUSE
### Livingston Avenue and Oak Tree Road, Tappan

The most notable of George Washington's four visits to this house was from September 28 to October 7, 1780, during the trial and subsequent execution of Major John André, the British spy. André had conspired with Benedict Arnold; Washington, recognizing his treachery as "treason of the blackest dye," had ordered the trial. The brick and stone house, Dutch Colonial in style, was built in 1700 and is now open to the public as a museum.

## PALISADES INTERSTATE PARK
### West bank of the Hudson River (Orange and Rockland Counties)

(Also in Bergen County, New Jersey—see entry under Orange County.)

## STONY POINT BATTLEFIELD
### Stony Point vicinity

In May 1779, British troops captured Stony Point and began to build fortifications on this steep promontory jutting into the Hudson River. On July 15 of that year, patriots led by General "Mad Anthony" Wayne attacked just before midnight and, within 20 minutes, won a victory over the surprised British. This was the last military action of any consequence in the northern theater during the Revolution. Washington abandoned the post three days later. The British held Stony Point briefly, but not in sufficient strength to threaten West Point, and abandoned it late in September 1779. The contours of the fortifications are still evident in this state historic site.

## ■ Saint Lawrence County

### ADIRONDACK FOREST PRESERVE
**(Clinton, Essex, Franklin, Fulton, Hamilton, Herkimer, and Saint Lawrence Counties)**

(See entry under Clinton County.)

## ■ Saratoga County

### CANFIELD CASINO AND CONGRESS PARK
**Roughly bounded by Spring and Circular Streets, Park Place, and Broadway, Saratoga Springs**

Saratoga Springs, "Queen of the Spas," gained fame both as a health resort and as a gambling center during the 19th century, thanks to these two adjoining properties. Dr. John Clarke purchased Congress Spring in the 1820s, began bottling and selling Saratoga water, and developed a park around the spring. The Casino, begun in 1866, was the inspiration of ex–heavyweight boxer John Morrissey. In 1894, Richard Canfield, "the Prince of Gamblers," bought and enlarged it. Like Morrissey before him, Canfield helped turn Saratoga into the Monte Carlo of America.

### PETRIFIED SEA GARDENS
**42 Petrified Gardens Road, Saratoga Springs**

Petrified Sea Gardens is significant in the history of North American geology as the area where stromatolite fossils were first recognized, described, and interpreted. Questions about the origin of these organisms that had puzzled geologists for more than a century were now answered. The property is also significant for its association with Winifred Goldring, a pioneering woman geologist, who conducted the most exhaustive study of the site. Goldring interpreted the ecology and environmental setting of these important, once widespread ancient life forms that flourished half a billion years ago.

### SARATOGA SPA STATE PARK
**Vicinity of U.S. Route 9 and New York Route 50, Saratoga Springs**

By the end of the 19th century the water table at Saratoga Springs had been drastically lowered by extensive use of the waters in carbonated beverages. To counteract this trend and to preserve the mineral waters for public benefit, New York state established a commission in 1909 to create a reservation, or park. The major group, constructed in the 1930s, includes a hotel, bathhouses, a swimming pool, a bottling plant, and an administration and research center, as well as a grand Hall of Springs built in the European style. The park attests to the state's involvement in protecting and promoting one of its important natural resources.

## ■ Schenectady County

### GENERAL ELECTRIC RESEARCH LABORATORY
**General Electric (GE) main plant, Schenectady**

Established in 1900, this is recognized as the first industrial research facility in the United States. Under the 30-year leadership of Willis R. Whitney, the laboratory made major contributions to scientific knowledge, especially in the areas of physics and chemistry. Beginning in a small garage with a dozen workers, the facility now employs hundreds. "We bring good things to life," GE proudly proclaims. Many of those good things first came to life here.

### IRVING LANGMUIR HOUSE
**1176 Stratford Road, Schenectady**

From 1919 to 1957 this large house was home of the distinguished General Electric (GE) chemist and inventor Irving Langmuir. Langmuir joined the GE Research Laboratory in 1909 and remained until 1950. In 1932 he was awarded the Nobel Prize in chemistry for his work in surface kinetics. The director of the laboratory, speaking of Langmuir, once declared that "few scientists, in either university or industry have made as many, and as significant, contributions to scientific progress."

## NOTT MEMORIAL HALL
**Union College campus, Schenectady**

Completed in 1876 to serve as a museum, Nott Memorial Hall is a bold and colorful representative of the High Victorian Gothic style. With its open interior, the building is essentially a 16-sided stone cylinder, 891 feet in diameter, supporting a cast-iron drum and dome. Nott Memorial was built as the focal point of a long-unrealized plan for Union College, founded in 1795. After serving in several capacities, it was restored in the 1990s and is now used for meetings and exhibitions.

■ *Schoharie County*

## OLD BLENHEIM BRIDGE
**New York Route 30 over Schoharie Creek, North Blenheim**

Appearing as if it belonged in a Currier and Ives print, this is one of the longest single-span wooden covered bridges in the world, stretching 210 feet across Schoharie Creek. Old Blenheim Bridge was constructed in 1855 by Vermonter Nicholas Montgomery Powers, who received $6,000 for his work. The bridge was in use until 1932, when a new span was built downstream alongside it.

■ *Schuyler County*

## LAMOKA
**Address Restricted, Tyrone**

This type site for the Lamoka phase has been described as "the largest recorded Archaic site in New York State and probably in the whole Northeast." Excavations conducted here in the 1920s provided the first clear evidence that an Archaic hunting and gathering culture existed in the northeast ca. 3000 B.C., thousands of years before European contact. At the time, this was far from being a generally accepted concept. The site, on a shallow stream between two lakes, is privately owned.

■ *Seneca County*

## ROSE HILL
**Route 96A, Fayette**

Rose Hill is one of the finest and best-preserved domestic examples of Greek Revival architecture in the United States. Built in 1837–1839, the U-shaped frame mansion is fronted by a monumental Ionic portico. A square belvedere astride the ridge of the roof provides views over Lake Geneva, which the house faces. Big, bold, beautiful—Rose Hill is a vivid testament to the prosperity the Erie Canal brought to western New York. After a period of decline, Rose Hill was restored in the 1960s and is now open as a historic house museum.

## ELIZABETH CADY STANTON HOUSE, (NPS)
**32 Washington Street, Seneca Falls**

Elizabeth Cady Stanton, one of the great figures in the struggle for women's rights, initiated the suffragette movement. While living in this simple frame house, she and Lucretia Mott organized the first women's rights convention, held in Seneca Falls in 1848. They composed a "Declaration of Sentiment," drafted in the style of the Declaration of Independence, for the convention. At Stanton's insistence it included a resolution advocating women's right to vote. Her Seneca Falls home is now the major component of the Women's Rights National Historical Park. (See Elizabeth Cady Stanton House, Bergen County, New Jersey.)

■ *Suffolk County*

## FIRST PRESBYTERIAN CHURCH
**44 Union Street, Sag Harbor**

Sag Harbor was a booming whaling port in the first half of the 19th century, and this church, built in 1843–1844 by wealthy ship owners, captains, and businessmen, reflects the town's aspirations. Designed by Minard Lafever, the clapboarded building is one of the most important examples of the Egyptian Revival style in the country. Unfortunately, the original 185-foot steeple, said to have been modeled on a mariner's spyglass, was destroyed by a hurricane in 1938 and not rebuilt.

## FORT CORCHAUG ARCHEOLOGICAL SITE
**Address Restricted, Cutchogue, Town of Southold**

Resources at Fort Corchaug Archeological Site shed light on occupations in the Historic Contact period in Montauk country, an area encompassing the whole of eastern Long

*Thomas Moran House, East Hampton, Suffolk County, 1964. Courtesy of NPS.*

Island within present-day Suffolk County. Contributing cultural resources include an exemplary assemblage of deposits documenting social, political, and economic relations between Corchaug Indian people and colonists during the first half of the 1600s.

## THOMAS MORAN HOUSE
### 229 Main Street, East Hampton

Thomas Moran introduced Americans to the natural splendors of the West through paintings such as *The Grand Canyon of the Yellowstone* and *The Chasm of the Colorado.* These grand views were done after he returned from western expeditions in 1871 and 1873 and were so acclaimed that the U.S. Congress purchased them to hang in the Capitol. Moran built this shingled house and studio in 1884, living and working here for more than 30 years. The building is privately owned.

## WILLIAM SYDNEY MOUNT HOUSE
### Stony Brook Road and New York Route 25-A, Stony Brook

William Sydney Mount is noted for his genre paintings that capture and reflect his deep feeling for the land and people of his native Long Island. His bucolic works, painted in the mid–19th century, were extremely popular, and many of his paintings were reproduced in engravings and lithographs. Toward the end of his career Mount wrote, "Paint pictures that will take with the public—never paint for the few, but the many." Most of his work was produced in this shingled, vernacular house, a portion of which his maternal grandfather built as a tavern.

## OLD HOUSE
### New York Route 25, Cutchogue

"Old House" seems a singularly uninspiring name for this singularly distinguished example of early American domestic architecture. John Budd built the frame house in 1649, and when his daughter married ten years later, he moved it ten miles away and presented it to her as a wedding present. Details reflect the work of a master builder, and the casement window frames are considered among the finest of their type in the country. Old House was restored in 1940 and is now a historic house museum.

## JACKSON POLLOCK HOUSE AND STUDIO
### 830 Fireplace Road, East Hampton

From 1945 until his death in 1956, Jackson Pollock lived in this unpretentious shingled house and worked in its backyard studio, a former barn that he moved to the site in 1946. Pollock is considered one of the most revolutionary figures in the history of 20th-century art, and it was here that he mastered the technique of pouring and propelling paint through the air. Pollock's famous canvases are among the most forceful and challenging oeuvres of their time. The property is now operated by the Stony Brook Foundation as a study center.

*Jean Hasbrouck House, New Paltz, Ulster County, 1967. Courtesy of NPS (Charles W. Snell).*

■ *Sullivan County*

### DELAWARE AND HUDSON CANAL
**(Orange, Sullivan, and Ulster Counties)**

(Also in Wayne County, Pennsylvania — see entry under Orange County.)

■ *Tompkins County*

### MORRILL HALL, CORNELL UNIVERSITY
**Cornell University campus, Ithaca**

Ezra Cornell, founder of the university that bears his name, offered money to establish the institution if New York would grant it the state's share of federal lands available from the Morrill Land Grant Act of 1862. Morrill Hall, dating from 1866–1868, is the original building, and its opening marked a revolution in American higher education. Training was offered on the basis of equality among various disciplines to prepare students for useful careers in the post–Civil War era. Students could select courses, and subjects such as political science and modern literature became the peers of traditional studies such as Greek and Latin.

■ *Ulster County*

### JOHN BURROUGHS RIVERBY STUDY
**Between New York Route 9W and the Hudson River, West Park**

In 1865, the *Atlantic Monthly* published the first significant nature essay by a virtually unknown author. From then until his death in 1921, John Burroughs wrote about the natur-

al world, presenting his chosen subject in interesting, nonpedantic fashion to thousands of avid readers. In 1881 he built this small frame study in the yard of his "Riverby" estate overlooking the Hudson, and it served as his only writing studio until 1895. The study is within the John Burroughs Nature Sanctuary. (See also Slabsides and Woodchuck Lodge, Delaware County.)

### DELAWARE AND HUDSON CANAL
**(Orange, Sullivan, and Ulster Counties)**

(Also in Wayne County, Pennsylvania — see entry under Orange County.)

### JEAN HASBROUCK HOUSE
**Huguenot Street opposite the junction with North Street, New Paltz**

Built in two stages — a one-room house in 1694 that was enlarged in 1712 to become both home and store — this stone structure survives as the best example of a Flemish Colonial house in the country. Jean Hasbrouck was a native of Calais and member of a group of French Huguenots from Flanders and the Lower Rhine who settled in the New Paltz area. The Huguenot Historical Society maintains the house as a historic house museum.

### HUGUENOT STREET HISTORIC DISTRICT
**Huguenot Street, New Paltz**

This historic district consists of five stone houses that together form a remarkable picture of an early-18th-century Huguenot community. In 1677, refugees from Flanders and the Lower Rhine purchased the site of New Paltz from the Esopus Indians with 40 kettles, 40 axes, and lots of wampum.

## HURLEY HISTORIC DISTRICT
### Bounded by Hurley Street, Hurley Mountain Road, and Schoonmaker Lane, Hurley

Old Hurley is Dutch in everything but name, and it used to be Dutch in name as well; when it was established in 1661, the settlement was matter-of-factly named Nieuw Dorp (New Village). The district centers on ten stone houses that illustrate the 17th- and 18th-century Dutch heritage. Also included in the district, but outside the village cluster, are the ca. 1750 Hardenbergh House, early home of Belle Hardenbergh (better known as Sojourner Truth), and the Matthias Ten Eyck House, representative of the Dutch farmsteads that once surrounded Hurley.

## LAKE MOHONK MOUNTAIN HOUSE
### Northwest of New Paltz

Begun in the 1870s by the Smiley family as a healthful vacation retreat, Lake Mohonk has grown into a major resort. The Mohonk Mountain House, a Victorian confection embellished with porches, balconies, towers, and turrets, hugs the rugged shore of a glacial lake and is the centerpiece of a 7,500-acre nature preserve. Over the years the resort has hosted a number of conferences related to

humanitarian causes and world peace, reflecting the ideals of its Quaker founders.

## SLABSIDES
### West of West Park

From 1895 until 1921 this was the summer residence and retreat of noted scientist and nature writer John Burroughs. In 1865, the *Atlantic Monthly* published his first significant nature essay, and he continued to write at a prolific rate until his death in 1921. More than any writer of his time, Burroughs created a receptive climate for conservation legislation. His cabin is called "Slabsides" because of its bark-covered siding. (See also John Burroughs Riverby Study and Woodchuck Lodge, Delaware County.)

## ■ *Warren County*

## OWL'S NEST
### New York Route 9L, Lake George, Joshua's Rock

Edward Eggleston, one of America's earliest realistic novelists, was among the first to tap the literary potential of the country's frontier experience. He grew up along the Ohio River and became a Methodist circuit rider in Minnesota. He recalled his experiences in his novel *The Circuit Rider*, which appeared first in serial form in 1873–1874. After serving from 1874 to 1879 as a Unitarian pastor, Eggleston retired to Owl's Nest to devote his full attention to writing. His stone library,

*Slabsides, Ulster County. Courtesy of NPS.*

built in 1883, and the adjoining house, built a few years later, remain in private ownership.

## RADEAU *LAND TORTOISE*
### Address Restricted, Lake George

*Radeau,* French for "raft," refers to a craft whose flat-bottomed, platform-like construction and simple planking are suggestive of this most elementary, utilitarian type of vessel. As the only known survivor of its type, *Land Tortoise* is unique, and although it now lies at a depth of more than 100 feet, the radeau is remarkably well preserved. Built in 1758 by British and provincial forces to be used during the French and Indian Wars, it was deliberately scuttled within two days of its launching on Lake George, to be recovered the following year. That never happened, and in spite of its name, *Land Tortoise* has remained on the bottom of the lake ever since. It is accessible to the diving public as a New York State Submerged Heritage Preserve.

*Armour-Stiner House, Irvington, Westchester County. Courtesy of HABS (Thom Loughman).*

### ■ *Washington County*

## LEMUEL HAYNES HOUSE
### Route 149, South Granville

This little frame house, built in 1793, was the home of Lemuel Haynes from 1822 until his death in 1833. Haynes was a member of the Green Mountain Boys during the Revolution but gained fame afterward as the first ordained black minister in the United States and the first black to minister to a white congregation. A Congregationalist, Haynes was known both as a pulpit orator and as a scholarly theologian. He began his South Granville pastorate when he was 69 years old and is buried in the town cemetery a mile from his home.

### ■ *Westchester County*

## ARMOUR-STINER HOUSE
### 45 West Clinton Avenue, Irvington

Looking as if it might have landed from a Victorian version of outer space, perhaps something Jules Verne might have imagined, this is the only fully domed octagonal residence in the country. It is one of the largest examples of a unique building type inspired by Orson Squire Fowler, author of *A Home for All; or, a New, Cheap, Convenient and Superior Mode of Building.* Fowler also wrote books on sex, temperance, tight lacing, and matrimony.

## BOSTON POST ROAD HISTORIC DISTRICT
### Boston Post Road and Milton Harbor, Rye vicinity

This well-preserved district along the old Boston Post Road on the shore of Long Island Sound contains three architecturally significant houses, the Jay family cemetery, and the Marshlands Conservancy. One of the houses, the Gothic Revival "Whitby," was built in 1854 from designs by architect Andrew Jackson Davis. The district is closely associated with the family of John Jay, first chief justice of the U.S. Supreme Court and second governor of the State of New York, who is buried in the Jay cemetery.

## CROTON AQUEDUCT (OLD)
### Between Croton and New York City (Bronx, New York, and Westchester Counties)

(See entry under Bronx County.)

## JOHN W. DRAPER HOUSE
### Draper Park, 407 Broadway, Hastings-on-Hudson

John Wesley Draper, well known in mid-19th-century scientific circles, made significant contributions in physics and chemistry and authored important works in intellectual history. He is remembered for his pioneering work in photochemistry, especially for discoveries that contributed to the study of light diffraction and spectrum analysis. Draper was the first person to photograph the moon and the solar spectrum. The restored house in which he lived from 1840 until his death in 1882 is now the home of the Hastings Historical Society and open to the public twice a week.

## DUTCH REFORMED CHURCH
### North edge of Tarrytown on U.S. Route 9, North Tarrytown

Built ca. 1697 of rubblestone by the Philipse family, "Lords of the Manor" of Philipsborough, this early church is a reminder of the Dutch influence in colonial America. Its modest belfry topped with a weathervane contains a bell cast in Holland in 1685. In later years the old building gained fame when Washington Irving, who lies buried in its churchyard, wrote "The Legend of Sleepy Hollow." As the favorite haunt of the "headless horseman," the church and graveyard have ever since been associated with him and his victim—poor, hapless, gawky Ichabod Crane.

## JAY GOULD ESTATE
### 635 South Broadway, Tarrytown

Lyndhurst is one of the nation's finest examples of Gothic Revival architecture. Built of brick but faced in marble, it was built in 1838 for William Paulding, former mayor of New York City. A. J. Davis was the architect, and he designed enlargements for the second owner as well. In 1880, Jay Gould, a freewheeling financier in the era of unrestrained capitalism after the Civil War, purchased the estate. Gould is still remembered, and still vilified, for his attempt to corner the nation's gold market. In 1961 his daughter bequeathed the estate to the National Trust for Historic Preservation, and it is now open to the public.

## JOHN A. HARTFORD HOUSE
### 75 Grasslands Road, Valhalla

John Hartford, son of a founder of the Great Atlantic & Pacific Tea Company (A&P), the nation's first chain store, was the firm's merchandizing genius. With Hartford's no-nonsense policies of low inventory, low prices, no deliveries, and cash only, A&P's outlets grew from 480 in 1912, to 4,500 in 1920, to 15,700 in 1930. Hartford completed this stone Tudor Revival mansion in 1932 and lived here until his death in 1951. Still maintaining its residential character, Hartford Hall is now administrative headquarters for Westchester Community College.

*Dutch Reformed Church, North Tarrytown, Westchester County, 1967. Courtesy of NPS (Charles W. Snell).*

## JOHN JAY HOMESTEAD
### Jay Street, Katonah

John Jay was a major figure in the political history of our nation during its formative years, serving as president of the Continental Congress, secretary of foreign affairs, and first chief justice of the U.S. Supreme Court. He began his country house in February 1787, and its simple, unostentatious lines reflect the ideals of the man. "Here I enjoy liberty in a comprehensive sense and leisure which is neither vicious nor useless," he once declared. Now owned by the State of New York, Jay's house is open as a state historic site.

## THOMAS PAINE COTTAGE
### 20 Sicard Avenue, New Rochelle

Thomas Paine, pamphleteer and propagandist extraordinaire for both the American and French revolutions, first came to attention when he published *Common Sense* in January 1776. In his work, Paine urged the American colonies to unite against Britain, and he practiced what he preached by enlisting in the Continental army. With the outbreak of the French Revolution, he became a self-appointed missionary of world revolution. His *Rights of Man and The Age of Reason,* published in the 1790s, were further expressions of his beliefs. Paine spent the last seven years of his life, from 1802 until 1809, at this farm that the State of New York had given him. He is buried here, and his cottage is open as a historic house museum.

## PHILIPSBURG MANOR
### 381 Bellwood Avenue, Upper Mills

Frederick Philipse, associate of Peter Stuyvesant, came to the New World as official "carpenter" of the Dutch West Indies Company and founded an estate that eventually included some 90,000 acres. In the 1680s, at about the time he built Philipse Manor Hall downstream on the Hudson, he built a portion of this stone house, Philipsburg Manor, and a mill. By 1749 the house had doubled in size, and it was further enlarged after the Revolution, under new ownership. In 1951, thanks to John D. Rockefeller's philanthropy, the property was purchased, subsequently restored, and is now open to the public.

Philipsburg is interpreted as an illustration of a working Dutch-English manor at the height of its importance, ca. 1730–1740.

## PHILIPSE MANOR HALL
### Warburton Avenue and Dock Street, Yonkers

Erected in stages between 1682 and 1758, this brick and fieldstone house is one of the most notable relics of the Dutch colonial era in the country. The house was begun by Frederick Philipse and served as the social and administrative center of his Philipse Manor, or Manor of Philipsburg, which extended 20 miles along the Hudson River. The Manor Hall is open to the public as a state historic site.

## PLAYLAND AMUSEMENT PARK
### Playland Parkway and Forest Avenue, Rye

Conceived by the Westchester County Park Commission and opened in 1928, this first totally planned amusement park in America was designed specifically to accommodate automobile travelers. After more than 70 years, its Art Deco and Spanish Revival attractions remain essentially unaltered, and most of its original rides—the Whip, the Dragon Coaster, and the Derby Racer—continue to thrill. With its well-planned layout and attractive landscaping, Playland has served as a prototype for many contemporary theme parks. Its popularity continues, although annual attendance now seldom approaches the 3.8 million visitors who came in 1932 at the height of the Depression.

## JOHN D. ROCKEFELLER ESTATE
### Pocantico Hills, Mount Pleasant

Think what you will of the man and his methods, John Davison Rockefeller was responsible for epochal accomplishments in American industry, finance, and philanthropy. He grew wealthy in post–Civil War America by controlling the nation's oil industry, and when he retired as president of Standard Oil in 1896, he was considered the world's richest man. Rockefeller devoted his retirement years to worthy causes, focusing on institutions that advanced knowledge and human welfare. From 1893 until his death in 1937, Kykuit (from the Dutch for "lookout") in the

Pocantico Hills was his primary residence. Considering the means of its builder, the mansion was far less ostentatious than those built by other barons of the Gilded Age. Rockefeller's son Nelson willed Kykuit to the National Trust for Historic Preservation in 1979, and it is now open to the public.

## SUNNYSIDE
### Sunnyside Lane, Tarrytown

When Washington Irving returned home in 1832 after a 17-year European sojourn devoted largely to writing, he found himself regarded as America's foremost prose author. In 1835 he purchased an old stone house on the eastern bank of the Hudson and subsequently enlarged and remodeled it into Sunnyside, a charmingly romantic dwelling in what might be called a "faux Dutch" style. Irving published his first book, *A History of New York,* in 1809 under the pseudonym Diedrich Knickerbocker. He is best remembered for his 1819–1820 work, *The Sketch Book,* with its unforgettable characters. Rip Van Winkle, Ichabod Crane, and the headless horseman all gallivanted, or slept, not very far from Sunnyside. Irving's home is open to the public.

## VAN CORTLANDT MANOR
### U.S. Route 9, north of the intersection with U.S. Route 9A, Croton-on-Hudson

Begun in the late 17th century and finally occupied full-time in 1749, this manor house is nationally important as a document of colonial frontier culture in the Hudson Valley. Unlike larger Dutch manors downstream, it reflects the simpler and more rugged life of the frontier. The house, restored and open to the public, is an unusually fine, well-preserved specimen of Dutch-influenced colonial architecture.

## VILLA LEWARO
### North Broadway, Greenburgh

Villa Lewaro was designed by a prominent black architect for a black entrepreneur, who intended it to show what members of her race could accomplish. This winning twosome were Vertner Woodson Tandy, a 1909 graduate of Cornell who became New York's first licensed black architect, and cosmetics manufacturer Madame C.J. Walker, who accounted for her success by claiming, "I got myself a start by giving myself a start." The large Mediterranean style villa was completed in 1918 and is surrounded by lavish Italian style gardens, also designed by Tandy.

*Sunnyside, Westchester County. Courtesy of HABS (Patrick M. Burkhart).*

# NORTH CAROLINA

■ *Beaufort County*

## PALMER-MARSH HOUSE
### Main Street, Bath

One of North Carolina's oldest houses, this is a well-preserved example of a substantial building designed as both a place of business and a residence. At the time it was built in the mid-18th century, Bath was an important port. Now owned by the state, the handsome frame house, noted for its immense brick chimneys, is open to the public.

■ *Buncombe County*

## BILTMORE ESTATE
### U.S. Highway 25, Asheville

In 1888, George W. Vanderbilt, capitalist, conservationist, and amateur architect of sorts, began purchasing land in the mountains of western North Carolina, eventually amassing an estate of more than 125,000 acres. Frederick Law Olmsted helped develop the property, and in 1891 Vanderbilt appointed

*Palmer-Marsh House, Bath, Beaufort County, 1962. Courtesy of HABS (Jack E. Boucher).*

Gifford Pinchot superintendent of forestry management. Pinchot, fresh from studying managed forests in Europe, soon proved for the first time in America that scientific forest management was profitable. In 1898, Vanderbilt established the Biltmore Forest School, the first of its kind in the country. Vanderbilt's princely mansion, Biltmore House, was designed by Richard Morris Hunt and built between 1890 and 1895. Resembling a French chateau, the house, now open to the public, is one of the nation's most impressive and best-preserved mansions of the Gilded Age.

## THOMAS WOLFE HOUSE
### 48 Spruce Street, Asheville

Of all the major American novelists, Thomas Wolfe was perhaps the most autobiographical. He composed many passages, and created many characters, based on boyhood remembrances experienced in this large, rambling frame house. His mother bought it in 1906 and operated it as a boarding house, which she named "The Old Kentucky Home." Wolfe lived here until 1916, when he entered the University of North Carolina. Among his best-known works are *Look Homeward, Angel* (1929) and *You Can't Go Home Again* (1940). The state restored the house and furnished it as a memorial to its most famous occupant, but a fire in July 1998 caused extensive damage.

■ *Cabarrus County*

## REED GOLD MINE
### 11 miles southeast of Concord

Nuggets of "heavy yellow metal" found on John Reed's farm in 1799 set off the first gold rush in the United States and led to the opening of the earliest documented gold mining operation in the nation. North Carolina mines furnished much of the gold minted in Philadelphia before 1829, when gold was discovered in Georgia. The Reed mine was largely depleted by 1860. The property was purchased by the State of North

Chowan County
Courthouse,
Edenton, Chowan
County. Courtroom,
1940. Courtesy of
HABS (Thomas T.
Waterman).

Carolina in 1971 and designated a state historical site. Portions of the underground tunnels have been restored for guided tours.

■ *Caswell County*

## UNION TAVERN
### Main Street, Milton

This building, erected as a tavern, later became the workshop of Thomas Day, who moved to Milton in 1823. Day, a free black cabinetmaker, achieved recognition and success with the superior quality of his craftsmanship. By the mid-19th century, his workshop had the largest production and greatest number of apprentices in the state. Day counted among his clients the governor of North Carolina and many of the region's wealthy planters. In addition to furniture, Day crafted interiors, and a number of area homes display his workmanship. The tavern was extensively damaged by fire in 1989, but it is being restored by Thomas Day/Union Tavern Restoration, Incorporated.

■ *Chowan County*

## CHOWAN COUNTY COURTHOUSE
### East King Street, Edenton

This colonial courthouse, begun in 1767, is one of the most impressive Georgian public buildings in the south. Magnificently sited at the head of a broad lawn, or green, facing Edenton Bay, the brick structure is topped by a clock tower and cupola and is notable for its perfect proportions and chaste lines. Little altered, it retains its elaborate interior paneling and is still used for the purpose for which it was built.

## CUPOLA HOUSE
### 408 South Broad Street, Edenton

Dating from the 1750s, this extraordinary timber-framed house is a superb illustration of the transition from earlier Jacobean architecture to 18th-century Georgian. In all the southern states, it is the only house extant that carries a Jacobean "jetty," or overhang, at the second story. The roof is crowned by a large octagonal wooden cupola, giving the house its name. The house was restored in 1964–1966 and is open to the public.

## HAYES PLANTATION
### East Water Street Extension, Edenton

This imposing plantation house, dating from 1814–1817 and designed by William Nichols, is one of the South's most accomplished examples of a five-part Palladian villa. Built of frame, it has a central block with dependencies connected by curved hyphens, and a large belvedere above the central block provides expansive views across Edenton Bay. Hayes was built on the site of an earlier home that belonged to Samuel Johnston, who had been

*Cape Hatteras Light Station, Buxton vicinity, Dare County, ca.1893. Courtesy of U.S. Light House Board (Bamber).*

a major political leader in North Carolina during the War for Independence. He was president of the North Carolina Convention that ratified the U.S. Constitution and served as governor, and then U.S. senator, as well. Although it was long assumed that the present mansion was directly associated with Samuel Johnston, it was actually built by his son, James C. Johnston, after his father's death. Hayes, nationally significant architecturally, is privately owned.

## ■ *Cumberland County*

### MARKET HOUSE
**Market Square, Fayetteville**

Built in the 1830s, this structure is important as one of the few American examples of a familiar English building type: a combination market and town hall. Farmers and merchants sold produce and meat under the open first-floor arcade, and the second floor served as the town hall and general meeting place. The Market House is centrally located where four of Fayetteville's major streets converge, and its cupola bell still rings not only the hours, but also the times for breakfast, dinner, sundown, and curfew.

## ■ *Dare County*

### CAPE HATTERAS LIGHT STATION
**Cape Hatteras, Buxton vicinity**

Cape Hatteras is a prominent projection on North Carolina's famous Outer Banks—the long, low stretches of sandy beaches that protect the state's mainland, but have been the bane of existence for mariners for centuries. Protection was provided at the "Graveyard of the Atlantic," as the cape has been known for years, in 1803 when the first lighthouse was built. In 1854 it was heightened to 150 feet, and in 1870 the current brick tower was erected. Its height of 208 feet makes it the tallest lighthouse in the nation, and its well-known black and white spiral banding, its daymark, makes it a prominent landmark during daylight hours. In addition to the lighthouse, supporting structures—including the oil house and both the principal and assistant keeper's dwellings—also survive. All are popular daytime visitor attractions at the Cape Hatteras National Seashore, but at night the lighthouse continues to serve its prime purpose, guiding navigators around the cape. During the summer of 1999, the lighthouse was moved—inch by inch—to a new location a quarter mile from the original site. The move was necessitated by extensive beach erosion that threatened to destroy the lighthouse.

## MONITOR
### Address Restricted, Cape Hatteras

The short-lived USS *Monitor* launched on January 30, 1862, steamed into history the following March when it did battle with CSS *Virginia* (formerly the USS *Merrimac*) in Virginia's Hampton Roads channel. This was the first time two ironclad warships had fought, and *Monitor* soon became a legend as the "ship that saved the Union." Although that claim is an exaggeration, *Monitor* is rightly commemorated as the prototype of a class of ironclad, turreted warship that altered both naval technology and marine architecture in the 19th century. Designed by Swedish engineer John Ericsson, *Monitor* contained nascent innovations that helped revolutionize warfare at sea. It now rests in the "Graveyard of the Atlantic," off North Carolina's Cape Hatteras, having sunk on December 31, 1862, a month shy of its first birthday.

## ■ *Davie County*
### COOLEEMEE
#### Mocksville Vicinity

Constructed in 1850–1855, this monumental Italian villa is a prime example of the influence of mid-19th-century pattern books in the diffusion of architectural styles across the country. In this instance, Plate 32 in Volume I of W. H. Ranlett's *The Architect* was the model. Built in the form of a modified Greek cross, the stuccoed-brick house has four equal wings extending from a central octagonal core topped by an octagonal cupola. The cupola lights the central hall, which is dominated by an imposing spiral stairway.

## HINTON ROWAN HELPER HOUSE
### Mocksville vicinity

Hinton Helper's 1857 volume, *Impending Crisis in the South and How to Meet It,* condemned the institution of slavery on an economic, rather than a moral, basis. In his treatise, Helper argued that the planter oligarchy, the "lords of the lash," benefitted from slavery, while the majority of whites were left "in galling poverty and ignorance." Printed in large numbers, the treatise was used by Republicans in the 1860 elections and had an influence far more potent than *Uncle Tom's Cabin*. Helper lived here for the first 20 years of his life and returned in later years. The original log structure is now clapboarded and has modern frame additions.

## ■ *Durham County*
### W. T. BLACKWELL AND COMPANY TOBACCO FACTORY
#### 201 West Pettigrew Street, Durham

Bull Durham Smoking Tobacco was the first truly national brand of tobacco. From 1874 to 1957 it was manufactured, bagged, and labeled in this brick building, considered at one time the world's largest tobacco factory. W. T. Blackwell and Company introduced production, packaging, and marketing techniques that made Bull Durham part of American industrial history and folklore. At one time the famous trademark was emblazoned on the Egyptian pyramids.

## DUKE HOMESTEAD AND TOBACCO FACTORY
### 2828 Duke Homestead Road, Durham

This frame farmhouse, with its attendant log and frame buildings constructed for processing tobacco, was the home of the Dukes, the family most responsible for the development of the tobacco industry in the post–Civil War South. Here Washington Duke and his son James Buchanan Duke founded a family business that emerged into the American Tobacco Company, the nation's preeminent tobacco firm in the late 19th and early 20th centuries. The homestead was acquired by Duke University in 1931 and deeded to the state in 1973. The property is open to the public.

## NORTH CAROLINA MUTUAL LIFE INSURANCE COMPANY
### 114–116 West Parish Street, Durham

This 1921 building was the second home office of the North Carolina Mutual Life Insurance Company, founded in 1898. The company evolved out of a tradition of mutual benefit societies and fraternal organizations that had become second only to the church as an institution in African-American society by the early 20th century. From the time it was organized by its seven founders, North Carolina Mutual symbolized racial progress and the legacy of racial solidarity and self-help. The company eventually came to be regarded as the "World's largest Negro Business," and won Durham its reputation as the "Capital of the Black Middle Class."

## ■ Edgecombe County

## COOLMORE
### Route 3, Tarboro vicinity

Coolmore survives as one of the largest, finest, and best-documented examples of a mid-19th-century Italian villa in the South. The frame house was built in 1859–1861 from designs by Baltimore architect E. G. Lind, who gave it such characteristically Italianate features as arched window heads, bracketed cornices supporting broad eaves, and an ornamental cupola, or belvedere, astride its roof. The interior is particularly elaborate, with a profusion of wooden and plaster ornamentation, an elliptical stairway, and trompe l'œil paintings. A complete set of original plantation outbuildings surrounds the mansion, providing a vivid picture of antebellum life.

## ■ Forsyth County

## BETHABARA
### 2147 Bethabara Road, Winston-Salem

Moravians established Bethabara on their Wachovia lands in 1753. The community, whose name means "House of Passage," was the first colonial town in the Carolina Piedmont, but was intended to be a temporary settlement from which Salem and outlying farming villages would develop. However, Bethabara continued long after Salem was established. Archeological investigations have contributed to a significant understanding of Moravian culture, in particular the manufacture of pottery.

## OLD SALEM HISTORIC DISTRICT
### Winston-Salem

This remarkably well-preserved district is the center of Salem, a community established in 1766 by Moravians from Pennsylvania. This was a congregational town; its lands, plan, buildings, and industries were controlled by a governing board of church officials. The buildings, many open to the public, reflect in their architecture the German origin and communal organization of their builders, as well as the gradual absorption of both into American culture. Salem, the central community of Wachovia, a 100,000-acre tract of land bought by church officials in 1753, developed into the leading commercial center of Piedmont North Carolina. In 1849, Moravians sold 51 acres immediately north of Salem to found the Forsyth County seat of Winston, and in 1913 the two were joined as Winston-Salem.

## SALEM TAVERN
### 800 South Main Street, Winston-Salem

Built in 1784 to replace an earlier tavern, this substantial structure is an outstanding example of an 18th-century colonial ordinary (tavern). Salem's leaders wisely realized that a tavern was a necessity for the town to develop as a trading center, and this is reputed to have been the community's first brick building. Like everything else in Salem, it was built by the Moravian congregation, who kept title to the building and leased its operation to a tavern keeper. Among its other distinctions, the tavern can honestly claim that "George Washington slept here." On his Southern tour of 1791, he spent two nights in the northeast corner chamber. The restored tavern is now open to the public as a museum.

## SINGLE BROTHERS' HOUSE
### South Main and Academy Streets, Winston-Salem

The older half of this large building dates from 1768–1769 and is an outstanding example of Germanic half-timbered construction. It is also the oldest major building remaining in Salem, which had been established in 1766. As its name implies, this was a domicile for Moravian boys, who moved here when they were about 14 and remained until they married. The house also served as a trade school in which young apprentices learned their trades from master craftsmen. In 1786 growth of the community dictated an addition, which was built of brick and reflects the lessening of Germanic architectural tradi-

Coolmore, Edgecombe County, 1940. Courtesy of HABS (Thomas T. Waterman).

Old Salem Historic District, Winston-Salem, Forsyth County, North Carolina. Lick-Bonner House, 1969. Courtesy of NPS.

tions. Portions of the Single Brothers' House are open to the public as a museum.

### ■ Guilford County

### BLANDWOOD

**447 West Washington Street, Greensboro**

Blandwood is one of the nation's earliest Italian villas and is regarded as an important prototype of the Italianate style. In 1844, Governor John Motley Morehead hired architect Alexander J. Davis to remodel the frame farmhouse he had owned since 1827. Davis transformed the building into a Tuscan villa, complete with central tower, broad overhanging eaves, and twin dependencies connected by arcades. The house was threatened with demolition in the 1960s but was purchased by the Greensboro Preservation Society and restored. It is open to the public.

### ■ Henderson County

### CONNEMARA (NPS)

**North Carolina Route 1123, west of Flat Rock**

Carl Sandberg was the only American to receive Pulitzer Prizes in two different fields: biography—for *Abraham Lincoln: The War Years* (1939), and poetry—for *Complete Poems* (1950). In 1945 he moved with his family to this farm and remained until his death in 1967. The house, a mid-19th-century frame structure, was built for C. G. Memminger, secretary of the treasury for the Confederacy. It is now open to the public as the Carl Sandberg Home National Historic Site.

## ◾ *Johnston County*

### BENTONVILLE BATTLEFIELD

**Along North Carolina Routes 1008 and 1009, Newton Grove and Bentonville**

The Civil War Battle of Bentonville, lasting from March 19 through March 21, 1865, was the last time the Confederate army mounted an all-out offensive against Union forces. The Confederates, led by General Joseph Johnson, were trying to stop General William Sherman, who had run rampant from Atlanta to the sea and then turned north into the Carolinas. Their loss at Bentonville was the Confederacy's death knell, for it fatally weakened their last mobile field army. More than 90,000 combatants participated in the largest battle ever fought on North Carolina soil. A portion of the field is now a North Carolina Historic Site.

## ◾ *Montgomery County*

### TOWN CREEK INDIAN MOUND

**Address Restricted, Mount Gilead**

This site contains the remains of a temple mound, a minor temple, and a mortuary hut, all enclosed by a palisade. Excavations uncovered burials containing grave items, and domestic artifacts were found nearby, supporting the theory that there was an associated village at the site. It is believed that the complex was a major ceremonial center for outlying villages. Town Creek's remains also reflect the cultural changes western-migrating Native Americans experienced during the 16th to 18th centuries.

## ◾ *Moore County*

### PINEHURST HISTORIC DISTRICT

**Vicinity of the junction of North Carolina Routes 5 and 2, Pinehurst**

Pinehurst was founded in 1895 as an active recreational resort community by captains of American commerce, finance, and industry. Golf was the prime attraction, and the North Carolina sandhills proved a perfect spot for the many courses that Donald James Ross, a Scottish-born golf pro, designed and developed between 1900 and 1948. In addition to the courses that make Pinehurst the prototype of the American golf resort, the community has preserved its original network of curvilinear roads that embrace the village green and are lined with late-Victorian, Colonial Revival, and bungalow style houses, hotels, stores, and churches. Nearby, tennis courts, bowling greens, croquet courts, horse stables, and a racetrack beckon to non-golfers who seek other recreational activities.

## ◾ *New Hanover County*

### FORT FISHER

**U.S. Route 421, 18 miles south of Wilmington**

For nearly four years this earthen Confederate stronghold near the mouth of the Cape Fear River guarded the important port of Wilmington and protected the blockade runners on which the Confederacy relied to supply its troops. After the fall of Fort Morgan in Mobile Bay in August 1864, it became the last major coastal fortification in the Confederacy. When it fell in January 1865, the Confederacy was virtually isolated from the outside world, and the end was soon at hand. In the 1960s, the State of North Carolina acquired the fort and subsequently stabilized it. The site is open to the public.

### NORTH CAROLINA

**West bank of Cape Fear River, Wilmington**

The first launched, and subsequently the namesake, of a class of American battleships built just prior to World War II, USS *North Carolina* set a standard for shipbuilding technology combining high speed and powerful armament. Its superior performance during the Battle of the Eastern Solomons in August 1942 established the new primary role of this battleship class as the protector of aircraft carriers. *North Carolina* has the most impressive war record of any surviving American battleship that served in the Pacific during World War II, earning 15 battle stars for its service. "The Big Ship with the Big Past," now resting in the Cape Fear River across from downtown Wilmington, is open to an admiring public.

## ◾ *Orange County*

### NASH-HOOPER HOUSE

**118 West Tryon Street, Hillsborough**

This frame house was built in 1772 by Francis Nash, Revolutionary War hero and general who was killed at the Battle of Germantown. In 1782 it was bought by William Hooper and was his home until his death in 1790. Hooper, attorney general of North Carolina in 1770–1771, served in the colony's five provincial congresses and was a delegate to the Continental Congress from 1775 to 1777. He was also a North Carolina signer of the Declaration of Independence.

## OLD EAST
### Cameron Avenue, University of North Carolina, Chapel Hill

The first of the first, this brick structure is the first building constructed on the campus of the first state university in the nation to open its doors to students. Although the University of North Carolina was chartered in 1789, three years after the University of Georgia, it was the first to commence classes. For many years after Old East was completed in 1795, this single building housed the entire institution. Its present appearance dates from a mid-19th-century enlargement and alteration by architect Alexander Jackson Davis. Old East now serves as a dormitory.

## PLAYMAKERS THEATER
### Cameron Avenue, University of North Carolina, Chapel Hill

Completed in 1850, this small, perfectly proportioned Grecian temple is considered one of architect Alexander Jackson Davis's masterpieces. The building is of brick, stuccoed, and its portico columns have capitals composed of carved representations of wheat, corn, and tobacco, instead of the usual acanthus leaves of the Corinthian order. The building has been used for a number of purposes, including ballroom, library, chemistry lab, bathhouse (serving 500 students), and law classrooms. In 1925 it was dedicated as Playmakers Theater and has housed the Carolina Playmakers ever since.

## ■ Stanley County
## HARDAWAY SITE
### Address Restricted, Badin

During the Paleo-Indian to Early Archaic periods (12,000–6000 B.C.), prehistoric Indians journeyed to this promontory to exploit its lithic resources for manufacture of projectile points and stone tools. Over the years these activities created stratified cultural deposits as much as four feet in depth. Excavations at Hardaway have played a significant role in the development of archeological method and theory. The site has advanced understanding of the sequential development of prehistoric cultures in the eastern United States, particularly in regard to the earliest periods of human occupation.

## ■ Wake County
## CHRIST EPISCOPAL CHURCH
### 120 East Edenton Street, Raleigh

In 1847, when Christ Church was under construction, its minister wrote to its architect, Richard Upjohn, expressing the hope that the new building would "be the means of introducing a new style of church architecture in the south." His hopes were fulfilled. Designed in the early–English Gothic style, Christ Church set a precedent that was followed for many years in the region. The exemplary Gothic Revival building with its steeply pitched rooflines and stone tower and spire is considered one of Upjohn's finest exercises in the style. Excellently maintained, the church remains an ornament on Raleigh's Capitol Square and provides a fascinating architectural contrast with the Greek Revival Capitol across the way.

## JOSEPHUS DANIELS HOUSE
### 1520 Caswell Street, Raleigh

Josephus Daniels served as President Wilson's secretary of the navy from 1913 to 1921. During those pivotal years, he instituted policies aimed at making the Navy "a training school for democracy." Among his innovative and farsighted changes were introducing schooling for illiterate sailors, instituting vocational training, opening the Naval Academy to enlisted men, and enlisting women. Daniels began construction of this expansive Georgian Revival mansion in 1920, and it was his home until his death in 1948. It was acquired by the Masonic Order in 1950 and, with a large wing added in 1956–1958, continues to serve as a Masonic Temple.

## STATE CAPITOL
### Capitol Square, Raleigh

Built between 1833 and 1840 from granite quarried nearby, North Carolina's State Capitol is Greek Revival architecture at its most sophisticated and erudite. Details were inspired by various ancient prototypes, but the overall form and proportions were determined by the functions it was designed to house. The cruciform plan, imposing rotunda, two-story legislative chambers, rich detail, and superb stonework distinguish the building. The Capitol stands as an important representative work of three major 19th-century architects: Ithiel Town and Alexander Jackson Davis, who received the commission, and their Scottish collaborator, David Paton, who was in charge of construction. The building, still housing executive offices of the state's government, is open to the public.

# NORTH DAKOTA

### ■ Burleigh County

## MENOKEN INDIAN VILLAGE SITE
### Address Restricted, Menoken vicinity

This site includes the remains of some 20 earthen lodges, identified by depressions, most of which were enclosed by palisades inside a fortification ditch. Archeological significance is drawn from several possibly pre-Mandan artifacts and from architectural remains that may reflect transitional Mandan construction methods. It has been suggested that this was the village that La Verendrye first encountered during his 1738 expeditions into the northern Great Plains.

### ■ Mercer County

## BIG HIDATSA VILLAGE SITE (NPS)
### Address Restricted, Stanton vicinity

Occupied from about 1740 to 1850, this was the largest of three Hidatsa villages near the mouth of the Knife River and Fort Mandan, the 1804–1805 winter headquarters of the Lewis and Clark Expedition. The 15-acre site provides evidence of the effects of nearly a century of interaction with whites, primarily in connection with the fur trade. Big Hidatsa Village is thought to contain the best-defined earth lodge depressions of any major Native American site in the Great Plains.

### ■ Morton County

## HUFF ARCHEOLOGICAL SITE
### Address Restricted, Huff vicinity

The Huff Village is one of the best-known and best-preserved sites of the Mandan people, who had come to occupy such villages by ca. A.D. 1500, after having developed extensive trading networks over the previous 200 years. Located on the Missouri River, the village had a bastioned fortification system and a dense and regular arrangement of

*Huff Archeological Site, Huff Vicinity, Morton County. Palisade excavation, ca. 1961. Courtesy of the State Historical Society of North Dakota (Ray Wood).*

houses. Remains of these and a wide variety of material culture attest to the Mandan way of life. A large central house facing an open plaza gives evidence of a ritual space, reflecting the complex spiritual and ideological world the Mandan have maintained since historic contact.

## ■ Williams County

### FORT UNION TRADING POST (NPS)
**Fort Union Trading Post National Historic Site, Buford vicinity**

For four decades, from 1828 to 1867, this was the principal fur trading depot in the upper Missouri River region. Fort Union was the center of a vast trading empire that exchanged goods for hides with the Assiniboian, Crow, Blackfeet, Cree, Ojibwa (Chippewa), Mandan, Hidatsa, and Arikara tribes. The palisaded fort, measuring some 240 by 220 feet, was also the most solidly constructed post on the Missouri. During most of its existence, the American Fur Company operated it. The fort was dismantled in 1867, and its timbers used to enlarge the nearby army post of Fort Buford.

# OHIO

## ■ Adams County

### SERPENT MOUND
**5 miles northwest of Locust Grove on Ohio Route 73**

This giant earthen snake effigy, the largest and finest of its type in the country, probably dates from the Adena period (1000 B.C.–A.D. 200). The serpent extends a quarter of a mile in seven deep curves and is depicted in the act of uncoiling. The site, one of the first in the United States to be set aside because of its archeological value, is preserved and open to the public as Serpent Mound State Park.

## ■ Allen County

### MIAMI AND ERIE CANAL DEEP CUT
**2 miles south of Spencerville on Ohio Route 66**

Begun in 1825, the Miami and Erie Canal was the westernmost element in Ohio's extensive system of canals in the 19th century. Extending from Cincinnati to Toledo on Lake Erie, via Dayton, it was instrumental in bringing settlers into western Ohio and providing market access to farmers. The Deep Cut, a man-made trough cut through the earth, remains as one of the most important and best-preserved vestiges of the canal.

## ■ Ashtabula County

### JOSHUA R. GIDDINGS LAW OFFICE
**112 North Chestnut Street, Jefferson**

For most of his professional life, abolitionist and congressman Joshua Reed Giddings had his law office in this small two-room frame building. Giddings served in Congress from 1838 to 1859, and during that time his unwavering objective was to eliminate slavery by whatever means it might take. As a biographer has stated, although he was a "political pariah for much of his career, and a maverick for all of it, no Northern political figure did more to channel and move institutions against slavery."

## ■ Athens County

### MANASSEH CUTLER HALL
**Ohio University, Athens**

Begun in 1816 and completed in 1819, this three-story brick structure, whose wooden tower and cupola serve as a symbol for Ohio University, is the oldest college building in the Old Northwest. It was named for Manasseh Cutler, the eminent New England physician, botanist, and minister who wrote the university's charter and founded it in 1804. The building, which once contained the entire institution, now houses administrative offices.

■ *Brown County*

## U. S. GRANT BOYHOOD HOME
### 219 East Grant Avenue, Georgetown

From 1823, when he was brought here as an infant, until he left to enter the U.S. Military Academy in 1839 at age 17, this was the home of Ulysses Simpson Grant, 18th president of the United States. A typical middle-class brick town house of its period, it was built by Jesse R. Grant, Ulysses's father. Privately owned, the house has been restored and is open to the public as a historic house museum.

## JOHN P. PARKER HOUSE
### 300 Front Street, Ripley

A former slave, John Parker was one of many African-American conductors on the Underground Railroad, the means of escape for countless members of his race in the decades preceding the Civil War. His unflagging and heroic efforts to rescue escaped slaves from the "borderlands" along the Ohio River underscore the fact that African Americans were not only slaves and fugitives in these clandestine operations, but rescuers as well. Parker repeatedly slipped secretly back into slave territory to lead others to safety and freedom on the Ohio side of the river. He lived and operated an iron foundry at this site from ca. 1853 until his death in 1900.

## JOHN RANKIN HOUSE
### 6152 Rankin Road, Ripley

John Rankin's brick house stands high on a bluff overlooking the village of Ripley, the Ohio River, and northern Kentucky beyond. This pivotal location—coupled with the activities of its owner—made it one of the first stops on the Underground Railroad. From 1822 to 1865, Rankin, a Presbyterian minister, and his family assisted hundreds of escaped slaves on their trek to freedom. In addition, his 1826 *Letters on American Slavery* became standard reading for abolitionists throughout the country. Rankin related to Harriet Beecher Stowe the true story of one slave's dramatic escape to his house, and the tale of Eliza's crossing the ice-bound Ohio River became one of the most dramatic episodes in her *Uncle Tom's Cabin*. The

Rankin House is now operated as a state historic site and museum.

■ *Butler County*

## DONALD B
### 3106 Old A & P Road, East, Georgetown

Towboats have been an important part of the American transportation system since the 1850s and have moved barges on all the navigable waters of the Western Rivers. Built in 1923 as the first towboat for Standard Oil of Ohio, and first named *Standard,* this towboat inaugurated modern oil operations on the Ohio River. *Standard* was sold and renamed for the oldest son of its new owner in 1940. *Donald B* is now the only known 1920s diesel sternwheel towboat remaining in unchanged condition in the country, and continues to ply its trade on the Ohio River and its tributaries.

## LANGSTROTH COTTAGE
### 303 Patterson Avenue, Oxford

Apiculture, the art and science of caring for colonies of honeybees, is one of humankind's oldest forms of animal husbandry. In 1851, Lorenzo Lorraine Langstroth, Congregational minister, teacher, and apiarist, discovered the principle of "bee space" and invented a movable frame, making it possible to remove honey-laden combs from a hive without destroying it. From 1858 to 1887, Langstroth lived in this brick cottage, given him by his brother-in-law. Here he wrote *The Hive and the Honeybee,* the treatise explaining his work and discovery, the single most important innovation in the history of apiculture.

## WILLIAM H. MCGUFFEY HOUSE
### 401 East Spring Street, Oxford

William McGuffey built this two-story brick house and lived here from 1833 to 1836, during the period he was a professor of languages at Miami University. While living in the house, McGuffey compiled the first four of his six McGuffey Readers, elementary school texts that were printed in huge numbers and reached generations of Americans. Admonitions on thrift, hard work, and patriotism—all profusely illustrated—filled their pages, and helped revolutionize the nation's elementary education. The house is owned by Miami University and is maintained as a museum, library, and research center for material related to McGuffey. (See William H. McGuffey Boyhood Home Site, Mahoning County.)

## JOHN B. TYTUS HOUSE
### 300 South Main Street, Middletown

This large brick Romanesque Revival mansion was the lifetime home of John Butler Tytus, who invented and developed a practical hot, wide-strip, continuous steel-rolling process. His work was conducted during the 1920s and contributed significantly to the growth of the steel industry. By the 1930s sheet steel produced by the continuous mill process was in use throughout America, particularly in the automobile and electric appliance industries.

## ■ *Columbiana County*

## BEGINNING POINT OF THE U.S. PUBLIC LAND SURVEY
### On the Ohio-Pennsylvania boundary, East Liverpool

This is the point where the rectangular-grid land survey system established for "disposing of lands in the western territory" (the Old Northwest) began. As directed by the Ordinance of 1785, public lands were to be divided into townships six miles square, and each township was then subdivided into 36 sections of 1 square mile each. This was the first mathematically designed system adapted by any modern country, and its imprint remains indelible on the American landscape. The actual beginning point, on the northern shore of the Ohio River on the border between Ohio, Pennsylvania, and West Virginia (then Virginia), is now inundated, but a nearby marker commemorates the site. (Also in Beaver County, Pennsylvania.)

## ■ *Cuyahoga County*

## CLEVELAND ARCADE
### 401 Euclid Avenue, Cleveland

Begun in 1888 and completed in 1890, this is one of the few 19th-century glass-covered shopping arcades remaining in America. An engineering marvel in its day, the arcade comprises a grand 300-foot-long esplanade surrounded by five tiers of galleries. The intricate glass-and-steel skylight that crowns the composition is 290 feet long, 60 feet wide, and 104 feet above the ground. To ensure commercial success, the site was carefully chosen to connect two of Cleveland's major commercial arteries: Euclid Avenue and Superior Street. The arcade, a forerunner of today's indoor shopping malls, stands in remarkably unchanged condition.

*Cleveland Arcade, Cleveland, Cuyahoga County, 1966. Courtesy of HABS (Martin Linsey).*

## *COD*
### North Marginal Drive, Cleveland

This Gato class submarine was launched in March 1943 and dispatched to the western Pacific, where it operated out of Australia and the Philippines. *Cod* made seven war patrols, sinking 10 warships, 30 merchant ships, and damaging 7 other vessels. It was awarded seven battle stars for service in World War II. *Cod* remains in virtually original condition on Cleveland's Lake Erie waterfront. It is open to the public during summer months, and visitors have to climb down an access hatch, just as the submarine's wartime crew once had to do, to come aboard.

## OHIO AND ERIE CANAL (NPS)
### Ohio Route 631, Valley View Village

Completed in 1832, this eastern element of Ohio's 19th-century canal network united Cleveland and Portsmouth and connected Lake Erie to the Ohio River. Ohio's canals helped the state develop rapidly, spurring growth in population, industry, and commerce. One of the best-preserved sections of the Ohio and Erie Canal is this 1½-mile-long stretch south of Cleveland, including locks, an aqueduct, mills, and houses. The canal is now part of the Cuyahoga Valley National Recreation Area.

## ROCKET ENGINE TEST FACILITY
### Lewis Research Center, Cleveland

Built in 1956–1957, this facility at the Lewis Research Center pioneered the technology necessary to employ hydrogen as a rocket fuel. This work was critically important in the development of major vehicles such as the Centaur rocket and the upper stages of the Saturn V. The facility is not operational and not open to the public.

## ZERO GRAVITY RESEARCH FACILITY
### Lewis Research Center, Cleveland

This facility at the Lewis Research Center is the only one in the inventory of the National Aeronautics and Space Administration (NASA) where the physics of handling liquids in a zero-gravity environment are studied. Knowledge of characteristics of liquids in a low-gravity environment is essential in spacecraft design and crucial to the successful performance of high-energy, liquid-fuel spacecraft. Successful development of the Viking, Voyager, and Mariner spacecrafts was made possible by results of studies obtained here.

## ■ *Erie County*

## THOMAS A. EDISON BIRTHPLACE
### Edison Drive, Milan

This small brick cottage was the 1847 birthplace of Thomas Alva Edison, one of America's most illustrious and "inventive" inventors. His accomplishments in the development of the telegraph and the telephone, among others, are legion, and in 1929 the U.S. Congress awarded him a gold medal for

*Ohio and Erie Canal, Cuyahoga County. Tender's house and inn. Courtesy of HAER (Louisa Taft Cawood)*

his contributions to mankind. Although he left Milan in 1854, Edison always cherished the memory of this house; in 1906 he acquired it from his sister. It is now open to the public as a museum honoring him.

## HOTEL BREAKERS
### Cedar Point, Sandusky

Constructed in 1905, this is a major turn-of-the-century American summer resort hotel. Designed after the owner had visited the Loire Valley, it somewhat resembles a French château, but its overall impression is Victorian. Unlike many hotels of its type, the Breakers was built in conjunction with an amusement park. The hotel is of particular interest to football buffs: In the summer of 1913, Knute Rockne and Gus Dorais were lifeguards here, and they perfected the forward pass on the Lake Erie beach in front of the Breakers.

## SPACECRAFT PROPULSION RESEARCH FACILITY
### Lewis Research Center, Sandusky

Dating from 1968, this 38-foot-diameter by 55-foot-high stainless steel vacuum chamber is significant because of its association with the development of the Centaur rocket, which has launched some of America's most important space probes. The unique technical capabilities of the facility enabled engineers to hot-fire full-scale Centaur engines in simulated space conditions. The facility continues to test launch systems for the National Aeronautics and Space Administration, the U.S. Air Force, and other aerospace organizations.

## ■ *Fairfield County*
## JOHN SHERMAN BIRTHPLACE
### 137 East Main Street, Lancaster

John Sherman worked for his country in a number of capacities during his long career in public service: congressman, senator, secretary of the treasury, and secretary of state. He is remembered primarily because of two bills he introduced during his Senate career: the Sherman Anti-Trust Act (1890), the first

*Ohio Theater, Columbus, Franklin County. Courtesy of HABS.*

attempt by the federal government to regulate industry, and the Sherman Silver Purchase Act, passed the same year. Sherman's older brother, William Tecumseh Sherman, Union army general, was also born here. The house—much of it postdating Sherman's birth and occupancy—is maintained as a museum, largely devoted to the Civil War era.

## ■ *Franklin County*
## OHIO STATEHOUSE
### Broad and High Streets, Columbus

Considered one of the outstanding statements of the Greek Revival style in America, Ohio's capitol was begun in 1839 but not completed until 1861. Announcement of an architectural competition for its design resulted in more than 60 entries, and a number of America's foremost architects of the mid–19th century—including Henry Walters, Alexander J. Davis, and Isaiah Rogers—offered their talents. The statehouse is in the Doric order and is built of limestone. It is unusual in that the circular drum above the main block is not capped with a dome.

## OHIO THEATER
### 39 East State Street, Columbus

Built in 1928, this massive Spanish Baroque structure was designed during the "Golden

Age" of the movie palace by Thomas W. Lamb, one of America's most prolific and best-known theater architects. When the theater opened, *Motion Picture News* gushed that the "auditorium is probably as rich an interior as will be found in the country." Now fully refurbished after being threatened with demolition in 1969, the Ohio remains a magnificent example of one of the country's most extravagant building types ever conceived.

## CAPTAIN EDWARD V. RICKENBACKER HOUSE
### 1334 East Livingston Avenue, Columbus

From 1895 to 1922 this little shingled house was the residence of Edward Vernon Rickenbacker. A leading racecar driver prior to the First World War, Rickenbacker became a hero as an aviator. His feat of shooting down 26 German aircraft in less than six months established him as the "American Ace of Aces" and made him the idol of a whole generation of American youth. After the war, Rickenbacker devoted his energies to the developing commercial airline industry.

### ■ *Greene County*

## HUFFMAN PRAIRIE FLYING FIELD
### Wright-Patterson Air Force Base, Fairborn vicinity

After making aviation history in Kitty Hawk, North Carolina, where their *Wright Flyer I* made the world's first powered, sustained, and controlled airplane flight, Wilbur and Orville Wright returned to Dayton to conduct further tests and make refinements. During 1904 and 1905, they made 150 flight starts in what was then a 100-acre cow pasture east of Dayton. Here they perfected the technique of flying and developed an airplane able to bank, turn, circle, make figure eights, withstand repeated takeoffs and landings, and remain airborne for more than half an hour. The field, now within the Wright-Patterson Air Force Base, remains much as it did when the Wrights knew it. (See Hawthorn Hill, Wright Cycle Company and Wright and Wright Printing, *Wright Flyer III*, Montgomery County.)

## COLONEL CHARLES YOUNG HOUSE
### Columbus Pike between Clifton and Stevenson Roads, Wilberforce

Charles Young was the third African American to graduate from the U.S. Military Academy at West Point, the highest-ranking black officer in World War I, and the first black military attaché in American history. In addition to his military achievements, he was an accomplished musician and linguist. Young lived in this house while teaching at Wilberforce University from 1894 to 1898. The National Afro-American Museum was established on the campus of the university.

### ■ *Guernsey County*

## S BRIDGE, NATIONAL ROAD
### On U.S. Route 40, 4 miles east of Old Washington

Constructed in 1828, this single-arch stone structure carried the National Road over Salt Fork. Originally ending at Wheeling, on the Ohio River, the National Road was extended through Ohio between 1825 and 1837 and became one of the major thoroughfares for settlement and development in what had been the Old Northwest Territory. The bridge's span over the stream is straight, but the approach curves on either side, giving the appearance of the letter *S* in plan.

### ■ *Hamilton County*

## BAUM-TAFT HOUSE
### 316 Pike Street, Cincinnati

One of the earliest grand mansions in Ohio, this elegant Federal style villa was built ca. 1820 by Martin Baum, one of Cincinnati's prominent entrepreneurs. It stands as an eloquent reminder of the prosperous times when Cincinnati was known as "The Queen City of the West." The house later served as the home of Charles Phelps Taft, whose half-brother, William Howard Taft, accepted the presidential nomination from the portico in 1908. Charles Phelps Taft bequeathed the house and the family's collections of paintings, oriental porcelains, and sculpture to the city of Cincinnati. The house is open to the public.

S Bridge, National Road, Old Washington, Guernsey County. Courtesy of NPS.

## CAREW TOWER-NETHERLAND PLAZA HOTEL

### West Fifth Street and Fountain Square, Cincinnati

Built at the beginning of the Great Depression, this hotel/office/shop complex is one of the finest examples of Art Deco, skyscraper modernism in America. Chicago architect Walter W. Ahlschlager, who had already designed dramatic theater spaces such as the flamboyant Roxy in New York, provided equally impressive decorations and vistas here. These public spaces virtually epitomize the 1920s Jazz Age, an embodiment of speed, high style, and a mass-market machine age. The block-square complex cost $33 million, an enormous sum for the time, and was finished in 13 months by crews working 7 days a week, 24 hours a day. Most of the decorative work had been created in France several years prior to construction in Cincinnati and was exhibited at the 1925 Exhibition of Decorative Art in Paris. The complex continues to operate in its original functions.

## CINCINNATI MUSIC HALL

### 1243 Elm Street, Cincinnati

This mammoth Victorian Gothic structure, built in 1878 from designs by Cincinnati architect Samuel Hannaford, included a central auditorium—the music hall—and wings that contained industrial exhibition halls. It was, in short, an early example of a civic center. The Music Hall also illustrates the musical traditions of the German-American *Saengerfests,* or Singing Festivals, essential components of the cultural tradition of Germans who settled in the United States in the 19th century.

## CINCINNATI OBSERVATORY

### 3489 Observatory Place, Cincinnati

In the late 19th century, the Cincinnati Observatory was known worldwide for its endeavors in the field of proper motions, gravitational studies, and sidereal astronomy, including double stars, nebulae, and clusters. It is nationally significant for the publication of *Stellar Proper Motions,* which provided data important in determining the structure and rotation of the Milky Way and data utilized in modern cosmological theories, such as the "Big Bang." It is also significant for its association with internationally renowned astronomer Paul Herget, who was director of the observatory from 1946 to 1978.

## CINCINNATI UNION TERMINAL

### 1301 Western Avenue, Cincinnati

One of the last grand-scale railroad terminals in the world, this huge Art Deco masterpiece was designed by the New York firm of Fellheimer and Wagner, who employed Paul Cret as aesthetic adviser. The terminal, built between 1929 and 1933 and originally covering 287 acres, was conceived to replace a

*Cincinnati Union Terminal, Cincinnati, Hamilton County. Courtesy of the Cincinnati Preservation Association Collection (Richard N. P. Stewart).*

*Covington and Cincinnati Suspension Bridge, Covington, Kenton County, Kentucky, and Cincinnati, Hamilton County, Ohio. Courtesy of HAER (Jack E. Boucher).*

number of decaying stations serving different rail lines. Beautifully engineered, it was planned to accommodate 17,000 people and 216 trains daily. The terminal, a distinctive round-arched, semispherical dome, still serves a reduced volume of rail traffic, and its major spaces now contain a variety of innovative museum exhibits.

## CINCINNATI ZOO HISTORIC STRUCTURES
### Vine Street, Cincinnati

The second-oldest zoo in the country, the Cincinnati Zoo opened to the public in September 1875, 14 months after the Philadelphia Zoo. Significant for the antiquity and richness of its collections and for its continuing efforts in the propagation and nurturing of rare and endangered species, it was well known as the home of "Martha," the last passenger pigeon, who died in 1914. The Aviary, where she lived, and the original Monkey House and Herbivore (Elephant) House are the zoo's earliest surviving structures. Their exotic architecture reflects the fact that they were designed to house out-of-the ordinary inhabitants.

## COVINGTON AND CINCINNATI SUSPENSION BRIDGE
**Spanning the Ohio River between Covington, Kentucky, and Cincinnati**

At the time of its completion in 1867, this suspension bridge, with its 1,057-foot span, was the longest in the world, taking the honor from the Wheeling Suspension Bridge upstream on the Ohio. John A. Roebling, who went on to design an even longer span with his Brooklyn Bridge, was its architect/engineer. Cables supporting the span are hung from huge stone towers with open arches 75 feet high and 30 feet wide. The bridge continues to provide a link between Kentucky and Ohio and is maintained by the Kentucky Department of Highways. (Also in Kenton County, Kentucky.)

## GLENDALE HISTORIC DISTRICT
**Ohio Route 747, Glendale**

Established in 1851, concurrently with the railroad on which it depended, this is one of the first residential subdivisions in America, certainly the oldest in Ohio, that remains a separate and complete entity, with its original layout—and many of its original houses—intact. Glendale's curvilinear street plan, based on topographical considerations, was a radical departure from the typical grid patterns generally employed at the time.

## MAJESTIC
**Ohio River below Central Bridge, Cincinnati**

"Showboat's a'coming, there's dancing tonight." Between 1831 and the 1920s, more than 50 showboats carried circuses and dramatic productions to towns large and small lining the rivers of America. Their eagerly awaited arrivals, generally announced by the sounds of the calliope, were occasions for celebration. Now only two survive: *Majestic* and *Goldenrod*. Built in 1923, *Majestic* brought pleasure to towns on the Mississippi and Ohio Rivers and their tributaries until World War II. The City of Cincinnati bought *Majestic* in 1967 and refurbished it for waterfront performances. (See *Goldenrod*, Saint Louis City, Missouri.)

## GEORGE HUNT PENDLETON HOUSE
**559 East Liberty Street, Cincinnati**

From 1879 until his death ten years later, George Hunt Pendleton lived in this brick house high on Cincinnati's Liberty Hill. Parker, a lawyer and politician, gained national fame during his term as a U.S. senator (1879–1885) by spearheading civil service reform. Meeting in this house in 1882, he and his Senate subcommittee drafted the Pendleton Act, creating the civil service merit system. The Civil Service Commission met here for the first two years of its existence.

## PLUM STREET TEMPLE
**Eighth and Plum Streets, Cincinnati**

"Moorish cathedral" may be a contradiction in terms, especially when applied to a synagogue, but it seems to fit the bill in describing this imposing and unusual building with its twin minarets towering above the facade. Built in 1865–1866, from designs by Cincinnati architect James Keys Wilson, Plum Street Temple is one of the nation's most significant and best-preserved Moorish Revival buildings. Dr. Isaac Mayer Wise, rabbi at the time of construction, was an important figure in American Judaism. Under his leadership, Cincinnati became a center for Reform Judaism in America.

## ALPHONSO TAFT HOME (NPS)
**2038 Auburn Avenue, Cincinnati**

This is the birthplace and boyhood home of William Howard Taft, 27th president of the United States (1909-1913). Taft's administration was noted for dissolving monopolistic trusts and for passage of notable reform legislation. After he retired from the presidency, Taft became a law professor at Yale University, his alma mater, and was later appointed chief justice of the U.S. Supreme Court. His

Auburn Avenue house is now open to the public as the William Howard Taft National Historic Site.

## ■ *Jefferson County*

## BENJAMIN LUNDY HOUSE
**Union and Third Streets, Mount Pleasant**

During his brief stay in this brick row house in 1820–1821, abolitionist Benjamin Lundy established his influential antislavery newspaper, *Genius of Universal Emancipation*. Lundy's paper was one of the germinal chronicles of the antislavery movement in America, and he is regarded as the most important figure in antislavery reform during the decade of the 1820s. At a time when few were willing to confront the issue, he was "virtually the only person in the entire land willing to make antislavery agitation his career."

## ■ *Lake County*

## JAMES A. GARFIELD HOME (NPS)
**1059 Mentor Avenue, Mentor**

From 1876 until his death five years later, James Abram Garfield, 20th president of the United States, called Lawnfield home. He enlarged the house soon after his purchase by adding a second story and an attic, as well as the famous "front porch" from which he conducted his presidential campaign. Garfield had been selected by the Republican Party in 1880 as its "dark horse" candidate for the presidency. His small campaign office, where he received news of his presidential victory via telegraph, stands in the yard. What sort of president he would have made is unknown. Four months after his inauguration, on July 2, 1881, Garfield was fatally wounded by an assassin and died on September 19. Lawnfield is open to the public as a historic house museum.

## KIRTLAND TEMPLE
**9020 Chillicothe Road, Kirtland**

Built from 1833 to 1836 by members of the Church of Jesus Christ of Latter Day Saints, or Mormons, during their brief sojourn in Ohio, this structure combines Federal and Gothic Revival design elements. The exterior resembles New England meetinghouses of the period, but the interior arrangements, dictated by Mormon tenets, are quite different. The temple contains two auditoriums, each with several pulpits, and displays excellent craftsmanship. Brigham Young, soon to lead the Saints, worked on the building as a plasterer and glazier. The temple is maintained by the Reorganized Church of Jesus Christ of Latter Day Saints and is open to the public.

## ■ *Licking County*

## NEWARK EARTHWORKS
**Roughly bounded by Union, 30th, James, and Waldo Streets, and Ohio Route 16, Newark**

These earthworks provide mute testimony to the building skills of the Hopewell people. Notable for the precision of their layout and their great size — the earthworks likely covered some two square miles — they consisted of circular, rectangular, and polygonal works connected by parallel walls. Numerous mounds are also present. The Hopewell culture flourished from ca. 300 B.C. to ca. A.D. 250 and was centered in this area. The earthworks are now in the Mound Builders State Memorial.

*Kirtland Temple, Kirtland, Lake County. Elevated pulpits. Courtesy of HABS.*

*Newark Earthworks, Newark, Licking County. Courtesy of NPS (Francine Weiss).*

## ■ *Lorain County*

### WILSON BRUCE EVANS HOUSE
**33 East Vine Street, Oberlin**

Constructed in 1854–1856, this Italianate brick house was the home of Wilson Bruce Evans, a leading African-American abolitionist and member of Oberlin's commercial and educational communities. Evans and his brother Henry participated in the dramatic 1858 Oberlin-Wellington Rescue, saving an escaped slave who had been captured and was to be taken back to his owner in Kentucky. This was one of several well-publicized confrontations resulting from the Fugitive Slave Act of 1850 and was significant in fueling the nation's sectional differences prior to the Civil War.

### JOHN MERCER LANGSTON HOUSE
**207 East College Street, Oberlin**

John Mercer Langston was the first African American known to have been elected to public office. In 1855 he was chosen as township clerk in Brownhelm, Ohio, but a year later he moved to Oberlin, where he foresaw greater opportunities for his law practice. From 1856 to 1867 he lived with his family in this simple clapboard structure. Langston later served in the Freedman's Bureau and was the first dean of the Howard University Law School, which he organized. President Hayes

appointed him minister to Haiti in 1877. When he returned to the United States, he became a member of Congress from Virginia, the first African American to be elected from the Old Dominion.

### OBERLIN COLLEGE
**Tappan Square, Oberlin**

Founded in 1833 as Oberlin Collegiate Institute, Oberlin developed into a socially and politically influential college during the years immediately preceding the Civil War. Oberlin made the education of African Americans and women a matter of institutional policy. The admittance of four women in 1837 marked the beginning of coeducation on the collegiate level in the United States. Free African Americans were admitted on the same basis as whites, and John Mercer Langston (see the preceding entry) was one of the school's first black graduates.

## ■ *Lucas County*

### FALLEN TIMBERS BATTLEFIELD
**On U.S. Route 24, 2 miles west of Maumee**

The Battle of Fallen Timbers was the culminating event in the nation's efforts to secure control of the Old Northwest Territory from Native Americans. "Mad Anthony" Wayne's victory here on August 20, 1794, asserted American sovereignty and led to the Treaty

*Paul Laurence Dunbar House, Dayton, Montgomery County. Courtesy of NPS (Joseph S. Mendinghall).*

of Green Ville, in which the Indians ceded their claims. The battle and treaty ensured a period of peaceful settlement in the Ohio Country. The battlefield site is administered by the Ohio Historical Society as a memorial and is open to the public.

### EDWARD D. LIBBEY HOUSE
**2008 Scottwood Avenue, Toledo**

Edward Drummond Libbey revolutionized the American glass industry. One of the world's most successful glass manufacturers, he set standards for the industry as head of the Libbey Glass Company, the Owens Bottle Company, and Libbey-Owens Sheet Glass. Under his aegis, glass manufacture was transformed from an operation depending on procedures that had prevailed for centuries, to a machine age process. From 1895 until his death in 1925, Libbey lived in this Queen Anne–Shingle Style house designed by David L. Stine, the same architect who had designed the Libbey pavilion at the 1893 Columbian Exposition in Chicago.

### ■ *Mahoning County*

### WILLIAM H. MCGUFFEY BOYHOOD HOME SITE
**McGuffey Road, Coitsville Township**

In 1802, the McGuffey family moved from Pennsylvania to Ohio. William Holmes McGuffey was then two years old, and he remained here until 1817, when he left for further schooling. Later a college professor, McGuffey achieved fame as the author of the McGuffey Readers, a six-volume series of texts that had an enormous influence on the nation's elementary education. They were in common use across the nation for more than 70 years, and some 122 million copies were sold. (See William H. McGuffey House, Butler County.)

### ■ *Marion County*

### WARREN G. HARDING HOME
**380 Mount Vernon Avenue, Marion**

Warren Gamaliel Harding, 29th president of the United States (1921–1923), lived in this clapboarded two-story house for most of his adult life. He and his wife had designed it a year before their marriage in 1891. Like an earlier president from Ohio, James A. Garfield, Harding conducted his campaign largely from the expansive front porch of his home. Like the Garfield House, Harding's home has a one-story building in the yard that served as official campaign headquarters. Mrs. Harding bequeathed the house to the Harding Memorial Foundation, which operates it as a museum and memorial.

### ■ *Montgomery County*

### PAUL LAURENCE DUNBAR HOUSE
**219 North Summit Street, Dayton**

For the last three years of his life, from 1903 until 1906, this brick house was home to

Paul Laurence Dunbar, the distinguished African-American poet. His poetic use of dialect to convey both the joys and sorrows of an oppressed people brought him national acclaim. Dunbar was only 34 when he died, and a sense of his frustration at the end of the day is revealed in the two lines of a poem he never finished:

*I have asked so little of life.*
*How strange that she should deny it.*

His mother maintained the house in his native Dayton until her death in 1934. It was then bought by the State of Ohio; it is open to the public and is preserved as a loving memorial to the "poet laureate of his race."

## HAWTHORN HILL
### 901 Harmon Avenue, Oakwood

Fronted by a giant-order Ionic portico, this large white-brick Georgian Revival mansion clearly reveals the wealth and fame Wilbur and Orville Wright achieved after their invention—and successful first flight—of the airplane. Wilbur and Orville both helped design Hawthorne Hill; however, Wilbur died in 1912, two years before it was completed. Many of the mechanical features were designed by Orville, who lived here until his death in 1948, entertaining the greats and near greats in the history of American aviation. After his death, the National Cash Register Corporation bought the mansion for use as a guest house for visiting dignitaries. (See Wright Cycle Company and Wright and Wright Printing, *Wright Flyer III;* Huffman Prairie Flying Field, Greene County.)

## CHARLES F. KETTERING HOUSE
### 3965 Southern Boulevard, Kettering

From 1914 until his death in 1958, Charles Franklin Kettering, founder of the Dayton Engineering Laboratories Company (Delco), lived in this handsome Tudor Revival mansion. More than anyone else, Kettering, who headed the General Motors Research Corporation from 1920 to 1947, influenced the technological developments of the automobile. He developed the first electric starter, was responsible for the promotion of the gasoline engine, and also helped make

possible the conversion of the nation's railroads from steam to diesel power. American transportation as we know it is largely due to Kettering. In 1994 the original house burned down; the reconstructed house is now a conference center for the Kettering Medical Center.

## SUNWATCH SITE
### 2301 West River Road, Dayton

Sunwatch, formerly known as the Incinerator Site, is located on the west bank of the Great Miami River within the city limits of Dayton. Ceramics found on the site, radiocarbon dates, and other evidence indicate that the site was probably occupied for fewer than 25 years during the late 12th and early 13th centuries A.D., though the village was carefully laid out and encircled by a stockade. The site is one of the best-preserved and most completely excavated and analyzed archeological village sites associated with the post–Archaic Eastern Farmers. It is now operated as a museum.

## WRIGHT CYCLE COMPANY AND WRIGHT AND WRIGHT PRINTING
### 22 South Williams Street, Dayton

From 1895 to 1897, Wilbur and Orville Wright manufactured bicycles on the first floor of this brick building and operated a printing shop on the second floor. The two years they spent working with sprockets, spokes, chain drives, tires, metals, and machines were of inestimable value in preparing the brothers for their subsequent success with gliders and flying machines. In addition, the profits they realized here helped finance their later experiments. The shop, integral to the development of the airplane, has been restored and is open to the public. (See Hawthorn Hill, *Wright Flyer III;* Huffman Prairie Flying Field, Greene County.)

## *WRIGHT FLYER III*
### Carillon Park, 2001 South Patterson Boulevard, Dayton

This muslin-over-wood biplane, constructed in 1905, was one of the three experimental flyers the Wright brothers designed and built in their quest to develop a practical airplane.

With *Flyer III* they perfected a plane completely controlled by the pilot, capable of banking, turning, circling, and even making figure eights in the air. For all practical purposes, they had completed their conquest of the air. Over the years, *Flyer III* was disassembled and its parts put on display at several locations. In 1947, with Orville Wright providing direct supervision, the parts were reassembled, replacement elements fabricated where necessary, and *Flyer III* was reconstructed. The plane that ushered in the age of aviation is on display in Wright Hall at Dayton's Carillon Park. (See Hawthorn Hill, Wright Cycle Company and Wright and Wright Printing, Huffman Prairie Flying Field, Greene County.)

### ◼ *Ottawa County*

## JAY COOKE HOME
**Put-in-Bay, Gibraltar Island**

One of Jay Cooke's popular sobriquets was the "Napoleon of Finance." Like the diminutive Corsican, Cooke was brilliant and daring in his campaigns—although his were monetary, not military. His Civil War bond selling campaigns gave important financial support to the Union cause. An idea of the scope of his influence is gleaned from the fact that his banking firm's failure caused the national financial panic of 1873. Cooke was forced to sell this Italianate stone house on Gibraltar Island in Lake Erie, where he had summered since 1865. "Our Modern Midas," as he was also called, later recovered his fortune and repurchased the house in 1880. His last entry in the property's record book states "God be praised for the happiness we have enjoyed here." Cooke died a year later, in 1905. The island is now owned by Ohio State University, and his house is a men's dormitory.

## JOHNSON'S ISLAND CIVIL WAR PRISON
**Sandusky Bay**

Johnson's Island in Sandusky Bay, an arm of Lake Erie, was a major federally operated prisoner of war camp during the Civil War. The wooded island was close to Sandusky, where provisions could be obtained, and small enough to be easily managed. The prison was designed to house 1,000 prisoners, but at times more than 3,000 Confederates, most of them officers, were confined on the island. Much of the island has been developed in recent years, but significant archeological sites remain, and the Confederate cemetery serves as a poignant reminder of Johnson's Island's place in history.

*Jay Cooke Home, Ottawa County, 1965. Courtesy of NPS.*

## ■ Ross County

### HOPETON EARTHWORKS (NPS)
**Address Restricted, Hopetown**

These earthworks, part of a large Hopewell-ian ceremonial center, are a fine example of the work of the Hopewell people (300 B.C.–A.D. 250). Although the structures have been reduced by erosion and cultivation, they are discernible from the air. The site ranks among the largest of the Hopewellian earth-work centers and represents a truly monumental investment of labor in public architecture. Hopeton relates to the Mound City Group, across the Scioto River, and has been a unit of Hopewell Culture National Historical Park since 1980. Together the two sites are important for the information they have revealed about the Hopewell culture.

## ■ Sandusky County

### SPIEGEL GROVE
**1337 Hayes Avenue, Fremont**

Completed in 1863 and later enlarged, Spiegel Grove was first the summer home, and later the year-round home, of Rutherford Birchard Hayes, 19th president of the United States. A library/museum housed in a separate structure built in the 1930s preserves family memorabilia and serves as the repository for Hayes documents. Both the president and his wife are buried on the estate, which is open to the public as the Rutherford B. Hayes State Memorial.

## ■ Shelby County

### PEOPLE'S FEDERAL SAVINGS AND LOAN ASSOCIATION
**101 East Court Street, Sidney**

Completed in 1918 from designs by architect Louis Sullivan, this architectural gem—small in scale, exquisite in detail, colorful in material—makes a strong and individualistic architectural statement in its small-town Midwestern setting. The building was executed late in Sullivan's career and is one in the series of commissions that profoundly influenced 20th-century architecture. He considered it one of his best works, and it remains in virtually pristine condition, continuing to serve its original use. Patrons still enter under a mosaic panel inscribed with a single word: *Thrift*.

*William McKinley Tomb, Canton, Stark County. Courtesy of AASLH (George R. Adams).*

## ■ Stark County

### WILLIAM MCKINLEY TOMB
**Westlawn Cemetery, Canton**

This large circular, domed mausoleum, completed in 1907, is the resting place of William McKinley, 25th president of the United States (1897–1901). McKinley's election in 1896 began an era of Republican dominance and of American expansion in the Caribbean and the Far East. On September 6, 1901, he was wounded by an assassin while standing in a reception line at the Pan-American Exposition in Buffalo, New York, and died a week later.

## ■ Summit County

### STAN HYWET HALL
**714 North Portage Path, Akron**

This outstanding example of Tudor Revival architecture was built in 1911–1915 by Frank Augustus Seiberling, founder of the Goodyear Tire and Rubber Company and the Seiberling Rubber Company. Seiberling was, along with Harvey Firestone and B. F. Goodrich, a titan in the American rubber industry. Stan Hywet (the words mean "stone hewn" in Anglo-Saxon) was named because of the sandstone quarry on the property. The mansion, of brick and half-timber on a stone foundation, was designed by Charles S. Schneider of Cleveland, who used a well-known English house, Compton Wynyates, as a model. Stan Hywet is open to the public as a historic house museum.

## ■ *Trumbull County*
### HARRIET TAYLOR UPTON HOUSE
**380 Mahoning Avenue, NW, Warren**

Harriet Taylor Upton, a nationally prominent figure in both the suffrage movement and the Republican Party, lived in this house on Warren's "Millionaires' Row" from 1883 to 1931. From 1903 to 1909 her home served as headquarters of the National American Woman Suffrage Association (NAWSA). Upton, whose father was a prominent congressman, joined the NAWSA in 1890 and put her political resources at the disposal of the organization, where her congressional connections and her astute organizational skills ensured her rapid rise through the ranks. Currently, the Upton Association operates the house as a museum.

## ■ *Warren County*
### FORT ANCIENT
**On Ohio Route 350, 7 miles southeast of Lebanon**

This hilltop area with large surrounding earthworks was inhabited by people of the Hopewell culture (ca. 300 B.C.–A.D. 250). Hundreds of years after the site had been abandoned by the Hopewell, the Fort Ancient people (1200–1600) settled here. They were prehistoric farmers, supplement-

ing their diet with game, fish, and wild plants. Fort Ancient is the type site of the Hopewell culture and an Ohio State Memorial.

## ■ *Washington County*
### W.P. SNYDER, JR.
**Muskingum River off 601 Second Street, Marietta**

Towboats have moved barges on all the navigable waters of the Western Rivers and have been vital components in America's transportation system since the 1850s. *W.P. Snyder, Jr.,* launched in 1918 as *W.H. Clingerman,* is one of the very few paddlewheel towboats in the country. In 1945, the Crucible Steel Company bought the vessel and named it for the company president. *Snyder* towed barges on the Ohio and its tributaries until 1954 and was donated to the Ohio Historical Society the next year. Now moored at Marietta, *Snyder* is a museum vessel.

## ■ *Wood County*
### FORT MEIGS
**1 mile southwest of Perrysburg**

Built by General William Henry Harrison during the War of 1812, this stockade withstood a nine-day British siege the next year. The siege marked the zenith of both the British advance in the west and that of Native American forces under the leadership of the Shawnee chief, Tecumseh. Fort Meigs was abandoned in 1815, after the Treaty of Ghent was signed. It is now an Ohio State Memorial, and a replica of the fort has been constructed on the site.

# OKLAHOMA

## ■ *Bryan County*
### FORT WASHITA
**Oklahoma Route 199, Durant vicinity**

Fort Washita was established in 1842 as the westernmost United States frontier defense. It was founded because of treaty commitments to protect the Chickasaw and Choctaw from

the more violent Plains tribes. The fort also became an important way station for immigrants and traders on the southern Overland Trail. Union troops abandoned it in 1861, and Confederates subsequently held it throughout the Civil War. Abandoned in 1865, it was acquired by the Oklahoma Historical Society in 1962. Its buildings have

*Cherokee National
Capitol, Tahlequah,
Cherokee County.
Courtesy of HABS
(Walter Smalling, Jr.).*

been stabilized or restored, and the fort is open to the public.

## ■ *Cherokee County*

### CHEROKEE NATIONAL CAPITOL
**Tahlequah**

This two-story brick structure served as the council meeting place of the Cherokee National Council from 1869 until 1907, when Oklahoma became a state. A typical example of the Italianate style, the capitol stands as a symbol of the Cherokee's ability to adjust their culture to prevailing customs of the times. After its use as a tribal capitol ceased, it became the Cherokee County Court House.

### MURRELL HOME
**4 miles south of Tahlequah**

This two-story frame dwelling with its two-story porch, built in 1845 just south of the Cherokee capital of Talequah, markedly resembles houses of its period in Piedmont Virginia. The resemblance is hardly accidental: Virginian George Murrell, who married the niece of Cherokee leader John Ross, built it. The settlement at Park Hill became an early cultural center of the Cherokee, and the Murrell house, with many of its original furnishings intact, now stands as the sole reminder of this once prosperous community. It was purchased by the State of Oklahoma in 1948 and is open to the public.

## ■ *Cimarron County*

### CAMP NICHOLS
**Address Restricted, Wheeless vicinity**

This camp was established by Kit Carson in 1865 to offer protection to wagon trains using the Cimarron Cutoff of the Santa Fe Trail. Although used less than a year (from May to September 1865), it included some 25 buildings of local sandstone, adobe, and sod construction. Only ruins now mark the location of the most important Santa Fe Trail site in Oklahoma.

## ■ *Comanche County*

### FORT SILL
**Highway 62**

Fort Sill was begun on January 8, 1869, with General Philip H. Sheridan in charge. Construction of the first stone buildings was accomplished by black troops of the 10th Cavalry, the famous "Buffalo Soldiers." Also associated with the fort is Henry Ossian Flipper, first black graduate of West Point, who designed and built "Flipper's Ditch," a drainage system that alleviated the malaria that had plagued the fort in its early years. Troops stationed at Fort Sill were active in campaigns against Southern Plains tribes in the late 1800s. The fort has expanded over the years and has continued to be an important army post in the 20th century.

*Guthrie Historic District, Logan County. Courtesy of Susan Kline.*

■ *Kay County*

## 101 RANCH HISTORIC DISTRICT
**Oklahoma State Highway 156, 13 miles southwest of Ponca City**

This was once the largest diversified farm and cattle ranch in the country. It was also the home base of the 101 Wild West Show that operated from 1904 to 1916, and again from 1925 to 1931, setting national standards for rodeo entertainment. Among the performers who captivated audiences in America and Europe were Tom Mix, Will Rogers, and Bill Pickett, the well-known African American cowboy who invented "bulldogging" steer wrestling and was elected to the Cowboy Hall of Fame. A picnic area now commemorates the 101 Wild West Show.

## DEER CREEK SITE
**Address Restricted, Newkirk vicinity**

This is a fortified village site believed to have been occupied by the Wichita or related Indian groups in the first half of the 18th century. It was also the site of a French trading post that existed ca. 1725 to 1750, judging from artifacts uncovered at the site. Deer Creek is important in providing information on early European–Native American contact on the Plains and the beginnings of Plains Indian acculturation.

## ERNEST WHITWORTH MARLAND MANSION
**901 Monument Road, Ponca City**

Few have contributed as much to the development of a single American industry as Ernest Whitworth Marland did to petroleum. Beginning as a wildcatter, he came to control, through his Marland Oil Company, one-tenth of the world's supply of oil. He also served as Oklahoma's governor and was instrumental in establishing the 1935 Interstate Oil Compact to conserve petroleum reserves. From 1928 until his death in 1941, he lived in this impressive stone mansion, modeled by architect John Duncan Forsyth on a Florentine palace. Now owned by the city, the mansion is a showplace of fine arts.

■ *Logan County*

## GUTHRIE HISTORIC DISTRICT
**Roughly bounded by Oklahoma Avenue, Broad Street, Harrison Avenue, and railroad tracks, Guthrie**

Constituting the core of the city, this historic district contains mostly two- and three-story commercial buildings of red brick and/or sandstone, constructed between 1889 and 1910. This outstanding collection of commercial architecture displays the aspirations of the city's founders to create a city worthy of its distinction as the first and only territorial capital of Oklahoma (from 1890 to 1907) and then as the first state capital (from 1907 to 1910). Guthrie is also significant for its association with the opening of the last frontier to non-Indian settlement

## ■ *McCurtain County*

### WHEELOCK ACADEMY
**Off U.S. Route 70, Millerton vicinity**

This academy, housed in several buildings, began as a mission school in 1832. It became the prototype for tribal school systems established by the Five Civilized Tribes in the Indian Territory and set the precedent for some 35 academies and seminaries over the years. Wheelock, named for the founder of Dartmouth College, existed as a Choctaw tribal school until 1932, when it became a regular United States Indian School. It merged with Jones Academy in 1955. In 1997, the Choctaw Nation began repairing and restoring the property.

## ■ *Muskogee County*

### FORT GIBSON
**Fort Gibson**

Fort Gibson was established in 1824. It was garrisoned by troops whose mission was to protect Cherokee, Creek, and Seminole Indians, who had been removed from the Southeast, against the Plains tribes. It rapidly became one of the most important frontier administrative outposts. Fort Gibson was abandoned prior to the Civil War but was reoccupied by Union troops in 1863 and helped to strengthen the loyal element of the Cherokee Nation. The fort was originally a log stockade with log buildings, but beginning in 1837 stone buildings were constructed. Several of these remain, and the State of Oklahoma, which maintains the fort as a shrine, has built replicas of the early log structures.

## ■ *Okfuskee County*

### BOLEY HISTORIC DISTRICT
**Roughly bounded by Seward Avenue, Cedar Street, the original southern boundary of the city limits, and Walnut Street**

Boley was founded in 1903 as a camp for African Americans employed in constructing the Fort Smith and Western Railway. Located on a fertile site, it soon became the largest of several towns established in Oklahoma to provide African Americans with opportunities for self-government. Advertisements lured a number of settlers from Southern states during the era of white supremacy and segregation, and by 1911 Boley had a population of 4,000. Crop failures in the 1920s and the Depression hurt the community, and its population dwindled. A number of significant public and private buildings dating from its early days survive.

## ■ *Okmulgee County*

### CREEK NATIONAL CAPITOL
**Sixth Street and Grand Avenue, Okmulgee**

This two-story sandstone building, topped by a rectangular cupola, was built in 1878 to serve as the meeting place of the Creek Indian Council. The Creek Nation modeled its government on that of the United States, and the building contained halls for the two legislative houses, the House of Warriors and the House of Kings, as well as the Supreme

*Fort Gibson, Muskogee County. Courtesy of Robison and Associates Architects, 2927 The Paseo, Oklahoma City, OK 73103 (Jenny Woodruff).*

Court. After Oklahoma became a state in 1907, the capitol became the Okmulgee County Courthouse. It is now open to the public as a museum of Creek culture and history.

### ■ Roger Mills County
### WASHITA BATTLEFIELD (NPS)
**U.S. Route 283, Cheyenne vicinity**

On November 27, 1868, troops under command of Lieutenant Colonel George A. Custer made a surprise attack on a sleeping Cheyenne village here and virtually destroyed it and its inhabitants. The aim was to force the Plains Indians to settle on reservations, and the battle demonstrated the effectiveness of winter campaigns against the Indians, who traditionally fought only in spring and summer. In the larger sense, Washita was fought because of inalienable differences between two cultures, one accustomed to adapt to nature, the other attuned to conquering and subduing it. The opposing philosophies were like flint and steel; when they met, sparks flew. Washita Battlefield is now a unit of the National Park System.

### ■ Sequoyah County
### SEQUOYAH'S CABIN
**Sequoyah's State Park, Sallisaw vicinity**

This hewn-log cabin, built in 1829 and now restored, protected by a stone structure and open to the public, was the frontier home of Sequoyah (George Gist, or George Guess). Born of a Cherokee mother and a white, or half-blood, father, he never learned the English language, but in 1821 he invented an 85-character syllabic alphabet, making it possible to read and write the Cherokee language. With this gift of literacy, the Cherokee Nation developed a written constitution, began to govern themselves according to Anglo-American standards, and committed their tribe to education. Similar renditions of languages of the other Civilized Tribes soon followed the Cherokee's lead. Sequoyah's statue stands in Statuary Hall in the U.S. Capitol; he is honored as one of 12 alphabet inventors on the doors of the Library of Congress, and the giant sequoia trees of California are named for him.

### ■ Texas County
### STAMPER SITE
**Address Restricted, Optima vicinity**

One of the few excavated sites of the North Canadian River branch of the Panhandle Culture, this is a Plains village/agricultural complex somewhat modified by contacts with the Pueblo peoples to the west. Dating from about A.D. 1200 or 1250 to 1450, the life-style and general artifact assemblage reflect some similarities to those of the Central Plains cultures, but the architecture exhibits a Puebloan character.

### ■ Tulsa County
### BOSTON AVENUE METHODIST EPISCOPAL CHURCH
**1301 South Boston, Tulsa**

The Boston Avenue Methodist Episcopal Church is an outstanding example of the Art Deco style. Heralded as "a building that is a voice of the 20th century," it was built in 1927–1929 from designs by architect Bruce Goff. Sculptor Robert Garrison's terra-cotta figures are also notable, and represent a Methodist iconography with their depictions of early church leaders on horseback as circuit riders. The church is also distinguished for its application of new structural materials—primarily steel—in a religious building, and for the prominence the plan gives to educational facilities.

### ■ Washita County
### MCLEMORE SITE
**Address Restricted, Colony vicinity**

This was a small village of the Plains agricultural complex, dating from about A.D. 1000 to 1400, called the Washita River Focus. As one of the better-known sites of the type, it remains a key location for the interpretation of Southern Plains prehistory. House patterns, refuse and storage pits, numerous burials, and associated artifacts that have been uncovered furnish details on relationships between the Washita River Focus and other cultures. The site was first reported in 1955 and was excavated in the 1960s.

# OREGON

■ *Clackamas County*

### TIMBERLINE LODGE

**Mount Hood National Forest, Portland vicinity**

Situated on the south slope of Mount Hood at an altitude of 6,000 feet above sea level, this rustic hotel within the Mount Hood National Forest is widely regarded as the finest example of 1930s Works Progress Administration "mountain architecture." Broad sloping roofs above stone and timber walls were designed to harmonize with the mountain and its ridges—and to withstand heavy alpine winds and deep snows. The interiors are beautifully appointed, with carvings capturing the spirit of Indian cultures of the Northwest, and hand-crafted furnishings paying tribute to the pioneer heritage. The lodge still serves the purpose for which it was designed and built.

■ *Clatsop County*

### FORT ASTORIA SITE

**15th and Exchange Streets, Astoria**

Fort Astoria was planned in 1811 by John Jacob Astor, who had formed the Pacific Fur Company in an effort to break the British monopoly on fur trading in the Pacific Northwest. The fort's establishment also represented an important American claim to the Oregon Territory, but this early effort was unsuccessful. In 1813, Astor's supply ships failed to arrive with trading goods, and he was forced to sell the site to his competitor, the British Northwest Company. From 1813 to 1825, as Fort George, it was the principal western depot of the British operations. Today, a reconstructed blockhouse in the heart of Astoria marks the site.

### LIGHTSHIP WAL-604, *COLUMBIA*

**Columbia River Maritime Museum, Astoria**

The 1950 lightship WAL-604 is, with its sister ship WAL-605, the best representative of the last class of lightships built under the auspices of the U.S. Coast Guard. Although these vessels resembled earlier lightships in external appearance, they were distinctly different in construction, with all-welded hulls. Of the lightships built after 1939, WAL-604, or *Columbia,* remains the least changed. It

*Timberline Lodge, Clackamas County, 1973. Courtesy of the Oregon State Highway Travel Division.*

375

*Lightship WAL-604, Columbia,* Astoria, Clatsop County, *ca. 1965. Courtesy of the U.S. Coast Guard, 13th District.*

was retired in 1979 as the last Columbia station lightship, and the last on the Pacific coast. It is now displayed at the Columbia River Maritime Museum.

## ■ *Jackson County*

### JACKSONVILLE HISTORIC DISTRICT
**Jacksonville**

Founded as a gold-mining town in 1852, Jacksonville remains one of the West's most extensive and complete examples of a 19th-century community. It was the principal financial center of southern Oregon until 1884, when the California and Oregon Railroad bypassed it. That—and the removal of the Jackson County seat to nearby Medford in 1927—helped preserve the town. Some 60 commercial and residential structures, running the gamut of architectural styles popular in its heyday, remain, along with open spaces and landscapes. Together they constitute a matchless ensemble, provid-

ing an authentic picture of times long past—the 19th-century West.

## ■ *Josephine County*

### OREGON CAVES CHATEAU (NPS)
**Oregon Caves National Monument, Cave Junction vicinity**

Completed in 1934, this lodge is a grand example of rustic architecture. It is especially significant for its creative adaptation to an extremely limited site that spans a gorge (part of the stream runs through an artificial brook in the dining room). The château, with its shaggy-bark cedar finish, retains a high degree of integrity, as do its furnishings. Landscape features include stone retaining walls, fish ponds, waterfalls, and walkways, all adding to the sense of rustic intimacy and total harmony with nature.

## ■ *Klamath County*

### CRATER LAKE SUPERINTENDENT'S RESIDENCE (NPS)
**Crater Lake National Park, Munson Valley vicinity**

Built in 1932, this building represents the best elements of the rustic style so typical of National Park Service design and construction of its time. The battered walls of the chaletlike residence are composed of huge boulders, topped with steeply pitched gable roofs with dormers. Its unusual method of construction was devised for the extremely short building season (often of only 12 weeks' duration) at this alpine altitude. The residence, now used to house visiting researchers, is part of a group of rustic buildings serving as park headquarters. Award-winning adaptive reuse and rehabilitation projects have provided new uses for many of the structures while retaining their significant architectural features.

### LOWER KLAMATH NATIONAL WILDLIFE REFUGE
**Lower Klamath Lake, Dorris vicinity**

This first large area of public land to be reserved as a wildlife refuge was, in 1908, superimposed on an existing federal reclamation project to drain the Klamath Basin wetlands for agricultural purposes. In 1940 mea-

*Crater Lake Superintendent's Residence (NPS), Klamath County. Courtesy of NPS (Laura Soulliere Harrison).*

sures were initiated to bring the refuge back to productivity, and with the introduction of scientific management principles into wildlife conservation, it again attracts migratory waterfowl in great numbers. The refuge provides an outstanding illustration of conflicts between reclamation and conservation interests and their potential resolution. (Also in Siskiyou County, California.)

### ■ *Lake County*

## FORT ROCK CAVE
**Address Restricted, Fort Rock**

The earliest occupation of this site dates to 11,000 B.C.; the "Fort Rock sandals," oldest manufactured articles found in the Western Hemisphere, were discovered here. Investigations at Fort Rock Cave, which has a continuous, stratified sequence of artifacts ranging over 10,000 years, have been invaluable in the interpretation of environmental changes and prehistory in the Great Basin. The site is now the Fort Rock State Monument.

### ■ *Lane County*

## DEADY AND VILLARD HALLS
**University of Oregon, Eugene**

Completed in 1876 and 1886, respectively, Deady and Villard Halls are the first and second buildings of the University of Oregon. Deady Hall combines Italianate detailing with Second Empire forms and is identified by its twin towers and dormered mansard roofs. Villard Hall, with four short corner towers, is a more formal Second Empire composition and one of the few surviving academic buildings of its era in the western United States. Standing next to each other at the heart of the university, the two buildings are familiar and cherished symbols to all alumni.

### ■ *Multnomah County*

## BONNEVILLE DAM HISTORIC DISTRICT
**On the Columbia River**

When this mammoth federal project was built by the U.S. Army Corps of Engineers in the 1930s, no other water impoundment or diversion structure in the country was comparable to it. Located at the western end of the Columbia River Gorge, Bonneville Dam was designed to generate hydroelectric power and was the first dam built with a "hydraulic drop" capable of developing more than 500,000 kilowatts of electric power. Other associated structures in the district include a powerhouse, the navigation lock, built to allow river boats to travel around the dam, the fishways, designed so that salmon and steelhead trout can reach their spawning grounds upstream, and the fish hatchery. (Also in Skamania County, Washington.)

## PIONEER COURTHOUSE
**555 Southwest Yamhill Street, Portland**

Completed in 1875, Portland's U.S. Courthouse, Customhouse, and Post Office was one of the first monumental buildings to be constructed in the Pacific Northwest. The classical building, capped by a domed octagonal cupola, was designed by Alfred B. Mullet, supervising architect of the Treasury Department. Over the years compatible additions have been made, and the building was restored in the 1970s. Its name, Pioneer Courthouse, was given in 1937 when it was reactivated after several years of disuse.

## SKIDMORE/OLD TOWN HISTORIC DISTRICT
**Burnside Street to the Willamette River, Portland**

This 20-block commercial district marks the site where Portland began and where it first flourished. Buildings, dating mostly from the mid-to-late 19th century, represent a variety of Victorian-era architectural styles. Many feature cast-iron fronts, constituting one of the most impressive collections of this particular building type on the West Coast. The ornate Skidmore Fountain, dating from 1888, centers the district, and gives it its name.

## SUNKEN VILLAGE ARCHEOLOGICAL SITE
**Address Restricted, Portland vicinity**

Sunken Village, a water-saturated site on the lower Columbia River floodplain between Vancouver, Washington, and Portland, contains the archeological remains of a Chinook settlement (A.D. 1250–1750) that is extraordinarily well preserved. The Chinook were a cosmopolitan people who practiced a successful, complex hunter-gatherer economy that permitted densely occupied villages and extensive trade relations.

■ *Wallowa County*

## WALLOWA LAKE SITE
**Oregon Route 82, Joseph vicinity**

This traditional Nez Perce campsite, with spectacular views of a high, glaciated lake and surrounding mountains, is a symbol of the homeland from which Chief Joseph and the Wallowa band were driven in 1877, thus precipitating the Nez Perce War. On the slope above the lake, a small cemetery contains the grave of Old Chief Joseph, whose dying words fueled his son's determination to hold onto the Wallowa country: "This country holds your father's body. Never sell the bones of your father and your mother."

# PENNSYLVANIA

■ *Adams County*

## DWIGHT D. EISENHOWER FARMSTEAD (NPS)
**Gettysburg vicinity**

This farm adjoining the Gettysburg National Military Park served Dwight D. Eisenhower, 34th president of the United States (1953–1961), as a retreat during those years, and as his principal residence during retirement. The Eisenhowers commissioned Washington, D.C., architect George S. Brock to enlarge the brick farmhouse, which is now open to the public as the Eisenhower National Historic Site.

■ *Allegheny County*

## ALLEGHENY COUNTY COURTHOUSE AND JAIL
**Fifth, Grant, Ross, and Diamond Streets, Pittsburgh**

When architect Henry Hobson Richardson realized his days were numbered, he wrote: "Let me have time to finish Pittsburgh and I should be content without another day." He was referring to the massive buildings he had designed for Allegheny County in 1883, which were then being built. The jail—most rugged and solid of Richardson's designs—was completed in 1886, and the adjoining courthouse—more specifically Romanesque

*Allegheny County Courthouse and Jail, Pittsburgh, Allegheny County. Courthouse with the "Bridge of Sighs," 1963. Courtesy of HABS (Jack E. Boucher).*

in its stylistic allegiance — was completed in 1888, a year after his death. The stone group is rightly considered among the truly great examples of his individual architectural style, the Richardsonian Romanesque.

## BOST BUILDING
### 621–623 East Eighth Avenue, Homestead

Between June 29 and November 21, 1892, much of the nation followed the events of a labor strike outside Pittsburgh, Pennsylvania, that pitted the Carnegie Steel Company against one of the strongest labor unions at the time. During the strike at the Homestead Steel Works, the Bost Building served as union headquarters and as the base for newspaper correspondents reporting the events. The confrontation turned bloody when Pinkerton guards approached the steelworks on barges, but failed to reclaim it. The Bost Building is the best surviving structure associated with this important strike.

## FORKS OF THE OHIO
### Point Park, Pittsburgh

This spot, where the Allegheny and Monongahela Rivers converge to form the Ohio, was one of the most strategic sites in the early exploration and settlement of North America. Control of the forks meant control of the rich Ohio Valley and, ultimately, of the Mississippi Valley beyond. The French erected Fort Duquesne in 1754; the British replaced it with Fort Pitt in 1758, and Pittsburgh grew under its protection. Now part of Point Park, the site of Fort Pitt has been excavated and marked. A museum operated by the Pennsylvania Historical and Museum Commission contains displays that attest to the significance of this historic spot over the years.

## KENNYWOOD PARK
### 4800 Kennywood Boulevard, West Mifflin

Opened to the public in 1899 as a "trolley park," Kennywood survives from an era when street railway companies (in this instance the Monongahela Street Railway Company) built suburban amusement parks. An example of enlightened self-interest, such parks not only provided recreational opportunities to thousands, they also ensured increased patronage of the streetcar lines leading to them. Because it has had 11 roller coasters over the years, Kennywood has been called the "Roller Coaster Capital of the World." Also billed as "America's greatest traditional amusement park," it retains many other rare attractions.

## OAKMONT COUNTRY CLUB
### Hulton Road, Oakmont and Plum Boroughs, Oakmont

In 1903, 100 men and 25 teams of horses transformed a pastureland some 12 miles northeast of Pittsburgh into a golf course. Fairways were built as narrow as possible, and greens were built large. The result was a challenging 6,600-yard course, considered one of the most difficult in the world. Now, lengthened to 6,989 yards but with its original layout virtually intact, Oakmont is the oldest top-ranked golf course in the United States. It has hosted 13 major national championships and 6 U.S. Opens over the years. The course

Smithfield Street Bridge, Pittsburgh, Allegheny County, 1974. Courtesy of HABS (Jack E. Boucher).

still punishes imprecise shots and remains the epitome of penal golf course design.

## SMITHFIELD STREET BRIDGE
### Smithfield Street at the Monongahela River, Pittsburgh

One of the first steel truss bridges in the country, the Smithfield Street Bridge was constructed in 1883 and widened in 1890. Gustave Lindenthal, a young engineer from Germany who became one of America's foremost civil engineers of the early 20th century, chose the Pauli lenticular truss for his span. The flowing trusses are as strong as they are graceful and have allowed the bridge to function safely for more than a century.

## WOODVILLE
### On Pennsylvania Route 50, south of Heidelberg

John Neville played an important role throughout the Revolution, climaxing his career in September 1783 when he was appointed brigadier general. His postwar career was less spectacular. As revenue inspector, he had the unenviable job of collecting the excise tax on whiskey in western Pennsylvania. In 1794 participants in the Whiskey Rebellion, protesting the tax, burned the home he was living in at the time. Woodville, a frame house that Neville had built in 1785, survives as the property most closely associated with him.

■ *Beaver County*

## BEGINNING POINT OF THE U.S. PUBLIC LAND SURVEY
### On the Ohio-Pennsylvania boundary

This is the point where the rectangular-grid land survey system established for "disposing of lands in the western territory" (the Old Northwest) began. As directed by the Ordinance of 1785, public lands were to be divided into townships 6 miles square, and each township was then subdivided into 36 sections of 1 square mile each. This was the first mathematically designed system adapted by any modern country, and its imprint remains indelible on the American landscape. The actual beginning point, on the northern shore of the Ohio River on the border between Ohio, Pennsylvania, and West Virginia (then Virginia), is now inundated, but a nearby marker commemorates the site. (Also in Columbiana County, Ohio.)

## OLD ECONOMY
### Pennsylvania Route 65, Ambridge

The Harmonists were among the most peripatetic of America's 19th-century religious societies. They arrived in Pennsylvania in 1804 (see Harmony, Butler County), and after a sojourn in Indiana (see New Harmony, Posey County), returned east in 1824 to found Economy, their third "terrestrial home." Economy was one of the most successful of 19th-century American utopian communities and achieved national recognition for its wool, cotton, and silk industries. A number of communal buildings survive and are maintained by the Pennsylvania Historical and Museum Commission and open to the public.

## MATTHEW S. QUAY HOUSE
**205 College Avenue, Beaver**

U.S. Senator Matthew Stanley Quay was one of the most representative and effective of the professional politicians who dominated late-19th-century American politics. Through his powerful machine, he quietly and ably served his party, and in 1888, as Republican national chairman, he organized and managed Benjamin Harrison's successful presidential campaign. Featuring tricks and bribery, this was then the most expensive presidential campaign ever waged. From 1874 until his death in 1904, Quay lived in this solid brick house in Beaver.

### ■ *Bedford County*

## BEDFORD SPRINGS HOTEL HISTORIC DISTRICT
**U.S. Business Route 220 and Township Road 408, Bedford Township**

During the 19th and early 20th centuries, Americans "took to the waters" in droves, congregating in fashionable spas to recuperate from what ailed them, to relax, and—most especially—to "see and be seen." Bedford Springs was one of these well-known summer resorts, and its many buildings and extensive grounds conjure up a vivid image of spa architecture and life-style. Bedford Springs was also an important political gathering place during the mid–19th century. Pennsylvanian James Buchanan, 15th president of the United States, used the resort as a summer White House during his administration.

## DAVID ESPY HOUSE
**123 Pitt Street, Bedford, Bedford County**

During the 1794 Whiskey Rebellion, David Espy, a local official, owned this 2½-story fieldstone house. He made it available for use by President Washington from October 19 to 20, when he came with the militia to sup-

press the rebels. The house is also significant as the only extant property associated with Arthur Saint Clair, Revolutionary War general and first governor of the Northwest Territory. From 1771 to 1772, Saint Clair maintained it as his office when he was an official of the newly created Bedford County.

### ■ *Berks County*

## GRUBER WAGON WORKS
**On Red Covered Bridge Road, Reading**

Until the automobile came into general use in the early 20th century, Americans depended on wagons, carriages, and horsecars for most of their transportation. The family-owned Gruber Wagon Works produced both standard farm wagons and custom vehicles from 1882 to the 1950s. Its fully preserved machinery and tools make the works an outstanding example of a once essential American industry. When its original site was inundated by a flood-control project, the Wagon Works was dismantled in 1976–1977, rebuilt at a new site resembling the old, and opened as a museum in Tulpehocken Creek Valley Park.

## CONRAD WEISER HOUSE
**2 miles east of Womelsdorf on U.S. Route 422**

Johann Conrad Weiser was the principal agent in the arbitration and implementation of colonial Pennsylvania's Indian policy. His wise counsel helped maintain peace on the frontier and ensured friendly relations between the colonists and the powerful Six Nations of the Iroquois during the French and Indian War. From 1729 until his death, he lived in this small stone farmhouse, now open to the public as a museum honoring this early-day keeper of the peace.

### ■ *Blair County*

## ALLEGHENY PORTAGE RAILROAD OF THE PENNSYLVANIA CANAL (NPS)
**12 miles west of Altoona on U.S. Route 22, Cresson (Blair and Cambria Counties)**

This first railroad over the Allegheny Mountains operated from 1834 to 1854 and was considered a technological marvel of its time. An inclined plane, it carried canal boats over a 36-mile mountain divide between the eastern and western sections of the Pennsylvania Canal. The canal, with its railroad, was Pennsylvania's main transportation line to the West for more than two decades and played a critical role in opening the interior of the country to trade and settlement. A portion of the route is included in the Allegheny Portage Railroad National Historic Site.

## CHARLES B. DUDLEY HOUSE

**802 Lexington Avenue, Altoona**

Charles B. Dudley, fresh out of Yale's Sheffield Scientific School, went to work for the Pennsylvania Railroad Company in 1875. His employment marked the first time a major American company hired a scientist purely to conduct research. Dudley immediately proved his mettle by studying the physical properties of steel rails and suggesting improvements that were soon implemented. Thanks to him, research and development— R & D—are now integral components of American companies. Dudley lived in this Altoona town house from 1898 until his death 11 years later.

## HORSESHOE CURVE

**5 miles west of Altoona on Pennsylvania Route 193, Altoona**

Placed in service in 1854, Horseshoe Curve is a notable early example of railroad engineering and construction. It was built to gain distance and reduce the grade in crossing the Alleghenies and required huge cuts and fills before tracks could be laid. Completion of the Horseshoe Curve marked the joining of the eastern and western divisions of the Pennsylvania Railroad, traversing the state on one continuous line. The curve is still a vital link and has been widened from two to four tracks. A small park and a museum are at the curve's apex.

## LEAP-THE-DIPS

**700 Park Avenue, Altoona**

Leap-the-Dips, the last known extant example of a Side-Friction Figure Eight roller coaster in the country, represents a significant development in the technological evolution of roller coasters. Roller coasters developed in tandem with amusement parks in the late 19th and early 20th centuries and were usually signature attractions at these popular recreational spots. Leap-the-Dips was constructed in 1902 at Lakemont Park, which had been developed in the 1890s by the Altoona and Logan Valley Electric Railway Company.

### ■ *Bucks County*

## ANDALUSIA

**1.4 miles north of Philadelphia on State Road, Philadelphia**

Andalusia was the residence of Nicholas Biddle, head of the Second Bank of the United States from 1823 to 1836 and famous as President Jackson's opponent. Biddle's defeat in the epic political-economic struggle that had its impetus in renewing the bank's charter paved the way for Jacksonian democracy. To the original house at Andalusia, whose north front remains an outstanding American example of the Regency style, Biddle added a Greek Revival temple front, with a portico modeled on the Parthenon, to the south, or river, front. Designed by Thomas U. Walter and built in 1834, this is one of the earliest and most pristine examples of the Greek Revival style in the country.

## PEARL S. BUCK HOUSE

**Southwest of Dublin on Dublin Road, Hilltown Township, Dublin**

Noted American novelist Pearl S. Buck maintained this mid-19th-century stone farmhouse in Bucks County as her principal residence from 1933 until her death in 1973. She purchased the farm with royalties from *The Good Earth,* her story of a Chinese family. The novel won the 1932 Pulitzer Prize, and in 1938 Buck won the Nobel Prize for literature "for rich and genuine epic portrayals of Chinese life, and for masterpieces of biography." Buck's work interpreted the East for the West and did much to dispel the traditional myth of the inscrutable orient.

## DELAWARE CANAL

**Paralleling the west bank of the Delaware River from Easton to Bristol (Bucks and Northampton Counties)**

Completed in the early 1830s and in operation for a century, the Delaware Canal

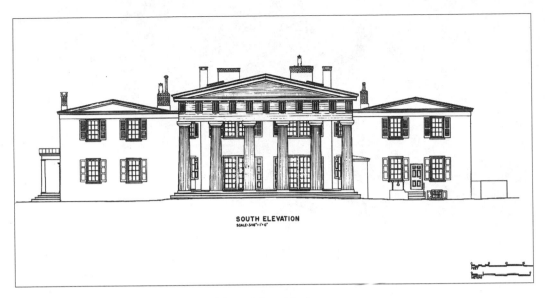

SOUTH ELEVATION
SCALE 3/16"=1'-0"

*Andalusia, Bucks County. Courtesy of HABS (Martin J. Rosenblum).*

*Fonthill, Mercer Museum, and Moravian Pottery and Tile Works, Doylestown, Bucks County, Fonthill, 1966. Courtesy of HABS (Jack E. Boucher).*

extended 60 miles from Bristol to Easton, paralleling the Delaware River. It was part of the state's extensive early-19th-century canal system, and its particular purpose was to transport anthracite coal mined in the Lehigh Valley to markets throughout Pennsylvania and New York. When the canal was returned to the state by the Lehigh Coal and Navigation Company in 1931, Pennsylvania developed it as Roosevelt State Park. It retains a great deal of integrity throughout its length and provides a nostalgic reminder of a once vital transportation link.

## FONTHILL, MERCER MUSEUM, AND MORAVIAN POTTERY AND TILE WORKS

### Court Street and Swamp Roads, Pine and Ashland Streets, Doylestown

These three buildings were designed by Henry Chapman Mercer, antiquarian, proponent of the Arts and Crafts movement, and visionary architect and builder. Mercer "designed" as he proceeded. At his home, Fonthill (1907–1912), he planned each room, then assembled blocks of clay as models to determine the appearance and form the

exterior would take. Mercer was one of the nation's first designers to work with reinforced concrete as a building material, and also revived the Pennsylvania German craft of tile making. The floors of the State Capitol in Harrisburg were made at the Tile Works, which is now a museum illustrating Mercer's techniques. All three buildings are open to the public.

## HONEY HOLLOW WATERSHED
### South of the Delaware River, New Hope

Honey Hollow Watershed is a 700-acre natural basin where numerous streams drain into a central waterway: Honey Hollow Creek. In 1939 six farmers established the nation's first watershed in multiple use and private ownership here. It soon proved that cooperative local action, supported by federal technical assistance, could achieve national goals in water, soil, wildlife conservation and flood prevention. Honey Hollow has served as a prototype for thousands of similar areas across the country.

## SUMMERSEAT
### Clymer Street and Morris Avenue, Morrisville

George Clymer was one of the first advocates of America's complete independence from England. He was a three-term member of the Continental Congress, a signer of both the Declaration of Independence and the Constitution, and a member of the first United States Congress. After his long and fruitful efforts to see his country established, he purchased this large Georgian mansion in 1806 and lived out his well-deserved retirement here. The house is unusual in that it has a brick facade, stuccoed end walls, and a stone rear elevation.

## WASHINGTON'S CROSSING
### On the Delaware River, County Route 546, New Hope

Here, on Christmas night, 1776, General George Washington and his troops crossed the Delaware River on their way to capture Trenton, then held by British forces. Thanks largely to the famous painting by Emanuel Leutze, the crossing has assumed almost legendary proportions in American history. It was actually a realistic and carefully planned maneuver, whose success gave the colonials a much-needed taste of victory at the war's lowest ebb. State parks on both banks of the river, one in New Jersey, one in Pennsylvania, memorialize the event, as does an annual reenactment. (Also in Mercer County, New Jersey.)

■ *Butler County*

## HARMONY HISTORIC DISTRICT
### Pennsylvania Route 68, Harmony

Harmony was the first home of the Harmonie Society, a utopian community that George Rapp established in 1805. One of the most successful of early America's religious settlements, it became a prosperous agricultural and manufacturing center, noted especially for its production of wine, whiskey, and woolens. By 1814, there were 700 members, but the village was sold the next year when the Society decided to move to Indiana in search of more fertile land. A number of buildings, including the church and the Great House, remain and are open to the public. (See Old Economy, Beaver County.)

(See Old Economy, Beaver County.)

## ■ Cambria County

### ALLEGHENY PORTAGE RAILROAD OF THE PENNSYLVANIA CANAL (NPS)
**12 miles west of Altoona on U.S. Route 22, Cresson (Blair and Cambria Counties)**

(See entry under Blair County.)

### CAMBRIA IRON COMPANY
**Along Conemaugh River, Johnstown**

Founded in 1852 to supply iron rails for the nation's burgeoning railroad network, the Cambria Iron Company grew to be America's largest ironworks by the 1870s. As it expanded during the late 19th century, Cambria attracted leading engineers, innovators, and managers to Johnstown, and the city became a leader in technological innovations in the iron and steel industry. Bethlehem Steel Company purchased the plant in 1923, and under the stewardship of the country's second-largest steel company it continued to expand. The plant's history reflects the nationwide evolution of the iron and steel industry.

### STAPLE BEND TUNNEL
**State Route 3035 and Mineral Point, Conemaugh Township vicinity**

The first railroad tunnel in the country was constructed between November 1831 and June 1833 to carry the Allegheny Portage Railroad through a 900-foot promontory of shale, sandstone, and silt stone. Part of the Pennsylvania Canal, both tunnel and railroad were considered engineering marvels in their day, affording a means of crossing the Allegheny Mountains. The link they provided with the eastern seaboard helped redirect Pennsylvania's western trade and commerce from the Ohio and Mississippi River basins, thus helping Philadelphia to maintain its position as a major port.

## ■ Carbon County

### ASA PACKER MANSION
**Packer Road, Jim Thorpe**

This is one of the most perfectly preserved mid-19th-century Italian villas in America. Little changed from the time it was completed in 1852, the mansion still contains its original furniture, chandeliers, and silver. A huge orchestrion—a giant Swiss "music maker" with organ, bells, and drum—is a prize exhibit. Asa Packer, one of America's leading early coal and railroad magnates, built the Lehigh Valley Railroad and founded Lehigh University. His daughter lived in the house until 1911. It was then donated to the borough and is open as a historic house museum.

### SAINT MARK'S EPISCOPAL CHURCH
**Race and Susquehanna Streets, Jim Thorpe**

Richard Upjohn designed this extraordinarily picturesque stone church late in his career. Built in 1867–1869, it occupies a commanding hillside site, standing on a platform overlooking downtown Jim Thorpe. Asa Packer, one of America's richest men of his time, commissioned the church and insisted that its appointments be the finest obtainable. Mahogany pews, brass pulpit, marble font and altar, and stained-glass windows by Tiffany enhance Upjohn's fine Gothic design. They provide comfortable Victorian assurance that "God's in his heaven—All's right with the world!"

## ■ Chester County

### CEDARCROFT
**North of Kennett Square**

From 1859 to 1874 this was the residence of James Bayard Taylor, poet, novelist, Civil War correspondent, and translator of *Faust*. Although the bulk of his prolific work is perhaps deservedly forgotten, he is memorable for the fact that his contemporaries believed him to be one of the great American writers of his day. Taylor did much of his writing in this still privately owned house, which he built himself.

## WHARTON ESHERICK HOUSE AND STUDIO
### 1520 Horseshoe Trail, Malvern

From 1926 to 1966 this was the home and workplace of Wharton Esherick, noted artist, craftsman, carpenter, and architect. Esherick agreed with Frank Lloyd Wright that a house should appear to grow from its site and not be encumbered with superfluous ornament. His idiosyncratic stone and frame building contains furnishings that bridge the gap between utility and art; the stairway has been well described as "functional sculpture." His house and studio are open to the public.

## LUKENS HISTORIC DISTRICT
### South First Street, Coatesville

Rebecca Lukens owned and managed the Brandywine Ironworks (later Lukens Steel Company), one of the industry's major firms in the decades before the Civil War. Following the deathbed wish of her husband to continue the business that her father had started and he had managed, she became the only woman in the antebellum period to head a heavy industry with interstate and international interests. The house she lived in and worked from, two later family houses, and a later main office building are included within this historic district.

## HUMPHREY MARSHALL HOUSE
### 1407 South Strasburg Road/Pennsylvania Route 162, Marshalltown

Constructed in 1773–1774 and enlarged in 1801, this 2½-story house served as home, office, warehouse, conservatory, and laboratory for Humphrey Marshall. Along with his cousin John Bartram, Marshall was one of colonial America's most noted botanists. He authored *Arbustum Americanum,* the first account of trees and shrubs native to the United States. The unique plan of the house attests to the numerous uses Marshall made of it. The property, including Marshall's garden, was willed to the Chester County Historical Society in 1982.

## VALLEY FORGE (NPS)
### Norristown (Chester and Montgomery Counties)

Every American shivers at the thought of Valley Forge, conjuring up vivid images of ragged, hungry soldiers huddled around campfires outside log huts during a bitterly cold winter. At the end of an eight-day march, Washington's battered and dispirited troops staggered into camp here on December 19, 1777, after the British captured Philadelphia. Valley Forge represents the nadir of the Revolution, but thanks to the military training and discipline that General von Steuben imposed, rejuvenated troops emerged in the spring of 1778 as a real army and reoccupied Philadelphia in June. Now a National Historical Park, Valley Forge contains replicas of the soldiers' huts and several stone buildings that officers used during the winter of their discontent. (See Washington's Headquarters, Montgomery County.)

## GENERAL FRIEDRICH VON STEUBEN HEADQUARTERS (NPS)
### Pennsylvania Route 23, Valley Forge State Park

From February to June 1778, Baron Friedrich Wilhelm Ludolf Gerhard Augustin von Steuben trained the ragged Continental army at Valley Forge. Formerly a Prussian staff officer and aide-de-camp to Frederick the Great, von Steuben had come to America at Benjamin Franklin's request to assist the American cause. His service was invaluable, and Washington's last official act before relinquishing command of the army in December 1783 was to write him a letter of commendation. Since 1976 this building has been included in Valley Forge National Historical Park as a memorial to Von Steuben.

## WAYNESBOROUGH
### 2049 Waynesborough Road, Paoli

From his birth in 1745 until 1791, five years before his death, Anthony Wayne lived in this large stone house. Brash, brave, and impetuous, this brigadier general of the Continental army fought in many of the pivotal battles of the Revolution and later subdued the Indian tribes of the Northwest Territory. His actions and attitude earned him the sobriquet "Mad," now almost thought of as his first name. The house, still privately owned, was originally constructed in 1724 by Wayne's grandfather and has been enlarged several times over the years.

## ■ *Cumberland County*

### CARLISLE INDIAN SCHOOL
**East edge of Carlisle on U.S. Route 11**

Founded in 1879 at the Carlisle Barracks, a U.S. military reservation, the Carlisle Indian Industrial School pioneered federal educational programs for Native Americans. The school became a model for similar institutions, whose programs were based on the premise of "civilizing" Indians into white man's ways, preferably at locations removed from their reservations and their own cultures. Sports were an important part of the curriculum under athletic director Glen S. "Pop" Warner. Baseball star Joseph "Chief" Bender and the legendary Jim Thorpe, who won both the Olympic pentathlon and decathlon in 1912, were among the stars who brought fame to Carlisle. A number of buildings, as well as the athletic field and grandstand, attest to the school's many years of service.

### OLD WEST, DICKINSON COLLEGE
**Carlisle**

Old West is the oldest structure at Dickinson College. Benjamin H. Latrobe, one of America's first professional architects, designed it in 1803, contributing his time and talents without charge. Because of funding problems, the stone structure was built in increments and was completed only in 1822. The handsome Federal style building is capped with an open cupola, and the mermaid weathervane that tops the cupola has become the college symbol. Dickinson College was founded by Dr. Benjamin Rush and counts President James Buchanan among its alumni.

## ■ *Dauphin County*

### SIMON CAMERON HOUSE
**219 South Front Street, Harrisburg**

Simon Cameron's national political career included pre– and post–Civil War terms in the U.S. Senate, appointment as secretary of war under Abraham Lincoln, minister to Russia, and chief member of U.S. Grant's "kitchen cabinet." On the state level, Cameron was a master "spoilsman," who built the patronage system and installed antireform "Stalwarts" as the dominant faction in Pennsylvania's Republican party. From 1863 until his death in 1889, except when he was in Washington, Cameron maintained his home in Harrisburg. The oldest part of the stone mansion fronting on the Susquehanna was built in 1764–1776 by the city's founder, John Harris. The John Harris Mansion/Simon Cameron House is open as a historic house museum.

### HARRISBURG STATION AND TRAINSHED
**Aberdeen Street, Harrisburg**

Built in 1885–1887 for the Pennsylvania Railroad, the Harrisburg train shed is one of

*Old West, Dickinson College, Carlisle, Cumberland County, 1961. Courtesy of NPS (C. E. Shedd).*

*1704 House, Delaware County, 1967. Courtesy of NPS (Charles W. Snell).*

the earliest extant examples of the Fink roof truss, a form of major significance in the history of American civil engineering and industrial building. Albert Fink, engineer for the Baltimore & Ohio Railroad, patented the prototype in 1854. In addition to their being used in roof construction, as in this instance, Fink trusses were especially effective for long-span bridges.

## MILTON S. HERSHEY MANSION
**Mansion Road, Hershey**

Few individuals have contributed as much to satisfying America's "sweet tooth" as Milton S. Hershey. In the first half of the 20th century his company became the world's largest manufacturer of chocolate, and the Hershey Bar became virtually a generic term. Hershey built a model company and town and lived in this house on Chocolate Avenue from 1908 to 1945. Colonial Revival in style, it is constructed of locally quarried limestone. In 1930, Hershey donated the house to a newly formed country club, reserving only a small second-floor apartment for himself. In 1977 the company he founded purchased the house for its corporate headquarters.

■ *Delaware County*

## 1704 HOUSE
**Dilworthtown**

This early stone house, named for its date of construction, was built by William Brinton, a Chester County Quaker. Representative of

early Delaware Valley manor houses, it has a distinctly medieval flavor, with its steeply pitched roofs, brooding dormer windows, and diamond-pane windows with leaded sash. Local Pennsylvania building traditions, such as the pent eaves between first and second stories on the two long facades, blend with the earlier English-inspired features. The house was enlarged and altered late in the 19th century but was restored in the 1950s. It is open to the public.

## BRANDYWINE BATTLEFIELD
**Brandywine Battlefield Park, Chadds Ford**

On September 11, 1777, Washington's Continentals met British forces under Lord Howe in a major battle of the Revolution. The battle, which took place over a huge tract of farmland and woodland and around several small towns, was an American defeat, but the Continentals demonstrated a newly won ability to withstand the determined attack of British regulars, even while sustaining heavy losses. Still, at the end of the day, the British were only 30 miles from Philadelphia and only 14 days away from capturing it. A 50-acre park maintained by the Commonwealth of Pennsylvania contains a reconstruction of Washington's headquarters.

## MERION GOLF CLUB
**Ardmore Avenue, Ardmore (Haverford Township)**

The Merion Golf Club's east and west courses (1911 and 1914, respectively) were among the first in this country to incorporate a combination "penal" and "strategic" design, less demanding of golfers than earlier designs that punished any variation from prescribed pathways between tee and cup. Hugh I. Wilson designed the two courses, and over the years golf pros have pronounced them among the best in the country. The Merion Golf Club has hosted many national championship tournaments over the years.

## THE PRINTZHOF
### Taylor Avenue and Second Street, Essington

Constructed in about 1643 of hewn logs, the Printzhof was the residence of Johan Printz, governor of New Sweden, the first permanent European settlement in what became Pennsylvania. A gargantuan man (he weighed more than 400 pounds), Printz took his commission seriously—to make New Sweden show a profit. His success sparked resentment from the Dutch, who eventually captured the Swedish colony. Today, the Printzhof's stone foundations are the only visible remains of the settlement.

## BENJAMIN WEST BIRTHPLACE
### Swarthmore College campus, Swarthmore

This stone house, with its typical Pennsylvania pent between the first and second stories, was the birthplace of Benjamin West. A noted artist of early America in his own right, West is now remembered mostly for the encouragement and training he provided fledgling American artists who sought him out after he moved to England in 1763. Among those he assisted were Gilbert Stuart, Charles Willson Peale, Thomas Sully, and John Trumbull. West's birthplace is on the Swarthmore College campus and is used as a faculty residence.

## N. C. WYETH HOUSE AND STUDIO
### Murphy Road, Chadds Ford Township

Newell Convers Wyeth's illustrations have excited the imagination of generations of readers. In a career that spanned the first half of the 20th century, Wyeth illustrated some

90 books and countless stories for such prestigious magazines as *Harpers, McClure's, Saturday Evening Post,* and *Scribner's.* Wyeth lived and worked in the several buildings that make up this historic district and planted his roots so deep in the Chadds Ford soil that two succeeding generations of Wyeth artists have found nourishment here. His son, Andrew, and grandson, James, both began their art training in his studio. The property is open to the public.

### ■ *Fayette County*

## FALLINGWATER
### West of Pennsylvania Route 381, Mill Run

Fallingwater may well be the most famous 20th-century house in the world. Frank Lloyd Wright designed it as a summer home for a Pittsburgh department store owner, Edgar J. Kaufmann, in the 1930s. The house is cantilevered over a waterfall, dramatically exploiting its site. Fallingwater has few rooms, but these are expanded by balconies and terraces. In 1963, the Kaufmann family presented the house, contents, and grounds to

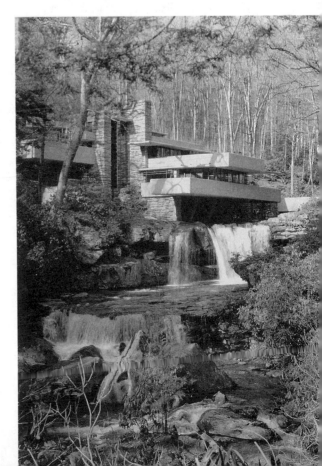

*Fallingwater, Mill Run, Fayette County. Courtesy of HABS (Jack E. Boucher).*

the Western Pennsylvania Conservancy, which preserves and maintains them and opens them to the public.

## ALBERT GALLATIN HOUSE (NPS)
**3 miles north of Point Marion on Pennsylvania Route 166**

Swiss-born Abraham Alfonse Albert Gallatin, American financier, politician, and idealist, served in the U.S. House of Representatives from 1795 to 1801, and as secretary of the treasury from 1802 to 1814. During his tenure at the Treasury Department, he sought to abolish the national debt in order to free funds to focus on needed internal improvements, but expenses incurred during the War of 1812 prevented him from achieving that goal. During his long stint of government service, Gallatin made his permanent residence at Friendship Hill, which he bought in 1788 and then enlarged. In 1978 the site became the Friendship Hill National Historic Site.

## ISAAC MEASON HOUSE
**Route 119, Dunbar Township**

Built by Isaac Meason, a wealthy ironmaster and businessman, this dressed-sandstone manor is a remarkably sophisticated structure for its time (1802) and place (west of the Alleghenies). Essentially a Palladian villa, the five-part composition consists of a two-story main block with one-story wings connected by hyphens. Beyond the wings, two identical offices add to the symmetry. Meason brought craftsman/architect Adam Wilson from England to design and build his house, which stands virtually unaltered.

## SEARIGHTS TOLLHOUSE, NATIONAL ROAD
**West of Uniontown near U.S. Route 40**

In 1831 the federal government turned over to Pennsylvania that portion of the National Road within the state. Four years later the Commonwealth authorized the construction of six tollhouses, two of which survive. The 20-foot, two-story tower on this hexagonal brick structure (1836) provided the tollhouse keeper with excellent views of the road in both directions, and the one-story wings afforded living space. The tollhouse, recently restored, is owned by the Pennsylvania Historical and Museum Commission and is maintained as a museum.

## ■ *Huntingdon County*

## EAST BROAD TOP RAILROAD
**U.S. Route 522, Rockhill Furnace**

One of the oldest narrow gauge lines in America, this railroad was established in 1871 and operated for more than 80 years as a coal-carrying line in the heart of Pennsylvania's bituminous coal mining region. In addition to carrying coal, the 33-mile line transported timber, sand, rock, general freight, and passengers. The railroad ceased operations in 1956, but much of the track and several engines have been preserved. Steam engines now provide nostalgic excursions on a restored portion of this rare vestige of a once common type of railroad.

## PULPIT ROCKS
**Old Huntingdon—Hollidaysburg Turnpike**

Pulpit Rocks, a dramatically picturesque group of sandstone pillars, is a prime example of the findings of the seminal First Geological Survey of Pennsylvania. Conducted between 1836 and 1842, the survey established the framework for all future geological work in the Appalachian Mountains and for stratigraphy throughout the eastern United States. It was at this site that surveyors first recognized the order in which sedimentary rocks of central Pennsylvania had been deposited, and where they discovered that there were three separate sandstone formations. Pulpit Rocks remains remarkably undisturbed and unchanged from the time it was first surveyed.

## ■ *Lackawanna County*

## TERENCE V. POWDERLY HOUSE
**614 North Main Street, Scranton**

This Victorian-era frame house was the longtime home of Terence Vincent Powderly, who headed the Knights of Labor from 1879 to 1893. The Knights, an early national labor organization, flourished under his leadership, and Powderly dominated the American labor movement during the 1880s. The Knights counted women and African Americans as members at a time when such inclusiveness was not the norm. The organization failed in the 1890s, largely because it opposed strikes, which soon became the labor movement's modus operandi.

## ■ Lancaster County

### JAMES BUCHANAN HOUSE
**1120 Marietta Avenue, Lancaster**

From 1849 until his death in 1868, James Buchanan, 15th president of the United States, maintained his primary residence at Wheatland, a 17-room brick house. Buchanan served as president from 1857 to 1861, years during which the nation moved inexorably toward disunion and civil war. After Abraham Lincoln was elected, Buchanan retired to Wheatland, where he wrote *Mr. Buchanan's Administration Upon the Eve of Rebellion*. Wheatland contains many Buchanan items and is open as a historic house museum.

### EPHRATA CLOISTER
**Junction of U.S. Routes 322 and 222, Ephrata**

Erected between 1740 and 1746, these mostly frame buildings with their steep, expansive gabled roofs and long shed-roofed dormers are among the most pronounced Germanic buildings erected in colonial America. They housed members of the Seventh Day Baptists, a pietistic monastic community that Conrad Beissel founded in 1732. During the Revolution, members of the Ephrata community nursed some 500 wounded soldiers from the Battle of Brandywine here. Now administered by the Pennsylvania Historical and Museum Commission, Ephrata Cloister is open to the public.

### FULTON OPERA HOUSE
**12–14 North Prince Street, Lancaster**

This early-Victorian structure was built in 1852 to serve several civic purposes and was remodeled in the Italianate style in 1873 by architect Samuel Sloane as the Fulton Opera House. It was named in honor of Robert Fulton, native of Lancaster County whose statue centers a niche in the facade. The opera house was restored in the 1960s and continues in use as an active theater.

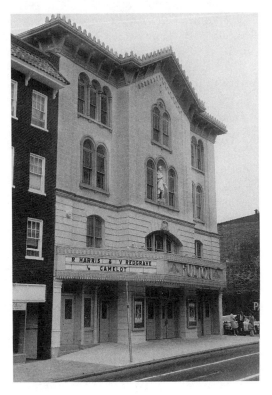

*Fulton Opera House, Lancaster, Lancaster County, 1968. Courtesy of NPS.*

### ROBERT FULTON BIRTHPLACE
**8 miles south of Quarryville on U.S. Route 22**

This stone house was the birthplace of Robert Fulton, artist, civil engineer, and inventor. A multifaceted genius, Fulton is best remembered for designing the *Clermont* (a.k.a. "Fulton's Folly"), the first commercially successful American steamboat. When it was launched in August 1807, a new era in water-borne transportation was opened. The Commonwealth of Pennsylvania acquired Fulton's birthplace in 1969 and subsequently restored it. The house is open to the public.

### STIEGEL-COLEMAN HOUSE
**Pennsylvania Route 501 and U.S. Route 322, Brickerville**

William Stiegel built the first part of this expansive stone complex in 1756–1758, near his Elizabeth Furnace that produced war material to aid in the Revolution. After Stiegel's death, Robert Coleman bought the property, constructed a large addition, continued the furnace operations, and amassed one of the largest fortunes in post-Revolutionary Pennsylvania. Both men were significant early industrialists, and the property is associated with more than a century of American iron manufacturing.

### ■ Lebanon County

### BOMBERGER'S DISTILLERY

**7 miles southwest of Newmanstown off Pennsylvania Route 501**

Dating from 1753, when it was operated by John and Michael Shenk, Bomberger's—later Michter's—was the nation's oldest distillery when it was designated a National Historic Landmark. Under its several names, it represented the transformation of whiskey

distilling from a small agricultural enterprise into a large-scale industry. The still house, warehouse, and jug house date from about 1840. Faced with financial problems, the distillery closed in 1981, and the property has since deteriorated.

### CORNWALL IRON FURNACE

**Rexmont Road and Boyd Street, Cornwall**

Cornwall represents the type of furnace that produced most of America's iron from prior to the Revolution until after the Civil War. Producing pig iron from 1742 to 1883, Cornwall is one of the best-preserved charcoal furnaces in the country. Nearby, the Cornwall Ore Banks, mined continuously

*Cornwall Iron Furnace, Cornwall, Lebanon County. Courtesy of NPS (Constance M. Greiff).*

*Union Canal Tunnel, Lebanon, Lebanon County. Courtesy of NPS (Robie Lange).*

Henry Antes House, Upper Frederick Township, Montgomery County. Courtesy of NPS (George E. Thomas).

from 1742 to 1974, constituted the largest known iron ore deposits in America until the discovery of Minnesota's Mesabi Range in 1887. The miners' village and ironmaster's house also remain as part of this historic district. Administered by the Pennsylvania Historical and Museum Commission, the restored furnace is open to the public.

## UNION CANAL TUNNEL
**Tunnel Hill Road, Lebanon vicinity**

Tunnel technology in the early 19th century was crude, arduous, and dangerous, but, as proven here, it could be successful. Dug, drilled, and excavated between 1825 and 1827 as part of an 80-mile canal, the Union Canal Tunnel is the oldest extant canal tunnel in the United States. The canal linked the Susquehanna and the Schuylkill Rivers, and provided swift, cheap, and easy transportation for passengers and freight between Philadelphia and Pennsylvania's resource-rich interior. The tunnel is located at the canal's highest elevation, taking it under Pansy Hill.

## ■ *Lehigh County*
## GEORGE TAYLOR HOUSE
**Front Street, Catasauqua**

George Taylor came to Pennsylvania in 1736 as an indentured servant. Put to work at an iron furnace, he soon became manager, and—almost as soon—husband of his for-

mer employer's widow. He produced cannon and cannon balls for the Revolutionary cause, to which he also pledged his support as a signer of the Declaration of Independence. From 1768 to 1776 he lived in this two-story stone house, now a historic house museum.

## ■ *Montgomery County*
## HENRY ANTES HOUSE
**Colonial Road, Upper Frederick Township**

This stone house, with its sparse fenestration, three-room plan, central chimney, and steep gabled roof, easily recalls the homeland of its builder, Henry Antes. Built in 1736, it is one of the best remaining representatives of a colonial house type once prevalent in Pennsylvania and in other areas settled by Germans. Antes held frequent evangelical and political meetings here to promote understanding among colonists of different religions, cultures, and races. He became the Moravian Church's chief architect and builder, directing work in Pennsylvania and in North Carolina. The Moravian school established in the house was one of the first interracial, nonsectarian schools in the state.

## AUGUSTUS LUTHERAN CHURCH
**Seventh Avenue East and Main Street, Trappe**

Dedicated in September 1745, this distinctive structure with polygonal apse and gambrel

*Augustus Lutheran Church, Trappe, Montgomery County, 1967. Courtesy of NPS (Charles W. Snell).*

roof is one of the country's best examples of vernacular German ecclesiastical architecture. It is also the oldest extant Lutheran church in the nation. Exterior walls, of sandstone, have been stuccoed since 1814. Most of the original interior fittings remain, including the pulpit and the balcony railing, with its cutout heart figures.

## GRAEME PARK
### Keith Valley Road, Horsham

This gambrel-roofed stone mansion, long and narrow in plan, is noted for its rich Georgian interiors. The building is actually an early example of a major architectural remodeling. It was built in 1721–1722 as the malt house for a brewery established by provincial governor William Keith. Between 1739 and 1740, his son-in-law, Dr. Thomas Graeme, remodeled it into a dwelling, and the interior woodwork dates from that time. Remarkably unchanged since then, Graeme Park is open to the public as a historic house museum managed by the Pennsylvania Historical and Museum Commission.

## GREY TOWERS
### Easton Road and Limekiln Pike, Glenside

Constructed in 1893, this American "castle" typifies the architectural image that families of great wealth and pretensions sought at the

turn of the century. Architect Horace Trumbauer designed the huge stone pile for sugar refiner William Welsh Harrison, drawing on a number of European structures for inspiration. It was Trumbauer's first major project and inaugurated a career that included a number of commissions from other Americans of similar wealth and aspirations. Beaver College purchased Grey Towers in 1929, two years after its builder's death, and it remains, by far, the most imposing structure on campus.

## MERION CRICKET CLUB
### Montgomery Avenue and Grays Lane, Haverford

Founded in 1865 and located at this site since 1892, the Merion Cricket Club is among a handful of properties that illustrate the history of cricket, English in origin but once a major American sport. After 1900 the club's members assumed a vigorous role in promoting the new sport of lawn tennis, and in 1939 the great lawn in front of the clubhouse was the setting for the Davis Cup competition. Frank Furness, one of Philadelphia's premier Victorian-era architects, designed the main portion of the stone and brick clubhouse.

## MERION FRIENDS MEETING HOUSE
### 615 Montgomery Avenue, Merion Station

Merion Friends Meeting House is the building most closely associated with the "Merioneth Adventurers," a group of Welsh Quakers who came to Pennsylvania in 1682. The earliest known migration of Celtic-speaking Welsh people in the Western Hemisphere, they came in response to the egalitarian policies that William Penn established in his colony. The building is the second-oldest Friends meeting house in the country, having been started ca. 1695 and completed by 1714. The stone-walled church, now stuccoed, is in the form of a T and is a rare survivor of Welsh-inspired vernacular architecture.

## MILL GROVE
**Pawling Road, Audubon**

From 1804 to 1808 this native fieldstone house was home to the fledgling naturalist and artist John James Audubon. Like the birds he painted, however, Audubon flitted from place to place throughout his career. His father, who owned Mill Grove, sent his Haitian-born, French-bred son here at age 18, likely so that he would avoid Napoleon's draft. Here Audubon first observed the birds of America, experimented in banding, practiced taxidermy, and began painting. Now open to the public as a museum, the house contains a rare collection of the artist's work. Fittingly, the surrounding acreage is a wildlife sanctuary.

## M. CAREY THOMAS LIBRARY
**Bryn Mawr College, Bryn Mawr**

Completed in 1907, this library honors M. Carey Thomas, who broke new ground by establishing academic opportunities for women at Bryn Mawr that paralleled the highest standards in higher education for men. As first dean of the college that was founded in 1885, and as its second president—from 1894 to 1922—Thomas established entrance exams, made the study of Latin and Greek mandatory, and created a curriculum offering subjects previously unavailable to women. In addition, she inaugurated a far-reaching building campaign that resulted in Bryn Mawr's becoming the first college in the country where the Collegiate Gothic Style predominated.

## VALLEY FORGE (NPS)
**Norristown (Chester and Montgomery Counties)**

(See entry under Chester County.)

## WASHINGTON'S HEADQUARTERS, VALLEY FORGE (NPS)
**Valley Creek Road, near junction of Pennsylvania Route 252 and 23, Valley Forge State Park**

This stone farmhouse served as Washington's headquarters from Christmas Eve 1777 to June 1778, during the Continental army's Valley Forge encampment. From February through June, Martha Washington left the comforts of Mount Vernon to join her husband here. The house, built by Isaac Potts, a Quaker, has a surprisingly elaborate Georgian interior. Restored and open to the public, it has been included in Valley Forge National Historical Park since 1976.

## WOODMONT
**1622 Spring Mill Road, Gladwyne**

Woodmont was designed by architect William Lightfoot Price and built in the 1890s for industrialist Alan Wood, Jr. Along with its support buildings, it is a superb example of a large country estate of its time. The house, imitating a medieval French château, is replete with turrets and towers, oriels and gargoyles. In 1952, the Reverend M. F. Divine, better known as Father Divine, made Woodmont his home and headquarters. A charismatic African-American preacher, he had great success in breaking down color lines and fostered integration long before the national civil rights movement. Father Divine is buried on the property, which is open to the public.

■ *Northampton County*

## 1762 WATERWORKS
**East Bank of Monocacy Creek, Bethlehem**

Begun in 1754 and enlarged in 1762, the Bethlehem Waterworks is thought to be the first municipal pumping system to provide drinking and washing water in the United States. The system served the city until 1832. By the 1960s the area had become an automobile junkyard. The stone pumphouse was restored in the 1970s, and the waterwheel and pumps were subsequently reconstructed based on the original plans that had been preserved in the Moravian Archives in Germany.

## DELAWARE CANAL
**Parallels the west bank of the Delaware River from Easton to Bristol (Bucks and Northampton Counties)**

(See entry under Bucks County.)

## GEMEINHAUS–DE SCHWEINITZ RESIDENCE
**West Church Street, Bethlehem**

This was the birthplace and longtime home of Lewis David de Schweinitz, Moravian minister and naturalist. During the early 19th century he made significant contributions to the study of botany in America and abroad. While serving as general agent of the southern province of the Moravian Church, he wrote *The Fungi of North Carolina* (1818), containing descriptions of more than 1,000 species. He followed this work with "A Synopsis of North American Fungi," published in *Transactions,* the journal of the American Philosophical Society, in 1834. Of the 3,000 species it described, de Schweinitz had discovered 1,200. His log house, dating from 1733–1743, is Bethlehem's oldest, and is open to the public.

## ■ *Northumberland County*
### JOSEPH PRIESTLEY HOUSE
**Priestley Avenue, Northumberland**

Joseph Priestley, trained as a minister, became increasingly interested in chemistry, and most especially in gases, while still in England. In the early 1770s he identified carbon dioxide and established a simple method for its extraction, but his chief fame derives from his identifying oxygen in 1776. An amateur scientist, Priestly never realized the importance of discovering what he called "dephlogisticated air." In 1794 he set sail for America, and "imported" carpenters from Philadelphia to build this frame house. Priestley continued his experiments during his Pennsylvania years

and discovered carbon monoxide while working here. The Pennsylvania Historical and Museum Commission maintains the house, which is open to the public.

## ■ *Philadelphia County*
### ACADEMY OF MUSIC
**Broad and Locust Streets, Philadelphia**

Opened in 1857, this is the country's oldest auditorium retaining its original form and serving its original purpose. Architect Napoleon Le Brun was influenced by European opera houses in designing this Renaissance Revival structure of brownstone and brick. The elegant auditorium is known around the world for its fine sight lines and acoustics. Since the turn of the 20th century, the "Grand Old Lady of Broad Street" has been the home of the Philadelphia Orchestra.

## AMERICAN PHILOSOPHICAL SOCIETY HALL (NPS)
**Independence Square, Philadelphia**

Since 1789 this two-story late-Georgian brick building has housed the fortnightly meetings of one of America's oldest and most honorable learned societies. The organization traces its origins to 1743, when Benjamin Franklin publicly urged the creation of an institution to stimulate interest in learning. Over the years the Society has counted America's intellectual elite among its members. Thomas Jefferson was one, and at his urging, the records of the Lewis and Clark Expedition are preserved in the Hall. The Society's journal, *Transactions,* continues as the country's oldest scholarly periodical.

## ATHENAEUM
**219 South Sixth Street, Philadelphia**

Built between 1845 and 1847, this is one of the first Renaissance Revival buildings in the nation. Architect John Notman, who won the design competition, described the facade as "an excellent specimen of the Italian style of architecture," and the commission helped him gain a reputation as one of the leading architects of his time. Notman's use of brownstone was also innovative and helped promote the material in Philadelphia and beyond. The Athenaeum was founded in 1814 and continues as a major force in the intellectual life of the city and the nation.

## JOHN BARTRAM HOUSE
### 54th Street and Eastwick Avenue, Philadelphia

John Bartram was America's first native botanist of note, and through his extensive correspondence and travels, he brought native plants to the attention of botanists around the world. In 1765 he was appointed botanist to King George III. Bartram built this stone house between 1730 and 1731 and surrounded it with extensive gardens filled with rare and exotic plants. His son later enlarged the gardens, and both house and grounds are now preserved and open to the public.

## BECUNA
### Penn's Landing, Delaware Avenue and Spruce Street, Philadelphia

An example of the standard Fleet type, Balao class, submarines that could operate at a test depth of 400 feet, *Becuna* was commissioned in 1944 and served as the submarine flagship of the Pacific Fleet in World War II under command of General Douglas MacArthur. It is credited with sinking 3,888 tons of Japanese shipping and received four battle stars for its World War II service. *Becuna* was decommissioned in 1969 and is now berthed at Penn's Landing in Philadelphia, where it serves as an educational resource and tourist attraction alongside the cruiser *Olympia*.

## BOATHOUSE ROW
### 1–15 East River Drive, Philadelphia

Situated on the bank of the Schuylkill, these 15 private clubhouses are a sports and social center for many Philadelphians. The parent organization, the Schuylkill Navy, was formed in 1858 and continues as the nation's oldest amateur governing body in sports. The Navy restricts its contests to amateurs, and its rules have helped clarify distinctions between amateur and professional sports. One of the buildings houses the oldest club in the United States, another the oldest women's club. Architect Frank Furness designed the Undine Barge Club, which partisans consider—architecturally speaking— "the best little oar house."

## CARPENTERS' HALL (NPS)
### 320 Chestnut Street, Philadelphia

Erected between 1770 and 1773 as a guild hall for the Carpenters' Company of Philadelphia, this jaunty two-story brick building with its prominent cupola is one of the country's finest examples of late Georgian public architecture. Robert Smith, originally from Scotland and a member of the organization that promoted fellowship along with good design and craftsmanship, provided the design. The First Continental Congress met in the Hall in 1774, and it served as a hospital for both British and American troops in the Revolution. It later became the temporary office of both the First and Second Banks of the United States. Carpenters' Hall is still owned and used by the group for whom it was built.

## CHRIST CHURCH, PHILADELPHIA (NPS)
### Second Street, between Market and Filbert Streets, Philadelphia

This elegant brick building is the most ornate colonial church in America, and one of the largest. Its Georgian design, verging on the Baroque, makes it also one of the most distinguished architecturally, although the prominent tower that once dominated Philadelphia has been dwarfed by later, taller buildings. The church, third on its site, was constructed between 1727 and 1754, when the steeple was completed. It houses a still-active parish that was organized in 1695.

## CHURCH OF THE ADVOCATE
### 18th and Diamond Streets, Philadelphia

Built between 1887 and 1897 with a private bequest and from designs by architect Charles M. Burns, Jr., this church was intended to serve as the Episcopal Cathedral of Philadelphia. The church and its attendant buildings are remarkable documents of late Gothic Revival architecture, with notable sculpture and stained glass, the latter executed by the English firm of Clayton & Bell. In the late 20th century, the Church of the Advocate promoted extensive social reform and embraced the causes of civil rights. It housed the third annual National Conference on Black Power in 1968 and the first

*Cliveden, Philadelphia, Philadelphia County, 1967. Courtesy of NPS (Charles W. Snell).*

ordination of women in the Episcopal Church in 1974.

## CLIVEDEN
### Germantown Avenue, between Johnson and Cliveden Streets, Philadelphia

Cliveden, completed in 1764, survives as a superb example of late-Georgian architecture, and as the most important landmark associated with the Battle of Germantown. The stuccoed-stone house, its gabled roof decorated with arched dormers and urns, was the country estate of Benjamin Chew, attorney general of Pennsylvania. The battle that raged around it on October 4, 1777, left its scars when Washington ordered a full-scale assault on a British contingent. Although Germantown was an American defeat, it was not a disaster. Impressed with Washington's strategic ability—aided by the victory at Saratoga that same month—the French decided to help the American cause. Cliveden has been restored and is open to the public as a historic house museum.

## COLONIAL GERMANTOWN HISTORIC DISTRICT
### Germantown Avenue, between Windrum Avenue and Upsal Street, Philadelphia

Late-17th-century religious persecution in Europe led to the establishment of this first German settlement in the New World.

Francis Daniel Pastorius arrived in August 1683, and other settlers followed in October. Soon a sizeable settlement, encouraged by William Penn's Quaker doctrine of "live and let live," was flourishing several miles northwest of colonial Philadelphia. This linear historic district, now incorporated within Philadelphia's city limits, stretches several miles along Germantown Avenue and contains a number of houses built by several generations of German colonists.

## JOHN COLTRANE HOUSE
### 1511 North 33d Street, Philadelphia

Tenor saxophonist and American jazz pioneer John Coltrane lived here from 1952 until his death in 1967. A musician and composer, Coltrane played a central role in the development of jazz during the 1950s and 1960s. He took the American jazz tradition as it had developed by the late 1940s, with its established forms and harmonies, and radically transformed it, pioneering modal harmonies and incorporating influences from a variety of international sources. Along with Louis Armstrong and Charlie Parker, Coltrane was one of the most influential performing soloists in the history of jazz.

## EDWARD D. COPE HOUSE
### 2102 Pine Street, Philadelphia

The building at 2102 Pine Street, a unit in a

group of stone row houses, was the home of Edward Drinker Cope from 1880 until his death in 1897. Cope was one of America's most prolific and creative 19th-century geologists and paleontologists. He is credited with some 1,300 titles, and his entry in the National Academy of Science's *Biographical Memoir Series* runs to 60 pages.

## THOMAS EAKINS HOUSE
### 1729 Mount Vernon Place, Philadelphia

Born in Philadelphia in 1844, Thomas Eakins lived in this brick row house from the age of two until his death in 1919. One of America's greatest painters, Eakins was often rebuffed and scorned, even by—often especially by—those who sat for him. His unrelentingly realistic, often uncomplimentary, portraits eschew surface expression to focus on inner truth and character. Walt Whitman initially disliked his 1887 portrait, but came to understand that "The more I get to realize it, the profounder seems its insight." The house is now a community arts center.

## EASTERN STATE PENITENTIARY
### 21st Street and Fairmount Avenue, Philadelphia

"The exterior...should convey to the mind a cheerless blank indicative of the misery that awaits the unhappy being who enters within its walls." With this ominous directive, architect John Haviland designed a mammoth stone complex that remains the prime example of the Pennsylvania system of imprisonment, one that had limited influence in the United States but was widely studied and applied abroad. Haviland's architectural expression of a system that emphasized solitary confinement, but hoped to reform rather than purely punish, incorporated a radial plan around a central rotunda. The first prisoner arrived in 1829, and the last left when it ceased operations in 1970. The Pennsylvania Prison Society now gives tours of the penitentiary.

## ELFRETH'S ALLEY HISTORIC DISTRICT
### Between Second and Front Streets, Philadelphia

This block-long alley was opened between 1702 and 1704 by mutual agreement of two

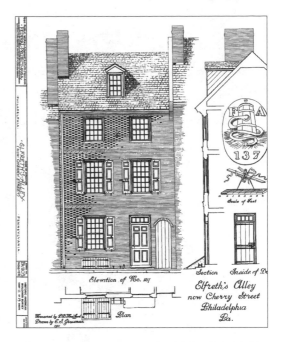

*Elfreth's Alley Historic District, Philadelphia, Philadelphia County. No. 137, 1940. Courtesy of HABS (C. S. Grossman).*

adjoining landowners on Front Street. It now survives as the oldest unchanged and continuously inhabited street in Philadelphia. Its narrow two- and three-story dwellings, their facades flush on the narrow sidewalks, were occupied by artisans and tradesmen and are remarkable survivors of colonial America's largest city. The Elfreth's Alley Association, established in 1934, safeguards the unique character of this charming urban enclave, a living vestige of the past.

## FAIRMOUNT WATER WORKS
### East bank of the Schuylkill River, Philadelphia

This engineering triumph and architectural masterpiece was built to supplement Philadelphia's first water system. It opened in 1815 as the nation's first municipal waterworks to use paddle wheels to pump water. Later, it was the first to replace that system with more efficient turbine engines. The impressive machinery was housed within a picturesque group of four Greek Revival buildings standing on a terrace above the Schuylkill. The grounds were landscaped to form one of the first parks—as opposed to town squares and commons—in the country.

*Fairmount Water Works, Philadelphia, Philadelphia County. Courtesy of HAER (Jack E. Boucher).*

*First Bank of the United States, Philadelphia, Philadelphia County. Courtesy of the Independence National Historical Park Collection.*

## FIRST BANK OF THE UNITED STATES (NPS)

### 116 South Third Street, Philadelphia

The proposal to charter this institution provoked the first great debate over a strict versus expansive interpretation of the Constitution. Congress and President Washington, following Secretary of the Treasury Alexander Hamilton's argument for an assumption of implied powers, chartered the bank and helped to ensure the new nation's survival and continuing growth. Samuel Blodgett designed the impressive headquarters, likely the first example of the use of marble on the facade of a major building in the country. The First Bank was built in 1794–1797 and is now a unit of Independence National Historical Park.

## FORT MIFFLIN
**Marina and Penrose Ferry Roads, Philadelphia**

This fort on Mud Island in the Delaware River was begun in 1772 by the British to defend the water approach to Philadelphia. American forces captured it during the Revolution, and in 1777 a small garrison resisted some of the heaviest bombardments of the war. Their action delayed the British occupation of Philadelphia, but Americans were eventually forced to burn and evacuate the fort. Fort Miflin was rebuilt during John Adams's administration, was manned in the War of 1812, and served as a Confederate prison during the Civil War. It was disarmed in 1904 and is now open to the public except during winter months.

## FOUNDER'S HALL, GIRARD COLLEGE
**Corinthian and Girard Avenues, Philadelphia**

This building represents an outstanding example of philanthropic support for education in the United States and is one of the finest examples of Greek Revival architecture in the country. In 1831, wealthy merchant Stephen Girard bequeathed property worth more than $6 million to establish an educational institution to be operated by the city. Girard College opened in 1848 in this magnificent Corinthian structure, designed by architect Thomas U. Walter.

## FRIENDS HOSPITAL
**4641 Roosevelt Boulevard, Philadelphia**

Friends Hospital opened in 1817 as the first private, nonprofit hospital in the United States devoted exclusively to treating mentally ill patients. The social and medical concerns of Quakers regarding psychiatric problems influenced the physical site plan and the methodology of treatment for "such of our members who may be deprived of the use of their reason." These approaches became the model for similar facilities in the 19th and early 20th centuries. The hospital's design, based on William Tuke's York Retreat in England, but with better ventilation and light as suggested by Philadelphia Friend Thomas Scattergood, also became a model for other American mental facilities.

## FURNESS LIBRARY, SCHOOL OF FINE ARTS, UNIVERSITY OF PENNSYLVANIA
**34th Street below Walnut Street, Philadelphia**

Completed in 1890, this is a major work by an important late-19th-century architect, Frank Furness. The overall appearance of the stone-trimmed red-brick structure is ecclesiastical, with both Romanesque and Gothic elements, including gargoyles and distinctive, monumental foliate carving. The interior plan is considered one of the most innovative of its time, with separate reading rooms and stacks. The stack wing was designed so that the rear wall could be removed and new bays added as the book collections grew.

## GERMANTOWN (MANHEIM) CRICKET CLUB
**5140 Morris Street, Philadelphia**

Founded in 1855, this is the second-oldest cricket club in the United States. Whereas its namesake sport dominated club activities in the 19th century, tennis gained prominence in the early 20th. William T. "Big Bill" Tilden, an international tennis star of the 1920s, was a member. The imposing brick clubhouse is an accomplished example of early Georgian Revival architecture and was designed by Charles F. McKim of McKim, Mead and White. Completed in 1891, it served as a prototype for numerous area buildings designed in the same style.

## FRANCES ELLEN WATKINS HARPER HOUSE
**1006 Bainbridge Street, Philadelphia**

Frances Ellen Watkins Harper was born of free black parents in Baltimore in 1825. She became a writer and social activist and participated in the abolitionist, black rights, women's suffrage, and temperance movements. Harper began her career as an abolitionist spokesperson in 1854 when the Maine Anti-Slavery Society hired her to lecture in New England and lower Canada. After her death, W. E. B. Du Bois stated that she deserved most to be remembered "for her attempts to forward literature among colored people." Harper lived in this Philadelphia row house from 1870 until her death in 1911.

## HILL-KEITH-PHYSICK HOUSE
### 321 South Fourth Street, Philadelphia

This impressive free-standing brick town house was the home of Philip Syng Physick from ca. 1815 until his death in 1837. Physick has been called the father of American surgery. He designed a number of innovative surgical instruments and achieved fame as a lecturer at the Pennsylvania Hospital and the University of Pennsylvania. Many of his students went on to occupy leading positions in medicine throughout the country. His home is now a historic house museum.

## INSTITUTE OF THE PENNSYLVANIA HOSPITAL
### 111 North 49th Street, Philadelphia

Begun in 1854 and completed in 1859 from plans by Dr. Thomas Story Kirkbride, this hospital introduced innumerable innovations in the treatment of the mentally ill. Kirkbride believed that patients suffering from mental illness should be treated with the same consideration as those suffering from other sicknesses. Fresh air, proper ventilation, light, and adequate supervision were among the needs he specifically addressed. Kirkbride also authored a book on the subject of hospitals for the mentally ill. It—and the Institute—influenced the design of hospitals that followed the "Kirkbride Plan" in more than 31 other states.

## INSURANCE COMPANY OF NORTH AMERICA (INA) BUILDING
### 1600 Arch Street, Philadelphia

The Insurance Company of North America (INA) is the oldest capital stock insurance company in the United States. Founded in 1792 and incorporated in 1794, the company pioneered many forms of insurance, in particular marine underwriting. INA was also the first American firm to insure the *contents* of houses against fire, in addition to the structures themselves. This imposing 16-story steel-framed office building, faced in brick with limestone trim, was completed in 1925 as the company's ninth home office.

## JOHNSON HOUSE
### 6306 Germantown Avenue, Philadelphia

Philadelphia was a center of the 19th-century American movement to abolish slavery, and the Johnson House was an important station on the Underground Railroad that helped lead so many to freedom. From 1770 to 1908, five generations of the Quaker Johnson family, leading abolitionists and reformers, lived in this colonial stone house. Among the oldest structures in Germantown, it later served as a women's club and is now a historic house museum. The house is within the Colonial Germantown National Historic Landmark District.

*Institute of the Pennsylvania Hospital, Philadelphia, Philadelphia County, ca. 1856. Thomas S. Kirkbridge, On Hospitals (Philadelphia, 1880).*

## LAUREL HILL CEMETERY
### 3822 Ridge Avenue, Philadelphia

Designed by John Notman in 1835–1836, Laurel Hill is one of America's oldest "romantic" cemeteries. Although its primary purpose was obvious, it was also intended to be a place where mourners and tourists alike could seek comfort and solace (not only from their grief, but also from the increasing urbanism around them) as they wandered along winding walkways among its elaborate tombs and landscaped grounds. Andrew Jackson Downing cited Laurel Hill as a model for large urban parks, at a time when city dwellers were in desperate need of green space. The cemetery is open to the public.

## J. PETER LESLEY HOUSE
### 1008 Clinton Street, Philadelphia

From 1869 until 1896, J. Peter Lesley, one of America's foremost geologists, had his residence and office here. Lesley served as geologist for the State of Pennsylvania and was director of the Second Geological Survey of Pennsylvania from 1874 to 1896, an extraordinary survey that eventually resulted in 120 volumes. Lesley is regarded as the father of the science of topographic geology, and he achieved acclaim for mapping the state's anthracite districts. His detailed and precise maps were put to practical use in mining operations.

## JAMES LOGAN HOME
### 18th and Courtland Streets, Philadelphia

Stenton was built in 1728 as the country seat of James Logan, who was recognized in his lifetime as "a universal man in the Renaissance tradition." Arriving in Philadelphia in 1699 as William Penn's secretary, Logan occupied pivotal roles in the colony's government—including that of governor—for 50 years. He assembled one of the best libraries in colonial America, discovered the vital role of pollen in the fertilization of corn (an achievement that caused Linnaeus to consider him "among the demigods of science"), and amassed a fortune in the fur trade. His house, now open as a historic house museum, is an outstanding example of early American Georgian architecture.

## MEMORIAL HALL, PHILADELPHIA
### West Fairmount Park, Philadelphia

The only major structure now remaining from those built specifically for the 1876 Philadelphia Centennial Exposition, Memorial Hall served as the fair's art gallery. At the time, only three American cities had art museums, and those in Boston and New York were still under construction. Memorial Hall, most pretentious of the lot, was designed by 30-year old Herman Joseph Schwartzmann, who also planned the exposition's grounds and 33 other buildings at the fair. His Beaux-Arts arrangement of a central block with corner pavilions, embellished with coupled columns and niches filled with statues, established the architectural character for American art museums for decades.

## MOTHER BETHEL A.M.E. CHURCH
### 419 Sixth Street, Philadelphia

Founded in 1793 in a frame building on the site, Mother Bethel is the mother church of its denomination, the African Methodist Episcopal church. It was founded by former slave Richard Allen, who left Saint George's Methodist Church in protest against its segregated worship practices. The church Allen founded attempted not only to answer religious needs, but to deal with the political, social, and economic affairs of its members. The present church, fourth on the site, is a monumental granite-faced building dating from 1889. Richard Allen is buried in its crypt.

## MOUNT PLEASANT
### East Fairmount Park, Philadelphia

Completed in 1762, this is one of the finest examples of late-Georgian domestic architecture in the Middle Colonies and the most opulent of the villas that once surrounded Philadelphia. Built of stone, stuccoed, with brick trim, Mount Pleasant consists of a large central block flanked by identical pavilions—a familiar Palladian arrangement. Sea captain and privateer John MacPherson built the house, which is now a historic house museum furnished primarily with fine Philadelphia pieces.

*Mount Pleasant, Philadelphia, Philadelphia County, 1967. Courtesy of NPS (Charles W. Snell).*

## NEW CENTURY GUILD
### 1307 Locust Street, Philadelphia

This building has served the New Century Guild from 1906 to the present. Founded in 1882, the Guild was one of the earliest, largest, and most successful organizations created to deal with issues that arose as more and more women entered the nation's work force at the end of the 19th century. The Guild's goal was to address specific needs of "self-supporting women," a bold step when many Americans believed that no self-respecting woman would work for pay outside her home. Among the innovative services the Guild offered its clients were a newspaper (founded in 1887 and still published), evening classes, a staffed library, a restaurant, guest rooms, and— definitely not least — a health insurance plan.

## NEW MARKET
### South Second Street, between Pine and Lombard Streets, Philadelphia

This rare survivor of a once common urban amenity was established in 1745 in response to the city's burgeoning population, particularly in the Society Hill area. Like the older Market Street Market it supplemented, the New Market is simple and utilitarian in design, with two parallel rows of brick pillars supporting a gable roof. Unlike most of its type, which disappeared as neighborhood groceries took their place, New Market survived. So did its "head house," an attached firehouse built in 1804. Now restored, New Market is an important component of a renewed Society Hill and a visual reminder of how colonial Americans obtained their daily produce.

## *OLYMPIA*
### Pier 40, at the foot of Chestnut Street, Philadelphia

The oldest steel-hulled American warship afloat, *Olympia* served as Commodore Dewey's flagship in the Battle of Manila Bay (1898). The cruiser was born out of a shipbuilding program of the 1880s and 1890s that aimed to create a "new navy." *Olympia* is the last ship remaining of the "Great White Fleet" and is also the sole surviving combatant of the Spanish-American War. At the end of World War I, *Olympia* returned home from France carrying the body of the Unknown Soldier. Now retired and restored to its 1898 appearance, this honored warrior is open to the public at Penn's Landing along with other ships.

## CHARLES WILLSON PEALE HOUSE
### 2100 Clarkson Avenue, Philadelphia

From 1810 to 1820, this was the home of Charles Willson Peale, the country's preeminent painter during its early national period.

Peale, remembered for his miniatures and portraits of notable Americans, painted seven likenesses of George Washington. Called by John Adams "a tender, soft, affectionate creature," Peale married three times, and had a dozen children by his first two wives. Siblings Raphael, Rembrandt, and Reubens Peale were among his children who also achieved fame as artists in their time.

## PENNSYLVANIA ACADEMY OF THE FINE ARTS
**Broad and Cherry Streets, Philadelphia**

Philadelphia architect Frank Furness was noted for his controversial designs, and this exuberant Victorian structure is the best preserved of his remaining buildings. It was completed in 1876, in time to be a focal point of the Philadelphia Centennial Exhibition. The Academy's broad polychromed facade on Broad Street is centered with an ornate, deeply recessed Gothic window above a double entrance. A list of the various materials that assail the eye — brownstone, sandstone, polished granite, red and black brick —hints at its rich exterior. Well-lit galleries of the fireproof structure contain one of the country's leading art collections.

## PENNSYLVANIA HOSPITAL
**Eighth and Spruce Streets, Philadelphia**

This prominent institution is the nation's oldest public hospital. Pennsylvania's colonial legislature authorized it in 1751, and it has been at its present location since 1756. The hospital was conceived by Dr. Thomas Bond, an eminent 18th-century Philadelphia physician, who attempted, but failed, to gain sufficient financial support. Benjamin Franklin came to the rescue and secured the necessary funds through efforts that included a promotional booklet, *Some Account of the Pennsylvania Hospital*. Although the hospital has been greatly enlarged over the years, the handsome exterior of the original Georgian structure survives remarkably unchanged.

## PHILADELPHIA CITY HALL
**Penn Square, at Broad and Market Streets, Philadelphia**

Designed by John McArthur, Jr., begun in 1872 and completed in 1901, Philadelphia's City Hall is the largest and most elaborate center of municipal government ever built in America. It is also one of the nation's finest examples of the Second Empire style. Alexander Milne Calder and assistants carved the hundreds of sculptures that adorn the building and were intended "to express American ideas and develop American genius." The central tower is topped by a 37-foot bronze statue of William Penn that, when it was hoisted into place, was the world's largest sculpture on a building.

## PHILADELPHIA CONTRIBUTIONSHIP
**212 South Fourth Street, Philadelphia**

In 1752, Benjamin Franklin founded and organized the Philadelphia Contributionship for the Insurance of Houses from Loss by Fire. It was the first fire insurance company in the United States and originated the practice of setting rates according to the quality of the risk. The Contributionship became a pioneer in the development of the insurance industry across the nation — despite the fact that it has never issued a policy beyond Philadelphia's immediate environs. Since 1836 this 3½-story red brick building, designed by architect Thomas U. Walter, has been the company's headquarters.

## PHILADELPHIA SAVINGS FUND SOCIETY (PSFS) BUILDING
**12 South 12th Street, Philadelphia**

This 36-story steel-framed structure, completed in 1932, is among the most important skyscrapers built in America in the period between the Chicago School, which flourished in the 1880s and 1890s, and the International Style of the 1950s. Designed by Philadelphian George Howe and Swiss-born William Lescaze, it represents an American synthesis of European Modernist architectural theories. Among its remarkable architectural qualities is its timelessness; even now most observers would be hard-pressed to guess from its sleek, streamlined appearance that the PSFS, as it is universally known, is almost three-quarters of a century old.

## PHILADELPHIA SCHOOL OF DESIGN FOR WOMEN
### 1346 North Broad Street, Philadelphia

From 1880 to 1959 this building housed the Philadelphia School of Design for Women, the first institution of its sort in the United States. Led by numerous prominent art educators, the school graduated women who became leaders in the fields of industrial design as well as the fine arts, helping America achieve independence from European dominance. The house that formed the nucleus of the school was once the home of the noted Shakespearean actor Edwin Forrest.

## PHILADELPHIA'S MASONIC TEMPLE
### 1 North Broad Street, Philadelphia

Dedicated in 1873, this Norman Romanesque style building contains some of the most ornate and beautifully detailed interiors of any Victorian structure in the nation. As is usual in Masonic Temples of this scale and caliber, individual halls are decorated in specific architectural styles: Egyptian, Ionic, Corinthian, Gothic, and Renaissance, among others. Philadelphia architect James Windrim, who later became supervising architect of the U.S. Treasury Department, designed the temple. George Herzog, who gained fame for his work at the 1876 Centennial Exposition, decorated the interiors.

## EDGAR ALLAN POE HOUSE (NPS)
### 532 North Seventh Street, Philadelphia

From 1842 to 1844, this narrow brick town house was home to Edgar Allen Poe, one of America's most famous writers. Poe authored some of his best-known works, including *The Murders in the Rue Morgue* and "The Raven" in the house. It was also while living here "that the last vestiges of his prosperity disappeared and that the swift descent into the whirlpool of despair took on an accelerated motion." Poe left in the spring of 1844 with his ailing wife, mother-in-law, aunt, and $4.50 in his pocket. The property became the Edgar Allan Poe National Historic Site in 1978 and is open to the public.

## RACE STREET MEETINGHOUSE
### 1515 Cherry Street, Philadelphia

Race Street Meetinghouse, built in 1856, served as the site of the Hicksite Yearly Meeting from 1857 to 1955 and was at the forefront of women's involvement in both the Quaker religion and American political activism. Many leaders in the women's movement were associated with this meetinghouse, among them abolitionist and activist Lucretia Mott, peace activist Hannah Clothier Hull, and suffrage leader Alice Paul.

## READING TERMINAL AND TRAINSHED
### 1115–1141 Market Street, Philadelphia

Completed in 1893, this is the largest single-span (259-foot, 8-inch), arched-roof train shed in the world. A monument in engineering history, it once covered 13 tracks and 8 platforms. Utilitarian in the extreme, it is attached to the rear of the more florid, eight-story "head house" terminal that contained waiting room and offices above. Joseph M. Wilson designed the shed for the Philadelphia and Reading Railroad, and because viaducts brought trains into the station's second-floor level, was able to incorpo-

*Reading Terminal and Trainshed, Philadelphia, Philadelphia County, 1974. Courtesy of HABS (Jack E. Boucher).*

rate a large market at street level. The market still exists, but the rest of the complex now serves as part of the Philadelphia Convention Center.

## REYNOLDS-MORRIS HOUSE
### 225 South Eighth Street, Philadelphia

Built between 1786 and 1787, this 3½-story brick house is one of the finest surviving examples of a Georgian town house in the nation. It was built by brothers John and William Reynolds and was one of the first houses of its caliber to be erected in its neighborhood. In the economic slump following the Revolution, the house was sold to Luke Wistar Morris, and it remained in that family for seven generations.

## RITTENHOUSETOWN HISTORIC DISTRICT
### 206–210 Lincoln Drive, Philadelphia

An important industrial community that spans the 17th, 18th, and 19th centuries, Rittenhousetown is the core of a village that grew up around the first paper mill in British North America, established by William Rittenhouse in 1690. At one time the village included more than 40 industrial, agricultural, institutional, and domestic structures; today, six houses and a barn survive. One of the houses, the William Rittenhouse House, is open to the public.

## SAINT JAMES THE LESS EPISCOPAL CHURCH
### Hunting Park Avenue at Clearfield Street, Philadelphia

This is the first example of a stylistically pure English parish church in America. Its plans, based on the 13th-century Cambridgeshire church of Saint Michael's, Long Stanton, were provided by the English Ecclesiological Society (the Cambridge Camden Society), whose mission was to spread the Gothic architectural gospel to the New World. Robert Ralston, wealthy landowner and merchant, was the major contributor to the church, which was consecrated in 1850. As he and his British cohorts had hoped, the church did indeed have a profound influence on the Gothic Revival in America.

## SAINT MARK'S EPISCOPAL CHURCH
### 1625 Locust Street, Philadelphia

In 1847 the vestry of Saint Mark's parish commissioned architect John Notman to design a "town church" of brownstone. Mindful that his work must follow ecclesiological dictates, Notman sent his plans to the Cambridge Camden Society for approval. The result, which contains elements modeled on several English churches, is one of the nation's finest examples of what has been termed "the archeological phase" of the

*Rittenhousetown Historic District, Philadelphia, Philadelphia County. View of 207 and 207A Lincoln Drive. Courtesy of NPS (George Thomas).*

Gothic Revival. The church is now surrounded by taller buildings in downtown Philadelphia, but with its stone tower and spire, this accomplished building—figuratively if not literally—still tops them all.

## SAINT PETER'S CHURCH
### Third and Pine Streets, Philadelphia

Constructed between 1758 and 1764, Saint Peter's Protestant Episcopal Church was designed by Philadelphia architect/builder Robert Smith. It is an outstanding—and extremely well-preserved—example of high-style Georgian architecture. The interior displays an innovative and rare architectural response to 18th-century Anglican liturgical requirements; the altar is at the east end and the pulpit is on axis at the west end, giving equal weight to the liturgy and the spoken word. The extraordinarily tall tower, designed by William Strickland, was built in the 1840s.

## SECOND BANK OF THE UNITED STATES (NPS)
### 420 Chestnut Street, Philadelphia

Completed in 1824, this huge temple of finance, modeled on the Parthenon, is one of the finest examples of Greek Revival architecture in the country. Seminal in its influence, it was designed by William Strickland. Congress chartered the Second Bank of the United States in 1817, and under Nicholas Biddle's leadership it became, for a while, an effective regulator of the national economy. Following the determined leadership of President Andrew Jackson, Congress allowed the bank's charter to expire in 1836. The building is now a unit of Independence National Historical Park and is open to the public.

## THOMAS SULLY RESIDENCE
### 530 Spruce Street, Philadelphia

Thomas Sully was one of the best-known American portraitists of his time, producing a phenomenal 2,600 works. English born, he lived and worked in several major cities along the eastern seaboard before settling in Philadelphia in 1808. For a short period, from 1828 to 1829, he lived in this brick row house. Except for trips abroad—one of which he took to do a portrait of Queen Victoria—he remained in the city until his death in 1872.

## HENRY O. TANNER HOMESITE
### 2903 West Diamond Street, Philadelphia

This row house, greatly altered from its original appearance, was the boyhood home of Henry Ossawa Tanner, one of America's best-known black artists. Tanner studied in Philadelphia under Thomas Eakins, and although he subsequently spent most of his productive life in Europe, many of his works, including his well-known *Banjo Lesson* (1893), reflect the black experience in

*Second Bank of the United States, Philadelphia, Philadelphia County. Courtesy of the Independence National Historical Park Collection.*

America. In 1927, New York's National Academy of Design elected Tanner as its first black academician.

## UNITED STATES NAVAL ASYLUM
**Grays Ferry Avenue at 24th Street, Philadelphia**

Completed in 1833, the Naval Asylum was designed to provide a home and hospital for disabled and destitute naval officers and seamen. Considered one of architect William Strickland's finest works, the Greek Revival main building is noted for its Ionic portico, which gives great distinction to an otherwise strictly utilitarian design. The complex is also noteworthy for its service as the country's first formal naval training school until 1845, when Annapolis became the facility's permanent home. The asylum was declared surplus after its personnel moved to a new facility in 1976.

## WAGNER FREE INSTITUTE OF SCIENCE
**17th Street and Montgomery Avenue, Philadelphia**

The Wagner Free Institute is an unparalleled survivor of a rare, almost extinct species: a privately endowed 19th-century scientific society. Philadelphia merchant, philanthropist, and amateur scientist William Wagner formally established it in 1855. Wagner selected John McArthur to design the building, which opened in 1865 and contains a lecture hall, library, and museum. The Institute is also significant for its association with Dr. Joseph Leidy, one of the most prominent biologists of the 19th century. It was one of the earliest proponents of adult education in the country and still offers a broad range of courses, lectures, and symposia.

## WALNUT STREET THEATRE
**Ninth and Walnut Streets, Philadelphia**

This is one of the oldest surviving theaters in the country. It opened in 1809 as the Olympic Theater and originally housed a circus, but within two years legitimate drama had taken center stage. Architect John Haviland remodeled the theater in 1828, and the current facade is patterned after his work.

Most of the major historic figures of the American stage—Sarah Bernhardt, Ellen Terry, Sir Henry Irving, Richard Mansfield, John Drew, and Maude Adams—have trod its boards.

## JOHN WANAMAKER STORE
**Juniper and Market Streets, Philadelphia**

Designed by Daniel H. Burnham and built in three stages between 1902 and 1910, this 12-story masonry-clad, steel-frame structure housed one of America's great retail firms. Although John Wanamaker did not found the modern department store, his far-reaching innovations, especially in advertising, were essential contributions to its evolution. Built on the site of his earlier "Grand Depot," this temple to retailing (it contains more than 45 acres of floor space) is known for its grand interior court, its huge pipe organ (largest in the world when it was installed in 1911), and its nine-foot bronze eagle with 5,000 feathers.

## WOODFORD
**East Fairmount Park, Philadelphia**

Begun in 1756, this is the first of the opulent Georgian villas built just outside Philadelphia, then the largest city in the colonies. William Coleman, a wealthy merchant and Pennsylvania Supreme Court judge, built the first story. The second story, with its handsome Palladian window, was added in 1772. Woodford, noted for its interior woodwork, is one of several houses in Fairmount Park that have been preserved and opened as historic house museums.

## WOODLANDS
**40th Street and Woodland Avenue, Philadelphia**

This two-story stone house is one of the earliest and most advanced examples of the Adamesque style in the country. The features that give it architectural distinction date from 1788 to 1790, when William Hamilton enlarged the house after his return from England. A handsome attenuated Doric portico graces the river facade, and semicircular projections on each end hint at intricate room arrangements within. In the 1840s the acreage surrounding the house was developed as a rural cemetery, with the natural, romantic landscaping then coming into vogue. The house became the caretaker's residence and is now surrounded by a notable collection of tombstones.

## WYCK
### 6026 Germantown Avenue, Philadelphia

Begun in 1690 by Hans Millan, a German immigrant recently arrived in Germantown, Wyck was subsequently enlarged, rebuilt, and lived in by nine generations of his family. The stone house, furnishings, and a rare collection of family papers survive to provide an unexcelled portrait of an American family's way of life through two centuries. The house was sensitively altered in 1824 by architect William Strickland and is now a historic house museum.

## ▪ Pike County

### MINISINK ARCHEOLOGICAL SITE
**Address Restricted, Bushkill vicinity**

Minisink was the most important Munsee Indian community during most of the 17th and 18th centuries. The Munsee lived in an area stretching from southern New York across northern New Jersey to northeastern Pennsylvania. Archeological resources found on this upper Delaware River island site have yielded information on their contact with colonial traders and settlers. Minisink is one of the most extensive, best-preserved, and most intensively studied archeological sites in the Northeast. (Also in Sussex County, New Jersey.)

### GIFFORD PINCHOT HOUSE
**West edge of Milford, Milford**

For 60 years this large stone mansion, styled by architect Richard Morris Hunt after a French château, was associated with Gifford Pinchot. Built in 1884–1886 as a summer home by his parents, it became the permanent home of their son and his wife in 1915. Pinchot, twice governor of Pennsylvania, is best remembered for his role as conservationist and forester. He established the nation's first graduate school of forestry at Yale, his alma mater, and created the U.S. Forest

Service in 1905. In 1963, the 100-acre estate was turned over to the U.S. Forest Service for use as a conference center.

## ▪ Venango County

### DRAKE OIL WELL
**Drake Well Memorial Park, 3 miles southeast of Titusville**

Great oaks from little acorns grow—and barrels of oil from little derricks flow. In the summer of 1859, Edwin L. Drake drilled the world's first successful oil well near the community of Titusville. The boom that followed made northwestern Pennsylvania the oil center of the United States for the next quarter-century. Now administered by the Pennsylvania Historical and Museum Commission, the site includes a museum and replicas of the first oil derrick and attendant machinery.

## ▪ Washington County

### EDWARD G. ACHESON HOUSE
**908 Main Street, Monongahela**

From 1890 to 1895 this brick house was the home of scientist Edward G. Acheson. In all probability it is also the site where, in 1891, he conducted experiments that led to his invention of Carborundum, the name he gave to silicon carbide. A mixture of clay and powdered coke, fused by means of an electrical current, Carborundum was then—and for 50 years remained—the hardest known artificial substance in the world. It has been used in countless industrial processes, primarily as an abrasive, over the years. Acheson's achievements are all the more remarkable in that he was self-educated and worked independently.

### DAVID BRADFORD HOUSE
**175 South Main Street, Washington**

Constructed in 1788, this 2½-story stone house was the residence of lawyer David Bradford, most prominent rebel leader in the famous Whiskey Rebellion of 1794. Bradford, envisioning himself a new George Washington called to lead his backwoods countrymen to victory, organized a march on Pittsburgh, but the insurrectionists sobered up when federal militia, ordered by the real president, Washington, appeared. The incident proved Washington's resolve to enforce the laws of the land and helped establish the principle that redress must be sought through legal means, not through force. Bradford was ultimately pardoned, and his house is now a museum owned by the Commonwealth of Pennsylvania.

## F. JULIUS LE MOYNE HOUSE
### 49 East Maiden Street, Washington

This handsome stone mansion was the residence of Dr. F. Julius LeMoyne from 1827 until his death in 1879. LeMoyne represents the mainstream of antislavery activity and thought before 1850. His philosophy was one of legitimate activism, and his house served as a depot for antislavery literature distributed throughout the Ohio Valley. The house was a station on the Underground Railroad, as letters of thanks from many who stopped here on their way to freedom attest. It now serves as headquarters and museum of the Washington County Historical Society.

### ■ *Wayne County*
## DELAWARE AND HUDSON CANAL
### Homesdale

Completed in 1828, the 108-mile canal was the main waterway connecting the anthracite coal fields of northeastern Pennsylvania with the furnaces of New York. Enormously profitable, the canal helped fuel America's industrial growth when coal was the nation's major source of power. The growth of the railroads led to the canal's demise in 1899. A number of vestiges, including locks and the Roebling Aqueduct spanning the Delaware River, remain and are included in this discontiguous National Historic Landmark. (Also in Orange, Sullivan, and Ulster Counties, New York.)

### ■ *Westmoreland County*
## BUSHY RUN BATTLEFIELD
### 2 miles east of Harrison City on Pennsylvania Route 993

Fought in August 1763, the two-day Battle of Bushy Run was a decisive Anglo-American victory during "Pontiac's Rebellion," the most determined and dangerous Indian campaign against the colonial frontier. Colonel Henry Bouquet feigned retreat, drawing the Indians into disorganized pursuit, then turned and attacked their flank. His victory ended the siege of Fort Pitt and demonstrated his ability to conduct warfare in the wilderness. The site is now Bushy Run Battlefield State Park.

# PUERTO RICO

### ■ *Dorado County*
## *ANTONIO LÓPEZ*
### Address Restricted, Dorado vicinity

The SS *Antonio López* is significant as the most important blockade runner and shipwreck of the Spanish-American War. Although several other Spanish vessels were lost in the conflict between Spain and the United States, the *Antonio López* is the only shipwreck in the Caribbean from that war that has been scientifically located and investigated. The ship is also significant in marine engineering and architecture of the late 19th century, with its steel construction and electric lighting system.

### ■ *San Juan County*
## CAPARRA ARCHEOLOGICAL SITE
### Museo y Parque, Highway 2, Guaynabo vicinity

The Caparra Site contains archeological remnants of Puerto Rico's first capital, the oldest known European community now under United States jurisdiction. The inland town was founded in 1508 by Juan Ponce de Leon, first governor of the island, but was abandoned in 1521 for San Juan, a more felicitous site on the harbor. A museum operated by the Institute for Puerto Rican Culture is part of the complex, now surrounded by Villa Caparra, a suburb of San Juan.

*Caparra Archeological Site, Guaynabo. Courtesy of the Puerto Rico State Historic Preservation Office (Eric Toledo).*

## LA FORTALEZA
### Between San Juan Bay and Calle Recinto Oeste

La Fortaleza was begun in 1533 as part of the city of San Juan's fortifications. It was largely destroyed by a Dutch invasion in 1625 and was later damaged by fire. Reconstruction began in 1640, but because the island's governors had already begun to reside here, the rebuilding was more along domestic than military lines. La Fortaleza was further remodeled and enlarged in subsequent centuries, and in 1822 was declared the official governor's residence, more than a century after it was first used as such. Its present neoclassical appearance dates from an 1846 remodeling. In 1983, La Fortaleza and the adjoining San Juan National Historic Site were added to the United Nations Educational, Scientific, and Cultural Organization's (UNESCO) World Heritage List.

## ■ *Utuado County*

## CAGUANA SITE
### Caguana Indian Ceremonial Park and Museum, New Mexico Highway 11, Utuado vicinity

The Caguana (Capa) Site, dating from A.D. 1200 to 1500, is the largest and most complex ceremonial site in Puerto Rico and the West Indies. Constructed by the Tiano Indians, the site consists of a ceremonial dance area and ten earth-and-stone–lined ball courts. Investigation of the site in the early 20th century demonstrated the sophistication of Taino ceremonialism and organization during Late Prehistoric and Early Contact periods and provided the basis for defining the Capa phase. The site is operated as an archeological park by the Institute for Puerto Rican Culture.

# RHODE ISLAND

## ■ *Bristol County*

## JOSEPH REYNOLDS HOUSE
### 956 Hope Street, Bristol

Built between 1698 and 1700, this frame house is a fine example of the transition from 17th-century design and building practices to those of the 18th. It may be the earliest wooden structure of its form extant in New England. Exposed internal structural members are cased, and there is a wealth of robust early paneling. In addition to its architectural distinction, the house has historical associations; it served as Lafayette's headquarters in September 1778 when he was quartered in Bristol.

## Kent County

### GENERAL NATHANIEL GREENE HOMESTEAD
**40 Taft Street, Anthony**

General Nathaniel Green, one of the military geniuses of the Revolution, began his service in October 1774 when, as a private, he helped organize the Kentish Guards. He ended his career when he resigned from the Continental army in November 1783 as a major general. During the interim he participated in battles from Massachusetts to South Carolina, often in concert with Washington, whom he served as second in command. From 1774 to 1783 this two-story clapboard dwelling, which Greene designed and built, was his residence, although he obviously spent most of those years in the field. It is now a historic house museum.

## Newport County

### ISAAC BELL, JR., HOUSE
**70 Perry Street, Newport**

Edna Villa, built in 1881–1883 for a Southern cotton broker, marked a turning point for the architectural firm of McKim, Mead and White and a milestone in the development of American architecture. Along with their nearby Newport Casino, its contemporary, the Bell House is one of the earliest examples of the Shingle Style. This peculiarly American architectural style, a winning combination of Colonial and Queen Anne motifs, is generally clad, as here, in shingles of many patterns. Open, informal plans, expansive verandas, and horizontal outlines characterize the style, which found its perfect expression in large summer cottages such as this. The Preservation Society of Newport County acquired the Bell House in 1994, and it is open to the public.

### BELLEVUE AVENUE HISTORIC DISTRICT
**Roughly bounded by the Atlantic Ocean, Easton Bay, Coggeshall Avenue, Spring Street, and Memorial Boulevard, Newport**

Few American avenues are bordered by such an impressive assemblage of buildings as Bellevue. Leading southward from the colonial town, it was *the* address to have during the late 19th and early 20th centuries, when Newport developed as the nation's most

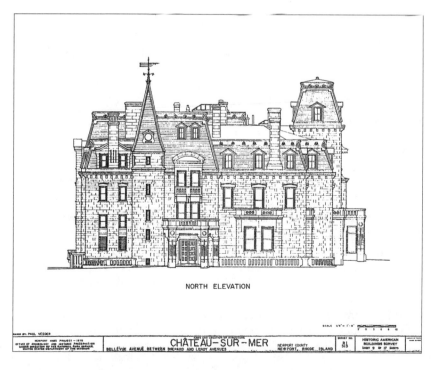

*Bellevue Avenue Historic District, Newport, Newport County. Château-Sur-Mer, 1970. Courtesy of HABS (Paul Veeder).*

NORTH ELEVATION

CHÂTEAU–SUR–MER

exclusive summer resort. Architects such as Richard Upjohn, Richard Morris Hunt, McKim, Mead and White, and Horace Trumbauer left their marks here with Gothic Revival villas, Stick Style and Shingle Style summer houses, and great marble palaces, all known in Newport's peculiar parlance as "cottages."

## THE BREAKERS
### Ochre Point Avenue, Newport

If, as has been posited, the Gilded Age could be represented by a single structure, that structure would have to be The Breakers. Representing American domestic design at its most opulent, this Beaux-Arts palace was designed by Richard Morris Hunt for Cornelius Vanderbilt II, member of a family noted for prominence in the world of finance, as patrons of the arts, and as vanguards of international society. In 1895, the year it was completed, The Breakers, now open to the public, was the largest and most elegant of the "cottages" at America's most fashionable summer resort—and still is.

## BRICK MARKET
### Thames Street and Washington Square, Newport

Peter Harrison, one of colonial America's most important architects, designed the Brick Market. Inspired by a plate from an English architectural book, Harrison displayed an awareness of correct classical proportions and details seldom realized in America at the time. Above an arcaded ground floor, giant Ionic pilasters divide the bays of the two upper stories and support a full entablature below a shallow hipped roof. The Market was under construction for 11 years, from 1761 to 1772. Now restored, it is a museum.

## THE ELMS
### Bellevue Avenue, Newport

The Elms, coal magnate Edward J. Berwind's Newport "cottage," was designed by Philadelphia architect Horace Trumbauer and built between 1899 and 1901. Trumbauer modeled the house on the Château d'Asnieres in France and was lauded for achieving such "a rich simplicity" in his design. Its architecture and landscape design

(also by Trumbauer) reflect a perfect unification of house and garden. The estate is owned by the Preservation Society of Newport County and is open to the public.

## FORT ADAMS
### Fort Adams Road at Harrison Avenue, Newport

Constructed between 1824 and 1857, Fort Adams stands as a superlative example of 19th-century American military engineering and technology. One of the country's largest seacoast fortifications, the pentagon-shaped granite fort protected the entrance to Narragansett Bay from both sea and land attacks. Fort Adams was designed by Simon Bernard, and its construction was supervised by Joseph G. Totten, both preeminent 19th-century engineers, who based their work on French military design. During the opening months of the Civil War, the U.S. Naval Academy was located here. In 1964, Fort Adams became a state park, but only portions are open to the public.

## HUNTER HOUSE
### 54 Washington Street, Newport

This large frame house is one of the finest examples of early-Georgian domestic architecture in the country. Presumably begun for Deputy Royal Governor Jonathan Nichols, Jr., it was completed sometime around 1767. A 2½-story building, it is covered with a balustraded gambrel roof, and the facade is highlighted by a doorway with a broken, curved pediment and carved pineapple, traditional symbol of hospitality. The house was acquired by the Preservation Society of Newport County in 1945 and is open as a historic house museum.

## EDWARD KING HOUSE
### Aquidneck Park, Spring Street, Newport

Andrew Jackson Downing, an expert on 19th-century American architecture, described this villa as "one of the most successful specimens of the Italian style in the United States." Designed by Richard Upjohn, it was constructed between 1845 and 1847 and is among America's earliest examples of the style. Built of brick, the house has asymmetrical massing, arched win-

FRONT SOUTH ELEVATION

dow heads, and a prominent tower, all typical features of Italianate design. The King House is now a senior citizens' center.

## KINGSCOTE
### Bellevue Avenue, Newport

Kingscote, begun in 1839, is one of Newport's oldest summer "cottages." It was a precursor of the mansions that came to line Bellevue Avenue, only a dusty lane when this house was built. Richard Upjohn was

the architect, and Andrew Jackson Downing the landscape architect. The charming Gothic Revival frame house in its picturesque setting helped to promote the cause of romantic design across the country, and to promote the careers of both men as well. Architect Stanford White enlarged the house in the 1880s, more than doubling its size and allowing it to hold its own with its new neighbors along now-fashionable Bellevue Avenue. In 1972, Kingscote was bequeathed to the Preservation Society of Newport County, which maintains it as a historic house museum.

## NEWPORT CASINO
### 186–202 Bellevue Avenue, Newport

America's answer to Wimbledon, the Newport Casino is almost as important to architectural history as it is to the history of tennis. Built in 1880 as a private gentlemen's club, the casino was designed by McKim, Mead & White and is a seminal example of the Shingle Style. The grass tennis courts have been in use since 1880, and the first U.S. Lawn Tennis Championship was held here in 1881. The casino hosted these championship tournaments until they were moved to Forest Hills in 1915, and it is now the International Tennis Hall of Fame.

## NEWPORT HISTORIC DISTRICT
### Bounded roughly by Van Zandt Avenue and Farewell, Sherman, High, Thomas, Golden Hill, Thames, Marsh, and Washington Streets, Newport

From ca. 1740 until the Revolution, when it was occupied by the British, Newport flourished as a port and mercantile center and as Rhode Island's colonial capital. The district's Georgian public buildings and mansions are among the most stylistically advanced of any erected in colonial America, but rows of small dwellings and shops give the area its primary architectural identity—a harmonious ensemble composed of buildings that relate to each other in scale, texture, mass, and materials. Providence became the capital and the state's most important urban center after the Revolution, and Newport was left to slumber until it prospered as a summer resort in the 19th century.

## OCEAN DRIVE HISTORIC DISTRICT
### Ocean Drive, Newport

This large historic district includes the southwestern tip of Rhode Island—not the state, but the island on which Newport is built. It has a rugged, informal character, as compared with the formal aspect of the Bellevue Avenue Historic District. It includes early farms and elaborate summer homes, as well as landscapes designed by nationally famous Frederick Law Olmsted to accord with the natural contours of rocky cliffs, green hills, and pastures.

## OLD STATE HOUSE, NEWPORT
### Washington Square, Newport

Dating from 1739–1741, this 2½-story brick structure was built to house the Rhode Island General Assembly and is considered one of the finest and least-altered examples of an early-Georgian public building in the country. On July 20, 1776, citizens gathered outside to hear the Declaration of Independence proclaimed from its balcony, and delegates met inside in 1790 to ratify the Constitution. From 1776 to 1900, the Old State House served as one of Rhode Island's two state capitols; the General Assembly met here in May and in Providence in January. After 1900 it became the Newport County Court House, and is now open as a museum.

## ORIGINAL U.S. NAVAL WAR COLLEGE
### Coaster's Harbor Island, Newport

This institution was established in 1884 to offer advanced courses for naval officers. Alfred Thayer Mahan became its second president two years later, and his effective leadership gave the college influence and stature that affected naval policy around the globe. Luce Hall, a granite-faced building, was erected between 1891 and 1892, and other buildings were added in the 20th century. Founders Hall now houses the Naval War College Museum.

## REDWOOD LIBRARY
### 50 Bellevue Avenue, Newport

Completed in 1750, this is one of the oldest library buildings in continuous use in the country. It was the first building designed by Peter Harrison, a notable 18th-century American architect, and is the country's earliest example of Palladian architecture. The library is fronted by a Doric portico, and the full entablature extends around the entire building. Walls are frame, but are cut and scored to resemble ashlar stone blocks. Large additions to the side and rear do not detract from Harrison's original work.

## WILLIAM WATTS SHERMAN HOUSE
**2 Shepard Avenue, Newport**

Constructed in 1874–1876, this is one of architect Henry H. Richardson's masterpieces of domestic architecture. With its bold massing, multigabled facade, variety of materials, and tall chimneys, it is an early American example of the Queen Anne style. Soon after the house was completed, Stanford White redecorated several rooms, and a large addition was made to the side and rear in the early 20th century. The house became a Baptist home for the elderly in 1950 and is now owned by Salve Regina University.

## SITE OF THE BATTLE OF RHODE ISLAND
**Lehigh Hill and Rhode Island Route 21, between Medley and Dexter Streets, Portsmouth**

The August 29, 1778, Battle of Rhode Island, the Narragansett Bay island on which Newport and Portsmouth are located, was the only Revolutionary War engagement in which African Americans participated as a distinct racial group. The First Rhode Island Regiment had been in training only three months when the battle took place, and although the 138 soldiers fought valiantly, the tide turned in favor of the British. When the colony of Rhode Island sought to recruit African Americans into service, the legislature passed a law that any who passed muster would be "absolutely FREE, as though he had never been encumbered with any kind of servitude or slavery."

## TRINITY CHURCH, NEWPORT
**141 Spring Street, Newport**

Erected between 1725 and 1726 by Newport's master carpenter/builder, Richard Munday, this early-Georgian frame church closely resembles Boston's Old North Church, and—in turn—Christopher Wren's famous London churches. In short, it is one of the most architecturally distinguished churches of colonial America. In 1762 the church was lengthened to accommodate larger congregations. Trinity still houses an active parish and is open to the public.

## VERNON HOUSE
**46 Clarke Street, Newport**

The symmetrical appearance of this academically correct late-Georgian house belies the fact that it is the product of two separate building campaigns. The first portion was built early in the 18th century, the second in 1758. Noted for its fine interior trim and stairway, the house served as headquarters for the Count de Rochambeau when French allies were quartered in Newport during the American Revolution.

## WANTON-LYMAN-HAZARD HOUSE
**17 Broadway, Newport**

Dating from the last years of the 17th century, this is Newport's oldest house and an excellent example of architectural transition from the 17th century to the 18th. The steep pitch of the roof and massive central chimney typify the former; the symmetrical five-bay facade and pedimented doorway hint at the formality of the latter. The house was damaged by Stamp Act riots in 1765, when it was occupied by a Tory stampmaster. It was purchased by the Newport Historical Society in 1927, was restored, and is now a historic house museum.

## ■ *Providence County*

## NELSON W. ALDRICH HOUSE
**110 Benevolent Street, Providence**

From 1891 until his death in 1915, Nelson Wilmarth Aldrich lived in this elegant Federal frame mansion on College Hill. Few men have exercised as much power from his U.S. Senate seat as Aldrich did from 1881 to 1911. As Republican Senate "boss," he maintained virtual veto power over any legislation. Aldrich held the view that business and government should combine to lead the country, but if a choice had to be made between the two, business should play the leading role. The Aldrich house currently serves as the Rhode Island Museum and home of the Rhode Island Historical Society.

## ARCADE
**130 Westminster Street and 65 Weybosset Street, Providence**

Constructed between 1827 and 1828, this

elegant Greek Revival commercial structure imitates European business arcades. It is also an important example of early monolithic granite construction. The arcade extends through a city block, with Ionic porticos opening onto each sidewalk. The open interior, lined with three floors of shops, is lit by a skylight.

## ELEAZER ARNOLD HOUSE
### Great Road, Lincoln

This post-Medieval farmhouse is a fine example of a regional building type known as a stone-ender. Although the rest of the house is frame, the chimneys of the hall and kitchen are combined on one end to form a stone wall. In this instance the chimney stack above the gabled roof is of brick, one of the most elaborate in New England. The original structure was erected in 1687, enlarged in the 18th century, and restored in the 20th. The Society for the Preservation of New England Antiquities maintains it as an architectural study house.

## JOHN BROWN HOUSE
### 52 Power Street, Providence

Providence flourished in the years immediately after the Revolution, as its sea captains and merchants grew rich in the profitable China trade. John Brown was chief among them, and he built one of the city's finest mansions. Designed by his brother Joseph and built between 1786 and 1788, this is a perfect example of late-Georgian–early-Federal design. John Quincy Adams was so impressed by the three-story brick house, trimmed with brownstone, that he called it "the most magnificent and elegant private mansion that I have ever seen on this continent." The Rhode Island Historical Society now maintains it as a historic house museum.

## COLLEGE HILL HISTORIC DISTRICT
### In the vicinity of Benefit Street, between Sheldon and Olney Streets, Providence

College Hill Historic District, located on the eastern bank of the Providence River, contains the core of the original town that Roger Williams established in 1636. Its architectural character derives from its unrivaled collection of more than 300 structures dating from ca. 1730 to 1825, when Providence grew as a major city and port. Centered on Benefit Street, which forms the spine of the district, College Hill is also significant for its 20th-century preservation efforts and achievements.

## CORLISS-CARRINGTON HOUSE
### 66 Williams Street, Providence

Begun by John Corliss between 1810 and 1811, this superb example of a large brick Adamesque Federal style town house was completed when Edward Carrington added a third story in 1812. Since then it has remained largely unaltered. The facade is dominated by a two-story porch, and a balustrade above the cornice hides the shallow deck-on-hip roof from view. The house is privately owned.

## CRESCENT PARK LOOFF CAROUSEL
### Bullock's Point Avenue, East Providence

Built ca. 1895, this is the earliest, most elaborate, and probably best-preserved of the few remaining carousels built by Charles I. D. Looff, one of the foremost manufacturers of carousels in the United States. The Crescent Park Carousel served as a "showroom" when his operations were headquartered in East Providence from 1905 to 1910, and Looff embellished it during those years with additional carved horses. The original 14-sided shed and early-20th-century band organ and lighting fixtures also survive.

## FIRST BAPTIST MEETINGHOUSE
### North Main Street, between Thomas and Waterman Streets, Providence

Erected between 1774 and 1775, this handsome frame building is an important example of late-Georgian church design. Joseph Brown, its architect, based its components on plates from English architect James Gibbs's *Book of Architecture*. The sanctuary, large for its time, has been used for Brown University's commencements since 1776. One of Brown's graduates, John D. Rockefeller, Jr., sponsored a rehabilitation in 1957–1958 that returned the church to a close approximation of its original appearance.

*Governor Henry Lippitt House, Providence, Providence County. Courtesy of HABS.*

## FLEUR-DE-LYS STUDIOS
**7 Thomas Street, Providence**

Fleur-de-Lys Studios is a prime monument of the American Arts and Crafts movement. Constructed in 1885, the building's design resulted from a collaboration between painter Sydney R. Burleigh and architect Edmund R. Wilson. They modeled Fleur-de-Lys on a half-timbered building that Burleigh had admired in Chester, England. The studios, with their overhanging eaves and cozy interiors, were envisioned as a place where artists could find relief from the "hard edges of industrialization and the visual pollution of an urbanizing city space" — a statement that amounts to a virtual credo of the Arts and Crafts movement.

## GOVERNOR STEPHEN HOPKINS HOUSE
**15 Hopkins Street, Providence**

Stephen Hopkins, royal governor of Rhode Island from 1755 to 1757, later became a member of both Continental Congresses and a signer of the Declaration of Independence. He was also first chancellor of Rhode Island

College, now Brown University, and was instrumental in having the institution moved from Warren to Providence in 1770. He built the main portion of this house in 1742 and lived here until his death in 1785. Carefully restored in 1927–1928, it is now a historic house museum.

## THOMAS P. IVES HOUSE
**66 Power Street, Providence**

Erected during 1803–1806, this privately owned 3½-story brick residence with balustraded roof is a magnificent example of a large town house designed in the Adam-esque Federal style. Such mansions were favored by newly rich sea captains and merchants throughout New England in the early days of the Republic. Providence contains a notable collection of them.

## GOVERNOR HENRY LIPPITT HOUSE
**199 Hope Street, Providence**

This well-preserved mansion was built during the Civil War years for Henry Lippitt, who became governor of Rhode Island in 1875. The house combines traditional form — in this instance the square, three-story brick houses that characterized Providence a generation or two earlier — with up-to-date Italianate details. Inside, architect/builder Henry Childs provided lavish and colorful decorations that are among the best of their kind in the country. The Heritage Trust of Rhode Island maintains the house as a museum.

## NIGHTINGALE-BROWN HOUSE
**357 Benefit Street, Providence**

One of the truly distinguished mansions of the early Republic, this elegant frame house summarizes and concludes late-Georgian–early-Federal architecture in Providence. In size and quality it is distinguished even among its neighboring structures, which have been called "one of the great groups of early post-Republican houses in the country." The house was built in 1791 for Colonel Joseph Nightingale. Nicholas Brown purchased it in 1814, and it housed generations of his family until 1985. It is now preserved and open, under the administration of Brown University, as the John Nicholas Brown Center for the Study of American Civilization.

Old Slater Mill, Pawtucket, Providence County, 1974. Courtesy of NPS (Blanche H. Schroer).

## OLD SLATER MILL
### Roosevelt Avenue, Pawtucket

Pawtucket, "the place of the waterfalls," has been called the birthplace of America's industrial revolution. If so, then this mill is its cradle. Samuel Slater, who perfected the country's first successful water-powered spinning machine in 1790, helped build the first unit of this mill three years later. It became the country's first successful cotton mill, which launched the textile industry, and was enlarged again and again over the years. The mill was restored in 1924 and is now open as a living history museum.

## UNIVERSITY HALL
### Brown University, Providence

Dating from 1771, this is the oldest building at the nation's seventh-oldest college. Until 1832, it was the only structure on campus and housed the entire institution. Standing four stories tall, University Hall contained dormitory rooms, lecture and recitation rooms, chapel, library, and dining hall. Now used for administrative offices, the Hall is also significant for its association with Horace Mann, one of the founders of the American system of free public schools. Mann was an 1819 graduate of Brown and returned to his alma mater as a Latin and Greek tutor.

■ *Washington County*

## BLOCK ISLAND SOUTH EAST LIGHT
### South East Light Road, New Shoreham

Block Island South East Lighthouse has been

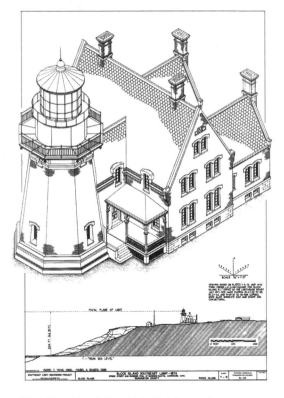

Block Island South East Light, Lighthouse Cove, Washington County. Courtesy of HAER (Isabel C. Yang and Mabel A. Baiges).

a major aid to navigation since it was first lit in 1874. High atop Mohegan Bluff and visible for miles along a busy sea lane, the tower and attached keeper's house were planned as showpieces for the U.S. Lighthouse Bureau. The dramatic setting and picturesque keeper's house combine to provide a powerful expression of the romanticism so often associated with lighthouses. As it turned out, the original setting was all too dramatic. The structures became threatened with collapse by continuous erosion of the bluff and had to be moved some 360 feet in August 1993. A museum is now maintained at the station, but the primary function is—as always—to help steer navigators safely around Block Island's southeastern corner.

## COCUMSCUSSOC ARCHEOLOGICAL SITE
### Address Restricted, North Kingstown

After establishing Providence in 1636, Rhode Island's founder, Roger Williams, settled the next year on a tract of land given him by the Naragansett sachem (chief) Canonicus. Williams established the colony's first trading post here, carrying on a lively commerce with his Indian neighbors until he sold the property in 1651. Archeological remains dating to the Historic Contact period are associated with Richard Smith, Sr., who purchased the site from Williams in 1651, and his son, Richard Smith, Jr., who operated the post from 1662 to 1692.

## FLYING HORSE CAROUSEL
### Terminus of Bay Street, Watch Hill

Dating from about 1876, this may be the oldest carousel in the nation, and is definitely the oldest of its type. Twenty horses, arranged two abreast, are suspended from a center frame. New York's Charles W. F. Dare Company, a major carousel manufacturer from 1866 to 1901, constructed the carousel, which is one of only two examples of their work that remain. The carousel was originally operated by real horsepower: a nag who spent the summers walking in circles. The carousel was first housed in a canvas tent but is now protected by a hipped-roof pavilion supported by cobblestone columns. The flying horses are carefully preserved, restored when the need arises, and ready to ride each summer at this resort community.

## GILBERT STUART BIRTHPLACE
### Gilbert Stuart Road, Saunderstown

Gilbert Stuart, one of America's most famous portraitists, was born in this gambrel-roofed frame building in 1755. Intended by his father to serve in the dual capacity of home and mill, the house was built between two streams and has a waterwheel attached to one side. The son showed artistic talent from his youth, and after returning to America from a long sojourn in England, Stuart painted George Washington—time after time after time. His uncompleted portrait became the most popular likeness ever done of Washington, and Stuart copied it whenever he needed money, referring to the copies as his "hundred-dollar bills." Today we know the portrait from a lesser denomination: the one dollar bill. Stuart's birthplace was restored in the 1930s and is maintained as a memorial to the artist.

*Gilbert Stuart Birthplace, Saunderstown, Washington County, 1974. Courtesy of NPS (Blanche Higgins Schroer).*

# SOUTH CAROLINA

## ■ *Abbeville County*

### BURT-STARK MANSION
**North Main and Greenville Streets, Abbeville**

Robert E. Lee surrendered the Army of Northern Virginia to Ulysses S. Grant at Appomattox on April 9, and General Joseph E. Johnston surrendered his army on April 26. Even so, President Jefferson Davis, staying with his longtime friend Armistead Burt in his handsome pillared mansion while on his retreat southward, believed he could rally troops to continue the struggle for an independent Confederate States of America. On the afternoon of May 2, 1865, he called a "council of war" to meet in the parlor. When officers in attendance convinced him that all was indeed lost, the war was finally over. Eight days later Davis was captured in Georgia. The house that heard the death knell of the Confederacy is now open to the public as a museum.

## ■ *Aiken County*

### GRANITEVILLE HISTORIC DISTRICT
**Along South Carolina Route 19 and Gregg Street, Graniteville**

William Gregg, perhaps the most significant figure in the development of cotton mills in the antebellum South, preached and practiced a gospel of industrialization. He started work on his mill in 1846, and when it was completed three years later, its 8,400 spindles could turn out more than 13,000 yards of cloth daily. In addition to establishing his model mill, steam-heated and solidly built of granite, Gregg supervised construction of an adjoining town, the prototype of the Southern cotton mill village. Gregg refused to hire children under the age of 12, required his teen-aged workers to attend school, and forbade them—and their parents—to drink or dance. Gregg died of pneumonia in 1867, brought on by exposure while working in waist-deep water to help repair the mill's dam. The industry he introduced to the

South developed primarily after the Civil War, and the company he founded in Graniteville continues.

## ■ *Bamberg County*

### WOODLANDS
**3 miles south of Bamberg on South Carolina Route 78**

William Gilmore Simms is considered the central literary figure of the antebellum South. Best known for romantic novels such as *The Yemassee* (1835) and *Eutaw* (1856), he earned a nationwide reputation and a secure place in the mainstream of American fiction. He moved to the banks of the Edisto River in 1836 and lived here until his death in 1870. He rebuilt his one-story brick house on several occasions, and a later generation of the family added a second floor.

## ■ *Beaufort County*

### BEAUFORT HISTORIC DISTRICT
**Bounded by the Beaufort River and Bladen, Hamar, and Boundary Streets, Beaufort**

Beaufort, after Charleston the oldest settlement in South Carolina, has preserved a number of distinctive "low-country" houses from the 18th and early 19th centuries. Beaufort never grew as large or became as crowded as Charleston or nearby Savannah, and its typical houses—standing tall on masonry foundations—are generally freestanding with spacious two-story verandas, essentially plantation houses brought to town. Several are built of tabby, a regionally important building material composed of oyster shells, lime, and sand mixed with seawater.

### MARSHLANDS
**501 Pinckney Street, Beaufort**

This clapboarded frame house raised on an English basement is a fine example of early Beaufort architecture. A piazza supported by masonry piers and arches surrounds the house on three sides, perhaps reflecting West

Indian influence. Marshlands was built ca. 1814 for Dr. James Robert Verdier, who discovered a treatment for yellow fever. During the Civil War, the U.S. Sanitary Commission maintained the house as its headquarters.

## PENN SCHOOL HISTORIC DISTRICT
### 1 mile south of Frogmore

When Union forces captured Saint Helena Island in 1861, plantation owners fled to the mainland, leaving their slaves behind. In 1862, Northern missionaries arrived to assist them, organizing one of the first Southern schools for emancipated slaves and pioneering in health services and self-help programs. The oldest existing structure is the Brick Church, built in 1855 for the island's Baptist planters, but utilized after they left as the first school for the newly freed slaves. It and later buildings make up Penn Center Community Services, the successor institution to Penn School and still the heart and soul of this rural island community.

## ROBERT SMALLS HOUSE
### 511 Prince Street, Beaufort

This large frame house was the residence of Robert Smalls, born a slave, who served in the South Carolina legislature from 1868-1874, was a United States congressman from 1875 to 1881, and was customs collector of the Port of Beaufort from 1889 to 1913. Smalls first came to national attention when, on May 13, 1862, he organized the abduction of the *Planter,* a Confederate steamer based in Charleston Harbor. He purchased the house, in which he had lived as a slave, at a tax sale in 1863.

### ■ *Berkeley County*

## MIDDLEBURG PLANTATION
### About 2 miles southwest of Huger on the east branch of the Cooper River

Built ca. 1699 by a French Huguenot planter, this two-story plantation house is one of the oldest frame structures in South Carolina. Its exterior is a picture of simplicity, with its clapboarded walls, plain fenestration, and unadorned hipped roof. The one-story verandas, or piazzas, on the long facades are 18th-century additions. Inside, heavy corner posts and girts reflect postmedieval construction, and the single-room plan, providing needed ventilation in the hot climate of the Carolina low country, may be regarded as a prototype for the Charleston "single-house" plan.

## MULBERRY PLANTATION
### Off U.S. Route 52 on the Cooper River, Moncks Corner

Stylistically, Mulberry is one of the most distinctive early-18th-century houses in the nation and has been called everything from

*Mulberry Plantation, Moncks Corner, Berkeley County, 1969. Courtesy of NPS.*

Jacobean, Queen Anne, and Baroque to early Georgian. It is, in a word, unique: a rare example of a transitional house combining diverse 17th-century forms into a unified ensemble foretelling the arrival of 18th-century Georgian formality. The brick plantation house was built for Thomas Broughton, later royal governor of the colony, and is identified by its dormered, steeply pitched gambrel roof and the attached square brick pavilions at its four corners.

## POMPION HILL CHAPEL
**0.5 miles southwest of intersection of South Carolina Routes 41 and 402, Huger**

This miniature Georgian masterpiece was constructed in 1763–1765 on the site of South Carolina's first Anglican church built outside Charleston. The brick, and likely the design, with its arched fenestration and clipped gable roof, were provided by Zachariah Villepontoux. The master mason was William Axson, and the initials of both men are carved on the walls. The interior woodwork and nearly all furnishings are original. The pulpit, constructed of red cedar, is a model of its type, with its wineglass shape and domed sounding board.

## SAINT JAMES CHURCH, GOOSE CREEK
**South of Goose Creek, Goose Creek**

Built in 1713–1719 by planters originally from Barbados, this is one of the first Georgian churches in the English colonies. The stuccoed-brick building is rectangular and one story high, has prominent corner quoins, and is covered with a jerkin-head roof. Above the main entrance is a stucco relief of a pelican piercing her breast with her beak to nourish her young—the symbol of the Society for the Propagation of the Gospel, the Anglican group that helped fund construction. The interior is one of the finest of America's small 18th-century country churches. A colorful lion and unicorn—the Royal Arms of George I—have now pranced between the broken, scrolled pediment for more than 2½ centuries.

## SAINT STEPHEN'S EPISCOPAL CHURCH
**On South Carolina Route 45, Saint Stephens**

Erected in 1767–1769, this Georgian style brick church is distinguished by a high gambrel roof with Jacobean gables. Providing a distinctive and unusual profile to the exterior, these features were apparently built so that the interior could accommodate a tray ceiling, likely modeled after the similar feature at Saint Michael's Church in Charleston, then recently completed. The interior of this handsome country church is original, and the reredos, with its Tablets of the Law (the Ten Commandments) is particularly impressive.

*Saint Stephen's Episcopal Church, Saint Stephens, Berkeley County, 1969. Courtesy of NPS.*

■ *Charleston County*

## WILLIAM AIKEN HOUSE AND ASSOCIATED RAILROAD STRUCTURES
**456 King Street, Charleston**

These structures are associated with William Aiken, Sr., founder of the South Carolina Canal and Railroad Company, and commemorate the birth of regular steam locomotive passenger service in the United States. When the 136-mile railroad, linking Charleston with Hamburg, South Carolina, was completed in 1833, it was the longest operating railroad in the world. Aiken's line was the first to use steam from the beginning of its operations, the first to use an American-made locomotive, and the first railroad to carry the U.S. mail. Portions of the railroad structures are incorporated into the Charleston Visitor Center.

## WILLIAM BLACKLOCK HOUSE
**18 Bull Street, Charleston**

Constructed in 1800, this hipped-roof brick house is a refined example of the Adamesque style. Its fine proportions and sophisticated details make it an exemplar of its type. The entrance is centered on the facade above a high English basement and reached by a stairway on either side. An elliptical fanlight, a particularly handsome and delicate feature, extends to cover sidelights that flank the front door.

## MILES BREWTON HOUSE
**27 King Street, Charleston**

The famous Miles Brewton House is often considered the country's most distinguished colonial town house. Built between 1765 and 1769, the almost-square two-story brick house is fronted by a two-story portico. The center-hall plan, with two rooms on either side, is known in Charleston as a "double house" to distinguish the type from the narrower "single houses." The Miles Brewton House is particularly notable for its interior woodwork, carved by Ezra White, and its formal second-story drawing room with a coved ceiling rising to a height of 17 feet. Leaders of armed forces, who seem to have a penchant for choosing the best places to occupy, chose the Brewton House on two occasions. During the Revolution, British general Sir Henry Clinton made it his headquarters, as did Union officers in the last days of the Civil War.

## ROBERT BREWTON HOUSE
**71 Church Street, Charleston**

Miles Brewton built a Charleston double house for himself, but for his son Robert he erected what is now the city's earliest known example of a single house. It remains one of the best examples of the type. Dating from ca. 1730, the three-story stuccoed structure is one room wide, with the narrow end facing the street and the front doorway midway on one of the long side walls. This arrangement, so often found in Charleston and so necessary in the city's notoriously hot climate, ensured that three sides of a house would be exposed to cooling breezes.

## BRICK HOUSE RUINS
**South of Edisto Island**

Constructed ca. 1725, this two-story house with a high pitched roof exhibited French Huguenot influence on South Carolina's colonial architecture. Built of brick imported from Boston and lumber aged seven years prior to construction, the house was the focal point of a 300-acre plantation. In 1929 a fire burned all but its shell. Its walls with stuccoed quoins and trim remain, still providing eloquent testimony to the architectural finesse the house once displayed.

## CHARLESTON HISTORIC DISTRICT
**Incorporating most of the area south of Bee, Morris, and Mary Streets to the waterfront, Charleston**

According to Charlestonians, their city was founded in 1670 where "the Ashley and Cooper Rivers merge to form the Atlantic Ocean." It grew to become colonial America's largest and most prosperous metropolis south of Philadelphia, and its major Southern port. By some strange alchemy, Charleston has prospered whenever "good" architecture has been in vogue, and has been too poor to build whenever "bad" design was in favor. A phenomenal number of early buildings survive, many displaying impressive adaptations

*Drayton Hall, Charleston County. Courtesy of HABS (Ken Breuer).*

to the oppressively humid climate of the Carolina low country. Charleston is also recognized as an icon in the country's preservation annals. The zoning ordinance passed in 1931 to protect its historic areas was the nation's first and became a model for subsequent historic district ordinances throughout the country. Charleston has endured wars, fires, an earthquake, and hurricanes. Long may it prosper—at least when good architecture is in the ascendency.

## *CLAMAGORE*
### Patriot's Point, Mount Pleasant

A Balao class submarine, *Clamagore* was one of 132 fleet submarines built during World War II for the U.S. Navy as part of the major submarine construction program following the Japanese attack on Pearl Harbor. The submarine warfare subsequently pursued by the United States was instrumental in securing an American victory in the Pacific. One of nine submarines converted to a Guppy III in 1947, *Clamagore* is now the only surviving example of its type. *Clamagore* is currently on exhibit just outside Charleston at Patriot's Point Naval and Maritime Museum.

## COLLEGE OF CHARLESTON
### Glebe, George, Saint Philip, and Green Streets, Charleston

Three antebellum structures on this urban campus are of architectural significance: the main building (1829; 1852), a large Classical Revival edifice fronted by a monumental Ionic portico, was designed by William Strickland and enlarged by Edward B. White; the gate lodge (1852), also Classical Revival, was designed by White; and the library (1856), with Italianate details, is the work of George Walker, like White, an architect of Charleston. The three buildings achieve architectural unity through their Pompeian-red stuccoed walls and together form a notable example of a 19th-century academic complex.

## DRAYTON HALL
### 12 miles west of Charleston on South Carolina Route 61

Unquestionably one of the oldest and finest plantation houses in America, this noble Georgian building was completed in 1742. Its brick facade is centered by a two-story portico—one of the first of its type in the country—reached by a double flight of stairs. Inside, the entrance hall, with its elaborate stair arrangement, paneled walls, and ornamental ceiling, is one of colonial America's finest rooms. Drayton survived the Civil War unscathed through its legendary use as a smallpox hospital and was never altered or "updated" in subsequent years. Owned by the National Trust for Historic Preservation since 1974, Drayton Hall is presented as a museum with emphasis on its outstanding architecture and workmanship.

## EXCHANGE AND PROVOST
**East Bay Street, Charleston**

Built between 1767 and 1771, this Georgian public building has served as customhouse, mercantile exchange, military prison and barracks, and post office. During its multifaceted career, it has witnessed scenes important in the history of the city, state, and nation. Rather than throwing their tea overboard, Charlestonians confiscated it and stored it here in 1774. In 1790, the South Carolina legislature met in the Exchange to ratify the new state constitution, and in 1791, George Washington was welcomed on its steps. The building was badly damaged by Union artillery fire during the Civil War and by the great earthquake of 1886. It was repaired after each occasion, was restored in the late 20th century, and is now open as a museum.

## FARMERS' AND EXCHANGE BANK
**14 East Bay Street, Charleston**

Completed in 1854 from designs by Charleston architects Edward C. Jones and Francis D. Lee, this is one of the nation's best examples of Moorish design, perhaps the least familiar and least employed of the many revival styles that characterized mid-19th-century American architecture. The brownstone facade displays horseshoe arches and other motifs based on Eastern designs. The idea of clothing a bank in Islamic vestments may have come from illustrations in Washington Irving's popular story *The Alhambra,* published in 1851. Whatever its source, the building is a charming anomaly in a city noted primarily for far more traditional architecture.

## FIREPROOF BUILDING
**100 Meeting Street, Charleston**

Completed in 1827 from designs by Robert Mills, this strong masonry structure with iron casement window sash is believed to be the first building of supposedly fireproof construction erected in the United States. It was commissioned by the State of South Carolina to be the Charleston District Record Building. Architecturally, the Greek Revival

building is a good example of the work of Mills; massing and basic forms give character, while spare and simple details provide a few embellishments. The building is now the home of the South Carolina Historical Society.

## WILLIAM GIBBES HOUSE
**64 South Battery, Charleston**

This late-Georgian town house, constructed in 1779, was remodeled in 1794 when elaborate Adam style interiors were installed. It exemplifies the Charleston double house as expressed in frame construction, and is one of colonial America's most notable town houses. A double stairway in front of a stone-faced English basement leads to the central entrance, a broad frontispiece with a triangular pediment stretching over the door and sidelights. On a larger scale, this motif is repeated in the attic pediment that extends over the three central bays.

## HAMPTON PLANTATION
**8 miles north of McClellanville**

Erected in 1735, enlarged in 1757 and again in 1791, Hampton evolved from a modest frame structure built by a Huguenot settler into a large Georgian plantation house. The monumental Roman Doric portico that centers the south facade dates from the last phase of the building's evolution and is one of the first domestic examples of its type in America. After the death of its last private owner, poet Archibald Rutledge, the house was acquired by the State of South Carolina and is now the Hampton Plantation State Park.

## DUBOSE HEYWARD HOUSE
**76 Church Street, Charleston**

From about 1919 to 1924, this narrow tile-roofed house was the residence of DuBose Heyward, author of the 1925 novel *Porgy,* which inspired George and Ira Gershwin's famed opera, *Porgy and Bess.* Heyward, who worked on the Charleston waterfront as a cotton checker, chose the black community of his hometown as the setting for his novel, and "Catfish Row" is only a stone's throw from the house. Porgy is a crippled beggar whose struggle is treated with sensitivity and insight by the author, himself a victim of polio. *Porgy* was the first widely popular novel to present the Southern African American not as a vehicle for comic relief or social protest, but on his own terms.

## HEYWARD-WASHINGTON HOUSE
### 87 Church Street, Charleston

From 1777 to 1794 this three-story brick double house was the home of Thomas Heyward, Jr., a signer of the Declaration of Independence. The stark exterior belies its elegantly paneled interiors, and as testament to the caliber of its accommodations, the City of Charleston rented it for a week in 1791 to house President George Washington when he visited the city on his famous "southern tour." Known ever since by its hyphenated name honoring Thomas Heyward and its most famous visitor, the house was acquired by the Charleston Museum in 1929 and is open as a historic house museum.

## HIBERNIAN HALL
### 105 Meeting Street, Charleston

Completed in 1840 from designs by Philadelphia architect Thomas U. Walter to house a social and charitable organization, this Greek Revival structure is the only extant building associated with the Democratic Convention of 1860. This was one of the most critical political assemblies in the history of the United States, with Hibernian Hall

serving as headquarters for the faction supporting Stephen A. Douglas, the pivotal personality of the convention. An observant reporter passing by after Douglas failed to gain the nomination saw "the Douglas delegation...from Illinois seated mournfully on the steps....They were pensive and silent." Failing to secure a two-thirds majority for any candidate here, and at a subsequent convention in Baltimore, the Democrats were too fractured to agree on a nominee. By the time Douglas was finally selected, his party was so divided that the Republican candidate, Abraham Lincoln, was ensured victory later that year.

## HUGUENOT CHURCH
### 136 Church Street, Charleston

Completed in 1845, this was Charleston's first major Gothic Revival building and the first Gothic design by local architect E. B. White. The exterior of the brick building is stuccoed, with buttresses between each bay. The interior is noted for its ceiling, imitating in plaster the stone groin vaults of true Gothic construction. The church is the third on its site, replacing structures erected in 1687 and 1800.

## *INGHAM*
### 40 Patriots Point Road, Mount Pleasant

Christened in 1935 and completed the next year, the 327-foot U.S. Coast Guard cutter *Ingham* is one of two surviving examples of

Ingham, *Mount Pleasant, Charleston County, 1944. Courtesy of the U.S. Naval Institute.*

*Kahal Kadosh Beth Elohim, Charleston, Charleston County. Courtesy of HABS (Louis Schwarz).*

Secretary class cutters. This class proved significant as a response to the German U-boat coastal threat in World War II. *Ingham* escorted convoys across the North Atlantic, Mediterranean, and Caribbean, earning the Presidential Unit Citation. In 1942 it sank *U-626* with a single depth charge. Transferred to duty in the Pacific, *Ingham* spearheaded the liberation of Corregidor and other Philippine territory. In 1968 it returned to combat off Vietnam. When its career ended in 1988, *Ingham* was the oldest commissioned U.S. warship afloat. *Ingham* is now a museum vessel at Patriots Point.

## KAHAL KADOSH BETH ELOHIM
### 90 Hassell Street, Charleston

Charleston's Beth Elohim synagogue is regarded as the birthplace, in 1824, of Reform Judaism in America. Originated by German Jews early in the 19th century, the movement first sought to modernize traditional worship by introducing choral singing and organ music, and using languages other than Hebrew in services. Eventually a critical reevaluation of Jewish theology developed from the movement. Beth Elohim's congregation was established in 1749 and had become the largest Jewish community group in the country by the end of the 18th centu-ry. The Greek Revival temple, dating from 1840, is the third-oldest synagogue extant in the United States.

## LAFFEY
### East side of Charleston Harbor, Mount Pleasant

The only surviving Allen M. Sumner class destroyer and the only surviving World War II destroyer that saw service in the Atlantic, *Laffey* acted as escort to convoys to Great Britain and on D Day bombarded Utah Beach at Normandy. Sent to the Pacific, *Laffey* was involved in one of the most famous destroyer-kamikaze duels of the war. It earned five battle stars and a Presidential Unit Citation for its service and is now on display at Patriots Point.

## JOSEPH MANIGAULT HOUSE
### 350 Meeting House, Charleston

Charleston-born architect Gabriel Manigault designed this three-story brick mansion for his brother. Dating from 1790, the fine Adam-style house has a bowed piazza on one end, matched by a bowed stairwell projection on the other. These curved appendages exemplify the Adamesque fondness for shapes other than the traditional squares and rectangles that characterized the earlier Georgian style.

The Manigault House is maintained and displayed as a house museum by the Charleston Museum.

## MARKET HALL AND SHEDS
### 188 Meeting Street, Charleston

Constructed in 1841 from designs by architect Edward B. White, this is one of a small number of 19th-century American market complexes extant. The Market Hall, facing Meeting Street, is raised above an arcaded ground story and provides an imposing frontispiece with its Doric portico, elaborate ironwork, and stuccoed masonry walls. Particularly appropriate are the bull and rams heads that decorate the entablature. Classically correct, they also provided an early instance of "theme advertising" for butchers and purveyors of meat. Behind Market Hall, six single-story brick sheds, stretching eastward, constitute the market proper.

## CLARK MILLS STUDIO
### 51 Broad Street, Charleston

This building, now adapted for office use, was the residence of self-taught American sculptor Clark Mills. In 1848 his ambitious design for a statue in Washington, D.C., to honor Andrew Jackson was selected over other proposals. Mills built his own foundry and furnace to melt bronze cannons Jackson had captured in 1814, and on his sixth casting, achieved success. The statue, dedicated in 1853, is the first equestrian statue cast in the United States and remains the centerpiece of Washington's Lafayette Square. (See Lafayette Square Historic District, Washington, D.C., and Jackson Square, Orleans Parish, Louisiana.)

## OLD MARINE HOSPITAL
### 20 Franklin Street, Charleston

This is one of several U.S. military hospitals that Robert Mills designed for indigent seamen who had become public charges. All were built with the same general plan, but in different styles. This example is Gothic, with pointed arches and clustered columns supporting a two-story veranda. Originally the building was larger, but rear wings were damaged following a fire and removed during

renovation. Currently, the former hospital houses the administrative offices of the Charleston Housing Authority.

## PARISH HOUSE OF THE CIRCULAR CONGREGATIONAL CHURCH
### 150 Meeting Street, Charleston

Built ca. 1806, the parish house of this church is a small Greek Revival temple with graceful twin stairways leading to its second-floor portico. It is a good example of Robert Mills's ability to provide a monumental appearance for a building of modest size and scale. At the time the parish house was built, Mills also designed the congregation's church, named for its then-unusual shape and thought to be the first domed church in America. The present church, an impressive Romanesque Revival building standing in front of the parish house, is an 1892 replacement of Mills's original building.

## POWDER MAGAZINE
### 79 Cumberland Street, Charleston

This tiny multigabled brick building with a bright-red tile roof is one of Charleston's most beloved and most venerable structures. Completed in 1713 to store and keep gunpowder and ammunition secure for the defense of the city, it is a visible reminder of the era of the Lord Proprietors, a time when not only the English, but also the French and Spanish, were pressing their claims for control of North America. The building was apparently constructed in haste, and a year after it was completed, repairs had to be made to keep the city's powder dry. By 1721 the magazine was reported as being "very dry, clean and in good order." The large iron tie-rods were inserted in the gables after the 1886 earthquake damaged the walls. In 1899, the National Society of the Colonial Dames in America purchased the magazine, and the Society has maintained it as a museum since then.

## ROBERT BARNWELL RHETT HOUSE
### 9 East Battery, Charleston

This large frame dwelling was the residence of Robert Barnwell Rhett, the "Great Secessionist." Rhett was one of the most effective and prominent members of his circle of proslavery "fire-eating" radicals, and in 1850 he launched a carefully programmed campaign to sever slave-holding states from the Union. He used his newspaper, the *Charleston Mercury,* as a vehicle to expound his policies, and his efforts bore fruit a decade later when, in 1860, South Carolina was the first state to pass an ordinance of secession. As might be expected, Rhett himself had a major influence on the ordinance, and he influenced other states to follow South Carolina's example with a report titled "Address to the Slave Holding States."

## ROBERT WILLIAM ROPER HOUSE
### 9 East Battery, Charleston

This brick residence of grand scale and monumental features is one of the architectural treasures of Charleston. Located on fashionable East Battery, it is easily identified among a group of imposing houses by its giant-order Ionic portico, rising high above an arcaded ground floor. At the opposite end of the facade, the front doorway is surrounded by an architrave frame carved in a rope molding, an ingenuous reference to the first owner's last name. An indication of the quality of construction is the fact that the Flemish bond walls of the Roper House were unscathed by the earthquake of 1886 that wreaked such havoc on Charleston.

## NATHANIEL RUSSELL HOUSE
### 51 Meeting Street, Charleston

This three-story brick residence, built ca. 1809 by a wealthy Charleston merchant, is one of the finest examples of the Federal style in the country. Its rooms employ various shapes, typical of the Federal fondness for spaces other than squares and rectangles, and the elliptical stairway is unmatched in its delicacy. Adamesque motifs are found throughout the interior. Russell was justifiably proud of his mansion, which cost $80,000 in early-19th-century dollars, and had his monogram wrought into the iron balcony above the entrance. After use as a dwelling and as a school for young ladies, the Russell House is now owned and maintained as a house museum by the Historic Charleston Foundation.

## EDWARD RUTLEDGE HOUSE
### 117 Broad Street, Charleston

Edward Rutledge, leader of the South Carolina delegation to the Second Continental Congress and a signer of the Declaration of Independence, lived in this large frame house from 1787 until his death in 1800. Rutledge staved off action on the Declaration for almost a month, fearing that the "low Cunning and those leveling Principles" of New England might prevail over the South if a strong federal government were established. A prisoner of war during the Revolution, Rutledge later became a state senator and was serving as governor of South Carolina at the time of his death.

## JOHN RUTLEDGE HOUSE
### 116 Broad Street, Charleston

John Rutledge, Edward's older brother, lived in this three-story brick double house from 1763 until his death in 1800. Like his brother, John devoted much of his adult life to the service of his state and nation in their formative years. He was a delegate to both Continental Congresses, a signer of the federal Constitution, governor of South Carolina from 1779 to 1782, and senior associate justice of the United States Supreme Court from 1789-1791. He resigned from that position to become chief justice of South Carolina. A number of alterations have been made on the house since Rutledge's time, but the basic form and plan survive.

## SAINT JAMES CHURCH, SANTEE
### 17 miles south of Georgetown on the Santee River

Constructed in 1768, this little-altered Georgian building is a fine example of the architectural sophistication achieved in South Carolina's Anglican parishes. The hip-roofed brick church has pedimented porticos front and rear, supported by brick columns that display both diminution (the diameter of the base is larger than that of the capital) and entasis (a swelling of the shaft), classical refinements not often found—much less expected—in a small country church. Although the original interior arrangement has been revised, much original trim, woodwork, and even hardware, remain. Still in a pristine country setting, Saint James' Santee appears almost as a time capsule from colonial days.

## SAINT MICHAEL'S EPISCOPAL CHURCH

### 80 Meeting Street, Charleston

One of the great Georgian churches of America, St. Michael's provides dramatic architectural evidence of Charleston's wealth and taste in colonial times. The white-painted stucco-over-brick church was completed in 1761, and the giant-order Roman Doric portico that dominates the facade was the first of its type on any American church. Impressive as the portico is, it pales in comparison to the magnificent tower, rising in receding stages to culminate in a steeple 185 feet high. During the Revolution the tower was painted black in a misguided effort to hide it from offshore British gunners. Inside, box pews, galleries, pulpit, and handsome tray ceiling are all original. Saint Michael's holds and preserves the indominable spirit of Charleston more than any other building in the city.

## SAINT PHILIP'S EPISCOPAL CHURCH

### 146 Church Street, Charleston

Saint Michael's may be the oldest Episcopal church *building* in Charleston, but members of Saint Philip's like to point out that theirs is the older *parish,* the oldest in South Carolina, in fact. The parish was established in 1670, and this is its third church. Built of brick, stuccoed, the body of the church was completed in 1838, and the imposing spire was added a decade later. The Georgian lines of church and tower, architecturally conservative for their time, reflect an attempt to replicate the lines of the early-18th-century church it replaced. Three pedimented Tuscan porticoes contribute to the design of this handsome church.

## SIMMONS-EDWARDS HOUSE

### 12–14 Legare Street, Charleston

Constructed ca. 1800, this three-story brick dwelling is one of Charleston's finest examples of a single house. The house is also notable in a city of notable houses for its fine wrought-iron decoration and for its landscaping. As is typical of Charleston's high-style single houses, the door from the sidewalk does not lead directly into the house, but onto the first level of the two-story piazza.

## SNEE FARM

### About 6 miles west of Mount Pleasant off U.S. Route 17

Charles Pinckney was one of the youngest members of the Continental Congress and one of the leaders of the Constitutional Convention. He advocated a strong national government, and many of the articles of the Constitution are credited to him. Under the new government, he was a devoted Federalist. He served three terms as governor of South Carolina, was a United States senator, and was twice the Federalist presidential candidate. Snee Farm interprets Pinckney's role in American history, as well as the history of African Americans on the property. The house where the interpretive exhibits are displayed postdates Pinckney's ownership of the property.

## STONO RIVER SLAVE REBELLION SITE

### West bank of the Wallace River, Rantowles vicinity

On September 9, 1739, approximately 51 escaped slaves attacked a warehouse here, killing two guards and seizing the weapons stored within. The group, led by an Angolan called Jemmy, then set off for freedom in the Spanish province of Florida, burning plantations and murdering all whites they encountered along the way. Their attempt was thwarted by a Colonial militia, which overtook the swelling band (by this time the group had grown to include 80 slaves) and killed or captured those involved. The insurrection that began here was one of the most serious slave revolts of the colonial period. As a result, the South Carolina legislature soon enacted one of the most comprehensive slave codes in the English colonies.

## COLONEL JOHN STUART HOUSE

### 104–106 Tradd Street, Charleston

Built in 1772 by Colonel John Stuart,

Britain's royal commissioner for Indian Affairs in the South, this is one of the finest examples of a three-story Georgian frame town house in the Southern colonies. Unfortunately, its builder had little time to enjoy it. In June 1775, South Carolina's colonial authorities ordered Stuart's arrest, charging him with attempting to incite the Catawba and Cherokee to assist the British. He fled to Florida, where he died in 1779. In 1930, the Minneapolis Museum of Art purchased and removed the woodwork of two rooms, a sure sign of the high quality of the interior decorations. These have since been replicated within the house.

## UNITARIAN CHURCH
### 6 Archdale Street, Charleston

Begun in 1772, and "Gothicized" by Francis D. Lee between 1852 and 1854, this is a good example of how the mid-19th-century mood of romanticism and picturesqueness came to dominate the art and architecture of the time. Lee added a four-story tower, with buttresses and crenellations, to the front of the church but saved his most ornate decoration for the interior. The stunning "vaulted" ceiling replicates late medieval English fan tracery, but is executed in lath and plaster, not in stone. Structural it is not, but showy it certainly is.

## DENMARK VESEY HOUSE
### 56 Bull Street, Charleston

This small frame house was the residence of Denmark Vesey, free black Charleston carpenter, whose 1822 plans for a slave insurrection created mass hysteria throughout the Carolinas and beyond. Until then, owners may have feared revolts from their slaves, but thought they had little cause to expect trouble from free blacks. Free to travel around Charleston on his own, Vesey carefully selected a group of followers and planned his rebellion for July 14. A slave informant betrayed the news to his owner, and the plot was thwarted. Ultimately 313 alleged participants were arrested, 67 were convicted, and 35 of those were executed. Vesey was sentenced to death on July 2, two weeks before his revolt was to have taken place.

## YORKTOWN
### Charleston Harbor, Mount Pleasant

This aircraft carrier was the second of the nation's Essex class, the corps of the fast carrier task forces in the Pacific. *Yorktown* supported American ground troops in the Philippines, at Iwo Jima, and at Okinawa and participated at Truk and in the Marianas. It received 11 battle stars and a presidential citation for its World War II service. *Yorktown* arrived in Charleston in 1975 and is on display at Patriots Point.

## ■ *Darlington County*

## COKER EXPERIMENTAL FARMS
### West of Hartsville on South Carolina Route 151

Here, following the example of his father, David Robert Coker conducted crop-improvement experiments on the family plantation at the turn of the 20th century. Beginning with 30 experimental cotton selections and methodically applying the latest techniques in the scientific breeding of crops, Coker Experimental Farms played a great role in the agricultural revolution in the South. Tirelessly spreading the information he obtained throughout the South, Coker, through his experiments, helped mesh agriculture, science, and industry for better and more efficient use of the land.

## ■ *Dorchester County*

## MIDDLETON PLACE
### 10 miles southeast of Summerville on South Carolina Route 61

The expansive grounds of Middleton Place constitute the first landscaped gardens in America. Begun in 1741 by Henry Middleton, they comprised 16 acres of lawn and 45 acres of gardens and took ten years to complete. Most of the original ca. 1738 house they surrounded was burned by Union troops in 1865, but one wing, dating from 1755, survives. Middleton Place was the estate of its namesake family, members of whom achieved prominence in American history. Henry Middleton became president of the First Continental Congress, and his son Arthur was a delegate to the Second Continental Congress and a signer of the

Declaration of Independence. Both men are buried in their beloved and beautifully maintained gardens, which are still owned by descendants and are open to the public.

### ■ *Florence County*

## SNOW'S ISLAND

### Address Restricted, Johnsonville

From approximately December 1780 to late March 1781, this isolated spot served as headquarters for forces led by Francis Marion, the celebrated and colorful South Carolina militia officer known to history as the "Swamp Fox." Employing guerilla war tactics, Marion significantly contributed to the American war effort by conducting numerous raids on British outposts, then retreating to the secure, swampy terrain of Snow's Island.

### ■ *Georgetown County*

## ATALAYA AND BROOKGREEN GARDENS

### U.S. Highway 17, Murrells Inlet vicinity

These contiguous properties honor the distinguished career of American sculptor Anna Hyatt Huntington, whose work spanned a period of 70 years. The beachfront Atalaya was her winter home and studio, while Brookgreen Gardens, which she designed and helped establish in 1931, was the first public garden in the country to display sculpture in appropriate natural settings. Huntington specialized in studies of animals and in heroic themes. Her work gained internation-

*Atalaya and Brookgreen Gardens, Murrells Inlet, Georgetown County. Don Quixote. Courtesy of National Coordinating Committee for the Promotion of History (Jill Mesirow).*

al recognition, and in 1922 she was made a Chevalier of the French Legion of Honor. In 1923 she married Archer Huntington, heir to a shipbuilding fortune, whose resources paid for the house and garden. Brookgreen is open to the public as a sculpture garden and as a museum dedicated to the preservation and study of flora and fauna native to the southeast.

## HOPSEWEE
**12 miles south of Georgetown on U.S. Route 17**

Thomas Lynch, Jr., whose signature on the Declaration of Independence is one of the most poignant of all, was born and grew up in this house on the Santee River. Lynch was appointed a delegate to the Continental Congress, in part to care for his father, also a delegate, who had suffered a stroke. The senior Lynch was too ill to sign, and he died in Annapolis on the way home. Dating from the 1740s, the frame building, a fine example of a Carolina "low country" plantation house, is fronted by a two-story piazza and covered with a dormered hip roof. Hopsewee remains in private ownership.

## JOSEPH H. RAINEY HOUSE
**909 Prince Street, Georgetown**

Joseph Hayne Rainey, the first African American elected to the United States House of Representatives, served from 1870 to 1879, longer than any of his black contemporaries. The election of Rainey and of Hiram R. Revels, who began his term in the United States Senate the same year, marked the beginning of active African-American participation in the federal legislative process. Rainey's association with this pre-Revolutionary frame house was lifelong. He is said to have been born in it, and he launched his political career from it. It was his principal residence from 1866 to 1870 and served as his district headquarters when he was in Congress. He lived in it again from 1879 to 1881, and from 1886 until his death the next year.

## ▪ Greenwood County
### NINETY SIX AND STAR FORT (NPS)
**2 miles south of Ninety Six between South Carolina Routes 248 and 27**

First a trading post, then a village with a district courthouse, Ninety Six received its name because it was 96 miles south of the Cherokee Indian village of Keowee. Ninety Six was of prime importance in the settlement of South Carolina's "up country," and

during the Revolution was a focal point of violent Patriot-Tory strife. The first land battle of the Revolution south of New England occurred here late in 1775, and in 1781, Americans under Nathaniel Green's command conducted a 27-day siege of British-held Star Fort, a palisaded stockade adjacent to the village. The settlement was renamed Cambridge after the Revolution, but declined in importance during the 19th century. Earthworks of the fort remain at the site, which is administered by the National Park Service and open to the public.

## ▪ Kershaw County
### BETHESDA PRESBYTERIAN CHURCH
**502 Dekalb Street, Camden**

Dedicated in 1822, this is an important ecclesiastical example of the work of architect Robert Mills. Its neoclassical temple form represents Mills's work as a maturing architect influenced by Jeffersonian classicism. The simple interior, with its floor sloping toward the central pulpit, reflects the importance of the sermon over liturgy in Presbyterian worship. Mills also designed the Dekalb monument in front of the church. The monument, whose cornerstone was laid by Lafayette in 1825, marks the final resting place of German Baron Johann DeKalb, major general in the Revolution, who died at the Battle of Camden.

## CAMDEN BATTLEFIELD
**5 miles north of Camden on U.S. Routes 521 and 601**

On August 16, 1780, a Continental contingent under the command of General Horatio Gates, victor at Saratoga the year before and a favorite of the Continental Congress, was routed here by a British army half its size. The British victory, led by Lord Charles Cornwallis, climaxed a series of disasters in the southern theater of war and marked a low point in the colonial struggle for independence. The valiant Major General Baron DeKalb was killed in the battle, and Gates was replaced by Nathaniel Greene. Greene's appointment marked a turning point, and within two years he had driven the British from Georgia and the Carolinas.

## ■ *Lancaster County*

### LANCASTER COUNTY COURTHOUSE
**104 North Main Street, Lancaster**

The design of this two-story brick building has been attributed to Robert Mills, who provided architectural services for a number of buildings in his native state, and who—as a member of the South Carolina Board of Public Works from 1820 to 1830—was referred to as "State Engineer and Architect." Raised on a high English basement, the brick structure is fronted by a pedimented portico and characterized by Palladian symmetry. It has served in continuous use as a courthouse since its completion in 1828.

### LANCASTER COUNTY JAIL
**208 West Gay Street, Lancaster**

Completed in 1823, this jail reflects a number of innovations advocated by architect Robert Mills for proper housing of prisoners. Among these were adequate ventilation and air circulation (achieved here by placing barred cells in the centers of rooms), incorporating an apartment for the jailer in the building, and arranging prisoners according to their crime (debtors were incarcerated on the first floor, others above). The jail, a handsome stuccoed masonry building with stone quoins and belt courses and recessed arches on the ground floor, stands a block from the county courthouse.

*Lancaster County Courthouse, Lancaster, Lancaster County. Courtesy of HABS (Jack E. Boucher).*

## ■ *Pickens County*

### FORT HILL
**Clemson University campus, Clemson**

From 1825 to 1850 this was the residence of John Caldwell Calhoun, best remembered for his vigorous defense of states' rights. Calhoun's long political career included terms in the U.S. House and Senate, and as secretary of war, vice president, and secretary of state. At Fort Hill during the congressional recess of 1828, he wrote his famous "South Carolina Exposition," embodying the doctrine of nullification. Calhoun's son-in-law willed the house to the state as a site for a college to teach agricultural and mechanical arts, with the proviso that Fort Hill "shall never be torn down or altered." Clemson

University, established in 1889, continues to preserve the large, rambling frame dwelling, a fine example of a South Carolina "up-country" plantation house, which is open as a museum honoring Calhoun.

## ■ *Richland County*

### CHAPELLE ADMINISTRATION BUILDING
**1530 Harden Street, Columbia**

Completed in 1925, this imposing Georgian Revival building is one of the finest works of John Anderson Lankford. An 1896 graduate of Tuskegee Institute, with honors in mechanical engineering and mechanical drawing, Lankford opened the first black architectural firm in America in Jacksonville, Florida, in 1899. Early in the 20th century he moved to Washington, D.C., where he continued his practice, obtaining commissions throughout the country, helping gain recognition for African Americans in the architectural profession. Constructed as the main

building of Allen University, Chapelle continues as its administrative center.

## FIRST BAPTIST CHURCH
### 1306 Hampton Street, Columbia

On December 17, 1860, the 159 delegates to the South Carolina Convention of the People met here and unanimously approved the resolution, "That it is the opinion of this Convention that the State of South Carolina should forthwith secede from the Federal Union, known as the United States of America." By this vote, South Carolina was the first Southern state to declare its separation from the union and took a pivotal step on the path toward civil war. The Greek Revival church, built in 1859, continues to house the congregation for which it was built.

## MILLS BUILDING, SOUTH CAROLINA STATE HOSPITAL
### 2100 Bull Street, Columbia

Designed by Robert Mills, for whom it is named, and constructed between 1822 and 1827, this is the oldest building in the country to be used continuously as a mental institution. With an appropriation of $30,000, it was the nation's third mental hospital built with public funds. Mills saw to it that the building incorporated concepts aimed at a more humane treatment than was usual at the time for mental illness. Rooms faced

south, providing maximum fresh air and sunlight, and—according to a report published while the hospital was being built—"the iron bars [took] the similitude of sashes" in an attempt to provide a familiar and comfortable domestic appearance and feeling.

## ROBERT MILLS HOUSE
### 1616 Blanding Street, Columbia

This two-story brick mansion was built for wealthy Columbia merchant Ainsley Hall from designs by Robert Mills, native South Carolinian, first federal architect and the designer of the Washington Monument in Washington, D.C. Now a monument to Mills, the house is furnished to reflect the period of its construction, the 1820s. The Robert Mills House and Park are open to the public.

## SOUTH CAROLINA STATE HOUSE
### Capitol Square, Columbia

Begun in 1851 but not completed until 1907, this Neoclassical building demonstrates the disruptive effects of the Civil War and Reconstruction on Southern development. It was here, between 1869 and 1874, that the only legislature in American history with an African-American majority met. The State House also provided the setting for James Shepherd Pike's *The Prostrate State: South Carolina under Negro Government* (1874), an influential book that fostered the image of

*Robert Mills House, Columbia, Richland County, 1970. Courtesy of HABS (Cortlandt V.D. Hubbard).*

Reconstruction as an era of black domination, corruption, and misrule. Two years later, in 1876, the State House was the scene of disputes about state elections, which ultimately resulted in the removal of federal troops from the state and the return to power of the Democrats under the leadership of Wade Hampton. The building still serves in its originally intended function, as the capitol of South Carolina.

### ■ *Sumter County*

### BOROUGH HOUSE
**1 mile north of State Route 261 and State Highway 76/378, Stateburg**

The Borough House Plantation complex contains the oldest and largest collection of "high-style" *pise de terre* (rammed earth) buildings in the United States. Six of the 27 dependencies and portions of the five-part main house were constructed in 1821 with the use of this ancient technique, which is accomplished by tamping moist earth between forms and covering the hardened soil with stucco. The method was introduced to this country in 1806 in *Rural Economy* by S. W. Johnson. The Borough House and several dependencies are fronted by handsome

Greek Revival porticos. Lieutenant General Richard H. ("Fighting Dick") Anderson, one of the Confederacy's leading officers of the Civil War, was born and raised in this family home, which remains in Anderson ownership.

### CHURCH OF THE HOLY CROSS
**South Carolina Route 261, Stateburg**

Built in 1850, this structure was designed by Charleston architect Edward C. Jones in the Gothic Revival style. The cruciform building is a distinguished example of its style and gains added significance because its walls are constructed of *pise de terre* (rammed earth), thus forming—with the Borough House group across the road—the largest complex of such buildings in the country. Inside, the church contains a rare organ, Bohemian stained-glass windows, and the original carved walnut pews.

### MILLFORD PLANTATION
**2 miles west of Pinewood on South Carolina Route 261**

Scarlet O'Hara would have loved living here. Millford epitomizes the popular "Gone With the Wind" image of antebellum architecture of the American South—so often attempted,

*Borough House, Stateburg, Sumter County. Courtesy of HABS (Jack E. Boucher).*

*Millford Plantation,
Sumter County, 1973.
Courtesy of the South
Carolina State Historic
Preservation Office,
South Carolina
Department of Archives
and History.*

so seldom achieved. Dating from 1839, the house is fronted with a magnificent, giant-order Corinthian portico, and one-story verandas connect the main block to dependencies on both sides. An unsupported flying spiral staircase is an outstanding interior feature. Millford, in the High Hills of the Santee, was the seat of an important—and obviously profitable—cotton plantation. Now beautifully restored and maintained, it remains in private ownership as the centerpiece of an extensive acreage.

# SOUTH DAKOTA

## ■ Buffalo County

### CROW CREEK SITE
**Crow Creek Sioux Reservation, Chamberlain**

This large fortified prehistoric Native American village site on the east bank of the Missouri River represents two occupations. The older is an Initial Middle Missouri Tradition component, dating from ca. A.D. 1100–1150, and referred to as Crow Creek. The village was surrounded by a defensive ditch, but ca. A.D. 1325 another people, competing for the same scarce resources as the Crow Creek people, attacked the village and massacred its inhabitants. Their mass grave holds the remains of more than 486 individuals. The second occupation is an Initial Coalescent Tradition component called Wolf Creek, dating from ca. A.D. 1400 to 1550.

### FORT THOMPSON MOUNDS
**Address Restricted, Fort Thompson**

Fort Thompson Mounds is a discontiguous district containing more than four dozen prehistoric mounds. This is the largest concentration of remaining Northern Plains burial mounds and provides evidence of possible communication with eastern cultures, as indicated by trade items that have been uncovered. Surprisingly, no evidence of any supporting village or campsite has been found to supply information on the occupation, which is culturally connected to the Plains Woodland tradition (A.D. 1–900) through burial patterns and artifacts. The mounds are located on the Crow Creek Indian Reservation.

## ■ Campbell County

### VANDERBILT ARCHEOLOGICAL SITE
**Address Restricted, Pollock vicinity**

Archeological information about the earliest history of today's Mandan and Hidatsa peoples is preserved in the Vanderbilt Village Site. They began to transform their environment along the Missouri River floodplain near the Cannonball River about A.D. 1000 by expanding a horticultural economy with permanent villages, substantial houses, and more complex technologies. By A.D. 1400, the Vanderbilt Village was a well-established, dynamic community; its people traded, hunted, fished, and created a highly developed clan tradition with neighboring villages.

## ■ Davison County

### MITCHELL SITE
**Mitchell Prehistoric Indian Village and Archeodome, Indian Village Road, Mitchell**

Mitchell Site is the only reliably dated site (ca. A.D 1000) pertaining to the Lower James River phase (Initial Variant) of the migration of late Woodland-Mississippian culture to the Middle Missouri Valley. The site that supported a farming and hunting society of as many as 1,000 people was surrounded by a defensive ditch and, later, palisades. Overcrowding and declining resources forced the inhabitants to abandon the area. The site is particularly known for the information obtained from its burials. Mitchell Site is open to the public.

## ■ Dewey County

### MOLSTAD VILLAGE
**Address Restricted, Mobridge**

A tiny fortified prehistoric village site containing five circular house rings enclosed by a ditch, Molstad appears to represent a period of transition. Dating from ca. A.D. 1550, it represents the time when Central Plains and Middle Missouri cultural traits were combining to form the basis for Mandan, Hidatsa, and Arikara cultures as they existed at the time of the first contact with Europeans.

## ■ Hanson County

### BLOOM SITE
**Address Restricted, Bloom**

This site is a well-preserved example of a prehistoric fortified Over Focus Indian village (ca. A.D. 1000). About 25 depressions mark the locations of rectangular houses. Prior to their destruction by cultivation, some 50 burial mounds, ranging up to 200 feet in diameter and from 3 to 10 feet in height, also marked the site. As a representative of the Over Focus, the Bloom site may have been the home of a group of ancestral Mandans as they moved from the eastern prairies toward the Missouri River valley.

## ■ Hughes County

### ARZBERGER SITE
**Address Restricted, Pierre**

The northernmost outpost of the Central Plains tradition (ca. A.D. 1500), this fortified village site is atop a low mesa overlooking the Missouri River. The village was extraordinarily large; the site covers some 70 acres. The fortification had 24 bastions, and 44 circular house rings have been noted. The village likely represents the Arikara Indians at the time they were differentiating from the parent Pawnee.

## ■ Lawrence County

### DEADWOOD HISTORIC DISTRICT
**Deadwood**

Wild Bill Hickock, Calamity Jane, Deadwood Dick, Poker Alice, Preacher Smith, and Crooked Nose Jack McCall—the list of famous and infamous characters who once inhabited this wide-open town of the Wild West is endless. The site of a rich gold strike in 1875, Deadwood emerged the next year as a hastily built tent and log cabin settlement, and by June 1876 it had a population of 2,000. Although fires took their toll in the early days, Deadwood still retains a number of buildings dating from its heyday and maintains the atmosphere of a western mining town. That atmosphere is amplified, during the tourist season, with reenactments of Jack McCall shooting Wild Bill, and his subsequent trial.

### FRAWLEY RANCH
**Interstate 90 and U.S. Highway 85, vicinity of Spearfish**

When the 160-acre homestead concept that helped populate so much of the west proved a failure in the rugged Black Hills of South Dakota, Henry J. Frawley purchased a number of the unsuccessful farms. By 1913 the lawyer had developed his 5,000-acre spread into one of western South Dakota's largest, best run, and most profitable cattle ranches. Many sites and buildings from both eras remain, testament to what can happen when man works with mother Nature, and what can result when he doesn't.

*Deadwood Historic District, Deadwood, Lawrence County, 1954. Courtesy of NPS (George Grant).*

■ *Lincoln County*

## BLOOD RUN SITE

**Junction of Blood Run Creek and the Big Sioux River**

This extensive site, which also continues across the Big Sioux River into Iowa, contains the remains of an Oneota Indian village and numerous conical mounds. Limited archeological investigations of the mounds indicate that the site may have been occupied as early as A.D. 1300. Occupation over many centuries by different tribes has left abundant cultural remains. (Also in Lyon County, Iowa.)

■ *Lyman County*

## LANGDEAU SITE

**Address Restricted, Lower Brule**

Remains from the Langdeau Site, a small prehistoric village containing housepits and other habitation features, date to a single occupation from A.D. 1000 to 1140. Possibly the earliest reliably dated village of the Missouri Trench, Langdeau Site represents the full emergence of the Plains Village traditions in the Middle Missouri cultural area. Evidence suggests that the people of Langdeau introduced horticulture to a region previously occupied by hunter/gatherers and participated in trade with cultures as far away as the Gulf of Mexico and the lower Ohio River.

■ *Meade County*

## BEAR BUTTE

**Bear Butte State Park, Northeast of Sturgis**

Bear Butte was associated with several Plains Indian tribes, primarily with the Cheyenne. Their name for the towering mountain was Nowahawus, "the place where the people were taught." It was here that agents of Maheo, the All Father, imparted to Sweet Medicine, the most revered Cheyenne prophet, the knowledge from which the tribe derived their religious, political, social, and economic customs. In essence, Bear Butte was the Cheyenne's Mount Sinai. Bear Butte was also a well-known sentinel to explorers and frontiersmen. It is now the centerpiece of Bear Butte State Park.

■ *Shannon County*

## WOUNDED KNEE BATTLEFIELD

**11 miles west of Batesland, Pine Ridge Indian Reservation**

On December 29, 1890, the last major clash between Native Americans and U.S. troops in North America occurred here, in what has been called the Massacre at Wounded Knee. In the period following the introduction of the Ghost Dance religion among the Lakota and the killing of Sitting Bull, a band of his Sioux followers (120 men and 230 women and children) led by Big Foot left the Cheyenne River Reservation. Intercepted by

*Bear Butte, Sturgis, Meade County, ca. 1939. Courtesy of NPS.*

U.S. cavalry troopers, they gave themselves up and were escorted to an army encampment on Pine Ridge Reservation, where they were to be disarmed. During the disarming, tempers flared and a shot rang out. The ensuing struggle, short but bloody, resulted in a number of army casualties (mostly from other troopers' fire) and the virtual massacre of Big Foot's band. The mass grave of the Indians is marked, and a museum provides interpretation of this site. As one of the Indian survivors recalled years later, "A people's dream died there." For soldiers and settlers, Wounded Knee marked the passing of the frontier.

## ■ Stanley County

### FORT PIERRE CHOUTEAU SITE

**South Dakota Route 1806, 4 miles north of Fort Pierre**

Perhaps the most significant fur trade/military fort on the western American frontier, Fort Pierre Chouteau was the largest (almost 300 feet square) and best-equipped trading post in the northern Great Plains. John Jacob Astor's American Fur Company built the fort in 1832 to support its expansion into the Upper Missouri region. From then until 1857, when the fort was abandoned, activities between traders and settlers on one hand,

and native cultures on the other, exemplified the commercial alliances critical to the success of the fur business, and to the acculturation of both societies. When the U.S. Army abandoned Fort Pierre, usable buildings were transported to Fort Randall and the remaining timber was used as fuel for steamboats plying the Missouri River.

### VERENDRYE SITE

**Between Second and Fifth Streets and Second and Fourth Avenues, Fort Pierre**

François and Louis Joseph de la Verendrye, seeking a northwest passage to the Pacific, were the first Europeans to explore the Northern Plains region of the present United States. Here, in late March 1743, 61 years before the Lewis and Clark Expedition, they buried a lead plate beneath a pile of stones, claiming the region for France. This served as the basis for French sovereignty on the Upper Missouri, defining the bounds of French Louisiana to include the entire Mississippi River drainage. The tablet, uncovered in 1913, is the first written record of white men in South Dakota. A granite monument, framed by three flagpoles that fly the banners of France, the United States, and South Dakota, now marks the site.

# TENNESSEE

## ■ Carter County

### SYCAMORE SHOALS

**2 miles west of Elizabethton on the Watauga River**

Sycamore Shoals, picturesque rapids of the Watauga River, marks the location of events important in America's early westward expansion. By the terms of a treaty signed here in March 1775, the Cherokee sold 20 million acres of their land. The tract, known as Transylvania, included much of Tennessee and Kentucky. Five years later the shoals were the rendezvous point for 900 frontiersmen, known as the Overmountain Men,

before they marched to Kings Mountain, where they contributed to the defeat of the British army. The State of Tennessee acquired Sycamore Shoals in 1975 and has since developed it as a state park.

## ■ Cheatham County

### MONTGOMERY BELL TUNNEL

**Harpeth River and Bell Bend Road, White Bluff vicinity**

By tunneling through a 290-foot-wide limestone ridge in 1818–1819, slaves belonging to Montgomery Bell created the first known large-diameter tunnel in the United States.

*Jubilee Hall, Fisk University, Nashville, Davidson County, 1965. Courtesy of NPS.*

The diversion tunnel, connecting two sections of the meandering Harpeth River, served as a man-made water flume with an approximate 16-foot drop of water. It was constructed by hand drilling, with the use of hammers and chisels and black powder, which was ignited and exploded, causing the stone to fracture and break. Bell hoped that once he provided water power, the U.S. government would purchase his property and establish an armory that Congress had recently authorized. When that hope failed to materialize, he established an iron forge at the site to utilize the water power. The tunnel is now part of the Montgomery Bell State Park.

## ■ *Davidson County*

### GEORGE PEABODY COLLEGE FOR TEACHERS

#### 21st Avenue South and Edgehill Avenue, Nashville

Financier and philanthropist George Peabody established the Peabody Education Fund in 1867 to rebuild the shattered public education system of the post–Civil War South, and to train teachers to carry on the work. The University of Nashville, organized in 1826, was the first college to receive aid from the fund. In 1875 the university began to function as a state normal school. After 1889, it was known as Peabody Normal College and in 1909 was incorporated as the George Peabody College for Teachers. Peabody College moved to its present campus in 1914. Its designation as a National Historic Landmark serves as a tribute to George Peabody and the contributions his fund made to the advance of education in the South.

### THE HERMITAGE

#### 12 miles east of Nashville on U.S. Route 70, Nashville

From 1804, when he bought a farm here, until his death in 1837, Andrew Jackson called the Hermitage home. He and his wife Rachel first lived in a log house, then began building a brick house in 1819. On two occasions Jackson enlarged and remodeled the house until, by the time he retired in March 1837 from his second term as the nation's seventh president, it reached its present form—a handsome Greek Revival mansion with porticos front (in the Corinthian order) and rear (in the Doric order). Earlier, Jackson had built a domed pavilion guarding the monument over Rachel's tomb. Still remaining in the house is a mantelpiece fashioned of hickory sticks, alluding to Jackson's nickname, "Old Hickory." The Hermitage and its grounds are open to the public.

## JUBILEE HALL, FISK UNIVERSITY
### 17th Avenue North, Nashville

Fisk University was founded by the American Missionary Society in 1865 and named for the administrator of the Freedmen's Bureau in Tennessee. Initially intended as a normal school to train black teachers after the Civil War, Fisk evolved into a liberal arts college—in contrast with the vocational approach of Tuskegee and Hampton—and is now recognized as one of the country's leading historically black universities. Jubilee Hall, a large Victorian Gothic brick building, dates from 1873–1876. The oldest structure on campus, it was built with money obtained by the college choir, the Jubilee Singers, on their tours around the country to obtain funds for the fledgling institution.

## NASHVILLE UNION STATION AND TRAINSHED
### 10th Avenue South at Broadway, Nashville

Completed in 1900, this is one of the largest single-span gable-roof trainsheds in the United States. Built by the Louisville and Nashville Railroad, it has a clear span of 200 feet. It marks the apogee of gabled-roof trainshed construction, and the significant contribution such engineering feats made to modern building practices. The station to which the deteriorating shed is connected is a large stone structure designed in the Romanesque Revival style and dominated by a tall clock tower.

## OLD FIRST PRESBYTERIAN CHURCH
### Nashville

"Karmac on the Cumberland" is the affectionate name given one of the country's largest and most important Egyptian Revival buildings. William Strickland designed it late in his career, during the time he was engaged on the construction of the Tennessee State Capitol. By 1849, when the church was begun, he had become one of the foremost architects in the country. The exterior of the brick church has distinctive twin towers flanking a portico supported by deeply fluted pillars with lotus blossom capitals. The dramatic and colorful interior, full of Egyptian

*Old First Presbyterian Church, Nashville, Davidson County, 1970. Courtesy of HABS (Jack E. Boucher).*

motifs (including stained-glass windows depicting palm trees and lotus plants) dates from the 1880s. Strickland never saw it, but one wonders if Cecil B. deMille might have.

## TENNESSEE STATE CAPITOL
### Capitol Hill, Nashville

Tennessee's State Capitol, located high on an acropolis overlooking downtown Nashville, is one of the nation's most impressive—and most individualistic—Greek Revival public buildings. Constructed of limestone between 1845 and 1859, it was designed by one of the most noted architects of the time, William Strickland. He copied the Ionic order of the Erectheum in Athens for the building's four porticos, and the monument of Lysicrates, also in Athens, for the round tower that centers the pedimented roof. Strickland, who also supervised construction, died in 1854, shortly before the capitol was completed, and is buried in a vault in the north portico. His son finished the work he started.

■ *Fentress County*

## ALVIN CULLOM YORK FARM
**U.S. Route 127, 7 miles north of Jamestown, Pall Mall**

From 1922 until 1964 this was the residence of Alvin Collum York, known to history as "Sergeant York." On October 8, 1918, during the Battle of the Argonne Forest, this mountaineer marksman fought a virtually one-man battle against the opposing German army, killing 25 soldiers, taking 132 prisoners, and capturing 35 machine guns. For his actions, York was awarded the Congressional Medal of Honor and the French Croix de Guerre. He magnified his legend by refusing to capitalize on it, saying that he had served his country as his duty, not for money. A grateful State of Tennessee presented him with the 396-acre farm on which the house was built. It is now the Sgt. Alvin C. York State Historic Park.

■ *Hamilton County*

## MOCCASIN BEND ARCHEOLOGICAL DISTRICT
**Address Restricted, Chattanooga**

This large peninsula formed by the Tennessee River opposite Chattanooga contains the most compact, diverse, and best preserved samples of archeological remains known in the Tennessee River valley. Evidence has been found of occupation by Native American groups of the Archaic, Woodland, and Mississippian periods. Spanish trade and gift items, dating from the 16th century, have also been unearthed, evidence of the early contact period in the Southeast. Also included are Civil War earthworks associated with the battle of Chattanooga. Obviously, as is currently proved by the existence of Chattanooga itself, this has been an important crossroads of commerce and trade for centuries.

■ *Hardeman County*

## SIEGE AND BATTLE OF CORINTH SITES
**On the Hatchie River, south of Pocahontas**

Two important trunk railroads passed through Corinth, making it a vital transportation hub of the western Confederacy. The Union siege

from April 28 to May 30, 1862, forced the Confederates to evacuate, and a Southern attack was repulsed at the Battle of Corinth on October 3–4. This Union triumph, following a summer of Southern victories that appeared to presage recognition of the Confederacy by the United Kingdom, helped to end that prospect. Well-preserved earthworks, batteries, rifle pits, houses used as military headquarters, and the Corinth National Cemetery, with more than 5,600 Civil War interments, most of them unknown, remain (also in Corinth and Alcorn Counties, Mississippi).

■ *Hardin County*

## SHILOH INDIAN MOUNDS SITE (NPS)
**East of Hurley in Shiloh National Military Park**

Located in Shiloh National Military Park, the site is the largest extant fortified Mississippian ceremonial mound complex in the Tennessee River valley and is important as a source for testing the chronology of other sites in the region. The site consists of six Late Mississippian temple mounds, one Late Woodland burial mound and an associated village site, and a low earth embankment that once served as a foundation for a wooden palisade.

■ *Knox County*

## WILLIAM BLOUNT MANSION
**200 West Hill Avenue, Knoxville**

William Blount was appointed governor of the territory south of the Ohio River (commonly known as the Southwest Territory) in 1790, and he built this frame house and office soon afterward. For its time and place, it was definitely a "mansion": weatherboards were shipped by water from North Carolina, and window panes by pack train from Virginia. Blount, who already represented North Carolina in the Continental Congress and had signed the U.S. Constitution when he moved here, was president of the convention that met in January 1796 to proclaim the transformation of the territory into the state of Tennessee. He then became one of the new state's first U.S. senators. Blount's Knoxville home was acquired by an association formed in 1926 to preserve it, and it is open to the public.

### ■ *Lauderdale County*

## FORT PILLOW
### Tennessee Route 87, Fort Pillow

Constructed by Confederate engineers to hinder Union gunboats on the Mississippi, this earthwork fort was captured by Union troops in June 1862, then recaptured by Confederate forces under Major General Nathan Bedford Forrest in April 1864. At that time it was garrisoned by some 570 Union troops, of whom 262 were African Americans — ex-slaves recruited in Tennessee and Alabama. In the savage fight, Confederates aimed their fury particularly at the African Americans, killing 229 rather than accepting their surrender. News of the fight, labeled a massacre, had a profound effect: "Remember Fort Pillow" became a battle cry of black soldiers, and the fort itself their Alamo. The fort is now the centerpiece of Fort Pillow State Historic Park.

### ■ *Madison County*

## PINSON MOUNDS
### 460 Ozier Road, Pinson

This large site includes three distinct mound groups, earthen embankments, and several village sites, originally partially enclosed by a palisade. The site was occupied during several periods, beginning as early as 5000 B.C. Surprisingly, unlike other sites of its magnitude, it was situated on a minor drainage system instead of a major stream. The Pinson Mounds are also significant because they are near the often-posited center of the origin of the Mississippian culture. The mounds are now part of Pinson Mounds State Archeological Area with a visitor's center and museum.

### ■ *Maury County*

## JAMES K. POLK HOUSE
### West Seventh and South High Streets, Columbia

Constructed in 1816, this two-story brick house was, for a time, the home of James Knox Polk, 11th president of the United States. The house was built by Polk's father, and the future president lived here until 1819, when he went to Nashville to read law. Admitted to the bar a year later, Polk returned to open his practice in Columbia. His term as president (1845–1849) was marked by rapid expansion of the territorial boundaries of the United States. The house in which he spent his young manhood was purchased by the State of Tennessee in 1929 and is open to the public.

## RATTLE AND SNAP
### Tennessee Route 43, Columbia vicinity

This flamboyant brick mansion is one of the most distinguished Greek Revival houses in America. Its entrance facade is highlighted by a giant-order Corinthian portico with ten columns. The portico's arrangement and pro-

*Rattle and Snap, Columbia Vicinity, Maury County, 1971. Courtesy of HABS (Jack E. Boucher).*

Rhea County Courthouse, Dayton, Rhea County. Courtroom, 1972. Courtesy of Tennessee Historical Commission (Frank Glass, Jr.).

portions, along with the arched windows that flank the doorways it protects, show a freedom from the archeological correctness that characterized earlier Greek Revival designs. The house was built in 1842–1845 by George Knox Polk, a cousin of President Polk, and his wife Sallie Hilliard, on land inherited from his Revolutionary War–hero father, Colonel William Polk of North Carolina. The name, as flamboyant in its way as the house itself, refers to the fact that Colonel Polk won the land in a game of "rattle and snap," a game of chance much like craps, but played with beans rather than dice.

## ■ *Monroe County*

### FORT LOUDOUN

**U.S. Route 411, Vonore vicinity**

Begun in 1756 at the request of the western Cherokee and occupied until 1760, Fort Loudoun was instrumental in allying the Indians with the English during the most critical years of the French and Indian War. Once relations between colonial settlers and the Cherokee deteriorated, however, the Indians attacked the fort and laid siege to it. Its commander surrendered on August 7, 1760, and it was burned the next year. Using archeological evidence, the palisaded log fort, in an irregular shape resembling a four-pointed star, has been reconstructed and is open to the public.

## ■ *Carter County*

### RHEA COUNTY COURTHOUSE

**Market Street between Second and Third Avenues, Dayton**

From July 10 to July 21, 1925, the eyes of the world focused on this red brick courthouse, or at least on what was transpiring inside. John Thomas Scopes, a Dayton public school teacher, was on trial for teaching Darwin's theory of evolution, in violation of a Tennessee state law passed earlier that year. The famous Scopes "Monkey Trial" was a battle between two great lawyers — William Jennings Bryan for the prosecution versus Clarence Darrow for the defense — and a symbol of the clash between fundamentalist and modernist thought in science, theology, philosophy, and politics. Reverberations from the trial continue to resound.

## ■ *Roane County*

### X-10 REACTOR, OAK RIDGE NATIONAL LABORATORY

**Oak Ridge National Laboratory, Oak Ridge**

When it went into operation on November 4, 1943, this was the world's first full-scale nuclear reactor and the first to produce significant amounts of heat energy and measurable amounts of plutonium. In 1946 the reactor became the first to produce radioactive isotopes for medical therapy. For many years,

X-10 was the principal atomic research facility in the United States. The reactor, located in Building 3001 at the Oak Ridge National Laboratory, was the world's oldest operating reactor when it was shut down in 1963. It was opened to the public in 1968.

## Shelby County

### BEALE STREET HISTORIC DISTRICT
**Beale Street, from Main to Fourth Streets, Memphis**

Beale Street helped give birth to the "blues." With its bars, night clubs, gambling halls, and pawn shops, this once rowdy entertainment district provided a vibrant environment that fostered the development of this peculiarly American form of music in the early 20th century. The blues affected the transition of black music from the vocal to the instrumental realm and influenced jazz, rock, pop, and even symphonic music. W. C. Handy, reputed "father of the blues," habituated Peewee's Saloon, where he composed "Memphis Blues," "Saint Louis Blues," and—of course—"Beale Street Blues." He is honored with a statue in Handy Park, located in the center of the district.

### CHUCALISSA SITE
**1897 Indian Village Drive, Memphis**

Chucalissa is the best-preserved civic/ceremonial center complex of the Walls phase (A.D. 1400–1500), one of the best-known Late Mississippian phases in the Central Mississippi Valley. The site includes a large platform mound and an extensive village area surrounding the central core and is known for its excellent preservation of architectural, floral, faunal, and human remains. Chucalissa (from a word translated as "abandoned house") is within T. O. Fuller State Park and is open to the public.

## Sullivan County

### LONG ISLAND OF THE HOLSTON
**South fork of Holston River, Kingsport vicinity**

Located just east of the confluence of the North and South Forks of the Holston River, Long Island was a sacred council and treaty ground of the Cherokee Nation. The island also figured significantly in early American exploration and settlement. Starting at Long Island in March 1775, Daniel Boone led a team of 30 axmen to open a trail through the Cumberland Gap, which gained fame as the Wilderness Road. Between 1775 and 1795, more than 200,000 emigrants passed along the trail. In recent decades the island has lost much of its integrity, and its illustrious past exists more in memory than in reality.

## Sumner County

### ISAAC FRANKLIN PLANTATION
**U.S. Route 31, 4 miles south of Gallatin**

Isaac Franklin was a principal in the largest slave-trading firm in the antebellum South. At its height, Franklin & Armfield had offices in Alexandria, Virginia; Natchez, Mississippi; and New Orleans, Louisiana; agents in every important Southern city and its own fleet of sailing ships; and trafficked in thousands of slaves annually. Franklin built Fairvue in 1832 when he decided to leave the profitable but unsavory trade to live the more genteel life of a planter. The 2½-story red-brick house with its associated outbuildings, among them four slave houses and an overseer's house, reflects the life-style of wealthy antebellum planters in the upper South. (See Franklin & Armfield Office, Alexandria, Virginia.)

### WYNNEWOOD
**Tennessee Route 25, Castalian Springs**

Wynnewood, consisting of a main house and five dependencies, constitutes one of the finest and most fully developed pioneer log complexes in the country. The 110-foot main house, built of white oak logs in 1828 to serve as an inn, consists of several individual log units, or pens, and utilizes both of the two traditional ways of joining them: "saddle bag" and "dog trot." The dependencies, more or less contemporary with the main house, are of oak, cedar, walnut, and ash logs.

## Williamson County

### FRANKLIN BATTLEFIELD
**South of Franklin on U.S. Route 31**

One of the bloodiest battles of the Civil War

*Wynnewood, Castalian Springs, Sumner County, 1971. Courtesy of NPS.*

occurred here. Early on the afternoon of November 30, 1864, Confederate General John Bell Hood, against the advice of his staff, ordered his Army of Tennessee to attack Union forces under the command of Major General John M. Schofield and his field commander, General Jacob D. Cox. Each of the numerous assaults made against the entrenched Federals was repulsed. The huge losses (more than 6,000 casualties) sustained by Hood's army helped doom his Tennessee campaign. The Carter House, Cox's command post during the battle and one of the four noncontiguous properties included in this National Historic Landmark, is open to the public.

## HIRAM MASONIC LODGE NO. 7
### South Second Avenue, Franklin

The 1830 Treaty of Franklin, which provided for the removal of Chickasaw Indians from their eastern homelands to a region beyond the Mississippi, was signed in this building. Although it was never actually ratified, as the first Southern removal treaty it became a prototype for the eventual removal of the five "civilized" Indian nations. President Andrew Jackson personally opened the proceedings, the only time a U.S. president journeyed to an Indian council for the purpose of making a treaty. The Lodge, a tall brick building with rudimentary Gothic Revival detailing, is the oldest Masonic hall in continuous use in Tennessee.

# TEXAS

■ *Armstrong County*

## J A RANCH
### Palo Duro Canyon, Palo Duro

Charles Goodnight, soldier, plainsman, trail-blazer, and pioneer cattleman of the Panhandle's staked plains, dominates the history of the cattle frontier of Texas. He arrived in this area in 1876, only a year after it had been wrested from the Kiowa and the Comanche. In 1877, Goodnight formed a partnership with John G. Adair—who provided financial backing—and under his direction, the J A Ranch grew to encompass 700,000 acres of grassland supporting 40,000 head of cattle. The nine major buildings of the headquarters, including a ranch house that incorporates a pre–Civil War log homestead as its nucleus, still preside over a huge cattle spread.

## ■ Bastrop County

### BASTROP STATE PARK
**East of Bastrop between State Routes 21 and 71**

Bastrop State Park is one of the finest illustrations of the legacy and influence of architect Herbert Maier's work as a regional director of the Civilian Conservation Corps (CCC) and as the leading spokesperson on architecture for the National Park Service's effort to assist state parks during the 1930s. Bastrop was established as a showplace for state park design and construction in Texas and was one of the most extensive state parks developed during the New Deal. Facilities constructed by the CCC—all well preserved—include roadways, picnic tables, refectory, bridges, cabins, and a nine-hole golf course.

## ■ Bexar County

### ALAMO
**Alamo Plaza, San Antonio**

On February 24, 1836, during the Texan War for Independence, some 5,000 Mexican soldiers under command of Antonio Lopez de Santa Anna laid seige to a garrison of 145 Texans and their supporters who had sought refuge within the stone walls of this mission chapel. On March 1, thirty-two reinforcements arrived, but on March 6, Santa Anna's forces stormed the Alamo, killing all of its 187 defenders—among them famed fron-

tiersmen James Bowie and David Crockett—then burning their bodies. The defeat won sympathy and support for the Texan cause in the United States, and the battle cry "Remember the Alamo" strengthened the Texan will to throw off Mexican domination. The Alamo, standing within a landscaped park at the heart of San Antonio, is now open to the public as a museum and shrine to the Texas patriots who died within its walls.

### ESPADA AQUEDUCT (NPS)
**Espada Road, just east of U.S. Route 281, San Antonio**

Probably constructed between 1731 and 1745, this sturdy masonry aqueduct, carrying water across Piedra Arroyo, was once part of an irrigation system serving the Spanish missions of San Antonio. During the height of activity at Espada Mission, nearly 1,000 acres were under cultivation. Now the only remaining Spanish structure of its type in the United States, the five-mile long aqueduct and dam are included in San Antonio Missions National Historical Park.

### FORT SAM HOUSTON
**North edge of San Antonio**

Authorized in 1875 and completed in 1879 on a 92-acre site donated by the city of San Antonio, this was the U.S. Army's principal

*Alamo, San Antonio, Bexar County, 1961. Courtesy of HABS (Jack E. Boucher).*

*Fort Sam Houston, San Antonio, Bexar County. Watch tower. Courtesy of HABS (David J. Kaminsky).*

supply base in the Southwest. "Fort Sam" supplied the Rough Riders in 1898, furnished most of the men and matériel for Pershing's campaign against Pancho Villa in 1916, and provided training facilities for thousands of troops in World War I. Experiments with the Wright biplane here led to the establishment of the Signal Corps Aviation Section in 1914. Many historic structures—including officers quarters, barracks, and the 1879 Quadrangle—remain on this active military post that has grown to approximately 35,000 acres, or 54 square miles.

## HANGAR 9, BROOKS AIR FORCE BASE
### Inner Circle Road, San Antonio

Erected in 1918 for the U.S. Army Signal Corps Aviation Section on one of its hastily established World War I training fields, this wood-trussed frame structure is the country's oldest Air Force aircraft storage and repair facility. Now a museum, the hangar symbolizes the Army's early efforts to create an effective air force and the rapid progress made toward that goal in response to the impetus of war.

## MAJESTIC THEATRE
### 230 East Houston Street, San Antonio

Designed by Chicago architect John Elberson, the Majestic opened to rave reviews in June 1929. One of the great movie palaces of its era, the theater occupies parts of 6 floors of a 15-story office building but gives little exterior hint at the riches to be found within. The auditorium, originally seating 3,700 patrons, has side walls replicating a Spanish village, with columns, oriels, balconies, latticework, sculpture, and trailing vines—all silhouetted against a ceiling that appears to be a vaulted blue sky with twinkling (electric) stars. This fantasy world, into which anyone could escape for a few hours to forget the harsh realities of the Depression that followed months after it opened, closed its doors in 1974. Fortunately, it was restored to its original splendor and reopened as a venue for live theater and symphony concerts in 1989.

## MISSION CONCEPCION (NPS)
### 807 Mission Road, San Antonio

Established in 1731 by Franciscan friars, this is the best preserved of the Texas missions. The massive masonry church, with its full cruciform plan, is designed in Mexican Baroque style and is fronted by twin bell towers flanking the entrance. The church and adjacent mission buildings were used by the U.S. Army in 1849, but in 1887 repairs were made and the church was reopened as a place of worship. Mission Concepcion is included in San Antonio Missions National Historical Park.

## SPANISH GOVERNOR'S PALACE
### 105 Military Plaza, San Antonio

This large Spanish Colonial town house is the only remaining example in Texas of an aristocratic 18th-century Spanish residence. Constructed ca. 1749, it was originally intended as the residence of the commanding officer of the presidio. Except for an elaborately carved and dated keystone over the

*Spanish Governor's Palace, San Antonio, Bexar County. Interior plaza, 1968. Courtesy of NPS (Charles W. Snell).*

main entrance, the Palace presents a plain facade to the street. The building was restored in 1929 and is now open to the public as a museum of Spanish Colonial History.

## ■ *Blanco County*

## LYNDON BAINES JOHNSON BOYHOOD HOME (NPS)
### Ninth Street, Johnson City

Beginning in 1913, when he was five years old, Lyndon Baines Johnson spent most of his growing-up years in this small one-story frame house in the heart of the Texas hill country. Johnson's grandfather began raising cattle in the area in the 1850s, and Johnson City was later named for the Johnson family pioneers. The future president's father built the house in 1886, and it was restored by the president and his family during the time he was serving as the 36th president of the United States (1963–1969). More than most men, Johnson is associated with the place that nurtured him. Throughout his years of public service in many places the hill country of Texas was always home. His boyhood home is open to the public as part of the Lyndon B. Johnson National Historical Park.

## ■ *Cameron County*

## CABOT
### At the foot of Jackson Street, Port Isabel

Reflecting the exigencies of World War II, *Cabot* (1943) is the sole survivor of a unique class of light carriers built atop the incomplete hulls of cruisers of the President class. Constructed as hasty replacements for carriers lost early in the war, the Independence class carriers served with distinction in nearly every major naval engagement of the War in the Pacific from 1943 on. *Cabot* earned nine battle stars and the prestigious Presidential Unit Citation. In 1967 the ship was turned over to Spain and recommissioned SNS *Dedalo*, but was returned to the United States in 1989.

## FORT BROWN
### Off International Boulevard, Brownsville

The first U.S. military post in Texas, Fort Taylor, was established in 1846, soon after Brigadier General Zachary Taylor arrived to occupy territory claimed by Mexico and the United States. Taylor left the fort and a garrison of 50 men under the command of Major

Jacob Brown, but returned to end a Mexican siege after defeating forces at Palo Alto and Resaca de la Palma. Learning that Major Brown had been killed, Taylor renamed the fort in his honor. Later, troops stationed at Fort Brown fought the last battle of the Civil War, a month after Appomattox. The fort served as the center for troop activity during the Mexican bandit trouble of 1913–1917 and continued as a regular army post until 1944. Buildings representing many eras of the fort's history remain.

## PALMITO RANCH BATTLEFIELD
**South of Texas State Highway 4 (Boca Chica Highway), Brownsville vicinity**

Although this battlefield is famous as the site of the last land engagement of the Civil War, its greater significance derives from its strategic position at the mouth of the Rio Grande, which defined the Confederacy's only international border. Throughout the war, Confederates could trade with Mexico and with foreign ships anchored offshore, ensuring a necessary lifeline throughout the conflict. The lower Rio Grande valley was a vital outlet for southern cotton, and the Gulf of Mexico a source of guns and ammunition from Europe. It was the collapse of the Confederacy elsewhere that led to defeat at Palmito Ranch in May 1865—a month after Lee had surrendered at Appomattox.

## PALO ALTO BATTLEFIELD (NPS)
**6 miles north of Brownsville on Farm Road 511**

Here, on May 8, 1846, Brigadier General Zachary Taylor and 2,300 U.S. Army soldiers engaged 3,300 Mexican troops commanded by Major General Mariano Arista in the first of two important battles of the Mexican War fought on American soil. The Mexicans attacked twice, but were repelled both times and were forced to retreat. After additional losses the next day at Resaca de la Palma, they recrossed the Rio Grande to return to Mexico. Taylor's victory here made the invasion of Mexico possible.

## RESACA DE LA PALMA BATTLEFIELD
**North edge of Brownsville on Parades Line Road**

Along with Palo Alto, this is one of only two important battles of the Mexican War fought on American soil. In the early hours of May 9, 1846, after losing at Palo Alto, Mexican forces under Major General Mariano Arista retreated to the ravine of this creek just north of Brownsville. Brigadier General Zachary Taylor and his army gave pursuit; Taylor ordered his cavalry to charge the Mexican position, sending the enemy into disarray and, ultimately, back across the Rio Grande. All the Mexican artillery and supplies fell to the victorious Americans.

■ *Dallas County*

## DEALEY PLAZA HISTORIC DISTRICT
**Roughly bounded by Pacific Avenue and Market and Jackson Streets, Dallas**

Because of the tragic event that took place here on November 22, 1963, Dealey Plaza is forever imprinted in America's national memory. A landscaped park dating from 1934–1940, it served as an impressive gateway to downtown Dallas from the west, and was, formerly, a focus of civic pride. At 12:29 P.M. on his way to a luncheon, President John F. Kennedy, his wife Jacqueline beside him, entered the plaza in a motorcade. A minute later shots rang out from the Texas School Book Depository, just to the north. The president, mortally wounded, died that afternoon at a Dallas hospital. An exhibition commemorating Kennedy's assassination and legacy has been established on the sixth floor of the Depository. Few places in America—Ford's Theatre comes to mind—summon the emotions as Dealey Plaza does.

## FAIR PARK TEXAS CENTENNIAL BUILDINGS
**Northeast of the intersection of Perry and Second Avenues, Dallas**

Texas celebrated its 1936–1937 centennial in a big way. "Big D" won out over Houston and San Antonio as host for the exposition by offering a 200-acre site (the State Fairgrounds, along with the Cotton Bowl) and issuing municipal bonds to fund construction. Influenced by the recently completed "Century of Progress" in Chicago, architect George Dahl, with Paul Cret as consultant, provided a collection of exemplary International Style buildings, many embellished with Art Deco motifs and bas-relief sculptures. Most remain in what is now one of the largest intact groups of exposition buildings remaining in the nation. The grounds continue to be used for the Texas State Fair and were restored for the Texas Sesquicentennial in 1986.

## ■ Fannin County

### SAMUEL T. RAYBURN HOUSE
**1.5 miles west of Bonham on U.S. Route 82**

Samuel Taliaferro Rayburn, "Mr. Sam," served in the U. S. House of Representatives almost a half-century, from 1913 until his death in 1961. For 17 years he was Speaker of the House, serving twice as long in that position as any other individual. His astute political sensitivity helped preserve the delicate balance between factions of the Democratic Party. Rayburn is particularly remembered for saving the peacetime draft bill in 1941 and for obtaining appropriations for the Manhattan Project, both contributing greatly to American victory in World War II. From 1916 until his death, this farmhouse—known as the Home Place—was his primary residence. It is now a museum honoring one of Texas's best-known, and best-loved, statesmen.

## ■ Galveston County

### EAST END HISTORIC DISTRICT
**Irregular pattern, including both sides of Broadway and Market Streets, Galveston**

Galveston, for many years the state's largest city, flourished as a port, financial center, and trading emporium, with all of Texas as its hinterland. Many of its 19th-century nabobs built impressive houses in the east end of the city, especially along Broadway. The ornate Gresham House, or Bishop's Palace (1887–1893), is one of the grandest. It and many other houses in the area were designed by Nicholas J. Clayton, the state's first professional architect.

### ELISSA
**Pier 21, The Strand, Galveston**

Built in 1877 in Aberdeen, Scotland, the bark Elissa carried various cargoes during its century-long career, beginning with a shipload of Welsh coal that it took to Brazil. It put into Galveston in 1883, bringing bananas in and taking cotton out. In 1970, about to be scrapped, Elissa was instead saved and ultimately restored to complement Galveston's historic waterfront. The official "Tall Ship of Texas," it is now considered the second-oldest operational sailing vessel in the world and one of the three oldest merchant vessels still afloat. Open and accessible to the public, Elissa allows visitors to participate as working crew members, providing a firsthand perspective on square-riggers, maritime culture, seafaring, and maritime preservation.

### STRAND HISTORIC DISTRICT
**Roughly bounded by Avenue A, 20th Street, the alley between Avenues C and D, and the railroad depot, Galveston**

Galveston's Strand was the city's primary commercial area during the second half of the 19th century. A thriving, energetic, and prosperous district, it developed alongside the shipping channel and port that helped make the city the largest metropolis in the state during those years. Galveston's prominence began to taper off in the early 20th century as the Houston Ship Canal diverted port traffic. Fortunately, the growth of its rival, Houston, meant the survival of a number of buildings that might otherwise have been demolished for larger replacements. Remaining buildings, many of them restored in recent years, display the range of architectural styles popular during the Victorian period.

## ■ Gillespie County

### HA-19
**340 East Main Street (Admiral Nimitz Museum), Fredericksburg**

Built as part of Japan's expansion of its armed forces in the 1930s, Haramaki (HA-19) is an early example of an Imperial Japanese Navy midget submarine. A participant in the attack on Pearl Harbor on December 7, 1941, HA-19 was the only Japanese vessel captured intact. After its capture, HA-19 was visited by millions of Americans during a War Bond tour of major cities across the country. For a time, HA-19 was on display in Key West, Florida, but can now be seen at the Admiral Nimitz Museum of the Pacific War.

■ *Goliad County*

## PRESIDIO NUESTRA SEÑORA DE LORETO DE LA BAHIA

**1 mile south of Goliad State Park on U.S. Route 183**

Constructed at various times in the second half of the 18th century, Our Lady of Loreto at Bahia, renamed Goliad in 1829, is one of the country's finest remaining examples of a Spanish presidio. The fort's stone walls form a one-story quadrangle, and the impressive chapel with its tower at the northwest corner rises high above to dominate the complex. Spanish soldiers garrisoned here protected nearby missions, and as the main link between Mexico and East Texas from San Antonio to the Rio Grande, this presidio was the principal military post under Spanish and Mexican rule. On Palm Sunday 1836, several hundred Americans were massacred here under orders of Santa Anna, making Goliad, like the Alamo, a symbol and rallying point for Texan independence. The presidio was restored in the 1930s and now serves as a museum. The chapel is an active parish church.

■ *Hale County*

## PLAINVIEW SITE

**Address Restricted, Plainview**

Excavations at this site demonstrated the antiquity of a type of spear point commonly found throughout the Plains region. It had long been suspected that such points were associated with ancient hunters, but this was not proven until they were found at this kill site with the remains of an extinct species of bison. This is the type site for the Plainview point, which dated from 7800–5100 B.C.

■ *Harris County*

## APOLLO MISSION CONTROL CENTER

**Lyndon B. Johnson Space Flight Center, Houston**

This control center represents the importance of the Johnson Space Center in the U.S. manned space-flight program. Nine Gemini flights, all Apollo flights, Apollo-Soyuz, and space shuttle flights have been monitored from this facility. The center exercised full mission control of *Apollo 11,* from lift-off at the Kennedy Space Center, through the first landing of men on the moon in July 1969, to splashdown in the Pacific.

## SAN JACINTO BATTLEFIELD

**San Jacinto Battleground State Park, 22 miles east of Houston**

Here, on April 21, 1836, the decisive battle of the Texas Revolution was fought and the independence of the Republic of Texas

*Presidio Nuestra Señora de Loreto de la Bahia, Goliad County, 1968. Courtesy of NPS.*

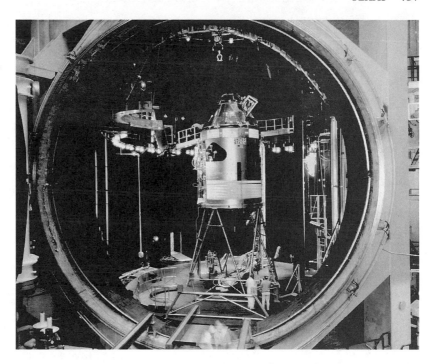

*Space Environment Simulation Laboratory, Houston, Harris County. Chamber A with Apollo spacecraft, 1968. Courtesy of NASA.*

ensured. Nine hundred men, led by General Sam Houston, commander in chief of all Texas forces, surprised 1,200 Mexicans commanded by President Antonio Lopez de Santa Anna. The Texans, raising the war cry "Remember the Alamo!" routed the enemy in a decisive victory after a battle that lasted only 18 minutes. The following day, Santa Anna, dressed as a Mexican private, was captured and held hostage against further Mexican attack. In 1936, as part of the Texas Centennial celebration, a towering granite monument was built, with a museum at its base and a Lone Star at its tip. The battlefield is a Texas state park, and numerous markers explain the battle.

## SPACE ENVIRONMENT SIMULATION LABORATORY
### Lyndon B. Johnson Space Flight Center, Houston

Constructed in 1965, this laboratory was designed, built, and used for thermal-vacuum testing for all U.S. manned spacecraft during the Apollo-era programs. The large size of the two chambers that form the laboratory meant that full-scale flight hardware could be tested here to ensure the safety of astronauts and the success of the space program. The two chambers, along with instrumentation and data systems and support facilities, are housed in Building 32 at the Lyndon B. Johnson Space Center.

## TEXAS
### San Jacinto Battleground State Park, 22 miles east of Houston

USS *Texas,* sole survivor of six American "dreadnoughts," was built between 1911 and 1912 by the Newport News (Virginia) Shipbuilding and Dry Dock Company. *Texas* participated in the American landings at Vera Cruz, then served during World War I as a member of the Atlantic Fleet, hunting down German warships. Between the two world wars, *Texas* was the first battleship to launch an aircraft from its decks. During World War II, the ship led major troop convoys across the Atlantic and bombarded enemy shore positions during the invasions of North Africa, Normandy—taking a position off Omaha Beach—and southern France. Late in 1944, *Texas* proceeded to the Pacific, where it participated in the bombardment of Iwo Jima and Okinawa. Decommissioned in 1948 after a distinguished career, *Texas* is now moored as a museum vessel at San Jacinto Battleground State Park.

## ◼ *Jack County*

### FORT RICHARDSON
**South of Jacksboro on U.S. Route 281, Jacksboro**

Established in 1867 to replace the recently abandoned Fort Belknap as the northernmost fort in the Texas chain of fortifications, Fort Richardson played an important role in the protection of American lives and property during the post–Civil War Kiowa-Comanche conflict. Troops from Fort Richardson participated in the Red River War of 1874–1875, which broke the power of the Indians, after which they were confined to reservations in Oklahoma. That accomplished, the fort was abandoned in 1878. Its former hospital now houses a museum.

## ◼ *Jeff Davis County*

### FORT DAVIS (NPS)
**Junction of Texas Routes 17 and 118, Fort Davis**

Named for then–secretary of war Jefferson Davis, this West Texas fort was established in 1854 to guard the San Antonio–El Paso road and to provide protection against predatory bands of Apache and Comanche. Located on the southern route to California, the fort became a popular way station for settlers. Fort Davis was originally built of log, but after the Civil War it was rebuilt in adobe and stone. By 1891, having outlived its usefulness, it was abandoned. It is now maintained by the National Park Service as Fort Davis National Historic Site, and its many buildings—some restored, some semiruinous—in a pristine mountain landscape, are among the most extensive and impressive of any Western frontier fort.

## ◼ *Jefferson County*

### LUCAS GUSHER, SPINDLETOP OIL FIELD
**3 miles south of Beaumont on Spindletop Avenue**

More than any other single word, the name "Spindletop" stands out in the history of oil in America. On January 10, 1901, at Spindletop, a little knoll rising out of a swampy prairie a few miles north of the Gulf of Mexico, a great gusher roared in, spewing mud and gas, before a steady six-inch stream of oil rose more than 100 feet above the derrick. Lucas Gusher, named for mining engineer Anthony F. Lucas, signaled the opening of the vast oil deposits of the coastal plains of Texas and Louisiana and the beginning of the modern era of the American petroleum industry. A tall monument, topped by a star, was dedicated on the 50th anniversary of the gusher to commemorate this pivotal moment in history.

## ◼ *Kaufman County*

### PORTER FARM
**2 miles north of Terrell on Farm Road 986**

Here, in 1903, Dr. Seaman A. Knapp, special agent of the U.S. Department of Agriculture, organized the first cooperative farm demonstration designed to help local cotton farmers deal with the boll weevil. Walter C. Porter agreed to let 70 acres of his farm be used for the demonstration. He followed Knapp's instructions on disking and fertilizing, and the results were phenomenal. From this one demonstration, the entire nationwide Agricultural Extension Service has developed. Boy's Corn Clubs, Ladies' Canning Societies, 4-H Clubs, and intensified county fair activities in large measure all stem from the extension work begun on the Porter Farm.

## ◼ *Kennedy and Kleberg Counties*

### KING RANCH
**Kingsville and its environs (Kennedy, Kleberg, Nueces, and Willacy Counties)**

This vast, almost legendary spread ranks as one of the most outstanding and best-known of all the cattle enterprises in the Southwest. Founded in 1852 by Richard King, who purchased a Spanish land grant of 75,000 acres, the ranch grew steadily to include more than one million acres. Extending over four counties in southern Texas, it became the largest ranch in the country. The famous Santa Gertrudis breed of cattle, named for the original Spanish land grant, was developed here.

## Lubbock County

### LUBBOCK LAKE SITE
**2401 Landmark Drive, Lubbock**

Discovered in the 1930s, this site in Yellow House Canyon has revealed an extremely well-defined stratified sequence of human habitation spanning 11,000 to 12,000 years. Evidence of occupation during Clovis, Folsom, Plainview, Late Paleo-Indian, Archaic, Ceramic, and historic periods has been found. Over the centuries, the site was used as a camp, a kill/butchering locale, and a processing station. Now a state park with a state-of-the-art museum, Lubbock Lake Site is open to the public.

## Nueces County

### KING RANCH
**Kingsville and its environs (Kennedy, Kleberg, Nueces, and Willacy Counties)**

(See entry under Kennedy County.)

## Oldham County

### LANDERGIN MESA
**Address Restricted, Vega**

Landergin Mesa is a major Late Prehistoric village site (A.D. 1200–1500) near the western limit of the Antelope Creek Focus region. The ruins consist of a series of buildings atop a steep-sided mesa on the east side of East Alamosa Creek. Landergin is one of the largest, best-stratified, least-damaged, and most spectacularly located ruins of Panhandle culture.

## Starr County

### ROMA HISTORIC DISTRICT
**Properties along Estrella and Hidalgo Streets between Garfield Street and Bravo Alley, Roma**

Roma is significant as a rare surviving community with an outstanding architectural fabric illustrating the history and evolution of Southwestern American vernacular traditions. Roma is also the only intact U.S. settlement that derives from the mid-18th-century town planning efforts of José de Escandon, who fostered colonization of the remote frontier

along the Rio Grande. Roma's buildings form a virtual "living catalog" of different building technologies along the lower Rio Grande in the 19th century.

## Tom Green County

### FORT CONCHO
**San Angelo**

Established in 1867 to protect the frontier, Fort Concho served "as a shield across the very heart of Texas." Until it was abandoned in 1889, it also served as a point of departure for southern travel to the Far West and helped extend the frontier westward. Soldiers from the fort waged campaigns against the Kiowa and Comanche in 1870–1875. Fort Concho was a large post, and some 39 buildings were erected during its first decade. In 1929, the City of San Antonio began purchasing the fort property and has since restored a number of the remaining stone structures. Still retaining a great deal of flavor of the period when it was an active military post, Fort Concho is open to the public.

## Travis County

### GOVERNOR'S MANSION, AUSTIN
**1010 Colorado Street, Austin**

This handsome Greek Revival mansion, standing on a knoll near the Texas State Capitol, was begun in 1854 and completed two years later. Austin architect/builder Abner Cook constructed it and embellished its facade with a giant-order Ionic portico. Its first occupant, Governor Elisha M. Pease, moved in on June 15, 1856, and every other governor of the Lone Star State has also called it home during his (or her) term of office. The Texas Governor's Mansion is among the nation's oldest houses built for the chief executive of a state.

### TEXAS STATE CAPITOL
**Congress Avenue and 11th Street, Austin**

When Texas dedicated its new state capitol in 1888, it was the largest state capitol in the country. That, along with the fact that the dome rose four feet taller than the U.S. Capitol, demonstrates how Texans wished the

*Governor's Mansion, Austin, Travis County, 1966. Courtesy of HABS (Jack E. Boucher).*

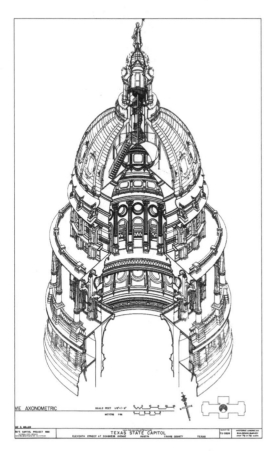

*Texas State Capitol, Austin, Travis County. Courtesy of HABS (Murray G. Miller).*

nation to perceive their state. Like its prototype, the United States Capitol in Washington, the building is dominated by a huge Renaissance-inspired dome resting on a masonry drum. Above the lantern, the figure of Liberty holds a lone star. The capitol is faced with quarry-faced Texas red granite, giving it a rough-cast appearance and a distinctive warm hue. This building represents the high water mark in the career of architect Elijah E. Myers, who also designed capitols for Michigan and Colorado. A long-term restoration was begun in the 1980s, along with an addition that is mostly underground. The building is open to the public and stands as an enduring symbol of the Lone Star State.

## ■ *Uvalde County*

### JOHN NANCE GARNER HOUSE
#### 333 North Park Street, Uvalde

From 1920 to 1952 this was the residence of John Nance Garner, who served in the U.S. House of Representatives for 30 years, from 1903 to 1933. As speaker from 1931 to 1933, he led efforts to combat the Depression in cooperation with President Hoover. He lost the Democratic presidential nomination to Franklin D. Roosevelt in 1932, but continued his public service as Roosevelt's vice president from 1933 to 1941. It was largely due to his efforts and talents (and the many friendships he had garnered during his years as a legislator) that Roosevelt's New Deal policies became law. After his wife's death in 1952, Garner moved back to the modest frame house where the couple had begun their married life. Both are included in the National Historic Landmark designation; the larger house is open to the public as the Garner Memorial Museum.

## ■ *Walker County*

### WOODLAND
**Avenue L, Sam Houston University, Huntsville**

In the minds of many Americans, Texas and Sam Houston are virtually synonymous, and for good reason. Houston led the Texas army to victory at San Jacinto, was elected first president of the Republic of Texas (1836–1838), served a second term from 1841 to 1844, and represented the new state in the U.S. Senate (1846–1859). During his years in Washington, he tried vainly to stem the inexorable tide of Southern secession. His last public post was as governor of Texas (1859–1861). He was removed from office for refusing to support the state's secession from the Union. From 1847 to 1859, Woodland, a small log house covered with clapboards, was home for Houston and his family. Now restored, it is open to the public as a museum honoring this great Texan and great American.

## ■ *Willacy County*

### KING RANCH
**Kingsville and its environs (Kennedy, Kleberg, Nueces, and Willacy Counties)**

(See entry Kennedy County.)

## ■ *Young County*

### FORT BELKNAP
**1 mile south of the junction of Texas Routes 24 and 251**

Fort Belknap was the anchor of a chain of forts stretching from the Red River to the Rio Grande. It was established in 1851 following the Mexican War, when the Texas frontier was being ravished by Comanche-Kiowa raids, and was initially of log construction. Until 1865 it was the key post in the protection of the exposed frontier. It bore the brunt of Indian assault and during the Civil War served as a base for campaigns against Comanche-Kiowa raiders. The 1852 stone arsenal is the only original building, but others were reconstructed during the Texas Centennial of 1936. Fort Belknap is now a state park.

### HARRELL SITE
**Address Restricted, South Bend**

First excavated in 1938–1939, this site at the confluence of the Brazos and Clear Fork Rivers is the type site for the Henrietta Focus, a southern Plains village agricultural complex. It is located in a region between the Puebloan and Mississippian cultures, and trade items from those groups, as well as from related Plains groups, are among the many artifacts that have been found. The village may have been occupied before A.D. 1400, and then abandoned in early historic times, ca. 1600. Its inhabitants hunted bison and other game, grew maize, and fished with bone fishhooks.

## ■ *Zapata County*

### TREVIÑO-URIBE RANCHO
**Uribe and Treviño Streets, San Ygnacio**

The Jésus Treviño-Blás Uribe Rancho is an exceptional survivor of vernacular Mexican architectural and ranching traditions on the northern, or American, side of the Rio Grande. Evolving from a simple one-room stone shelter, built ca. 1830 by Jésus Treviño, who maintained his principal residence in Mexico, the complex grew during four, possibly five, building campaigns, into a large ranch headquarters forming an enclosed quadrangle. Although the last addition dates from 1871, traditional building patterns were maintained, illustrating the persistence of Hispanic culture along the borderlands long after Texas had become part of the United States. Largely in original condition, the rancho vividly portrays the Mexican/Texan frontier experience.

# UTAH

## ■ *Carbon and Emery Counties*

### DESOLATION CANYON
**Green River (Carbon, Emery, Grand, and Uintah Counties)**

John Wesley Powell, one-armed Civil War veteran, naturalist, and explorer, led a Smithsonian expedition down the Colorado River in 1869. In the previously unexplored canyon, he met and conquered natural perils and gave enduring names to mountains, rapids, streams, and other natural features never before visited by white men. Except for the presence of an occasional abandoned ranch, Desolation Canyon is little changed from the time Powell and his group first saw it.

## ■ *Garfield County*

### BRYCE CANYON LODGE AND DELUXE CABINS (NPS)
**Bryce Canyon National Park**

Built between 1924 and 1929, this group consists of a lodge and 15 nearby cabins, all of stone, frame, and log construction. Designed by Gilbert Stanley Underwood, the complex is an excellent example of the rustic architecture encouraged by the National Park

Service to appear as if the buildings had been constructed by craftsmen with primitive hand tools. The Park Service provided the design and the site, but the Union Pacific Railroad/Utah Parks System constructed the buildings and operated them as a concession. With necessary modifications and modernizations, the buildings continue in their original functions.

## ■ *Grand County*

### DESOLATION CANYON
**Green River (Carbon, Emery, Grand, and Uintah Counties)**

(See entry under Carbon County.)

## ■ *Salt Lake County*

### BINGHAM CANYON OPEN PIT COPPER MINE
**16 miles southwest of Salt Lake City on Utah Route 48**

Initiated in 1904, this was the first open pit copper mine in the world. It grew—and deepened—over the years to become the largest. As of the 1980s, the mine was more than 2.3 miles wide and 0.5 miles deep. The

*Fort Douglas, Salt Lake City, Salt Lake County. Officers' duplexes, 1968. Courtesy of HABS (P. Kent Fairbanks).*

mine is terraced into approximate 50-foot levels, with ramps providing access to each, and with ore removed by railroad cars. A visitor observation point provides a comprehensive view of this enormous pit that still supplies a large percentage of the nation's copper.

## EMIGRATION CANYON
### East edge of Salt Lake City on Utah Route 65

"This is the place." With those words, uttered on July 24, 1847, Brigham Young signaled to his Mormon followers that their journey was over. They had left the Missouri Valley that spring to find a place where they could practice their beliefs without interference. From a small knoll in the canyon, which forms a natural passage from the Wasatch Mountains, Young obtained his first unobstructed view of the fertile Salt Lake Valley. In 1947, the Mormons erected an impressive monument, designed by a grandson of Brigham Young, to mark the spot.

## FORT DOUGLAS
### Fort Douglas Military Reservation, Salt Lake City

Fort Douglas was established in 1862 in the foothills of the Wasatch Mountains overlooking Salt Lake City. Ostensibly, the installation was an effort to protect telegraph lines and transportation routes from hostile Indians,

but it also gave the government a new advantage in its continuing struggle to compel Utah's predominantly Mormon population to cooperate with federal officials and federal laws, especially regarding polygamy. The post newspaper, *The Union Vedetee,* first non-Mormon journal in Utah, reported soldiers' discoveries of gold, silver, and lead, helped to promote mining efforts in the state, and encouraged non-Mormons to settle in Utah. A number of buildings from various eras remain, and a former barracks built in 1875 now houses a museum.

## OLD CITY HALL
### State Street, Salt Lake City

Erected between 1864 and 1866, this red-sandstone structure served in the joint capacity of city hall and Utah Territorial Capitol until 1894. In the latter capacity, it was a focal point for confrontations between federal officials and Mormon leaders. Between 1961 and 1962 the building was taken down from its original location, rebuilt, and restored on the grounds of the Utah State Capitol. It currently houses the Utah Travel Council.

## TEMPLE SQUARE
### Temple Square, Salt Lake City

This ten-acre square is the "holy of holies" for members of the Church of Jesus Christ of

*Temple Square, Salt Lake City, Salt Lake County. Mormon Tabernacle, 1971. Courtesy of HAER (Jack E. Boucher).*

Latter-Day Saints—familiarly known as Mormons. Here are the temple (1853–1893), the tabernacle (1863–1867), and the assembly hall (1877–1882). The temple is open only to members of the faith, but the ellipsis-shaped tabernacle is open to all. The shape of this marvel of 19th-century engineering was dictated by church leader Brigham Young, but the man responsible for its intricate roof system was Henry Grow. Utilizing a system of wooden lattice trusses, based on a type patented by Ithiel Town—which in this instance were fastened with wooden pegs and rawhide bindings—Grow created the largest hall in the world unsupported by columns. The tabernacle, renowned for its superb acoustics, houses a famous organ and is the home venue of the Mormon Tabernacle Choir.

## BRIGHAM YOUNG COMPLEX

**63–67 East South Temple Street, Salt Lake City**

Brigham Young, who joined the Mormon Church in 1832, became its second president after Joseph Smith was murdered in 1844. Young led the Mormons westward, founded Salt Lake City in 1847, and for the next 30 years, until his death in 1877, was the predominant political and religious figure in Utah Territory. Included in this group of buildings are the Beehive House (Young's own house), the Lion House (where several of his wives and children lived), and the office where he presided over church and state affairs. The Beehive House, named for its distinctive cupola (the beehive is the symbol of Mormon industry), is open to the public as a house museum.

## ◼ San Juan County

### ALKALI RIDGE

**Address Restricted, Monticello**

This large area, comprising some 70 square miles, contains vestiges of the earliest traditionally recognized Puebloan architecture—above-ground dwellings built around a central courtyard with associated underground kiva. The ridge is considered the type location of the Pueblo II period (A.D. 900–1100),

a transitional time between life focused within scattered pit dwellings and a true sedentary life-style with multistory structures, irrigation agriculture, and high-quality ceramics.

## ◼ Tooele County

### DANGER CAVE

**1 mile east of Wendover on U.S. Route 40**

Excavations at Danger Cave provided the first continuous record of a prehistoric occupation spanning 10,000 years in the Great Basin. The deep, stratified deposits permitted Professor Jesse D. Jennings to develop a chronological framework that, when coupled with information from other sites, documents the long-lived Desert Archaic culture. This life-style was based on cyclic wanderings of small groups, following game and seasonal patterns of vegetation. Access to the cave may be obtained only by permission of the Utah Division of Parks and Recreation.

## ◼ Uintah County

### DESOLATION CANYON

**Green River (Carbon, Emery, Grand, and Uintah Counties)**

(See entry under Carbon County.)

## ◼ Utah County

### REED O. SMOOT HOUSE

**183 East 100 South, Provo**

Reed O. Smoot served his state for 30 years (1903–1933) as a United States senator. From 1904 to 1907, Senate hearings were conducted in an attempt to unseat this high-ranking Mormon apostle in what became the last major national Mormon-gentile conflict. A member of the conservative "stand pat" wing of the Republican party, Smoot played a leading role in the drafting and passage of the Hawley-Smoot Tariff in 1930. This measure raised American import duties to an all-time high and invited retaliation by other nations, actions that most scholars believe exacerbated the Great Depression. Smoot lived in this little-altered brick mansion from 1892 until his death in 1941.

# VERMONT

■ *Addison County*

## ROBERT FROST FARM
**3 miles east of Ripton**

Distinguished 20th-century American poet and winner of four Pulitzer Prizes, Robert Frost achieved both popular readership and critical acclaim. From 1940 until his death in 1963, he spent summers and autumns at this farm in Vermont's Green Mountains. Frost occupied a small log cabin at the edge of the woods and rented the farmhouse to his secretary. Middlebury College now owns the property. (See also Robert Frost Homestead, Rockingham County, New Hampshire.)

## MOUNT INDEPENDENCE
**On Lake Champlain opposite Fort Ticonderoga, Orwell**

This site was fortified by Colonial troops in 1776–1777 in an attempt to prevent the British from penetrating to the Hudson River through the Champlain Valley. It formed the heart of a great defensive complex known as "the Gibraltar of the North." When the fortifications fell in July 1777, George III is said to have exclaimed, "I have beat them! I have beat all the Americans." Although he spoke too soon, the American defeat did lay the northern colonies open to General Burgoyne's invasion. The site is now owned by the state of Vermont and the private Fort Ticonderoga Association.

## ROKEBY
**U.S. Route 7, Ferrisburgh**

Rokeby, a Robinson family farmstead for four generations, is significant for its role in the Underground Railroad. Rare surviving documentation kept by the Robinson family attests to its use as a stop and provides accurate insights into an understandably shadowy segment of American history. In 1851 a former slave who had escaped to Canada wrote to one of the Robinsons, "[I am] at work at my trade getting a living looking through the glasses you gave me for which I never shall forget to be thankful. I think that I shall soon be able to send for my family if I conclude to stay here." Of all the known Underground Railroad sites, Rokeby is unrivalled in its historical integrity and in the poignancy of the stories its documents tell. It is open to the public as a museum.

## EMMA WILLARD HOUSE
**131 South Main Street, Middlebury College campus, Middlebury**

From 1809 until 1819 this two-story brick house was the home of Emma Hart Willard, an influential pioneer in women's education.

*Robert Frost Farm, Ripton, Addison County, 1974. Courtesy of NPS (Polly M. Rettig).*

*Round Church,
Richmond,
Chittenden County.
Courtesy of Vermont
Division for Historic
Preservation.*

Her 1818 *Address to the Public... Proposing a Plan for Improving Female Education* has been called the Magna Carta of its subject. It was based on experiences she gleaned from the Middlebury Female Seminary, which she founded in 1814, and which was housed in this building. The house, her former home and school, is now the admissions office for Middlebury College, chartered in 1800, which first admitted women in 1883.

### ■ *Caledonia County*
### SAINT JOHNSBURY ATHENAEUM
**30 Main Street, Saint Johnsbury**

Horace Fairbanks, member of the town's wealthiest family and later a governor of Vermont, built this combination library/art gallery in 1868–1873. It is one of the earliest and least-altered examples of a privately endowed small-town athenaeum and contains the original books and paintings that Fairbanks provided, many of them bought directly from the artists. Paintings are hung as they were in 1891, and the collection is considered the nation's oldest in its original condition. The unaltered building retains a strong Victorian flavor, and residents still come to it to hear lectures, poetry readings, and musical performances, to read books, and to look at the paintings.

### ■ *Chittenden County*
### ROUND CHURCH
**Bridge Street, Richmond**

The "Round" Church, built in 1812–1813 by a local blacksmith and builder, is a well-preserved 16-sided meetinghouse. Although the plan is highly unusual, the church's typical Federal style details follow examples from popular builders' pattern books. Inside, the unusual shape gives all listeners close contact with the "spoken word." Box pews on the ground floor and in the horseshoe gallery all focus on a raised pulpit. The church has been restored and is open to the public.

### *TICONDEROGA*
**Shelburne Museum, Shelburne**

*Ticonderoga*, the only unmodified side-paddle-wheel lake boat extant in the United States, symbolizes an era of travel that has all but vanished from the country's waterways. From its completion in 1906 until 1953, the coal-powered vessel plied the waters of Lake Champlain, carrying day passengers, freight, and excursion groups. Built at Shelburne Harbor, Vermont, *Ticonderoga* was purchased by the Shelburne Museum in the 1950s, lifted from the lake, and restored. Now set within a simulated drydock, it houses displays illustrating steamboat history on Lake Champlain.

## ■ Orange County

### JUSTIN S. MORRILL HOMESTEAD
**South of the Common, Strafford**

Justin Smith Morrill, member of the U.S. House of Representatives from 1855 to 1867 and U.S. senator from 1867 to 1898, sponsored the Land Grant College Acts of 1862 and 1890. The initial legislation called for federal lands in each state to be set aside to provide endowments for colleges to educate "farmers, mechanics, and all those who must win their bread by labor." His 1890 legislation provided additional cash subsidies for the colleges. Every state in the Union can claim at least one land grant institution. Morrill designed and constructed this Gothic Revival house in 1848–1851 and owned it throughout his career. The house and associated outbuildings are open to the public as a state-owned historic site, honoring one of the best friends American higher education ever had.

## ■ Washington County

### VERMONT STATEHOUSE
**State Street, Montpelier**

Set against a backdrop of wooded hills, the Vermont Statehouse is one of the most picturesque state capitols in the country. The Greek Revival building, constructed of Vermont granite, is fronted by a giant order Doric portico and topped by a dome. A 14-foot statue of Ceres, Roman goddess of agriculture, crowns the dome. Ammi B. Young, a Vermonter who became supervising architect of the U.S. Treasury Department, designed the original building, which was nearly destroyed in an 1857 fire. His portico remains, but the rebuilding followed the plans of architect Thomas Silloway. The Statehouse was restored in the 1990s, retains its original use, and is open to the public.

## ■ Windham County

### NAULAKHA
**Kipling Road, Dummerston**

Rudyard Kipling, first English-language author to win the Nobel Prize for literature (1907), built Naulakha for himself and his American bride. Kipling once said that helping to plan and build this large Shingle Style house gave him "a life-long taste for playing with timber, stone, concrete and such delightful things." Despite the brevity of his residence in Vermont (1893–1896), Kipling wrote several of his best-known works here, including *The Jungle Books* and *Captains Courageous*. The house was named (with slightly different spelling) after a book that Kipling authored jointly with his American brother-in-law. The Landmark Trust (USA) owns and operates the property.

## ■ Windsor County

### CALVIN COOLIDGE HOMESTEAD DISTRICT
**Off Vermont Route 100A, Plymouth Notch**

Few places speak as eloquently of a native son as Plymouth Notch speaks of "Silent Cal." Calvin Coolidge was born in this New England hamlet in 1872, in a house attached to his father's general store. In 1876 the family moved across the road, and it was here in 1923, while on a vacation, that Vice President Coolidge received word of President Harding's death. His father, a justice of the peace, administered the oath of office to the nation's 30th president in the sitting room. Six generations of Coolidges, including the president, are buried in the cemetery just south of the village. Most of Plymouth Notch is now owned, maintained, and open to the public as a state-owned historic site.

### GEORGE PERKINS MARSH BOYHOOD HOME (NPS)
**54 Elm Street, Woodstock**

George Perkins Marsh, lawyer, philologist, and diplomat, made a significant contribution to American conservation with his writings, especially *Man and Nature* (1864). Until he attended Dartmouth College in 1816, he lived in this house that his father had built in 1805–1807. A later owner, Frederick Billings, president of the Northern Pacific Railroad Company, transformed the house into a Queen Anne style mansion and added a number of buildings to form an exemplary country estate. The house is now part of the Marsh-Billings National Historical Park. Other portions of the property are now operated as the Billings Farm and Museum.

## ROBBINS AND LAWRENCE ARMORY AND MACHINE SHOP
### South Main Street, Windsor

The Robbins and Lawrence firm contributed enormously to America's industrial revolution in the 1840s. Machine tools perfected in the shop stimulated mass production and accelerated the country's position as a world leader in industrial processes. The 3½-story brick building is now open as a museum illustrating the history of machine tools and the products their development made possible.

## STELLAFANE OBSERVATORY
### South of North Springfield off Breezy Hill Road, Springfield

Stellafane Observatory played a pioneering role in the development of popular astronomy in the United States. The site contains the original clubhouse of the Springfield Telescope Makers, Inc. (1924), and the first large optical telescope (1930) built and owned by an amateur society. Annual conventions held here attract thousands of amateur telescope makers and astronomers from many countries.

# VIRGIN ISLANDS

■ *Saint Croix*

## COLUMBUS LANDING SITE (NPS)
### Salt River Bay National Historical Site and Ecological Preserve

On November 14, 1493, on his second voyage to the New World, Christopher Columbus sighted an island, called by the Tainos Ay Ay, which he christened Santa Cruz. A party of his men landed and attacked a group of Carib natives, killing one and capturing the others. The site thus marks the earliest place under the United States flag associated with Christopher Columbus, and the first recorded conflict between Europeans and Native Americans.

## FORT FREDERIK
### South of the junction of Mahogany Road and Route 631, Frederiksted

Fort Frederik was erected in the mid-18th century to protect Danish interests in the Caribbean and to defend the western end of Saint Croix against incursion from other European powers. It is nationally significant as an early surviving building associated with Dutch settlement, and because it was the setting of two important events that led to the dissolution of the slave-based economy of the Virgin Islands. First, the Emancipation Revolt of 1848 ended slavery in the Danish West Indies, but inaugurated a 30-year period of serfdom based on contract labor that ensured continuing control by plantation owners. Then, in 1878, escalating tensions erupted into the Labor Riot and Fireburn, which brought an end to the contract system. Restored in the 1970s, Fort Frederik is maintained as a historical site.

■ *Saint Thomas*

## FORT CHRISTIAN
### Saint Thomas Harbor, Charlotte Amalie

Although modified in the 18th and 19th centuries, initial construction dating from the late 17th century makes this fortification the oldest extant structure in the Virgin Islands. It was the nucleus of early Dutch settlement, serving as military and administrative headquarters, and housed governors and Lutheran ministers as well as providing protection for settlers. The fort now houses the Virgin Islands museum.

## SAINT THOMAS SYNAGOGUE
### Crystal Gade No. 16AB, Queens Quarters, Charlotte Amalie

Saint Thomas Synagogue, built in 1833, is the second-oldest synagogue and longest in continuous use now under the American flag. The synagogue, fourth on its site, was built to house a congregation founded in 1796 by Sephardic Jews who had come to the Caribbean Basin to finance trade between Europe and the New World. The congrega-

Skytsborg (Blackbeard's Castle), Charlotte Amalie, Saint Thomas Island. Courtesy of NPS (Cherrie Wallace).

tion reached its zenith in the mid–19th century, declined in the late 19th and early 20th centuries with the fortunes of the Danish Virgin Islands, and grew again in the late 20th century.

## SKYTSBORG

### No. 38 Dronningens Gade, King's Quarter, Charlotte Amalie

Skytsborg, or Blackbeard's Castle, is a masonry tower constructed in 1679 by the Danish colonial government as part of a network of defensive fortifications to protect Saint Thomas. It is the best remaining example of 17th-century Danish colonial military architecture now under the American flag, and is the only unmodified 17th-century fortified tower in the Caribbean. Now situated within a modern hotel complex, the tower contains a gift shop on the ground floor and guest rooms above. By the way, the notorious Captain Edward Teach, better known to history as the pirate Blackbeard, was never known to have visited Saint Thomas.

# VIRGINIA

## ■ Albemarle County

## MONTICELLO

### 2 miles south of Charlottesville on Virginia Route 53

Except for the White House and Mount Vernon, Monticello is likely the most famous and recognizable house in America. Thomas Jefferson began work on his "Little Mountain" in 1770 and spent a good portion of the rest of his life perfecting its design, enjoying his favorite pursuit of "putting up and pulling down." What emerged was a creative amalgam of motifs inspired by Roman, Palladian, and French sources, executed in Virginia red brick. Monticello and its contents were sold after Jefferson's death in 1826, and inventories taken at the time proved invaluable in refurnishing the house to reflect his occupancy. The house and its grounds and gardens, which Jefferson also planned, embody the spirit of its creator.

Beautifully preserved and interpreted, Monticello is open to the public and is listed on the United Nations Educational, Scientific, and Cultural Organization's World Heritage List.

## SHACK MOUNTAIN

### 2 miles northwest of Charlottesville, near the junction of Virginia Routes 657 and 743

Fiske Kimball, one of the greatest and most complex figures in the history of American art and architectural history and a pioneer in the restoration movement, built Shack Mountain in 1935–1936 as his retirement home. With his 1916 book *Thomas Jefferson, Architect,* Kimball established his subject's reputation as a major early American architect. Shack Mountain is a miniature distillation of the architectural forms and details that Jefferson created, and that Kimball admired. Like Jefferson's Monticello, it commands extensive views of Albemarle County from its mountain setting.

## ■ *Alexandria City*

## ALEXANDRIA HISTORIC DISTRICT

From the mid–18th century until the Civil War, Alexandria was northern Virginia's principal seaport, tobacco market, and commercial center. The district, also known as Old Town, includes significant examples of colonial and Federal urban architecture. Interspersed among rows of modest houses are more imposing mansions, and colonial churches and meetinghouses set in graveyards provide variety to the streetscape. Several buildings within the district are listed individually as National Historic Landmarks.

## CHRIST CHURCH
**Southeast corner of Cameron and Columbus Streets**

Completed in 1773 from plans by James Wren, this is a little-altered, continuously used, late-Georgian brick church. Its two-story height and rectangular form were typical of Anglican churches in northern Virginia. The eastern wall is highlighted by a large Palladian window, whereas the western tower was a later addition. George Washington often attended services here, as did Robert E. Lee.

The church houses a large, active parish and welcomes visitors throughout the week.

## GERALD R. FORD, JR., HOUSE
**514 Crown View Drive**

From 1955 to 1974 this suburban brick-and-frame house was home to Gerald R. Ford, Jr., and his growing family. These years constitute the major part of Ford's long career as a U.S. representative from Michigan, his years as vice president, and his first ten days as the 38th president of the United States. After his term was over, Ford settled in California and sold the house. Mrs. Ford remarked, "Leaving the White House wasn't nearly so much of a wrench as leaving our house in Alexandria.... We had built the place, the children had grown up there, [and] all our neighbors were friends." The house remains in private ownership.

## FRANKLIN & ARMFIELD OFFICE
**1315 Duke Street**

Between 1828 and 1836, Isaac Franklin and John Armfield created the largest-scale slave trading operation in the antebellum South. Alexandria was a convenient location because of a surplus of slaves from the nearby tobacco districts of Virginia and Maryland. Armfield bought slaves, and Franklin sold them to cotton planters at the firm's New Orleans and

*Alexandria Historic District, Alexandria. Gadsby's Tavern, 1969. Courtesy of NPS.*

Charles Richard Drew House, Arlington County. Courtesy of the Afro-American Bicentennial Corporation.

Natchez offices. The firm had agents in most southern cities and trafficked in thousands of slaves annually. After the firm disbanded, this brick town house that served as their office continued as a slave market until 1861; during the Civil War, captured Confederate soldiers were held in it. (See Isaac Franklin Plantation, Sumner County, Tennessee.)

## GADSBY'S TAVERN
### 128 North Royal Street

Comprising two adjoining brick buildings, this was one of the best-known 18th-century inns in the country. John Gadsby operated the inn from 1796 until 1808. In 1798, a year before his death, Washington reviewed troops for the last time from the tavern's doorway, after a dinner of canvasback duck and hominy, accompanied by Madeira wine. Restored during the nation's 1976 Bicentennial, Gadsby's operates once again as a tavern, and duck is still occasionally on the menu.

## ■ *Amelia County*

### SAYLER'S CREEK BATTLEFIELD
#### Vicinity of Farmville and Burkeville (Amelia and Prince Edward Counties)

After the April 2–3, 1865, evacuation of Richmond and Petersburg and the flight of the Confederate government, General Robert E. Lee attempted to move his Army of Northern Virginia to North Carolina, where he hoped to join forces with General

Joseph E. Johnston. A logistical mix-up caused a one-day delay at Amelia Court House, allowing time for Union forces to cut off his line of retreat. The three distinct battles fought on April 6 in the valley of Sayler's Creek form the last major engagement between armies commanded by Lee and Grant, which led to the Confederate surrender at Appomattox Court House three days later. Much of the battlefield is preserved as a Virginia state park.

## ■ *Arlington County*

### BENJAMIN BANNEKER SW-9 INTERMEDIATE BOUNDARY STONE
#### 18th and Van Buren Streets

This small sandstone boundary marker commemorates the accomplishments of Benjamin Banneker: farmer, mathematician, inventor, astronomer, writer, surveyor, scientist, and humanitarian. Perhaps colonial America's most famous African American, Banneker helped Major Andrew Ellicott survey the District of Columbia. This stone, carved with the date 1791, was one of 40 erected to mark each mile along the boundary of the "ten mile square" federal reservation, formed from the states of Maryland and Virginia. Now protected by a metal grille, the stone is in a small park.

### CHARLES RICHARD DREW HOUSE
#### 2505 South First Street

From 1920 to 1939, this two-story clap-

*The Homestead, Hot Springs, Bath County. Courtesy of the Homestead.*

boarded structure was the residence of Charles Richard Drew. A surgeon who taught at Howard University, Drew is best remembered for his pioneer work in discovering the means to preserve blood plasma. During World War II he directed the Plasma for Britain program, using reserves that had accumulated in America's Blood Bank to save thousands of lives. Drew had the distinction of being the first African American in the nation to earn the Doctor of Science in Medicine degree, which he received from Columbia University.

## FORT MYER HISTORIC DISTRICT
### Arlington Boulevard (U.S. Route 50), Arlington

This installation close to the nation's capital has been intimately associated with the main currents of American military history. In 1908–1909, the Wright brothers conducted their earliest experiments in military aviation on its parade ground, which led to the army's development of the airplane as a military component.

## PENTAGON
### Virginia Route 110 at Interstate 395

The Pentagon, the world's largest office structure, was completed in 1943 to house the rapid expansion of the military during World War II. It became headquarters for the Department of Defense when that department was created in 1947. More than describing a building, the term "Pentagon" has now become a synonym and generic term for America's military establishment. Throughout its history, it has been associated with people and events that have shaped America's geopolitical role as a superpower.

## QUARTERS 1, FORT MYER
### Grant Avenue, Arlington

The northernmost of six large brick residences on "Generals' Row," Quarters 1 was completed in 1899. Since the early 20th century, it has been the residence of all U.S. Army chiefs of staff. Douglas MacArthur, George C. Marshall, Dwight D. Eisenhower, Omar Bradley, and William Westmoreland are counted among its distinguished occupants.

### ■ *Bath County*

## THE HOMESTEAD
### U.S. Route 220, Hot Springs

From its beginnings in the mid-18th century, the Allegheny Mountain spa of Hot Springs was known for its healing waters. With the construction of the Homestead in 1902, Hot

Springs became known more as a resort than simply a place to seek healing. The Cincinnati architectural firm of Elzner and Anderson designed the Colonial Revival hotel, and Olmsted Brothers of Boston landscaped the grounds. The resort continues to provide luxurious accommodations, fabulous golf (Sam Snead learned to play on one of its several courses), excellent cuisine, and beautiful natural scenery for its guests.

## ■ Bedford County

### POPLAR FOREST
**Lynchburg vicinity**

If any great American deserves to be commemorated by two houses, Thomas Jefferson certainly does. Poplar Forest was his "other home," which he designed and built to serve as a villa retreat once he left the presidency. An octagonal brick house, it was begun in 1805 and represents the culmination of his mature architectural style. He once described it as "the best dwelling house in the state, except for Monticello," then went on to posit that it was perhaps preferable because it was better proportioned to the needs of a private citizen. The house remained in private ownership until the 1980s, when the Corporation for Jefferson's Poplar Forest purchased it. Poplar Forest, currently being restored to the most exacting professional standards, is open to the public.

## ■ Caroline County

### CAMDEN
**Port Royal vicinity**

Built shortly before the Civil War, this exemplary Italian villa featured such state-of-the-art innovations as a central heating system, gas lights, inside toilets, and shower baths. The flat, fertile lowlands where Camden was built had been the site of much earlier human occupation. John Smith visited as early as 1608, and a few decades later the area was set off as a preserve for Native Americans. Excavations have uncovered silver medals that colonial officials presented to "Ye King of Machotick," and "Ye King of Patomeck," chiefs of Native American tribes whose confidence they hoped to gain.

## ■ Charles City County

### BERKELEY
**8 miles west of Charles City Courthouse on Virginia Route 5**

This early 18th-century brick Georgian house was the birthplace and lifelong home of Benjamin Harrison V, member of the Continental Congress (1774–1778), signer of the Declaration of Independence, and governor of Virginia. Berkeley was also the birthplace and boyhood home of his son, William Henry Harrison, ninth president of the United States. During the Civil War the surrounding plantation served as a Union supply base, and it was here, in 1862, that General Daniel Butterfield composed the bugle call "Taps." Berkeley is open to the public as a historic house museum.

### SHIRLEY
**Virginia Route 5, Hopewell vicinity**

Completed in the 18th century on property patented in 1660, Shirley remains in the hands of descendants of its builder. The mansard-roofed main house, flanked by dependencies and formal brick farm buildings, is noted for its interior paneling and dramatic "flying" staircase, a tour de force of colonial craftsmanship. Shirley was the birthplace, in 1773, of Anne Hill Carter, who became the mother of Robert E. Lee. The house is open to the public, and with its accumulation of furnishings and portraits acquired over the centuries, presents a remarkable picture of an important Virginia plantation house and family — the Carters.

### JOHN TYLER HOUSE
**4 miles east of Charles City Court House on Virginia Route 5**

John Tyler purchased this plantation in 1842, and, because he considered himself something of a modern-day Robin Hood or political outlaw, named it Sherwood Forest. He added long wings to the existing frame house, and by the time he finished, the one-room-wide house stretched a distance of 300 feet. Tyler was elected vice president under William Henry Harrison, but became the nation's tenth president after Harrison caught pneumonia on Inauguration Day and died a month later. At the time of his own death in 1862, Tyler had just been elected to the Confederate Congress. Members of the Tyler family still own Sherwood Forest, which is open to the public.

## WESTOVER
**7 miles west of Charles City Court House on Virginia Route 5**

Architecture is seldom more refined than this. The epitome of early-Georgian design, Westover on the James River is one of Virginia's most familiar and recognizable early plantation houses. Built by William Byrd II, the brick mansion dates from the first half of the 18th century. Byrd was one of the wealthiest planters of his day, and he embellished the grounds of his home with wrought-iron gates, and the interior with marble mantels—all imported from England. Planter, land speculator, public official, and—above all—Virginia gentleman, Byrd lies buried under an imported marble tomb in the gardens at his beloved Westover. The house is privately owned, but the grounds are open to the public.

### ■ *Charlottesville City*

## ROTUNDA, UNIVERSITY OF VIRGINIA
**University Avenue at Rugby Road**

This centerpiece and symbol of the university he founded is one of Thomas Jefferson's most impressive architectural achievements. He designed the Rotunda when he was in his seventies, and it was finished in 1826, the year he died. Jefferson modeled the building on the Pantheon of ancient Rome but reduced its proportions by half. The Rotunda, originally the university's library, was largely reconstructed after a fire in 1895 but was restored to something more akin to its original appearance in the 1970s. It is open to the public.

## UNIVERSITY OF VIRGINIA HISTORIC DISTRICT
**University and Jefferson Park Avenues, Hospital and McCormick Roads**

Although Thomas Jefferson had long envisioned a state university for Virginia, it was not until he was in his seventies that he saw

*Westover, Charles City County, 1969. Courtesy of NPS.*

his dream become a reality. Jefferson designed its buildings, superintended their construction, planned the landscaping, established the curriculum, and directed the hiring of its first faculty. In fact, Mr. Jefferson—as he is known in Charlottesville—was so intimately associated with "The University"—as it is known throughout Virginia—that it has been called "the lengthened shadow of one man." The district focuses on The Lawn—his original "academical village" (1817–1827) with ten professors' pavilions, student rooms, and the Rotunda. The University of Virginia is listed on the United Nations Educational, Scientific, and Cultural Organization's World Heritage List.

## ■ Chesapeake City
### SEQUOIA
**Atlantic Yacht Basin, Great Bridge**

One of four surviving presidential yachts, *Sequoia* was used by nine chief executives between 1931 and 1977. *Sequoia* was the setting for social and recreational activities (President John F. Kennedy's last birthday party was held aboard), but also witnessed crucial domestic and foreign policy meetings and decisions, especially during Richard M. Nixon's presidency. *Sequoia* is currently in private ownership.

## ■ Clarke County
### GREENWAY COURT
**1 mile south of White Post on Virginia Route 277**

For 30 years, from 1751 to 1781, this was the estate of Thomas Fairfax, sixth Baron Fairfax of Cameron. The only English peer residing in the colonies, Fairfax inherited his five-million-acre Virginia land grant from his mother, a daughter of Lord Culpepper. Fairfax was George Washington's first employer, hiring him as a teenager to help survey his vast estate. A lifelong bachelor, he lived in a hunting lodge at Greenway Court. A later brick house replaces the lodge, but Fairfax's stone land office remains.

### SARATOGA
**Boyce vicinity**

Colonel Daniel Morgan began this gray

limestone mansion in 1779 after resigning from the Continental army, naming it after the 1777 Battle of Saratoga, in which he had demonstrated his military prowess. Morgan was recalled to duty in the summer of 1780 and promoted to the rank of brigadier general. In January 1781, with an unorthodox but brilliant disposition of troops, he achieved his best-known victory at Cowpens in South Carolina. The next month, plagued with ill health, he returned to Saratoga, and finished the house in 1782. Likely built by Hessian prisoners of war, Saratoga remains in private hands and in excellent condition.

## ■ Dinwiddie County
### FIVE FORKS BATTLEFIELD (NPS)
**12 miles west of Petersburg on County Route 627 at Church Road**

The battle that took place here on April 1, 1865, at the juncture of five country roads has been called the Waterloo of the Confederacy. Union troops under Philip Sheridan's command defeated the Confederates under General George Pickett, who had been sent to protect the Southside Railroad, Robert E. Lee's last supply line. The Union victory broke the siege of Petersburg and led to the fall of Richmond. Lee consequently had to abandon his Richmond-Petersburg defenses and began his retreat westward. Appomattox was only eight days away. Five Forks is now part of the Petersburg National Battlefield.

## ■ Fairfax County
### GUNSTON HALL
**15 miles south of Alexandria on Virginia Route 242, Lorton vicinity**

Gunston Hall was the home of George Mason, gentleman, planter, and patriot. Mason authored the 1776 Virginia Declaration of Rights—a document that influenced Thomas Jefferson when he drafted the Declaration of Independence—and much of the Virginia Constitution. Mason brought William Buckland from England to Virginia to build his mansion and released him from his indenture when it was completed in 1758. Buckland later went to Annapolis, where he became one of colonial

*Gunston Hall, Fairfax County, 1974. Courtesy of NPS (Benjamin Levy).*

*Patowmack Canal Historic District, Fairfax County. Lock No. 1. Courtesy of HAER (Jack E. Boucher).*

America's most noted architect/builders. The brick house, with its wealth of intricate interior detail and extensive formal gardens, was recently restored. Gunston Hall is maintained by the National Society of the Colonial Dames and is open to the public.

## MOUNT VERNON
### 7 miles south of Alexandria on George Washington Memorial Parkway

George Washington's home stands as an icon of American architecture, history, and preservation. Washington inherited a small frame house and by 1787 had enlarged it to its present form with its elegant piazza overlooking

the Potomac. The property remained in family hands after his death, but the house was near collapse by 1858 when Ann Pamela Cunningham organized the Mount Vernon Ladies' Association to purchase it. This was one of the first instances of an organized preservation effort in the country. Over the years the Association has restored and furnished the house with Washington pieces, relandscaped the extensive grounds, and rebuilt dependencies. Open to the public, Mount Vernon provides an authentic portrait of the personality and interests of the man who so well deserves the title "Father of His Country."

## PATOWMACK CANAL HISTORIC DISTRICT (NPS)
### Great Falls Park, Great Falls

This district consists of the remains of an impressively engineered canal built in 1785–1802 to carry boats around the Great Falls of the Potomac River, linking Georgetown (Maryland) with Harpers Ferry (Virginia). George Washington was first president of the company that undertook the enterprise, which, because the Potomac is the boundary between Maryland and Virginia, was a notable early instance of interstate cooperation. The district, with its numerous remains, is preserved and interpreted by the National Park Service.

## WOODLAWN
### Richmond Highway, Alexandria vicinity

Woodlawn was built between 1800 and 1805 for Major Lawrence Lewis and his wife, Eleanor (Nelly) Parke Custis, on land that George Washington, his uncle and her step-grandfather, willed them. The brick house, designed by Dr. William Thornton, architect of the U.S. Capitol, integrates Georgian and Federal features in its design. Woodlawn is also a pivotal monument in the evolution of the historic preservation movement in America. In 1948 a group was formed specifically to save it and soon served as a prime example of the purposes for which the National Trust for Historic Preservation was created. In 1951, the Trust accepted Woodlawn as its flagship property. The mansion is open to the public.

## ■ Fauquier County
### GENERAL WILLIAM ("BILLY") MITCHELL HOUSE
#### 0.5 miles south of Middleburg on Virginia Route 626 (Fauquier and Loudoun Counties)

From 1926 to 1936 this handsome country estate was the residence of General William "Billy" Mitchell, dominant figure in American military aviation between the two world wars. Mitchell recognized the strategic value of air power, especially in bombing missions, and foresaw the likelihood of an air attack on Pearl Harbor 17 years before it happened. His efforts to persuade America to "wake up" went unheeded. He was court-martialed in 1925 for his views and for not channeling articles he wrote through proper military chains of command. Mitchell died in 1936, shortly before his ideas were vindicated.

## ■ Fluvanna County
### BREMO HISTORIC DISTRICT
#### Bremo Bluff vicinity

These early-19th-century houses and farm buildings associated with the Cocke family are significant architecturally and socially. Upper Bremo incorporates Palladian architectural features popularized by Thomas Jefferson, whose advice General John Hartwell Cocke sought on the design. Bremo Recess and Lower Bremo are Jacobean Revival in style. A Temperance monument and an impressive stone barn with Tuscan portico and cupola are also part of the district. Cocke was president of the American Temperance Union in 1836, but is better remembered for assisting Jefferson at the University of Virginia, where he served on the Board of Visitors from 1819 until 1852.

## ■ Frederick County
### CEDAR CREEK BATTLEFIELD AND BELLE GROVE
#### On Interstate 81 between Middletown and Strasburg (Frederick and Warren Counties)

On October 19, 1864, General Philip Sheridan rallied his badly routed force of 31,000 Union soldiers to win a crucial victory over a smaller force of Confederates commanded by General Jubal Early. The battle was the climax of the struggle for the Shenandoah Valley and raged around Belle Grove, which served as Union headquarters. Isaac Hite, Jr., James Madison's brother-in-law, built the stone house in the 1790s. Belle Grove is open to the public.

## ■ Fredericksburg City
### KENMORE
#### 1201 Washington Avenue

Kenmore was built in the mid–18th century by Fielding Lewis, member of the Virginia House of Burgesses, for his bride, Betty, who was George Washington's sister. The dignified, restrained exterior of the brick Georgian style house contrasts with its interior, which contains the most elaborate colonial plasterwork in the country. In the 1920s, Kenmore was purchased by the Kenmore Association, formed specifically to protect the mansion and its grounds. In the years since then, Kenmore has emerged as one of the most impressive historic house museums in the country.

## JAMES MONROE LAW OFFICE
### 908 Charles Street

From 1786 to 1789, long before he became the nation's fifth president, James Monroe practiced law in Fredericksburg. He left in 1790 to fill a vacancy in the U. S. Senate and went on to serve continuously in state and national offices until the end of his second term as president in 1824. This small brick building, its original section a good example of a Federal period attorney's office, is adjacent to the site of Monroe's actual office. It is open as a museum illustrating his life and career.

## RISING SUN TAVERN
### 1306 Caroline Street

Charles Washington, George's youngest brother, built this tidewater cottage ca. 1760 as his home. In 1792 it was converted into a tavern known as the Golden Eagle. It is now restored and serves to interpret 18th-century tavern life, specifically as a museum commemorating Fredericksburg's Rising Sun Tavern, believed to have been located elsewhere in the city. Once one of the town's leading hostelries, the Rising Sun was a favorite stopover and meeting place for southern leaders on their way to the Continental Congress in Philadelphia.

### ■ Gloucester County
## ROBERT R. MOTON HOUSE
### Off Rural Route 662, Capahosic

In 1935, Robert Russa Moton retired to Holly Knoll, a large 2½-story Georgian Revival house on the York River, and spent the remaining five years of his life there. A nationally prominent black educator, Moton was chosen to succeed Booker T. Washington as principal of Tuskeegee Institute in 1915. During the next 20 years he transformed the institute from a vocational and agricultural school to a fully accredited collegiate and professional institution. "Major Moton," as he was called, was also a founder of the National Urban League. He received the Harmon Award in Race Relations in 1930 and the Spingarn Medal in 1932. Holly Knoll is now operated as an executive conference center.

### ■ Goochland County
## TUCKAHOE
### River Road, southeast of Manakin

Tuckahoe, one of the first Virginia plantations established above the fall line—where the Tidewater changes into the Piedmont—is an outstanding example of early Georgian architecture. Home of the Randolph family, the H-shaped frame house was the result of several building operations and was likely completed after 1734. A remarkable "street" of plantation buildings also survives from the 18th century. From 1745 to 1752, the young Thomas Jefferson lived here while his father was serving as guardian for Thomas Mann Randolph, son of a deceased kinsman. Tuckahoe, beautifully preserved and interpreted by members of the family that acquired it in the 1930s, is open to the public.

### ■ Grayson County
## RIPSHIN FARM
### Troutdale vicinity

Sherwood Anderson reintroduced subjectivity into American literature through his self-revealing novels. By so doing, he set a powerful example for those who followed him: William Faulkner, Katherine Ann Porter, and Eudora Welty, to name a few. He decided to move to southwestern Virginia in the 1920s, soon after the 1919 publication of his masterpiece, *Winesburg, Ohio*. His memoir, titled *I Build a House,* records the construction of Ripshin, the rustic stone-and-log dwelling he completed in 1927. Anderson lived here until his death in 1941.

*30- by 60-Foot Full Scale Tunnel, Hampton City. Test section with Vought 03U-1 airplane, 1931. Courtesy of NASA-Langley Research Center Archives.*

## ■ *Halifax County*

### BERRY HILL
#### South Boston vicinity

Far more reminiscent of plantation houses in the Deep South than in Virginia, Berry Hill dates from 1842–1844 and is fronted by a giant-order, octastyle Doric portico modeled on the Parthenon. Two smaller buildings, also fronted with Doric porticos, flank the main house. Architect John E. Johnson designed the group for James Coles Bruce, a wealthy tobacconist. Berry Hill, recently restored and adapted as a corporate conference center, is one of Virginia's last great plantation houses and one of its purest examples of Greek Revival architecture.

## ■ *Hampton City*

### 30 BY 60 FOOT FULL SCALE TUNNEL
#### Langley Research Center

Constructed in 1929–1931, this is the first full-scale wind tunnel the National Advisory Committee for Aeronautics built. It was designed to test large-scale and full-scale aircraft at actual flight speeds, and during its 64 years of operation contributed to the design of an entire new generation of aircraft. Almost all World War II fighters were tested in what was then the world's largest wind tunnel. The National Aeronautics and Space Administration terminated its operations in 1995 and turned the facility over to Old Dominion University for use as an engineering research laboratory.

### EIGHT-FOOT HIGH SPEED TUNNEL
#### Langley Research Center

Finished in 1936, this is a significant example of the research facilities created by the National Advisory Committee for Aeronautics, parent agency of the National Aeronautics and Space Administration. It was the first continuous-flow high-speed wind tunnel able to test large models and actual working parts of airplanes. It is also important in wind tunnel design for the "slotted throat" that was added in 1950. This feature makes it possible to obtain accurate test results in the transonic range. The tunnel was phased out of operation in 1956.

### FORT MONROE
#### Old Point Comfort

Fort Monroe, the country's largest coastal fort, was constructed between 1819 and 1834 to protect Hampton Roads, entrance to the Chesapeake Bay. Pentagonal in shape, it covers 63 acres and is guarded by a moat. During the Civil War, it was the closest continuously occupied Union installation to Richmond, the Confederate capital, and served as a con-

stant threat to the South. On March 9, 1862, spectators stood on its ramparts to watch the USS *Monitor* and the CSS *Virginia* exchange fire in the first battle in history between iron-clad vessels. Several casements now house museums telling various aspects of the fort's history; one commemorates the imprisonment of ex–Confederate president Jefferson Davis from 1865 to 1867.

## HAMPTON INSTITUTE
### Off U.S. Route 60, on the east side of Hampton Creek

Founded by the American Missionary Association to train selected young black men and women to "teach and lead their people," Hampton Normal and Industrial Institute opened in April 1868 with two teachers and 15 students. The Institute served as a model for numerous black industrial schools subsequently established to aid freedmen; Booker T. Washington, founder of Tuskeegee Institute, was one of its early graduates. The campus includes several notable buildings, among them Virginia Hall, designed by Richard Morris Hunt and built by students in 1873. Hampton is now a fully accredited university with an international faculty and student body.

## LUNAR LANDING RESEARCH FACILITY
### Langley Research Center

Constructed in 1965, this facility helped pre-pare U.S. astronauts for their journey to, and landing on, the moon. It employed a mock Lunar Excursion Module attached to a fixed facility. The experience gained here proved that astronauts could master the skills needed to land the Apollo lunar excursion module, or LEM, on the moon. Both Neil Armstrong and Edwin Aldrin spent many hours training at this facility.

## RENDEZVOUS DOCKING SIMULATOR
### Langley Research Center

Constructed in 1963, this full-scale facility was designed to train pilots in the controlled docking techniques of various types of space vehicles. It simulated docking procedures for Gemini and Apollo astronauts and was indispensable in accomplishing the goal of landing men on the moon in 1969. Only after the Apollo astronauts had successfully mastered rendezvous and docking skills here did the National Aeronautics and Space Administration give permission to proceed to the final stage, the actual moon landing.

## VARIABLE DENSITY TUNNEL
### Langley Research Center

Constructed between 1921 and 1923, this was the first wind tunnel in the world to use the principle of variable density air pressure to test scale model aircraft. It was also the first research facility to establish the technical competence of the National Advisory

Committee for Aeronautics, parent agency of the National Aeronautics and Space Administration. The tunnel was a technological quantum leap and helped to restore America's preeminence in aircraft design after it had fallen behind European countries prior to World War I.

## ■ *Hanover County*

### HANOVER COUNTY COURTHOUSE
**On U.S. Route 301, Hanover**

Hanover County still uses the courthouse its colonial justices ordered to be built in 1735. The small T-shaped Georgian brick structure, fronted by an arcade and covered by a hipped roof, is a perfectly preserved example of a type widely used in colonial Virginia. In 1763 a relatively unknown local lawyer first gained notice here when he argued and won "the Parson's Cause." The case dealt with the colony's practice of paying ministers in tobacco, then a legal medium of exchange. Patrick Henry turned what has been described as a bad legal case into a popular appeal for religious liberty and independence from royal control. The rest, as they say, is history.

### MARLBOURNE
**11 miles northeast of Richmond on U.S. Route 360**

Marlbourne, Edmund Ruffin's home, is now his final resting place. Ruffin used his plantation as an experimental laboratory in his efforts to correct the soil-depleting agricultural practices of the antebellum South. Marl pits provided fertilizer and gave the property its name. In addition to his agricultural interests, Ruffin was an ardent secessionist. He fired the first shot against Fort Sumter in 1861, thus inaugurating the Civil War. After the Confederacy's collapse, he took his own life at Marlbourne.

### SCOTCHTOWN
**10 miles northwest of Ashland on Virginia Route 685**

From 1771 to 1777 this large 1½-story frame house was the residence of Patrick Henry. While living here, Henry made his most famous speeches and served in the Continental Congress. It was also while resident at Scotchtown that Henry was elected the first nonroyal governor of Virginia (1776). Before his tenure the house had been the childhood home of Dolley Payne, later to become the wife of James Madison. Scotchtown was restored in 1958–1962 and is now a museum.

## ■ *Henrico County*

### VIRGINIA RANDOLPH COTTAGE
**2200 Mountain Road, Glen Allen**

This small brick cottage honors Virginia E. Randolph, a notable black teacher. Because of her exemplary work at Henrico County's Mountain Road School, she was asked in

*Lunar Landing Research Facility, Hampton City. LEM testing, 1965. Courtesy of NASA-Langley Research Center Archives.*

1908 to become the country's first Jeanes Supervising Industrial Worker, or instructor. The Jeanes program, officially titled the Negro Rural School Fund, was established to improve vocational training in schools. Randolph's success made her a role model for thousands of others in a program that was instituted throughout America and abroad. The cottage, built in 1937 with federal funds as the home economics building of the training school named for her, is now a museum.

### ■ Isle of Wight County

## SAINT LUKE'S CHURCH

**4 miles south of Smithfield on Virginia Route 10, Benn's Church**

This brick building is one of the nation's premier architectural links with its medieval British heritage. Likely dating from the last quarter of the 17th century, the church has a prominent tower, lancet-arched windows, wall buttresses, and a traceried east window—all hallmarks of English Gothic architecture. The church, no longer serving an active parish, was restored in the 1950s and is open as a historic and religious shrine.

### ■ James City County

## CARTER'S GROVE

**Southeast of intersection of U.S. Route 60 and Virginia Route 667, Williamsburg vicinity**

Built in 1750–1755 for Carter Burwell, this brick manor is one of colonial America's most impressive examples of Georgian archi-

tecture. The interiors are especially rich, and the segmental arch framing the walnut stair is one of many handsome features. In 1928–1931 the roof was heightened to accommodate a dormered third floor, and the formerly freestanding dependencies were enlarged and connected to the central block. The house is owned by the Colonial Williamsburg Foundation and is open to the public. The mansion and a reconstructed slave quarter on the grounds illustrate both sides of 18th-century plantation life.

### ■ King William County

## ELSING GREEN

**Tunstall vicinity**

Overlooking the Pamunkey River, this large two-story, U-shaped Georgian manor was likely built by Carter Braxton between 1760 and 1767. It is the only surviving structure associated with Braxton, one of Virginia's signers of the Declaration of Independence. Braxton served earlier in the House of Burgesses and later in the Virginia General Assembly. Elsing Green is privately owned.

### ■ Lancaster County

## CHRIST CHURCH, KILMARNOCK

**3 miles south of Kilmarnock on Virginia Route 3, Irvington**

Christ Church stands near the top of any list of America's most significant—and best-preserved—Georgian structures. Built in the 1730s by Robert "King" Carter, wealthiest

*Carter's Grove, James City County, 1969. Courtesy of NPS (Charles W. Snell).*

Virginian of his time and progenitor of a distinguished family, the cruciform church with its prominent hipped roof is noted for its superbly executed Flemish-bond brickwork and its unaltered interior. At the rear of the church, the builder lies under an elegant marble tomb between those memorializing his two wives. Christ Church is beautifully maintained and is open to the public.

### ■ Lexington City

## BARRACKS, VIRGINIA MILITARY INSTITUTE
**Virginia Military Institute**

Virginia Military Institute (VMI) opened its doors in 1839 as the first state-supported military institution in the country. French-born engineer Claudius Crozet, its first president, modeled the fledgling institution on the U.S. Military Academy, where he had taught. Consequently known as the "West Point of the South," VMI contributed a number of leaders to the Confederate army. Most of the campus, including the barracks—the largest individual structure—was designed by Alexander Jackson Davis in an appropriately military version of the Gothic Revival, with fortified towers and crenellations. Federal troops burned the Institute in June 1864, but it was rebuilt. The barracks still serves its original use. (See Virginia Military Institute Historic District.)

## LEE CHAPEL, WASHINGTON AND LEE UNIVERSITY
**Washington and Lee University**

This simple Romanesque Revival chapel commemorates the years (1865–1870) when Robert E. Lee, former Confederate commander, served as president of Washington College, now Washington and Lee University. Lee suggested the college build a chapel and helped supervise its construction in 1867. Colonel Thomas Hoomes Williamson, engineering professor at nearby Virginia Military Institute, was the architect. Lee was buried in the chapel crypt in 1870, and in 1883 a rear extension was built to house his recumbent statue, sculpted by Edward V. Valentine. The building—a shrine to "Marse Robert," Southern gentleman and

hero incarnate—still serves as the university chapel. (See Washington and Lee University Historic District.)

## VIRGINIA MILITARY INSTITUTE HISTORIC DISTRICT

The first state-supported military college, Virginia Military Institute (VMI) was formally organized in 1839. It provided leaders for the Confederate army and has supplied men for all subsequent wars in which the United States has participated. During World War II, 4,100 graduates, including 62 officers of general or flag rank, made VMI proud. For years the institute admitted only men, and the camaraderie established by its rigid discipline during the first, or "rat," year was expressed by alumni who, throughout life, called other members of their graduating class "Brother Rat." The district encompasses most of the Gothic-inspired buildings that constitute the campus. (See Barracks, Virginia Military Institute.)

## WASHINGTON AND LEE UNIVERSITY HISTORIC DISTRICT

The historic core of the Washington and Lee campus is composed of a group of architecturally harmonious and spatially related Neoclassical buildings. Because they are connected by a continuous covering, the group is known collectively as "the Colonnade." Although the buildings were erected over a 150-year span, beginning in 1824, the Colonnade forms one of the most dignified and unified academic complexes in the nation. Lee Chapel, itself a National Historic Landmark, faces the Colonnade across a sloping lawn.

### ■ Loudoun County

## BALL'S BLUFF BATTLEFIELD AND NATIONAL CEMETERY
**Leesburg vicinity**

In October 1861, Major General George B. McClellan ordered Union troops stationed along the Potomac above Washington to make "a slight demonstration" and draw out the Confederate force based in Leesburg. His plan backfired, and the demonstration became a debacle. The disaster was one in a string of Union defeats and led to the creation of the Joint Committee on the Conduct of the War. This was the first major exercise of Congressional authority to oversee and investigate operations of the federal executive branch. Commemorative monuments and the Ball's Bluff National Cemetery mark the battle site.

## GENERAL GEORGE C. MARSHALL HOUSE
**217 Edwards Ferry Road, Leesburg**

George Catlett Marshall, Jr., one of the most important military figures of his time, lived here from 1941 until his death in 1959. Winston Churchill recalled that Marshall was the only individual in World War II upon whom all leaders of the Western powers conferred unqualified praise and admiration. He is particularly remembered for his role in developing the postwar European Recovery Program, better known as the Marshall Plan. After World War II, Marshall served as U.S. secretary of state and secretary of defense. Dodona Manor, named after a Greek oracle, is now operated by the George C. Marshall International Center, and the house is being restored.

## GENERAL WILLIAM "BILLY" MITCHELL HOUSE
**0.5 miles south of Middleburg on Virginia Route 626 (Fauquier and Loudoun Counties)**

(See entry under Fauquier County.)

## OAK HILL
**8 miles south of Leesburg on U.S. Route 15**

James Monroe inherited this property from his uncle in 1808 and began construction of the present mansion in the 1820s. His two-term administration as fifth president of the United States (1817–1825) was marked by calm and prosperity and has been called "the era of good feeling." His serene Classical Revival house, with its handsome Roman Doric portico overlooking formal gardens, seems the perfect architectural expression of those times. Monroe made Oak Hill his home until 1830, when he left to join his daughter in New York. The house, enlarged since then, is still the centerpiece of a prosperous country estate.

## OATLANDS
**Leesburg vicinity**

George Carter designed this notable Federal style mansion and began its construction in 1804. In 1827 he added the two-story Corinthian portico that now fronts the stuccoed-brick house. Oatlands, with its elegant gardens and numerous dependencies, formed one of the nation's most elaborate country seats of the early Republic. In 1965 members of the Corcoran family presented the estate to the National Trust for Historic Preservation. House and grounds are open to the public.

## WATERFORD HISTORIC DISTRICT
**Waterford**

Waterford was established by Quakers from Pennsylvania about 1730. By the 1830s it was described as a flourishing village of 400 people, with 70 houses, a tannery, and a boot and shoe manufacturer. Except for the industries, no longer active, the description still seems to apply. Set in a rolling, verdant landscape, this Virginia "Brigadoon" comes as a fresh surprise every time one visits. Log, stone, frame, and brick houses, informally arranged on several streets, are remarkably preserved, as are their surroundings. Since 1943, the Waterford Foundation has spearheaded efforts to preserve the village and its almost pristine setting.

## ◼ Louisa County

## GREEN SPRINGS HISTORIC DISTRICT (NPS)
**Northeast of Zion Crossroads on U.S. Route 15**

This large rural district is characterized by fields, pastures, and woodlands—and by a number of architecturally significant structures that the rich lands enabled their owners to build. The 1849 Westend, with its Roman temple front, displays the continuity of Thomas Jefferson's architectural influence in Piedmont Virginia, and the 1851 Hawkwood, now ruinous after a fire in 1982, was one of Alexander Jackson Davis's best Italian villas. Green Springs was settled early in the 18th century, grew over the years, and continues to flourish as an important center of agricultural production.

Savannah, *Newport News. Courtesy of NPS (James P. Delgado).*

## ■ *Lynchburg City*

### CARTER GLASS HOUSE
**605 Clay Street**

From 1907 to 1923 this was the residence of Carter Glass, one of the most influential shapers of U.S. financial policy in the first half of the 20th century. Glass served in the U.S. House of Representatives (1902–1918), as secretary of the treasury (1918–1920), and as U.S. senator (1920–1946). He authored the Glass-Owen Act (1913), which established the Federal Reserve system. Glass enlarged his Lynchburg town house, a handsome brick structure dating from 1827, soon after his purchase. It now serves as the parish house for the adjacent Saint Paul's Episcopal Church and has been restored following a fire in 1986.

## ■ *Madison County*

### CAMP HOOVER (NPS)
**Shenandoah National Park, Graves Mill vicinity**

This wooded retreat was developed from 1929 to 1932 as a "summer White House" for President Herbert Hoover. Three of 13 original buildings remain, along with trails, stone bridges, trout pools, and a massive outdoor stone fireplace. Both Hoover and his wife were geologists and put great value on the beneficial effects of natural surroundings. Hoover wrote in 1930, "The joyous rush of the brook...forest and mountain all reduce our egotism, smooth our troubles and shame our wickedness." The camp, built on land the Hoovers owned, is now within the boundaries of Shenandoah National Park and is undergoing restoration. As Hoover requested, it is still available to the president of the United States as a summer weekend retreat.

## ■ *Newport News City*

### *SAVANNAH*
**James River Reserve Fleet, Fort Eustis**

Designed and constructed in the late 1950s as the first nuclear-powered merchant ship, this combination cargo/passenger vessel was developed as part of President Eisenhower's Atoms for Peace initiative. Although the market for such vessels never materialized, the ship's design and operation represented major technological breakthroughs. *Savannah* was also a success in a unique public relations role, serving as a floating exhibit to demonstrate possible peacetime uses of nuclear energy. In this role *Savannah* sailed one-half million miles and was boarded by 1.5 million people. This exposure is credited with helping to ease the world's anxieties over nuclear energy.

## ■ *Orange County*

### MONTPELIER

**4 miles west of Orange on Virginia Route 20**

For 76 years this was the residence of James Madison, "father of the Constitution," secretary of state, fourth president of the United States, and husband of the indomitable Dolley. Madison habitually spent summers at home rather than in hot, humid Washington, and in one letter written to President Jefferson at Monticello, he gave his return address as "U.S. Dept. of State, Orange County, Va." From 1809 to 1812, with Jefferson's advice, Madison enlarged the house that his father had built in 1755. A later owner, William du Pont, more than doubled its size ca. 1900. In 1984, Montpelier and its extensive acreage became the property of the National Trust for Historic Preservation. James and Dolley Madison are buried on their much-loved estate, and their much-altered house is open to the public.

## ■ *Patrick County*

### REYNOLDS HOMESTEAD

**Virginia Route 798, Critz vicinity**

Richard Joshua Reynolds introduced "the first modern cigarette." His company, named after him, and now identified simply by his initials, RJR, first marketed Camels in 1913. Before that time, smokers had to "roll their own." Reynolds's innovation gave the company 50 percent of the cigarette market by the 1920s. From his birth in 1850 to 1874, Reynolds lived in this red-brick farmhouse, learning the myriad tasks associated with tobacco culture and manufacture. The house has been restored and is open to the public, and the surrounding farmland is now the Reynolds Homestead Research Center for the study of forestry and wildlife management.

## ■ *Petersburg City*

### EXCHANGE

**15–19 West Bank Street, Petersburg**

This two-story Greek Revival structure with a Doric portico is a rare survivor of an unusual building type. It was built in 1841 by a group of citizens to display and auction tobacco and cotton, two commodities that helped antebellum Petersburg flourish as a regional commercial center. During the first half of the 20th century the Exchange was Petersburg's police department, but in the 1970s it was converted into a museum commemorating the city's traumatic Civil War years.

## ■ *Pittsylvania County*

### PITTSYLVANIA COUNTY COURTHOUSE

**U.S. Business Route 29, Chatham**

This small antebellum brick courthouse became an important site in constitutional history in 1878. After county judge J. D. Coles denied black citizens of Pittsylvania County the right to serve as grand or petit jurors, he was arrested on charges of violating the Civil Rights Act of 1875. Coles countered by filing a petition with the U.S. Supreme Court. The court's ruling in *ex Parte Virginia* represented one of the few victories for African Americans in the post–Civil War era. Although its immediate impact was limited, the decision pointed toward the promise of the future.

## ■ *Portsmouth City*

### DRYDOCK NO. 1

**Norfolk Naval Shipyard**

The Norfolk Naval Shipyard, established prior to the Revolution, is the oldest in the country. Drydock No. 1, constructed between 1827 and 1834, is built of large blocks of granite shipped in from Massachusetts. During the Civil War the shipyard was in Confederate hands, and here the Union frigate USS *Merrimack* was reconfigured to become the ironclad CSS *Virginia*. The drydock is still in use, virtually unchanged from its original design.

### LIGHTSHIP NO. 101 *PORTSMOUTH*

**London Slip, Elizabeth River**

Now known as *Portsmouth*, Lightship No. 101 is one of a small number of American lightships that have been preserved. Lightships were essential partners with lighthouses as aids to navigation and were first used in the 1820s. No. 101 was built in 1916 as one of two vessels from the same plan, and during the course of a long career it served at least five stations, helping to guide vessels into the Chesapeake Bay and Delaware Bay, and within Nantucket Bay. *Portsmouth* was retired in the 1960s and is now owned and operated as a museum exhibit by the City of Portsmouth.

## ■ *Prince Edward County*

### ROBERT RUSSA MOTON HIGH SCHOOL
**Intersection of South Main Street and Griffin Boulevard, Farmville**

This one-story, U-shaped brick building was built in 1939 as Prince Edward County's high school for black students. It later became a focus of the battle to integrate the nation's public schools. A student strike in 1951 led to a state district court case that, on appeal, was combined with four other appellate school segregation cases. These were argued before the U.S. Supreme Court in 1954 under the rubric *Brown v. Board of Education of Topeka*. The court's decision struck down the "separate but equal" principle. Instead of integrating, Prince Edward County embarked on a policy of "massive resistance," closing all its public schools from 1959 until 1964. Remarkably unchanged from the 1950s, the school is now a study center for civil rights in education and a museum recording a half-century of progress toward those rights in Southside Virginia.

### SAYLER'S CREEK BATTLEFIELD
**Vicinity of Farmville and Burkeville (Amelia and Prince Edward Counties)**

(See entry under Amelia County.)

## ■ *Prince George County*

### BRANDON
**Bank of the James River at the end of Virginia Route 611, Burrowsville vicinity**

Brandon, completed ca. 1765–1770 for Nathaniel Harrison, is a superb Palladian villa with a complex plan and form that may have incorporated fabrics of earlier structures. The estate is also noted for its gardens, an early and extensive example of colonial landscaping. The land on which the house stands was patented in 1616 and is still worked as an extensive farm, likely representing the longest continuous agricultural enterprise in the country. The gardens and grounds are open to the public.

## ■ *Richmond City*

### CONFEDERATE CAPITOL
**Capitol Square**

The Virginia State Capitol, designed by Thomas Jefferson with help from noted French architect Louis Clérisseau, was modeled on the Maison Carrée, a well-preserved Roman temple in Nimes, France. Begun in 1785, the capitol introduced the Classical Revival to America. From July 1861 to April 1865, the Confederate congress met here, but the building also continued to house Virginia's state legislature and governor during the Civil War. In the first decade of the 20th century, matching wings were added to either side, providing larger quarters for the two houses of the Virginia General Assembly, the oldest legislative body in the Americas.

### EGYPTIAN BUILDING
**East Marshall and College Streets**

Completed in 1846, this is the oldest building of the Medical College of Virginia, and one of the oldest medical college buildings in the South. It was designed by Philadelphia architect Thomas Stewart, who selected the exotic Egyptian Revival as his style of choice. With its bold cavetto cornice and lotus-leaf columns, it is considered one of the finest expressions of this style in the country. A small front yard is protected by a cast-iron fence whose posts are stylized mummies, with rather unexpected bare feet protruding from the bases.

### ELLEN GLASGOW HOUSE
**1 West Main Street**

From 1888 until her death in 1945, Ellen Glasgow lived in this sedate Greek Revival town house. Glasgow's novels reveal much about Virginia society from the 1850s through the 1940s. Her primary concern was not the manners of her home state, but human nature and the survival of essential values in the face of adversity, pretension, and change. Her 1941 book *In This Our Life* won the Pulitzer Prize for literature.

*Main Street Station and Trainshed, Richmond, 1971. Courtesy of HAER (Jack E. Boucher).*

## JACKSON WARD HISTORIC DISTRICT
**Roughly bounded by Fifth, Marshall, and Gilmer Streets and the Richmond-Petersburg Turnpike**

By the turn of the 20th century, Richmond was one of the foremost black business communities in the country, and Jackson Ward was its hub. Here were banks, clubs, insurance companies, and commercial and social institutions. Notable residents included Maggie L. Walker, who established the Saint Luke Penny Savings Bank, and actor and dancer Bill "Bojangles" Robinson. Jackson Ward suffered a decline in the mid-20th century, but many of the Greek Revival and Italianate houses that line the neighborhood's streets are now being revitalized.

## MAIN STREET STATION AND TRAINSHED
**1520 East Main Street**

Constructed in 1900–1901, Main Street Station shows the Beaux-Arts influence in American architecture, whereas the shed, one of the last gable-roofed train sheds in the nation, is significant in the history of American engineering. Both have Pennsylvania antecedents: The station was designed by the Philadelphia architectural firm of Wilson, Harris, and Richards, and the shed was fabricated by that state's Pencoyd Iron Works. The complex now serves as state offices and storage facilities.

## JOHN MARSHALL HOUSE
**Ninth and East Marshall Streets**

John Marshall lived in this late-Georgian style brick town house for 45 years, from 1790 until his death in 1835. After a brief stint as secretary of state (1800–1801) under John Adams, Marshall became the fourth chief justice of the U.S. Supreme Court. "The great Chief Justice" participated in more than a thousand decisions during his 30 years on the bench, writing more than half of them himself. More than any other individual, Marshall established the Supreme Court as an equal partner with the executive and legislative branches of the federal government. The home of this great American jurist is furnished with many family pieces and is open to the public.

## JAMES MONROE TOMB
**Hollywood Cemetery, 412 South Cherry Street**

President James Monroe is entombed beneath a flamboyant monument that is a masterpiece of Gothic Revival design and cast-iron artistry. Richmond architect Albert Lybrock designed it, and Wood and Perot of Philadelphia cast it. Monroe died in New York in 1831, and his remains were buried there until the 1850s, when the governor of New York asked the governor of Virginia if he wished Monroe to be reinterred in his native state. Both governors spoke at the 1858 service honoring Monroe's return home on the centennial of his birth.

## MONUMENTAL CHURCH
### 1224 East Broad Street

Constructed between 1812 and 1814, this church was built as a memorial to the 72 people, including the governor of Virginia, who burned to death while attending a performance in a theater on the site. In designing the building, architect Robert Mills produced one of the nation's earliest and most distinctive Greek Revival churches. A shallow dome covers an octagonal sanctuary, and a portico holds a memorial urn. The ashes of those who perished remain in a crypt below the church. Monumental Church served an Episcopal parish until 1965, then became a chapel for the adjacent Medical College of Virginia. The Historic Richmond Foundation now holds title and opens the church for special tours.

## MONUMENT AVENUE HISTORIC DISTRICT
### From the 1200 block of West Franklin Street to the 3300 block of Monument Avenue

Monument Avenue was proposed in 1887 both to provide an appropriate setting for a major memorial to Robert E. Lee and to encourage residential development west of downtown Richmond. The broad tree-lined

*James Monroe Tomb, Richmond, 1969. Courtesy of HABS (Edward F. Heite).*

avenue with its double roadway inspired prominent Richmonders to erect the mansions now flanking it. The houses were, in turn, matched by a series of monumental public sculptures that commemorate other heroes of the Confederacy. In the late 20th century a statue honoring native Richmonder Arthur Ashe, noted black tennis player, was added to the group and stands as a testament to the city's having outgrown its past. Monument Avenue is the country's only grand-scaled boulevard with such a series of impressive memorials.

## OLD CITY HALL
### Bounded by 10th, Broad, 11th, and Capitol Streets

Completed in 1894 from designs by Elijah E. Myers, Richmond's monumental city hall is a prime example of the High Victorian Gothic style. It was Richmond's first major post–Civil War structure and is noted for its multiplicity of ornamental gables, dormers, and finials, presided over by a tall corner tower. The building is solidly built of granite, and when it was dedicated, the *Richmond Dispatch* noted, "There is no question that it was built to stay." It ceased to function in its original use when a new city hall was built in the 1970s and now serves as quality office space.

## SAINT JOHN'S EPISCOPAL CHURCH
### East Broad Street between 24th and 25th Streets

"Give me liberty or give me death!" Patrick Henry delivered his "Liberty or Death" speech on March 23, 1775, and whether or not he actually ended his address with those ringing words, his firm declamation galvanized members of the Virginia General Assembly. They had convened in the largest meeting space in the village of Richmond to decide what direction Virginia should take in its growing disputes with Britain. Their tone was conciliatory at first, but Henry persuaded the members to pass the resolutions he introduced for the colony's defense. Saint John's has been altered since Henry pointed the way here, but the building still maintains an aura of long-ago times. The church houses an active parish and is open to the public.

## TREDEGAR IRON WORKS
### 500 Tredegar Street

Established in 1837 and named for a foundry in Wales, the Tredegar Iron Works was one of the largest iron works in the United States from 1841 to 1865. During the Civil War, Tredegar was the Confederacy's largest ordnance foundry, supplying the South with a major share of the iron products that helped it sustain four years of war. After the company left its original site on the banks of the James River, the ruinous complex was stabilized by the Ethyl Corporation.

## VIRGINIA GOVERNOR'S MANSION
### Capitol Square

Located on Capitol Square, this is the nation's oldest "purpose built" governor's mansion that continues in its original use. A finely proportioned Federal style house, designed by New England architect Alexander Parris, it was completed in 1813. A polygonal bay that contains the dining room on its main floor was added in the first decade of the 20th century. The mansion, currently being restored, for the most part, remains as it was first envisioned—a handsome, unpretentious residence for Virginia's chief executives.

## MAGGIE LENA WALKER HOUSE (NPS)
### 110 East Leigh Street

Maggie Lena Walker, daughter of an ex-slave mother and a Northern abolitionist father, was founder and later president of the successful Saint Luke Penny Savings Bank. A Richmond community leader, Walker moved to the Jackson Ward neighborhood in 1904. Her brick row house is now open to the public as the Maggie L. Walker National Historic Site. (See Jackson Ward Historic District.)

## WHITE HOUSE OF THE CONFEDERACY
### East Clay and 12th Streets

From 1861 to 1865, this white-stuccoed brick structure was the residence of Jefferson Davis, president of the Confederate States of America. The Southern "White House" was originally built in 1818 but later remodeled.

It presents an austere facade to the street, but a handsome giant portico looks onto the garden at the rear. The house was acquired by the Confederate Memorial Literary Society in 1893 and was restored in the 1980s. Along with the adjacent Museum of the Confederacy, it is open to the public.

## WICKHAM-VALENTINE HOUSE
### 1005 East Clay Street

One of Richmond's finest Federal style residences, notable for its fine proportions and impressive spiral staircase, this stuccoed-brick house was designed by Alexander Parris and built in 1812 for noted constitutional lawyer John Wickham. Wickham gained fame as the successful defense counsel in Aaron Burr's celebrated treason trial, held in Richmond in 1807. Mann Valentine II, who bought the house in 1882, willed it to the city for use as a museum. The Wickham House is open to the public as a historic house museum, and adjacent buildings contain the Valentine Museum's other displays and collections.

## ▪ Richmond County

## MENOKIN
### About 4 miles northwest of Warsaw

Francis Lightfoot Lee and his 17-year-old bride, Rebecca, received a handsome present when they were married in 1769. Rebecca's father, Colonel John Tayloe of nearby Mount Airy, gave them Menokin: a two-story stone house, complete with dependencies, and a large plantation. Lee soon joined the cause of American independence, serving in the Continental Congress from 1775 to 1779 and signing the Declaration of Independence and the Articles of Confederation. Both Lee and his wife died in 1797, and Menokin all but disappeared over the ensuing years. Somehow, as an eminent architectural historian has stated, it "tenaciously defies complete obliteration." The interiors were removed and preserved before the roof collapsed, and plans are currently under way for a restoration or reconstruction.

## MOUNT AIRY
### 1 mile west of Warsaw on U.S. Route 360

Constructed in the mid-18th century by

John Tayloe II, this five-part mansion represents the high-water mark of neo-Palladianism in Virginia's Georgian architecture. Unique in the Tidewater, where frame and brick are the norm, Mount Airy is built of sandstone obtained from the Tayloe family's Aquia Creek quarry. In the best tradition of Palladian villas, the two-story central block is connected by curved one-story hyphens to two-story dependencies, creating a formal, commanding architectural presence on the landscape. The house remains in family ownership.

## SABINE HALL
**Warsaw vicinity, Tappahannock**

Built ca. 1735 by Landon Carter, son of Robert "King" Carter, Sabine Hall is an exemplary manifestation of early Georgian architecture. The two-story brick mansion is noted for its fully paneled central hall. The imposing north portico is a later addition, as are the hyphens that now connect the central block with originally detached dependencies. Sabine Hall is still owned by descendants of its builder, and portions of its original terraced gardens remain.

### ■ *Rockbridge County*

## CYRUS MCCORMICK FARM AND WORKSHOP
**South of Staunton, Steele's Tavern vicinity**

In July 1831, Cyrus McCormick demonstrated to a group of neighbors a new agri-

*Sabine Hall, Richmond County, 1969. Courtesy of NPS.*

*Cyrus McCormick Farm and Workshop, Rockbridge County, 1963. Courtesy of NPS.*

cultural machine that he, and his father before him, had been tinkering with for years. This was a reaper, and because it permitted farmers to easily harvest all the grain they could sow, it revolutionized American agriculture. McCormick began production of his reapers here at Walnut Grove, then moved gradually westward until 1847, when he located his operations permanently in Chicago. His farmhouse and workshop are preserved, the latter serving as a museum. The land where he put his machine into practical service now serves quite fittingly as an experimental farm and research station, managed by Virginia Polytechnic Institute and State University.

## NATURAL BRIDGE
### Intersection of Routes 11 and 130, Natural Bridge vicinity

During colonial times and into the early days of the Republic, Natural Bridge was considered one of the most notable natural wonders of the New World. It was a source of inspiration for writers and artists, who regarded it as

one of the most awesome and sublime landscapes in America. Thomas Jefferson once owned the bridge, kept it open to the public, constructed a cabin for the comfort of visitors, and directed that nothing be done to interfere with its beauty or cause it harm. The first sight of the bridge spanning a rocky, wooded ravine and creek still causes sensitive hearts to skip a beat. The bridge is open to the public.

### ■ Stafford County

## AQUIA CHURCH
### Intersection of U.S. Route 1 and Virginia Route 610, Stafford vicinity

Completed in 1757, this is one of Virginia's finest and least-altered colonial churches. The exemplary Georgian structure is built of brick, with quoins and door frames of locally quarried Aquia Creek sandstone. The unusual plan is a true Greek cross, with all four "arms" extending the same length. The finely crafted interior contains its original Ionic altarpiece and three-level pulpit with sounding board high above. Aquia still houses an active Episcopal parish.

## GARI MELCHERS HOME
### Off U.S. Route 1, Falmouth

Gari Melchers, distinguished American landscapist and portraitist, lived and worked at Belmont from 1916 until his death in 1932. Among his best-known works are the companion allegorical murals, *Peace* and *War*, which he completed for the Library of Congress. A popular artist, Melchers helped spark a great interest in American art—both at home and abroad. His widow left Belmont to Mary Washington College in Fredericksburg, and it is now open as a museum.

### ■ Staunton City

## WOODROW WILSON BIRTHPLACE
### North Coalter Street between Beverly and Frederick Streets

Thomas Woodrow Wilson, educator, author, governor, and 28th president of the United

*Natural Bridge, Rockbridge County. Courtesy of Frazier Associates.*

States, was born in this two-story Greek Revival brick house in 1856. The house had been built in 1846 as the parsonage of Staunton's First Presbyterian Church, where Wilson's father became pastor in 1855. In 1857 the family left for Augusta, Georgia, when the Reverend Wilson accepted the call to a new pulpit. Now restored, the house and grounds are open to the public as a museum honoring this great American and, albeit just barely, great Virginian.

## ■ Surry County

### BACON'S CASTLE
**Off Virginia Route 10, Bacon's Castle**

This venerable brick house speaks volumes about Virginia's early years—the trials colonial settlers endured and the triumphs they enjoyed. Dating from the 1660s, it is the state's best domestic example of authentic postmedieval architectural forms. Major Arthur Allen built it, but the house gained its name from its use as a rebel fortress during Bacon's Rebellion (1676–1677), the first instance of violent resistance to British exploitation in colonial America. After serving as a private home for centuries, Bacon's Castle was acquired by the Association for the Preservation of Virginia Antiquities in 1973. It has been restored and is open as a historic house museum.

## ■ Tazewell County

### POCAHONTAS EXHIBITION COAL MINE
**Route 659, Reedsville Hollow, Pocahontas**

Pocahontas Mine Number 1 was opened in the spring of 1882 to tap an extraordinarily thick seam of high-quality semi-bituminous coal. The opening inaugurated development of the Pocahontas/Flat Top Field. Coal from this field was especially adapted to steam generation, and the U. S. Navy used it exclusively for its ships during World War I. In 1938, when active mining ceased, Mine Number 1 achieved another "first." It became the first exhibition coal mine in the country. It continues to provide an unrivaled glimpse of conditions under which miners worked in this dangerous but profitable enterprise.

*Cape Henry Lighthouse, Virginia Beach, 1961. Courtesy of NPS.*

## ■ Virginia Beach City

### CAPE HENRY LIGHTHOUSE (NPS)
**Atlantic Avenue at U.S. Route 60**

This stalwart stone sentinel atop a high sand dune is the first lighthouse erected by the federal government. Marking the southern entrance to Chesapeake Bay, the 90-foot tower was completed and its oil-burning lights were first lit in October 1792. The beacon was in constant use until 1881, when a new lighthouse was constructed nearby. The lighthouse is currently administered as part of Colonial National Historical Park.

### ADAM THOROUGHGOOD HOUSE
**1636 Parish Road**

In 1632, Adam Thoroughgood obtained title to the property on which his son or grandson likely built this house. A story-and-a-half tall, the brick house has large, nonmatching end chimneys and irregularly spaced fenestration, typical of the postmedieval design that prevailed before Georgian symmetry became the norm. The house was restored in the 1950s and is open to the public as a museum illustrating the life-style of Virginia's early colonists.

### ■ *Warren County*

## CEDAR CREEK BATTLEFIELD AND BELLE GROVE

**On Interstate 81 between Middletown and Strasburg, Middletown (Frederick and Warren Counties)**

(See entry under Frederick County.)

## THUNDERBIRD ARCHEOLOGICAL DISTRICT

**Address Restricted, Limeton vicinity**

This extraordinarily important archeological district consists of three sites—Thunderbird Site, the Fifty Site, and the Fifty Bog. Together they provide a stratified cultural sequence spanning Paleo-Indian cultures (9500 B.C.) through the end of Early Archaic times (6500 B.C.), with scattered evidence of later occupation. Thunderbird is the first undisturbed Paleo-Indian site discovered in eastern North America, and the Fifty Site is the first known stratified Paleo-Indian-to-Early-Archaic hunting-processing camp. Fifty Bog is the only Late Pleistocene/ Early Holocene habitat in eastern North America associated with human occupation that contains well-preserved organic materials.

### ■ *Westmoreland County*

## SPENCE'S POINT

**On Sandy Point Neck on Virginia Route 749, Westmoreland vicinity**

For much of his life, John Roderigo Dos Passos was associated with this property. Acclaimed as one of the most influential of modern American writers, he based his early works on his World War I experiences, stripping war and military life of the romanticism with which they had traditionally been viewed. In his *USA,* a trilogy (1930–1936), Dos Passos invented a new form of storytelling, one in which social history itself became the dynamic drive of the work, not merely its framework. The writer summered at this 1806 Federal style house in his youth, then lived here permanently from 1949 until his death in 1970.

## STRATFORD HALL

**1 mile northeast of Lerty on Virginia Route 214**

Stratford's distinctions seem virtually endless. It was the home of the Lees of Virginia, two of whom—brothers Richard Henry Lee and Francis Lightfoot Lee—signed the Declaration of Independence. They were both born at Stratford, and the house later became the birthplace and childhood home of Confederate general Robert E. Lee. The brick house, completed ca. 1730 and now restored, is a unique example of early Georgian architecture; H-shaped in plan, it is noted for its dra-

*Stratford Hall, Westmoreland County, 1969. Courtesy of HABS (Jack E. Boucher).*

matic pair of clustered chimney stacks and its paneled, tray-ceilinged great hall. A number of important plantation buildings survive as well. Stratford, located in a pristine rural setting and the centerpiece of a vast acreage that is still a working farm, is open to the public.

## YEOCOMICO CHURCH
### 0.5 miles southwest of Tucker Hill on Virginia Route 606

This small early-18th-century brick church displays a blend of medieval and classical features that make it a significant example of transitional colonial architecture. The "wicket door" (a smaller opening set within a larger one) is a common enough feature in English medieval design, but is unique in America. The modillion cornice, on the other hand, heralds the approach of the Georgian style. Named for a nearby river that was, in turn, named for an Indian tribe, Yeocomico Church is preserved in a wooded setting, likely even more tranquil now than it was in colonial times.

## ■ Williamsburg City
## BRUTON PARISH CHURCH
### Duke of Gloucester Street

Bruton Parish, "court" church of colonial Virginia, was likely designed by Royal Governor Alexander Spottwood. The body of the brick building was completed in 1715 and was among the earliest structures in the colonies to display elements of Georgian design. The tower was added in 1769. The church has added significance because one of its 20th-century rectors, Dr. William A. R. Goodwin, inspired John D. Rockefeller to begin the restoration of the entire city of Williamsburg, including the church, to its colonial appearance. One of Williamsburg's most familiar buildings, the church houses a large parish and is regularly open to visitors.

## PEYTON RANDOLPH HOUSE
### Intersection of Nicholson and North England Streets

This elegant frame house, built in three stages during the 18th century, was home to Peyton Randolph from 1745 until his death in 1775. A member of colonial Virginia's House of Burgesses from 1766 to 1775, Randolph served on the national level as first president of the Continental Congress in 1774. His house, overlooking the court green in the center of this restored community, is a vital element in the townscape and plays a major role in Colonial Williamsburg's interpretive programs.

## JAMES SEMPLE HOUSE
### South side of Francis Street, between Blair and Walker Streets

Likely dating from the 1770s, this is a formal frame house whose design may have been influenced by Thomas Jefferson. The two-story central block with a pedimented gable, flanked by one-story wings, is similar to Monticello as first built. The house may be

*James Semple House, Williamsburg, 1969. Courtesy of NPS (Charles W. Snell).*

Wren Building, College of William and Mary, Williamsburg, 1969. Courtesy of NPS.

seen as the prototype of a number of houses of the same form that were built in Virginia and in nearby North Carolina. The Semple House, owned by Colonial Williamsburg, is easily visible but is not open to the public.

## WILLIAMSBURG HISTORIC DISTRICT
### Francis, Waller, Nicholson, North England, Lafayette, and Nassau Streets

As capital of the largest English colony in America, Williamsburg witnessed, and helped bring about, many of the stirring events that led to the Revolution and American independence. Virginia's government moved here from Jamestown in 1698, then moved to Richmond in 1780. Williamsburg mostly slumbered until the 1920s, when John D. Rockefeller began to rouse it. Starting with a few selected houses, Rockefeller eventually sponsored the restoration and rebuilding of the entire colonial capital. Williamsburg was a milestone in historic preservation in America, and its able leaders and staff continue to refine our definitions of restoration and interpretation.

## WREN BUILDING
### College of William and Mary

The Wren Building, first building of the second-oldest institution of higher learning in the country, was begun in 1695, two years after the College of William and Mary was chartered. Although it remains uncertain whether English architect Sir Christopher Wren actually designed the building, which housed the entire college for many years, his

name has long been associated with it. Sixteen members of the Continental Congresses, four signers of the Declaration of Independence, and three future presidents of the United States studied, slept, dined, prayed, and played within its solid brick walls.

## WYTHE HOUSE
### West side of Palace Green

From 1755 to 1791 this fine Georgian brick town house was home to George Wythe, signer of the Declaration of Independence and mayor of Williamsburg. Wythe was the first professor of law in an American college, and among the students he influenced at William and Mary were Thomas Jefferson, John Marshall, and James Monroe. In 1937 Colonial Williamsburg acquired his house, which it subsequently restored. It is open as a historic house museum.

## ■ Winchester City

## STONEWALL JACKSON'S HEADQUARTERS
### 415 North Braddock Street

In the months preceding his famous Shenandoah Valley campaign in the spring of 1862, Confederate Major General Thomas J. (Stonewall) Jackson used this Gothic Revival house as his home and headquarters. Jackson's rapid maneuvers and diversions in the valley kept federal forces occupied and prevented them from joining and assisting in the peninsular assault on Richmond. The City of Winchester owns the house and maintains it as a museum.

# WASHINGTON

■ *Franklin County*

## MARMES ROCKSHELTER
**Address Restricted, Lyons Ferry**

This is one of the most outstanding archeological sites yet discovered in the Northwest. Excavations conducted in the 1960s revealed the earliest known burials in the Pacific Northwest (ca. 5500–4500 B.C.) and what were heralded as some of the oldest human remains yet encountered in the Western Hemisphere (ca. 11,000–9000 B.C.). The eight strata at the site all contain cultural materials, and the sequence of human occupation ranges over a period of 11,000 years. The site was protected before waters of the Lower Monumental Reservoir inundated it, and it still offers research potential.

■ *Jefferson County*

## FORT WORDEN
**Cherry and West Streets, Port Townsend vicinity**

Fort Worden commemorates the remarkable Endicott system of coastal defenses constructed in the 1890s and early 1900s. The system was named for Grover Cleveland's secretary of war, William C. Endicott, who chaired a board that recommended the construction and/or strengthening of forts at strategic coastal defenses. This fort, one of the largest posts in the system, remains one of the least altered and is a superb example of military design and technology of its time. The fort is owned by the State of Washington and is open to the public as a state park.

## PORT TOWNSEND
**Bounded by Scott, Walker, Taft, and Blaine Streets and the waterfront, Port Townsend**

First settled in the 1850s, Port Townsend soon became the seat of Washington Territory's Jefferson County and headquarters of federal customs operations on Puget Sound. These functions, along with its development as a lumber town and port, made it grow and flourish, particularly in the 1880s. The local economy collapsed in 1890, following an over-ambitious boom in land speculation. Although Port Townsend eventually recovered, the townscape is identified primarily by the many structures that survive from its glory days during the second half of the 19th century. The district includes houses, stores, schools, and churches, not to mention the courthouse and the customhouse, that reflect the enormous variety of architectural styles and materials available during that time.

*Port Townsend, Jefferson County. Starrett House. Courtesy of NPS (Jake Thomas).*

Arthur Foss, Kirkland, King County. Courtesy of NPS (James P. Delgado).

## ■ King County

### ADVENTURESS
#### Lake Union Drydock, Seattle

A schooner yacht and pilot boat, *Adventuress* is a significant example of the "fisherman profile" favored by Bowdoin B. Crownin-shield, a noted early-20th-century American naval architect whose work was influential in the development of American yachts and fishing schooners. Built in 1913 for private Arctic exploration and fishing expeditions, *Adventuress* was acquired by the San Francisco Bar Pilots in 1914 and worked until 1952 as a pilot boat. Its main occupation was the adventurous task of guiding maritime traffic across the treacherous San Francisco Bar into the busy port of San Francisco. *Adventuress* is now operated as a sailing school vessel.

### ARTHUR FOSS
#### Central Waterfront at Moss Bay, Kirkland

Built in 1889 as *Wallowa* and renamed *Arthur Foss* in 1934, this is the only known wooden-hulled 19th-century tugboat left afloat and in operating condition in the United States. *Foss* towed lumber and grain-laden square-rigged ships across the Columbia River, thus participating in the Pacific Coast lumber trade and the international grain trade. While under charter to the U.S. Navy, *Foss* was the last vessel to successfully escape Wake Island before Japanese forces attacked and captured that Pacific outpost in 1942. Life was not always so serious, however. In another role in its varied career, *Wallowa* starred in the 1933 film *Tugboat Annie*.

### DUWAMISH
#### Lake Washington Ship Canal, Chittenden Locks, Seattle

*Duwamish* is an excellent example of the typical fireboat found in major American port cities through much of the 20th century. Although there may be earlier vessels that were modified and adapted from existing tugboats to be used as fireboats, *Duwanish* (1909) is the country's second-oldest surviving fireboat built specifically as a fire-fighting vessel. It was designed to conform to Seattle's waterfront; built as a shallow-draft vessel, without an external keel, it could navigate the shallow waters and mudflats of the city's harbor with ease.

### FIR
#### 1519 Alaskan Way, Seattle

Lighthouses, often necessarily built on remote, rugged, inhospitable shores, from their beginnings have required tenders to service and maintain them. *Fir*, launched in 1938, and a workhorse of the waters if ever there was one, spent most of its active career operating out of Seattle, transporting light-house keepers, bringing supplies, mail, and fuel, as well as servicing lightships, moving buoys, and participating in search and rescue efforts. Until October 1991 this essentially unmodified cutter was the last working member of the U.S. Coast Guard's Lighthouse Service fleet. *Fir*'s decommissioning that month signaled the end of an era.

## LIGHTSHIP NO. 83, *RELIEF*
### Central Waterfront at Moss Bay, Kirkland

Known by its last official designation, *Relief,* No. 83 was built (1904) to serve as one of the first four lightships on the Pacific coast. *Relief* guided mariners to three major ports— Eureka on Humboldt Bay, San Francisco, and Seattle. No. 83 and its sister, No. 76, are the earliest surviving examples of American lightships. *Relief* is currently owned and being restored by the Northwest Seaport Maritime Heritage Center in Seattle.

## PIONEER BUILDING, PERGOLA, AND TOTEM POLE
### First Avenue, Yesler Way, and Cherry Street, Seattle

The Richardsonian Romanesque Pioneer Building, completed in 1892, is one of the best-preserved structures clustering around Pioneer Square, once the commercial heart of Seattle. The cast-iron pergola in the center of the square reminds visitors that Seattle once had cable cars; it was built in 1909 as a shelter for passengers awaiting the arrival of cars. The totem pole is a reproduction of one that burned in 1938. Its predecessor was unveiled in 1899, having been brought to town by participants in a chamber of commerce excursion to Alaska, where they had stolen it from the Tlingit Indians. Together these disparate elements provide a vivid picture of a vibrant early Seattle.

## SEATTLE ELECTRIC COMPANY GEORGETOWN STEAM PLANT
### King County Airport, Seattle

Erected between 1906 and 1908, this substantial reinforced-concrete building houses the last operational examples of the world's first large-scale steam turbines. These Curtis Vertical Steam Turbo generators, patented by Charles G. Curtis and manufactured by the General Electric Corporation, marked the end of an era of reciprocating steam engine–driven generators. The new technology established General Electric as a leader in the manufacture of steam turbines. The plant itself is also significant as an example of the "fast track" construction process.

## *VIRGINIA V*
### 4455 Shilshole Avenue, Seattle

*Virginia V* is one of two surviving members of the American "mosquito fleet"—the large unlicensed steamers that worked the inland waters of United States, flitting around like mosquitoes. *Virginia V* was built in 1922 for the West Pass Transportation Company, whose steamers carried passengers, produce, and mail on the waters of Puget Sound. Now owned by the Virginia V Foundation, it is an excursion steamer still plying the waters of Puget Sound, still earning its keep.

## ■ *Kitsap County*
## PORT GAMBLE HISTORIC DISTRICT
### Northwest end of Kitsap Peninsula, Port Gamble

Port Gamble was one of the earliest and most important lumber-producing centers on the Pacific coast. It began in 1853 when Captain William C. Talbot, looking for a likely spot to build a sawmill, began a lumber camp on a heavily forested peninsula in the heart of one of the world's most important stands of timber. By the mid-1860s, the settlement owned by the Puget Sound Mill Company, of which Talbot was a partner, was named Port Gamble. The mill closed down in 1997, but the community remains a little-spoiled example of a mid-19th-century company town.

## PUGET SOUND NAVAL SHIPYARD
### Roughly bounded by Mahan Avenue, Coghlan Road, and Cottman Road, Bremerton

Puget Sound Naval Shipyard was the principal repair facility for the U.S. Navy's battle-damaged Pacific Fleet during World War II. Five of the eight battleships bombed at Pearl Harbor on December 7, 1941, were refitted here and returned to duty. These were but 5 of the 26 battleships (some limped into harbor more than once), 18 aircraft carriers, 13 cruisers, and 79 destroyers that were repaired at Bremerton. In all, more than 30,000 workers at the shipyard built, fitted out, restored, overhauled, or modernized nearly 400 fighting ships between 1941 and 1945.

### ■ *Lewis County*

### MOUNT RAINIER NATIONAL PARK (NPS)

**Tahoma Woods–Star Route, Ashford vicinity (Lewis and Pierce Counties)**

The initiation of the National Park Service (NPS) master planning process at Mount Rainier National Park in the late 1920s was a major step in the design and management of scenic reservations in the 20th century. In addition to being the first fully developed example of NPS master planning, Mount Rainier also remains the most complete example of the results of such planning. The park has retained most of the facilities— buildings, roads, trails, even woodsheds— built during the historic period.

### ■ *Pacific County*

### CHINOOK POINT

**Chinook vicinity, off U.S. Route 101**

Robert Gray, fur trader and American sea captain, discovered the Columbia River in May 1792 by sailing upstream from Deception Bay and landing at Chinook Point. This gave the United States a strong claim to the Pacific Northwest, as international law held that discovery and entrance into the mouth of a river gave the discovering nation sovereignty not only over the water, but also over its valley, watershed, and adjacent coast. Great Britain disputed the claim, which was finally resolved by the Oregon Treaty of 1846.

### ■ *Pierce County*

### FIREBOAT NO. 1

**Marine Park on Ruston Way, Tacoma**

Although *Fireboat No. 1,* built in 1929, operated only on Puget Sound, it is representative of most fireboats built prior to the Second World War throughout the United States. One of only ten fireboats more than 50 years old in the country, and one of only five dating from the 1920s, *Fireboat No. 1* is the least modified and best preserved of all. Owned by

the City of Tacoma, it is preserved and open to the public as a museum exhibit.

### FORT NISQUALLY GRANARY

**Point Defiance Park, Tacoma**

Fort Nisqually, an outpost of the Hudson's Bay Company, was the first permanent Anglo-American settlement on Puget Sound and served as a communications and supply center for the company's other trading posts in British Columbia. The fort's one-story granary, built in 1843 of log construction, and the factor's house are the only surviving original examples of Hudson's Bay Company buildings in the United States. Moved in 1934 from their original site to Point Defiance Park, both structures have been restored and are open to the public.

### LONGMIRE BUILDINGS (NPS)

**Mount Rainier National Park, Longmire**

This group of three structures at Mount Rainier National Park, built between 1927 and 1929, contributed substantially to the development of rustic architecture in the National Park system. The structures— administration building, community building, and service station—use natural materials (log and stone) and were designed to respect and blend with their awesome surroundings. The rounded glacial boulders that form the first floor of the administration building appear to rise naturally out of the ground.

### MOUNT RAINIER NATIONAL PARK (NPS)

**Tahoma Woods-Star Route, Ashford vicinity (Lewis and Pierce Counties)**

(See entry under Lewis County.)

### PARADISE INN (NPS)

**Mount Rainier National Park, Paradise**

This rustic hotel, dating from 1916–1917, was the first major concession structure built by the Rainier National Park Company and helped to set the architectural stage for future construction at this popular national park. Built of stone and cedar, the latter having weathered naturally "on the stump" for 30 years before being used in the hotel, Paradise Inn fits handsomely and naturally into its

Paradise Inn, Pierce County. Courtesy of NPS (Laura Soulliere Harrison).

Yakima Park Stockade Group, Sunrise, Pierce County. North Blockhouse. Courtesy of NPS (Laura Soulliere Harrison).

scenic surroundings. Inside, the lobby utilizes log decor to the maximum degree; even a piano and its bench, as well as a grandfather clock, are constructed of logs. The inn is also significant as one of the earliest ski resorts in the United States.

## YAKIMA PARK STOCKADE GROUP (NPS)
### Mount Rainier National Park, Sunrise

Constructed between 1930 and 1943, this group of buildings is a classic example of the exaggerated rustic style that National Park Service architects practiced at the time. The complex, consisting of three buildings and a vertical log "stockade" fence enclosing a utility yard, was designed to reflect the frontier architecture of the Pacific Northwest. No actual frontier fort ever existed here; in fact, the site was once a summer campground and rendezvous spot for the Yakima and other tribes. Somehow, even if the justification for a pseudo-fort at the site seems a bit far fetched, the result seems just right.

## ■ San Juan County

## AMERICAN AND ENGLISH CAMPS, SAN JUAN ISLAND (NPS)
### Friday Harbor vicinity

These sites are associated with the mid-19th-century quarrel between America and Britain concerning the water boundary between Vancouver Island, British Columbia, and the Oregon Territory. Events came to a head in 1859 when an American settler shot a British pig (a black boar, to be precise). Words were exchanged, armed forces of both sides faced off at San Juan Island, and the

"Affair of the Pig" almost led to war. After skillful, if belated, negotiations, the two nations agreed to joint occupation, and for a dozen years both maintained armed forces at these two camps on San Juan Island. The 1871 Treaty of Washington finally provided for a peaceful settlement. At last, for the first time in the history of the United States, there was no boundary dispute with Great Britain.

■ *Skagit County*

### W. T. PRESTON
**Anacortes waterfront, at the foot of Seventh Street on R Avenue, Anacortes**

*W. T. Preston* (1929), known as "the last of the Puget Sound sternwheelers," is one of two surviving U.S. Army Corps of Engineers snagboats and bucket dredges. Snagboats were part of a nationwide, decades-long commitment by the Army Corps to improve rivers and harbors throughout the country. *W. T. Preston* worked nearly 11 months of each year removing large pieces of driftwood, waterlogged pilings and logs, derelict boats, ships, airplanes, and debris from Puget Sound.

■ *Skamania County*

### BONNEVILLE DAM HISTORIC DISTRICT
**Columbia River**

When this mammoth federal project was built by the U.S. Army Corps of Engineers in the 1930s, no other water impoundment or diversion structure in the country was comparable to it. Located at the western end of the Columbia River gorge, Bonneville Dam was designed to generate hydroelectric power and was the first dam built with a "hydraulic drop" capable of developing more than 500,000 kilowatts of electric power. Other associated structures in the district include a powerhouse, the navigation lock—built to allow river boats to travel around the dam, the fishways—designed so that salmon and steelhead trout could reach their spawning grounds upstream, and the fish hatchery. (Also in Multnomah County, Oregon.)

# WEST VIRGINIA

■ *Brooke County*

### CAMPBELL MANSION
**East of Bethany on West Virginia Route 67**

Alexander Campbell, founder of one of America's largest indigenous religious movements, the Disciples of Christ, was also a formidable debater, political reformer, and philosopher, as well as prolific author, successful businessman, and agriculturalist. Likewise a pioneer in American education, Campbell founded Bethany College in 1840 and served as its president until his death in 1866. His charmingly informal house, built in stages between 1793 and 1840, is furnished with many family pieces and is open to the public. The small hexagonal study where he prepared his sermons and wrote copy for his newspaper, the *Millennial Harbinger,* stands in the yard.

### OLD MAIN
**Bethany College, Bethany**

This impressive brick structure has been the dominant architectural presence in Bethany since it was erected between 1858 and 1871. It is one of the country's earliest large-scale examples of collegiate Gothic design. Old Main also represents Bethany College's pivotal historical role as the headquarters of Alexander Campbell, principal founder of the Disciples of Christ. As such, Bethany may be seen as the progenitor of colleges and universities established throughout the country when "Campbellites" who were trained here helped to settle the American frontier.

## ■ Cabell County

### CLOVER SITE
**Address Restricted, Lesage**

This site includes the extraordinarily well-preserved remains of an Indian town dating from ca. A.D. 1550 to 1600. The site pertains to the Fort Ancient culture, descendants of the cosmopolitan Hopewell trading societies and related to the other great urbanizing mound builders of the Mississippian period. Clover Site is on the second terrace of the southern bank of the fertile lowlands of the Ohio River.

## ■ Greenbrier County

### THE GREENBRIER
**U.S. Route 60, White Sulphur Springs**

"America's Premier Resort" is how the Greenbrier thinks of itself, and there is much truth in the slogan. One of the country's oldest resorts, White Sulphur catered to wealthy Southerners in the antebellum era and counted Henry Clay and John Tyler among its guests. The main hotel, the Greenbrier, was built in 1913 and enlarged over the years. Prisoners of war were accommodated here during World War II. During the Cold War secret underground chambers were built to accommodate the U. S. Congress in the

event that a nuclear catastrophe necessitated the evacuation of Washington. Today the 6,500-acre resort continues in its traditional peacetime role of providing luxury accommodations, superb golfing, and excellent cuisine to its well-heeled guests.

## ■ Jefferson County

### TRAVELLER'S REST
**On West Virginia Route 48, Kearneyville**

Horatio Gates moved to this property in 1773. He offered his services to the Continental Congress in 1775 and in October 1777 led patriot troops that forced General Burgoyne's army of almost 6,000 men to surrender at Saratoga. This was the first great American victory of the Revolution, but it was counterbalanced for Gates when Cornwallis defeated him at the Battle of Camden, South Carolina, in 1780. In 1790, Gates sold Traveller's Rest, emancipated his slaves, and moved to New York. Except for alterations made to equip the still privately owned house for 20th-century use, it remains remarkably unchanged from the time Gates knew it.

## ■ Lewis County

### WESTON ASYLUM
**River Street, Weston**

One of the largest hand-cut stone buildings in America, this phenomenal structure was

*Traveller's Rest, Kearneyville, Jefferson County, 1972. Courtesy of NPS.*

conceived in 1858 when Virginia's legislature authorized the Trans–Alleghany Lunatic Asylum. Architect Richard Snowden Andrews of Baltimore designed the hospital to conform to principles propounded by Dr. Thomas Kirkbride. Individual wards and pavilions accommodated patients according to their illnesses and needs and were designed to provide the maximum amount of light and ventilation. Although not presently used, the building remains well preserved.

## ■ *Marshall County*

### GRAVE CREEK MOUND
**Tomlinson and Ninth Streets, Moundsville**

Dating to ca. 500 B.C, this is one of the largest and oldest burial mounds of the Adena culture in the United States. The mound is also one of the most famous ancient constructions in the country. Located near the Ohio River, it was seen, and commented on, by almost every explorer who passed by. Early accounts testify that it was once the focal point of an extensive network of mounds and earthworks. The mound is now preserved by the state, and the adjacent Delf Norona museum contains exhibits pertaining to the site and the mound builders.

## ■ *Mingo County*

### MATEWAN HISTORIC DISTRICT
**Roughly bounded by McCoy Alley, the Mate Creek Railroad Bridge, Railroad Street, and Warm Hollow, Matewan**

The "Matewan Massacre" of May 19, 1920, resulted from escalating tensions between miners and coal company owners. Striking miners demanded that companies recognize the United Mine Workers of America, and management retaliated by bringing in armed guards to evict miners from the mines, and families from company houses. Police chief Sid Hatfield threatened the guards with arrest on the grounds that they had no eviction warrants. The ensuing conflict that left ten people dead was a pivotal event in the subsequent end of coal company control in West Virginia. Buildings remain from the time of the massacre.

## ■ *Monongalia County*

### ALEXANDER WADE HOUSE
**256 Prairie Street, Morgantown**

Alexander Wade, a teacher and superintendent of the Monongalia County school system, introduced important innovations in grading, promotion, and graduation procedures in 1874. These received such rave reviews from

*Wheeling Suspension Bridge, Wheeling, Ohio County. Courtesy of HAER (Jack E. Boucher).*

the National Education Association in 1879 that the organization passed a resolution commending his plan, which was soon adopted in schools throughout the country. From 1872 until he died in 1904, Wade lived in this mansard-roofed brick house.

## ■ *Ohio County*

### WEST VIRGINIA INDEPENDENCE HALL
**16th and Market Streets, Wheeling**

When this Renaissance Revival structure, designed by Ammi B. Young to serve as "Custom House, Post Office, and Court Room," was built in 1857–1859, Wheeling was one of antebellum Virginia's largest cities. The building soon served in a totally unexpected role, as the birthplace of a new state. Conventions held here created the Restored Government of Virginia, and offices of the governor were located in this building. A constitutional convention followed, and West Virginia became the 35th state of the union on June 20, 1863. The building then reverted back to its original use and later became an office building. The state purchased it in 1964 and subsequently restored it to serve as a museum.

### WHEELING SUSPENSION BRIDGE
**10th and Main Streets, Wheeling**

When this first bridge across the Ohio River was completed in 1849 to carry the National Road over the main channel, it was the world's longest suspension bridge. Charles Ellet, Jr., designed it and made repairs after it collapsed in 1854. In 1859, William McComas rebuilt it. The century-and-a-half-old bridge remains the oldest major long-span suspension bridge in the world, with a span of more than 1,000 feet. One of the nation's most significant antebellum engineering structures, it still carries traffic, although it has long since ceased to be the only bridge across the Ohio at Wheeling.

## ■ *Pocohontas County*

### REBER RADIO TELESCOPE
**National Radio Astronomy Observatory on West Virginia Route 28, Greenbank**

Designed and built in 1937 by Grote Reber,

*Reber Radio Telescope, Green Bank, Pocohantas County. Telescope with the inventor, ca. 1960. Courtesy of National Radio Astronomy Observatory.*

this was the first parabolic antenna specifically designed and built to aid research in the newly emerging field of radio astronomy. Depending on interstellar radio waves rather than light wavelengths, the development liberated astronomers from the confines of optical astronomy, allowing them to penetrate the universe as never before. An amateur astronomer and electronics expert, Reber was the world's only active radio astronomer from 1937 until after World War II. In 1959–1960 his telescope was relocated from the backyard of his home in Illinois and reassembled on the grounds of the National Radio Astronomy Observatory.

## ■ *Preston County*

### ELKINS COAL AND COKE COMPANY HISTORIC DISTRICT
**Off West Virginia Route 7, Bretz**

This complex of structures, dating from 1906 to 1919, contains what is probably the nation's largest group of beehive coke ovens. Coke, produced by burning coal at high, controlled temperatures, is essential in the manufacture of iron and steel. Of the 400 domed brick ovens originally here, 140 survive, built into the hillside facing the Baltimore & Ohio Railroad tracks. Thanks to blast furnace ovens such as these, America became the world's leading producer of iron and steel in the late 19th and early 20th centuries.

■ *Randolph County*
## DAVIS AND ELKINS HISTORIC DISTRICT
**Davis and Elkins College campus, Elkins**
This historic district contains West Virginia's two grandest Gilded Age mansions. Graceland, begun in 1891, was the home of Senator Henry Gassaway Davis, the senior and Democrat member of a bipartisan duo that dominated West Virginia business and politics at the turn of the 20th century. Nearby Halliehurst, begun in 1890, was the summer home of Davis's Republican counterpart and son-in-law, Stephen Benton Elkins. Elkins became a major figure in Republican presidential politics of the 1880s and served as senator from West Virginia from 1895 until his death. Davis and Elkins College now owns the mansions, maintains

them in prime condition, utilizes Graceland as a conference center, and welcomes the public to both properties.

■ *Taylor County*
## ANDREWS METHODIST EPISCOPAL CHURCH
**11 East Main Street, Grafton**
From Philadelphia, Anna M. Jarvis sent 500 carnations to this church, which she had attended as a youth, to be distributed at morning services on Sunday, May 10, 1908, to honor mothers. Philadelphia merchant John Wanamaker, who had joined her cause to establish Mother's Day, held an afternoon service in his store the same day. The movement, a combination of religious and commercial interests, grew rapidly, and in 1914 President Woodrow Wilson proclaimed that the second Sunday in May would be observed annually as Mother's Day throughout the nation. The church where it all began is now the International Mother's Day shrine and is open to the public. Its Victorian-era interior, with stained-glass windows, paintings, organ pipes, and pressed-tin ceilings, is little changed from that seminal second Sunday in May 1908.

# WISCONSIN

■ *Adams County*
## FOURTH STREET (MEIR) SCHOOL
**333 West Galena Street, Milwaukee**
Milwaukee's Fourth Street School is the American building most closely associated with Golda Meir, who from 1969 to 1974 was prime minister of Israel. Fleeing the pogroms of their native Russia, Mrs. Meir's family came by steerage to America in 1906 and soon settled on Walnut Street in Milwaukee. The young Golda attended the Fourth Street School, where she learned English and exhibited an early talent for leadership; in 1912, she graduated valedicto-

rian. The school continues to serve the students of Milwaukee, and on a return visit from Israel decades later, Mrs. Meir visited and recalled that "it had not changed very much in all those years."

■ *Columbia County*
## FARMERS' AND MERCHANTS' UNION BANK
**159 West James Street, Columbia**
One of architect Louis Sullivan's jewel-like small-town banks, this example dates from 1919. Small and compact, it manages to impart a look of permanence and safety—so

important in the philosophy of bank design at the time—at the same time displaying some of the most florid, inventive, and beautiful decorative motifs that Sullivan ever composed. Perhaps a reason for its aura of perfection is that Sullivan not only designed it, he also supervised construction. This was the last of the eight banks he designed throughout the Midwest.

■ *Crawford County*

## ASTOR FUR WAREHOUSE
**Water Street, Saint Feriole Island, Prairie du Chien**

Constructed ca. 1828 by Joseph Rolette, this plain stone building is the only known original fur trade warehouse in the Upper Mississippi Valley. It was one of the principal posts of John Jacob Astor's American Fur Company and recalls the time when Prairie du Chien, a short distance north of the spot where the Wisconsin River flows into the Mississippi, was one of the most important fur trading posts of the region. The building has been restored and is open as a museum illustrating the history of fur trading and the Upper Mississippi Valley.

## BRISBOIS HOUSE
**Water Street, Saint Feriole Island, Prairie du Chien**

This stone house, built ca. 1840, is Prairie du Chien's largest and most pretentious house of its time, reflecting the prosperity that fur trading brought to the community. It was built by the son of Michail Brisbois, a French-Canadian who had been one of the town's first permanent settlers in 1781.

## DOUSMAN HOTEL
**Water Street, Saint Feriole Island, Prairie du Chien**

When it was built between 1864 and 1865, this three-story buff-colored brick structure was the largest and most luxurious hotel in town and showed just how far Prarie du Chien had come from its origins as a frontier outpost. It was sponsored by the Milwaukee and Mississippi Railroad, which did its part in helping make the town an important travel terminus. The hotel was used as a stopping point by thousands of emigrants to the West after the Civil War but closed ca. 1925. It later became a meat packing plant.

## SECOND FORT CRAWFORD MILITARY HOSPITAL
**Rice Street at South Beaumont Road, Prairie du Chien**

Fort Crawford, the strongest of a chain of forts built along the upper Mississippi after the War of 1812, was the center of federal authority in the Old Northwest. The fort was relocated to higher ground in 1829, and the hospital was built ca. 1835. Fort Crawford was abandoned in 1856, reactivated during the Civil War, and sold in 1872. In the 1930s a Works Progress Administration team reconstructed the hospital around its remaining foundations, and it now serves as a museum of medical history. Dr. William Beaumont, post surgeon during the 1820s, conducted important experiments in digestive processes at Fort Crawford, but it is doubtful that he was associated with the second fort's hospital.

## VILLA LOUIS
**Saint Feriole Island, Prairie du Chien**

Hercules Louis Dousman I, prominent fur agent for the American Fur Company, adviser to the government on matters ranging from Indian affairs to land surveys, owner of river steamboats and proponent of the railroads, left a fortune sufficiently large for his son, Hercules Louis Dousman II, to build this large Italianate villa, designed by Milwaukee architect Edward Townsend Mix, in 1870. The house stands on a mound—believed to be a Hopewell site—which was also the location of two early forts, one of them the first Fort Crawford. A predecessor house that the first Hercules Dousman built was also on the site. Villa Louis is open to the public as a house museum.

■ *Dane County*

## HAROLD C. BRADLEY HOUSE
**106 North Prospect Street, Madison**

Constructed in 1909, the Bradley House is one of two residences by Louis Sullivan dating between the years he achieved fame as a designer of commercial structures and his death in 1924. He poured his creative energy into the design of this large house. Notable features include a cantilevered second-story porch and Sullivan's signature ornamentation. George Grant Elmslie, then Sullivan's chief draftsman, also contributed his talents. The house has been restored and is now a University of Wisconsin fraternity house.

## ROBERT M. LA FOLLETTE HOME
### 733 Lakewood Boulevard, Maple Bluff

Robert M. La Follette served in the U.S. House of Representatives from 1885 to 1891, but did not emerge as a major force in governmental reform until his time of service as governor of Wisconsin, from 1901–1906. As a four-term U.S. senator (1906–1925), he continued to champion "progressive" causes and was the Progressive Party's candidate for president in 1924, the year before his death. He lived the last 20 years of his life in this suburban Madison house.

## NORTH HALL
### University of Wisconsin, Madison

This austere four-story sandstone structure is the oldest building on the University of Wisconsin campus. It opened on September 17, 1851, and represents the progressive ideas that have emanated from the institution it

serves. The University of Wisconsin pioneered in extension work, particularly in agricultural programs, and in the involvement of scholars in legislative and regulatory affairs on a nonpartisan basis. Known as the Wisconsin Idea, the university's innovative cooperative programs stemmed from the Jacksonian concept that an enlightened public would best ensure a progressive America. Built as a dormitory, North Hall became a classroom and office building after 1884.

## UNIVERSITY OF WISCONSIN ARMORY AND GYMNASIUM
### 716 Langdon Street, Madison

This massive Romanesque Revival structure was the site of the 1904 Wisconsin Republican Convention, a seminal event in the history of the Progressive movement. At the convention, Robert M. La Follette's Progressives defeated the Stalwarts for control of the Wisconsin Republican Party. Widespread favorable publicity launched La Follette on the national scene. The controversy and legal suit engendered by the "Gymnasium Convention" and La Follette's subsequent vindication by the supreme court of Wisconsin led the Progressives to victory that November, giving them a majority in the state legislature the following year. This allowed the enactment of substantial reforms,

*Robert M. La Follette Home, Maple Bluff, Dane County. Courtesy of NPS.*

University of Wisconsin Armory and Gymnasium, Madison, Dane County. Courtesy of NPS (Greg Gent).

many of which were subsequently adopted by states across the nation.

## UNIVERSITY OF WISCONSIN SCIENCE HALL
### 550 North Park Street, Madison

Science Hall is associated with Charles R. Van Hise, the first geologist in the nation to apply microscopic lithology to the extensive study of crystalline rocks, and to use those results in the formulation of geological principles. Van Hise's emphasis on the quantitative application of physical and chemical laws to geological problems was one of his greatest contributions to his field. His influential 1904 monograph, *A Treatise on Metamorphism,* moved geology out of the science of classification and into formulating principles. As a teacher, Van Hise earned a reputation for training geologists who matched his own high standards in scientific research. (See Van Hise Rock, Sauk County.)

## ■ *Door County*

### NAMUR HISTORIC DISTRICT
**Roughly bounded by County Road K, Brussels Road, Wisconsin Route 57, Belgian Drive, and Green Bay shoreline**

Among the many nationalities that helped to settle our country, Belgians are seldom counted. This rural district in northeastern Wisconsin proves that they, too, added spice to the ingredients that went into the American melting pot. Namur is the nation's largest known concentration of farmhouses, barns, woodsheds, granaries, and other structures that reflect a distinctive Belgian influence. French-speaking Walloons from Brabant Province first arrived here in the 1850s, but most of the buildings postdate a forest fire that swept the area in 1871. In addition to the built environment, the Belgian heritage of the region is preserved in fairs and festivals.

## ■ *Fond Du Lac County*

### LITTLE WHITE SCHOOLHOUSE
**Blackburn and Blossom Streets, Ripon**

As the painted legend on the gable of this simple one-room, frame schoolhouse proudly proclaims, this is the "Birthplace of the Republican Party." On March 20, 1854, 53 petitioners called a meeting to protest the U.S. Senate's passage of the Kansas-Nebraska Act, which permitted the extension of slavery beyond the limits of the Missouri Compromise. The meeting resulted in the formation of a new, albeit local, party, drawn from the ranks of dissatisfied Whigs, Free Soilers, and Democrats. Subsequent meetings held by other dissatisfied local groups were held, and a national political party emerged.

No matter whether party principles that first developed here have remained steadfast, the building itself has been quite peripatetic. It now rests at its fourth location, close to, but not on, the original site.

## ■ *Iowa County*

### TALIESIN EAST

#### 2 miles south of Spring Green

A superb example of Frank Lloyd Wright's organic architecture, growing out of his Prairie Style work, Taliesin was the second great center of his activity (after Oak Park, Illinois). The principal surviving complexes are Taliesin III (1925), Hillside Home School (1902, 1933), and Midway Farm (1938); additions include those done by architects who studied under Wright after the founding of the Taliesin Fellowship in 1932. Wright lived here each summer until his death in 1959, and the complex is fully representative of the theories and taste of this most famous of American architects. It continues to be the summer headquarters of the Taliesin Fellowship and is open to visitors. (See also Taliesin West, Maricopa County, Arizona.)

*Little White Schoolhouse, Ripon, Fond du Lac County, 1973. Courtesy of NPS (Donald A. Anderson).*

*Hamlin Garland House, West Salem, La Crosse County, 1971. courtesy of NPS.*

## ■ *Jefferson County*

### AZTALAN

**Aztalan State Park, near Lake Mills on Wisconsin Route 89**

This large stockaded temple mound site, first discovered in 1836, is the northernmost of the major Mississippian culture archeological sites. The largest such site in Wisconsin, it was occupied ca. A.D. 1100–1300. The site is now incorporated in Aztalan State Park, and portions of the complex have been reconstructed.

## ■ *La Crosse County*

### HAMLIN GARLAND HOUSE

**357 West Garland Street, West Salem**

This rambling frame dwelling is associated with author Hamlin Garland, who purchased it for his parents in 1893. Garland's early fiction exploded the romantic myths of the West and exposed the hard lot of the pioneers and frontiersmen. He has been hailed as one of the country's most important regional authors, and in his realism has helped shape the technique and philosophy of modern American fiction. His 1922 work, *A Daughter of the Middle Border*, won him the Pulitzer Prize. Garland visited his parents regularly and accomplished a great deal of writing during his lengthy stays at what he described as a "plain spacious old house."

## ■ *Manitowoc County*

### *COBIA*

**809 South Eighth Street, Manitowoc**

USS *Cobia*, a World War II-era Gato class submarine, was launched in 1943. During its six war patrols, *Cobia* sank 13 Japanese ships and earned four battle stars for its service. In 1970 the people of Wisconsin dedicated *Cobia* as an International Memorial to submariners throughout the world. *Cobia* is now a museum, berthed at the Wisconsin Maritime Museum.

## ■ *Marquette County*

### FOUNTAIN LAKE FARM

**County Highway F and Gillette Road, Rural Montello**

John Muir, pioneering advocate of natural preservation, lived at Fountain Lake Farm as a teenager from 1849 to 1856, and periodically from 1862 to 1864. Late in life he traced the formation of his conservation philosophy to the years he spent here. Although no structures associated with Muir's period of residence exist, a natural meadow, spring, and lake remain. They are now encompassed in John Muir Memorial County Park.

## ■ *Milwaukee County*

### DR. FISK HOLBROOK DAY HOUSE

**8000 West Milwaukee Avenue, Wauwatosa**

The Day House, architecturally a wonderful example of Victorian eclecticism, is important for its association with amateur geologist Dr. Fisk Holbrook Day. Day and other naturalists of his time unselfishly assembled large collections of natural history specimens, made detailed observations on a local scale, then passed them along to professional scientists who examined them and deciphered their significance on the national level. In such a manner, the Dr. Days of their time played key roles in the progress of 19th-century American science. Dr. Day's particular contribution was a large and outstanding collection of Silurian fossils, which now forms an important part of the paleontology collection in the Museum of Comparative Zoology at Harvard University.

### THOMAS A. GREENE MEMORIAL MUSEUM

**3367 North Downer, Milwaukee**

Like Dr. Day in nearby Wauwatosa, Thomas A. Greene was the sort of amateur naturalist who played a crucial role in the development of 19th-century science by accumulating extensive collections of natural history specimens. From 1878 to 1894 he assembled a comprehensive collection of minerals from around the world, along with an unparalleled group of fossils from reefs of the Milwaukee-Chicago area. His work stimulated further research by professional geologists, and his collections provided abundant material for them to study. Greene's heirs constructed a museum building to house his collections in 1913. The University of Wisconsin-Milwaukee, present owner of the remarkable holdings he assembled, has moved the collection to new quarters.

## PABST THEATER
### 144 East Wells Street, Milwaukee

This is the best-preserved German-American theater in the United States, and a tangible reminder of a time when German-Americans thought of Milwaukee as the "Deutsche Athen" (German Athens). Constructed in 1895, the theater is conservative in design, with little specifically German in its architectural makeup. Its exterior belies the fact that its technical aspects—acoustics, stage facilities, and fireproof construction—were quite advanced for their time. Inside, the drum of the shallow dome that covers the auditorium contains plaques with names of celebrated artists, musicians, and writers, among them Wagner, Goethe, and Beethoven. The theater was closed in 1967 but was restored in the 1970s to appear as it had on opening night, November 9, 1895. At that celebration, patrons had been treated to a specially composed orchestral number, the "Pabst Theater Festival March," and then saw *Zwei Wappen,* a comedy about a romance between the daughter of an American sausage maker and the son of a German baron.

## SCHOONMAKER REEF
### North of West State Street between North 66th Street extended and North 64th Street extended, Wauwatosa

Schoonmaker Reef, a 425-million-year-old fossil reef, is significant in the history of geology in the United States. In 1862, this and several other nearby sites were first investigated and interpreted as fossil reefs, making the group the first fossil reefs recognized in North America. Collections taken from Schoonmaker by amateur naturalists Fisk Holbrook Day, Thomas A. Greene, and others are found in geological museums across the country. Eminent professional geologists used data collected from the reef to formulate theories fundamental in the study of geology.

## SOLDIERS' HOME REEF
### Clement J. Zablocki Veterans Affairs Medical Center, Milwaukee

This rock mound in the Menomonee River valley near Milwaukee was discovered by Increase A. Lapham, Wisconsin's first scientist, in the 1830s. In 1862, James Hall was the first to recognize and interpret this and several other nearby mounds as fossil reefs, making the group the first ancient reefs described in North America and among the first described anywhere in the world. Thomas C. Chamberlin used this reef and others in formulating his paleoecological and sedimentological model of reef development, which was published in his classic 1877 work, *Geology of Eastern Wisconsin.*

## TURNER HALL
### 1034 North Fourth Street, Milwaukee

Founded in early 19th-century Germany, the *Turnverein* was a gymnastic association that emphasized harmonious development of mind and body. As Germans migrated to America, the movement came with them, and Milwaukee's Turner Hall, built in 1882, survives as one of the nation's major buildings associated with this influential organization. It exemplifies the major place Milwaukee—the "German Athens" of America—held in the association and represents the group's unheralded role in political reform. From the days of the antislavery movement in the 1850s, before this clubhouse was built, through the era of progressive municipal reform, Milwaukee's Socialist Party mayors, who were known for their efficient leadership, were members of Turner Hall.

■ *Oconto County*

## OCONTO SITE
### Copper Culture State Park, Oconto

At this prehistoric burial ground, implements of the Old Copper Culture people, who occupied the northern Midwest about 2500 B.C., have been found in association with human burials. The name Old Copper Culture derives from the fact that these people fashioned arrowheads, spears, bracelets, and other objects out of copper. The site forms the Copper Culture State Park.

■ *Racine County*

## ADMINISTRATION BUILDING AND RESEARCH TOWER, S.C. JOHNSON COMPANY
### 1525 Howe Street, Racine

Frank Lloyd Wright's Depression-era design for the Johnson Wax Company's Administra-

*Administration Building and Research Tower, S.C. Johnson Company, Racine, Racine County, 1969. Courtesy of HABS (Jack F. Boucher).*

tion Building and Research Tower was so radical that local building commissioners refused to approve it without a test. At issue were Wright's novel "mushroom" columns, intended to carry loads varying from 2 to 12 tons. When a sample was built and withstood a load of 60 tons, the permit was granted. A classic of modern office design, the complex, which opened in 1939, continues to serve its original functions, and still contains original furnishings that Wright designed. Widely published, it was recognized for its importance even before it was completed, and helped the architect to gain a number of commissions.

## HERBERT JOHNSON HOUSE
### 33 East Four Mile Road, Racine

Built in 1937–1938 for the president of the S. C. Johnson Wax Company, "Wingspread" was considered by Frank Lloyd Wright to be the finest (and most expensive) house he had designed up to that time. Its name befits its plan; a large Prairie Style house, it has four radiating arms, or wings, that fan out from

the central core. Each wing has a defined function, and the arrangement allows easy access from all rooms to a patio or balcony. Beautifully sited and crafted, as was typical of Wright's work, Wingspread served as the Johnsons' home until 1978. Now a conference center devoted to educational and cultural affairs, it has been virtually unchanged over the years and still contains its original furnishings.

### ■ *Rock County*

## MILTON HOUSE
### 18 South Janesville Street, Milton

This tall hexagonal building, constructed of concrete grout and covered with plaster, is nationally significant not because of its unusual shape and construction, but because of its antebellum usage. Built as a hotel, it and the nearby log Goodrich Cabin served as stops on the Underground Railroad. Fugitive slaves could enter the cabin, open a trapdoor, and make their way through a tunnel to the Milton House, where the Goodrich family provided food, shelter, and assistance to reach their next stop on their way to freedom. This property, open to the public as a museum, also illustrates the westward spread of abolitionism and its transformation from a moral to a political issue. Joseph Goodrich, founder of Milton and proprietor of the hotel, had moved from New York state to Wisconsin. He was one of many who brought the reform movement and its ideals westward.

### ■ *Sauk County*

## RINGLING BROTHERS CIRCUS WINTER QUARTERS
### Bounded by Water, Brian, Lynn, and East Streets, Baraboo

From 1884 until 1918, the structures in this complex served as the winter headquarters for the Ringling Brothers Circus. By 1900, the Ringling Brothers had built their circus into one of the largest on the circuit; in 1907, with the purchase of the Barnum and Bailey Circus, they owned the largest circus combine in history. The two circuses were operated separately until 1919, when the brothers consolidated their holdings. The structures are currently part of the Circus World Museum complex.

## VAN HISE ROCK

**State Highway 136, approximately .75 mile north of State Highway 154, Rock Springs vicinity**

Located in the picturesque Upper Narrows of the Baraboo River near Ableman, this small outcrop provides an inordinate amount of geologic information about metamorphism, Precambrian rocks, and structural geology, all subjects to which Charles Van Hise, for whom the rock is named, made early and significant contributions. Work by Van Hise and others made the Baraboo area famous among structural geologists around the world, and Van Hise Rock is still used regularly by universities to train geology students. (See University of Wisconsin Science Hall, Dane County.)

# WYOMING

### ■ Big Horn County

## MEDICINE WHEEL

**Bighorn National Forest, Kane**

Medicine Wheel is one of the most interesting and mysterious remains of late-period aboriginal culture. It is composed of loose, irregularly shaped, whitish flat stones, with 28 linear spokes, 70 to 75 feet in length, radiating from a central hub to an encircling stone "rim." Thought to date from ca. A.D. 1800, it seems little modified from its original construction, yet its builders and function remain unknown.

### ■ Carbon County

## TOM SUN RANCH

**6 miles west of Independence Rock on Wyoming Route 220, Independence Rock (Carbon and Natrona Counties)**

This ranch, in the Sweetwater Valley alongside the Oregon Trail, is one of the best-preserved medium-sized cattle ranching operations of the open range period of the 1870s and 1880s. As early as 1882, the *Cheyenne Daily Leader* remarked that if any easterner happened to ask "his friends out west...what a ranch is like [he] would find his answer in a description of Tom Sun's." Sun was a French-Canadian frontiersman who became a pioneer cattleman after trying prospecting without much luck. The log house he built in 1872 and numerous outbuildings remain.

### ■ Fremont County

## SOUTH PASS

**10 miles southwest of South Pass City on Wyoming Route 28**

In the winter of 1823–1824, fur trapper Jedediah Smith learned, from the Crew Indians, of an area rich in beaver and in March 1824 set out to find it. On his way he discovered an easy pass through the Rocky Mountains; so easy, in fact, that many who followed on the Oregon Trail were unaware of exactly when they crossed the Continental Divide here. From the time Smith discovered it, South Pass was heavily used by westbound settlers, fur traders, and miners. The traffic through the Pass helped establish an effective U.S. claim to the Pacific Northwest, but also led to increased "Indian trouble," as Native Americans realized the immigrants were coming to stay. For the countless thousands who crossed South Pass, their successful passage marked the entrance into the Oregon Country, or, as one traveler put it: "Here Hail Oregon!"

### ■ Johnson County

## FORT PHIL KEARNY AND ASSOCIATED SITES
**Story vicinity**

One of the most significant and dramatic campaigns in the history of the West occurred in and around this fort. Established in 1866 to protect travelers along the

Bozeman Trail, the fort was under virtual siege throughout the "Red Cloud War" of 1866–1868. The Sioux successfully kept Anglo-Americans out of their hunting grounds and off the Bozeman Trail. Nearby Fetterman and Wagon Box sites commemorate two notable engagements of the war. The 1868 Treaty of Fort Laramie resulted in the closing of the trail and the abandonment of its forts, which the Indians jubilantly destroyed. This was one of the few instances when the army abandoned a region it had occupied.

### ■ *Laramie County*

### FORT D. A. RUSSELL
**West side of Cheyenne**

Fort Russell was established in 1867 to protect workers for the Union Pacific Railroad, then under construction across the country, from hostile Indians. It was home of the Pawnee Scout battalion in 1871, and troops from the fort participated in the Sioux War of 1876. None of the original frame fort buildings exists, but a number of brick quarters, offices, and stables survive from the 1880s and later. Fort Russell now forms part of the Francis E. Warren Air Force Base, and its slogan "From Mustang to Missile" capsulizes the dramatic changes in military operations that have occurred here over the years.

### WYOMING STATE CAPITOL
**24th Street and Capitol Avenue, Cheyenne**

Even as a territory, Wyoming was at the forefront of the national women's suffrage movement, in large part because of Esther Hobart Morris, who lobbied members of the territorial council. When Wyoming achieved statehood in 1890, it became the first state to grant women full suffrage, thanks to an all-male group that drafted the state constitution. The State Capitol, an imposing sandstone structure capped by a gold-leafed dome, represents this seminal achievement in the women's suffrage movement. A statue of Esther Morris, a replica of that in the U. S. Capitol in Washington, D.C., stands in front of the building's main entrance.

### ■ *Lincoln County*

### J. C. PENNEY HISTORIC DISTRICT
**J. C. Penney Avenue and South Main Street, Kemmerer**

James Cash Penney stands tall in the history of American retailing. Although not the first to establish a chain of department stores, he was the first to do so on a national scale. It started in Kemmerer in 1902, when he opened his Golden Rule emporium. Handling only merchandise that had a general demand and selling only for cash (it was, after all, his middle name), Penney achieved great success and soon expanded operations to other small

*Fort D. A. Russell, Laramie County. Fifth Cavalry Veterinary Barn. Courtesy of the Wyoming Division of Cultural Resources.*

*J. C. Penney Historic District, Kemmerer, Lincoln County. J. C. Penney House. Courtesy of the Wyoming Division of Cultural Resources.*

towns. By 1928, the J. C. Penney Company had 1,023 stores across the country. This district contains his original Golden Rule Store and the small frame cottage where the Penneys lived from 1902 until 1909.

■ *Natrona County*

### INDEPENDENCE ROCK
**60 miles southwest of Casper on Wyoming Route 220**

This rounded granite outcropping, 1,900 feet long and 850 feet wide, thrusting upward from a level plain, had been a well-known landmark for years, even before the Oregon Trail passed nearby. By 1840 it was regarded as "the great registry of the desert," because so many travelers painted or carved their names on it. One of the earliest graffiti artists inscribed the word "Independence," thus providing a name for those who followed.

### TOM SUN RANCH
**6 miles west of Independence Rock on Wyoming Route 220 (Carbon and Natrona Counties)**

(See entry under Carbon County.)

■ *Park County*

### HORNER SITE
**Address Restricted, Cody**

This site, considered the Cody Complex type site, is the first location where a distinctive

tool kit, including knives and several projectile points, was found in a context indicating its association with a single prehistoric flint tool industry. The Horner Site dates to approximately 5000 B.C. and contains evidence suggesting use of a corral for procuring and butchering at least 200 bison.

### NORRIS, MADISON, AND FISHING BRIDGE MUSEUMS (NPS)
**Norris Geyser Basin, Madison Junction, and Fishing Bridge, Yellowstone National Park (Park and Teton Counties)**

Built between 1929 and 1931, these three museums are located in different areas of Yellowstone National Park. Architect Herbert Maier took great pains to make them harmonize with their surrounding landscapes. All display bold stone foundations, seemingly part of natural rock outcroppings. The frame and log constructions above are often exaggeratedly rustic. These naturalistic, or rustic, designs served as models for hundreds of state and county park structures built by Works Progress Administration workers during the Great Depression.

### OBSIDIAN CLIFF (NPS)
**Approximately 13 road miles south of Mammoth, Yellowstone National Park, on the east side of U.S. Route 89, just south of the Obsidian Cliff**

Obsidian Cliff is the source of one of the most extensively traded and highly prized materials utilized by prehistoric peoples throughout the Northern Plains. For nearly 12,000 years Native Americans worked and traded this volcanic "glass," fashioning it into tools sharper than modern surgical scalpels or into jewel-like precious objects. Obsidian objects have been found as far away as the Ohio River valley and Southern California. In addition to the actual cliff, the site in Yellowstone Park includes intact mining features, workshops, and campsites of what can be considered one of the first industrial workshops on the North American continent.

## WAPITI RANGER STATION
**Shoshone National Forest, Wapiti vicinity**

Built in 1903, this was the first forest ranger station in the United States. It is located within the first national forest reserve (Shoshone National Forest), established by President Benjamin Harrison in 1891 as the Yellowstone Timberland Reserve. The station, a single-story log cabin with several additions, represents the beginnings of forest conservation in the country.

### ■ Platte County

## LAKE GUERNSEY STATE PARK
**1 mile northwest of Guernsey**

Lake Guernsey State Park represents an early and successful collaboration between the National Park Service and the Bureau of Reclamation (BOR) in developing what came to be known as "recreation areas." Lake Guernsey, a BOR project, was filled in 1927, and the park, designed by NPS personnel and constructed by the Civilian Conservation Corps, began in 1934. Intended as a showplace of state park design in Wyoming, it maintains an extremely high degree of integrity. The museum, constructed of massive sandstone blocks that seem to rise naturally out of a rock-strewn landscape, is a masterpiece of rustic design and still contains its original Works Progress Administration–era displays.

## OREGON TRAIL RUTS
**0.5 miles south of Guernsey**

Few "bumpy roads" evoke any sense of history, but this one surely does. Worn from two

to six feet deep in an eroded sandstone ridge on the south side of the North Platte River, these ruts give clear physical evidence of the Oregon Trail, the route that thousands of 19th-century pioneers took on their westward trek across the plains. The trail's first recorded use was in 1812, and it continued in use until completion of the Union Pacific Railroad in 1869 provided a shorter, surer, safer journey.

## SWAN LAND AND CATTLE COMPANY HEADQUARTERS
**East side of Chugwater**

Organized in Scotland in 1883, the Swan Company was one of the largest of several foreign livestock concerns that flourished in the West. It had more than 113,000 head of cattle in 1886, but the severe winter of 1886–1887 reduced that number by half. The company went bankrupt, then recovered, but never again reached the numbers it had in the profitable 1880s. It operated for more than 70 years, primarily as a sheep ranch after 1904. Surviving buildings include the ranchhouse, the barn, and the commissary.

### ■ Sheridan County

## SHERIDAN INN
**Broadway and Fifth Street, Sheridan**

When the Sheridan Inn opened in 1893, it was considered the finest hotel between Chicago and San Francisco, or at least the finest on the line of the railroad that built it, the Chicago, Burlington, and Quincy. The hotel immediately became the social center of the Big Horn country, and represented the taming of the "Wild West." William F. ("Buffalo Bill") Cody operated it from 1894 to 1896, adding barns and livery stables to accommodate big game hunters, who were the inn's primary clientele. A long frame building with two tiers of dormer windows on its expansive sloping roof, the hotel has been restored.

### ■ Sublette County

## UPPER GREEN RIVER RENDEZVOUS SITE
**On Green River above and below Daniel**

Of all the rendezvous sites associated with

the Rocky Mountain fur trade, this was by far the most popular. Of the 15 annual meetings held by the mountain men from 1825 to 1840, eight took place in the vicinity of Daniel, Wyoming. The "rendezvous" was a colorful trade fair, where trappers, traders, and Indians congregated to exchange furs and goods, the latter brought in by supply caravans from Saint Louis. Kit Carson and Jim Bridger, and a number of missionaries were among those who participated. The rendevouz is commemorated annually on the second Sunday in July by a reanactment that serves as a tribute to the mountain men.

■ *Sweetwater County*

## EXPEDITION ISLAND
### Near the east bank of the Green River

On May 22, 1871, at a small clearing somewhere on this island, Major John Wesley Powell and his men embarked on their expedition down the Green and Colorado Rivers. The site may also have served the same purpose for his 1869 trip. On these trips, Major Powell explored the last large land area unknown to European-Americans in the mainland United States. A scientist as well as an explorer, Powell studied the fragile ecology of the area, and when he became director of the U. S. Geological Survey in 1881, he sought to institute intelligent policies for land and water use.

■ *Teton County*

## NORRIS, MADISON, AND FISHING BRIDGE MUSEUMS (NPS)
### Norris Geyser Basin, Madison Junction, and Fishing Bridge, Yellowstone National Park (Park and Teton Counties)

(See entry under Park County.)

## OLD FAITHFUL INN (NPS)
### Yellowstone National Park, Old Faithful

This superb hotel is the first building in a national park constructed in a style designed to be harmonious with the grandeur of the surrounding natural landscape. The Northern Pacific Railroad built it, between 1903 and 1904, adjacent to one of Yellowstone's most popular attractions. The hotel reflects an architectural style that had been used often in rustic vacation camps in the Adirondacks of New York state. Here, the idiom was enlarged to enormous proportions; the seven-story-high lobby, constructed of gnarled logs and rough-sawn lumber, is a veritable wonderland of wood. Old Faithful Inn has a sense of place as identifiable as the park it graces and the geyser it stands beside.

*Old Faithful Inn, Old Faithful, Teton County. Courtesy of the Wyoming Division of Cultural Resources.*

# OTHER JURISDICTIONS

## ■ *American Samoa*

### BLUNTS POINT BATTERY
**Matautu Ridge, Pago Pago vicinity, Eastern District**

After the attack on Pearl Harbor, a Japanese invasion of Samoa — the critical link in the Allies' Pacific lifeline to Australia and New Zealand — seemed imminent. Marines were rushed to strengthen island defenses, and American Samoa became the largest Marine Corps installation in the Pacific. This two-gun battery and magazine at Blunts Point, overlooking the entrance to Pago Pago Harbor, are rare survivors and wartime symbols. After the Battle of Midway, invasion of Samoa was no longer considered a threat, but the site continued in use during World War II as an advanced training center and staging area.

### GOVERNMENT HOUSE
**U.S. Naval Station Tutuila, Eastern District**

Built by the U.S. Navy to serve as a residence for the naval governor in 1903, only three years after the United States annexed Eastern (American) Samoa, this two-story frame house is the most enduring land-based symbol of American naval and diplomatic might in the South Pacific. In essence the capitol of American Samoa through much of its history, the house has served as the official residence of civilian governors since 1951.

## ■ *Commonwealth of the Northern Marianas Islands*

### LANDING BEACHES, ASLITO-ISLEY FIELD AND MARPI POINT
**Chalan Kanoa, Saipan Municipality**

On June 15, 1944, U.S. Marines stormed the southwestern shores of this island in the center of the Marianas chain; on July 9, after furious combat, Saipan was declared secured. The assault on Saipan formed Phase I of an operation whose aim was to capture the Marianas and breach Japan's inner defense line, thus opening the way to the Home Islands. In the last nine months of World War II, Army Air Force B-29s conducted long-range raids against Japanese industrial and urban targets from Saipan.

Blunts Point Battery, American Samoa. Six-inch naval gun, overlooking Pago Pago harbor. Courtesy of NPS (E. N. Thompson).

*Tinian Landing Beaches, Ushi Point and North Fields, Tinian Island. Atomic bomb loading pit. Courtesy of NPS (E. N. Thompson).*

## TINIAN LANDING BEACHES, USHI POINT AND NORTH FIELDS
**Tinian Village, Tinian Municipality**

In late July 1944 two Marine divisions succeeded brilliantly in a difficult amphibious operation and captured this island in the Northern Marianas. By assaulting two small beaches, the Marines confused Japanese commanders and established a beachhead at little cost of American lives. Tinian's North Field provided American forces with valuable airstrips from which to mount raids on Japan; ultimately, the island served as the base from which the atomic bomb attacks on Hiroshima and Nagasaki were staged.

■ *Federated States of Micronesia*

## NAN MADOL
**East side of Temwen Island, Pohnpei Freely Associated State**

Nan Madol, known as the Venice of the Pacific, is a complex of man-made basalt islands built atop an atoll on Pohnpei's eastern coast. The name roughly translates as "between the intervals" and refers to the network of islands and canals that were the means of travel and communication for the occupants of the 200-acre site. The district's core was the seat of Pohnpei's ruling Sau Deleur dynasty in prehistoric times. Archeological investigations have helped in

understanding and interpreting the development of the island's "chief" hierarchy, one of the most complex in the Pacific islands.

## TRUK LAGOON UNDERWATER FLEET
**Truk Atoll, Truk Freely Associated State**

Considered one of the best anchorages in the world, Truk Lagoon served as the base of operations for Japan's Combined Fleet from July 1942 to early February 1944. After the fleet had withdrawn because of the threat of American attack, a U.S. Navy carrier strike on February 17–18, 1944, destroyed virtually all remaining Japanese ships in the lagoon and heavily damaged Japanese air and land defenses. This action allowed U.S. forces to bypass Truk and to strike at Japan's inner defenses in the Marianas. Between 30 and 60 sunken ships, now adorned with coral, sponges, and algae, constitute the "underwater fleet."

■ *Kingdom of Morocco*

## AMERICAN LEGATION
**8 Zankat America (Rue d'Amerique), Tangier**

An elaborate Moorish style complex of stuccoed masonry, the American Legation at Tangier evolved from a small stone building presented to the United States in 1821 by Sultan Moulay Suliman. This was the first property our nation acquired abroad, and it housed the legation and the consulate for 140 years, the longest period any building has served as a U.S. foreign diplomatic post. The building is symbolic of the 1786 Morocco-U.S. treaty of friendship, still in force today. During World War II it served as headquarters for U.S. intelligence agents. In 1961 a new legation was acquired, and this building became a school. It was later converted into a museum and study center, its current use.

## ■ *Republic of the Marshall Islands*

### KWAJALEIN ISLAND BATTLEFIELD
Kwajalein Island

In early February 1944, U.S. Army amphibious troops captured Kwajalein after four days of bitter fighting, making this the first Japanese territory in the Pacific that army troops took by battle in World War II. Kwajalein, the world's largest coral atoll, was the scene of a devastating land, sea, and air bombardment that virtually changed the face of the island. Ruins of many reinforced-concrete Japanese structures remain on the battlefield, now part of the U.S. Army's Kwajalein Missile Range.

### ROI-NAMUR

U.S. Marines captured Roi-Namur from the Japanese in 1944, in coordination with the U.S. Army attack on Kwajalein Island. The 4th Marine Division, in its first combat action, took Roi Island in the short span of 6 hours and seized Namur Island, connected to Roi by a sandbar and causeway, in 26 hours. The simultaneous victories here and at Kwajalein allowed American forces to accelerate the schedule for further advances in the Central Pacific during World War II.

## ■ *Republic of Palau*

### PELELIU BATTLEFIELD
Peleliu Island, Peleiu Municipality

The battle for Peleliu, gateway to the Philippines, was the longest and one of the hardest-fought amphibian operations of the entire Central Pacific theater in World War II. In contrast to other islands, where the Japanese were unsuccesful in annihilating advancing enemy troops on the beaches, here they established their main-line defenses inland. Although the Japanese troops lost the battle, their new tactics enabled them to inflict heavy losses on U.S. Marine and Army forces and to hold out for 74 days before surrendering.

## ■ *U.S. Minor Islands*

### WAKE ISLAND

Wake Island became a symbol of hope and a morale booster for Americans when marines stationed here repulsed Japanese attacks three days after Pearl Harbor. The Japanese recaptured Wake just before Christmas, 1941, removing a threat to their line of defense from Tokyo to the Marshall Islands. The landmark includes World War II–related resources on Peale, Wilkes, and Wake Islands. These three islands in the coral atoll, surrounded by a reef, that form Wake, still an active military base.

### WORLD WAR II FACILITIES AT MIDWAY
Sand and Eastern Islands, Midway Islands

The Japanese launched an attempt to capture these islands in June 1942. American carrier forces, ordered by Admiral Nimitz to intercept the Japanese, retaliated with air power after the Japanese fleet had begun its attack. All four of the Japanese carriers were sunk and 332 of their planes were lost, along with more than 2,000 pilots and sailors. The Japanese navy never fully recovered from the American victory in this battle, which restored American naval power in the Pacific. The Battle of Midway proved to be the turning point of the Pacific theater in World War II. Since 1997, the U.S. Fish and Wildlife Service has had jurisdiction over Midway.

# INDEX OF NATIONAL HISTORIC LANDMARKS

# GENERAL INDEX

*Subentries include an abbreviated reference to individual landmark entries.*